TWENTIETH
CENTURY
CULTURE

*American Culture
After World War II*

DICTIONARY OF

TWENTIETH CENTURY CULTURE

American Culture After World War II

Edited by

Karen L. Rood

Associate Editors

Kathryn Bennett   Ina Rae Hark   Darren Harris-Fain
Jolyon Helterman   Louise E. Peake   Leigh D. Soufas

A MANLY, INC. BOOK

 Gale Research Inc.

DETROIT • WASHINGTON, D.C. • LONDON

TABLE OF CONTENTS

TOPICAL TABLE OF CONTENTS

LITERATURE

Agee, James
Algren, Nelson
American Booksellers Association
American Literature
Angelou, Maya
Asimov, Isaac
Baldwin, James
Baraka, Amiri
Barth, John
Beat Generation
Bellow, Saul
Berrigan, Ted
Berryman, John
Best-seller Lists
Black Aesthetic
Black Arts Movement
Black Humor
Black Mountain College
Blume, Judy
Bly, Robert
Book Clubs
Books on Tape
Bradbury, Ray
Brat Fiction
Brautigan, Richard
Bread Loaf Writers' Conference
Burroughs, William S.
Capote, Truman
Carver, Raymond
Censorship
Chain Bookstores
Confessional Poetry
Cozzens, James Gould
Creative-Writing Programs
Creeley, Robert
Cultural Literacy
Deconstruction
Dickey, James
Didion, Joan
Doctorow, E. L.
Duncan, Robert
Eliot, T. S.
Ellison, Ralph
Esquire
Evergreen Review
Faulkner, William
Feminist Criticism
Ferlinghetti, Lawrence
Fiedler, Leslie
Fitzgerald, F. Scott
Frost, Robert
Gates, Henry Louis, Jr.
Ginsberg, Allen
Giovanni, Nikki

Gothic Fiction
Grove Press
Harper's Magazine
Heinlein, Robert A.
Heller, Joseph
Hellman, Lillian
Hemingway, Ernest
Horror Fiction
Imprint Publishing
Iowa Writers' Workshop
Irving, John
Jarrell, Randall
Jones, James
Jong, Erica
Kerouac, Jack
Kesey, Ken
King, Stephen
Lee, Harper
Levertov, Denise
Literary History of the United States
Lowell, Robert
Macdonald, Ross
MacDowell Colony
Mailer, Norman
Malamud, Bernard
McMurtry, Larry
Metafiction
Michener, James A.
Minimalism
Modern Language Association of
   America, The
Moore, Marianne
Morrison, Toni
Multiculturalism
Nabokov, Vladimir
National Endowment for the Hu-
   manities
New Criticism
New Directions
New Formalism
New Historicism
New Journalism
New Yorker, The
New York Review of Books
New York School
New York Times Book Review
Oates, Joyce Carol
O'Connor, Flannery
O'Hara, John
Olson, Charles
Paperback Books
Paris Review
Plath, Sylvia
Poet Laureate of the United States
Police Procedural

Poststructuralism
Pound, Ezra
Postmodernism
Projective Verse
Pynchon, Thomas
Ramparts
Reader's Digest Condensed Books
Rice, Anne
Roethke, Theodore
Rolling Stone
Romance Fiction
Roth, Philip
Salinger, J. D.
Science Fiction and Fantasy
Semiotics
Sendak, Maurice
Seuss, Dr.
Sexton, Anne
Shaw, Irwin
Singer, Isaac Bashevis
Skinner, B. F.
Spillane, Mickey
St. Mark's Church-in-the-Bowery
Stanford Writing Program
Steinbeck, John
Steinem, Gloria
Stevens, Wallace
Styron, William
Susann, Jacqueline
Thompson, Hunter S.
Tyler, Anne
Updike, John
Village Voice
Vonnegut, Kurt, Jr.
Walker, Alice
Warren, Robert Penn
Welty, Eudora
Wilbur, Richard
Williams, William Carlos
Wolfe, Tom
Yaddo
Young Adult Fiction

DRAMA AND FILM

Abbott, George
Academy of Motion Picture Arts
   and Sciences
Actors Studio
Actors Theatre of Louisville
Adler, Stella
Albee, Edward
Allen, Woody
Altman, Robert
American Film Institute
American Theatre Wing

Anderson, Robert
Arena Stage
Atkinson, Brooks
Auteur Theory
Bailey, Pearl
Barnes, Clive
Beatty, Warren
Bennett, Michael
Bergman, Ingrid
Brando, Marlon
Broadway Musicals
Brooks, Mel
Burton, Richard
Canby, Vincent
Cinema Verit
Clift, Montgomery
Comden, Betty, and Adolph Green
Connery, Sean
Coppola, Francis Ford
Corman, Roger
Costner, Kevin
Crowther, Bosley
Day, Doris
Dean, James
De Niro, Robert
Disney, Walt, Productions
Douglas, Kirk
Drive-in Theaters
Eastwood, Clint
Fierstein, Harvey
Film Noir
Fonda, Jane
Ford, Harrison
Fosse, Bob
Gardner, Ava
Grant, Cary
Guare, John
Gurney, A. R.
Guthrie Theater
Haight-Ashbury
Hansberry, Lorraine
Happenings
Hellman, Lillian
Henley, Beth
Hepburn, Audrey
Herman, Jerry
Heston, Charlton
Hitchcock, Alfred
Hoffman, Dustin
Holden, William
Howe, Tina
Hudson, Rock
Huston, John
Inge, William
Ives, Burl

Jones, Quincy
Kael, Pauline
Kanin, Garson
Kazin, Elia
Kelly, Gene
Kelly, Grace
Kerr, Walter
Kopit, Arthur
Kramer, Stanley
Kubrick, Stanley
Lancaster, Burt
Lee, Spike
Lemmon, Jack
Lerner, Alan Jay, and Frederick
    Loewe
Lewis, Jerry
Loesser, Frank
Lucas, George
Madonna
Mancini, Henry
Mamet, David
McNally, Terrence
Miller, Arthur
Mitchum, Robert
Mixed Media
Monroe, Marilyn
Newman, Paul
Nichols, Mike
Nicholson, Jack
Norman, Marsha
Pacino, Al
Papp, Joseph
Peck, Gregory
Peckinpah, Sam
Poitier, Sidney
Preminger, Otto
Presley, Elvis
Prince, Harold
Rabe, David
Redford, Robert
Rich, Frank
Robbins, Jerome
Rodgers, Richard, and Oscar
    Hammerstein II
Schwarzenegger, Arnold
Scorsese, Martin
Shepard, Sam
Simon, Neil
Sinatra, Frank
Siskel, Gene, and Roger Ebert
Sondheim, Stephen
Spielberg, Steven
Stallone, Sylvester
Stone, Oliver
Streep, Meryl

Streisand, Barbra
Taylor, Elizabeth
Wasserstein, Wendy
Wayne, John
Wilder, Billy
Williams, John
Williams, Tennessee
Wilson, August
Wilson, Lanford

MUSIC AND DANCE
Acid Rock
Acuff, Roy
Adams, John
Ailey, Alvin
Aleatory Music
American Ballet Theatre
Amram, David
Anderson, Laurie
Anderson, Marian
Armstrong, Louis
Atonal Music
Babbitt, Milton
Bacharach, Burt
Baez, Joan
Bailey, Pearl
Balanchine, George
Barber, Samuel
Baryshnikov, Mikhail
Basie, Count
Beach Boys, The
Beatles, The
Bebop
Belafonte, Harry
Bennett, Michael
Berberian, Cathy
Bernstein, Leonard
Berry, Chuck
Biggs, E. Power
Billboard
Black Mountain College
Blitzstein, Marc
Bluegrass Music
Bolcom, William
Boone, Pat
Bossa Nova
Boston Pops Orchestra
Boston Symphony Orchestra
Broadway Musicals
Brown, James
Brubeck, Dave
Bruhn, Erik
Bumbry, Grace
Cage, John
Caldwell, Sarah

Callas, Maria
Calypso
Carter, Elliott
Cash, Johnny
Charles, Ray
Chicago Lyric Opera
Chicago Symphony Orchestra
Cleveland Orchestra
Cleveland Quartet
Cliburn, Van
Cole, Nat King
Coleman, Ornette
Collins, Judy
Coltrane, John
Copland, Aaron
Corigliano, John
Crossover Music
Crumb, George
Cunningham, Merce
Davidovsky, Mario
Davis, Miles
Disco
Down Beat
Dylan, Bob
Electronic Music
Ellington, Duke
Farm Aid
Farrell, Suzanne
Fitzgerald, Ella
Folk Music
Foss, Lukas
Fosse, Bob
Fox, Virgil
Franklin, Aretha
Fusion Music
Gillespie, Dizzy
Glass, Philip
Gospel Music
Gould, Morton
Graham, Martha
Graphic Notation
Grateful Dead, The
Guthrie, Arlo
Haggard, Merle
Haight-Ashbury
Happenings
Heavy Metal
Heifetz, Jascha
Hendrix, Jimi
Herman, Jerry
Hines, Jerome
Horne, Marilyn
Horowitz, Vladimir
Hovhaness, Alan
Husa, Karel

Ives, Burl
Ives, Charles
Jackson, Michael
Jefferson Airplane
Joffrey Ballet
Jones, Quincy
Kelly, Gene
Knight, Gladys, and the Pips
Led Zeppelin
Lerner, Alan Jay, and Frederick
    Loewe
Liberace
Live Aid
Loesser, Frank
LP Records
Luening, Otto
Lynn, Loretta
Ma, Yo-Yo
Maazel, Lorin
MacDowell Colony
Madonna
Mancini, Henry
Marsalis, Wynton
Mehta, Zubin
Menotti, Gian Carlo
Menuhin, Yehudi, Sir
Minimalism
Mitropoulos, Dmitri
Mixed Media
Modern Jazz Quartet
Monk, Thelonious
Monroe, Bill, and the Blue Grass
    Boys
Motown
Muzak
New Age Music
New Wave Music
New York Metropolitan Opera
Nikolais, Alwin
Oliveros, Pauline
Ono, Yoko
Ormandy, Eugene
Parker, Charlie
Pavarotti, Luciano
Perlman, Itzhak
Peter, Paul & Mary
Postmodernism
Presley, Elvis
Previn, Andre
Price, Leontyne
Progressive Jazz
Punk Rock
Rap Music
Reggae
Reich, Steve

Robbins, Jerome
Rochberg, George
Rock 'n' Roll
Rodgers, Richard, and Oscar
    Hammerstein II
Rolling Stone
Rolling Stones
Rorem, Ned
Rosen, Charles
Ross, Diana, and the Supremes
Rostropovich, Mstislav
Salsa
San Francisco Opera
Schuller, Gunther
Serial Music
Serkin, Rudolf and Peter
Sessions, Roger
Sills, Beverly
Simon, Paul
Sinatra, Frank
Sondheim, Stephen
Soul Music
Springsteen, Bruce
Stern, Isaac
Streisand, Barbra
Taylor, Paul
Tharp, Twyla
Thomson, Virgil
Top 40
Tower, Joan
Tudor, Antony
Tudor, David
Turner, Ike and Tina
Twist, The
Varese, Edgard
Vaughan, Sarah
Watts, Andre
We Are the World
Welk, Lawrence
Williams, Hank
Williams, John
Woodstock
World Music
Wuorinen, Charles
Yaddo
Zappa, Frank
Zwillich, Ellen Taaffe

RADIO AND TELEVISION
ABC
All in the Family
Allen, Steve
American Bandstand
Berle, Milton
Brady Bunch, The

EDITORIAL PLAN

Culture is a broad term that has different meanings for different people. It is a word that is used variously to describe how we are alike, how we are different, and what we should aspire to know and appreciate. Thus the title of this work was the subject of careful deliberation by the advisory board at the initial planning meeting in 1990. At issue were basic definitions that determined the fundamental elements of the editorial rationale.

The consensus was that the *Dictionary of Twentieth-Century Culture (TCC)* should undertake to provide a ready reference for the vocabulary of culture, which the board defined as the broad language drawing on shared knowledge used by people of similar backgrounds to communicate with one another. A standard dictionary of language records the definitions of words used in verbal discourse; the advisory board agreed that such dictionaries are inadequate to define more complicated structures of meaning that *TCC* addresses. Communication is frequently extra-verbal, drawing on shared experiences, common concepts, communal notions about celebrities, and universally construed messages conveyed by certain images. Culture embraces all aspects of life, from the mundane to the sublime, from the knowledge of grocery-item brand names and the images they connote to a familiarity with classic works of literature, music, and art.

Cultural language is expressed orally, visually, musically, and physically in speech, art, music, and performance. It is frequently allusive, depending for its full meaning on symbols and metaphors, and thus meaning is layered. For example, the first anniversary-issue cover of Tina Brown's *New Yorker* on 21 February 1994 made a witty cultural statement: it depicted a Eustace Tilley descendant named Elvis Tilley, a street-punk reading a sex-show leaflet. The meaning of that statement was immediately clear to one segment of American society, who knew the history of Eustace Tilley and the circumstances of Ms. Brown's job; the allusive meaning was hopelessly obscure to others, though many could still appreciate the timeliness of the image, especially if they were familiar with the streets of New York City. We anticipate that the entry here on the New Yorker will provide the information necessary to decode the message.

Culture broadly construed is an unmanageable topic for a dictionary-type reference work. Comprehensive coverage would fill a large library. For practical reasons, it was necessary to narrow the scope of *TCC*. The advisory board elected to restrict the series to entries on people, places, terms, art forms, and organizations associated with creative expression in the humanities, those forms of creativity that seek to describe and interpret the human condition. Certainly physicists, chemists, physicians, mathematicians, jurists, and legislators are as creative in their own ways as writers, artists, actors, dancers, and musicians. But as specialists, they view the world from different, though no less important, perspectives than creative artists in the humanities do. Because we cannot do justice to all these world views in a single series, we have limited ourselves to the rich world of art, music, literature, drama, radio and television performance, movies, and dance. The advisory board elected not to include entries on individual works, because works are described in entries devoted to their creators. Both high and low art that meet the qualification of having made a lasting impression on society will be covered. Endurance is a matter of editorial judgment, and it will be left to volume editors and the editorial board make the necessary decisions about inclusion.

Obviously it is a distortion to suggest that creative expression occurs in isolation. Most art is not about art but about people from all walks of life and the ways they act, individually and in the company of others. The people, events, and ideas outside the arena of creative expression that stimulated artistic responses have a special significance in culture, and entries are provided to describe certain specific social and historical forces and the creative responses they prompted. Thus, in this volume there are entries on AIDS, the Civil Rights Movement, Feminism, and the Vietnam War; John F. Kennedy, Martin Luther King Jr., Timothy Leary, Betty Friedan, and Gloria Steinem, for example, because all have contributed in a basic way to our perception of the world.

The purpose of *TCC* is not to prescribe what people should know about modern culture; rather, *TCC* attempts to describe and define what people have collectively thought was significant. The purpose of *TCC* entries is definition rather than analysis. Entries are concise, in some cases as brief as a few sentences. In rare cases does an entry exceed 1000 words.

For the purposes of *TCC*, culture is normally defined geographically. There will be volumes on German culture, French culture, Latin-American culture, and Middle-Eastern Arab culture, for example. The decision to organize such volumes geographically was a difficult one, determined by practical considerations and by assumptions about the readership for the series. In fact, of course, there are several distinct cultural groups in most countries, defined sometimes by religion, sometimes by ethnicity, sometimes by socio-economics. Careful attention is due separate cultural groups around the world, but that responsibility must be left to another work. *TCC* is devoted to cultural commonality, not cultural diversity.

Related to the decision to take the broad view of distinct cultures is the advisory board's perception of the audience for *TCC*: American high-school and college students and the patrons of American public libraries. The board has assumed a certain ethnocentrism among the audience, and thus *TCC* will be disproportionately American in character. In addition to Post-WWII American culture, volumes on American culture before WWI, Afro-American culture, and Native-American culture are in progress. Other volumes will, in most cases, concentrate on the dominant cultures of a country. Unarguably comprehensive coverage of the topic is the work of lifetimes.

Certainly many significant entries could be added to those included here. Almost as certainly, entries that should have been included are inadvertently omitted. Significance is a subjective judgment, determined in large part by the cultural background to which the editors themselves are bound. There is some comfort in the anticipation that *TCC* will be a living project that continues its evolution after publication of this volume.

Richard Layman
Columbia, South Carolina
18 April 1994

DICTIONARY OF TWENTIETH-CENTURY CULTURE PUBLISHING PLAN

American Culture after World War II
American Culture before World War II
Russian Culture after World War II
Russian Culture before World War II
German Culture
African-American Culture
Arab Culture in the Middle East
Arab Culture in Northern Africa
French Culture
South American Culture

Italian Culture
British Culture after World War II
British Culture before World War II
Native American Culture
Japanese Culture
Chinese Culture
Africa South of the Sahara
Eastern European Culture
South East Asian Culture
Culture of India

ACKNOWLEDGMENTS

This book was produced by Bruccoli Clark Layman, Inc.

Production coordinator is George F. Dodge. Julie E. Frick is editorial associate. Photography editors are Edward Scott, Dennis Lynch, Josephine A. Bruccoli, and Joseph Matthew Bruccoli. Layout and graphics supervisor is Penney L. Haughton. Copyediting supervisor is Bill Adams. Typesetting supervisor is Kathleen M. Flanagan. The production staff includes Phyllis A. Avant, Ann M. Cheschi, Melody W. Clegg, Patricia Coate, Wilma Weant Dague, Brigitte B. de Guzman, Denise W. Edwards, Sarah A. Estes, Joyce Fowler, Laurel M. Gladden, Stephanie C. Hatchell, Rebecca Mayo, Kathy Lawler Merlette, Pamela D. Norton, Delores I. Plastow, Patricia F. Salisbury, Paul Savage, and William L. Thomas, Jr.

Walter W. Ross, Robert S. McConnell, Deborah M. Chasteen, and Everett Dague did library research. They were assisted by the following librarians at the Thomas Cooper Library of the University of South Carolina: Linda Holderfield and the interlibrary-loan staff; reference librarians Gwen Baxter, Daniel Boice, Faye Chadwell, Cathy Eckman, Gary Geer, Qun Gerry Jiao, Jean Rhyne, Carol Tobin, Carolyn Tyler, Virginia Weathers, Elizabeth Whiznant, and Connie Widney; circulation-department head Thomas Marcil; and acquisitions-searching supervisor David Haggard.

FOREWORD

It has traditionally been assumed that high culture — classic literature, art movies, serious drama, museum art, and concert music — is the expression of the best humanist thought and the most profound emotions in our civilization. Because the messages delivered by these art forms are complex, building associations and references from a defined body of aesthetic values, high culture was closed to the uninitiated. Initiation required, in unequal parts, a sufficient education, adequate intelligence, and correct instincts; a privileged social background was an asset, as well. Thus, much of the population was denied access to the most respected truths its culture had to offer, except through academic interpreters and classroom teachers, who exposed students to the ancient Greek and Roman, British, and Western European works that formed the intellectual foundation for American social structures.

Well into the twentieth century Americans were still uneasy about their own creative aptitude, feeling that native achievements were inadequate compared to British and European models. The frontier was frequently blamed. So much creative energy was required to tame the wilderness in America that little was left for refined pursuits, it was held. Music critic Deems Taylor summed up the situation in a 1922 review of the state of American civilization: "We spend more money upon music than does any other nation on earth. . . . We squander millions every year upon an art that we cannot produce." It was not until after World War II that American thought and American art began to gain respect. In 1952 Lionel Trilling, one of most respected teachers and literary critics in the United States observed, "For the first time in the history of the modern American intellectual, America is not to be conceived of as *a priori* the vulgarest and stupidest nation of the world."

American artists asserted their new status boldly. After the war several forces converged to form successive waves of assault on, disrespect for, and indifference to high culture. Abstract Expressionist artists rebelled against formal training, espousing theories of art that belittled the classical tradition, and pop artists appropriated icons of low culture to the purposes of high art. Rock 'n' roll musicians first captured the largest musical audiences in the history of the world, then proclaimed themselves serious artists, to the horror of classicists. The paperback book brought classic literature to a broader audience than had ever before been thought to be capable of appreciating it, yet paperback vendors displayed literary classics side by side with science fiction and Westerns on mass-market book racks. Off-Broadway, Off-Off-Broadway, and even regional theater challenged the monopoly of the centrist New York theater world with daring productions of controversial plays. Dance was democratized as an emotional expression of youthful energy divorced from formal models.

Mavens of high culture had traditionally ignored the issue of audience. Let the philistines gape and doze, they reasoned; serious art provided such profound benefits to society that its place was assured, even if its appreciation was restricted to the intellectual elite. That attitude was challenged after World War II changed the creative marketplace. The postwar economic boom brought new prosperity to an expanded middle class, fueling cultural aspirations. Budding savants had money to spend on culture; they had a naive confidence in the validity of their tastes; and they had a healthy disdain for foreign models and creative pretension. By the late 1950s there was plenty of money to support rock concerts, genre fiction, and comic-book art, but museums and symphony orchestras were begging. The wealthy upper class, the traditional funding source for high art, grew stingier as its share of the national wealth decreased. The problem grew so severe that in 1965 President Lyndon B. Johnson instituted the National Endowments for the Humanities and the Arts to provide federal funding for high culture. The message was clear: High art had to broaden its appeal if it was to survive.

By the late 1960s the intellectual caretakers were already murmuring doubts about the value of high cultural values, and they were scrambling to develop what turned out to be an ironic response to disdainful critics. They would save high culture by redefining it, democratizing it, attacking it, and, finally, declaring it nonexistent. Thus the intellectuals' priestly roles as interpreters were salvaged, and common tastes, now called popular culture, were granted legitimacy.

The theory that the essence of a creative work lay not with the singular vision of its creator but with individual perceivers, each of whose interpretations are equally valid, has roots in turn-of-the-century Acmeist and Futurist movements of prerevolutionary Russia, but the notion gained currency in the United States as a means of mitigating the assault of the middle class on cultural fortresses. Instead of being denied access to the temple of high-minded creativity, the uninitiated were embraced by the high priests of the new values. The border between high and low culture was stripped away, and the standards for judging creative values were redefined. The town-hall-meeting approach to culture, in which every person's tastes and opinions were held to have equal validity, gained prominence by the 1980s. Culture ceased to be high or low; it became an amalgam of whatever creative interests prevailed.

Since World War II the definition of art has changed. Mystery fiction came to be taught in American English departments with as much frequency as medieval literature. Painting and sculpture came to be appreciated for the abstract ideas they conveyed as well as for the

basic evocative power of their images. Jazz, the music of improvisation, was taught in music schools, and rock 'n' roll song lyrics were called poetry. Dance choreography came to emphasize fundamental emotive values rather than technical proficiency. Movies, the mass-entertainment medium of the period between the world wars, came to be called film and were hailed as high art.

Some critics assert that the democratization of culture is a dangerous trend that will result in the dilution of the best virtues of our traditional heritage. Others insist that classical works of art reflect a narrow perspective made all the narrower because they have been identified by elitists. Arguments about the wisdom of ignoring the classical foundations of our culture will not be resolved easily, but there is general agreement that postwar American society has contributed significantly to the broadening and the leveling of the cultural universe, asserting its own distinctive identity in the process.

—R.L.

TIMELINE: SELECTED WORKS AND EVENTS

1945

Historical Events
US planes drop the first atom bombs on Hiroshima and Nagasaki; with the end of World War II veterans flock to US colleges with education benefits granted under the first GI Bill.

Art & Architecture
Romare Bearden, *The Passion of Christ*

Dance
Antony Tudor, *Undertow*

Drama
Richard Rodgers and Oscar Hammerstein II, *Carousel*
Tennessee Williams, *The Glass Menagerie*

Film
The Lost Weekend

Literature
Wallace Stevens, *Esthétique du mal*

Music
Frank Sinatra, "Dream"

1946

Historical Events
The UN General Assembly meets for the first time; the US conducts atom-bomb tests at Bikini Atoll in the South Pacific.

Dance
George Balanchine, *Orpheus*

Drama
Garson Kanin, *Born Yesterday*

Film
The Big Sleep
The Killers
The Postman Always Rings Twice
Notorious

Literature
Robert Lowell, *Lord Weary's Castle*
Robert Penn Warren, *All the King's Men*
Eudora Welty, *Delta Wedding*
William Carlos Williams, *Paterson*, part 1

Music
Marc Blitzstein, *Airborne Symphony*
Nat "King" Cole, "For Sentimental Reasons"
Duke Ellington, *Deep South Suite*
Gian Carlo Menotti, *The Medium*
Bill Monroe and the Blue Grass Boys, "Blue Moon of Kentucky"

1947

Historical Events
The Marshall Plan to aid economic recovery in Europe is proposed; Jackie Robinson signs with the Brooklyn Dodgers, becoming the first black to play major-league baseball.

Art & Architecture
Andrew Wyeth, *Dodges Ridge*

Drama
Tennessee Williams, *A Streetcar Named Desire*

Film
Gentlemen's Agreement

Literature
James A. Michener, *Tales of the South Pacific*
Mickey Spillane, *I, the Jury*

Music
Roy Acuff, "Wabash Cannonball"
Duke Ellington, *Liberian Suite*
Virgil Thomson, *The Mother of Us All*

TV
Howdy Doody

1948

Historical Events
The USSR's blockade of land access to the Allied sectors of Berlin is broken by the Berlin airlift; Harry S Truman defeats Thomas E. Dewey in the presidential election.

Art & Architecture
Buckminster Fuller, Geodesic Dome
Andrew Wyeth, *Christina's World*

Dance
Martha Graham, *Errand in a Maze*

Film
The Treasure of Sierra Madre

Literature
Nobel Prize for Literature: T. S. Eliot
Truman Capote, *Other Voices, Other Rooms*
James Gould Cozzens, *Guard of Honor*
Literary History of the United States
Norman Mailer, *The Naked and the Dead*
Ezra Pound, *The Pisan Cantos*
Theodore Roethke, *Lost Son and Other Poems*
Irwin Shaw, *The Young Lions*
B. F. Skinner, *Walden Two*

Music
Milton Babbitt, *Composition for 4 Instruments*
Otto Luening, *Evangelina*

TV
The Ed Sullivan Show
Texaco Star Theatre

1949

Historical Events

The North Atlantic Treaty Organization (NATO) is founded; the USSR tests its first nuclear weapon; Communist forces backing Mao Ze-dong establish the People's Republic of China.

Art & Architecture

Robert Motherwell begins the *Elegies to the Spanish Republic* series

Barnett Newman, *Covenant*

Dance

George Balanchine, *Bourrée fantasque*

Drama

Arthur Miller, *Death of a Salesman*

Richard Rodgers and Oscar Hammerstein II, *South Pacific*

Film

All the King's Men

Literature

Nelson Algren, *The Man with the Golden Arm*

John O'Hara, *A Rage to Live*

Music

Leonard Bernstein, *Age of Anxiety*

TV

Your Show of Shows

1950

Historical Events

Sen. Joseph McCarthy charges that Communists have infiltrated American government; troops from Communist North Korea invade US-backed South Korea, and President Truman authorizes the use of US land troops with UN backing.

Art & Architecture

Jackson Pollock, *Number 1 (Lavender Mist)*

Mark Rothko, *Number 10*

Drama

T. S. Eliot, *The Cocktail Party*

Film

The Asphalt Jungle

Sunset Boulevard

Literature

Nobel Prize for Literature: William Faulkner

Isaac Asimov, *I, Robot*

Ray Bradbury, *The Martian Chronicles*

Dr. Seuss (Theodor Geisel), *If I Ran the Zoo*

Isaac Bashevis Singer, *The Family Moskat*

Wallace Stevens, *The Auroras of Autumn*

Music

Nat "King" Cole, "Mona Lisa"

Hank Williams, "Cold, Cold Heart"

1951

Historical Events

Julius and Ethel Rosenberg are sentenced to the electric chair for giving atomic-weapon secrets to the USSR; they are executed in 1953.

Art & Architecture

David Smith, *Hudson River Landscape*

Dance

George Balanchine, *La Valse*

Merce Cunningham, *Sixteen Dances for Soloist and Company of Three*

Martha Graham, *Judith*

Drama

Lillian Hellman, *The Autumn Garden*

Richard Rodgers and Oscar Hammerstein II, *The King and I*

Film

The African Queen

An American in Paris

Strangers on a Train

Literature

Isaac Asimov, *Foundation*

James Jones, *From Here to Eternity*

Robert Lowell, *The Mills of the Kavanaughs*

Marianne Moore, *Collected Poems*

J. D. Salinger, *Catcher in the Rye*

William Styron, *Lie Down in Darkness*

Music

John Cage, *Music of Changes*

Morton Feldman, *Projections*

Gian Carlo Menotti, *Amahl and the Night Visitors*

TV

The Honeymooners

I Love Lucy

See It Now

1952

Historical Events

Dwight D. Eisenhower defeats Adlai E. Stevenson in the presidential election.

Art & Architecture

Willem de Kooning, *Woman I* (1950–1952)

Helen Frankenthaler, *Mountains and Sea*

Film

Cry the Beloved Country

The Greatest Show on Earth

High Noon

Singin' in the Rain

Literature

Ralph Ellison, *The Invisible Man*

Ernest Hemingway, *The Old Man and the Sea*

Bernard Malamud, *The Natural*

Flannery O'Connor, *Wise Blood*

Paris Review founded

John Steinbeck, *East of Eden*

Kurt Vonnegut, Jr., *Player Piano*

Music

Leonard Bernstein, *Trouble in Tahiti*

John Cage, Mixed-Media Event at Black Mountain College and *Imaginary Landscape No. 5*

Otto Luening, *Fantasy on Tape*

George Rochberg, First String Quartet

Hank Williams, "Your Cheatin' Heart"

TV

Omnibus

National Educational Television (NET) established

1953

Historical Events

McCarthy becomes chair of the Senate Investigations Committee and opens hearings on alleged Communist infiltration of all aspects of American life; the Korean War ends.

Art & Architecture

Larry Rivers, *Washington Crossing the Delaware*

Dance

Alwin Nikolais, *Kaleidoscope*

Jerome Robbins, *Afternoon of a Faun*
Drama
Robert Anderson, *Tea and Sympathy*
William Inge, *Picnic*
Arthur Miller, *The Crucible*
Film
From Here to Eternity
Gentlemen Prefer Blondes
How to Marry a Millionaire
Niagara

Literature
James Baldwin, *Go Tell It on the Mountain*
Saul Bellow, *The Adventures of Augie March*
Ray Bradbury, *Fahrenheit 451*
William S. Burroughs (as William Lee), *Junkie*
Lawrence Ferlinghetti opens City Lights Pocket Bookshop in San Francisco
Charles Olson begins *The Maximus Poems* (1953–1975)
Theodore Roethke, *The Waking, Poems: 1933–1953*

1954

Historical Events
In *Brown vs. Board of Education, Topeka, Kansas* the Supreme Court strikes down the "separate but equal doctrine" of 1896, which allowed segregated public schools; the Senate condemns McCarthy for misconduct; the Geneva Accords end French rule in Indochina, dividing Vietnam into North and South sectors.
Art & Architecture
Morris Louis, *Veils*
Dance
George Balanchine, *Ivesiana*
Drama
George Abbott and Richard Russell, *The Pajama Game*
Film
The Caine Mutiny
Dial M for Murder

On the Waterfront
Rear Window
Literature
Nobel Prize for Literature: Ernest Hemingway
William Faulkner, *A Fable*
Wallace Stevens, *Collected Poems*
Music
Otto Luening and Vladimir Ussachevsky, *Rhapsodic Variations for Tape Recorder and Orchestra* and *A Poem in Cycles and Bells*
Gian Carlo Menotti, *The Saint of Bleeker Street*
Frank Sinatra, *In the Wee Small Hours of the Morning*
Edgard Varèse, *Déserts*
TV
Disneyland
The Tonight Show

1955

Historical Events
Civil war breaks out between the North and South Vietnamese; the Warsaw Pact of Communist countries is formed in opposition to NATO; Disneyland opens.
Art & Architecture
Jasper Johns begins his *Flag* and *Target* paintings
Fairfield Porter, *Katie and Anne*
Robert Rauschenberg, *Bed*
Drama
George Abbott, Douglass Wallop, Richard Adler, and Jerry Ross, *Damn Yankees*
William Inge, *Bus Stop*
Film
The Blackboard Jungle
East of Eden
The Man with the Golden Arm
Mr. Roberts
The Night of the Hunter

Rebel Without a Cause
The Seven Year Itch
To Catch a Thief
Literature
James Baldwin, *Notes of a Native Son*
Vladimir Nabokov, *Lolita*
Flannery O'Connor, *A Good Man Is Hard to Find*
John O'Hara, *Ten North Frederick*
Tennessee Williams, *Cat on a Hot Tin Roof*
Music
Marian Anderson is the first black to perform a solo role at the New York Metropolitan Opera
Chuck Berry, "Maybellene"
Tennessee Ernie Ford, "Sixteen Tons"
Bill Haley and the Comets, "Rock Around the Clock"
Elvis Presley, "Heartbreak Hotel"
TV
Gunsmoke

1956

Historical Events
The Montgomery, Alabama, bus boycott, led by Dr. Martin Luther King, Jr., results in a Supreme Court ruling that outlaws segregation of public transportation; Dwight D. Eisenhower defeats Adlai E. Stevenson in the presidential election.
Art & Architecture
Ellsworth Kelly, *Black Ripe*
Drama
Leonard Bernstein and Lillian Hellman, *Candide*
Alan Jay Lerner and Frederick Loewe, *My Fair Lady*
Film
Bus Stop
Giant

Literature
Nelson Algren, *A Walk on the Wild Side*
John Barth, *The Floating Opera*
John Berryman, *Homage to Mistress Bradstreet*
Allen Ginsberg, *Howl and Other Poems*
Richard Wilbur, *Things of This World*
Music
Johnny Cash, "I Walk the Line"
Elvis Presley, "Hound Dog"/"Don't Be Cruel" and "Love Me Tender"
Elvis Presley appears on *The Ed Sullivan Show*
Frank Sinatra, *Only the Lonely*
TV
The Mickey Mouse Club
Playhouse 90

1957

Historical Events
President Eisenhower sends federal troops to enforce school integration in Little Rock, Arkansas; the USSR launches *Sputnik I,* the first man-made satellite to orbit the earth.

Art & Architecture
Philip Guston, *The Mirror*
Dance
George Balanchine, *Agon*

Paul Taylor, *7 New Dances*
Drama
  William Inge, *The Dark at the Top of the Stairs*
  Arthur Laurents, Leonard Bernstein, and Stephen Sondheim,
    West Side Story
Film
  The Bridge on the River Kwai
  Paths of Glory
Literature
  James Agee, *A Death in the Family*
  James Gould Cozzens, *By Love Possessed*
  William Faulkner, *The Town*

Jack Kerouac, *On the Road*
Bernard Malamud, *The Assistant*
Theodore Roethke, *Words for the Wind*
Dr. Seuss (Theodor Geisel), *The Cat in the Hat*
Isaac Bashevis Singer, *Gimpel the Fool and Other Stories*
Robert Penn Warren, *Promises: Poems 1954–1956*
Music
  Milton Babbitt, *All Set*
  Pat Boone, "April Love"
  Elvis Presley, "Jailhouse Rock" and "All Shook Up"
TV
  American Bandstand

1958

Historical Events
  The US launches *Explorer,* its first earth satellite.
Art & Architecture
  Robert Frank, *The Americans*
  Morris Louis, *Point of Tranquility*
Dance
  Alvin Ailey, *Blues Suite*
  Martha Graham, *Clytemnestra*
Film
  The Long Hot Summer

Vertigo
Literature
  Truman Capote, *Breakfast at Tiffany's*
  Lawrence Ferlinghetti, *A Coney Island of the Mind*
  Bernard Malamud, *The Magic Barrel*
  John O'Hara, *From the Terrace*
Music
  Samuel Barber and Gian Carlo Menotti, *Vanessa*
  Frank Sinatra, "Witchcraft"

1959

Historical Events
  The Maharishi Mahesh Yogi introduces Transcendental Med-
    itation in the United States; Fidel Castro's revolutionary
    forces drive dictator Fulgencio Batista from Cuba.
Art & Architecture
  Allan Kaprow, *18 Piece Happening in 6 Parts*
Drama
  Edward Albee, *The Zoo Story*
  Lorraine Hansberry, *A Raisin in the Sun*
  Arthur Kopit, *Oh Dad, Poor Dad, Mama's Hung You in the Closet
    and I'm Feelin' So Sad*
  Richard Rodgers and Oscar Hammerstein II, *The Sound of
    Music*
  Tennessee Williams, *Sweet Bird of Youth*
Film
  Anatomy of a Murder
  Ben-Hur
  Butterfield 8

North by Northwest
On the Beach
Some Like It Hot
Literature
  William S. Burroughs, *Naked Lunch*
  William Faulkner, *The Mansion*
  Robert Lowell, *Life Studies*
  James Michener, *Hawaii*
  Philip Roth, *Goodbye, Columbus*
  John Updike, *The Poorhouse Fair*
  Kurt Vonnegut, Jr., *The Sirens of Titan*
Music
  John Coltrane, *Giant Steps*
  Miles Davis, *Kind of Blue*
  Gunther Schuller, *Seven Studies on Themes by Paul Klee*
  Ike and Tina Turner, "Fool in Love"
TV
  The Twilight Zone

1960

Historical Events
  Enovid is approved for use as an oral contraceptive; Students
    for a Democratic Society (SDS) is founded; the Student Non-
    violent Coordinating Committee (SNCC) is formed to coor-
    dinate sit-ins at segregated lunch counters; Timothy Leary
    begins research on psychedelic drugs; the USSR shoots down
    an American U-2 spy plane; John F. Kennedy defeats Rich-
    ard M. Nixon in the presidential election.
Art & Architecture
  Claes Oldenburg, *The Street*
Dance
  Alvin Ailey, *Revelations*
Drama
  Alan Jay Lerner and Frederick Loewe, *Camelot*
  Lillian Hellman, *Toys in the Attic*
Film
  The Apartment
  Elmer Gantry

The Hustler
Psycho
Spartacus
Literature
  John Barth, *The Sot-Weed Factor*
  Harper Lee, *To Kill a Mockingbird*
  Flannery O'Connor, *The Violent Bear It Away*
  Sylvia Plath, *The Colossus and Other Poems*
  Dr. Seuss (Theodor Geisel), *Green Eggs and Ham*
  Anne Sexton, *To Bedlam and Part Way Back*
  John Updike, *Rabbit, Run*
Music
  Joan Baez
  Elliott Carter, Second String Quartet
  Ray Charles, "Georgia on My Mind"
  Chubby Checker, "The Twist"
  Elvis Presley, "Are You Lonesome Tonight?"

1961

Historical Events
  US-backed Cuban counterrevolutionaries are defeated in the
    Bay of Pigs invasion; Soviet cosmonaut Yuri Gagarin is the
    first man in space, orbiting the earth; Alan Shepard is the
    first American in space, making a suborbital flight; Soviet

troops construct a wall to cut off movement between East
and West Berlin; 700 American military advisers in Vietnam
are joined by 200 more at year's end.
Art & Architecture
  The Art of Assemblage, Museum of Modern Art

Roy Lichtenstein, *Look, Mickey*
Claes Oldenburg, *The Store*
Andrew Wyeth, *Tenant Farmer*
Drama
Tennessee Williams, *The Night of the Iguana*
Frank Loesser and Abe Burrows, *How to Succeed in Business Without Really Trying*
Film
Judgment at Nuremberg
Little Shop of Horrors
A Raisin in the Sun
Splendor in the Grass
West Side Story

Literature
James Baldwin, *Nobody Knows My Name*
Robert Frost reads "The Gift Outright" at the inauguration of John F. Kennedy
Allen Ginsberg, *Kaddish and Other Poems, 1958–1960*
Robert A. Heinlein, *Stranger in a Strange Land*
Joseph Heller, *Catch-22*
J. D. Salinger, *Franny and Zooey*
Music
Ray Charles, "Hit the Road Jack"
Patsy Cline, "Crazy"
Henry Mancini, "Moon River"

1962

Historical Events
John Glenn is the first American to orbit the earth; The USSR backs down in a confrontation with the US over the presence of Soviet missiles in Cuba; *Ramparts* magazine, an influential voice of the New Left, is founded.
Art & Architecture
Roy Lichtenstein, *Takka Takka*
Andy Warhol, *100 Cans*
Dance
Paul Taylor, *Aureole*
Drama
Edward Albee, *Who's Afraid of Virginia Woolf?*
Film
Bird Man of Alcatraz
Cape Fear
The Days of Wine and Roses

Dr. No
Lolita
To Kill a Mockingbird
Literature
Nobel Prize for Literature: John Steinbeck
James Baldwin, *Another Country*
William Faulkner, *The Reivers*
Ken Kesey, *One Flew Over the Cuckoo's Nest*
Vladimir Nabokov, *Pale Fire*
Anne Sexton, *All My Pretty Ones*
William Carlos Williams, *Pictures from Breughel and Other Poems*
Music
Ray Charles, "I Can't Stop Loving You"
Aaron Copland, *Connotations*
Peter, Paul & Mary, "If I Had a Hammer"

1963

Historical Events
15,000 American troops in Vietnam; the US and USSR sign a nuclear-test-ban treaty; Martin Luther King delivers his "I Have a Dream" speech before 200,000 during the March on Washington to protest racial segregation; Betty Friedan publishes *The Feminine Mystique,* reviving the American feminist movement; President Kennedy is assassinated and is succeeded by Lyndon B. Johnson.
Art & Architecture
Roy Lichtenstein, *Drowning Girl*
Robert Rauschenberg, *Monogram*
Dance
Martha Graham, *Circe*
Alwin Nikolais, *Imago*
Drama
Neil Simon, *Barefoot in the Park*
Film
Cleopatra

Hud
The Lilies of the Field
Literature
James Baldwin, *The Fire Next Time*
New York Review of Books founded
Sylvia Plath, *The Bell Jar*
Thomas Pynchon, *V.*
Maurice Sendak, *Where the Wild Things Are*
Kurt Vonnegut, Jr., *Cat's Cradle*
Music
The Beach Boys, "Little Deuce Coupe" and "Surfin' U.S.A."
The Beatles, "I Want to Hold Your Hand"
Leonard Bernstein, *Kaddish*
Johnny Cash, "Ring of Fire"
Bob Dylan's "Blowin' in the Wind," recorded by Peter, Paul & Mary
Stan Getz, "The Girl from Ipanema"

1964

Historical Events
The Civil Rights Act bans segregation of public accommodations; Congress passes the Gulf of Tonkin Resolution, which leads to escalation of the Vietnam War; the Free Speech Movement at Berkeley sets the pattern for student protests over the next decade; Lyndon B. Johnson defeats Barry Goldwater in the presidential election; the Nobel Peace Prize is awarded to Martin Luther King.
Art & Architecture
Richard Anuszkiewicz, *Division of Intensity*
Romare Bearden, *Projections*
Andy Warhol, *Marilyn Monroe's Lips*
Drama
Edward Albee, *Tiny Alice*
Jerry Bock and Sheldon Harnick, *Fiddler on the Roof*
Jerry Herman, *Hello, Dolly!*
LeRoi Jones (Amiri Baraka), *The Slave* and *Dutchman*

Arthur Miller, *After the Fall*
Jules Styne and Bob Merrill, *Funny Girl*
Film
Dr. Strangelove
A Hard Day's Night
My Fair Lady
Literature
Saul Bellow, *Herzog*
John Berryman, *77 Dream Songs*
Ken Kesey, *Sometimes a Great Notion*
Robert Lowell, *For the Union Dead*
Theodore Roethke, *The Far Field*
Music
Milton Babbitt, *Philomel*
The Beach Boys, "I Get Around"
The Beatles appear on *The Ed Sullivan Show*
The Beatles, "Can't Buy Me Love," "A Hard Day's Night"

Bob Dylan, *The Times They Are a-Changin'*
The Supremes, "Where Did Our Love Go"

Roger Sessions, *Montezuma*

1965

Historical Events
Ken Kesey and the Merry Pranksters hold their first "Acid Test"; Martin Luther King leads a march from Selma to Montgomery, Alabama, to protest state regulations that limit black-voter registration; violent race riots involving roughly 10,000 people break out in the Watts section of Los Angeles; 40,000 antiwar protesters march in Washington, D.C.; by year's end there are 184,000 troops in Vietnam.

Art & Architecture
The Responsive Eye [Op Art], Museum of Modern Art

Drama
Neil Simon, *The Odd Couple*

Film
Help
The Sound of Music

Literature
Lenny Bruce, *How to Talk Dirty and Influence People*
Truman Capote, *In Cold Blood*

James Dickey, *Buckdancer's Choice*
Norman Mailer, *An American Dream*
Flannery O'Connor, *Everything That Rises Must Converge*
Sylvia Plath, *Ariel and Other Poems*
Tom Wolfe, *The Kandy-Kolored Tangerine-Flake Streamline Baby*

Music
Burt Bacharach and Hal David, "What the World Needs Now Is Love Sweet Love"
The Beach Boys, "Help Me, Rhonda"
The Beatles, "Eight Days a Week," "Ticket to Ride," and "Yesterday"
Leonard Bernstein, *Chichester Psalms*
James Brown, "I Got You (I Feel Good)"
The Rolling Stones, "(I Can't Get No) Satisfaction"
Gunther Schuller, *American Triptych*
Simon & Garfunkel, "The Sounds of Silence"
The Supremes, "Stop! In the Name of Love"

1966

Historical Events
Congress outlaws psychedelic drugs; the National Organization for Women (NOW) is founded; Huey P. Newton and Bobby Seale found the Black Panther Party, as Stokely Carmichael turns SNCC into a black separatist organization; 389,000 troops are in Vietnam by December.

Art & Architecture
Barnett Newman's *Stations of the Cross* (1959–1966) exhibited at the Guggenheim Museum
Edward Ruscha, *Every Building on the Sunset Strip*

Dance
Twyla Tharp, *Re-Moves*

Drama
Edward Albee, *A Delicate Balance*
Jerry Herman, *Mame*

Film
Who's Afraid of Virginia Woolf?

Literature
John Barth, *Giles Goat-Boy*
Bernard Malamud, *The Fixer*
Larry McMurtry, *The Last Picture Show*
Thomas Pynchon, *The Crying of Lot 49*

St. Mark's Poetry Project founded at St. Mark's Church-in-the-Bowery, New York
Anne Sexton, *Live or Die*
Jacqueline Susann, *Valley of the Dolls*
Hunter S. Thompson, *Hell's Angels: A Strange and Terrible Saga*

Music
Samuel Barber and Franco Zeffirelli, *Antony and Cleopatra*
The Beach Boys, "Good Vibrations"
The Beatles, "Eleanor Rigby"
The Grateful Dead, "Don't Ease Me In"
Jefferson Airplane Takes Off
Loretta Lynn, "Don't Come Home a-Drinkin' (With Lovin' on Your Mind)"
Steve Reich, *Come Out*
The Rolling Stones, "Paint It Black"
Barry Sadler, "The Ballad of the Green Berets"
Gunther Schuller, *Visitation*
The Supremes, "You Can't Hurry Love," "You Keep Me Hangin' On"
Velvet Underground, "Heroin"

TV
Star Trek

1967

Historical Events
20,000 people attend the Human Be-In in Golden Gate Park, San Francisco, to celebrate peace and love; Muhammad Ali is found guilty of draft evasion and stripped of the heavyweight boxing title; at least 50,000 antiwar demonstrators attend the March on the Pentagon; Sen. Eugene McCarthy announces that he will run for president on an antiwar platform; Dr. Benjamin Spock arrested for aiding draft resisters; 500,000 troops in Vietnam by the end of the year.

Art & Architecture
Richard Diebenkorn begins his *Ocean Park* series
Helen Frankenthaler, *Flood*
Eva Hesse, *Addendum*
Robert Motherwell begins his *Open* series

Dance
Antony Tudor, *Shadowplay*

Drama
Robert Anderson, *You Know I Can't Hear You When the Water's Running*
Galt MacDermot and Gerome Ragni, *Hair*

Film
Bonnie and Clyde

Cool Hand Luke
The Graduate
Guess Who's Coming to Dinner
In the Heat of the Night
To Sir with Love

Literature
Robert Bly, *The Light Around the Body*
Richard Brautigan, *Trout Fishing in America*
William Styron, *The Confessions of Nat Turner*

Music
The Beatles, *Sgt. Pepper's Lonely Hearts Club Band*
Country Joe and the Fish, "I-Feel-Like-I'm-Fixin'-to-Die Rag"
George Crumb, *Echoes of Time and the River*
Aretha Franklin, "Respect"
Arlo Guthrie, "Alice's Restaurant"
Gladys Knight and the Pips, "I Heard It Through the Grapevine"
Jefferson Airplane, *Surrealistic Pillow*
Jimi Hendrix Experience, "Purple Haze"
Rolling Stone magazine founded
The Rolling Stones, "Ruby Tuesday"

Frank Zappa and the Mothers of Invention, "We're Only in It for the Money"

TV
The Carol Burnett Show
Corporation for Public Broadcasting established

1968

Historical Events
Martin Luther King and presidential hopeful Robert F. Kennedy are assassinated; the Yippies (Youth International Party) are founded by antiwar activists Abbie Hoffman and Jerry Rubin; the Tet offensive in Vietnam demonstrates that the war is far from over; violence breaks out between antiwar demonstrators and Chicago police during the Democratic National Convention; Richard M. Nixon defeats Democrat Hubert H. Humphrey and third-party candidate George Wallace in the presidential election.

Drama
Robert Anderson, *I Never Sang For My Father*
Arthur Miller, *The Price*

Film
The Green Berets
Planet of the Apes
2001: A Space Odyssey

Literature
John Berryman, *His Toy, His Dream, His Rest*
Joan Didion, *Slouching Toward Bethlehem*
LeRoi Jones (Amiri Baraka) and Larry Neal, eds., *Black Fire*
Norman Mailer, *Armies of the Night*
Tom Wolfe, *The Electric Kool-Aid Acid Test*

Music
Joan Baez, *Any Day Now*
The Beatles, "Hey Jude"
James Brown, "Say It Loud (I'm Black and I'm Proud)"
Karel Husa, *Music for Prague*
Jimi Hendrix Experience, "All Along the Watchtower"
Steppenwolf, "Born to Be Wild"
Simon & Garfunkel, "Scarborough Fair," "Mrs. Robinson"
David Tudor, *Rainforest I*
Tammy Wynette, "Stand by Your Man"

TV
Laugh-In

1969

Historical Events
Neil Armstrong is the first man to set foot on the moon; the militant Weathermen seize control of SDS; Native American protesters take over Alcatraz Island; withdrawal of troops from Vietnam begins.

Art & Architecture
Christo, *Wrapped Coast – Little Bay, Australia*
Claes Oldenburg, *Lipstick (Ascending) on a Caterpillar Track*
Dennis Oppenheim, *Cancelled Crop*

Dance
Alvin Ailey, *Masekela Langage*
Jerome Robbins, *Dances at a Gathering*

Drama
Arthur Kopit, *Indians*

Film
Butch Cassidy and the Sundance Kid
Easy Rider
Midnight Cowboy
They Shoot Horses, Don't They?
The Wild Bunch
Yellow Submarine

Literature
Lillian Hellman, *An Unfinished Woman*

Vladimir Nabokov, *Ada*
Joyce Carol Oates, *them*
Ezra Pound, *Drafts and Fragments of Cantos CX–CXVII*
Philip Roth, *Portnoy's Complaint*
Anne Sexton, *Love Poems*
Kurt Vonnegut, Jr., *Slaughterhouse-Five*
Richard Wilbur, *Walking to Sleep, New Poems and Translations*

Music
Burt Bacharach and Hal David, "Raindrops Keep Fallin' on My Head"
The Beatles, *Abbey Road*
John Cage, *HPSCHD*
The Grateful Dead, *Live/Dead*
Merle Haggard, "Okie from Muskogee"
John Lennon and Yoko Ono, "Give Peace a Chance"
Frank Sinatra, "My Way"
Woodstock Art and Music Fair
Charles Wuorinen, *Time's Encomium*

TV
The Brady Bunch
Sesame Street

1970

Historical Events
Four students are killed and eight are wounded by National Guard troops during antiwar demonstrations at Kent State; an explosion in a Weatherman "bomb factory" in Greenwich Village damages the credibility of the New Left; 400,000 troops remain in Vietnam.

Art & Architecture
Dennis Oppenheim, *Reading Position for a Second Degree Burn*
Robert Smithson, *Spiral Jetty*

Film
Five Easy Pieces
M*A*S*H

Literature
Maya Angelou, *I Know Why the Caged Bird Sings*
James Dickey, *Deliverance*
Joan Didion, *Play It as It Lays*
Toni Morrison, *The Bluest Eye*
Irwin Shaw, *Rich Man, Poor Man*

Music
The Beatles, *Let It Be*
John Corigliano, *The Naked Carmen*
George Crumb, *Black Angels*
The Grateful Dead, *Workingman's Dead*
Loretta Lynn, "Coal Miner's Daughter"
Simon & Garfunkel, "Bridge Over Troubled Waters"

1971

Historical Events
Disney World opens; the National Women's Political Caucus is founded; eighteen-year-olds get the vote; publication of *The Pentagon Papers* further erodes confidence in the US war effort.

Art & Architecture
Chris Burden, *Shooting Piece*
Andrew Wyeth begins *The Helga Suite*

Drama
John Guare, *The House of Blue Leaves*
Terrence McNally, *Where Has Tommy Flowers Gone?*

David Rabe, *The Basic Training of Pavlo Hummel* and *Sticks and Bones*
Stephen Schwartz, *Godspell*
Neil Simon, *The Prisoner of Second Avenue*
Andrew Lloyd Webber and Tim Rice, *Jesus Christ Superstar*
Film
A Clockwork Orange
Dirty Harry
Klute
Play It Again Sam
Straw Dogs
Literature
E. L. Doctorow, *The Book of Daniel*
Addison Gayle, Jr., ed., *The Black Aesthetic*

Joyce Carol Oates, *Wonderland*
Flannery O'Connor, *The Complete Short Stories*
Anne Sexton, *Transformations*
John Updike, *Rabbit Redux*
Music
Joan Baez, *Blessed Are*
Leonard Bernstein, *Mass*
Elliott Carter, Third String Quartet
John Lennon, "Imagine"
The Ike and Tina Turner Revue, "Proud Mary"
The Rolling Stones, "Brown Sugar"
TV
All in the Family

1972

Historical Events
Ms. magazine is founded; President Nixon opens diplomatic relations with Communist China; Republican campaign functionaries break into Democratic national headquarters in the Watergate building in Washington, D.C.; George Wallace is shot while campaigning for the Democratic presidential election; Richard M. Nixon defeats George McGovern in the presidential election.
Art & Architecture
Judy Chicago and Miriam Schapiro, *Womanhouse*
Dance
Jerome Robbins, *Interplay*

Drama
Neil Simon, *The Sunshine Boys*
Stephen Sondheim, *A Little Night Music*
Film
The Godfather
Literature
Judy Blume, *Tales of a Fourth Grade Nothing*
Allen Ginsberg, *The Fall of America*
Eudora Welty, *The Optimist's Daughter*
Music
Joan Baez, *Come from the Shadows*

1973

Historical Events
The last US troops are withdrawn from Vietnam; the Supreme Court decision in *Roe v. Wade* legalizes abortion during the first six months of pregnancy; Senate hearings on the Watergate scandal begin; two Indians are killed during a ten-week Native American protest at Wounded Knee, South Dakota.
Dance
Twyla Tharp, *Deuce Coupe*
Drama
Lanford Wilson, *The Hot l Baltimore*
Film
American Graffiti

Mean Streets
Serpico
The Sting
Literature
Lillian Hellman, *Pentimento*
Erica Jong, *Fear of Flying*
Robert Lowell, *The Dolphin*
Toni Morrison, *Sula*
Thomas Pynchon, *Gravity's Rainbow*
Music
The Rolling Stones, "Angie"
Gladys Knight and the Pips, "Midnight Train to Georgia"
Eric Weissberg and Steve Mandell, "Dueling Banjos"

1974

Historical Events
Faced with impeachment for his role in the Watergate cover-up, Richard M. Nixon resigns the presidency and is replaced by Gerald R. Ford.
Film
Chinatown
The Godfather, Part II
Nashville

Young Frankenstein
Literature
Stephen King, *Carrie*
Music
Merle Haggard, "If We Make It Through December"
Patti Smith, "Hey Joe" and "Piss Factory"

1975

Historical Events
North Vietnamese and Vietcong forces complete their takeover of South Vietnam.
Dance
Martha Graham, *Lucifer* and *The Scarlet Letter*
Paul Taylor, *Esplanade*
Drama
James Kirkwood, Nicholas Dante, and Michael Bennett, *A Chorus Line*
Terrence McNally, *The Ritz*
Film
Dog Day Afternoon
Jaws

Love and Death
The Man Who Would Be King
One Flew Over the Cuckoo's Nest
Literature
John Ashbery, *Self Portrait on a Convex Mirror*
Saul Bellow, *Humboldt's Gift*
E. L. Doctorow, *Ragtime*
Music
Otto Luening, *Wisconsin Symphony*
Bruce Springsteen, *Born to Run*
TV
Saturday Night Live

1976

Historical Events
Jimmy Carter defeats Gerald Ford in the presidential election.
Art & Architecture
Christo, *Running Fence* (1972–1976)
Dance
Twyla Tharp, *Push Comes to Shove*
Drama
David Rabe, *Streamers*
Neil Simon, *California Suite*
Film
All the President's Men
Network
Rocky

Taxi Driver
Literature
Anne Rice, *Interview With the Vampire*
Anne Tyler, *Searching for Caleb*
Alice Walker, *Meridian*
Music
Joan Baez, "Diamonds and Rust"
Philip Glass, *Einstein on the Beach*
The Ramones, "Now I Wanna Sniff Some Glue"
Ned Rorem, *Air Music*
Paul Simon, "Fifty Ways to Leave Your Lover"

1977

Historical Events
President Carter pardons most Vietnam-era draft evaders.
Drama
David Mamet, *American Buffalo*
Neil Simon, *Chapter Two*
Charles Strauss and Martin Charnin, *Annie*
Film
Annie Hall
Julia
Star Wars

Literature
James Dickey reads "The Strength of Fields" at a celebration preceding the inauguration of President Carter.
Joan Didion, *A Book of Common Prayer*
Toni Morrison, *Song of Solomon*
Stephen King, *The Shining*
Music
Talking Heads, "Psycho Killer"
Richard Hell and the Voidoids, "(I Belong to) The Blank Generation"

1978

Historical Events
The Supreme Court refuses to allow strict quota systems in affirmative-action plans to establish racial equality in college and university enrollments.
Drama
Sam Shepard, *Buried Child*
Lanford Wilson, *5th of July*
Film
Blazing Saddles

Coming Home
The Deer Hunter
Manhattan
Literature
John Irving, *The World According to Garp*
James Jones, *Whistle*
Irwin Shaw, *Short Stories: Five Decades*
Music
The Police, "Roxanne"

1979

Historical Events
An accident at the Three Mile Island nuclear-power plant in Pennsylvania releases radiation into the environment; followers of the Ayatollah Khomeini occupy the American embassy in Teheran, Iran, and hold 52 Americans hostage.
Drama
Stephen Sondheim, *Sweeney Todd*
Lanford Wilson, *Talley's Folly*
Film
Apocalypse Now

The China Syndrome
Kramer vs. Kramer
Wise Blood
Literature
Norman Mailer, *The Executioner's Song*
William Styron, *Sophie's Choice*
Music
The Police, "Message in a Bottle"
The Sugar Hill Gang, "Rapper's Delight"

1980

Historical Events
President Carter announces a trade embargo against the USSR to retaliate for its invasion of Afghanistan; 8 Americans are killed in an abortive attempt to free the Iran hostages; Ronald Reagan defeats Jimmy Carter in the presidential election.
Drama
Beth Henley, *Crimes of the Heart*
Film
Coal Miner's Daughter
The Empire Strikes Back
First Blood
Ordinary People

Raging Bull
The Shining
Literature
Joyce Carol Oates, *Bellefleur*
John Kennedy Toole, *A Confederacy of Dunces*
Music
John Lennon and Yoko Ono, *Double Fantasy*
Dolly Parton, "Nine to Five"
Willie Nelson, "On the Road Again"
Joan Tower, *Petroushskates*
TV
CNN founded

1981

Historical Events
The AIDS virus is identified; the Iran hostages are freed; President Reagan is shot by a would-be assassin; Sandra Day O'Connor becomes the first female Supreme Court justice.

Drama
Harvey Fierstein, *Torchsong Trilogy*
Andrew Lloyd Webber, *Cats*

Film
The French Lieutenant's Woman
Raiders of the Lost Ark
Reds
Literature
Raymond Carver, *What We Talk About When We Talk About Love*
John Irving, *The Hotel New Hampshire*
Sylvia Plath, *Collected Poems*
Toni Morrison, *Tar Baby*

John Updike, *Rabbit Is Rich*
Music
Roger Sessions, *Concerto for Orchestra*
TV
Hill Street Blues
MTV

1982

Historical Events
The Equal Rights Amendment is defeated after a ten-year ratification struggle; Congress virtually eliminates busing to achieve racial integration of schools.
Drama
Sam Shepard, *True West*
Film
E.T.: The Extra-Terrestrial
Sophie's Choice
The Verdict

Literature
Joyce Carol Oates, *A Bloodsmoor Romance*
Isaac Bashevis Singer, *Collected Stories*
Alice Walker, *The Color Purple*
Music
Laurie Anderson, *Big Science*
Michael Jackson, *Thriller*
George Rochberg, *The Confidence Man*
Frank Zappa, "Valley Girl"

1983

Historical Events
The USSR shoots down a South Korean civilian airliner that has strayed into Soviet air space; a suicide bomber blows up a US Marine installation in Beirut, Lebanon, killing 241; US troops invade Granada, overthrowing its Marxist government.
Drama
Tina Howe, *Painting Church*
David Mamet, *Glengarry, Glen Ross*
Marsha Norman, *'night, Mother*
Sam Shepard, *Fool for Love*
Neil Simon, *Brighton Beach Memoirs*
Simon, *Biloxi Blues*
Film
The Big Chill

Return of the Jedi
Terms of Endearment
Yentl
Zelig
Literature
Raymond Carver, *Cathedral*
William Kennedy, *Ironweed*
Stephen King, *Pet Sematary*
Norman Mailer, *Ancient Evenings*
Bernard Malamud, *The Stories*
Music
Alabama, "The Closer You Get"
Laurie Anderson, *United States*
Talking Heads, "Burning Down the House"

1984

Historical Events
Ronald Reagan defeats Walter Mondale in the presidential election.
Dance
Alvin Ailey, *For Bird – With Love*
Drama
August Wilson, *Ma Rainey's Black Bottom*
Film
Amadeus
Birdy
Broadway Danny Rose

Indiana Jones and the Temple of Doom
The Terminator
Literature
Allen Ginsberg, *Collected Poems, 1947–1980*
Alison Lurie, *Foreign Affairs*
Jay McInerney, *Bright Lights, Big City*
Joyce Carol Oates, *Mysteries of Winterthurn*
Music
George Crumb, *Haunted Landscapes*
Michael Jackson, "Billy Jean"
Madonna, "Like a Virgin"

1985

Historical Events
Mikhail Gorbachev comes to power in the USSR.
Film
The Color Purple
Out of Africa
Prizzi's Honor
The Purple Rose of Cairo
Literature
E. L. Doctorow, *World's Fair*

Larry McMurtry, *Lonesome Dove*
Anne Rice, *The Vampire Lestat*
Anne Tyler, *The Accidental Tourist*
Music
Farm Aid
Live Aid
Bruce Springsteen, *Born in the U.S.A.*
Tina Turner, "What's Love Got to Do with It?"
USA for Africa, "We Are the World"

1986

Historical Events
The US space shuttle *Challenger* explodes on takeoff; the US bombs Libya in retaliation for its harboring terrorists; a major fire at the Chernobyl nuclear-power plant in the USSR releases clouds of radiation that affect all of Europe.
Film
The Color of Money

Empire of the Sun
Hannah and Her Sisters
Platoon
Drama
Tina Howe, *Coastal Disturbances*
Andrew Lloyd Webber, *The Phantom of the Opera*
August Wilson, *Fences*

Literature
Isaac Asimov, *Foundation and Earth*
Larry Heinemann, *Paco's Story*
Peter Taylor, *A Summons to Memphis*

Music
Madonna, *True Blue*
Run-D.M.C., *Raising Hell*
Paul Simon, *Graceland*

1987

Historical Events
Gorbachev announces a policy of domestic reform and openness toward the West.

Drama
Herbert Kretzmer, *Les Misérables*
Terrence McNally, *Frankie and Johnny at the Clair de Lune*
Neil Simon, *Broadway Bound*
Lanford Wilson, *Burn This!*

Film
Full Metal Jacket
Good Morning, Vietnam
Ironweed
The Last Emperor
The Untouchables
Wall Street

Literature
Truman Capote, *Answered Prayers*
James Dickey, *Alnilam*
E. D. Hirsch, *Cultural Literacy*
Stephen King, *Misery*
Toni Morrison, *Beloved*
Joyce Carol Oates, *You Must Remember This*
Philip Roth, *The Counterlife*
Tom Wolfe, *The Bonfire of the Vanities*

Music
John Adams, *Nixon in China*
The Grateful Dead, *In the Dark*

1988

Historical Events
The USSR begins to withdraw troops from Afghanistan; George Bush defeats Michael Dukakis in the presidential election.

Drama
Wendy Wasserstein, *The Heidi Chronicles*
August Wilson, *Joe Turner's Come and Gone*

Film
Rain Man

Literature
Pete Dexter, *Paris Trout*
Larry McMurtry, *Anything for Billy*
Anne Rice, *The Queen of the Damned*
Anne Tyler, *Breathing Lessons*
Richard Wilbur, *New and Collected Poems*

Music
William Bolcom, *Twelve New Etudes*
Ellen Taaffe Zwilich, *Sybolom*

1989

Historical Events
Chinese troops kill thousands of prodemocracy student demonstrators in Beijing; the Berlin Wall comes down as Communist rule of East Germany ends; Communist domination of Czechoslovakia and Rumania comes to an end.

Drama
A. R. Gurney, *Love Letters*
Terrence McNally, *The Lisbon Traviata*

Film
Born on the Fourth of July
Crimes and Misdemeanors
Do the Right Thing
Driving Miss Daisy
Indiana Jones and the Last Crusade

Literature
John Casey, *Spartina*
E. L. Doctorow, *Billy Bathgate*
Oscar Hijuelo, *The Mambo Kings Play Songs of Love*
Alice Walker, *The Temple of My Familiar*

Music
Martin Puryear, *Lever #3*

1990

Historical Events
Communists lose control of Bulgaria, Yugoslavia, Poland, and the USSR; East and West Germany are united; Iraq invades Kuwait, and the UN authorizes the use of force against Iraq.

Drama
John Guare, *Six Degrees of Separation*
Neil Simon, *Lost in Yonkers*
August Wilson, *The Piano Lesson*

Film
Batman
Dances with Wolves
Dick Tracy
The Godfather, Part III
Goodfellas
Mo' Better Blues

Literature
Robert Bly, *Iron John*
Charles Johnson, *The Middle Passage*
Thomas Pynchon, *Vineland*
John Updike, *Rabbit at Rest*

Music
John Corigliano, Symphony No. 1
Paul Simon, *Rhythm of the Saints*

1991

Historical Events
The Gulf War; the Union of South Africa repeals apartheid laws; fighting erupts in Yugoslavia as Slovenia and Croatia secede; the Warsaw pact is dissolved; the USSR breaks up, with most of its republics joining a loose Confederation of Independent States.

Drama
August Wilson, *Two Trains Running*

Film
Bugsy
Cape Fear
JFK
Jungle Fever
Mr. and Mrs. Bridge
The Prince of Tides
The Silence of the Lambs
Terminator 2: Judgment Day

Literature
Norman Rush, *Mating*
Jane Smiley, *A Thousand Acres*

Music
John Adams, *The Death of Klinghoffer*

1992

Historical Events
Fighting between Serbs and Muslims breaks out in Bosnia-Herzegovena as that country secedes from Yugoslavia; William Clinton defeats George Bush in the presidential election; US troops join a UN relief mission to Somalia.

Drama
David Mamet, *Oleanna*
Wendy Wasserstein, *The Sisters Rosensweig*

Film
Glengarry, Glen Ross
A League of Their Own
The Player
Scent of a Woman
Unforgiven

Literature
Robert Olen Butler, *A Good Scent from a Strange Mountain*
James Dickey, *The Whole Motion: Collected Poems 1945–1992*
Ken Kesey, *Sailor Song*
Cormac McCarthy, *All the Pretty Horses*
Toni Morrison, *Jazz*
Anne Tyler, *Saint Maybe*

Music
John Corigliano, *The Ghosts of Versailles*
Ice T, "Cop Killer"
Joan Tower, Violin Concerto

1993

Historical Events
450,000 Americans are infected with AIDS; President Clinton proposes a national health plan that would provide universal insurance coverage.

Drama
Terrence McNally, John Kander, and Fred Ebb, *Kiss of the Spider Woman*
Lanford Wilson, *Redwood Curtain*

Film
The Age of Innocence
A Few Good Men
Jurassic Park
Schindler's List
Short Cuts

Literature
Nobel Prize for Literature: Toni Morrison
Maya Angelou reads "On the Pulse of Morning" at Clinton's inauguration.
James Dickey, *To the White Sea*
Joyce Carol Oates, *Foxfire: Confessions of a Girl Gang*
E. Annie Proulx, *The Shipping News*
Philip Roth, *Operation Shylock: A Confession*

Music
Steve Reich, *The Cave*

TV
NYPD Blue

DICTIONARY OF

TWENTIETH
CENTURY
CULTURE

American Culture
After World War II

A

GEORGE ABBOTT

George Abbott (1887–) is a gifted, practical playwright, director, and producer of legendary longevity. He is best known as a director of **Broadway musicals:** between 1935 and 1962 twenty-two of the twenty-six musicals he directed were extremely successful. He also influenced many who worked under him, including **Michael Bennett, Bob Fosse,** and **Harold Prince.**

Abbott made his Broadway acting debut in 1913. His career took off with the enormous success of *Broadway* (1926), which he wrote and directed with Philip Dunning and which ran for 603 performances. Abbott's specialties were melodramas, farces, and musicals. Some of his most successful plays of the 1930s were collaborations with the musical team of Richard Rodgers and Lorenz Hart.

Abbott followed his pre–World War II successes with several hits. In 1944 he directed *On the Town;* written by **Betty Comden and Adolph Green** with music by **Leonard Bernstein** and choreography by **Jerome Robbins,** this musical ran for 462 performances. Abbott worked with the same team on *Wonderful Town* (1953; 559 performances). He also wrote and directed *Where's Charley?* (1948; 792 performances), with music by **Frank Loesser.**

Abbott's greatest successes came after he turned sixty. He wrote *The Pajama Game* (1954; 1,061 performances) with Richard Bissell and directed it with Robbins. He directed *Damn Yankees* (1955; 1,019 performances), which he wrote with Douglass Wallop, and he directed *A Funny Thing Happened on the Way to the Forum* (1962; 966 performances), a musical by Burt Shevelove and Larry Gelbart with music by **Stephen Sondheim.** With Stanley Donen, Abbott also directed the film versions of *The Pajama Game* (1957), which starred **Doris Day**, and *Damn Yankees* (1958). Though he never achieved this level of success again, he remained active in Broadway into his nineties. In 1983, seventy years after his first participation in the Broadway theater, Abbott directed a successful revival of *On Your Toes,* the Rodgers and Hart musical he had first directed in 1936.

REFERENCES:
George Abbott, *"Mister Abbott"* (New York: Random House, 1963);
Martin Gottfried, *Broadway Musicals* (New York: Abrams, 1979).
                                                                                                    – I.R.H.

ABC

ABC (American Broadcasting Company) was one of the "Big Three" television networks that dominated commercial television in America until the explosive growth of the cable-television industry in the 1980s.

ABC was formed as a radio network in 1943 when the U.S. government forced the Radio Corporation of America (RCA) to break up its alleged monopoly of the radio industry by selling one of its two networks. RCA kept the "NBC-red" network and sold the six "NBC-blue" radio stations, which became ABC, to Lifesavers candy magnate Edward J. Noble for $8 million.

When the radio networks began to expand to include the new medium of television in the late 1940s, ABC trailed its two chief rivals, **NBC (National Broadcasting Company)** and **CBS (Columbia Broadcasting System),** and began broadcasting television programs in April 1948. In 1953 ABC merged with the United Paramount Theaters company, which gave it the working capital necessary to survive the lean early years when other networks, such as DuMont and the Mutual Broadcasting System, fell by the wayside. In 1954 ABC achieved its first coup by broadcasting the Army-McCarthy hearings, Sen. **Joseph McCarthy**'s investigation into Communist infiltration of the armed forces. Over the next two years ABC contracted with the **Disney** and Warner Bros. studios to produce programs for the network, and its position as one of the Big Three was assured.

Throughout the 1960s ABC countered its competitors' more prestigious shows with highly successful violent melodramas such as *The Untouchables* (1959–1963). Also during the decade it took the lead in sports coverage, premiering the long-running *Wide World of Sports* in 1961. The network broadcast the Olympic games of the 1960s and 1970s, and in 1971 it brought professional sports to weekly prime time with *Monday Night Football,* which ran continuously and profitably for more than twenty years.

The high point of the network's success came in the 1970s. Fred Silverman, named president of ABC Entertainment in 1975, produced a string of lightweight but popular shows, including *Laverne & Shirley* and *Charlie's Angels.* The network's most important offering, however, was *Roots,* an ambitious production of Alex Haley's family history which ABC telecast over eight consecutive nights. Owing to the success of *Roots* (several of its episodes were the most-watched programs ever to that time), the network became the highest-rated network for the first time in 1977.

During the 1980s, an era of corporate mergers, the three major networks, weakened by the growing popularity of cable television, were ripe for takeover. In 1985 Capital Cities, a group of ABC affiliate stations that had also grown wealthy through investments in cable networks, took over its parent network for $3.5 billion.

REFERENCES:

Erik Barnouw, *Tube of Plenty: The Evolution of American Television,* revised edition (New York & Oxford: Oxford University Press, 1990);

Leonard H. Goldenson, *Beating the Odds* (New York: Scribners, 1991).

– C.D.B.

ABSTRACT EXPRESSIONISM

Abstract Expressionism was the first important twentieth-century movement in the visual arts to originate in the United States. With the development of the movement in the mid 1940s the center of the art world shifted from Paris to New York. Abstract Expression

Eight of the Abstract Expressionists whose works were included in the New American Painting exhibition at the Museum of Modern Art in 1958, with Dorothy Miller, organizer of the show, seated at center: (seated in front) Jack Tworkov, Barnett Newman, and Sam Francis; (back row) Theodore Stamos, James Brooks, Philip Guston, Franz Kline, and William Baziotes

dominated American painting through the late 1950s. Painters identified as Abstract Expressionists are usually grouped together as the **New York School.** The goal of these artists was to discover a new form of abstract painting that would be an advance on the French avant-garde work that had dominated the modern movement since before World War II.

The so-called first generation of New York School artists includes **Jackson Pollock, Willem de Kooning, Mark Rothko, Barnett Newman,** Hans Hofmann, **Philip Guston,** Clyfford Still, **Robert Motherwell,** Franz Kline, and Lee Krasner. Born during the first two decades of the twentieth century, they were friends and mentors to the second generation, which included **Helen Frankenthaler,** Larry Rivers, Joan Mitchell, and Elaine de Kooning, all of whom were born in the 1920s.

Although the term *Abstract Expressionism* covers a wide range of personal styles, most can be classified as action painting or color-field painting.

Action painters such as Pollock and Willem de Kooning spontaneously applied paint to their canvases, leaving visual records of the gestures they performed during the act of painting; thus action paint is alternately called gestural painting. Their method of creating abstract imagery largely relied on their physical movements, decisive strokes (which in de Kooning's case could also be endlessly revised), and a strong psychological involvement in the act of applying paint to canvas.

The hallmark of color-field painting, developed primarily by Rothko and Newman, was the use of a limited palette to create expansive yet simple areas of pure, flat color. Unlike action painting, these huge canvases create a sense of calmness, and their compositions were the result of a more premeditated approach. Rothko and Newman hoped to evoke profoundly emotional, even spiritual, responses in viewers through abstract imagery that was intended to be transcendental, as well as timeless. Both veins of Abstract Expressionism share a common source in the Surrealist belief in the use of the artist's unconscious to recognize and create artistic forms.

As Abstract Expressionism evolved through the late 1940s (when most of the first-generation artists found their mature styles) into the 1950s, many of its defenders perceived it as a heroic stand against bourgeois values. Critics such as **Clement Greenberg** and **Harold Rosenberg** hailed the Abstract Expressionists as ethically superior to American artists whose styles and subject matter were dictated by what the public seemed to want and were largely responsible for their widespread acceptance.

In 1958 the **Museum of Modern Art** organized a major Abstract Expressionist exhibition, New American Painting, which toured Europe for two years. By 1960 Abstract Expressionists had influenced critics, collectors and art schools in the United States to the extent that it seemed the only stylistic option for many painters. Much derivative work resulted. Yet in the late 1950s and early 1960s a host of insurgent, competing styles — including **Pop Art, Post-Painterly Abstraction, Happenings,** and **New Realism** — arose to challenge the dominance of Abstract Expressionism.

REFERENCES:

Clement Greenberg, *Art and Culture: Critical Essays* (Boston: Beacon Press, 1961);

Serge Guilbaut, *How New York Stole the Idea of Modern Art: Abstract Expressionism, Freedom, and the Cold War,* translated by Arthur Goldhammer (Chicago & London: University of Chicago Press, 1983);

Harold Rosenberg, "American Action Painters," *Art News,* 51 (December 1952): 22–23, 48–50;

Irving Sandler, *The New York School: The Painters and Sculptors of the Fifties* (New York: Icon/Harper & Row, 1978).

– K.B.

ACADEMY OF MOTION PICTURE ARTS AND SCIENCES

The Academy of Motion Picture Arts and Sciences (AMPAS) is probably the best-known professional arts organization in the world due to its sponsorship of the Academy Awards (Oscars). Since the annual ceremony was first televised in 1953, it has become an international event viewed by hundreds of millions of people worldwide.

Giving awards, however, was an afterthought for Academy founders. In early January 1927 Louis B. Mayer, head of Metro-Goldwyn-Mayer, along with actor Conrad Nagel, director Fred Niblo, and producer Fred Beetson, came up with the idea of creating an industry-wide body to deal with labor disputes, to improve the film community's public image, and to promote technical advances. A week later, on 11 January, Mayer presented the idea to thirty-six Hollywood executives (mostly producers) at a banquet at the Ambassador Hotel in Los Angeles, and the Academy was born. After many struggles with competing bodies, the Academy abandoned its attempts to be a labor-relations body in 1937. By then the Academy was well known for its annual awards.

The first awards, honoring films released between 1 August 1927 and 31 July 1928, were announced in February 1929 and presented at an awards banquet in May. *Wings* was named best picture. The distinctive statuette, designed by M-G-M art director Cedric Gibbons, was nicknamed Oscar in the early 1930s, probably by Margaret Herrick, the Academy librarian and later its executive director (1943–1970). The impressive Academy research library, which has extensive archives, is named in Herrick's honor. The Academy also maintains state-of-the-art projection facilities in its Samuel Goldwyn Theatre and publishes the casting director's bible, *The Academy Players Directory.* It sponsors student internships and, since 1973, the Student Film Awards Competition.

REFERENCES:

Richard Shale, *The Academy Awards Index: The Complete Categorical and Chronological Record* (Westport, Conn.: Greenwood, 1993);

Mason Wiley and Damien Bona, *Inside Oscar: The Unofficial History of the Academy Awards,* edited by Gail MacColl (New York: Ballantine, 1986).

– I.R.H.

ACID ROCK

Acid rock is a musical product of the so-called **hippie** drug culture of the late 1960s. It evolved from the psychedelic rock music that came out of the **Haight-Ashbury** area of San Francisco in 1965–1967. The

Haight-Ashbury bands, including the **Grateful Dead** and **Jefferson Airplane,** were the first to use light shows in their performances, which — during their early days in California — were intended to create a congenial atmosphere in which to take psychedelic drugs such as LSD (lysergic acid diethylamide), or acid. The best-known example of psychedelic rock is the **Beatles**' 1967 album, *Sgt. Pepper's Lonely Hearts Club Band,* influenced by the new "San Francisco Sound."

While psychedelic musicians experimented with effects that could be created with electronic instruments and sound equipment, acid rockers carried electronic audio distortions (including intentional audio feedback). The most notable acid rocker was Jimi Hendrix, who emerged in summer 1967 at the Monterey Pop Festival. He stunned audiences with his high-volume dramatic performances and the sounds he could create with an electric guitar, sometimes destroying one on stage. His drug-related death in 1970 essentially killed acid rock, but its influence is apparent in the heavy-metal sound of the early 1970s. The music of the California band Iron Butterfly, whose song "In-A-Gadda-Da-Vida" was a **Top 40** record in 1968, is sometime described as a transition between acid rock and **heavy metal**.

REFERENCES:

Curtis Knight, *Jimi: An Intimate Biography of Jimi Hendrix* (New York: Praeger, 1974);

Jim Miller, ed., *The Rolling Stone History of Rock & Roll* (New York: Rolling Stone Press/Random House, 1976);

Charles Shaar Murray, *Crosstown Traffic: Jimi Hendrix and the Post-War Rock'n'Roll Revolution* (New York: St. Martin's Press, 1989).

– L.D.S.

ACTORS STUDIO

Actors Studio, founded in 1947, took the lead in advocating the Method style of acting, which became a primary force in American drama and film during the 1950s and 1960s.

A professional performers' workshop, Actors Studio was started by Cheryl Crawford, **Elia Kazan**, and Robert Lewis. Lee Strasberg, who joined them in 1948, taught Method acting by adapting performance techniques originated by Russian director Konstantin Stanislavsky. In this style of acting the performer is taught to identify with the inner emotions of the character and to employ natural speech and movement.

Actors Studio, whose membership is limited and by invitation only, became a mecca for aspiring actors. The performers Strasberg trained include **Marlon**

Brando, Geraldine Page, **Montgomery Clift, James Dean**, Julie Harris, **Paul Newman,** Joanne Woodward, and Rod Steiger.

REFERENCES:

David Garfield, *A Player's Place: The Story of the Actors Studio* (New York: Macmillan, 1980);

Foster Hirsch, *A Method to their Madness: The History of the Actors Studio* (New York: Norton, 1984).

– I.R.H.

ACTORS THEATRE OF LOUISVILLE

Since the late 1970s the Actors Theatre of Louisville, Kentucky, has been a major regional theater, well known for launching new American plays that become successful nationwide.

The Actors Theatre of Louisville was created in 1964 by the merger of two recently established acting companies: Theatre Louisville, organized by Richard Block, and Actors, Inc., founded by Ewel Cornet. Block assumed full duties as artistic director in 1965. In 1969 Actors Theatre began on the road to national significance when its board of directors brought in Jon Jory, cofounder of the Long Wharf Theatre in New Haven, Connecticut, as producing director.

In 1977 Jory established the Festival of New American Plays, which has been funded by the Humana Corporation since 1979. Until 1986 Actors Theatre also sponsored an annual, nationwide Great American Play Contest, offering cash prizes for two full-length plays, which were later produced in the festival.

The first Festival of New American Plays, held in spring 1977, launched D. L. Coburn's *The Gin Game,* which went on to Broadway later that year and won the 1978 Pulitzer Prize for Drama. **Marsha Norman**'s *Getting Out,* a winner in the first Great American Play Contest, was produced in the second festival (1977–1978) and opened Off Broadway in 1978 for a successful run. **Beth Henley**'s *Crimes of the Heart* was a winner in the second contest and was staged in the 1978–1979 festival before it opened on Broadway in 1980 and won the 1981 Pulitzer Prize for Drama. Among the other new plays that went on to Broadway or Off Broadway after premiering in the Festival of New American Plays are James McLure's *Lone Star* (1978–1979 festival) and *Thanksgiving* (1982–1983 festival); John Pielmeier's *Agnes of God* (1979–1980 festival) and *Courage* (1982–1983 festival); William Mastrosimone's *Extremities* (1980–1981 festival); Wendy Kesselman's *My Sister in this House* (1980–1981 festival); Jane Martin's *Talking With* (1981–1982 festival); Kathleen Tolan's *A Weekend Near Madison* (1982–

1983 festival); John Patrick Shanley's *Danny and the Deep Blue Sea* (1983–1984 festival); Patrick Tovatt's *Husbandry* (1983–1984 festival); Mary Gallagher's *How to Say Goodbye* (1985–1986 festival); Deborah Pryor's *The Love Talker* (1986–1987 festival); and Constance Congdon's *Tales of the Last Formicans* (1988–1989 festival).

– I.R.H.

Roy Acuff

Widely acclaimed as the "King of Country Music," Roy Acuff (1903–1993) performed for more than half a century at the Grand Ole Opry in Nashville, Tennessee, and was one of the first country singers to develop a national following.

Born in Maynardsville, Tennessee, Acuff mastered the country fiddle and the guitar in his youth and formed his first band in 1933. When they began appearing with Acuff at the Grand Ole Opry in 1938, he named the group the Smoky Mountain Boys.

"The Great Speckled Bird," an old song with added verses that Acuff recorded in 1937, became a hit after Acuff performed it during his first Grand Ole Opry appearance, on 5 February 1938. The decision of **NBC** to air radio broadcasts of the Grand Ole Opry in 1939 created thousands of new **country-music** fans. During World War II, Acuff was more popular than **Frank Sinatra** with American soldiers, who delighted in blasting Acuff's music over loudspeakers at the Japanese. Acuff's distinctive, forceful vocal style — displaying his roots in Irish and English folk music — set him apart from the "crooners" who dominated country music at that time. Hundreds of his songs — such as "Precious Jewel," which he wrote and recorded in 1940, and his new renditions of old favorites, including "Night Train to Memphis" (1942) and "Wabash Cannonball" (Acuff's vocal version, 1947) — became hits and remained popular throughout his career.

Acuff was largely responsible for the success of the Grand Ole Opry, which in turn fostered the careers of the many young country singers who became well known in the 1950s and 1960s. Acuff-Rose Publications, founded by Acuff and songwriter Fred Rose in 1943, launched **Hank Williams**'s career and still produces many country and gospel standards. In 1962 Acuff was the first living person ever elected to the Country Music Hall of Fame.

REFERENCES:
Jack Hurst, *Nashville's Grand Ole Opry* (New York: Abrams, 1975);

Roy Acuff (right) teaching President Richard M. Nixon how to spin a yo-yo at the opening of the new Grand Ole Opry House in Nashville, Tennessee, 16 March 1974 (WSM photograph by Les Leverett)

Elizabeth Schlappi, *Roy Acuff: The Smoky Mountain Boy* (Gretna, La.: Pelican Publishing, 1978).

– L.D.S.

Ansel Adams

As a landscape photographer, master photographic technician, and conservationist, Ansel Adams (1902–1984) achieved a level of popular success and professional prestige rare among American photographers. Books, posters, and calendars brought his pristine images of American wilderness to a huge and appreciative mass audience, while in the late 1970s his photographs commanded the highest prices ever paid by dealers and collectors for prints by a living American photographer.

Adams's vision of the western landscape focused on its vastness, elemental purity, and irreplaceable value as a source of spiritual inspiration. Born in San Francisco, he took his first photographs of Yosemite Valley as a teenager in 1916 and returned there periodically throughout his life to explore, climb, and photograph. At twenty-six he became the official photographer for the Sierra Club, the preservationist organization (founded in 1892) that was largely responsible for the formation of the National Park Service. Throughout the late 1940s and the 1950s — aided by

Guggenheim Fellowships in 1946–1947, 1948–1949, and 1959–1961 — Adams created a formidable body of photographs taken in national parks and other wilderness areas. As his career progressed, he increasingly became identified as an important proponent of the preservationist ethic that made his photographs especially popular in the environmentalist climate of the 1970s.

Technically, Adams took the medium of black-and-white photography to extremes of definition and tonal range (contrasts between light and dark). He is important for his development of the "zone system," a method for controlling the tonal range of photographic prints. Dividing the shades of gray into numbered zones, the system essentially standardized many aspects of the photographic process, including exposure time and development method. The seminal technical manuals in his Basic Photo Series (1948–1956; revised, 1977–1981) continue to be influential.

During the last years of his life Adams was treated as an honored patriarch in photographic circles and beyond. In awarding him the Presidential Medal of Freedom in 1980, President Jimmy Carter called Adams "visionary in his efforts to preserve this country's wild and scenic areas, on film and on earth."

REFERENCE:

Ansel Adams, *Ansel Adams: An Autobiography* (Boston: Little, Brown, 1985).

– K.B.

John Adams

John Coolidge Adams (1947–) is a leader among the American composers who write in the eclectic style known as **minimalism**.

Having been chairman of the composition faculty at the San Francisco Conservatory (1971–1981) and composer-in-residence with the San Francisco Symphony Orchestra (1982–1985), Adams now enjoys international renown for his works. Among his many published compositions are *Shaker Loops* for string septet (1978; arranged for string orchestra, 1983) and *Phrygian Gates* for piano (1977). Adams's best-known works are two refreshingly contemporary operas in a minimalist vein: *Nixon in China* (1987), about President Richard M. Nixon's 1972 trip to China; and *The Death of Klinghoffer* (1991), dealing with the 1985 murder of Leon Klinghoffer, a wheelchair-bound passenger, on the hijacked cruise ship *Achille Lauro*.

As a composer, Adams is best described as a modernist among minimalists. He has emerged as one of the most original and provocative composers of the latter half of the twentieth century.

– L.D.S.

Stella Adler

Stella Adler (1901–1993), a distinguished actress and theatrical director, was one of the finest acting teachers in twentieth-century America.

The daughter of prominent performers in the Yiddish theater, Adler made her stage debut as a child. In 1931 she joined the acting company of the new Group Theatre, founded that year by Harold Clurman, Lee Strasberg, and Cheryl Crawford. Like Strasberg, who went on to teach acting at **Actors Studio,** Adler advocated a performance technique based on the principles developed by Konstantin Stanislavsky. Yet she disapproved of Strasberg's idiosyncratic "Method." Adler trained students to create characters by letting their imaginations react to the words in the play and the historical context of the plot, while Strasberg taught actors to inject their personal experiences into the portrayal of fictional characters.

Adler began to teach acting in the Erwin Piscator Dramatic Workshop at the New School of Social Research in New York (1940–1942). In 1949 she founded her own school, the Stella Adler Theatre Studio. It was renamed the Stella Adler Conservatory of Acting in 1960 and became affiliated with New York University in 1979. Some of its graduates are **Marlon Brando,** Eddie Albert, **Warren Beatty,** and **Robert De Niro.** Adler also taught acting at the Yale Drama School (1967–1968), and again at the New School of Social Research (1970–1972).

– I.R.H.

African-American Art

African-American artists have worked in a variety of styles since 1945, complicating the ongoing debate over defining black art and proving that knowledge of the maker's ethnic background offers only limited understanding of the work.

Figurative imagery that addresses American social conditions has always been employed in African-American art, as in the romantic-realist paintings of Hughie Lee-Smith (1914–) and the geometricized canvasses of Charles Alston (1907–1977). Since the 1930s, however, there have always been black artists who have self-consciously chosen other methods. Norman Lewis (1909–1979) and Hale Woodruff (1900–1980) were among those artists exploring personal means to apply Cubist, Surrealist, and **abstract-expressionist** techniques in their work.

By 1960 sculptor Richard Hunt (1935–   ), painter **Jacob Lawrence** (1917–   ), and collagist **Romare Bearden** (1911–1988) were among the most respected African-American artists in the nation.

Hunt's early works are welded steel figures. These abstract, linear, open constructions often include junked automobile parts and found objects. He was a twenty-year-old student at the Art Institute of Chicago when the **Museum of Modern Art** purchased *Arachne* (1956). Two years later *Extending Horizontal Form* sold to the Whitney Museum of American Art. During the late 1960s Hunt began making solid aluminum forms with twisted and distorted parts that assumed human, animal, or plant-like properties. Throughout his career Hunt has focused on the technical aspects of sculpture rather than social or political themes.

Jacob Lawrence employs simple color schemes, sharp angles, and strong designs in gouache and tempera paintings that recount the social history and protest of African Americans. His painting style has been linked to that of social realist Ben Shahn and early American modernist Arthur Dove. Several of his paintings have been reproduced in popular magazines such as *Fortune* and *Vogue*. In 1970 he became the first painter to receive the NAACP Spingarn Medal for his long-time commitment to portraying Black America.

Romare Bearden, who realized similar popularity, was a leading figure during the **Black Arts Movement** of the 1960s. In 1963 Bearden was a founder of the Spiral Group of black artists who met to discuss their role in the **civil rights movement.** Bearden wanted the group to collaborate on a collage made from cutouts each member selected from a large file of pictures he had compiled from various publications. Alone in his enthusiasm for this idea, Bearden adopted it himself and produced some of his best-known works. He describes his tightly composed collages as works that "redefine the image of man in terms of the Black experience I know best."

A large number of African American abstract artists emerged in the 1960s. Alma Thomas (1892–1978) and Sam Gilliam (1933–   ) were prominent figures within the Washington, D.C., school of color-field painting (see **Abstract Expressionism**). Al Loving (1935–   ), William T. Williams (1942–   ), and James Little (1952–   ) created geometricized compositions that drew considerable attention. Jack Whitten (1939–   ) and Howardina Pindell (1943–   ) constructed works using unconventional tools and methods indicating their interest in **process art.** Pindell, for example, built up compositions by pasting numbers punched from

canceled checks and personal communications onto paper or canvas.

The works of David Hammons (1943–   ), often constructed from trash and debris, are highly charged comments about present-day American society, forcefully challenging what it defines as *art.* First recognized for his racially political body prints, Hammons brings a fresh frame of reference to ordinary, often overlooked materials common to daily life.

Another African-American artist who drew on undesirable aspects of urban existence was Jean Michel Basquiat (1960–1988), a close associate of **Andy Warhol** and a prominent member of the New York–based young-artists group called the graffitists. Basquiat's work is a visual equivalent to **rap music,** using an eye-grabbing, scribbling style that has the immediacy of wall graffiti, the propagandistic force of billboards, and the haunting seriousness of a coded message. Hidden within his paintings and drawings are bits of ethnic commentary, predictions, and memories.

Black consciousness continues to motivate African-American artists, including some who never abandoned the figure. Benny Andrews (1930–   ) uses figurative line drawings and collages to depict his experiences as a black man in America, frequently linking his works to events in his hometown of Madison, Georgia.

While some African-American artists — including Andrews, Bearden, and Lawrence — were well known during the 1960s, their works were often omitted from the sort of large retrospective shows that can make an artist's reputation. A strong activist voice of that period, Andrews pressured mainstream galleries and museums, especially in New York, to consider works by black artists when planning major exhibitions. With the increasing emphasis on **multiculturalism** in the arts during the late 1980s, African-American artists such as Hammons, Martin Puryear, and Betty Saar have begun to establish major reputations within the mainstream of contemporary art.

REFERENCE:

Romare Bearden and Harry Henderson, *A History of African-American Artists, from 1792 to the Present* (New York: Pantheon, 1993).

                                                                 – A.A.

James Agee

The primary influence of James Agee (1909–1955) was on other writers, but it was pervasive enough to have affected a generation of readers who barely know his name. Many film scholars insist that he invented film criticism. Before him movies were reviewed rather than studied. In his movie review columns for *Time* (1939–1948) and the *Nation* (1942–1948) Agee applied literary standards to movies.

He is best known, though, for a magazine assignment gone haywire. In 1936 *Fortune* asked Agee and photographer Walker Evans to do a story on the poverty of tenant farmers in Alabama. They took three years to complete the work, and the result was so unconventional that the magazine rejected it. Agee and Evans involved themselves personally in their report and strayed from the objective viewpoint that reporters of the day were expected to observe. In 1941 the work was published in book form as *Let Us Now Praise Famous Men* and has since come to be regarded as a classic example of sensitive reportage. Moreover, literary historians view the work as a precursor of the **New Journalism** movement of the 1960s, in which reporters participated in their stories as principals, as active observers, or as sensitive reactors.

Agee's only novel, *A Death in the Family* (1957), won a Pulitzer Prize in 1958.

REFERENCES:

Laurence Bergreen, *James Agee: A Life* (New York: Dutton, 1984);

David Madden, ed., *Remembering James Agee* (Baton Rouge: Louisiana State University Press, 1974).

– R.L.

AIDS

Acquired immune deficiency syndrome (AIDS) is to contemporary American society what the plague was to fourteenth-century Europe — a devastating disease without a cure, fearsome both to victims it strikes, who may suffer a painful death, and to victims it threatens, whose dread of infection characteristically causes them to shun disease carriers cruelly and reassess their lives in a search for safeguards. The fatal disease was first identified in 1981, and by 1993 it was estimated that there were 450,000 infected Americans; death tolls varied widely from alarming to frightening.

AIDS is a particularly pernicious disease because the virus that causes it lies dormant in an infected person for an average of eight years, during which it produces no symptoms but can be transmitted to others. Since sexual contact and intravenous drug use are the primary means of infection and since an AIDS-virus carrier may exhibit no symptoms, every sexual partner outside a monogamous relationship is potentially deadly; and even monogamous partners risk infection if one is an intravenous drug user.

Public reaction to the AIDS epidemic was characterized by conservative, moralistic views of sex. Initially, in America, it was a disease of homosexuals and intravenous drug users who shared hypodermic needles. Medical researchers, supported primarily by federal funds, were slow to respond because most people with political clout felt the disease resulted from a degenerate lifestyle, and if the victims did not deserve the disease, they certainly had only themselves to blame for it.

As it became clear that AIDS could be spread by heterosexual sex, as well as other transfers of body fluids with an infected person, such as blood transfusions or certain medical procedures, the threat slowly took on a universal quality. Middle-class parents became anxious about the safety of their sexually active children, and extramarital indiscretions offered the possibility of penalties far more severe than a wronged spouse's anger.

AIDS forced Americans to accompany righteous preachments about sexual morality with a realistic confrontation of homosexuality, promiscuity, and drug use. Activists in schools and public health facilities, frustrated that warnings about dangerous behavior were ineffective, began programs to distribute condoms free to sexually active teenagers and to provide clean hypodermic needles to drug users. The result was an atmosphere of social revolution.

Homosexuals who saw, as if in a mirror, their friends and lovers dying horrible deaths took to the streets to demand public support of AIDS research and, at the same time, an end to homophobia and the discrimination it causes. In New York a Gay Liberation Day was proclaimed and marked by a parade with some one hundred thousand participants; similar gay pride demonstrations occurred in large cities all over the country. AIDS quilts, in which victims were memorialized individually in patchwork squares sewn by friends and pieced together for exhibition, were a particularly effective creative demonstration of grief for AIDS victims and support for the fight against the disease.

Creative artists, who were as a group hard hit by AIDS, promptly accepted the challenge of personalizing the suffering AIDS — and antihomosexual discrimination — causes as a means of generating support for the fight against the disease. In Los Angeles, Words Project for AIDS initiated annual awards in 1989 for books that promote understanding of the disease; art exhibits on the theme of AIDS traveled the country. In 1987 **Leonard Bernstein**, **Luciano Pavarotti**, and **Leontyne Price** staged a benefit for the Gay Men's Health Crisis at Carnegie Hall, which initiated a series of such concerts.

New York Memorial AIDS quilt in Central Park, 1988

Performing arts celebrities were equally active. **Madonna** and **Elizabeth Taylor** were among the movie stars who performed at AIDS benefits and attempted to persuade their fans to join them in the cause. By the early 1990s AIDS had become a potent political issue, and President William J. Clinton pledged a concerted federal effort to provide relief for victims and to find a cure.

REFERENCES:

James Kinsella, *Covering the Plague: AIDS and the American Media* (New Brunswick, N.J.: Rutgers University Press, 1989);

Robin Weiss, ed., *Confronting AIDS: Update 1988* (Washington, D.C.: National Academy Press, 1988).

– R.L.

ALVIN AILEY

Modern dancer and choreographer Alvin Ailey (1931–1989) founded the Alvin Ailey American Dance Theater, a true repertory company that regularly presents his work and that of other talented black choreographers such as Talley Beatty, Katherine Dunham, George Faison, Donald McKayle, and Pearl Primus.

Ailey first studied dance in 1949–1951 with the Los Angeles company of modern-dance pioneer Lester Horton. After Horton's death in 1953 Ailey became artistic director of the Lester Horton Dancers, taking them to the Jacob's Pillow Dance Festival in Massachusetts in summer 1954 and to New York that autumn.

In New York Ailey studied ballet with Karel Shook in 1954–1956 and acting with **Stella Adler** in 1960–1962. He danced in musicals, including the 1954 Broadway production of *House of Flowers* and the 1954 film version of *Carmen Jones*.

In 1958 Ailey founded his own dance group with a nucleus of performers drawn from Horton's company and went on to choreograph two of his best-known dances. *Blues Suite* (1958) details a joyous night in sporting houses along the Mississippi and the succeeding early-morning regret. *Revelations* (1960) celebrates the religious fervor of traditional African-American spirituals.

Ailey also choreographed *Antony and Cleopatra,* the **Samuel Barber** opera commissioned for the September 1966 opening of the New York Metropolitan Opera House in Lincoln Center, and **Leonard Bernstein**'s *Mass,* which opened the opera house at the Kennedy Center in Washington, D.C., in September 1971.

In 1969 Ailey choreographed a dance protesting the treatment of blacks in South Africa, *Masekela Langage,* using a score by the black South African trumpeter Hugh Masekela. Ailey cast an equally searching eye on the agonies of popular entertainers in a series of dances that includes *Quintet* (1968), *Flowers* (1971), and *For Bird — With Love* (1984). The last of these is dedicated to jazz innovator **Charlie Parker.**

Throughout his career Ailey's work displayed rhythmic vigor and clear narrative structure. Since his death in 1989 the Alvin Ailey American Dance Theater has been directed by dancer-choreographer Judith Jamison.

REFERENCES:

Joseph H. Mazo, *The Alvin Ailey American Dance Theater* (New York: Morrow, 1978);

Don McDonagh, *The Complete Guide to Modern Dance* (Garden City, N. Y.: Doubleday, 1976), pp. 125–132;

William Moore, "Alvin Ailey (1931–1989)," *Ballet Review,* 17 (Winter 1990): 12–17.

– D.M.

EDWARD ALBEE

Edward Albee (1928–) was considered the most promising playwright in America during the 1960s, largely on the basis of his first play, *The Zoo Story* (1959), which won an Obie (Off-Broadway) Award, and his first full-length play, *Who's Afraid of Virginia Woolf* (1962), which won two Antoinette Perry (Tony) Awards and a New York Drama Critics Circle Award. A successful movie adaptation in 1966 starred **Richard**

Burton and **Elizabeth Taylor,** who won an Academy Award for her performance.

Albee's first ambition was to write fiction and poetry. He began thinking about play writing in 1953 on the advice of playwright-novelist Thornton Wilder, but he produced nothing of note until 1958, when he wrote *The Zoo Story.* This one-act play introduces a theme that recurs throughout Albee's work: the necessity, at any cost, of a genuine connection between the individual and something or someone outside himself. After *The Zoo Story,* Albee wrote three one-act satires of American social values — *The Death of Bessie Smith* (1960), *The Sandbox* (1960), and *The American Dream* (1961) — before completing *Who's Afraid of Virginia Woolf?*

With *Tiny Alice* (1964) Albee began experimenting with absurdist methods of dramatic presentation. He won Pulitzer Prizes for *A Delicate Balance* (1966), *Seascape* (1975), and *Three Tall Women* (1994), and in 1980 he was awarded the Gold Medal for Drama by the American Academy and Institute of Arts and Letters. His plays of the 1980s — *The Lady from Dubuque* (1980), *The Man Who Had Three Arms* (1983), *Finding the Sun* (1983), and *Marriage Play* (1987) — have not attracted the large audiences that responded so enthusiastically to his early plays.

REFERENCES:
Richard E. Amacher, *Edward Albee,* revised edition (Boston: Twayne, 1982);
Matthew Charles Roudane, *Understanding Edward Albee* (Columbia: University of South Carolina Press, 1987).
— R.L.

ALEATORY MUSIC

During the 1950s and 1960s aleatory music, also referred to as "chance music" or "indeterminacy," challenged accepted notions of the composer's role. When playing a traditional piece of music, the performer follows the composer's written instructions, but in aleatory music elements of composition or performance are deliberately left to chance, creating a situation in which no two performances of a work are the same. For instance, throws of dice (the original meaning of *aleatory*) may be used to fix the choice of pitches, durations, dynamics, or sequence of events. Performers may be given alternatives in the written music to be determined by their choice, the day of the week, the hour of the day, audience voting, drawing cards, or various other methods. They may also be instructed to improvise in places or throughout. This radical freedom

spread to other arts, resulting in collaborations such as the mixed-media **happenings** of the 1960s.

Although precedents are found throughout Western musical history, aleatory music was developed principally by **John Cage.** His *Music of Changes,* written in 1951, was the first composition based on coin tosses and the use of the Chinese book of oracles, *I Ching.* His *Imaginary Landscape No. 4* (1951), which requires the simultaneous playing of twelve radios tuned to different stations, goes further in abandoning the composer's or performers' control over music.

Along with his friends **Morton Feldman** and Earle Brown, Cage aimed to remove the composer's traditional prerogatives of choice and self-expression and to allow sound — musical tone or noise — to "be itself." Cage's ideas were widely disseminated during the 1950s and 1960s and influenced a large number of younger American composers, among them Morton Subotnick, **Pauline Oliveros,** Gordon Mumma, and La Monte Young.

REFERENCES:
David H. Cope, *New Directions in Music,* fourth edition (Dubuque: William C. Brown, 1984);
Michael Nyman, *Experimental Music: Cage and Beyond* (London: Studio Vista, 1974).
— L.E.P.

NELSON ALGREN

One of the last American literary naturalists, Nelson Algren (1909–1981) depicted what he called the "luckless living" — losers and underdogs doomed hopelessly to struggle for position in a materialistic world. He was a Communist early in his career and was later influenced by French philosophers and thinkers, particularly his lover, Simone de Beauvoir, and her lover, Jean-Paul Sartre. Algren's fictional sympathies were always with the dispossessed.

Algren's writing career began in the early 1930s, when he drifted from his hometown Chicago to the Southwest, writing stories and planning his first novel. *Somebody in Boots* (1935), a hobo novel dedicated to "Those Innumerable Thousands: The Homeless Boys of America" demonstrated Algren's promise and helped him secure a job with the Federal Writers' Project until the start of World War II. Algren's second novel, *Never Come Morning* (1942), about the ruination of a young fighter and his girlfriend, and *Neon Wilderness* (1947), a collection of stories, were praised by critics. Both were set in Chicago, where Algren returned to live.

Nelson Algren in one of his customary poker games (photograph © Art Shay)

Algren did not receive widespread attention, though, until he was awarded the first National Book Award for *The Man with the Golden Arm* (1949), a convincing portrayal of Chicago street life that tells the story of drug addict Frankie Majcinek and his associates. **Ernest Hemingway** subsequently called Algren one of the best living American novelists. The 1955 film version of the novel, directed by **Otto Preminger** and starring **Frank Sinatra,** was controversial for its frank depiction of drug use, but Algren dismissed it because the movie showed "no respect for the book or the people in it."

Algren's next novel, *A Walk on the Wild Side* (1956), a substantial revision of *Somebody in Boots,* follows the fortunes of an illiterate drifter who struggles in vain to make his mark. A film version was released in 1962. This novel, *The Man with the Golden Arm,* and *Neon Wilderness,* are considered Algren's most enduring works.

Sartre's translation of Algren's *Chicago: A City on the Make* (1951), a nonfiction prose poem, was the beginning of Algren's substantial reputation in Europe, and *Neon Wilderness* was held up as a standard of American literary existentialism. Yet his American reputation declined rapidly after *A Walk on the Wild Side* as his variety of social realism became unfashionable with many readers and critics. His travel essays *Who Lost an American?* (1963) and *Notes from a Sea Diary* (1965), and a collection of stories, *The Last Carousel* (1977), were not well received, and his posthumously published novel based on the murder conviction of boxer Ruben "Hurricane" Carter, *The Devil's Stocking* (1983), was a failure. When not ignoring him altogether, critics have sometimes denigrated Algren's work as overly self-con-

scious and sentimental. Nevertheless, Algren's fiction attracted a faithful readership. He died in 1981 in Sag Harbor, New York.

REFERENCES:

Matthew J. Bruccoli, with the assistance of Judith Baughman, *Nelson Algren: A Bibliography* (Pittsburgh: University of Pittsburgh Press, 1985);

Martha Heasley Cox and Wayne Chatterton, *Nelson Algren* (Boston: Twayne, 1975);

H. E. F. Donohue, *Conversations with Nelson Algren* (New York: Hill & Wang, 1964);

Bettina Drew, *Nelson Algren: A Life on the Wild Side* (New York: Putnam, 1989).

– D.H.-F.

MUHAMMAD ALI

Muhammad Ali (1942–), who dominated the sport of boxing for most of the 1960s and 1970s, has been one of the most charismatic and controversial athletes in American history.

Born Cassius Marcellus Clay, he captured the public eye during the 1960 Olympic Games in Rome, where he won a gold medal in the light-heavyweight division, displaying the agile, lightning-quick style for which he would become famous. Out of the ring he soon became known for his flamboyant self-promotion, which often included impromptu poeticizing. (He described his boxing strategy as "float like a butterfly, sting like a bee.") Clay turned professional after the Olympics and took the world heavyweight title from Sonny Liston in 1964.

Just before the title fight Clay announced that he had become a Muslim and was changing his name to Muhammad Ali. In 1967, after he refused on religious grounds to be inducted into the army, he was stripped of his title and found guilty of draft evasion in federal court. His conviction was overturned in 1970 by the U.S. Supreme Court.

Ali returned to boxing and regained the heavyweight championship in 1974 by beating George Foreman in a bout described by **Norman Mailer** in *The Fight* (1975). In early 1978 Ali lost the title to Leon Spinks but won it back later that year. He retired in 1980, after losing to Larry Holmes.

Ali is the only fighter to have been world heavyweight champion three times.

REFERENCES:

Muhammad Ali, with Richard Durham, *The Greatest, My Own Story* (New York: Random House, 1975);

John Hennessey, *Muhammad Ali: "The Greatest"* (New York: Smithmark, 1991);

Norman Mailer, *The Fight* (Boston: Little, Brown, 1975).

– K.L.R.

ALL IN THE FAMILY

When it premiered in 1971, *All in the Family* stunned television viewers, who were accustomed to situation comedies about middle-class, suburban families whose lives were apparently untouched by current events. Inspired by a British television comedy, *Till Death Do Us Part,* producer **Norman Lear** created *All in the Family* as a satirical look at American life during a time when differences of opinion over race relations, women's rights, urban crime, and the **Vietnam War** were threatening to divide the nation into enemy camps.

The argumentative, opinionated Bunker family lived in Corona, a working-class section of the New York borough of Queens. The head of the family, Archie Bunker (played by veteran actor Carroll O'Connor), was a vulgar, loudmouthed bigot who managed to offend practically everyone. Sharing his home were his sweet but dim-witted wife, Edith (Jean Stapleton), his pretty, spunky daughter, Gloria (Sally Struthers), and Gloria's husband, Mike (Rob Reiner), a liberal graduate student. Mike's presence was especially galling to the ultraconservative Archie, who regularly received his comeuppance. Reiner and Struthers left the show in 1978. Stapleton was phased out of the series, at her request, during the 1979–1980 season, the first in which the show aired under a new name, *Archie Bunker's Place.* The last new episode was broadcast in 1983.

Though it got off to a slow start when it premiered as a replacement show in January 1971, *All in the Family* became extremely popular during summer reruns and became one of the most honored on television. While some critics praised the show for tackling sensitive social issues, others contended that it made racism appear harmless and humorous because O'Connor played Archie so sympathetically.

REFERENCES:

Richard P. Adler, *All in the Family: A Critical Appraisal* (New York: Praeger, 1979);

Donna McCrohan, *Archie & Edith, Mike & Gloria Revisited: A Retrospective Appreciation of All in the Family* (New York: Workman, 1987).

– C.D.B.

STEVE ALLEN

Steve Allen (1921–), whom playwright Nöel Coward once called "the most talented man in America," has achieved success in an assortment of professions: musician, songwriter, comedian, writer, and, above all, television personality.

Allen started out in radio in 1942 and moved on to **CBS** television in 1950, appearing on a series of shows before creating *The Tonight Show* for **NBC** in 1954. He hosted the late-night, Monday–Friday variety/talk show until mid January 1957, six months after NBC gave him his own weekly variety program, *The Steve Allen Show,* which ran until 1959. He later hosted the CBS game show *I've Got a Secret* (1964–1966).

From 1977 to 1981 Allen wrote and moderated the **PBS** series *Meeting of Minds,* which featured characterizations of historical personages in roundtable discussions. Actress Jayne Meadows, Allen's wife since 1954, was a frequent guest star on the program, portraying people such as Marie Antoinette, Cleopatra, and the Dark Lady of William Shakespeare's sonnets.

Allen has written more than three dozen books, including the novel *Murder on the Glitter Box* (1989). He has composed more than four thousand songs, among them "Impossible," first recorded by **Nat "King" Cole** in 1956, and "This Could Be the Start of Something Big," introduced by Les Brown and His Band of Renown on the *Steve Allen Show* in 1956. In 1955 he starred in the film *The Benny Goodman Story.*

REFERENCES:

Steve Allen, *Mark It and Strike It: An Autobiography* (New York: Holt, Rinehart & Winston, 1960);

Allen, *Hi-Ho Steverino!: My Adventures in the Wonderful Wacky World of TV* (Fort Lee, N.J.: Barricade, 1992).

– D.M.J.

WOODY ALLEN

Comedian Woody Allen (1935–) has become one of the best-known American filmmakers in the second half of the twentieth century.

Born Allen Stewart Konigsberg, he started out as a joke writer for various columnists and celebrities while still in his teens and began doing his own material as a self-deprecating stand-up comedian in 1961. In 1965 he wrote the script for *What's New Pussycat?,* in which he made his acting debut. The next year he helped to write English dialogue for a Japanese spy film and oversaw the process of turning it into *What's Up Tiger Lily?,* about a search for an egg-salad recipe, performing a speaking role in the new, dubbed-in sound track.

In 1969 Allen directed and acted in *Take the Money and Run* (1969), a parody of documentary and prison films, with a screenplay by Allen and Mickey Rose. Parody also dominated *Bananas* (1971), *Play It Again, Sam* (1971), *Everything You Always Wanted to Know About Sex (* but were afraid to ask)* (1972), and *Sleeper* (1973), in which he acted, as well as in most cases directing his own screenplay. Allen ended this early string of comedies with *Love and Death* (1975), an absurdist take-off on the works of the great nineteenth-century Russian novelists Leo Tolstoy and Fyodor Dostoyevski, which also manages to examine serious questions about the meaning of life.

Allen's next film, *Annie Hall* (1977), is the first of several highly praised movies in which he has concentrated on the romantic misadventures of cultured, well-to-do, and neurotic Manhattanites. *Annie Hall* won the 1978 Academy Award (Oscar) for best picture, brought Allen an Oscar for best director, and won the best original screenplay Oscar for Allen and Marshall Brickman. Allen's costar, Diane Keaton, was given the Oscar for best actress. Other Allen films in this genre include *Manhattan* (1979), *Hannah and Her Sisters* (1986), *New York Stories: Oedipus Wrecks* (1986), *Crimes and Misdemeanors* (1989), *Alice* (1990), *Husbands and Wives* (1992), and *Manhattan Murder Mystery* (1993).

Beginning in 1978 with *Interiors,* Allen has also written and directed brooding, philosophical films inspired by Swedish filmmaker Ingmar Bergman. He has not acted in these films, which also include *September* (1987) and *Another Woman* (1988), and they have had little commercial or critical success. Themes from these films, however, have appeared in many of his later successful comedies, and Bergman also inspired one of Allen's most optimistic comedies, *A Midsummer Night's Sex Comedy* (1982), which is rooted in Bergman's *Smiles of a Summer Night* (1955).

Allen has called *Stardust Memories* (1980) his personal favorite of his films. Yet this movie, about a famous film director (played by Allen) is among his least successful. In other films of the 1980s — *Zelig* (1983), *Broadway Danny Rose* (1984), *The Purple Rose of Cairo* (1985), and *Radio Days* (1987) — Allen managed to combine nostalgia and the parodic vein of his earlier films with a serious look at the concepts of fact versus fiction and dream versus reality.

In 1993 public reaction to Allen's personal life threatened to overshadow his professional reputation when it was revealed that he had had an affair with the twenty-year-old adopted daughter of his twelve-year companion, actress Mia Farrow.

REFERENCES:

Eric Lax, *Woody Allen: A Biography* (New York: Knopf, 1991);

Annette Wernblad, *Brooklyn Is Not Expanding: Woody Allen's Comic Universe* (Rutherford, Madison & Teaneck N.J.: Fairleigh Dickinson University Press, 1992).

– I.R.H.

ROBERT ALTMAN

Director/producer/screenwriter Robert Altman (1925–) was propelled into the vanguard of American film making by *M*A*S*H* (1970), a black comedy about a military field hospital. Although it is set during the Korean War, the film expressed the disillusionment of many Americans with the **Vietnam War.**

After service as a pilot during World War II, Altman worked as a writer/photographer/editor/director of industrial films in the late 1940s and early 1950s. His first two feature-length films — *The Delinquents* (1957) and a documentary, *The James Dean Story* (1957) — met with little success, and he turned to writing, producing, and directing episodes of television shows such as *Alfred Hitchcock Presents, Bonanza,* and *Combat.* He returned to feature-film making in 1964, but his efforts went virtually unnoticed until 1970.

*M*A*S*H* began a series of critical and popular successes that includes *McCabe and Mrs. Miller* (1971), *Thieves Like Us* (1974), and *Nashville* (1974). With the obscure *Three Women* (1977), the unfocused *A Wedding* (1978), and the grotesque, live-acting musical version of the cartoon *Popeye* (1980), Altman began to lose his audience. For nearly a decade he worked primarily on film and television adaptations of plays. *Tanner '88,* his HBO miniseries satirizing the 1988 presidential campaign, inspired renewed interest in Altman, who had major success with his 1992 movie, *The Player,* a darkly comic exposé of the film industry. His 1993 film, *Short Cuts,* loosely based on short stories by **Raymond Carver,** was also well received by critics.

Altman has cultivated an antiestablishment, non-Hollywood image. He has always been willing to alter a script to suit his personal vision and to allow actors to improvise according to their conceptions of their characters. Altman's trademarks —the diffuse narrative line, the large ensemble cast, and the complex layering of sound over sound — give his films a realistic, almost documentary style.

REFERENCES:

Helene Keyssar, *Robert Altman's America* (New York & Oxford: Oxford University Press, 1991);

Patrick McGilligan, *Robert Altman: Jumping off the Cliff, A Biography of the Great American Film Director* (New York: St. Martin's Press, 1989).

– I.R.H.

AMERICAN BALLET THEATRE

The American Ballet Theatre (ABT) is the oldest American ballet company still in existence and one of the most prestigious in the world. Originally called Ballet Theatre, it was renamed the American Ballet Theatre just before a 1964 tour of the Soviet Union. The company developed from the Mordkin Ballet, whose general manager was Richard Pleasant; Lucia Chase, a company member, provided financial support vital to its existence.

For its first performance the new company staged Michel Fokine's *Les Sylphides* and Mikhail Mordkin's *Voices of Spring* on 11 January 1940 at the Rockefeller Center Theatre in New York. It had eighty-five dancers, and its eleven choreographers included Adolph Bolm, Fokine, **Antony Tudor**, Anton Dolin, Andrée Howard, **Agnes de Mille**, and Eugene Loring. Other choreographers associated with Ballet Theatre in the 1940s were **George Balanchine** and **Jerome Robbins**, whose first ballet, *Fancy Free* (1944), was premiered by the company.

The ABT was innovative in its employment of several choreographers working in a variety of styles— from classical to modern and covering Russian, French, British, and American traditions. Most ballet companies have one staff choreographer, whose style dominates all their productions. The large and eclectic repertory that resulted at ABT was to become its trademark. The ABT was the first major company to establish itself as a national touring company without a fixed home. It practices in New York.

A bright roster of stars danced with ABT. Among the earliest were Dolin, Alicia Markova, Igor Youskevitch, Alicia Alonso, Nora Kaye, and John Kriza. Through the years it underwent many changes of personnel and even image. In the mid 1940s, Sol Hurok, a successful presenter of many musical and dance artists, emphasized the Russian ballets in the company repertory. Later Tudor's and Robbins's American ballets were featured. Financially, the company moved from crisis to crisis, with Chase faithfully stepping in with needed aid. Robbins choreographed a humorous musical about the financial woes of ABT, *Look, Ma, I'm Dancin'* (1948). He left to join the **New York City Ballet** in 1949, but returned in 1985 to choreograph a major production of the classical ballet *Les Noces*. Eliot Feld, another talented choreographer who rose from the company's ranks, left to form his own company. First-rate dancers also came and went, such

Rex Cooper, Harold Lang, Janet Reed, and Jerome Robbins in the first production of *Fancy Free,* choreographed by Robbins for the American Ballet Theatre (photograph by George Hurrell)

as Erik Bruhn, Carla Fracci, Rudolf Nureyev, Fernando Bujones, and **Mikhail Baryshnikov**. In 1980 Baryshnikov returned as artistic director, a position he held for most of the decade.

As the reputation of the ABT has grown, its repertory has remained eclectic. It continues to present great nineteenth-century classics such as *Swan Lake, The Sleeping Beauty,* and *Giselle* while performing newer works of compelling interest.

REFERENCES:

John Fraser, *Private View: Inside Baryshnikov's American Ballet Theatre* (Toronto: Bantam, 1988);

Charles Payne, *American Ballet Theatre* (New York: Knopf, 1978).

– D.M.

AMERICAN BANDSTAND

During the late 1950s and early 1960s the television show *American Bandstand* shaped the musical taste of American teenagers, bringing rock music to a large television audience.

Originally broadcast in 1952 as a local teenage dance show in Philadelphia, *American Bandstand* became a nationally broadcast, weekday afternoon program on the **ABC** network in August 1957. The first featured artist was rock musician Jerry Lee Lewis.

The host of *American Bandstand* for the duration of its national run was Dick Clark, a young Philadelphia disc jockey who took over the local program in 1955. The show featured clean-cut, nonprofessional, teenaged dancers. Some of the regulars, mostly from Philadelphia high schools, developed significant popular followings.

Many of the best-known rock musicians of the 1950s and early 1960s performed on *American Bandstand*. (**Elvis Presley** and Ricky Nelson are notable exceptions.) Fabian, Frankie Avalon, the Everly Brothers, and Paul Anka were frequent guests. In 1963 ABC moved *Bandstand* from its weekday lineup to Saturdays at noon, and the next year Clark took the show to Los Angeles to be closer to the popular music scene that had developed in California. Yet the program could not keep up with the changing tastes of American teenagers. It was shown on an increasingly irregular basis until its cancellation in December 1987.

REFERENCE:

Dick Clark, *Rock, Roll & Remember* (New York: Crowell, 1979).

– C.D.B.

AMERICAN BOOKSELLERS ASSOCIATION

One of the oldest American trade organizations, the American Booksellers Association (ABA) was created in 1900 to regularize bookselling practices. It promotes the well-being of booksellers through lobbying and seeks to improve their relationships with publishers and authors. Attendance at its national convention has increased from approximately 4,500 in 1970 to more than 25,000 in 1988.

The ABA has sought to adapt to changing markets, especially after World War II with the proliferation of **paperbacks,** increased prices for hardcover books, and the rise of **chain bookstores.** It has devoted much of its energy and influence to improving distribution and sales, sharing information on management and promotion among members, and encouraging sales of sideline items such as magazines, calendars, and **books on tape.** Since 1950 it has promoted reading by cosponsoring the National Book Awards. Beginning in the early 1970s it has fought earnestly against efforts at **censorship.**

REFERENCE:

Chandler B. Grannis, "More Than Merchants: Seventy-Five Years of the ABA," in *Bookselling in America and the World: Some Observations and Reflections*, edited by Charles B. Anderson (New York: Quadrangle/New York Times Books, 1975), pp. 65–108.

– D.H.-F.

AMERICAN FILM INSTITUTE

The American Film Institute (AFI) was chartered in 1965 to provide grants for filmmakers and preserve movies made in the United States, particularly those made on physically unstable nitrate film before the widespread adoption of nonflammable acetate film in the 1950s.

Established under President Lyndon B. Johnson's National Arts and Humanities Act, AFI opened its Washington, D.C., headquarters in 1967. Much of the funding for AFI comes from the National Endowment for the Arts.

By 1967 half of the films made in the United states had been lost or destroyed by physical deterioration. Yet the AFI has succeeded in locating and preserving many of those that survive through its film-preservation program at the Louis B. Mayer Library in Los Angeles, where films are available for study by scholars and the general public.

The AFI also encourages novice and independent filmmakers through its Center for Advanced Film and Television Studies in Los Angeles, and its ongoing *American Film Institute Catalog* will eventually include all films produced in the United States since 1890. The AFI journal, *American Film,* established in 1975, was discontinued in 1992 because of budget cutbacks.

Since 1973 the annual, nationally televised AFI Achievement Awards ceremonies have honored notable performers and filmmakers.

REFERENCE:

The American Film Heritage: Impressions from the American Film Institute Archives (Washington, D.C.: Acropolis, 1972).

– I.R.H.

AMERICAN LITERATURE

Since the first issue appeared in March 1929, *American Literature* has played a central role in defining the American literary canon: the body of writing that constitutes its major works.

The journal was founded by Duke University professor Jay B. Hubbell, a pioneer in the study of American literature, and published by Duke University Press in cooperation with the American Literature Group of the **Modern Language Association of America.** In 1929 academics were still debating whether the United States had a literary heritage distinct from that of Great Britain and whether the works of American writers were worthy of serious scholarly examination. American literature courses were relatively new additions to the curricula of American colleges and universities. *American Literature* enhanced the prestige of American writers, and, by the articles it accepted or rejected, it had a major influence on which authors were chosen as subjects of scholarly research. (For many years, for example, it did not accept articles on twentieth-century writers.) Authors who were written about in *American Literature* became important. Scholars passed on those judgments in the classroom, and a generally accepted canon of American literature gradually developed.

In the 1970s, however, feminist and minority critics began to challenge that canon, calling it a list of books by white males chosen by other white males. With the appointment of Cathy N. Davidson as head of its board of editors in 1991, *American Literature* signaled its intention to support the expansion of the traditional canon to include works by previously overlooked women and minority writers.

– K.L.R.

AMERICAN THEATRE WING

The American Theatre Wing is a group of writers, actors, directors, and other theater people. It is best known for its sponsorship since 1947 of the annual Antoinette Perry Awards (Tonys), the equivalent in Broadway theater to the Academy Awards in the film industry. Tony Award winners are elected by members of the New York theater community for outstanding achievement in acting, writing, stage and costume design, directing, and choreography.

The organization was started as Stage Women's War Relief during World War I. In 1940 the group changed its name in to the American Theatre Wing War Service. Among its many activities during World War II was its sponsorship of Stage Door Canteens to entertain soldiers in London, Paris, and eight American cities. Broadway performers and other entertainers often appeared at the canteens.

After the death in 1946 of actress and director Antoinette (Tony) Perry, who was chair and secretary of the American Theatre Wing board during the war, the Tony Awards were created in her memory. Other Theatre Wing activities include a Professional Training School in theater, radio, and television that boosted the careers of **Charlton Heston**, Gordon MacRae, and Tony Randall; theater seminars; and scholarships for performers and playwrights.

REFERENCES:

Lee Alan Morrow, *The Tony Award Book: Four Decades of Great American Theater* (New York: Abbeville, 1987);

Isabelle Stevenson, ed., *The Tony Award* (New York: Arno, 1975).

– I.R.H.

DAVID AMRAM

As a composer and performer, David Amram (1930–) has contributed much to bridging the gap between classical and popular styles in American music. He is one of the few French-horn players to perform jazz. As a conductor, he has directed concerts by the **New York Philharmonic Orchestra** (for which he was composer-in-residence in 1966–1967), a Brooklyn youth orchestra, and various jazz ensembles.

Collaborating with **Joseph Papp** in the New York Shakespeare Festival from 1956 to 1967, Amram composed a great deal of incidental theater music that is dramatic, romantic, and somewhat inspired by jazz. He wrote the score for Archibald MacLeish's *J. B.*, which won the Pulitzer Prize for Drama in 1959. In the same year Amram received an Obie (Off-Broadway) Award for the incidental music he wrote for the Shakespeare Festival and Phoenix Theatre productions. He has also composed scores for films, including *Splendor in the Grass* (1961) and *The Manchurian Candidate* (1962).

REFERENCE:

David Amram, *Vibrations: The Adventures and Musical Times of David Amram* (New York: Macmillan, 1968).

– L.E.P.

LAURIE ANDERSON

Laurie Anderson (1947–) is an avant-garde **performance artist** and composer whose primary goal has been to unite all the arts as they once existed in the theater of ancient Greece and Rome. Anderson learned to play the violin in her childhood, and in 1972 she earned an M.F.A. in sculpture from Columbia University, where she first began working with mixed artistic media.

In the 1970s she earned a reputation in the New York art world when she accompanied her films with live violin playing and storytelling. These experiments evolved into multimedia performances such as her eight-hour *United States,* combining music, stories, video, and film, first produced in its entirety in 1983, after four years of work.

Her breakthrough as a popular musician came in 1981 with her hit song "O Superman." This success led to her first commercial album, *Big Science* (1982), a selection of music from her *United States* show. The rock-influenced songs on *Big Science* and later albums comment on gender roles and Americans' obsession with technology. While her records are not top sellers, Anderson maintained a respectable following in the 1980s. In 1991 she toured colleges across the country, speaking out against **censorship** and the Persian Gulf War.

REFERENCES:

Laurie Anderson, *United States* (New York: Harper & Row, 1984);

Gillian G. Gaar, *She's a Rebel: The History of Women in Rock and Roll* (Seattle: Seal, 1992);

Janet Kardon, *Laurie Anderson, Works from 1969 to 1983: October 15 – December 4, 1983, Institute of Contemporary Art, University of Pennsylvania* (Philadelphia: Institute of Contemporary Art, 1983).

                                                        – L.D.S.

MARIAN ANDERSON

Marian Anderson (1897–1993), an African-American contralto, possessed "the voice that comes but once in a century," according to the great Italian conductor Arturo Toscanini. A performer in opera, oratorio, and song recitals, she was perhaps at her most compelling in her renditions of traditional African-American spirituals.

From her modest beginnings in a church choir in south Philadelphia to her farewell recital tour in 1964–1965, Anderson paved the way for later black American divas, including Leontyne Price, Grace Bumbry, Mattiwilda Dobbs, Shirley Verett, and Kathleen Battle. It was Anderson who broke the so-called color line at the Metropolitan Opera, where her appearance as Ulrica in Giuseppe Verdi's *Un ballo in maschera* on 7 January 1955 marked the first time a black sang there in a solo role.

Anderson battled racial discrimination throughout her career. In 1939, after the Daughters of the American Revolution (D.A.R.) refused Anderson's request to perform at their Constitution Hall in Washington, D.C., Eleanor Roosevelt intervened, and Anderson gave an Easter Sunday concert at the Lincoln Memorial to a throng of about seventy-five thousand people. (She sang at Constitution Hall four years later, invited by the D.A.R.) In 1958 Anderson's efforts to promote racial equality led President Dwight D. Eisenhower to appoint her an alternate delegate to the United Nations Human Rights Committee.

Anderson, who sang at Eisenhower's 1957 inauguration and at the inauguration of John F. Kennedy in 1961, went on a U.S. State Department–sponsored

Laurie Anderson performing in Chicago, May 1984 (photograph by David Tulsky)

ten-week tour of India and the Far East in 1957, giving twenty-four concerts in fourteen countries. She performed for American troops in Berlin in 1961, toured Australia in 1962, and sang at the Lincoln Memorial during the March on Washington for Jobs and Freedom in 1963. She began her farewell tour in October 1964 and gave her last public performance at Carnegie Hall in New York in April 1965.

President Lyndon B. Johnson awarded Anderson the Presidential Medal of Freedom in 1963. In 1976 the U.S. Congress authorized the striking of a commemorative gold medallion in her honor. The Marian Anderson Scholarship Fund, established in 1990, continues the exemplary work that she began in 1943, when she used the ten-thousand-dollar proceeds from the Bok Prize, awarded to her by the city of Philadelphia, to give financial aid to promising young singers.

REFERENCES:

Marian Anderson, *My Lord, What a Morning: An Autobiography* (New York: Viking, 1956);

Shirlee Petkin Newman, *Marian Anderson: Lady from Philadelphia* (Philadelphia: Westminster, 1966);

Kosti Vehanen, with George J. Barnett, *Marian Anderson: A Portrait* (New York & London: McGraw-Hill, 1941).

                                                        – L.D.S.

ROBERT ANDERSON

Robert Anderson (1917–) became well known during the 1950s for his plays about lonely and desperate people who reach out to others for some sort of emotional warmth or reassurance.

Anderson's first New York success was *Tea and Sympathy* (1953), about a sensitive young man who is accused of being homosexual by other boys at his prep school. To assuage the boy's fears about his masculinity, the headmaster's wife seduces him. In *Silent Night, Lonely Night* (1959), two strangers meet at an inn on Christmas Eve, talk, have sex, and then are able to face the problems in their unhappy marriages.

Although the four brief playlets in *You Know I Can't Hear You When the Water's Running* (1967), once again deal with troubled love relationships, three of them are comedies. Anderson's most recent Broadway success, *I Never Sang for My Father* (1968), is about the attempts of a middle-aged son to understand and come closer to his aging, demanding father.

Anderson has also written screenplays for the film versions of *Tea and Sympathy* (1956) and *I Never Sang for My Father* (1970), as well as screen adaptations of works by others, including Kathryn Hulme's *The Nun's Story* (1959), for which he received an Academy Award (Oscar) nomination, and Richard McKenna's *The Sand Pebbles* (1965). His screenplay for *I Never Sang for My Father* earned him a second Oscar nomination.

REFERENCE:
Thomas Adler, *Robert Anderson* (Boston: Twayne, 1978).
– I.R.H.

MAYA ANGELOU

Maya Angelou (1928–) is an African-American autobiographer and poet as well as a public speaker of extraordinary power. She appeared in the national spotlight when she read her "On the Pulse of Morning," a poem written for the occasion, at the 1993 inauguration of President William J. Clinton, a fellow Arkansan. Angelou was the first poet to read at a presidential inauguration since **Robert Frost** recited one of his poems at **John F. Kennedy**'s in 1961.

Angelou's first book, *I Know Why the Caged Bird Sings* (1970), was a commercial and critical success. Her best-known and most highly regarded work, it vividly chronicles her childhood in the segregated South. This autobiography was followed by four others: *Gather Together in My Name* (1974), *Singin' and Swingin' and Gettin' Merry Like Christmas* (1976), *The Heart of a*

Woman (1981), and *All God's Children Need Traveling Shoes* (1986). In these books, as Angelou describes her search for identity and the many obstacles she has faced, she also presents an examination of twentieth-century African-American experience. Covering her own eventful life up to the 1960s, she talks about her five years of silence after she was raped by her mother's boyfriend at age eight; her relationship with the son she bore in her teens; her work as a dancer, actor, singer, composer, and editor; her participation in the **civil rights movement**; and her experiences in Africa.

Angelou's six collections of poetry have been popular for their lyricism and affirmation, but her critical reputation rests mainly on her prose. Angelou has also written plays and screenplays. Her original screenplay for *Georgia, Georgia* (1972) was the first by an African-American woman to be filmed.

REFERENCES:
Jeffrey M. Elliot, ed., *Conversations with Maya Angelou* (Jackson: University Press of Mississippi, 1989);
Dolly A. McPherson, *Order out of Chaos: The Autobiographical Works of Maya Angelou* (London: Virago, 1991).
– D.H.-F.

DIANE ARBUS

In 1957 Diane Arbus (1923–1971) turned away from her successful career as a fashion photographer to pursue her own artistic projects, focusing increasingly on depictions of individuals living on the margins of conventional society. Over the next decade she became well known for her stark depictions of transvestites, nudists, midgets, and asylum inmates.

Arbus's choice of outsiders as subjects was less controversial than her unsentimental approach to them. Her photographs angered some critics, who charged that she held up for ridicule individuals who had trustingly let down their guard before her camera. Her admirers saw a rare artistic courage in her desire to confront middle-class society with the tragedies and vulnerabilities of human beings it generally avoided and labeled misfits.

By the late 1960s Arbus, Gary Winogrand, and Lee Friedlander were recognized as important forces in a new direction in American documentary photography. Although their approaches differ, they all photographed contemporary America without an explicit social agenda, emphasizing the artist's personal vision. Their works were shown together at the Museum of Modern Art in a 1967 exhibition called New Documents. In 1972, a year after her suicide, Arbus became the first American photographer to have her work represented at the Venice Biennale. Later that year there was a major retrospective exhibition of her photographs at the Museum of Modern Art, and another collection of her work traveled throughout the United States and Canada. Arbus continues to be considered a major twentieth-century American photographer.

REFERENCES:
Diane Arbus, Magazine Work (Millerton, N. Y. : Aperture, 1984);
Patricia Bosworth, *Diane Arbus: A Biography* (New York: Knopf, 1984).

– K.B.

ARENA STAGE

Arena Stage in Washington, D.C., is one of the oldest and most respected regional theaters in the United States. It was founded in 1950 by Zelda Fichandler, who retired in 1991 after four hundred plays and forty years of guiding the theater, which continues to prosper. In 1973 Arena Stage was the first American drama company to perform in the Soviet Union, and in 1976 it became the first theater outside New York to receive an Antoinette Perry (Tony) Award for distinguished theatrical achievement.

Since its beginnings, Arena Stage has balanced polished productions of plays from the Renaissance to the nineteenth century with productions of twentieth-century works by playwrights such as **Arthur Miller,** Tennessee Williams, and others. A few Broadway successes premiered at Arena, including Robert Anderson's *All Summer Long* (1953), Howard Sackler's *The Great White Hope* (1967), and Elie Wiesel's *Zalmen,* or *The Madness of God* (1974). Arena Stage is noteworthy for its emphasis on multicultural programming and its efforts to make theater widely accessible to the disabled.

REFERENCE:
Laurence Maslon, *The Arena Adventure: The First 40 Years* (Washington, D.C.: Arena Stage, 1990).

– I.R.H.

LOUIS ARMSTRONG

Trumpet player Louis Armstrong (1898–1971) was one of the finest **jazz musicians** of the twentieth century. Nicknamed "Satchmo" (a journalist's condensation of "Satchelmouth") in reference to his large mouth, Armstrong is credited with helping to transform jazz from black folk music to an American art form. Armstrong was the first jazz soloist to become known worldwide,

signaling a shift in emphasis from ensemble to solo improvisation.

Born in New Orleans, the "cradle of jazz," Armstrong learned to play the cornet in reform school, where he was sent at age thirteen after he fired a pistol in the air to celebrate the Fourth of July. He joined "Kid" Ory's Band in 1918 and was invited to Chicago to join "King" Oliver's Creole Jazz Band in 1922. Later in the 1920s Armstrong was a member of the Fletcher Henderson Orchestra in New York, before switching to trumpet and achieving stardom as a soloist with his own group, the Hot 5 (later the Hot 7). By 1930 Armstrong had achieved an international reputation as a trumpet virtuoso. He toured extensively and became known as "America's ambassador of goodwill" for his many international tours. He also made numerous guest appearances with other ensembles until just before his death.

After 1945 Armstrong sang more than he had during the first half of his career. He used his gravelly, scratchy voice to great effect during live performances as well as on his many recordings, including hits such as "Hello, Dolly!" (1964) and "What a Wonderful World" (1970). He also made many television and film appearances, most notably in movies such as *The Glenn Miller Story* (1954), *High Society* (1956), and *Hello, Dolly!* (1969). Though in his later career Armstrong relied on a set style and crowd-pleasing repertoire, he continued to be imitated by scores of jazz trumpeters, just as he influenced many earlier performers, such as pianist Earl Hines and saxophonist Coleman Hawkins.

REFERENCES:
Louis Armstrong, *Satchmo: My Life in New Orleans* (New York: Prentice-Hall, 1954);
James Lincoln Collier, *Louis Armstrong: An American Genius* (New York: Oxford University Press, 1983);
Hugues Panassié, *Louis Armstrong* (New York: Scribners, 1971).

– L.D.S.

ISAAC ASIMOV

Isaac Asimov (1920–1992) was important for his role in popularizing **science fiction.** He was born in Russia, and his family took up residence in Brooklyn, New York, when he was three. He attended Columbia University, where he received a Ph.D. in biochemistry in 1948.

In 1939, at the age of nineteen, Asimov fell under the influence of John W. Campbell, editor of the pioneering science-fiction pulp magazine *Astounding Science-Fiction,* and began a remarkable publishing career. As a frequent contributor to *Astounding Science-*

Louis Armstrong and Billie Holiday, 1946 (Estate of Louis Armstrong)

REFERENCES:

Jean Fiedler and Jim Mele, *Isaac Asimov* (New York: Ungar, 1982);

William F. Touponce, *Isaac Asimov* (Boston: Twayne, 1991).

– R.L.

ASSEMBLAGE

During the 1950s some of the American artists seeking alternatives to **Abstract Expressionism** turned to assemblage, the technique of combining various found materials to make a piece of sculpture.

Assemblage has its roots in Dada and Surrealism, especially in the "readymades" **Marcel Duchamp** had been creating since the second decade of the twentieth century. American artist Joseph Cornell, who associated with Duchamp and other Surrealists during the 1930s and 1940s, began constructing small boxes containing incongruously, but artfully, juxtaposed found objects in the 1930s. The term *assemblage*, coined in 1953 by French artist Jean Dubuffet, has also been applied to the large-scale sculptures that Louise Nevelson began creating in the mid 1950s by organizing scrap wood into large wooden structures that she then grouped together to form "atmospheres."

Artists such as **Robert Rauschenberg** and Richard Stankiewicz chose as their raw materials found objects from the street, scrap metal, and wood, transforming them into works of art which, unlike Abstract Expressionism, accepted and affirmed the concrete, often messy "real" world. Stankiewicz began making junk-metal sculpture in the early 1950s, achieving recognition later in the decade. Rauschenberg's mixed-media "combines" of the late 1950s blurred the distinction between painting and **sculpture.**

In 1961 William Seitz, then an associate curator at the Museum of Modern Art, organized a major international exhibition, The Art of Assemblage, in which he surveyed the history of the technique. In addition to including works by Duchamp, Cornell, Nevelson, Rauschenberg, and Stankiewicz, the exhibit showcased many young American artists who have since become well known. They included Lucas Samaras, **Jasper Johns, Edward Kienholz, John Chamberlain, and George Brecht.**

REFERENCES:

Barbara Haskell, *Blam! The Explosion of Pop, Minimalism, and Performance, 1958–1964* (New York: Whitney Museum of American Art/Norton, 1984);

William C. Seitz, *The Art of Assemblage* (New York: Museum of Modern Art, 1961).

– K.B.

Fiction, Asimov attracted an avid readership of science-fiction fans with classic stories such as "Nightfall" (1941) even before publication of his first book, *I, Robot* (1950), a collection from a ten-year-long series of stories about robots. Subsequently, he proved his ability to write books faster than most writers can produce short stories. Over the next forty years he wrote more than two hundred books, the most successful of which are science-fiction short stories and novels; these include his robot books, especially *The Caves of Steel* (1954) and *The Naked Sun* (1957), and the popular Foundation Trilogy, comprising five novelettes and four novellas collected in *Foundation* (1951), *Foundation and Empire* (1952), and *Second Foundation* (1953). Asimov continued the Foundation story decades later with *Foundation's Edge* (1982), *Foundation and Earth* (1986), and *Prelude to Foundation* (1988) and tied his two popular series together in *Robots and Empire* (1985). For the last of his books his publisher paid him more than $1 million.

During his long career Asimov also wrote an impressive number of volumes of mystery fiction, children's fiction, guides to Shakespeare and the Bible, and explanatory science books for children and adults. He won several Hugo and Nebula awards.

Brooks Atkinson

For more than thirty years, Brooks Atkinson (1894–1984), the drama critic for the *New York Times* from 1925 to 1960, was the most influential play reviewer in America.

During World War II Atkinson covered the war in China in 1942–1944 and was sent to Moscow in 1945. His series of reports on life in the Soviet Union won him the Pulitzer Prize for Foreign Correspondence in 1947. He returned to his position as drama critic for the *Times* in 1946.

In the 1950s, when most New York critics limited their coverage to plays on Broadway, Atkinson went Off-Broadway and found much to praise. He has been credited with helping to advance the careers of director Jose Quintero, producer **Joseph Papp,** and actors Geraldine Page, George C. Scott, Colleen Dewhurst, Jason Robards, and Ben Gazzara — all of whom he discovered Off-Broadway.

When Atkinson retired in 1960, the Mansfield Theatre on West 47th Street between Broadway and 8th Avenue was renamed the Brooks Atkinson Theatre in his honor. He continued to write a "Critic-at-Large" column for the *Times* until 1965. Fair-minded and gentlemanly even in disapproval, Atkinson collected some of his reviews and articles in *Broadway Scrapbook* (1947), *Tuesdays and Fridays* (1963), *Brief Chronicles* (1966), and *The Lively Years: Reviews and Drawings of the Most Significant Plays since 1920* (1973, with drawings by Al Hirschfield). He also wrote on theater history in *Broadway* (1970; revised, 1974).

– I.R.H.

Atonal Music

While most popular music is still defined by the major and minor keys, scales, and harmonies of "tonality," atonal music, which lacks the traditional tonal relationships, has been heard with increasing frequency since the beginning of the twentieth century.

Atonal composition often includes systems based on intervals between notes of a musical scale, creating melodic and harmonic structures. One of these systems is the twelve-tone method, developed in the 1920s by Arnold Schoenberg as a way of imposing order on the twelve pitches contained within one octave (the chromatic scale). This in turn led to systems of **serial music.**

Atonality, with or without serial structures, may be heard in **George Crumb**'s *Black Angels* (1970), an eclectic work using tonal and atonal methods, and in nearly all examples of aleatory music (as in the compositions of John Cage), electronic music, and progressive jazz. Milton Babbitt's *Three Compositions for Piano* (1947) and Roger Sessions's Third Symphony (1957) are serial American works.

REFERENCES:

Allen Forte, *The Structure of Atonal Music* (New Haven: Yale University Press, 1973);

John Rahn, *Basic Atonal Theory* (New York: Longman, 1980).

– L.E.P.

Auteur Theory

One of the most provocative and controversial developments in the history of American film after World War II was the emergence in the 1960s of the auteur theory, which acknowledged a select group of directors as the authors of their movies. The proponents of this theory asserted that despite the large number of creators necessary to produce a film, certain strong directors are able to impress their particular styles and personalities upon their movies, making these works unmistakably their own.

The auteur theory was developed in France in the 1950s, primarily by a group of young critics who wrote for the journal *Cahiers du Cinema*. Many of them, including François Truffaut and Jean-Luc Godard, later became film directors. In America film critic Andrew Sarris became the leading proponent of the auteur theory. His "Notes on the Auteur Theory in 1962" (*Film Culture,* Winter 1962–1963) prompted a heated response from movie reviewer **Pauline Kael,** who stressed the collaborative nature of film making.

Auteurists especially admired Hollywood directors who asserted their identities despite the controls placed on them by the studio system. When taken to extreme, this methodology rated directors who consistently manifested a personal style in a series of mediocre or insignificant films far above those anonymous craftsmen who directed collaborative masterpieces. Yet the auteur theory did bring about re-evaluations of directors such as **Alfred Hitchcock** who had been dismissed as commercial hacks. During the 1970s, after the breakdown of complete studio control over filmmakers, many American directors made conscious efforts to shape their films according to their own creative visions. Among the American auteurs who emerged in the 1970s are such widely acclaimed directors as Francis Ford Coppola, Martin Scorsese,

Steven Spielberg, and Robert Altman. Later American auteurs include David Lynch (*Blue Velvet,* 1986), and Tim Burton (*Batman,* 1989).

REFERENCES:

Andrew Sarris, *The American Cinema: Directors and Directions, 1949–1968* (New York: Dutton, 1968);

Diane Jacobs, *Hollywood Renaissance* (South Brunswick, N.J. & New York: A. S. Barnes, 1977).

– I.R.H.

RICHARD AVEDON

When the capital of fashion photography moved from Paris to New York City after World War II, two young American photographers — Richard Avedon (1923–) and **Irving Penn** — quickly rose to the top cf the field and stayed there for several decades. Avedon is considered one of the most successful and influential American photographers of the twentieth century.

Avedon's mentor was Alexey Brodovitch, the art director of *Harper's Bazaar* and a prime mover in experimental fashion photography and graphics. In 1945 Avedon became a staff photographer for *Harper's Bazaar* and remained at the magazine for two decades. In 1966 he joined the staff of *Vogue.* Early in his career Avedon began to react against the images of aloof and static models that appeared in the fashion photography of the previous generation. He abandoned the studio for city streets and other outdoor locations, creating glamorous imaginary scenarios and photographing his models in motion, creating a sense of playfulness and freedom. The fashion photographer in the movie *Funny Face* (1957), is based on Avedon during this period, and he served as a visual consultant during filming.

Over the years Avedon's style changed to incorporate new trends in popular culture and the visual arts, and in each decade there were signature Avedon models: sophisticated glamour with Suzy Parker in the 1950s, **Pop Art** goofiness with Twiggy and sensuality with Jean Shrimpton in the 1960s, and a new naturalness with Lauren Hutton in the 1970s. Avedon returned to photographing his models in the studio during the 1970s.

Avedon is also widely admired for his black-and-white portraiture, which he considers his most significant body of work. Many were shot in his studio with flat backdrops and harsh lighting, so that they seem to magnify his sitters physical flaws and expose their frailties with extraordinary honesty. He continues to take studio photographs, especially studies of famous people, and in December 1992 he became the first staff photographer for the *New Yorker* magazine.

REFERENCE:

Richard Avedon, *Autobiography* (New York: Random House/Rochester, N.Y.: Eastman Kodak, 1993).

– K.B.

B

Milton Babbitt

A pioneer in ways of thinking about music, composer Milton Babbitt (1916–   ) approaches it as a highly ordered and complex sound universe. Radically departing from Western musical tradition, he has provoked much criticism, and many of his compositions are virtually incomprehensible to listeners. His best-known article is titled "Who Cares If You Listen?" (*High Fidelity,* 1958). His demand for the composer's total control over all elements of sound has profoundly influenced numerous young composers in the United States and abroad.

Babbitt started out composing jazz and popular songs, but his early interest in mathematics and his studies with **Roger Sessions** soon led him to writing music according to Arnold Schoenberg's twelve-tone method, in which the twelve notes of an octave are arranged into a particular pattern. *Composition for 4 Instruments* (1948) was one of Babbitt's first consistent attempts to expand that system and to coordinate this twelve-tone set with similarly patterned sets of twelve different note lengths as well as twelve different instrumental sounds. This composition led to "total" **serial music** in Babbitt's later works. There texture, dynamics, time changes, and other aspects of sound are also "serialized," or preset.

In the mid 1950s Babbitt was one of the first composers to work with the RCA synthesizer Mark II, and since 1959 he has been director of the Columbia-Princeton Electronic Music Center. New **electronic music** resources made it possible for him to realize hitherto impossible degrees of precision and control.

Babbitt's approach to composition is rigorous whether he writes for electronic media, string quartet, large orchestra, or jazz ensemble. (*All Set* [1957] is a jazz piece based on one twelve-tone set.) Nevertheless, he does not neglect lyricism and expressiveness. Perhaps his most interesting and "listener-friendly" work is *Philomel* (1964), a combination of electronic sounds and live and taped vocal performance.

REFERENCES:

Andrew Washburn Mead, *An Introduction to the Music of Milton Babbitt* (Princeton: Princeton University Press, 1993);

Erich Salzman, "Babbitt and Serialism," *Twentieth-Century Music: An Introduction,* fifth edition (Englewood Cliffs, N.J.: Prentice-Hall, 1985).

– L.E.P.

Burt Bacharach

Songwriter Burt Bacharach (1928–   ) is one of the most successful popular-music composers of the postwar era. With lyricist Hal David, Bacharach wrote some of the best-selling pop hits of the 1960s. His music brought a more melodic and restrained sensibility to a decade dominated by raucous **rock 'n' roll.**

Bacharach was born in Kansas City, Missouri, and was forced by his parents to take piano lessons. He developed an interest in jazz while in high school, playing in local shows with **Dizzy Gillespie** and **Charlie Parker**. He studied music under Darius Milhaud and Henry Cowell and in the 1950s worked as a conductor and arranger for various record companies. He also worked as an accompanist to singers such as Vic Damone, Polly Bergen, and Steve Lawrence. From 1958 to 1961 he worked for Marlene Dietrich, serving as accompanist and arranger.

In 1957 Bacharach and David collaborated on two hit songs, "The Story of My Life," a top twenty hit for Marty Robbins, and "Magic Moments," a top five hit for Perry Como. The two did not work together again until

1962, when they and singer Dionne Warwick signed a contract with Scepter Records. The collaboration produced twenty-two top-forty hits from 1963 to 1970, including "Walk On By" (1964), "Alfie" (1967), "I Say a Little Prayer" (1967), "Do You Know the Way to San Jose?" (1968), and "I'll Never Fall in Love Again" (1970).

Bacharach and David also had success without Warwick, writing such well-known songs as the "What the World Needs Now [Is Love, Sweet Love]" (1965), "What's New, Pussycat?" (1965), and "The Look of Love" (1967). Their biggest hit was "Raindrops Keep Fallin' on My Head" (1969), which was featured in the film *Butch Cassidy and the Sundance Kid* (1970) and, recorded by B. J. Thomas, stayed in the number-one chart position for four weeks. Bacharach and David wrote the title songs for the movies *Wives and Lovers* (1964) and *Send Me No Flowers* (1964). Bacharach was also active on Broadway, writing an enthusiastically received score for *Promises, Promises* (1968).

By the 1970s musical tastes had changed, and the format of Bacharach's work was not as popular. In 1981 he cowrote the hit "Arthur's Theme" for the movie *Arthur*. In 1986 he wrote "That's What Friends Are For" with his wife, Carole Bayer Sager. The song, which was written to benefit **AIDS** research, was recorded by Warwick and spent four weeks at the number-one chart position. Bacharach's five-decade career marks him as one of the most enduring pop composers of the twentieth century.

–J.W.H.

Joan Baez

Folksinger and songwriter Joan Baez (1941–) is well known for her performance artistry and her nonviolent social activism. Often called the "Queen of the Folksingers," she contributed to the folk revival of the early 1960s. As an outspoken pacifist, she played an active and influential role in the **Vietnam War** protest movement.

The daughter of an Irish mother and a Mexican father, Baez grew up among whites and Mexicans in Redlands, California, developing early a sympathy for minorities. She began to play guitar when she was twelve and was initially influenced by such **rock 'n' roll** figures as **Elvis Presley** and Bill Haley. After she graduated high school, she moved with her family to Boston, where her father, a physicist, had taken a job at MIT. In Boston she added to her folk-song repertoire by spending her free time at a local **coffeehouse,** Tulla's Coffee Grinder. She was soon performing in

Boston coffeehouses, where her clear, pure soprano voice made her a local favorite.

After two successful performances at the Newport Folk Festival in Rhode Island, Baez signed with Vanguard and released her first LP, *Joan Baez,* in 1960. Baez became popular nationwide within a year, but instead of taking advantage of profitable offers, she spent much of her time appearing at charity concerts supporting the **civil rights movement** and the Vietnam War protest movement. In 1963 she refused to pay the portion of her federal income tax that would be spent to support the armed forces. In October 1967 she was arrested for demonstrating at the Oakland, California, Armed Forces Induction Center.

Throughout the turmoil of the 1960s and 1970s, her recordings continued to be popular. She won gold records for *Any Day Now* (1968), written by **Bob Dylan**, whom she had introduced to the folk-music scene by including him in a series of her concerts in the early 1960s, and *Blessed Are* (1971). In 1969 she was greeted with enthusiasm by the crowd at **Woodstock**. Her rendition of The Band's "The Night They Drove Ol' Dixie Down" (1972) became her biggest hit, reaching number five and staying on the charts for fifteen weeks. Baez made her songwriting debut in 1972 with the album *Come from the Shadows*. In December of that year she protested the Vietnam War by recording an LP in Hanoi, North Vietnam, while American planes bombed the city.

After the war Baez's music became more concerned with the events of daily life. In 1975 she toured with Bob Dylan. She continues to be an outspoken human-rights advocate and a popular folksinger.

REFERENCES:

Joan Baez, *And a Voice to Sing With: A Memoir* (New York: Summit Books, 1987);

Baez, *Daybreak* (New York: Dial, 1968);

Irwin Stambler and Grelun Landon, *Encyclopedia of Folk, Country, and Western Music,* second edition (New York: St. Martin's Press, 1984).

–J.E.F. and L.D.S.

Pearl Bailey

During the 1950s and 1960s Pearl Bailey (1918–1990) was one of a handful of black performers who established a large multiracial following. Her success as a singer and actress in the 1950s made her a popular figure on television in the 1960s, 1970s, and 1980s.

Bailey debuted as a singer in 1944 at the Village Vanguard in New York City. In the summer of that year she began an eight-month engagement at the exclusive Blue Angel nightclub in Manhattan, leaving to appear as the featured singer with Cab Calloway for a sixteen-week engagement at the Zanzibar club on Broadway.

Bailey moved to Broadway theater in 1946, appearing in Johnny Mercer and Harold Arlen's all-black musical *St. Louis Woman.* Her performance was singled out by critics as a highlight in a less-than-successful production, winning her the 1946 Donaldson Award as the best newcomer on Broadway. She then went on to Hollywood, appearing in *Variety Girl* (1947) and *Isn't It Romantic?* (1948).

In the 1950s Bailey primarily focused on movies and the concert circuit, although she did star in the **Truman Capote**–Harold Arlen musical *House of Flowers* (1954). Her film credits include appearances in *Carmen Jones* (1954), *That Certain Feeling* (1956), *St. Louis Blues* (1958), *Porgy and Bess* (1959), and *All the Fine Young Cannibals* (1960).

During the early and mid 1960s, Bailey concentrated almost entirely on her singing career. In 1967, however, she returned to the stage, taking over the title role in David Merrick's all-black production of *Hello, Dolly!* Bailey's performance was widely acclaimed and she was given a special Antoinette Perry (Tony) Award.

REFERENCES:

Pearl Bailey, *Between You and Me* (New York: Doubleday, 1989);

Bailey, *The Raw Pearl* (New York: Harcourt, Brace & World, 1968);

Bailey, *Talking to Myself* (New York: Harcourt Brace Jovanovich, 1971).

–J.W.H.

GEORGE BALANCHINE

George Balanchine (1904–1983), the most important and influential ballet master in the twentieth century, helped to broaden the audience for ballet in America. Schooled in classical ballet in his native Russia, he went on to expand the basic techniques of ballet and to establish the validity and the creative possibilities of nonnarrative ballet.

Balanchine began his career as a dancer. In 1924 he left Russia and began a decade of work as a choreographer in Europe. His technically innovative ballets drew the attention of ballet supporter Lincoln Kirstein, who invited him to the United States in 1933 to found a school and a company. In 1934 Balanchine helped to found and was an instructor at the School of American Ballet in New York, but

George Balanchine and Igor Stravinsky at a rehearsal for their 1957 ballet, *Agon* (photograph by Martha Swope)

early efforts at establishing a permanent company were disappointing. He began to choreograph **Broadway musicals** such as *On Your Toes* (1936) and films such as *The Goldwyn Follies* (1938). In 1946 he helped to establish **New York City Ballet** (then called Ballet Society) as part of the New York City Center for Music and Drama, with Balanchine as artistic director and choreographer.

During the 1940s Balanchine began to choreograph plotless ballets in which the relationship between dance and music was central. He did not entirely abandon ballets with stories, however. His *Orpheus* (1946) and *Agon* (1957), with music by his long-time collaborator Igor Stravinsky, are both based on Greek myth. Balanchine's most creative period occurred during the late 1940s and the 1950s, when he choreographed *Bourrée fantasque* (1949), *La Valse* (1951), *Ivesiana* (1954), and a score of other ballets. New York City Ballet became recognized as one of the leading international companies under his direction. He continued to create new, innovative ballets until the year before his death.

REFERENCES:
Don McDonagh, *George Balanchine* (Boston: Twayne, 1983);
Bernard Taper, *Balanchine* (New York: New York Times Books, 1984).

– D.M.

JOHN BALDESSARI

One of the earliest and most influential **conceptual artists** in the United States, John Baldessari (1931–) was one of the first American artist to reject the dogma of modernism and to adopt an approach later labeled as **postmodernist**. He reacted against what he called the "aesthetics of boredom": **Clement Greenberg**'s, art-for-art's-sake formalism and the uniformity of **minimalist** painting and sculpture.

Having lived in California all his life, Baldessari maintains that his relative isolation from the New York art world has allowed him to conduct his artistic experiments without the influence of critical doctrines and prejudices. In 1970 he burned his early paintings, placing the ashes in a book-shaped urn labeled "John Baldessari / 1953–1967." Thus liberated, he began to explore how people create meaning from the visual world. Much of his work combines photographs and text, breaking down traditional distinctions between fine-art photography and avant-garde art. Blurring the borders between artistic mediums was one of the first new directions in postmodernism in the visual arts.

Marcel Duchamp, whom Baldessari discovered in 1959 "as if I had come across a long-lost brother," may have influenced Baldessari's experiments in juxtaposing image and text. Baldessari was one of the first American artists to embrace the linguistic and critical theories of European writers such as Ludwig Wittgenstein, Ferdinand de Saussure, Claude Lévi-Strauss, and Roland Barthes. From such readings Baldessari drew the distinction between "semantic" meaning, which is rational and can be expressed in words, and "aesthetic" meaning, which is based in feelings and mental associations and resists verbal definition. His works often create tension between these two forms of meaning by playing one against the other.

An influential teacher, Baldessari was on the faculty at the California Institute of the Arts, one of the most avant-garde art schools in the United States from 1970 until 1989. His students included painters Eric Fischel and David Salle.

REFERENCES:
Coosje van Bruggen, *John Baldessari* (New York: Rizzoli International, 1990);

Marcia Tucker and Robert Pincus-Witten, *John Baldessari* (New York: New Museum, 1981).

– K.B.

JAMES BALDWIN

James Baldwin (1924–1987), one of the most influential African-American writers of the twentieth century, began his career during the last days of legalized segregation in the United States and became a significant literary voice of the **civil rights movement.** Yet in his fiction, plays, and essays Baldwin sought, and for the most part succeeded, in going beyond social issues "to reveal all that he can possibly discover concerning the mystery of the human being." He influenced African-American writers, including **Maya Angelou** and **Toni Morrison,** and white American writers such as **William Styron.**

Baldwin was born in Harlem, where his stepfather was a Pentecostal preacher. At fourteen he decided to follow in his stepfather's footsteps, but by the time he graduated from high school in 1942 he had become disillusioned and renounced the ministry. In 1948 he went to live in Paris. Although he lived abroad for most of the rest of his life, he always considered himself an American writer.

Baldwin's first, semi-autobiographical novel, *Go Tell It on the Mountain* (1953), describes his youth in Harlem, his religious conversion, and the experiences that led to his conviction that religion made African Americans passive victims of a racist, white-controlled society. Soon after completing the novel he began work on a play, *The Amen Corner,* which also focuses on life in Harlem and the black church. Students at Howard University staged the play in 1955; it was produced on Broadway in 1965. In his second novel, *Giovanni's Room* (1956), Baldwin, who was a homosexual, wrote about a young man torn between his fiancée and his male lover. The book is Baldwin's only work of fiction that includes no black characters.

As the civil rights movement gained momentum, Baldwin addressed racism and the black experience in America in essays collected in *Notes of a Native Son* (1955), *Nobody Knows My Name* (1961), and *The Fire Next Time* (1963). During the years 1957–1963 he spent most of his time in the United States. He gave speeches in the South, helped to launch a black-voter-registration drive in Selma, Alabama, and took part in the 1963 March on Washington led by **Martin Luther King, Jr.**

Baldwin's third novel, *Another Country* (1962), largely written during this period, deals with the controversial subject of interracial love. Set in New York during the 1950s, the novel was praised as "powerful" by some reviewers and attacked as "pornographic" by others. After completing this novel, Baldwin wrote *Blues for Mr. Charlie,* a play inspired by the 1955 murder of Emmett Till, a fourteen-year-old black from Chicago who was lynched by whites in Mississippi because he flirted with a white woman.

By the time the play opened on Broadway in 1964, a younger generation of African-American writers in the **Black Arts Movement** was beginning to view Baldwin as an elder statesman whose work was irrelevant to their goals. His later novels — *Tell Me How Long the Train's Been Gone* (1968), *If Beale Street Could Talk* (1974), and *Just Above My Head* (1979) — were dismissed by critics and largely ignored by the American reading public. Having become an expatriate to escape American racism, Baldwin had cut himself off from the way of life that lends such vitality to his early works. Yet those works continue to wield a powerful influence. After Baldwin's death from stomach cancer in 1987 LeRoi Jones (**Amiri Baraka**) praised Baldwin as "a man, spirit, voice — old and black and terrible .... [who] made us better, made us consciously human...."

REFERENCES:

James Campbell, *Talking at the Gates: A Life of James Baldwin* (New York: Viking, 1991);

Horace A. Porter, *Stealing the Fire: The Art and Protest of James Baldwin* (Middletown, Conn.: Wesleyan University Press, 1989);

Fred L. Standley and Louis H. Pratt, eds., *Conversations with James Baldwin* (Jackson: University Press of Mississippi, 1989).

– R.T.

AMIRI BARAKA

Born LeRoi Jones in Newark, New Jersey, Amiri Baraka (1934–) was the leading literary voice of the militant **Black Arts Movement** of the 1960s that expressed in revolutionary terms the rage of blacks at their social oppression. Grounded in the study of philosophy as a college student, Jones, who changed his name in 1969, lived in Greenwich Village during the 1950s, writing poetry, coediting little magazines, and writing leftist sociopolitical essays about race in America.

Beginning in the early 1960s, Jones became a proponent of agit-prop (agitation/propaganda) theater, one-act plays with a strong political message intended to arouse strong emotions. His *The Slave* (1964) and *Dutchman* (1964), which won an Obie as the best off-Broadway play of the year, were warnings to white audiences of a radical black consciousness that sought to replace white racism with black racism. These and other revolutionary plays seemed to advocate the most violent forms of racial revolution, and they encouraged the development of what was called a **black aesthetic** to create a value system based narrowly on black experience and black sensibilities.

In his essays of the period, collected in *Home: Social Essays* (1966) and *Raise Race Rays Raze: Essays Since 1965* (1971), Baraka laid the theoretical foundation for this call to arms. Politically, he saw himself as being aligned with racially oppressed peoples of the world, particularly in the West Indies and in Africa, and he was heavily influenced by the philosophy of Frantz Fanon and other Marxist theorists. By the early 1970s, Baraka had turned his attention to world conditions, promoting global action and seeking international solutions. As he lost his focus on national affairs, Baraka's strident voice was replaced by those of others who spoke more directly to domestic black issues. Baraka's poetry was collected in *Selected Poetry of Amiri Baraka/LeRoi Jones* (1979).

REFERENCES:

Amiri Baraka, *The Autobiography of LeRoi Jones* (New York: Freundlich, 1984);

Kimberly W. Bentson, ed., *Imamu Amiri Baraka (LeRoi Jones): A Collection of Critical Essays* (Englewood Cliffs, N.J.: Prentice-Hall, 1978);

Theodore Hudson, *From LeRoi Jones to Amiri Baraka: The Literary Works* (Durham, N.C.: Duke University Press, 1973).

– R.L.

SAMUEL BARBER

The works of Samuel Barber (1910–1981) are among the most frequently performed compositions by American composers. Barber is known mainly for his symphonic works and art songs. His music, mostly based on traditional European classical forms, possesses a lyric beauty influenced by Romanticism.

Barber began studying piano and cello at age six and wrote his first composition a year later. He entered the prestigious Curtis Institute in Philadelphia at fourteen and earned acclaim for his first compositions in 1933: an arrangement of Matthew Arnold's poem "Dover Beach" for baritone and strings (Barber sang at its premiere) and his *Overture to The School for Scandal*. The haunting *Adagio for Strings* (1938) is Barber's best-known work. Other works include his ballet *Medea* (1946); a piece for soprano and orchestra, *Knoxville: Summer of 1915* (1948); and his Piano Concerto (1962), which won a Pulitzer Prize — as did his 1958 opera *Vanessa,* libretto by **Gian Carlo Menotti.** His 1966 opera, *Antony and Cleopatra* (libretto by Franco Zeffirelli), which was commissioned by the **New York**

Gian Carlo Menotti, Jacqueline Kennedy, President John F. Kennedy, and Samuel Barber at the White House

Metropolitan Opera for the opening of its new Lincoln Center location in 1966, failed to impress audiences and critics.

REFERENCE:

Barbara B. Heyman, *Samuel Barber: The Composer and His Work* (New York: Oxford University Press, 1992).

                    – L.E.P.

CLIVE BARNES

Clive Barnes (1927–) is a longtime drama and dance critic in New York City, having worked at both the *New York Times* and the *New York Post*. He is one of the few critics to control a newspaper's opinion on two major art forms.

Barnes was born in London, England, and immigrated to the United States in 1965 to take over as dance critic at the *New York Times*. In 1967 he became the daily drama critic for the *New York Times* as well. This dual role caused concern among those with interests in the theater. Barnes would often-

times miss play openings in favor of conflicting dance performances, despite the fact that as the most powerful critical voice in New York City the opinion of the *New York Times* could cause a play to be a success or a failure.

Barnes's sensitivity to the power of his position at the *New York Times* seemed to affect the nature of his opinions. After he saw that a negative *New York Times* review could close a show overnight, Barnes became known as someone who would pull his punches. Barnes remained on the *New York Times* staff until 1977, when he joined the *New York Post*. He continues to review both dance and theater at the *Post,* but the diminished power of the *Post* as an opinion maker has made him much less influential as a critic.

REFERENCE:

William Goldman, *The Season: A Candid Look At Broadway* (New York: Harcourt, Brace & World, 1969).

                    –J.W.H.

JOHN BARTH

John Barth (1930–) is one of the leading advocates and practitioners of contemporary experimental fiction. His **postmodern,** highly intellectual works effectively employ **black humor** to comment on the absurdities of life and expand the potential of literature through **metafiction,** in which the author self-consciously reflects on the process of creating his book.

Barth's first two novels are fairly conventional. In *The Floating Opera* (1956), a man contemplates suicide because he is convinced that life has no meaning. Yet he gradually realizes that, if this belief is true, suicide is meaningless as well. Similarly, the protagonist of *The End of the Road* (1958) is paralyzed with indecision because no course of action is better than any other. When he does choose, the results are tragic. For all their apparent nihilism, these novels are surprisingly comic, highlighting Barth's use of black humor.

In *The Sot-Weed Factor* (1960) Barth rewrites the history of colonial Maryland and its poet laureate, Ebenezer Cooke, shifting from realism to a postmodern blend of fantasy, history, and myth while commenting on the fictionality of his own fiction. This novel, which brought Barth a wider readership, was followed by his first commercial success, *Giles Goat-Boy; or, The New Revised Syllabus* (1966). This metafictional fantasy set on a university campus further breaks down the wall between fiction and reality in Barth's work. For example, one of the editors of Giles's story is a writer named J.B. whose career parallels Barth's. This self-reflexiveness also appears in his only short-story collection, *Lost in the Funhouse:*

Mikhail Baryshníkov and Marianna Tcherkassky in the 1976 American Ballet Theatre production of Twyla Tharp's *Push Comes to Shove* (photograph by Martha Swope)

Fiction for Print, Tape, Live Voice (1968), which deals with the uncertainties of life and the distortions of art in a variety of narrative styles; *Chimera* (1972), a collection of three related novellas drawing on mythology; and his novel *Letters* (1979), in which Barth exchanges letters with characters from his previous works.

Barth's ongoing concern, outlined in his often-cited statement of a postmodern aesthetic, "The Literature of Exhaustion" (1967), is how to deal with outmoded narrative forms that assume a reality inaccessible to the contemporary writer. He addresses the problem in his fiction by using traditional narrative techniques and subverting them through framing devices, elaborate plots, blurring of past and present, and self-conscious narration. In short, the subject of most of Barth's fiction is fiction — its creation and reception. Barth's own reception has been mixed: some critics and readers have praised his playful inventiveness, while others have found it pointless and unreadable. Barth continues to enjoy respect in academe. His recent books include novels set in his native Maryland, *Sabbatical* (1982) and *Tidewater Tales* (1987), and the novel *The Last Voyage of Somebody the Sailor* (1991), in all of which he has continued to explore his fictional concerns. He has also published *The Friday Book: or, Book-Titles Should Be Straightforward and Subtitles Avoided: Essays and Other Nonfiction* (1984).

REFERENCES:

Stan Fogel and Gordon Slethaug, *Understanding John Barth* (Columbia: University of South Carolina Press, 1990);

David Morrell, *John Barth: An Introduction* (University Park: Pennsylvania State University Press, 1976).

– R.T.

MIKHAIL BARYSHNIKOV

Mikhail Baryshnikov (1948–) has been widely acclaimed as one of the greatest male ballet dancers in history. Like Rudolf Nureyev before him, Baryshnikov defected from the Soviet Union and became an American celebrity — a rarity for ballet dancers.

A natural actor and athlete, Baryshnikov began studying ballet in his teens and was a gold-medal winner in the international ballet competition held in Varna, Bulgaria, in 1966. He debuted with the Kirov Ballet in Leningrad in 1969 and quickly became recognized as an outstanding solo artist in the Soviet Union.

His unhappiness with life in his homeland and his feelings of frustration over the restricted repertoire he was permitted to dance were instrumental in his 1974 decision to remain in Canada, where he was appearing as part of a tour, rather than return to the Soviet Union. He joined **American Ballet Theatre** later that year and, ironically, was cast primarily in nineteenth-century classics — the very ballets he had left the Soviet Union to escape.

While he was with ABT, his quest for new challenges quickly led him to work with contemporary ballet choreographers such as Frederick Ashton, John

Neumeier, and **Jerome Robbins,** as well as modern dance choreographers **Alvin Ailey,** John Butler, Mark Morris, **Martha Graham,** and **Twyla Tharp.** Baryshnikov's most successful role was in Tharp's ABT piece *Push Comes to Shove* (1976), specifically created for him. It includes a mixture of modern dance and ballet accompanied by alternating Joseph Lamb's *Bohemia Rag* and Haydn's Symphony No. 82. He also choreographed and danced in successful productions of *The Nutcracker* (1976) and *Don Quixote* (1978) and appeared in television productions and three movies. He received an Academy Award nomination for best supporting actor for his first film, *The Turning Point* (1977), an engaging melodrama produced by Herbert Ross and Nora Kaye, former dancers with ABT.

Baryshnikov became artistic director of ABT in 1980, after a fifteen-month stay with **New York City Ballet** to study under **George Balanchine.** He staged several successful productions for ABT, including his versions of *Cinderella* (1984) and *Swan Lake* (1989). He left the position in 1989 to focus on his acting career and the White Oak Dance Project, a modern dance company.

REFERENCES:

Mikhail Baryshnikov with Charles Engell France, *Baryshnikov at Work: Mikhail Baryshnikov Discusses His Roles* (New York: Knopf, 1976);

John Fraser, *Private View: Behind the Scenes with Baryshnikov's American Ballet Theatre* (New York: Bantam, 1988);

Gennady Smakov, *Baryshnikov: From Russia to the West* (New York: Farrar Straus Giroux, 1981).

– D.M.

COUNT BASIE

William "Count" Basie (1904–1984) began his recording career in 1929, and his last album was recorded in 1981, when he was seventy-four. He was one of the dominant figures in American jazz during nearly half of the twentieth century. The famous Count Basie Orchestra was formed in 1935 and continued until just before his death. In the last years he came on stage in a motorized wheelchair, honking a bicycle horn to announce himself.

Basie's Orchestra, which, like all big jazz bands, endured a steady turnover in personnel, was one of the few to survive the Swing era of the 1930s. Along with **Duke Ellington,** he was able to adapt the jazz-orchestra format to the tastes of postwar audiences, but unlike Ellington, who was a musical pathfinder, Basie was a traditionalist. His signature recording was "One O'Clock Jump," named after an annoying pet dog. Featured performers included legendary jazz figures:

Count Basie autographing records for fans

Lester Young, Buck Clayton, Jay Jay Johnson, and Thad Jones. Over the years his band featured singers Billie Holiday, Billy Eckstine, **Sara Vaughan,** and **Ella Fitzgerald.**

Basie played piano, both with the orchestra and in ensemble groups. His uncluttered, one-finger style led unknowing listeners to conclude that he did not take the instrument seriously, but he was a skilled and pleasing pianist. Basie's demeanor was ever pleasant; critic Nat Hentoff said he smiled more and said less than anyone he had ever known. Nonetheless, Basie was a proven taskmaster, able over the years to manage groups of musicians not otherwise known for their discipline and to mold them into consistently stimulating big bands. Basie won many awards during his career. He was named a Kennedy Center laureate in 1981, and he was posthumously awarded the Presidential Medal of Freedom by President Ronald Reagan in 1985.

REFERENCES:

Count Basie, as told to Albert Murray, *Good Morning Blues* (New York: Random House, 1985);

Alun Morgan, *Count Basie* (Tunbridge Wells, U.K.: Spellmount / New York: Hippocrene, 1984).

– R.L.

The Beach Boys

The most successful American **rock 'n' roll** group of the 1960s, the Beach Boys are remembered for songs celebrating youth and the southern California lifestyle. Their distinctive sound combines layered, high-pitched vocals with simple melodies backed by guitars, drums, and electronic keyboards.

The group was created in 1961 when its members were in high school. Brothers Brian, Carl, and Dennis Wilson, their cousin Mike Love, and a friend, Alan Jardine, first toured as the Beach Boys in 1962, the year they produced their first album, *Surfin' Safari.* Their first hits, focusing on girls, surfing, and cars, include "Surfer Girl" (1963); "Little Deuce Coupe" (1963); "Surfin' U.S.A." (1963), based on **Chuck Berry**'s "Sweet Little Sixteen"; "Fun, Fun, Fun" (1964); and "I Get Around" (1964), their first number-one hit. Brian Wilson turned more to writing and producing for the group in 1964, leading to several replacements in the mid 1960s, most notably the addition of Bruce Johnston in 1965. The Beach Boys remained popular during this time: "Help Me Rhonda" (1965) was another number-one song, and "California Girls" was also popular. The group reached its peak in 1966 with its best-known album, *Pet Sounds,* which includes the hits "Wouldn't It Be Nice" and "Good Vibrations," their first song to sell more than a million copies. The album was a culmination of Brian Wilson's experiments with studio mixing and overdubbing (recording over other recordings), foreshadowing a growing trend in rock recording.

The popularity of the Beach Boys began to wane in the late 1960s, and in the 1970s the group turned more to touring with their hit songs of the past and making retrospective albums such as *Endless Summer* (1974). This album and their 1976 *15 Big Ones,* featuring songs by others, such as Berry's "Rock and Roll Music," sold well. The group continued to feature "classic" rock songs into the 1980s and 1990s and included Carl and Brian Wilson, Love, Jardine, and Johnston after Dennis Wilson's death by drowning in 1983. The Beach Boys were inducted into the Rock and Roll Hall of Fame in 1988.

REFERENCES:

John Milward, *The Beach Boys Silver Anniversary* (Garden City, N.Y.: Doubleday, 1985);

Byron Preiss, *The Beach Boys* (New York: Ballantine, 1979).

– D.H.-F.

Romare Bearden

Romare Bearden (1911–1988) drew on everyday African-American experiences to represent the rituals, customs, and social conditions of life in America in his art. Already one of the most respected African-American artists by 1960, Bearden went on during that decade to develop the innovative collage style for which he is now best known.

Born in Charlotte, North Carolina, Bearden spent most of his youth in New York City, where he moved with his family when he was about three, though the family made frequent visits to relatives in the South. After graduating from New York University (B.S., 1935) and studying under German proletarian caricaturist George Grosz at the Art Students League in New York (1936–1937), Bearden began exhibiting his work, often with that of fellow members of the "306 Group" of Harlem artists, including Henry Bannarn, Charles Alston, and **Jacob Lawrence.**

Major recognition came after his service in the U.S. Army during World War II. In 1945 a solo exhibition of his *The Passion of Christ* series at the Koontz Gallery in New York established him as an important modern painter. Following a 1950 trip to Paris financed by the GI Bill and two years composing jazz in his studio above the Apollo Theatre in Harlem, Bearden turned away from his early style, characterized by abstract, figurative designs with flat areas of color. He began to employ the splash, drip, and color-play techniques of **Abstract Expressionism.** The two approaches merged in the collage "paintings" of his next phase.

In the early 1960s he began to mix cutouts from painted paper, cloth, and magazines, newspapers, and other printed sources in his works. His goal was to create small works that suggest the quilt maker's block and the improvisation of jazz. His collages combine images from the popular media with references to a mythic Black culture based on his childhood memories of the rural South. Some of his earliest collages, photographically enlarged and called *Projections,* were shown in New York in 1964 and at the Corcoran Gallery of Art in Washington, D.C., in 1967, Bearden's first solo exhibit in a museum. The sizes of his collages vary (works dated 1967–1969 are huge) and have diverse themes. Yet all these works employ African-American cultural metaphors to speak a universal language.

REFERENCES:

Myron Schwartzman, *Romare Bearden: His Life & Art* (New York: Abrams, 1990);

M. Bunch Washington, *The Art of Romare Bearden: The Prevalence of Ritual* (New York: Abrams, 1973).

– A.A.

BEAT GENERATION

The Beat Generation was the most socially influential group of writers in the United States during the second half of the twentieth century. While other literary movements may have found as many followers among writers, the Beats changed the attitudes of succeeding generations toward authority and social convention in all aspects of their lives, paving the way for the **hippies** of the 1960s and 1970s.

In a period that valued conformity, the Beats wrote autobiographical fiction and poetry that dealt openly with heterosexuality and homosexuality, as well as the use of illegal drugs. They paired social criticism with a call for mystical detachment as a cure for **Cold War** tension, and they preached antimaterialism as an answer to the compulsion to "keep up with the Joneses."

The Beat movement began in 1944, when **William S. Burroughs, Jack Kerouac,** and **Allen Ginsberg** met in New York City. By the early 1950s Gregory Corso and Neal Cassady, whose lifestyles epitomized the self-conscious nonconformity of the Beats, had joined the group, and Kerouac and Burroughs had published novels describing the Beat scene. Yet most of the American public did not become aware of the Beats until later in the decade. In 1956 West Coast Beat poet **Lawrence Ferlinghetti,** who had just opened his City Lights Bookshop in San Francisco, published Ginsberg's *Howl and Other Poems*, and suddenly the Beats were in the news: a customs agent, deciding that Ginsberg's graphic indictment of the nation's ills was not fit reading for American children, seized copies Ferlinghetti had had printed abroad and had him arrested, setting in motion a highly publicized obscenity trial.

Ferlinghetti won. *Howl* became a best-seller. Ginsberg's sudden fame spilled over to other Beat writers. Kerouac's novel *On the Road* (1957), with a main character based on Cassady, and Burroughs's novel *Naked Lunch* (1959), which draws on his experience with drug addiction, were both best-sellers despite — or perhaps because of — widespread condemnation of their messages by the establishment. The mainstream media dubbed the group "beatniks" and parodied their apparent lack of motivation.

By the late 1960s the Beats' influence was readily apparent in the hippie lifestyle embraced by many young Americans, but their most significant contribution is less obvious. While they were not themselves social activists, the Beats encouraged freedom of expression, creating an atmosphere in which the **Civil Rights** and **Vietnam War** protest movements could flourish.

REFERENCES:

Ann Charters, *Scenes Along the Road: Photographs of the Desolation Angels, 1944–1960* (New York: Portents/Gotham Book Mart, 1970);

Charters, ed. *The Beats: Literary Bohemians in Postwar America, Dictionary of Literary Biography*, volume 16, 2 parts (Detroit: Gale Research, 1983);

John Tytell, *Naked Angels: The Lives and Literature of the Beat Generation* (New York: McGraw-Hill, 1976).

– K.L.R.

THE BEATLES

The most popular **rock 'n' roll** group in history, the Beatles exerted an appeal and influence in the 1960s that extended from England, their home country, to America. They led the "British invasion" that ended the dominance of American popular music in both countries.

John Lennon (1940–1980) and Paul McCartney (1942–), who began writing and performing together in 1957, were joined by George Harrison (1943–) the following year. After performing as the Quarrymen, Johnny and the Moondogs, and the Silver Beatles, the group became the Beatles in 1960, with Stuart Sutcliffe on bass and Pete Best on drums. Sutcliffe left the band in 1961, and in 1962 Best was replaced by Ringo Starr (born Richard Starkey, 1940–).

The Beatles were influenced by American rhythm and blues and rock stars such as Buddy Holly and **Chuck Berry.** Their early music, mostly love songs by Lennon and McCartney and a few songs by others, was accompanied by guitars and drums in simple arrangements. Their first recorded single, "Love Me Do" (1962), sold well, while their next, "Please Please Me" (1963), reached the top five on the British charts. "From Me to You," "She Loves You," and "I Want to Hold Your Hand" all hit number one on British charts in 1963. "I Want to Hold Your Hand" was their first number-one hit in the United States.

The Beatles' success rapidly caused worldwide "Beatlemania" as the group encountered screaming fans and extensive media coverage, setting fashion trends with their "mop-top" hairstyles and dark, collarless jackets. The "Fab Four," as they were known, became especially popular in America in 1964 after their manager, Brian Epstein, arranged an appearance on the **Ed Sullivan Show** and a tour of the country. In March 1964 Beatles songs held the top five positions on American charts. That year they appeared in their first film, *A Hard Day's Night,* about their constant touring. In the next few years they recorded many hits and made another movie, *Help* (1965).

Among the eight singles that reached number one on U.S. charts by 1966 were "Can't Buy Me Love"

(1964), "I Feel Fine" (1964), "We Can Work It Out" (1965), and "Paperback Writer" (1966). The last two belong to a transitional period, marked by the albums *Rubber Soul* (1965) and *Revolver* (1966), when, like many rock performers in the late 1960s, the Beatles began experimenting with new musical styles and with studio mixing and additional instruments in their recordings. They recorded more consciously "artistic" songs such as "Yesterday" (1965) and "Eleanor Rigby" (1966). This development — with their acceptance of experiments with drugs and their study of Transcendental Meditation under **Maharishi Mahesh Yogi** — culminated in the *Sgt. Pepper's Lonely Hearts Club Band* album in 1967, the year Epstein died. This period also marks the beginning of tensions within the band. Lennon's mystical "Strawberry Fields Forever" and McCartney's catchy "Penny Lane," which were combined into a single on *Sgt. Pepper,* highlight the writers' diverging styles, as did *The Beatles* (1968; known also as *The White Album* for its blank white jacket), which also featured songs by Harrison. The Beatles continued to record hit singles and albums such as "Hey Jude" (1968), "Lady Madonna" (1969), "Get Back" (1969), *Abbey Road* (1969), and *Let It Be* (1970), the making of which was the subject of the documentary film *Let It Be* (1970). They also provided the voices for the animated film *Yellow Submarine* (1969). The group split in 1970, and its members pursued individual careers.

Their music has remained extremely popular, and in 1987 all their albums were re-released on **compact disc.** In 1988 they were welcomed into the Rock and Roll Hall of Fame. The remaining Beatles reunited in 1994 and began work on a new album.

REFERENCES:
Mark Lewisohn, *The Complete Beatles Chronicles* (New York: Harmony Books, 1992);
Nicholas Schaffner, *The Boys from Liverpool: John, Paul, George, Ringo* (New York: Methuen, 1980).
                                                                    – D.H.-F.

WARREN BEATTY

Warren Beatty (1937–) began his film career as a 1960s equivalent to **Marlon Brando** or **James Dean** and then matured into a thoughtful actor-director who chooses his projects sparingly.

The brother of actress Shirley MacLaine, Beatty first gained attention as a regular on a television series, *The Many Loves of Dobie Gillis,* during its first season (1959–1960) and made his movie debut in *Splendor in the Grass* (1961). His star ascended rapidly after he played notorious robber Clyde Barrow in one of the most influ-

ential films of the New American Cinema, *Bonnie and Clyde* (1967), directed by Arthur Penn. The film was produced by Beatty, who received his first Academy Award (Oscar) nomination for best actor. He subsequently starred in, produced, and helped to write the screenplay for the highly successful *Shampoo* (1975), before receiving a second best-actor nomination for his role in *Heaven Can Wait* (1978), for which he was codirector and producer. He went on to produce, direct, and play the role of radical American journalist John Reed in *Reds* (1981), which earned him a third best-actor Oscar nomination and an Academy Award for best director.

After *Reds* Beatty did not make another film for six years, and his return vehicle, *Ishtar* (1987), a "road picture" costarring **Dustin Hoffman,** was one of the all-time Hollywood disasters, incurring multiple cost overruns and schedule delays and bringing in poor box-office returns. Beatty directed and played the title role in his 1990 film, *Dick Tracy,* which also failed to live up to expectations, but his 1991 performance as Benjamin Siegel in *Bugsy,* directed by Barry Levinson, brought him another Oscar nomination for best actor.

REFERENCES:
Susan Munshower, *Warren Beatty — His Life, His Loves, His Work* (New York: St. Martin's Press, 1983);
Lawrence J. Quirk, *The Films of Warren Beatty* (New York: Carol Publishing, 1990);
David Thomson, *Warren Beatty and Desert Eyes: A Life and A Story* (Garden City, N. Y.: Doubleday, 1987).
                                                                    – I.R.H.

BEBOP

Bebop, also known as rebop and simply as bop, is a jazz form developed in the early 1940s in New York City by a group of musical innovators who shut themselves off from outsiders. Minton's Playhouse on 118th Street in Harlem, where pianist **Thelonious Monk** and drummer Kenny Clarke were members of the house band in 1940, became an after-hours gathering place for talented jazz musicians attracted to late-night jam sessions. Notable among the regular visitors were **Charlie Parker, Dizzy Gillespie,** Denzil Best, Bud Powell, Don Byas, and Freddie Webster.

Keeping the quality of the sessions high, the regulars invented their own music, marked by unconventional harmonics, wildly syncopated rhythms, and frequent and unusual chord changes. Standards were a mainstay of bebop, but they were distorted and played in unusual keys. The purpose was a self-consciously weird music that was difficult to play. Those who played it, however, were some of the most accomplished jazz musicians of the day.

Their creativity attracted the attention of jazz fans and critics.

A so-called second generation of bebop musicians, led by such performers as **Miles Davis, John Coltrane,** and Julian "Cannonball" Adderley, produced a synthesis of bop and mainstream jazz, softening the strident tones of the 1940s while bringing a high level of sophistication to its music. Meanwhile talented newcomers such as Sonny Rollins and Sonny Stitt continued to work directly in the original bop tradition. But as bebop was attempted by other musicians of lesser caliber, it lost its energy and its creativity. As the stars died or turned their attentions to new forms, bebop lost its capacity to startle listeners — and thus its attraction.

Bebop made few concessions to its audience. Unlike pre–World War II swing bands, whose music was intended for a general dance audience, bebop was for hip listeners only. Bebop musicians were mostly black, and they celebrated their separateness. They adopted bohemian lifestyles and spoke a slang-filled hipster's language. Bebop and drug use were associated because most of the bebop stars were addicts at one time or another. As a result, bebop was considered unsavory by outsiders and maybe even immoral.

Bebop continued into the 1990s to be perhaps the most significant influence on contemporary jazz.

REFERENCES:

Xam Wilson Cartier, *Be-bop, Re-bop* (New York: Ballentine, 1987);

Raymond Horicks, *Dizzy Gillespie and the Be-bop Revolution* (New York: Hippocrene, 1984);

David Rosenthal, *Hard Bop: Jazz and Black Music: 1955–1965* (New York: Oxford University Press, 1992).

– R.L.

HARRY BELAFONTE

Harry Belafonte (1927–), a multi-talented performer, has been successful as a folk singer, an actor, and a producer. He is also a strong advocate and patron of young black musicians.

Belafonte began his career in New York City during the 1940s as a member of the American Negro Theater Workshop and a singer in jazz clubs. His first success came in 1951, when he began singing American and Caribbean folk songs in New York nightclubs,and in 1953 he starred in the film *Bright Road*. His performance in the play *John Murray Anderson's Almanac* on Broadway in late 1953 led Hollywood director and producer Otto Preminger to sign Belafonte as the lead in the all-black musical film *Carmen Jones* (1954). Crit-

ics praised his performance, and the film was entered in the Cannes Film Festival competition.

Belafonte was most successful in music. His great skill at finding and singing songs that used calypso and island rhythms corresponded with the listening public's fascination with Latin-American music in the 1950s. Belafonte had six top-forty hits in 1956 and 1957. The biggest was "Day O (The Banana Boat Song)," which reached number five on the pop chart in 1956.

After the end of the "calypso craze" in 1958, he continued his recording and acting career, though at a less frenetic pace. He used his earnings to found Belafonte Enterprises, which has as its goal the promotion and support of young black musicians, including South-African artist Miriam Makeba. In 1985 he played a leading role in the USA for Africa project, which raised millions of dollars in famine relief with its song and video **"We Are the World."**

REFERENCE:

Genia Fogelson, *Harry Belafonte* (Los Angeles: Melrose Square, 1991).

–J.W.H.

SAUL BELLOW

Saul Bellow (1915–), who was awarded the Nobel Prize in Literature in 1976, is in the first rank of postwar American novelists. His fiction is notable for its combination of humor, erudition, and realistic detail. While his protagonists — often Jewish intellectuals like himself — frequently explore philosophical issues, he writes in an accessible style, rejecting the pessimism of much modern literature and offering his readers a qualified sense of affirmation.

Bellow was born in Lachine, Quebec, of Russian–Jewish parents and spent the second half of his childhood in Chicago, where much of his fiction is set and where he now lives. The protagonist-narrator of his first novel, *Dangling Man* (1944), records his disappointments with family and friends, his failures as a writer, and his attempts to prepare himself for military service, as he waits for the draft board to work its way through the red tape created by the fact of his Canadian birth and induct him into the U.S. Army. (After much delay, Bellow himself was rejected by the draft board for medical reasons.)

In Bellow's next novel, *The Victim* (1947), the main character is blamed for causing a friend's downfall, raising the question of how to assign blame in an impersonal world where bad things can happen for no reason at all. Bellow followed these two early efforts with a series of novels that solidified his reputation. *The Adventures of Augie March* (1953) is an ambitious novel about a carefree hero who eventually learns to focus his energies on worthwhile ends but at the price of losing his youthful optimism and freedom. Like much of Bellow's work of this period, the title novella in *Seize the Day* (1956) features a man who finds partial fulfillment of his desire to free himself from the "anxious and narrow life of the average." His desire for simplicity and serenity is echoed by the comic, larger-than-life protagonist of *Henderson the Rain King* (1959), whose search for meaning takes him to Africa. There he learns the ironic lesson that the only way to conquer his anxiety about death and cosmic disorder is to embrace them.

Herzog (1964), which most critics call Bellow's most significant work, deals with its protagonist's vacillation between personal ties, with all their pain and pleasure, and a safe but sterile life of the mind. He finally realizes "that civilized individuals hate and resent the civilization that makes their lives possible" and embraces humanity. The bitter rejection of the modern world in *Mr. Sammler's Planet* (1970) makes this book the most pessimistic of Bellow's novels, but with *Humboldt's Gift* (1975) he returned to qualified affirmation. The novel is loosely based on Bellow's friendship with the late American poet Delmore Schwartz and examines the place of the artist in a materialistic culture.

Since Bellow received the Nobel Prize in Literature in 1976, he has written two novels and two novellas. His 1982 novel, *The Dean's December,* a series of pessimistic reflections on modern civilization, is narrated by a Chicago journalist-turned-academic and set in Bucharest, where he and his wife are tending her dying mother. The narrator of *More Die of Heartbreak* (1987) is also an academic. He and his scholarly uncle philosophize about life a great deal but avoid its attachments. In 1989 Bellow published two novellas. In *A Theft,* a fashion writer's vulnerability comes to the surface when a ring her lover gave her is stolen. In *The Bellarosa Connection* a man is rescued from the Nazis by Billy Rose's "Bellarosa Society" and the man's wife tries to force Rose to take responsibility for her husband's miserable life. Reviews of these books, while respectful, were mixed.

REFERENCES:

Malcolm Bradbury, *Saul Bellow* (New York: Methuen, 1982);

Robert R. Dutton, *Saul Bellow*, revised edition (Boston: Twayne, 1982).

– D.H.-F.

MICHAEL BENNETT

Dancer, choreographer, and director Michael Bennett (1943–1987) is best known for his phenomenally successful musical *A Chorus Line,* which ran continuously on Broadway for nearly twenty years (1975–1993).

Born in Buffalo, Bennett made his first Broadway show appearance as a dancer in *Subways Are for Sleeping* (1961). During the early 1960s he choreographed segments for television variety shows and performed Off Broadway. His first choreographic assignment in the theater was *A Joyful Noise* (1966). It flopped, as did *Henry, Sweet Henry* the following year. *Promises, Promises,* which Bennett choreographed in 1968, was his first successful show, and it was followed by another success, *Company* (1970).

Bennett received his first Antoinette Perry (Tony) Award for choreographing and codirecting *Follies* (1971). Hired to "doctor" *Seesaw* (1973) as he had done for other musicals without credit, he ended up rewriting the script, hiring a new cast, directing, and rechoreographing the show with Grover Dale and Tommy Tune, winning another Tony for choreography.

For *A Chorus Line,* Bennett taped interviews with scores of "gypsies," dancers who depend for their livelihoods on physically demanding, low-paying jobs in the chorus lines of musicals. All the dancers he interviewed called auditions their most difficult professional experiences. Bennett's play takes place during an audition, with information about his interviewees' personal lives, for the most part disguised, gradually emerging throughout the play. Bennett included some of his own experiences in the production, which dramatizes the hard life of the gypsy, who receives neither the high pay nor the posh amenities of the show's stars and whose career may be cut short or seriously curtailed by injury.

A Chorus Line opened Off Broadway in May 1975 and moved to Broadway in July. The play won a Pulitzer Prize and seven Tonies, including those for best musical, best director of a musical for Bennett, and best choreography for Bennett and Robert Avian. *A Chorus Line* has become the longest-running Broadway musical to date, reaching five thousand performances in August 1987, a little over a month after Bennett's death from **AIDS.**

Ballroom (1978), Bennett's next musical, was overshadowed by *A Chorus Line* but nevertheless earned Bennett and Avian another Tony for choreography. His last musical, *Dreamgirls,* loosely based on **Diana Ross and the Supremes,** opened on Broadway in December 1981 and closed in August 1985, after 1,522 performances, earning Bennett and Michael Peters a Tony for choreography.

REFERENCES:

Kevin Kelly, *One Singular Sensation: The Michael Bennett Story* (New York, London, Toronto, Sydney & Auckland: Doubleday, 1990);

Ken Mandelbaum, *A Chorus Line and the Musicals of Michael Bennett* (New York: St. Martin's Press, 1989).

– D.M.

Cathy Berberian

Cathy Berberian (1928–1983), an American soprano who performed avant-garde music, extended traditional vocal ranges and techniques.

She studied mime, opera, and creative writing before pursuing further voice training in Italy, where she made her professional debut in Naples in 1957. Possessing a three-octave vocal range, Berberian was especially sought out by modern experimental composers. Among those who wrote with her voice in mind were **John Cage** and Luciano Berio, whom Berberian married in 1950. Even after their divorce in 1966, Berberian and Berio remained on amicable terms. Pieces he composed for her to perform include *Circles* (1960); *Visage* (1961), an **electronic-music** piece with Berberian's voice on tape; the **aleatory** *Sequenza III* (1965); and *Recital I* (1972). Berberian had many other modern scores written for her, including Igor Stravinsky's *Elegy for J.F.K.* (1964). She was also active as a composer, writing works such as *Stripsody* (1966) for solo voice and *Morsicat(h)y* (1971) for piano.

Resenting being stereotyped as an exclusively modern performer, Berberian began performing more of the standard soprano repertory toward the end of her life. Several recordings of her later work, such as her album of Monteverdi arias and songs, attest to her diversity.

REFERENCE:

David Osmond-Smith, *Berio* (Oxford & New York: Oxford University Press, 1991).

– L.D.S.

Ingrid Bergman

Ingrid Bergman (1915–1982), an international film star of the 1940s, survived a potentially career-ending scandal toward the end of that decade to emerge as one of the most respected actresses in Hollywood.

Born in Stockholm, Sweden, Bergman studied at the Royal Dramatic Theater School in 1933–1934, leaving school after completing her first film, *The Count of the Monk's Bridge* (1934). Her role in the Swedish film *Intermezzo* (1936) was noticed by American producer David O. Selznick, who brought her to the United States to star in the Hollywood version (1939). She went on to play major roles in such classic films as *Casablanca* (1942), *For Whom the Bell Tolls* (1943), *Gaslight* (1944, for which she won an Academy Award [Oscar] for best actress), and *Notorious* (1946).

After Bergman fell in love with Italian director Roberto Rossellini in 1948 and abandoned her husband and daughter for him, Hollywood banished her. She made six mediocre films in Europe before making a Hollywood comeback in the title role of *Anastasia* (1956), which brought her a second Academy Award for best actress. She moved successfully into character parts in the 1970s and won a third Oscar, this time for best supporting actress, for her role as the timid Swedish governess in *Murder on the Orient Express* (1974). She died of cancer in 1982.

Bergman's daughter from her first marriage, Pia Lindstrom, became a successful television journalist, and one of Bergman's three children by Rossellini, Isabella Rossellini, made her mark as an international model and film actress.

REFERENCES:

Ingrid Bergman and Alan Burgess, *Ingrid Bergman: My Story* (New York: Delacorte, 1980);

Laurence Leamer, *As Time Goes By: The Life of Ingrid Bergman* (New York: Harper & Row, 1986).

– I.R.H.

Milton Berle

Milton Berle (1908–) was the first television star. His popular **NBC** comedy-variety series *Texaco Star Theatre* (1948–1956), which was broadcast every Tuesday evening at eight o'clock, helped establish home television as an entertainment medium during its early years, and Berle became known as "Mr. Television."

Berle acted as master of ceremonies and participant in the live musical-comedy show, which was filled with sight gags, songs, dancing, comedy skits, and jokes about current topics. For his signature routine Berle dressed as a woman. A manic sixty-minute broadcast for thirty-nine weeks a year, the show was live television at its best, but the hard work of writing, scoring, rehearsing, and producing the show is an example of why live television was so difficult to sustain. The show was popular from the beginning with both critics and audiences. Jay Gould of the *New York Times* called it television's "first smash hit."

Texaco Star Theatre was canceled in 1956 because of declining ratings, and Berle returned in 1958 with a new show on NBC. *The Kraft Music Hall,* which featured Berle until 1959, lacked the freshness and energy of *Texaco Star Theatre.*

REFERENCES:

Goodman Ace, "Berle's Still Berling," *Look,* 17 (7 April 1953): 52–54;

Milton Berle with Haskel Frankel, *Milton Berle: An Autobiography* (New York: Delacorte, 1974);

Alfred Bester, "The Good Old Days of Mr. Television," *Holiday,* 23 (February 1958): 97, 99–100, 102–103, 105.

– D.M.J.

LEONARD BERNSTEIN

Conductor, composer, and pianist Leonard Bernstein (1918–1990) combined several careers into one, achieving a renown that few other classically trained musicians have surpassed. The first conductor of a major orchestra to be born and trained in America, Bernstein used his considerable popularity to bring classical music to a large audience, influencing and supporting many younger artists.

Born in Lawrence, Massachusetts, Bernstein studied piano and composition in his youth. From 1940 to 1941 he studied at the Berkshire Music Center in Massachusetts under the legendary **Boston Symphony** conductor Serge Koussevitzky. In 1943 Bernstein became assistant conductor of the **New York Philharmonic Orchestra** and received an early opportunity to display his musical gifts when, on a few hours' notice, he replaced the ailing Bruno Walter, who was scheduled to conduct the orchestra in a nationwide broadcast concert.

Bernstein's success with this engagement brought him to the attention of the music world. While establishing himself as a composer, he conducted the New York City Center Symphony from 1944 to 1948 and taught part-time in the 1950s. In 1957, he was named conductor of the New York Philharmonic. He held this post for twelve years, stepping down in 1969 to accept guest conducting engagements around the world. He often combined his skills as a pianist with his conducting, performing at the keyboard while conducting the orchestra.

While Bernstein became famous as a conductor, especially for his exaggerated movements and facial expressions, he also achieved acclaim for a diverse body of compositions. In 1944 he completed *Jeremiah,* his first symphony, as well as the score for **Jerome Robbins**'s ballet *Fancy Free,* which was turned into the hit musical *On the Town* later that year by **Betty Comden and Adolph Green.** Bernstein wrote music for a second Robbins ballet, *Facsimile,* in 1946. His second

symphony, *Age of Anxiety,* premiered in 1949, and he completed his first opera, *Trouble in Tahiti,* in 1952. He teamed with Robbins and Comden and Green again for the musical *Wonderful Town* (1953) and wrote the scores for two more musicals: *Candide* (1956), written by **Lillian Hellman** with lyrics by **Richard Wilbur,** John Latouche, and Dorothy Parker and based on the novel by Voltaire; and the enormously successful *West Side Story* (1957), with lyrics by **Stephen Sondheim** and based in part upon William Shakespeare's *Romeo and Juliet.* Bernstein also wrote the score for the 1954 film *On the Waterfront.* His later compositions include his third symphony, *Kaddish* (1963); *Chichester Psalms* (1965), a choral work in Hebrew; and *Mass* (1971), a theater piece commissioned for the inauguration of the John F. Kennedy Center for the Performing Arts in Washington, D.C. He remained active as a composer and conductor until his death; on Christmas Day 1989 he conducted a recorded performance of Beethoven's Ninth Symphony with the orchestra seated in an area that spanned both sides of the dismantled Berlin Wall.

REFERENCES:

Shirley Bernstein, *Making Music: Leonard Bernstein* (Chicago: Encyclopædia Britannica, 1963);

John Briggs, *Leonard Bernstein: The Man, His Work, and His World* (Cleveland: World, 1961);

Joan Peyser, *Bernstein: A Biography* (New York: Beech Tree Books, 1987).

– L.D.S.

TED BERRIGAN

Often called a second-generation **New York School** poet or a second-generation **Beat** poet, Ted Berrigan (1934–1983) was one of the most prominent of the writers associated with the Poetry Project at **St. Mark's Church-in-the-Bowery,** New York City. Acknowledging New York School poets Frank O'Hara and James Schuyler as influences and counting Beat novelist **Jack Kerouac** as one of his heroes, Berrigan, who reviewed gallery openings for *ARTnews* during the 1960s, compared his comic-surrealist writings to the **Abstract Expressionism** of **Willem de Kooning.**

Berrigan arrived in New York in 1961 after the writers of the Beat movement and the New York School had started to disperse. Settling on the Lower East Side of Manhattan near St. Mark's Church-in-the-Bowery, he became part of the emerging **hippie** scene in the mid 1960s, often writing while high on drugs. The Poetry Project at St. Mark's, founded in 1966, brought together Berrigan and other writers in a group that became known as the Lower East Side poets.

Unorthodox and irreverent, Berrigan compared writing to "playing games." The lines in his poems appear interchangeable; in fact, he frequently rearranged and reused lines in various combinations within poems and often moved lines from one poem to another. Blatantly disregarding traditional notions of plagiarism, he also borrowed and transformed lines or entire works by other writers. He created his "cowboy novel," *Clear the Range* (1977), by crossing out and replacing words in a pulp Western novel. Believing that composer **John Cage** and his avant-garde friends took themselves too seriously, Berrigan constructed a 1967 "interview" with Cage by adding pieces of his friends' writings and his own jokes to a previously published interview with French playwright Fernando Arrabal.

REFERENCES:

Tom Clark, *Late Returns: A Memoir of Ted Berrigan, With 11 Letters from Berrigan to the Author* (Bolinas, Cal.: Tombouctou, 1985);

Stephen Ratcliffe and Leslie Scalapino, *Talking in Tranquility: Interviews with Ted Berrigan* (Bolinas, Cal.: Avenue B / Oakland, Cal.: O Books, 1991).

– K.L.R.

CHUCK BERRY

Elvis Presley was the greatest star in the history of American **rock 'n' roll**, but Chuck Berry (1926–) is the most enduring influence. For five years after his first recorded song, "Maybellene," which was a number-one hit on the *Billboard* "Hot 100," and number 5 on both the *Cashbox* "Top 100" and the *Billboard* rhythm-and-blues chart in 1955, Berry recorded a series of songs that after nearly forty years are among the most memorable of the era. When **The Beatles, The Rolling Stones,** and other British rock groups came to prominence in the mid 1960s, they pointed to Chuck Berry as a primary influence and recorded his songs. "Roll Over Beethoven," "School Days," "Rock and Roll Music," and "Johnnie B. Goode," all written by Berry and recorded by him between 1955 and 1958, are crystallized expressions of teenage sentiment and are regarded among the best rock 'n' roll recordings of the time.

Chuck Berry was at once a distinctive and an energizing performer. His stark, sure-fingered guitar playing, his witty lyrics smoothly sung, and his handsome appearance as he dance-hopped across the stage without missing a note — one leg stiff in front of him, the other deep-bent at the knee — were the elements of his appeal. Championed by disc jockey/impresario Alan Freed, partly in return for one-quarter credit as

composer of "Maybellene," Berry was, by virtue of his popularity, a leader in eliminating the race-music distinction from performances and recordings by black musicians.

Berry's career can be divided into phases by his terms in jail. In 1944 he was sentenced to ten years in a Missouri reform school for robbery. He was released two days after his twenty-first birthday in 1947 and began the most productive phase of his songwriting. In 1961 he was sentenced to three years in prison for violation of the Mann Act, having allegedly brought a fourteen-year-old across state lines for immoral purposes. Released on his thirty-seventh birthday he commenced the second phase of his career, still producing occasional hits but without the joy of his earlier work. In 1979 he was sentenced to three years, suspended on

Chuck Berry

serving 120 days, for income-tax evasion. While in prison he wrote his autobiography, a candid and enlightening account.

REFERENCE:
Chuck Berry, *The Autobiography* (New York: Simon & Schuster, 1987).

– R.L.

John Berryman

John Berryman (1914–1972) was viewed by his contemporaries as possibly the major poet of their generation, rivaled only by his friend **Robert Lowell**. The influential critic Edmund Wilson hailed Berryman's *Homage to Mistress Bradstreet* (1956) as "the most distinguished long poem by an American since *The Waste Land.*" Berryman's *77 Dream Songs* (1964) and *His Toy, His Dream, His Rest* (1968) — the two parts of *The Dream Songs* sequence — won Pulitzer Prizes and were widely recognized as important contributions to the **confessional-poetry** movement that dominated American poetry in the 1960s and 1970s.

Homage to Mistress Bradstreet draws on the life of Anne Bradstreet (1612 or 1613–1672), the first female American poet. Berryman's long, fifty-seven-stanza poem has two speakers: Bradstreet and the poet who is writing about her and sometimes distorting her biography to reveal his own concerns. This intrusion of the poet into his poem is a direct violation of **T. S. Eliot**'s call, in "Traditional and the Individual Talent" (1919), for the impersonality of the poet, and Berryman's poem led the way for the confessional poetry that he and others began writing in the mid 1950s.

Berryman's *Dream Songs*, written between 1955 and 1968, grew out of his analyses of 120 dreams he had in 1954 and 1955. While Berryman claimed that he was not his persona, Henry (also called Henry Pussycat, Henry House, and Mr. Bones), Berryman used *The Dream Songs* as a means of self-examination, splitting parts of himself into various facets of Henry's identity.

Critics, who had high expectations after the groundbreaking success of *Homage to Mistress Bradstreet* and *The Dream Songs*, were generally disappointed by Berryman's later poetry. His only novel, the unfinished, posthumously published *Recovery* (1973), is an autobiographical examination of his twenty-year struggle with alcoholism and the treatment he underwent in 1970. In 1972 Berryman, who was obsessed throughout his life by his father's suicide, killed himself by jumping from a bridge.

REFERENCES:
John Haffenden, *The Life of John Berryman* (Boston, London, Melbourne & Henley: Routledge & Kegan Paul, 1982);
Paul Mariani, *Dream Song: The Life of John Berryman* (New York: Morrow, 1990);
Ernest C. Stefanik, *John Berryman: A Descriptive Bibliography* (Pittsburgh: University of Pittsburgh Press, 1974).

– K.L.R.

Best-seller Lists

Best-seller lists are rankings of the books which have sold the most copies during a given period, usually weekly. The first list appeared in the February 1895 issue of the *Bookman*. Today a best-seller list is a fixture in almost all newspapers with a Sunday book section.

Major newspapers, such as the *New York Times, Washington Post,* and *Los Angeles Times,* compile lists for hardcover fiction and nonfiction books and for trade and mass-market paperbacks through reports from a carefully guarded and rotating list of designated bookstores and wholesalers. The lists are syndicated and thus reach a large audience. Some newspapers compile their own lists from reports by local stores.

Best-seller lists have generated controversy in publishing and book-selling circles. Adherents believe that the lists aid readers in their selections, since people like to read popular books. Critics argue that the lists are not accurate indicators of sales because bookstores may provide incorrect sales information, and the lists exclude sales from and to nontraditional sources (such as book clubs, libraries, and retail outlets other than bookstores). They also feel that reliance on the lists as indicators of merit causes other worthwhile books to be ignored.

The most influential best-seller list appears in *Publishers Weekly.*

REFERENCES:
Judith Appelbaum, "What's Really Wrong With Bestseller Lists," in *Dictionary of Literary Biography Yearbook: 1984,* edited by Jean W. Ross (Detroit: Gale Research, 1985), pp. 44–47;
"The Bestseller Lists: An Assessment," in *Dictionary of Literary Biography Yearbook: 1984,* pp. 38–44;
Alice Payne Hackett and James Henry Burke, *80 Years of Best Sellers: 1895–1975* (New York: Bowker, 1977).

– R.T.

E. Power Biggs

E. Power Biggs (1906–1977), an English-born American organist, popularized organ music in America through his many radio broadcasts, recordings, and concerts. Unlike his extroverted colleague **Virgil Fox,** he played the great baroque works for the instrument in a conservative style.

Biggs studied in London, immigrating to the United States in 1930 and becoming an American citizen in 1937. His weekly organ recitals, broadcast live from Harvard University on **CBS** radio (1942–1958), encompassed virtually the entire body of organ music suitable for concert performance. Biggs made a thorough study of antique organs and performance practice. He also commissioned many new works for organ: among the composers who wrote pieces for Biggs were Walter Piston and Benjamin Britten.

Afflicted with arthritis, Biggs reduced his concert activities toward the end of his life but continued to record organ works and to edit organ music for publication. He also recorded an album of ragtime pieces by Scott Joplin on the pedal harpsichord. Still, it was the traditional organ that was Biggs's first concern: he refused to perform on electronic organs, claiming that they distorted the true sound of the instrument and weakened the technique of the player. This view placed Biggs in the center of the traditionalists among organ performers, particularly when compared with Fox, who appreciated the power of electronic organs.

REFERENCE:

Barbara Owen, *E. Power Biggs, Concert Organist* (Bloomington: Indiana University Press, 1987).

– L.D.S.

BILLBOARD

Billboard magazine has been one of the most widely circulated weekly musical trade publications since its creation in 1894. It is the authoritative source for determining the rankings of popular-music performers in America, and it has subtly influenced the shape of American popular music by promoting the careers of some artists while criticizing or ignoring others.

Each issue features advertising, reviews of recorded music, and sales charts and figures for popular-music recordings in categories such as **rock 'n' roll,** country music, and jazz. It also has indicated examples of **crossover music,** when artists in one category appear on the charts of another. In addition, it has helped musicians through its up-to-date information about current trends in the music world.

REFERENCE:

Philip E. Ennis, *The Seventh Stream: The Emergence of Rocknroll in American Popular Music* (Hanover, N.H. & London:

Wesleyan University Press / University Press of New England, 1992).

– D.H.-F.

BIRTH CONTROL

While the attempt to control human birth can be traced to 1850 B.C., the modern birth-control movement in America dates from the period between the world wars. Three ideologies motivated birth-control activists. Women's rights advocates, led by Margaret Sanger, felt that women had the right to control their bodies. Sanger spoke for women who resisted the moralistic arguments against contraception based on romantic concepts of womanhood. Medical researchers and social psychologists, led by Dr. Robert L. Dickinson, felt that unwanted pregnancy disrupted the marriage relationship, damaging the family structure upon which our society is based. Dickinson, a gynecologist, brought the authority and support of the medical profession to the cause. Population theorists and sociologists, led by Dr. Clarence James Gamble, felt that uncontrolled population growth among lower social classes posed a threat to middle-class life and values. Gamble, a pharmacist-physician and a respected researcher in the field of population growth, brought financial clout (of Procter & Gamble) coupled with a specialist's knowledge. Together, Sanger, Dickinson, and Gamble started a social revolution.

Sanger was the pioneer. Seeking primarily to rally women to her cause, she founded the *Birth Control Review* in 1917 to disseminate information and established the American Birth Control League (1921) to organize the movement. Her activities led directly to the 1936 landmark U.S. Supreme Court decision *United States* v. *One Package*, which held that birth control was not an obscene subject and thus was immune from the Comstock Act of 1872 that prohibited sending obscene materials through the mail.

The Birth Control Federation of America, founded in 1939 and renamed the Planned Parenthood Federation of America in 1942, was the first broad-based organization with the goal of convincing the American public of the wisdom of birth control. With the endorsement of leading activists, including Sanger and Gamble, as well as the American Medical Association, Planned Parenthood mounted a public-relations campaign that attracted private and federal funding for birth-control education and research, particularly for an effective, unobtrusive, low-cost form of contraception.

In 1951 Sanger introduced Dr. Gregory Pincus, a Harvard-trained biologist who received Planned Parenthood funds for his research, to Katherine McCormick, a wealthy biologist who inherited the International Harvester fortune. With support from McCormick, Pincus convinced the research department at the pharmaceutical company G.D. Searle to commit itself to the development, under his direction, of an oral or injected contraceptive. The birth-control pill was announced in 1956, clinically tested by gynecologist John Rock in Puerto Rico in 1956 and 1957, and approved by the United States Food and Drug Administration (FDA) for treatment of menstrual cramps in 1957. In May 1960 the FDA approved Searle's Enovid for use as a contraceptive. "The Pill," as Enovid and its successors were called, took the sacrifice out of birth control, or so it seemed.

Easy as the pill was to use, it and all contraceptives were still against the law in parts of the United States, however. A Supreme Court case, *Griswold* v. *Connecticut* important in establishing a right of privacy, struck down the Connecticut law in 1966. Six years later, in *Eisenstadt* v. *Baird,* the court extended protection against laws prohibiting contraception to unmarried people.

Though birth control has often been construed narrowly as a women's issue, it has been an important factor in social, economic, and political matters as well. Studies released by the Princeton University Office of Population Research in the early 1940s showed increases in Third World populations that were startling to Americans. Fears mounted about the availability of food and living space should population growth continue unabated. Political scientists and sociologists warned of the implications for the world order. International organizations, led by the International Planned Parenthood Foundation (founded in 1952) and John D. Rockefeller III's Population Council (also founded in 1952) worked to find suitable methods of contraception for impoverished peoples. In 1967 federal law was amended to allow the purchase of contraceptives with foreign-aid funds.

Domestically, birth control was a catalyst for social change. It allowed women unprecedented participation in the workforce and in the corporate and political power structure, though social attitudes had to evolve first. At the same time, contraception was urged to stem the disproportionate increase in population among lower classes, which brought with it increased crime among unmanageable demands for federally funded welfare, among other effects. Such calls were met by civil-rights advocates with charges of racially motivated social engineering. Meanwhile, environmentalists were arguing that the earth can accommodate only so many people, and that capacity had been reached. Zero population growth was a goal promoted

with uncommon urgency. With the development of birth-control pills and advanced methods of contraception and sterilization, population growth in the United States showed signs of slowing by the mid 1970s.

As the **AIDS** epidemic reached crisis proportions worldwide in the late 1980s and became identified as a general threat, not limited to practicing homosexuals and intravenous drug users, activists' efforts toward both birth control and sexually transmitted disease control came to overlap more noticeably than in previous years. The words *safe sex* acquired a generally recognized dual meaning.

REFERENCE:

James Reed, *From Private Vice to Public Virtue: The Birth Control Movement and American Society Since 1830* (New York: Basic Books, 1978).

                                                                                                   – R.L.

BLACK AESTHETIC

The Black Aesthetic was a movement in the 1960s and early 1970s that provided theoretical support for the **Black Arts Movement**. Both sought to separate the goals and evaluation of black art from (white) Western ideals of art, instead celebrating black achievement and encouraging artists to direct their attentions to black audiences.

According to the Black Aesthetic, black life is distinct. Though its "essence" has been weakened by the dominant white culture, it can be reclaimed through political action and art, which are inseparable in the Black Aesthetic. Most Black Aesthetic writings called for a separate Black Nation within America. In general, the movement was prescriptive as well as descriptive: since black art should relate to the needs of all blacks, its advocates asserted, art should be representative of black life rather than personal, realistic rather than experimental. Nor could it be judged by Western aesthetic models, which were deemed inherently decadent, exclusive, and condescending. Like **feminist criticism**, one of the major contributions of the Black Aesthetic to modern criticism was its analysis of how value judgments are culturally conditioned and its challenges to the "universal" claims of "mainstream" culture.

Many Black Aesthetic critics were also writers, such as LeRoi Jones (later **Amiri Baraka**) and Larry Neal, who together edited the controversial and influential anthology *Black Fire* (1968). Its ideas also were spread in periodicals such as *Negro Digest* (renamed *Black World* in 1970) and in the essays collected by Addison Gayle, Jr., in *The Black Aesthetic* (1971). Despite opposition from traditional critics, the Black Aesthetic thrived and influenced later critics of African-American literature such as **Henry Louis Gates, Jr.**, and especially, Houston A. Baker, Jr. In the mid 1970s, however, the Black Aesthetic began to be criticized by black writers such as Ishmael Reed, who found the movement too restricting for black artists, and Baraka, who turned to Marxism. Others were uncomfortable with the tendency within the Black Aesthetic to criticize older black writers whose works were praised by white critics, the subordinate role the allied black-power movement assigned to women, and sweeping generalizations about blacks and whites alike. Slowly the Black Aesthetic agenda became less pressing with the gradual gains of the **civil rights movement**, and its concerns blended into **multiculturalism** and postcolonial criticism in the 1980s.

REFERENCES:

Jeffrey Louis Decker, ed., *The Black Aesthetic Movement, Dictionary of Literary Biography Documentary Series*, volume 8 (Detroit, New York & London: Gale, 1991);

Addison Gayle, Jr., ed., *The Black Aesthetic* (Garden City, N.Y: Doubleday, 1971).

– D.H.-F.

BLACK ARTS MOVEMENT

In 1968 black poet Don L. Lee wrote: "We must destroy Faulkner, dick, jane, and other perpetuators of evil. It's time for DuBois, Nat Turner, and Kwame Nkrumah. As Frantz Fanon points out: destroy the culture and you destroy the people." That was the language of the Black Arts Movement: urgent, unequivocal, isolationist. The theoriticians of the Black Arts Movement, BAM as it was known, preached that the exclusive role of the black artist was to advance the political aims of the movement. Art should promote the concept of black unity. It should educate and motivate, guided by the principles of the **Black Aesthetic**.

In practice writers and performers of the Black Arts Movement delivered their message in deliberately shocking, racist terms. The works of BAM were short, didactic dramas written to be performed on the street; agitating poems punctuated by profanity; and theoretical essays stipulating the duty of the artist to the movement.

The primary proponents of the Black Arts Movement were theorists Maulana Karenga, Don L. Lee (later Haki R. Madhubuti), and Larry Neal; essayist, poet, and dramatist LeRoi Jones (later **Amiri Baraka**); poets Sonia Sonchez and Nikki Giovanni.

REFERENCES:

LeRoi Jones and Larry Neal, eds., *Black Fire: An Anthology of Afro-American Writing* (New York: Morrow, 1968);

Larry Neal, "The Black Arts Movement," *Drama Review*, 12 (Summer 1968): 29-39.

– R.L.

BLACK HUMOR

Black humor is a term applied to post–World War II literature in which laughter is presented as the only available response to a painful and meaningless existence. It is humor with an angry edge that signals a refusal to give in to despair and death.

In the United States black humor was at its height in the 1960s, when it was employed in highly acclaimed experimental novels such as **John Barth**'s *The Sot-Weed Factor* (1960), **Joseph Heller**'s *Catch-22* (1961), **Thomas Pynchon**'s *V* (1963), John Hawkes's *Second Skin* (1964), and **Kurt Vonnegut, Jr.**'s *Slaughterhouse-Five* (1969). **Edward Albee**'s *Who's Afraid of Virginia Woolf?* (1962) is often called a black-humor play.

These works challenge the traditional view of an ordered world where human behavior is based on generally shared values. Presenting a grotesque, cynical picture of an absurd, chaotic world, they offer no possibility for heroism. At best their alienated protagonists are granted the limited affirmation that comes with laughing defiantly at their fate.

While characteristics of black humor can be identified in earlier literature, it is very much a phenomenon of the 1960s (when the term was coined), and it has appeared sporadically in literature since that decade.

REFERENCES:

Bruce Jay Friedman, ed., *Black Humor* (New York: Bantam, 1965);

Max F. Schulz, *Black Humor Fiction of the Sixties: A Pluralistic Definition of Man and His World* (Athens: Ohio University Press, 1973).

– D.H.-F.

BLACK MOUNTAIN COLLEGE

The academic outpost of the avant-garde during the ten years that followed World War II, Black Mountain College, a small unaccredited college in North Carolina, was the spawning ground for major innovations in art, architecture, music, and poetry.

The faculty included representatives from two of the most influential groups of twentieth-century abstract artists: the German Bauhaus school of art, architecture, and design, which was shut down by the Nazis in 1933, and the American **Abstract Expressionists**. Josef Albers — one of the many Bauhaus faculty who immigrated to the United States, where their ideas became widely accepted — was in charge of the art curriculum at Black Mountain from 1933 to 1949, attracting students and teachers from all over the country to the summer art and music "institutes" he started in 1944.

At a time when the Abstract Expressionists were still struggling for recognition, Albers hired **Robert Motherwell** (summer 1945) and **Willem de Kooning** (summer 1948) as visiting faculty. From the Bauhaus group he brought in artist Lyonel Feininger (summer 1945) and architect Walter Gropius, who was there frequently from 1944 until 1949.

Albers passed on his ideas about "how colors influence and change each other" when placed side by side — as well as the "Hard Edge" geometric shapes in his paintings — to Kenneth Noland, who studied at Black Mountain in 1946–1948 and summer 1950 and went on to be recognized as a major practitioner of **post-painterly abstraction**.

Robert Rauschenberg, who studied at Black Mountain in 1948–1949 and returned in summer 1952 with artist Cy Twombly, called Albers "the most important teacher I've ever had." Rauschenberg's biggest artistic breakthrough at Black Mountain may have been accidental. He awoke one morning to find a butterfly stuck to one of his paintings and invented his "combine" technique of creating works of art that were part painting and part sculpture.

The summer institutes continued to attract the Abstract Expressionists even after Albers's departure in 1949. **Jackson Pollock** and **Mark Rothko** taught at Black Mountain in summer 1950 (while **Helen Frankenthaler** was a visitor).

Inventor **Buckminster Fuller**, whose geodesic dome design seemed startlingly innovative to Americans in the 1960s, constructed the first full-size version of his dome with the help of students at Black Mountain in summer 1948. The project was literally a "flop," sending him back to the drawing board for further refinements.

Fuller and other institute participants took part in a performance of Erik Satie's *The Ruse of Medusa*, staged by composer **John Cage** and dancer **Merce Cunningham**. The two visited the school for the first time in April 1948 and were on the faculty for several subsequent summers. Cage did some of his most significant work on **aleatory music** at Black Mountain in 1952 and 1953. His 1952 **mixed-media event** — in

Buckminster Fuller and students erecting his first geodesic dome at Black Mountain College, 1948 (photograph by Beaumont Newhall)

which Cunningham, Rauschenberg, poets **Charles Olson** and Mary Caroline Richards, and pianist-composer **David Tudor** took part — was the first of the **Happenings** that became so popular in the 1960s.

After Olson came to Black Mountain full-time in 1951, writing began to dominate the curriculum. A charismatic, domineering, unorthodox teacher, Olson preached the doctrines of **Projective Verse**, gathering student disciples such as poets Edward Dorn, Joel Oppenheimer, Jonathan Williams, Michael Rumaker, and John Weiners. He also brought to the college the two writers who are now, with Olson, considered the major Black Mountain Poets. San Francisco poet **Robert Duncan** visited the school in 1955 and joined the faculty in 1956, the year the school was shut down for lack of funding. He took a position previously held by **Robert Creeley**, who before arriving at the school in March 1954 had joined with Olson to start the *Black Mountain Review*.

REFERENCES:

Martin Duberman, *Black Mountain: An Exploration in Community* (New York: Dutton, 1972);

Mary Emma Harris, *The Arts at Black Mountain College* (Cambridge, Mass.: MIT Press, 1987);

Mervin Lane, ed. *Black Mountain College: Sprouted Seeds* (Knoxville: University of Tennessee Press, 1990).

– K.L.R.

BLACK PANTHERS

The Black Panther Party was the most visible of the militant organizations of the late 1960s and early 1970s promoting a separate black nation within America. Many young urban blacks were attracted by their fearless confrontations with police and their high-profile "uniform" of leather jackets and black berets.

Huey P. Newton and Bobby Seale founded the Black Panther Party for Self-Defense in northern California in October 1966; it became simply the Black Panther Party in 1967. At first, the Panthers patrolled Oakland ghettos with weapons in "self-defense" against civil-rights violations by white police. In May 1967 they gained notoriety by marching into the California capitol with rifles to protest a bill that would make unconcealed weapons illegal. Tensions with the authorities led to a series of shootouts with the police; in October 1967 Newton was arrested for murdering an Oakland police officer. Control of the Black Panthers passed to Seale and to "minister of information" Eldridge Cleaver, who called for black offensive retaliation rather than self-defense. Their leadership was challenged early in 1968 by Stokely Carmichael, who encouraged black unity. Carmichael resigned his position in the party the following year, one sign of internal conflicts and confrontations with other groups that beset the party. The Panthers were further weakened by an April 1968 police shootout in Oakland that killed their seventeen-year-old treasurer, Bobby Sutton. As a result, authorities revoked Cleaver's parole. Rather than returning to prison, Cleaver went into hiding. Newton's 1968 conviction for voluntary manslaughter was overturned in 1970.

By 1968 the Black Panther Party had spread to cities across the country, but events such as the killing of two Chicago Panther leaders in a December 1968 police raid slowed its growth; by 1970 several Panther leaders were dead, in prison, or, like Cleaver, in exile. Newton tried to revive the party after his release in 1970 by rejecting a revolutionary stance and initiating a "Serve the People" program that provided free food and health clinics for children and the needy. In the mid-1970s Panthers even ran for political office. By this time, however, their influence was undermined by

claims that they had threatened and assaulted other blacks, and the party collapsed.

The Black Panthers combined militaristic discipline with an ideology that loosely mixed Marxism-Leninism with the ideas of Malcolm X and the Caribbean writer Frantz Fanon. The Black Panthers are credited with coining the 1960s slogans "Power to the people" and "Off the pigs!"—both of which were adopted by white protesters.

REFERENCES:
Todd Gitlin, *The Sixties: Years of Hope, Days of Rage* (Toronto, New York, London, Sydney, & Auckland: Bantam, 1987);

G. Louis Heath, *Off the Pigs! The History and Literature of the Black Panther Party* (Metuchen, N.J.: Scarecrow, 1976).

– D.H.-F.

MARC BLITZSTEIN

Composer and playwright Marc Blitzstein (1905–1964) is known for the radical political views expressed in his work and his 1952 translation of Bertolt Brecht and Kurt Weill's 1928 opera *Die Dreigroschenoper* as *The Threepenny Opera*.

Blitzstein studied composition in Europe under Nadia Boulanger and Arnold Schoenberg. He returned to the United States during the Great Depression and began writing music and plays. His most famous drama, *The Cradle Will Rock* (1937), is about the fight between a union and a steel executive. The play was controversial for its anticapitalism. Blitzstein's *Airborne Symphony* (1946) for speaker, tenor and baritone soloists, chorus, and orchestra is his most popular musical work. Conducted by **Leonard Bernstein** at its premiere, the piece combines Blitzstein's music — itself a combination of jazz influences and traditional classical styles — with text about the history of flight, based on Blitzstein's experience in the U.S. Army Air Corps during World War II. His opera *Regina* (1949) is based on **Lillian Hellman**'s 1939 play *The Little Foxes*, and his translation *The Threepenny Opera*, which maintains the sharp satire on middle-class society of the original, was highly praised by audiences and critics.

REFERENCE:
Eric A. Gordon, *Mark the Music: The Life and Work of Marc Blitzstein* (New York: St. Martin's Press, 1989).

– L.D.S.

BLUEGRASS MUSIC

Bluegrass music is a type of country music, with roots in **folk music**, created by musicians dedicated to preserving "hillbilly" or "old-time" music traditions. Its name derives from **Bill Monroe and the Blue Grass Boys,** a group founded in 1939 by Bill Monroe, a mandolin player who became known as "the Father of Bluegrass."

Monroe and his band played the old songs and dances with traditional acoustic string instruments such as the mandolin, guitar, banjo, and fiddle, but they performed them at a faster tempo and higher pitch than usual in country music, thus creating a new style. Bluegrass singing, which also includes **gospel** selections, emphasizes harmony. Although traditional bluegrass still prevails, two innovations appeared in the late 1960s and early 1970s: "progressive" bluegrass applies acoustic instruments and established styles to newer songs, including folk and **rock;** and "newgrass" uses electronically amplified instruments.

Bluegrass music was first widely heard in the 1940s on Grand Ole Opry radio broadcasts. Monroe and the Blue Grass Boys were among the most popular performers, and many bluegrass musicians either imitated them or learned under Monroe and moved on. Most notably, singer-guitarist Lester Flatt and banjo phenomenon Earl Scruggs left the Blue Grass Boys in 1948 to form the Foggy Mountain Boys. Before they ended their partnership in 1969, Flatt and Scruggs, as well as Monroe and the Blue Grass Boys and the Stanley Brothers, helped spread bluegrass beyond the Grand Ole Opry by performing at the folk-music and bluegrass festivals that were popular from the late 1950s through the 1970s. The Foggy Mountain Boys also gained wider attention for bluegrass with their 1962 recording of the theme for the television show *The Beverly Hillbillies* and their "Foggy Mountain Breakdown" (first recorded in 1949), which was featured in the 1967 film *Bonnie and Clyde.* The bluegrass tune "Dueling Banjos" — originally "Feuding Banjos," written and recorded in 1955 by Don Reno and Arthur Smith — also became popular after its use in the 1972 movie *Deliverance* (performed by Eric Weissberg and Steve Mandell).

REFERENCES:

Robert Cantwell, *Bluegrass Breakdown: The Making of the Old South Sound* (Urbana: University of Illinois Press, 1984);

Steven D. Price, *Old as the Hills: The Story of Bluegrass Music* (New York: Viking, 1975);

Neil V. Rosenberg, *Bluegrass: A History* (Urbana & Chicago: University of Illinois Press, 1985).

                                                          – L.E.P.

JUDY BLUME

Judy Blume (1938–) was among the first writers for adolescents to deal openly, and without moralizing, with adolescent concerns over sexuality and social relations. Though her approach has been controversial, she has been popular with young readers since the early 1970s.

Blume's first major success came with *Are You There God? It's Me, Margaret.* (1970), in which a twelve-year-old girl struggles with questions concerning her religious identity and the physical changes accompanying puberty. As with the majority of her later works, Blume injects frequent humorous episodes into the story and relies on colloquial, simple language. Her dramatic, accessible style has proved popular with young readers, though the treatment of Margaret's physical changes, including menstruation, has offended some critics.

Blume's realistic and often humorous treatment of juvenile and adolescent characters continued in works such as *Tales of a Fourth Grade Nothing* (1972), *Deenie* (1973), *Forever...* (1975), and *Tiger Eyes* (1981), which found large and appreciative audiences ranging in age from eight to sixteen. Despite the controversy over the sexual content and lack of traditional moralizing in Blume's books, their original approach to perennial adolescent problems has greatly influenced other writers in the field.

REFERENCE:

Maryann N. Weidt, *Presenting Judy Blume* (Boston: Twayne, 1990).

                                                          – S.B.

ROBERT BLY

Robert Bly (1926–) became famous after his bestselling *Iron John: A Book about Men* (1990) made him a leader in the so-called men's movement, aimed at helping men to find their innermost, essential selves. Yet Bly's poetry, translations, and criticism have been influential among literary people since the 1960s.

Bly began writing poetry in the tradition of **T. S. Eliot,** whose concept of the impersonal, objective poet had been embraced by two generations of British and American poets, but after reading European and Latin American Surrealist poetry in the mid 1950s, Bly changed his style. He began employing "deep images" intended, by a process of associations, to take the reader with the poet into the collective unconscious (the part of the mind that Carl Jung defined as the memories of a prehuman existence shared by all humankind).

In 1966 Bly helped to organize American Writers Against the **Vietnam War,** led antiwar "read-ins" on college campuses and edited two anthologies of antiwar poetry. He published many of his own antiwar poems in *The Light Around the Body* (1967). When this book won a National Book Award in 1968, Bly used the prize money to help draft resisters.

In 1970 Bly began an intensive study of Jungian and neo-Jungian psychology, which led to his examination of myths and fairy tales. By 1981, when he held the first of his popular seminars for men, he had focused his attention on stories illuminating the masculine side of the mind. Eventually he settled on the tale of Iron John — the story of a young prince's initiation into manhood by a mentor symbolizing man's essential masculine being — as the basis for his thinking about male identity.

Although Bly is now best known for his contribution to the men's movement, his long-term significance may lie in his championing of European and Latin American poetry as models for his contemporaries in the United States. Bly and poets such as James Wright, Louis Simpson, W. S. Merwin, Robert Kelly, and Jerome Rothenberg — are sometimes grouped together "deep-image poets" by critics who credit them with uniting an important European strain with the Whitmanic tradition in American poetry.

REFERENCES:

Victoria Frenkel Harris, *The Incorporative Consciousness of Robert Bly* (Carbondale & Edwardsville: Southern Illinois University Press, 1992);

Richard P. Sugg, *Robert Bly* (Boston: Twayne, 1986).

– K.L.R.

BODY ART

Combining aspects of **conceptual art** and **performance art,** body art, which emerged in late 1960s and early 1970s, made the artist's own body the artistic medium.

Los Angeles–based Chris Burden produced the most extreme versions of body art, often involving physical danger and implying masochism. In his *Shooting Piece* (1971) a friend shot him in the arm, causing a more serious injury than he had planned. In *Dead Man* (1972) he lay in the middle of a busy Los Angeles street with his body covered by a canvas tarpaulin. One of his goals was to confront viewers with moral decisions — such as whether or not to run over the "dead" body — forcing them out of the more passive role of the museumgoer.

Dennis Oppenheim, a conceptual artist and sculptor from California, created *Reading Position for a Second Degree Burn* (1970) by allowing selected areas of his skin to become sunburned, creating a vi-

sual analogy between skin pigmentation and a painter's colors. Unlike performance art, body art does not require a live audience. While Burden's body art occurred before often-unwitting spectators, it was usually photographed. Documentation through photographs and video was an essential element of much body art. Most American artists involved with body art in the 1970s have since moved in other directions.

REFERENCE:

RoseLee Goldberg, *Performance Art from Futurism to the Present* (New York: Abrams, 1989).

– K.B.

WILLIAM BOLCOM

William Bolcom (1938–) is an American composer and pianist who is especially known for his keyboard music and his advocacy of ragtime.

A native of Seattle, Bolcom studied in Paris with French composers Olivier Messiaen and Darius Milhaud. Bolcom's compositions are extremely challenging and eclectic, drawing on a variety of styles ranging from **serial music** to jazz and other popular idioms. His works include *Session 2* (1966) for violin and viola; *Black Host* (1967), a piece for organ, percussion, and tape; and *Twelve New Etudes,* which won the 1988 Pulitzer Prize for music. An accomplished pianist, Bolcom was one of the performers responsible for the "ragtime revival" of the late 1960s and the 1970s, and he has done much to raise respect for the piano works of Scott Joplin, Joseph Lamb, James Scott, and others. He is married to the American concert singer Joan Morris, who often appears with him in recitals devoted to American songs of the nineteenth and early twentieth centuries.

REFERENCE:

George Rochberg, *The Aesthetics of Survival: A Composer's View of Twentieth-Century Music,* edited, with an introduction, by William Bolcom (Ann Arbor: University of Michigan Press, 1984).

– L.D.S.

BOMB SHELTERS

Bomb shelters were a **Cold War** response to the possible threat of nuclear war with the former Soviet Union. They were especially popular in America during the 1950s and early 1960s. Some bomb shelters were planned by government agencies while others were built by individuals across the country.

In the early 1950s many people fearing nuclear attack were dissatisfied with government provisions for warning and evacuation. Taking matters into their own hands, some built private shelters, especially in California. Construction firms offered to build shelters ranging from cheap foxholes to one-room shelters complete with telephones, bunks, ventilation systems, and Geiger counters. Costs ran into the thousands of dollars, depending on accommodations. These underground shelters, loaded with emergency supplies and often with walls of reinforced concrete two to three feet thick, were supposed to be able to withstand an above-ground atomic blast. At the peak of the trend, there were an estimated two hundred thousand private bomb shelters in the United States. For such a serious topic, bomb shelters were a surprisingly cheerful subject in American culture of the 1950s: in 1959, for instance, *Life* ran a story about a couple who honeymooned for two weeks in their new shelter.

The government approached bomb shelters with greater reserve. Communities and a few states, such as New York, considered shelter plans, and deliberation about a national shelter program resulted in the creation of the Civil Defense Administration (CDA) in the mid 1950s. President Dwight D. Eisenhower and the military opposed the notion of bomb shelters, as did CDA official Val Peterson, who described them as "death traps" and "burial grounds" in 1957. Later that year, however, the CDA, which at first supported evacuation rather than shelter, reversed its position. This shift was encouraged by increasing knowledge that radioactive fallout would make evacuation futile and that developments in Soviet rocket technology, evidenced that year with the launch of the first Sputnik satellite (see **Space Race**), rendered early warning impossible. However, funding was limited by Congress, and only a handful of public buildings were designated as shelters in the late 1950s and early 1960s. To supplement such planning, many architects attempted to integrate shelters with new building designs, especially for schools.

While private bomb shelters enjoyed some popularity, many people opposed government shelters, fearing that they would be used if built. Also, as the **nuclear weapons** arsenals of the superpowers grew to massive proportions, many felt that no shelter could provide protection, and others ignored the threat of nuclear war altogether. By the mid 1960s the craze had largely passed; many people with private shelters used them for storage or children's playrooms instead. A small group of "survivalists" continued to maintain shelters, and a slight revival of general interest occurred in the 1980s.

REFERENCES:

James Gilbert, *Another Chance: Postwar America, 1945–1968* (Philadelphia: Temple University Press, 1981);

"Their Sheltered Honeymoon," *Life*, 46 (10 August 1959);

"Wonderful to Play In," *Time*, 57 (5 February 1951): 12.

– D.H.-F.

BOOK CLUBS

Book clubs have been an important force in American publishing since 1926, when Book-of-the-Month Club, the first major direct-mail trade-book merchandiser was organized. In the mid 1970s it was estimated that between eight and nine percent of all American book sales were through book clubs.

The success of book clubs can be attributed to two factors. First, they allow books to be marketed and sold directly to people who may not have ready access to one of the ten thousand or so American bookstores (as of the mid 1980s). Second, book clubs have effectively used the sales technique of negative option, which means that a featured book is automatically mailed to members periodically, usually every three weeks, unless the member mails the club a card instructing it not to send the book.

In 1980 there were some two hundred book clubs that fell into three categories: independents, such as the Book-of-the-Month Club; clubs affiliated with a magazine, as the *Playboy, Cosmopolitan,* and *Reader's Digest* book clubs are; and clubs affiliated with a publisher, as the Literary Guild and its various specialized spin-offs are with Doubleday. About seven million Americans belonged to book clubs in the mid 1970s.

The popularity of book clubs, which had steadily grown since they were introduced, seemed to reach a peak in the late 1970s and to decline modestly thereafter as intense competition and increasing marketing costs drove marginal clubs out of business. Meanwhile, the major clubs increased their dominance and their power. Trade-book publishers and booksellers continued to recognize that designation of a book as a selection of Book-of-the-Month Club or Literary Guild conferred upon it a distinction that increased non-club book sales.

REFERENCE:

John Tebbel, *A History of Book Publishing in the United States,* volume 4 (New York & London: Bowker, 1981), pp. 335–365, 740.

– R.L.

BOOKS ON TAPE

Books were recorded for the blind and for educational purposes for many years, but in the 1980s books on tape became popular as entertainment for the general public. This new trend was an outgrowth of the proliferation of cassette-tape players in America, including those in car stereos and portable players with headphones. Between 1983 and 1986 sales of books on tape rose from $25 million to $250 million a year. Many people listen to books on tape while traveling or driving to work.

Books on tape are often produced by publishers of current books, which are read by their authors or by actors. Nonfiction books — such as self-help books, foreign-language instruction, and books on business and health — are popular. Fiction books on tape also sell well, especially best-selling novels, other books by well-known authors, and genre fiction such as mysteries and **science fiction.** These books, which are usually abridged to one or two cassettes, often use music and sound effects. Some tapes are dramatized fiction, a throwback to radio shows before the age of television. Literary classics are also available on tape.

Thousands of titles are currently on tape, many of them at **chain bookstores.** Reviews and news of books on tape have appeared in *Publishers Weekly* since 1986, along with **best-seller lists** for taped fiction and nonfiction.

REFERENCES:

Ray Anello, "Heard a Good Book Lately?" *Newsweek,* 106 (29 July 1985): 55;

Books on Tape Catalog, 1993: World's Largest Selection of Audio Books, revised edition (Newport Beach, Cal.: Books on Tape, 1993);

Stefan Kanfer, "Heard Any Good Books Lately? Literature on Cassettes Is a Best-Selling Business," *Time,* 128 (21 July 1986): 71–72;

Anne McGrath, "Books That Speak for Themselves," *U.S. News & World Report,* 101 (14 July 1986): 49.

– D.H.-F.

PAT BOONE

For a few years in the 1950s, Pat Boone (1934–) ranked second only to **Elvis Presley** as a popular singer. Boone's image as a wholesome, clean-cut student contrasted with Presley's raw, sexual energy and contributed to his popularity with white middle-class audiences.

Boone began his career in Nashville, Tennessee, in the early 1950s. He won competitions on *Ted Mack's Original Amateur Hour* and *Arthur Godfrey's Talent*

Scouts in 1954 and signed a contract with Dot Records. At a time when many "white" radio stations did not play recordings by black musicians, record companies hired white performers such as Boone to record new "cover versions" of songs first recorded by black artists. Boone's versions of "Ain't That a Shame" (Fats Domino), "Tutti Frutti," and "Long Tall Salley" (both Little Richard) followed the release of the originals by mere days.

During 1955–1962 Boone had six number one hits, including "Ain't That a Shame" (1955), "I Almost Lost My Mind" (1956), "Don't Forbid Me" (1956), "Love Letters in the Sand" (1957), "April Love" (1957), and "Moody River" (1961). He also made movie appearances, starring in films such as *Bernadine* (1957) and *April Love* (1957). As **rock 'n' roll** became more accepted by the public and radio became less segregated, Boone's popularity waned. His last pop hit was "Speedy Gonzales" in 1962. Later in the 1960s and 1970s he recorded country and **gospel music.**

REFERENCE:

Pat Boone, *A New Song* (Carol Stream, Ill.: Creation House, 1970).

– L.D.S.

BOSSA NOVA

Deriving from the older samba, the bossa nova is a Brazilian musical style that originated during 1958-1959. The bossa nova differs from the samba in that it deemphasizes the role of the percussion, whereas the center of the samba is provided by the rhythmic pulse of the Latin-American percussion instruments. The term *bossa nova* first appeared as a lyric in the song

Pat Boone

"Desafinado" (1962), by Antonio Carlos Jobim, the composer most readily associated with the musical form. Its style is further characterized by unusual melodic and harmonic intervals and its integration of melody, harmony, and rhythm in equal proportions. Its vocals are usually unemotional, and the bossa nova is generally accompanied by acoustic guitar.

The style came to the United States in the late 1950s after musicians Bud Shank, a California saxophonist, and Laurindo Almeida, a Brazilian guitarist, brought some jazz-tinged sambas from Brazil. Stan Getz and Charlie Byrd returned from a Brazilian tour in the early 1960s with songs by Jobim and other Brazilian bossa-nova artists. Getz and Byrd had a hit in 1962 with their version of "Desafinado," which reached number fifteen on the pop chart. Jazz artist Herbie Mann was also instrumental in bringing the style from Brazil.

The high point of the bossa-nova craze in the United States was in 1963, when three pop songs with the bossa-nova beat reached the pop chart. Getz recorded Jobim's "The Girl from Ipanema," with vocals by João Gilberto. It reached number five on the pop chart. Eydie Gorme reached the chart with "Blame It on the Bossa Nova" and **Elvis Presley** hit with "Bossa Nova Baby." Although the bossa-nova craze faded, the fascination of the public and musicians with Latin-American rhythms did not. The bossa nova became part of American popular music.

– L.D.S.

Boston Pops Orchestra

The popular Boston Pops Orchestra provides an extension of the Boston musical season by giving performances of light classics and popular music from May through July, after the **Boston Symphony Orchestra** has completed its season. With the exception of its principal players, the Boston Pops is composed of members of the Boston Symphony. Its many recordings and its **PBS** broadcasts since 1970, *Evening at Pops,* have made it the best-known pops orchestra in America.

Its concerts, patterned after similar ventures abroad, began in 1885 as "Music Hall Promenade Concerts" to bring in and educate new audiences for classical music. They have been called "Pops" concerts since 1900, when the Boston Symphony first occupied Symphony Hall, its main performing site. Much of the credit for the success of the Boston Pops Orchestra is due to Arthur Fiedler, who led the group for nearly fifty years (1930–1979) and established a pattern for pops programs that has been adopted by similar ensem-

bles such as the Cincinnati Pops Orchestra. This formula divides a pops concert into three segments, with intermissions separating each: several light classics, such as opera overtures, preludes, and short orchestral pieces, open a concert; they are followed by a full-length concerto or comparable work featuring a soloist. The performance concludes with popular selections from **Broadway musicals, Top 40** hits, and other contemporary sources. Fiedler's perennial Pops encore was John Philip Sousa's "Stars and Stripes Forever," at the conclusion of which an American flag was unfurled from the ceiling of Symphony Hall to applause from the audience.

Near the end of the regular Pops season, the orchestra plays outdoor concerts on the banks of the Charles River. Called "Esplanade Concerts," these events were founded by Fiedler in 1930. After Fiedler's death in 1979 the ensemble was led by guest conductors before composer and conductor **John Williams** assumed the directorship in 1980. He stepped down in 1993.

REFERENCE:

Harry Ellis Dickson, *Arthur Fiedler and the Boston Pops: An Irreverent Memoir* (Boston: Houghton Mifflin, 1981).

– L.D.S.

Boston Symphony Orchestra

The Boston Symphony Orchestra is one of the oldest and most prestigious orchestras in America. Established in 1881 with an endowment from a wealthy Boston banker, the Boston Symphony had earned an enduring international reputation by 1945. The **Boston Pops Orchestra,** founded in 1885, is made up of musicians from the Boston Symphony Orchestra and performs in May and June, part of the Symphony Orchestra's off-season.

In keeping with its original mission to make quality performances available to the public, the Boston Symphony was the first orchestra to record a phonograph album in the United States (1917). It began a series of radio broadcasts in 1926, and it first toured Europe in 1952.

In addition to the classical European repertoire, the Boston Symphony has introduced works by contemporary composers, many of them American, especially under the baton of Serge Koussevitzky, who conducted the orchestra from 1924 to 1949. New music commissioned or premiered by the Boston Symphony includes works by **Samuel Barber**, Béla Bartók, Benjamin Britten, **Aaron Copland**, Sergey Prokofiev, Maurice Ravel, and Igor Stravinsky. The Boston Symphony

phony also founded the Berkshire Music Center, near Lenox, Massachusetts, where training sessions for musicians and composers have been held every summer since 1940. Two of its most successful students were **Leonard Bernstein** and **Lukas Foss**. The Tanglewood Music Festival is held there every summer.

Recent conductors of the Boston Symphony include Charles Munch (1949–1963), Erich Leinsdorf (1963–1968), William Steinberg (1968–1973), and Seiji Ozawa (1973–).

REFERENCES:

Janet Baker-Carr, *Evening at Symphony: A Portrait of the Boston Symphony Orchestra* (Boston: Houghton Mifflin, 1977);

Hugo Leichtentritt, *Serge Koussevitzky: The Boston Symphony Orchestra and the New American Music* (Cambridge, Mass.: Harvard University Press, 1946).

– D.H.-F.

RAY BRADBURY

Ray Bradbury (1920–) was the first American writer of **science fiction and fantasy** to be respected by literary critics and a wide general audience in addition to fans of genre fiction. He has also written realistic fiction as well as film and television scripts. Some critics feel he is not really a science-fiction writer, claiming he uses science-fiction trappings as background rather than as an essential part of his plots, making his works more poetic evocations of the past than extrapolations on the future. Given the low esteem in which many critics have held conventional science fiction, this deviation from the norm may at least partly account for Bradbury's positive reception.

Bradbury made his first professional sale to a pulp magazine in 1941 and soon began publishing in *Weird Tales,* one of the most popular of these periodicals. Many of his stories from the 1940s are fantasy and **horror;** several appear in his first book, *Dark Carnival* (1947). In the late 1940s Bradbury began writing more science fiction, and his fiction began to appear in mainstream publications such as *Harper's* and the *New Yorker.* Before Bradbury's success, **Robert A. Heinlein** was the only American science-fiction writer who had managed to place stories anywhere except for the science-fiction magazines with any regularity.

In the 1950s Bradbury's reputation grew: he was praised by writers such as Aldous Huxley and Christopher Isherwood for his lyrical style and social criticism, and his work was published in literary anthologies. *The Martian Chronicles* (1950) and *Fahrenheit 451* (1953) were among the first science-fiction books to receive widespread attention beyond science-fiction fandom.

The Martian Chronicles, more a collection of brief interrelated stories than a novel, deals with racism and the threat of nuclear war in human colonies on Mars. Bradbury condemns **censorship** and praises the magic of books in *Fahrenheit 451,* in which "firemen" burn books and rebels try to preserve them through memorization. During this decade Bradbury also coauthored the screenplay for **John Huston**'s *Moby Dick* (1956) and published short-story collections such as *The Illustrated Man* (1951) and *The Golden Apples of the Sun* (1953) and the realistic, nostalgic novel *Dandelion Wine* (1957).

Bradbury's success continued in the 1960s and 1970s, when he focused more on poetry and drama, and from 1985 to 1990 he wrote forty-two scripts for the *Ray Bradbury Theater* on **cable television**. Though some critics find his later fiction repetitive and sentimental, he has maintained a large audience.

REFERENCES:

Martin Harry Greenberg and Joseph D. Olander, eds., *Ray Bradbury* (New York: Taplinger, 1980);

David Mogen, *Ray Bradbury* (Boston: Twayne, 1986).

– D.H.-F.

THE BRADY BUNCH

The Brady Bunch was one of the last "family fun" situation comedies before the genre came to be dominated by more-socially conscious shows such as *All in the Family*. Its premise was that a widow with three daughters marries a widower with three sons, and they all live with a maid and a dog in a state of comic chaos. No one ever faced any serious problems, and the children invariably learned a simple moral lesson on such things as sharing or telling the truth.

The show has been an enduring success beyond its original run (1969–1974). Its most faithful fans are a younger generation familiar with it primarily through syndication. Several efforts to revive the show have been made, including a series of television movies, an hour-long soap opera, and a variety show. Episodes of the series have also been adapted for the stage, and a theatrical film has been considered. *Growing Up Brady*, by Barry Williams, who played the oldest son, Greg, was a best-selling book in 1992.

REFERENCES:

Andrew J. Edelstein, *The Brady Bunch Book* (New York: Warner Books, 1990);

Barry Williams, *Growing Up Brady* (New York: Harper, 1992).

– C.D.B.

MARLON BRANDO

A hero of rebellious youth in the 1950s and the best-known Method actor in Hollywood (see **Actors Studio**), Marlon Brando (1924–) achieved stardom when he played Stanley Kowalski in the 1947 Broadway premiere of **Tennessee Williams**'s *A Streetcar Named Desire*.

Born in Omaha, Nebraska, Brando made his Broadway debut in *I Remember Mama* (1944). He went on to study acting with both **Stella Adler** and Lee Strasberg, developing his much-imitated style of mumbling, naturalistic line delivery.

His film debut as a paraplegic in *The Men* (1950) was followed by a string of artistic triumphs that gained him Academy Award (Oscar) nominations four years in a row. *On the Waterfront* (1954), earned him an Oscar for best actor. Director **Elia Kazan,** who helped Brando create the role of Terry Malloy in *On the Waterfront*, had also collaborated with him on his highly acclaimed renditions of Stanley Kowalski in the film version of *A Streetcar Named Desire* (1951) and as the title character in *Viva Zapata!* (1952).

In the mid 1950s Brando began to accept roles unsuited to his talents (including Sky Masterson in the musical *Guys and Dolls,* 1955) and to play others eccentrically (most notoriously an effete Fletcher Christian in the 1962 remake of *Mutiny on the Bounty*). His triumphant return to acting brilliance as Don Vito Corleone in *The Godfather* (1972) won him a second Oscar for best actor. He sent a Native American to accept the award with a diatribe on white oppression of American Indians, underscoring his contempt for Hollywood and his unpredictability. Combined with burgeoning weight and family tragedies, Brando's radical politics and idiosyncratic behavior limited him to cameo parts from the mid 1970s on, and many felt that his acting degenerated into self-parody. Yet he turned even that perception to his advantage in the charming 1990 comedy *The Freshman*.

REFERENCES:

David Downing, *Marlon Brando* (New York: Stein & Day, 1984);
Richard Schickel, *Brando: A Life in Our Times* (New York: Atheneum, 1991).

– I.R.H.

BRAT FICTION

Brat fiction (or brat-pack fiction) is a term coined in the 1980s to describe novels and stories featuring adolescent or young-adult protagonists, in particular a lost generation of the 1980s caught up in a fast-paced lifestyle of parties, sex, and substance abuse.

Charlton Heston, Harry Belafonte, James Baldwin, and Marlon Brando at Martin Luther King, Jr's March on Washington, August 1963 (photograph by Jay Acton)

Described in the *Village Voice* as "socialite realism," brat fiction relies heavily on urban or private-school settings and a **minimalist** style combined with extensive detail (especially references to drugs, **rock 'n' roll** music, designer labels, and other elements of popular culture). Characters with unpromising futures, painful histories, and permissive or indifferent parents wander aimlessly, concerned only with fulfilling their own immediate urges. Brat fiction is often criticized for being as shallow and trendy as its self-indulgent characters, for whom many readers have little sympathy.

The most talented writer whose work is associated with the brat-fiction label, Jay McInerney (1955–), published his first book, *Bright Lights, Big City,* in 1984. The novel is narrated in the second-person present tense and deals with a young man in New York whose frenetic social life provides an inadequate escape from his desperation. Praised for its humor and its use of detail and dialogue, the novel was a **best-seller.** McInerney followed it with three novels: *Ransom* (1985), *Story of My Life* (1988), and *Brightness Falls* (1992). None received the acclaim of his first book, though his most recent fiction signals a growing maturity in his work.

Bret Easton Ellis (1964–) published his first novel, *Less Than Zero* (1985), while still in college. One critic called the book, a best-seller, "the first novel of MTV." It is filled with shocking depictions of rich

Los Angeles teens' hollow lives of casual sex, drugs, and violence. Like McInerney's protagonist in *Bright Lights, Big City,* in the end Ellis's main character distances himself from this sordid lifestyle. Ellis received less attention for his second novel, *The Rules of Attraction* (1987), but his third, *American Psycho* (1991), was briefly controversial due to its pornographic violence.

Other examples of brat fiction are Tama Janowitz's short-story collection *Slaves of New York* (1986), Jill Eisenstadt's *From Rockaway* (1987), Mark Lindquist's *Sad Movies* (1987), and Peter Farrelly's *Outside Providence* (1988). Brat fiction was satirized in *Spy* magazine's *Spy Notes on McInerney's* Bright Lights, Big City, *Janowitz's* Slaves of New York, *Ellis's* Less Than Zero ... and All Those Other Hip Urban Novels of the 1980s.

REFERENCES:

Spy Notes on McInerney's Bright Lights, Big City, *Janowitz's* Slaves of New York, *Ellis's* Less Than Zero ... and All Those Other Hip Urban Novels of the 1980s (New York: Dolphin/Doubleday, 1989);

Elizabeth Young and Graham Caveney, *Shopping in Space: Essays on America's Blank Generation Fiction* (New York: Atlantic Monthly Press/Serpent's Tail, 1993).

– D.H.-F.

RICHARD BRAUTIGAN

Poet and novelist Richard Brautigan (1935–1984) is often called a literary link between the **Beat Generation** writers who lived in the North Beach neighborhood of San Francisco in the late 1950s and the **hippies** of the **Haight-Ashbury** area of the city in the 1960s.

Though he published several volumes of poetry, the best known of which is *The Pill Versus the Springhill Mine Disaster* (1968), Brautigan's chief success came with his fiction, particularly his first three novels: *A Confederate General From Big Sur* (1964), *Trout Fishing in America* (1967), and *In Watermelon Sugar* (1968). Written in a whimsical style, these books exhibit a love of nature and nostalgic longing for a simple, pastoral life. As his characters search for a mythic American Eden, they find themselves repeatedly thwarted by the technology and pollution produced by modern American society. Brautigan became a hero to many college-age readers in the 1960s for his indictment of post–World War II American values as well as his love of nature.

He continued to write throughout the 1970s, enjoying a steady popularity among readers while the critical establishment tended to dismiss his work as facile and trendy. He was found dead, an apparent suicide, in September 1984, just as critics began to recognize his role in

the development of American **metafiction** and **postmodernism**.

REFERENCES:

Keith Abbott, *Downstream from* Trout Fishing in America: *A Memoir of Richard Brautigan* (Santa Barbara, Cal.: Capra, 1989);

Edward Halsey Foster, *Richard Brautigan* (Boston: Twayne, 1983).

– S.B.

BREAD LOAF WRITERS' CONFERENCE

Founded in 1926, the Bread Loaf Writers' Conference is the oldest and most prestigious summer workshop for writers, and the model for hundreds of imitators. Sponsored by Middlebury College, it is held for two weeks every summer in buildings belonging to the college at the foot of Bread Loaf Mountain, near Ripton, Vermont.

One reason for the long-standing popularity of Bread Loaf was the presence of **Robert Frost,** who taught there every summer from 1936 until 1962. Because of Frost and because for most of its existence it has been directed by poets — Theodore Morrison (1932–1955), John Ciardi (1956–1972), and Robert Pack (1973–)—the conference has always attracted poets. **Theodore Roethke,** May Swenson, **Anne Sexton,** X. J. Kennedy, and Diane Wakoski all received Bread Loaf fellowships. Yet the conference has become well known for its fiction offerings as well. **Carson McCullers, Eudora Welty,** and **Joan Didion** are among its alumni.

The faculty at Bread Loaf has always been distinguished. Since the 1960s it has included novelists John Hawkes, John Gardner, **John Irving,** Tim O'Brien, and Robert Stone, as well as poet Howard Nemerov.

– K.L.R.

BROADWAY MUSICALS

Broadway is the most prestigious venue for commericial theater in the United States. The term generally refers to the large-capacity New York theaters located in the Times Square area of Manhattan east and west of Broadway. The establishment of the Broadway area as a theatrical center dates from 1893, when the American Theatre opened at Forty-second Street and Eighth Avenue. Other houses soon followed, and the "Great White Way," so-called for its glittering electric marquees, became to American theater what Hollywood is to American movies. Broadway musicals, with their combinations of plays and songs, became popular early in the twentieth century.

Richard Rodgers and Oscar Hammerstein II's popular, trend-setting *Oklahoma!* (1943) set the stage for post–World War II Broadway musicals. *Oklahoma!* successfully integrated songs and plot, the best musical to do so since Jerome Kern and Hammerstein's *Show Boat* (1927), the first modern American musical. Rodgers and Hammerstein wrote three other musicals that passed the thousand-performance mark: *South Pacific* (1949), *The King and I* (1951), and *The Sound of Music* (1959), their final collaboration.

Other top musicals of the 1940s include Irving Berlin's *Annie Get Your Gun* (1946), his most popular Broadway musical, which was based on the life of Annie Oakley. The show starred Ethel Merman, whose run as the best-known leading lady on Broadway began in the early 1930s and extended into the 1960s. Another popular show was *Kiss Me, Kate* (1948), by composer/lyricist Cole Porter.

A new crop of composers wrote for Broadway during the 1950s. Frank Loesser's *Guys and Dolls* debuted in 1950; a Broadway revival of this show opened in 1992 and played through 1994. Richard Adler and Jerry Ross offered *The Pajama Game* (1954) and *Damn Yankees* (1955). Meredith Willson scored big with *The Music Man* (1957), and **Leonard Bernstein** and **Stephen Sondheim** broke new ground with *West Side Story* (1957), musically and dramatically, in its treatment of New York street life. Sondheim collaborated with composer Jule Styne on *Gypsy* (1959), starring Merman; the show was revived on Broadway in 1974 and 1989. The smash hit of the decade was **Alan Jay Lerner and Frederick Loewe**'s *My Fair Lady* (1956), starring Rex Harrison and based on Bernard Shaw's 1913 play *Pygmalion;* it ran for an unprecedented 2,717 performances and made Julie Andrews a star.

Lerner and Loewe worked together again for *Camelot* (1960), which featured Andrews, **Richard Burton,** and Robert Goulet. Jerry Bock and Sheldon Harnick's *Fiddler on the Roof* (1964) has had many New York revivals; it had an initial Broadway run of 3,242 performances. Jerry Herman's *Hello, Dolly!* (1964) ran for 2,844 performances, while his *Mame* (1966) established Angela Lansbury as Broadway's new grande dame. Styne and Bob Merrill's *Funny Girl* (1964) helped to launch **Barbra Streisand**'s career. *Hair* (1967) sounded a rebellious note amid the tradition and nostalgia of 1960s Broadway musicals: Galt MacDermot and Gerome Ragni's "American Tribal Love-Rock Musical" celebrated the **hippie** lifestyle, letting it "all hang out" with a full-cast nude scene at the end of the first act. This first rock musical was followed by others.

Andrew Lloyd Webber and Tim Rice's *Jesus Christ Superstar* (1971) and Stephen Schwartz's *Godspell* (1971) combined religion and popular music. Schwartz's *Pippin* (1972), directed and choreographed by **Bob Fosse,** ran for 1,944 performances. Sondheim established himself as the leading composer/lyricist on Broadway in the 1970s with *A Little Night Music* (1972), *Pacific Overtures* (1976), and *Sweeney Todd* (1979). Lloyd Webber and Rice's *Evita* (1978), about the Argentinian political figure Eva Peron, played for 1,567 performances. The two blockbusters of the 1970s were Charles Strouse and Martin Charnin's *Annie* (1977), based on the comic strip *Little Orphan Annie,* and Marvin Hamlisch and Edward Kleban's *A Chorus Line* (1975), which ran until 1993, becoming the longest-running musical on Broadway.

During the 1980s Lloyd Webber and Sondheim reigned as the leading composers for Broadway. Lloyd Webber's *Cats* (1981), inspired by poems by **T. S. Eliot,** and *The Phantom of the Opera* (1986) are still running in 1994. The elaborate staging of *Cats* and other productions of the 1980s set a new standard for Broadway. Sondheim's *Sunday in the Park with George* (1984) and *Into the Woods* (1987), both starring Bernadette Peters, enjoyed successful runs. Claude-Michel Schonberg and Herbert Kretzmer's *Les Misérables* (1987), based on the 1862 novel by Victor Hugo, is still running in 1994. In January 1994 attendance was off for all Broadway musicals except *Phantom of the Opera,* which continued to play to packed houses.

REFERENCES:

Martin Gottfried, *Broadway Musicals* (New York: Abrams, 1979);

Stanley Green, *Broadway Musicals: Show by Show* (Milwaukee: Leonard, 1985);

Arthur Jackson, *The Best Musicals: From "Show Boat" to "A Chorus Line"* (New York: Crown, 1977).

                                                          – D.M.J. and I.R.H.

MEL BROOKS

Mel Brooks (1926–) is a film producer and director, best known for his vulgar comedy and his parodies of film genres.

Brooks began as a television comedy writer, starting out with **Sid Caesar** on *The Admiral Broadway Revue,* later renamed *Your Show of Shows,* in 1949. He was part of one of the most talented staffs of comedy writers in television, including **Woody Allen, Neil Simon,** Carl Reiner, and Larry Gelbart. In the early 1960s Brooks and Reiner developed the comic interview form into a series of popular skits featuring a "2,000-year-old man." In 1965 he and Buck Henry created the television show *Get Smart*, a spoof of spy dramas that ran until September 1970.

In 1968 he directed his first movie, *The Producers,* which features the musical number "Springtime for Hitler." The movie has become a cult favorite and won for Brooks an Academy Award for best original screenplay. In 1978 he directed his parody of western movies, *Blazing Saddles,* which was a commercial success and secured Brooks's reputation as a director of comedies. *Young Frankenstein* (1974), a spoof of the horror genre, was a hit commercially and critically and was his most fully realized film parody.

His movies since then, which include *Silent Movie* (1976), *High Anxiety* (1977), *History of the World — Part I* (1981), *Spaceballs* (1987), *Life Stinks* (1991), and *Robin Hood — Men in Tights* (1993), have not been financially successful and were panned by most critics.

REFERENCES:

Bill Alder and Jeffrey Fineman, *Mel Brooks: The Irreverent Funnyman* (Chicago: Playboy Press, 1976);

William Holtzman, *Seesaw: A Dual Biography of Anne Bancroft and Mel Brooks* (Garden City, N.Y.: Doubleday, 1979);

Maurice Yacowar, *Method in Madness: The Comic Art of Mel Brooks* (New York: St. Martin's Press, 1981).

                                                              –J.W.H.

the assassination of **Martin Luther King, Jr.**, in 1968, Brown tried to soothe the anger of the black community, appealing for nonviolence. After the radical black leader Stokely Carmichael attacked Brown for being assimilationist, Brown responded to the charge by recording "Say It Loud (I'm Black and I'm Proud)." The highly charged rhythms and the racial pride expressed in that song, and in many others he recorded in the late 1960s and early 1970s, became a hallmark of funk music.

In the late 1980s and 1990s the distinctive rhythms and riffs in Brown's music were used by many **rap** musicians in their songs and performances. His arrest on drug charges and subsequent imprisonment in South Carolina in 1988 created an international furor which did nothing to diminish his status as a musical icon. Upon his release from prison in 1992 Brown resumed his recording and performing career. He continues to be one of the most influential popular musicians.

REFERENCES:

James Brown with Bruce Tucker, *James Brown: The Godfather of Soul* (New York: Macmillan, 1986);

Cynthia Rose, *Living in America: The Soul Saga of James Brown* (London: Serpent's Tale, 1990).

                                                              –J.W.H.

JAMES BROWN

The "Godfather of Soul" and "Soul Brother No. 1," James Brown (1928–), a leading **soul music** artist in the 1950s and 1960s and a creator of funk music in the late 1960s, has continued to be a major influence in black popular music.

Born in Barnwell, South Carolina, he started his music career in a **gospel** group. He formed his own soul group, James Brown and the Fabulous Flames, in the mid 1950s. Their first record, "Please Please Please" (1956), reached number six on the rhythm-and-blues (R&B) chart. Through 1964 he had twenty-nine R&B and pop hits, including "Try Me" (1958), "Think" (1960), "Night Train" (1962), and "Prisoner of Love" (1963). In 1963 he financed and released *The James Brown Show Live at the Apollo,* one of the first live albums featuring a rhythm-and-blues performer. While the majority of Brown's usual fans had been black, this album reached a white audience and stayed on the pop charts, which measured primarily white tastes, for sixty-six weeks.

In 1965 he released his two best-known songs, "Papa's Got a Brand New Bag" and "I Got You (I Feel Good)," both of which reached number one on the R&B chart and the top ten on the pop chart. After

DAVE BRUBECK

David Warren (Dave) Brubeck (1920–), a pianist and composer, was one of the most popular American jazz musicians of the late 1950s and 1960s. He won the piano division of the *Playboy* magazine jazz poll every year from 1961 to 1966, and his quartet was either first or second in the *Downbeat* magazine jazz poll throughout the late 1950s, until the quartet gradually dissolved in the mid 1960s.

Brubeck was trained as a pianist and composer under Darius Milhaud, and his jazz performances always reflected his respect for classical models. The Dave Brubeck Quartet was instrumental in the awakening of college audiences to concert jazz, partly because his music was technically innovative, particularly in its complicated rhythms and its polytonality. His best-known recording is the "Time Out" LP, which includes his composition "Blue Rondo a la Turk" in 9/8 time, and "Take Five" (in 5/4) by featured alto saxophonist Paul Desmond. The addition of technically accomplished drummer Joe Morello in 1956 enhanced the appeal of the Brubeck quartet to college audiences; yet at the same time critics complained that the group was overly intellectual and lacked spirit.

James Brown (photograph by David Ellis/Retna)

After the breakup of the quartet, Brubeck traveled extensively and concentrated on composition, writing works for musicians as diverse as the Cincinnati Symphony and the rock group New Heavenly Blue. During the 1960s he was commissioned to write a score for **American Ballet Theatre** (1961), the musical play *The Real Ambassadors* (1961), and the score for the CBS television show *Mr. Broadway* (1964–1965), in addition to other ambitious long works. In the 1970s he sometimes appeared in concert with his sons, pianist Darius, drummer Danny, and trombonist Chris.

REFERENCE:

Leonard Feather, *The Pleasures of Jazz* (New York: Horizon
    Press, 1976), pp. 134–137.

– R.L.

LENNY BRUCE

Lenny Bruce (1925–1966) was a pathetic hipster who, in the guise of stand-up comedian, became a foul-mouthed moralist preaching against the conformity and hypocrisy of his time. His voice was shrill and his criticisms were disturbing. When he died of a drug overdose at the age of forty, he was considered a martyr to the cause of social protest by some, an obscene blasphemist well silenced by others.

Until 1957 Lenny Bruce had worked primarily as a petty con man and as a master of ceremonies at burlesque shows. During a solo comedy job in San Francisco, he came to the attention of *Playboy* publisher Hugh Hefner, who gave Bruce the support he needed to gain national recognition. Two years later, at the insistence of host **Steve Allen,** Bruce appeared on the *Tonight Show* performing a sanitized act. He had already earned a reputation as a "sick comic" (*Time* magazine called him "the sickest of them all") because he considered no subject off limits. Bruce's stage routine consisted of his observations about the difference between what people said and what they did. Government, particularly law enforcement, and religion were frequent targets for his satiric bits, in which he also explored the meanings of words that might, for example, have sexual connotations in one usage but not in another. He sometimes repeated words that were considered obscene over and over to divorce the word from its meaning.

Bruce's career took on the characteristics of a crusade after the first of his many arrests for obscenity, in October 1961 at the Los Angeles Jazz Workshop, where he uttered a word on stage that offended a beat policeman. Afterwards the scenario was repeated often, sometimes at Bruce's insistence. The last years of his life were a series of arrests, trials, and legal appeals for onstage obscenity and for drug offenses. His defenses against those charges, along with his drug habit obsessed and consumed him. Bruce sometimes went on stage and simply read the transcript of one of his trials. By that time he was a cause célèbre intent on self-destruction.

Bruce's body was found naked in the bathroom at his home in Los Angeles, a hypodermic needle on the floor beside him. He died from acute morphine poisoning. About one thousand people attended the memorial service for him at Judson Memorial Church in New York. Among those who offered eulogies were **Allen Ginsberg,** the **rock 'n' roll** band The Fugs, and journalist Paul Krassner. The minister who presided observed that Bruce "exorcised the demons that plagued the body of the sick society." The generation of free-speech comedians that followed, notably George Carlin, Richard Pryor, and Eddie Murphy, benefited from Bruce's crusade.

REFERENCES:

Lenny Bruce, *How to Talk Dirty and Influence People: An Autobiography* (Chicago: Playboy, 1965);

Albert Goldman, *Ladies and Gentlemen Lenny Bruce!* (New York: Random House, 1974).

– R.L.

ERIK BRUHN

Dancer and choreographer Erik Bruhn (1928–1986) was one of the most technically polished ballet dancers of his generation — a fact attested to by Rudolf Nureyev, who traveled to Copenhagen to study with him in the early 1960s. Before Nureyev and **Mikhail Baryshnikov** joined **American Ballet Theatre** (ABT) in the 1960s and 1970s respectively, Bruhn was the male star of the company.

Most of Bruhn's career was spent outside his native Denmark. A product of the Royal Danish Ballet school, he traveled abroad at an early age and danced with a variety of companies but regularly returned home to appear with the Royal Danish Ballet. In 1947 he went to England to become a member of the short-lived Metropolitan Ballet. Bruhn danced with several companies but made his enduring reputation in the United States with American Ballet Theatre, which he joined in 1949. His first performance with ABT was in their 1950 production of John Taras's *Designs with Strings*. Later that year, he danced his first starring role: his performance opposite Alicia Markova in the classical ballet *Giselle* started him on the path to stardom. Among the twentieth-century works in which he made a special impression was the 1958 ABT production of Birgit Cullberg's *Miss Julie*. He danced the role of Jean, a well-mannered servant with whom the mistress of the household flirts, provoking a passionate response.

Though he stopped performing major roles in 1972, Bruhn remained active as a dancer through the 1970s. In 1975, for example, he danced with Cynthia Gregory and Nureyev in his revised version of the pas de trois from August Bournonville's *La Ventana* (1854), and in 1976 he premiered John Neumeier's *Hamlet Connotations* as Claudius, with Baryshnikov as Hamlet and Gelsey Kirkland as Ophelia.

Bruhn choreographed and restaged a variety of ballets for companies in Europe and the United States, including Harald Lander's *La Sylphide* in 1971. He also wrote about the Bournonville style, *Bournonville and Ballet Technique* (1961), with historian Lillian Moore. After his "retirement" from performing, he devoted his energies toward restaging nineteenth-century ballets, most often for the Swedish Ballet and the National Ballet of Canada, where he was artistic director.

REFERENCES:

Erik Bruhn, "Beyond Technique," *Dance Perspectives*, 36 (Winter 1968): 1–51;

John Gruen, *Erik Bruhn, Danseur Noble* (New York: Viking, 1979).

– D.M.

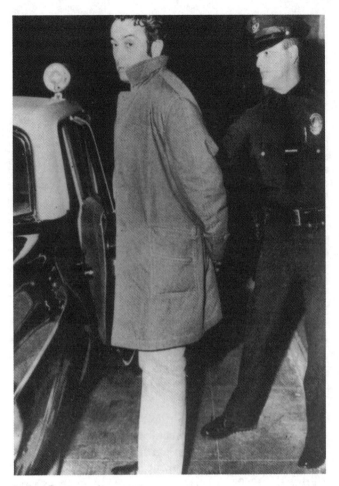

Lenny Bruce under arrest

GRACE BUMBRY

Grace Bumbry (1937–) is a noted African-American opera singer. The high point of her career occurred when she was invited in 1961 to appear as Venus in Richard Wagner's *Tannhäuser* at the Bayreuth Festival in Germany, becoming the first black soloist to appear at this prestigious event.

A native of Saint Louis, she studied with German-born soprano Lotte Lehmann in 1956. Bumbry was a cowinner (with Martina Arroyo) of the 1958 Metropolitan Opera Auditions. She debuted in 1960 in a production of Giuseppe Verdi's *Aida* in Paris. She has sung at Covent Garden, La Scala, Salzburg, Rome, and Vienna in addition to the **New York Metropolitan Opera.** Bumbry's acclaimed roles include Georges Bizet's Carmen, Richard Strauss's Salome, and Bess in George Gershwin's *Porgy and Bess*. She is also an accomplished lieder recitalist and has recorded much of her diverse repertory.

REFERENCES:

Alan Blyth, "Grace Bumbry," *Opera,* 21 (1970): 506;

Rupert Christiansen, *Prima Donna: A History* (London: Bodley Head, 1984).

– L.D.S.

CAROL BURNETT

Carol Burnett is best known as the host of *The Carol Burnett Show* (1967–1978), one of the most popular comedy-variety shows in television history.

She started in nightclub comedy during the mid 1950s, and in 1959 she starred in the Broadway production of *Once Upon a Mattress.* She was a regular on *The Garry Moore Show,* a television comedy-variety show from 1959 through 1962. In 1963 she began a series of network specials. *Julie and Carol at Carnegie Hall* (1963) and *Julie and Carol at Lincoln Center* (1972) with Julie Andrews, *Sills and Burnett at the Met* (1976) with Beverly Sills, and *Dolly and Carol in Nashville* (1978) with Dolly Parton were critical and popular successes.

The Carol Burnett Show debuted on CBS on 11 September 1967 and ran for eleven seasons in its Saturday-night slot. The show consisted of comedy sketches featuring guest stars and a cast of regulars: Harvey Korman, Vicki Lawrence, Tim Conway, and Lyle Waggoner. Burnett always opened the show by answering personal questions from the studio audience, a practice that endeared her to her many fans. Her good-humored personality defined the nature of the show and helped sustain its popularity for more than a decade, at a time when many other variety shows were being canceled. The show was also critically acclaimed: Burnett won three Emmy awards, and the show was nominated for ten others.

Burnett also appeared in movies, including *Who's Been Sleeping in My Bed* (1963), *Pete 'n' Tillie* (1972), *Front Page* (1974), *A Wedding* (1977), *Health* (1979), and *Four Seasons* (1981).

REFERENCES:

Carol Burnett, *One More Time: A Memoir* (New York: Random House, 1986);

J. Randy Taraborrelli, *Laughing Till It Hurts: The Complete Life and Career of Carol Burnett* (New York: Morrow, 1988).

– D.M.J. and J.W.H.

WILLIAM S. BURROUGHS

One of the original members of the **Beat Generation,** William S. Burroughs (1914-) willingly adopted the role of social outlaw in the 1940s, long before rebellion against the Establishment became widespread. He celebrated his Beat lifestyle in highly innovative and controversial fiction.

After several abortive career attempts, Burroughs began taking morphine in 1944 and drifted into drug use and other illegal activities, such as street hustling and theft. In the same year he befriended **Allen Ginsberg** and **Jack Kerouac** in New York and introduced them to his lifestyle, as well as to modern literature and avant-garde thought. The ideas and attitudes that emerged from their conversations became the basis of Beat Generation culture in the 1950s.

After 1946 Burroughs moved repeatedly to avoid scrapes with the law. In 1949 he and his wife, Joan, moved to Mexico City, where the next year he began his first novel, *Junkie,* an autobiographical account of life as a drug addict. In 1952 Ginsberg, acting as Burroughs's agent, sold the book to Ace Books, a paperback publishing house. It appeared in 1953 under the pseudonym William Lee.

In 1951, while still working on *Junkie,* Burroughs accidentally killed his wife while trying to shoot a glass balanced on her head. He was found not guilty of murder but was forced to leave Mexico in 1952. After traveling in South America, he settled in Tangier in 1953. There he could obtain morphine easily and live cheaply in a community of expatriate authors and artists. In this environment Burroughs produced nearly one thousand pages of fragmentary narrative episodes, which he called "routines." He underwent an apomorphine cure for his addiction in 1957 and with the help of several artist friends began to edit a selection of his routines. The result, *Naked Lunch,* was published in Paris in 1959 and radically broke with traditional novelistic form and content. Rather than a continuous narrative with a unifying plot, the book is a collection of arbitrarily juxtaposed episodes, with alternating prose styles, casts of characters, and points of view.

Though the lack of narrative continuity baffled many readers, the highly disturbing subject matter of *Naked Lunch* was most often the target of outraged critics. The work includes graphic descriptions of heroin addiction and life in the criminal underworld that surrounds it, as well as bizarre fantasies of murder and sadomasochistic sex and vicious satires of contemporary (and especially American) mores.

After **Grove Press** published the first American edition of *Naked Lunch* in 1962, officials in Los Angeles and Boston attempted to ban the book. These attempts at **censorship** failed and, ironically, helped to publicize the book, which became an underground success.

Burroughs drew from the remainder of the Tangier notes to produce the "sequel" to *Naked Lunch*, a science-fiction trilogy comprising *The Soft Machine* (1961), *The Ticket That Exploded* (1962), and *Nova Express* (1964). The trilogy portrays an ongoing struggle against alien-imposed systems of mental control and introduces the "cut-up" or "fold-in," a collage-like technique in which selected pages of text are cut up or folded and randomly arranged, then edited and rearranged until a satisfactory new order emerges. This technique is directly related to the narrative content of the three novels, as it successfully disrupts the controlling influences of language and logic. Yet this intentional disruption has alienated many readers, who find the cut-up passages incoherent.

In subsequent works, such as *The Wild Boys* (1971), and *Exterminator!* (1973), Burroughs has relied less on cut-up techniques and more on complex plots with utopian elements, balancing the bleak dystopian visions which dominated his earlier work.

REFERENCES:

Ted Morgan, *Literary Outlaw: The Life and Times of William S. Burroughs* (New York: Holt, 1988);

Jennie Skerl, *William S. Burroughs* (Boston: Twayne, 1985).

– S.B.

RICHARD BURTON

Richard Burton (1925–1984) was one of the finest natural actors on stage and screen during the second half of the twentieth century, drawing on strong inner emotions for powerful portrayals of characters with whom he could identify.

Born Richard Walter Jenkins, Jr., to an impoverished coal-mining family of thirteen children in Pontrhydfen, South Wales, he began his professional stage career while still in his teens and won a scholarship to Oxford University. After service in the Royal Air Force (1944–1947), he played stage and film roles, scoring his first major success as the lead in Christopher Fry's play *The Lady's Not for Burning* in London (1949) and New York (1950). He went to Hollywood in 1952 to appear in *My Cousin Rachel* and later played leading roles in films such as *The Robe* (1953), *Prince of Players* (1955), *Alexander the Great* (1956), and *Look Back in Anger* (1958). Returning to Broadway, he starred as King Arthur in **Alan Jay Lerner and Frederick Loewe**'s musical *Camelot* (1960). When he played another historical role, Mark Antony in the film *Cleopatra* (1963), his romance with costar **Elizabeth Taylor** made headlines. (Both actors were married to others at the time.) The two married in 1963, divorced in 1972, remarried in 1975, and divorced again in 1976. The notoriety surrounding their tempestuous relationship and Burton's problems with alcoholism began to overshadow his achievement as an actor. He continued to give fine performances during his marriage to Taylor — *Becket* (1964), *The Spy Who Came in from the Cold* (1965), and *Who's Afraid of Virginia Woolf?* (1966) with Taylor. Yet despite his major achievements, he never lived up to the great promise he displayed in his early career. His roles in the 1970s and 1980s (with the possible exception of *Equus,* 1977) were in substandard films or television movies. Burton was nominated for Academy Awards (Oscars) as best actor seven times before his death at age fifty-nine, but he never won.

REFERENCES:

Melvyn Bragg, *Richard Burton: A Life* (Boston, Toronto & London: Little, Brown, 1989);

Richard Jenkins, *Richard Burton, My Brother* (New York: Harper & Row, 1988).

– I.R.H.

C

CABLE TELEVISION

Cable television, which transmits a television signal over coaxial cable rather than the airwaves, has a history nearly as long as broadcast television itself. The first cable systems connected communities to a central antenna in order to improve reception in remote areas. In the early 1960s entrepreneurs discovered a more valuable use for cable: to bring subscribers shows they would not see on network television, including sporting events and first-run movies. Starting on the West Coast, subscription television quietly made its way across the country in the 1960s and 1970s.

In the late 1970s improved satellite technology paved the way for a greater expansion of the industry. Networks catering to specialized tastes for sports (ESPN), news **(CNN)**, movies (HBO), or adult films (the Playboy Channel) were launched. While the philosophy of the major networks had been to bring the family together around the television, the cable industry espoused what was called "narrowcasting": programming for each individual viewer's taste. Further, since cable viewers were voluntary subscribers, the industry was less constrained in terms of the contents of its shows. These factors led to some innovative programming, and several cable stations, most notably CNN and Music Television **(MTV),** have had significant cultural impact.

Throughout the 1980s and early 1990s the cable industry went through a series of growing pains and was compelled to accept government regulation of its subscription rates and, to some extent, the content of shows. Cable channels and the networks were asked to program possibly objectionable material more responsibly.

Industry experts have predicted that by the mid 1990s every home will be able to choose from hundreds of cable channels and that interactive television, which will allow cable subscribers to order programming from a menu, will customize the viewing experience even further. With the computer and telecommunications industries, cable television has laid the groundwork for an "information superhighway."

REFERENCES:

Erik Barnouw, *Tube of Plenty,* second revised edition (New York & Oxford: Oxford University Press, 1990);

Timothy Hollins, *Beyond Broadcasting: Into the Cable Age* (London: BFI, 1984).

– C.D.B.

SID CAESAR

Sid Caesar (1922–), one of the comic geniuses of television, earned his reputation on *Your Show of Shows* (1950–1954), generally considered the best comedy-variety show in television history.

Caesar got his start in comedy in the U.S. Coast Guard during World War II, when he wrote sketches and performed in two coast-guard musical-variety shows, *Six On, Twelve Off* and *Tars and Spars* in 1942.

After his discharge from the coast guard, Caesar performed in nightclubs until he got a part in Joseph Hyman's Broadway revue, *Make Mine Manhattan* (1948). On the basis of his performance he was signed to star with **Imogene Coca** on an **NBC** television show, the *Admiral Broadway Revue* (1949). The show had high ratings and was a success with critics, but it lasted only six months because of high production costs. Yet NBC soon signed Caesar to do a new live show with a similar format. *Your Show of Shows*

JOHN CAGE

Sid Caesar

debuted on 24 February 1950 and ran until 5 June 1954. Starring Caesar and Coca, the show also had a staff that included some of the best young comedy writers of the day: **Mel Brooks,** Larry Gelbart, **Woody Allen,** and **Neil Simon.**

After four seasons of high ratings and praise from television critics, NBC decided to produce three separate shows featuring cast members from *Your Show of Shows,* one with Caesar, one with Coca, and one with the musical director, Max Leibman. *Caesar's Hour* (1955–1958), with Nanette Fabray taking Coca's place, continued the format of *Your Show of Shows.*

Caesar's Hour was successful until the 1957–1958 season, when Caesar was in the midst of an acute problem with drugs and alcohol. By the time the show was canceled in 1958, filmed shows had largely replaced the live programs that had been so popular in the early years of television. Caesar continued to work in television, movies, and theater, but he never again attained the success he had during his years at NBC.

REFERENCES:

Sid Caesar, *Where Have I Been? An Autobiography* (New York: Crown, 1982);

Ted Sennett, *Your Show of Shows* (New York: Macmillan, 1977).

— D.M.J.

John Cage (1912–1992) was one of the most influential composers and writers in American avant-garde music. His works forced a radical rethinking of traditional definitions of music, and his collaborations with **Merce Cunningham,** which began in 1942 and continued into the 1960s, paved the way for revolutionary changes in all the performing arts.

By the late 1940s Cage had established his reputation as a musical innovator, mainly with compositions for percussion and pianos that he "prepared" by inserting rubber bands, wooden spoons, bits of paper and metal, and other small objects between the strings. The pianist then played the piano by plucking the strings and striking the keys.

Fascinated by Eastern philosophies and musical traditions, he studied Zen Buddhism and the *I Ching,* the Chinese book of changes. In 1951 he composed several pieces in which elements of chance were introduced into the process of creation or performance. He believed that in music, as in life, one should not try to shape the world according to one's desires or habits but make the best of it as it is: "Now structure is not put into a work, but comes up in the person who perceives it himself." Thus sound and silence, as well as musical tone and noise, are equally important. His philosophical and musical theories are presented in several books, the most famous of which is *Silence* (1961).

Concerts of his music were extremely controversial, but Cage found support and encouragement from musicians such as Morton Feldman, **David Tudor,** Earle Brown, and Christian Wolff, visual artists **Robert Motherwell, Robert Rauschenberg,** and **Jasper Johns,** and poet Mary Caroline Richards. In 1952, with his *Imaginary Landscape No. 5* and *Williams Mix,* Cage began to explore the possibilities of magnetic tape, chopping recorded passages into tiny fragments and reassembling them according to chance operations. During that summer, at **Black Mountain College,** he organized a piece of "concerted action" — involving simultaneous but uncoordinated performances of music, poetry, dance, film, and other media — that became the model for the many **Happenings** of the 1960s.

Reaction to Cage's music was initially hostile but gradually turned to general admiration. One of his most ambitious compositions is *Concert for Piano and Orchestra* (1958), in which any number of players may select anything from parts written with chance methods, coordinated only by time intervals signaled by the conductor (portions from a recorded performance are freely inserted into Cage's well-known lecture "Indeterminacy"). In another, *Atlas Eclipticalis,* conducted

John Cage preparing a piano for a performance of his music

by **Leonard Bernstein** with the New York Philharmonic Orchestra in 1964, microphones were attached to each instrument, the sounds mixed, altered, and transmitted to loudspeakers.

REFERENCES:

Richard Kostelanetz, ed., *John Cage: An Anthology,* revised edition (New York: Da Capo, 1991);

Michael Nyman, *Experimental Music: Cage and Beyond* (London: Studio Vista, 1974);

David Revill, *The Roaring Silence: John Cage, A Life* (New York: Arcade, 1992).

— L.E.P.

ALEXANDER CALDER

Sculptor Alexander Calder (1898–1976) became well known in the 1950s for the "mobiles" and "stabiles" that he created for display in public spaces worldwide.

Born in Lawnton, Pennsylvania, Calder was the son of sculptor Alexander Sterling Calder and painter Nanette Lederer Calder. His grandfather Alexander Milne Calder was also a sculptor. After spending much of his youth in California, where his father was chief sculptor for the 1915 San Francisco World's Fair, the third Alexander Calder earned a degree in mechanical engineering

from Stevens Institute of Technology in 1919. From 1923 to 1926 he took courses at the Art Students League in New York, studying painting with well-known artists such as John Sloan, George Luks, Guy Pene du Bois, and Thomas Hart Benton.

In 1932 Calder exhibited his first moving sculptures in Paris and New York. When artist **Marcel Duchamp** saw these works, he labeled them "mobiles," causing Alsatian painter Jean Arp, one of the founders of Dada, to comment that Calder's stationary sculptures should therefore be called "stabiles." From then on Calder assigned all his sculptures to one or the other of these categories.

Though Calder's best-known mobiles are large, some are small enough to fit into envelopes. Some of his early mobiles are hand-cranked or motorized, but most are moved by air currents. Typical Calder mobiles are groups of abstract metal or wood shapes painted in black, white, or primary colors and suspended from wires or rods. His stabiles also vary widely in size. The earliest are representational wire sculptures. Later stabiles are huge abstract shapes painted in the same colors as Calder's mobiles.

In the late 1930s Calder began to receive commissions for works to be displayed in public places. He designed a fountain for the 1937 Paris World's Fair and made a mobile to hang in the new Museum of Modern Art building completed in 1939. By the late 1950s his work was in great demand. In 1958 alone he completed commissioned works for the Brussels World's Fair, Idlewild (now Kennedy International) Airport in New York, and the UNESCO building in Paris. Later commissions included works for Spoleto, Italy, in 1962; Expo 67 in Montreal; and the defense complex in Paris in 1974. In the same year Calder made a huge mechanical mural for the Sears Tower in Chicago.

In addition to making mobiles and stabiles, Calder was a much-admired painter and jewelry maker. During his lifetime he had two major retrospective exhibitions of his works in New York, at the Guggenheim Museum in 1964 and the Whitney Museum in 1976.

REFERENCES:

Maurice Bruzeau, *Calder,* translated by I. Mark Paris (New York: Abrams, 1979);

Margaret Calder Hayes, *Three Alexander Calders: A Family Memoir* (Middlebury, Vt.: Eriksson, 1977);

Joan M. Marter, *Alexander Calder* (Cambridge & New York: Cambridge University Press, 1991).

— K.B.

SARAH CALDWELL

As the first woman to conduct the orchestra at a performance of the **New York Metropolitan Opera,**

Sarah Caldwell (1924–) laid to rest the notion that conducting is an exclusively male profession. She is one of the most respected opera producers and conductors in the United States today.

Caldwell studied violin and conducting and became interested in opera when she was in her early twenties. From 1953 to 1957 she was the head of the opera workshop at Boston University. In 1957 she established the Boston Opera Group (now the Opera Company of Boston). Under her direction, the company has given American premieres of many little-performed operas, such as Sergey Prokofiev's *War and Peace* (1943), Arnold Schoenberg's *Moses und Aron* (1932), Luigi Nono's *Intolleranza 1960* (1961), and **Roger Sessions**'s *Montezuma* (1964). Caldwell reached an important milestone in her career when she conducted Giuseppe Verdi's *La Traviata* (1853) at the **New York Metropolitan Opera** in 1976. She has conducted the New York Philharmonic in a concert devoted to women composers and has also been a guest conductor of the Pittsburgh Symphony Orchestra, the **Boston Symphony Orchestra,** and other major orchestras.

REFERENCE:
Lynn Gilbert and Gaylen Moore, eds., *Particular Passions: Talks with Women Who Have Shaped Our Times* (New York: C. N. Potter, 1981).

– L.D.S.

MARIA CALLAS

Called "La Divina" by her many fans, soprano Maria Callas (1923–1977) was respected for her skillful musicianship and acting in many opera roles. She used her celebrity status to revive many neglected Italian operas, thus changing the opera canon in the 1950s.

Born in New York of Greek ancestry, Callas began her early training in 1937 in Greece, where she studied with the distinguished soprano Elvira de Hidalgo. After her official debut in 1940 with the Athens Opera, Callas returned to America, where she found few singing opportunities. She returned to Europe, becoming a protégé of Italian industrialist and opera enthusiast Giovanni Battista Meneghini, to whom she was married for ten years (1949–1959). With Meneghini's assistance, Callas was able to gain a hearing with leading Italian conductors and eventually made her Italian opera debut in 1947 at the Verona Arena in the title role of Amilcare Ponchielli's *La Gioconda* (1876). Callas's ability to sing a wide-ranging repertoire, including Wagner, astonished musicians, opera lovers, and critics, including conductor Tullio

Serafin. He helped her obtain the role of Elvira in Vincenzo Bellini's *I Puritani* (1835) in 1948. This performance demonstrated Callas's remarkable bel canto singing, a lyrical technique that emphasizes precision and smoothness of tone rather than vocal forcefulness. She soon focused on such roles, her technical agility more than compensating for any flaws in her voice, and her fame grew. Callas first performed in America in 1954 for the opening of the **Chicago Lyric Opera,** and in 1956 she debuted at the **New York Metropolitan Opera,** where she reprised her Chicago performance in the title role of Bellini's *Norma* (1831). Callas's most successful roles (as well as the parts she sang most often) included Gaetano Donizetti's *Lucia di Lammermoor,* Giacomo Puccini's *Tosca,* Giuseppe Verdi's *Violetta,* and Luigi Cherubini's *Medea.*

Callas left the opera stage in 1965, when the quality of her voice began to decline, but she continued to record. She made a final concert tour in 1973–1974, and in 1977 she died in Paris. Her musical legacy survives in many fine recordings of complete operas and aria selections.

REFERENCES:
John Ardoin, *The Callas Legacy* (New York: Scribners, 1977);
George Jellenik, *Callas: Portrait of a Prima Donna* (New York: Ziff-Davis, 1960).

– L.D.S.

CALYPSO

Calypso is a form of **folk music** with African roots that comes primarily from the West Indies, especially Trinidad and Jamaica. Improvisational in nature and based on a handful of basic tunes, calypso often provides witty commentary on social customs and conditions. **Harry Belafonte** and other performers have done much to promote calypso. It enjoyed considerable popularity in the United States and internationally in the late 1940s and the 1950s, and it is a major influence in **reggae music** and **fusion** jazz.

The calypso was derived from the African *kalinda,* a duel in which musicians encouraged the combatants by providing rhythmic accompaniments to the warriors' movements. This origin accounts for the prominence of percussion instruments — particularly steel drums, claves, and maracas — in calypso music. Kalinda singers also supported the fighters by versifying the events of the duel, and the calypso has retained this spontaneity of improvisation. Calypso likely developed in the West Indies from a style of musical communication used by slaves forbidden to speak to one another. The calypso is also associated with the annual carnival season, a tradition in the West Indies. In keeping with the carnival atmosphere, calypso artists usually adopt colorful names, such as "the Mighty Sparrow," and wear flamboyant costumes.

REFERENCE:

Keith O. Warner, *Kaiso! The Trinidad Calypso: A Study of the Calypso as Oral Literature* (Washington, D.C.: Three Continents Press, 1982).

– L.D.S.

VINCENT CANBY

Because New York publications shaped national opinion, Vincent Canby (1924–   ), chief film critic for the *New York Times* from 1969 to late 1993, has been one of a the most influential movie reviewers in the United States.

Before going to work at the *Times,* Canby was assistant to the drama editor at the *Chicago Journal of Commerce* (1948–1951) and a critic and reporter for two show-business trade periodicals, *Motion Picture Herald* (1951–1958) and *Variety* (1959–1967). He became a member of the drama and film staff at the *Times* in 1967, and in 1969 he replaced **Bosley Crowther,** who had retired the previous year, as chief film critic. In December 1993 Canby became the Sunday theater critic at the *Times* and was replaced as chief film critic by Janet Maslin.

Because movies often open in New York before they are shown in most other areas of the country and because *New York Times* readers tend to be representative of the portion of the American population that has disposable income to spend on moviegoing, a bad review in the *Times* can do far more damage than hurting box-office receipts in the New York metropolitan area. Studios may decide to cut their losses by spending less on advertising the film, and theater bookings in other parts of the country may be limited.

Ironically, Canby has been accused of trying not to wield the power that comes with his position. For example, film scholar Raymond Carney has charged that Canby treats most films with humorous condescension, refusing to give good movies the serious consideration they deserve and failing to pan the truly bad ones.

REFERENCE:

Raymond Carney, "A Critic in the Dark: The corrupting influence of Vincent Canby and the *New York Times,*" *New Republic,* 194 (30 June 1986): 25–33.

– I.R.H.

TRUMAN CAPOTE

A creator of haunting, lyrical prose, Truman Capote (1924–1984) is, perhaps unfairly, remembered as a gifted self-promoter who became a victim of the fame he spent a lifetime cultivating.

Capote, who was born Truman Streckfus Persons in New Orleans, became Truman Garcia Capote when he was adopted by his mother's second husband in 1935. His mother often left him with relatives for extended periods of time, including slightly more than two years in 1930–1932, when he lived with middle-aged cousins in the tiny town of Monroeville, Alabama. Even after he joined his mother and stepfather in New York in 1932 and began to find friends his own age, Capote, who became aware of his homosexuality at an early age, felt lonely and alienated. Having decided when he was ten to become a famous writer, the young Capote began creating stories to deal with his sense of isolation. The short stories he began to sell to *Mademoiselle* and *Harper's Bazaar* in 1945 brought him instant acclaim in New York literary circles.

In Capote's first novel, *Other Voices, Other Rooms* (1948), which draws in part on his childhood in Alabama, thirteen-year-old Joel Knox, desperate for the love he cannot get from his dead mother or invalid father, turns to a male transvestite and accepts his own homosexuality. Notorious for its provocative dust-jacket photograph of Capote and its then-controversial theme, the book got mixed reviews but spent twenty-six weeks on the *New York Times* **best-seller list.**

While his first novel is often described as a dark and brooding example of Southern **gothic fiction,** Capote's second novel, *The Grass Harp* (1951), has been called sunny and nostalgic. Set once again in a town like Monroeville, it draws on happy childhood memories to portray a group of characters who retreat into an Edenic environment and return renewed to the outside world. The novel got better reviews than *Other Voices, Other Rooms* but sold about half as many copies.

Capote had far greater success with *Breakfast at Tiffany's* (1958). Often called the most perfect example of his prose style, this popular novella is the story of a Manhattan playgirl, Holly Golightly, who maintains an aura of innocence even when she accepts money from her dates and cures her anxieties by visiting Tiffany's. One of Capote's most popular works, *Breakfast at Tiffany's* was the basis for a 1961 movie starring Audrey Hepburn and George Peppard.

After writing *Breakfast at Tiffany's* Capote began to think about bringing "the art of the novelist together with the technique of journalism" to create a new genre: the nonfiction novel. In late

The photograph of Truman Capote that was published on the dust jacket of his *Other Voices, Other Rooms*

1959 he found his subject in a brief newspaper account of a multiple murder in Kansas. He spent five years researching and writing *In Cold Blood,* talking to townspeople, the killers, and everyone else involved with the case. *In Cold Blood* (1966) made Capote a millionaire and a national celebrity. He became a popular guest on late-night television shows. In November 1966 he created one of the major media events of the 1960s: his Black and White Ball at the Plaza Hotel in New York, with a guest list that read like a "who's who" of the beautiful, rich, and famous.

Having charmed his way into the New York elite when he was a young, little-known writer in the late 1940s, Capote had been observing high society for years. As early as 1958 he had planned *Answered Prayers* as an American version of *A Remembrance of Things Past* (1913–1927), Marcel Proust's fictional chronicle of salon society in Paris. Capote also used his novel to avenge real and imagined slights, including information friends had told him in confidence. This fact became apparent when chapters appeared in *Esquire* in 1975 and 1976. Increasingly ostracized by former friends who felt betrayed and suffering from addictions to drugs and alcohol, Capote died in 1984, never having completed any of the novel beyond the chapters published in 1975 and 1976.

The popularity of *Tru,* Jay Presson Allen's one-man show based on Capote's life, demonstrates Capote's continuing hold over the public imagination. Yet his lifelong willingness to create controversy for the purpose of achieving fame has made it difficult to look beyond the man to his real accomplishments as a gifted writer who never quite lived up to the promise of his early work.

REFERENCES:

Gerald Clarke, *Capote: A Biography* (New York: Simon & Schuster, 1988);

M. Thomas Inge, ed., *Truman Capote: Conversations* (Jackson: University Press of Mississippi, 1987).

– R.T.

ELLIOTT CARTER

Elliott Carter (1908–) is one of the most prestigious modern American composers. He is especially noted for his use of metric modulation, in which rhythms from different meters can shift and overlap, creating a layered, complex sound of "simultaneous streams of different things going on together."

Born in New York, Elliott Cook Carter, Jr., studied composition at Harvard University (1926–1932), where he was a pupil of Walter Piston and Gustav Holst. He then studied with Nadia Boulanger in Paris (1932–1935). His early compositions are neoclassical in style, but his mature compositions are more **atonal** and feature many innovations in rhythm and meter. In 1951 Carter began this experimental work with the first of his highly praised string quartets. His compositions became increasingly complex, usually featuring metric modulation and unusual time signatures such as 21/8 and 10/16. Such devices can be heard in the Double Concerto (1961) for harpsichord and piano with two chamber orchestras. Igor Stravinsky hailed the work as "the first true American masterpiece."

Carter has written prolifically in practically all classical-music genres and has won many prizes and awards for his works, including Pulitzer Prizes for his Second String Quartet (1960) and Third String Quartet (1971). Now in his eighties, Carter continues to receive numerous commissions and awards, including the National Medal of Arts conferred upon him in 1985 by President Ronald Reagan.

REFERENCES:

Allen Edwards, *Flawed Words and Stubborn Sounds: A Conversation with Elliott Carter* (New York: Norton, 1972);

Howard Pollack, *Harvard Composers: Walter Piston and His Students, from Elliott Carter to Frederic Rzewski* (Metuchen, N. J.: Scarecrow, 1992);

Charles Rosen, *The Musical Languages of Elliott Carter* (Washington, D.C.: Music Division, Research Services, Library of Congress, 1984).

– L.D.S.

RAYMOND CARVER

Raymond Carver (1938–1988) was widely considered a modern master of the short story. Variously labeled as "**minimalism**" or "dirty realism," his fiction was part of an American short-story renaissance in the late 1970s and the 1980s that also included Ann Beattie, Mary Robison, and Tobias Wolff. Carver's poetry, though less widely known, also earned him the respect of many poets and critics.

Loneliness, entrapment, and failed relationships are frequent topics in Carver's writing, and his characters are often unable to express their feelings or to understand what happens to them. While Carver wrote in a direct, spare style and employed a detached tone, there is no lack of sympathy for his characters.

Dealing with the working poor in small-town America, his stories reflect the harsh circumstances of his own life. The son of a laborer, Carver was married and a father of two by age twenty and was forced to work at several low-paying jobs to support his family. With little time to write early in his career, Carver focused on short forms such as poems and stories. His first books — two poetry collections, *Near Klamath* (1968) and *Winter Insomnia* (1970) — were published during the period when Carver began his fight with alcoholism. In 1976 he published a third volume of poetry, *At Night the Salmon Move*, and his first collection of stories, *Will You Please Be Quiet, Please?* Separated from his family, Carver stopped drinking in 1977.

He preferred writing poetry and stories even after the rewards of his increasing reputation in the late 1970s and the 1980s allowed him more time to write. Before his death in 1988 he published four more short-story collections — *Furious Seasons* (1977), *What We Talk about When We Talk about Love* (1981), *Cathedral* (1984), and *Where I'm Calling From* (1988) — and two books of poetry, *Where Water Comes Together with Other Water* (1985) and *Ultramarine* (1986). His stories have been translated into more than twenty languages. Some of them were the basis for the **Robert Altman** film *Short Cuts* (1993).

REFERENCE:

Arthur M. Saltzman, *Understanding Raymond Carver* (Columbia: University of South Carolina Press, 1988).

– D.H.-F.

JOHNNY CASH

One of the top male country-music performers in popularity and sales, Johnny Cash (1932–) helped to broaden the audience for country music from the 1950s to the 1970s through his many recordings and live performances, influencing many country artists after him. Cash's music is known for his powerful, throaty baritone and the traditionally spare country accompaniment.

A singer since his childhood in Arkansas, Cash began playing guitar and writing songs while in the U.S. Air Force (1950–1954). He settled in Memphis after his discharge and formed Johnny Cash and the Tennessee Two with guitarist Luther Perkins and bass player Marshall Grant. In 1955 they recorded their first singles with Sun Records: "Hey Porter" backed by "Cry, Cry, Cry," both written by Cash. His "I Walk the Line" (1956) reached the top ten on the country charts and became a **crossover** success, and "Folsom Prison Blues" was a **Top 40** hit. Cash and his group — which became the Tennessee Three with the addition of drummer Bill Holland — began recording with Columbia Records in 1958, and his first Columbia album, *Johnny Cash* (1959), sold more than four hundred thousand copies. His touring ensemble grew to include June Carter and other musicians in 1961. With Carter he wrote "Ring of Fire" (1963), another Top 40 hit. Carter helped Cash overcome his drug addiction of the mid 1960s, and they married in 1968; that year they recorded "Daddy Sang Bass" as a duet. Cash's live album *At Folsom Prison* (1968) and single "A Boy Named Sue" (1969), written by Shel Silverstein, both sold well, and Cash's popularity led to *The Johnny Cash Show,* on **ABC** television (1969–1971).

In the 1970s and 1980s Cash built on his success through tours, recordings, and television appearances. He also returned to his religious roots and increasingly performed **gospel music** as well as country and **folk music.** He was inducted into the Country Music Hall of Fame in 1980 and the Rock and Roll Hall of Fame in 1992. In 1986 he teamed with Kris Kristofferson, Waylon Jennings, and Willie Nelson for the album *Highwayman.*

REFERENCES:

Johnny Cash, *Man in Black* (Grand Rapids, Mich.: Zondervan, 1975);

Christopher S. Wren, *Winners Got Scars Too: The Life and Legends of Johnny Cash* (New York: Dial, 1971).

– D.H.-F.

CBS

CBS (Columbia Broadcasting System) is one of the "Big Three" television networks — with **NBC** and **ABC** — that dominated the medium before the explosive popularity of **cable television** in the 1980s. CBS began as a chain of largely unsuccessful radio stations purchased in 1927 by William S. Paley. During the lean years of the Depression, when the public relied primarily on radio for entertainment, the fledgling network began to prosper. It was still, however, far smaller than its chief rival, the Radio Corporation of America (RCA), with its two networks, NBC-red and NBC-blue (which became ABC).

CBS began experimental television broadcasts as early as 1931, but it was not until the late 1940s that the way was cleared for the industry to develop in earnest. CBS and what had become the single NBC network were the largest of a large number of adventurous companies that attempted to make their mark in the television industry. In the new medium CBS and NBC were on more equal footing. In fact, several CBS series were among the most popular of the 1950s: *I*

Love Lucy (1951–1961), *Gunsmoke* (1955–1975), and *The Honeymooners* (1955–1956).

Also during the 1950s Paley and David Sarnoff, head of NBC, pushed their networks to be the first to develop a viable color–television system. The government at first seemed to favor the CBS design, even though the CBS color television could not receive black-and-white broadcasts. Ultimately, however, the NBC-backed technology, which could receive both signals, became the standard for the industry.

By the 1960s the smaller networks had fallen by the wayside, leaving the "Big Three" in unquestioned control of the television medium. The most successful CBS shows of the decade were its silly, countrified situation comedies, including *The Beverly Hillbillies* (1962–1971) and *Green Acres* (1965–1971). Some of the network's more prestigious offerings of the same era include *The Smothers Brothers Comedy Hour* (1967–1969), a production of playwright Arthur Miller's *The Crucible* (1967), and *Mark Twain Tonight* (1967), starring Hal Holbrook. In 1967 the network premiered the news digest *60 Minutes,* one of its most durable successes, which maintained the news department reputation for integrity established by **Edward R. Murrow.** With **Walter Cronkite** as anchor, *The CBS Evening News* was the most-watched network news broadcast for several decades.

In the 1970s the network dropped many of its light situation comedies and revolutionized the genre with more mature offerings such as *All In the Family* (1971–1983) and *The Mary Tyler Moore Show* (1970–1977). Another CBS popular success, *Dallas* (1978–1991), started its own genre: the sexy, prime-time soap opera. For the 1974 season nine of the top-ten most-popular shows were on CBS.

In the 1980s the "Big Three" rivals faced common adversaries, the scores of cable "networks" that broadcast to a variety of specialized audiences. No longer could the networks count on being a viewer's preferred source for news, sports, or entertainment. Both NBC and CBS failed at their own cable ventures: a "culture channel" launched by CBS in the early 1980s cost the network tens of millions of dollars. Clearly, as the 1980s progressed, the era of television domination by the "Big Three" had ended. In 1985 the network was purchased by real-estate magnate Laurence Tisch.

REFERENCES:

Erik Barnouw, *Tube of Plenty,* second revised edition (New York & Oxford: Oxford University Press, 1990);

Ed Joyce, *Prime Times, Bad Times* (New York: Doubleday, 1988);

Robert Metz, *CBS: Reflections In a Bloodshot Eye* (New York: Playboy Press, 1975).

– C.D.B.

CENSORSHIP

Since World War II, government censorship has almost disappeared as a result of several controversial cases at national, state, and local levels. Edmund Wilson's book *Memoirs of Hecate County* (1946), for instance, was banned in New York and California for its depiction of sex in one of the stories; appealed to the U.S. Supreme Court, the ban was allowed to stand until state laws changed. On the other hand, while local and state governments often censored films until the 1950s, the Supreme Court in 1952 determined that movies were constitutionally protected as free speech. The same did not apply to comic books, which were considered a threat to children's morals and psyches and were investigated by Congress in the mid 1950s. In response, the industry imposed its own standards in 1954 through the Comics Code Authority, which most comics publishers followed until the 1980s.

The writers of the **Beat Generation** actually benefited from the free publicity that resulted from efforts to censor their works. In 1956 **Lawrence Ferlinghetti** was arrested for publishing **Allen Ginsburg**'s *Howl,* but the case was dismissed. A few years later Ginsberg testified to Congress that **William S. Burroughs**'s *Naked Lunch* (1959) was not obscene.

Government involvement in censorship decreased further with a 1957 Supreme Court decision that allowed for freer treatment of sex in print and the media but held that "obscenity" — a difficultly defined term referring to that which offends "community standards" — is not constitutionally protected. An indirect result of this decision was an increase in pornography and, according to some, a vulgarization of standards. Also significant was the court's admission of "value" — artistic, political, or scientific — as a bar to obscenity. Consequently, in 1959 the U.S. Post Office ban on distributing D. H. Lawrence's 1928 novel *Lady Chatterley's Lover* was lifted, as was the U.S. Customs ban on Henry Miller's 1934 novel *Tropic of Cancer* in 1961. Comedian Lenny Bruce was not so fortunate: his career was ruined when he was tried successfully for obscenity in 1964. As recently as 1990, a Cincinnati museum director was arrested for showing photographs by **Robert Mapplethorpe** depicting homoerotic and possibly pedophilic images, and the lead singer of the **rap** group 2 Live Crew was arrested in Florida for obscenity, but both were acquitted.

Though government censorship has considerably weakened in recent decades, de facto censorship has continued, from libraries removing books in response to Sen. **Joseph McCarthy**'s blacklists in the 1950s, to the self-imposed ratings system of the Motion Picture Association of America since 1968, to the many efforts to remove controversial **young adult** books and others from school libraries. Ironically, many such attempts at censorship have the opposite effect of publicizing books and movies that otherwise might not receive so much attention. It is also ironic that until recently most American censorship efforts have focused more on sex than violence, especially in television and film, whereas in many countries the reverse is true.

REFERENCES:

Lee Burress, *Battle of the Books: Literary Censorship in the Public Schools, 1950–1985* (Metuchen, N. J.: Scarecrow Press, 1989);

Edward de Grazia, *Girls Lean Back Everywhere: The Law of Obscenity and the Assault on Genius* (New York: Random House, 1992);

Richard S. Randall, *Censorship of the Movies: The Social and Political Control of a Mass Medium* (Madison & London: University of Wisconsin Press, 1968).

– D.H.-F.

CHAIN BOOKSTORES

Chain bookstores, which have existed since the turn of the century, began to dominate the retail book trade in the United States after World War II.

Soon after it opened its first store in New York in 1873, Barnes and Noble established shops in other locations, realizing that, by buying the same titles in bulk for several stores, it could reduce prices and draw customers away from small independent bookstores. The discount prices appealed to the consumer, and Barnes and Noble continued to expand, absorbing independent stores and smaller chains such as B. Dalton, Bookstar, Bookstop, Doubleday, and Scribner's.

Often engaging in extensive advertising campaigns that the independent bookstores cannot afford, chains appeal to the consumer looking for a discount. These national businesses are entirely profit-driven. They ensure mass sales by stocking best-sellers and books by popular authors, tending to avoid books with merit but limited sales potential and books from small publishers who cannot afford to give chains the sort of large discounts they get from big publishing companies.

Independent bookstores make up for their inability to give customer discounts by stocking books that cannot be found in the chains, including works of local interest, backlist books, and books that appeal to small, specialized markets. These stores tend to be staffed by knowledgeable readers who can offer assistance and recommendations and to have an on-site owner who is familiar with the stock and has created an environment that encourages the customer to browse.

The independent bookstore is usually a small establishment in a neighborhood shopping area. The chain store is either in a major shopping mall or a superstore, a large stand-alone that offers products such as tapes, magazines, stationery, and posters, as well as books, in a setting like a supermarket.

Two of the biggest chain bookstores are Barnes and Noble and Waldenbooks. Barnes and Noble has two hundred superstores. Waldenbooks, which opened its first bookstore in 1962, is owned by the K-Mart Corporation and has twelve hundred stores. This chain also owns Brentano's and Borders, and it is now developing Waldenbooks Kids, large children's bookstores attached to Waldenbooks stores in shopping malls. Other major chains include Crown, Books-a-Million, and Waterstone.

–J.A.B.

RAY CHARLES

Frank Sinatra called blues singer and piano player (and occasional saxophonist) Ray Charles (1930–) "the only genius in the business." Charles has been known as the Genius or, alternately, the High Priest of Soul. Unlike any other performer he was able to combine the influences of black **gospel music,** rhythm and blues, country music, and jazz into a distinct form that has appealed to white and black pop-music audiences.

Charles had a blues background. He was born into a poor rural Georgia family; at the age of six he watched his brother drown in a backyard washtub in which his mother did take-in laundry. Soon thereafter he began losing his sight due to glaucoma. By fifteen both his father and mother were dead, and he left a special school for the deaf and blind to play music on the road. At sixteen he began using heroin, a habit that continued until 1965, when at the peak of his career he was arrested and forced into a year-long stay in a rehabilitation center.

He drew on his troubled life for his music, playing soulful blues attributed to genuine emotion. In 1957 he added the Raelettes, three (later four) female vocalists to his band, and together they recorded some of the most memorable pop hits of the late 1950s and early 1960s. "What'd I Say" and the instrumental "One Mint Julep" demonstrated the earthiness of Charles's interplay with the Raelettes on the one hand and his sophisticated keyboard style on the other. "Georgia on My Mind" (1960) is the most popular example of Charles's tender and dis-

tinctive singing voice. In 1962 he recorded two albums of classic country and western songs, demonstrating his **crossover** appeal to diverse audiences.

After his drug arrest Charles continued to refine the style he had developed in his most creative years, and he has been considered a musical star and an innovative artist of the first rank.

REFERENCES:

Ray Charles, *Brother Ray: Ray Charles' Own Story* (New York: Dial, 1978);

Sharon Bell Mathis, *Ray Charles* (New York: Crowell, 1973).
–R.L.

CHICAGO 8

One of the most publicized events of the **Vietnam War** era was the trial of the Chicago 8, indicted for their role in the antiwar demonstrations that turned violent during the 1968 Democratic National Convention, held in Chicago during 25–29 August. They were the first defendants charged under a recent federal law making it a felony to conspire and to cross state lines for the purpose of inciting a riot.

The eight defendants were a diverse group. Abbie Hoffman and Jerry Rubin were **Yippies.** David Dellinger, a committed pacifist since World War II, was chairman of the National Mobilization to End the War in Vietnam (Mobe), the group that had coordinated the March on the Pentagon in October 1967. Tom Hayden and Rennie Davis, **New Left** veterans of Students for a Democratic Society (SDS), were the Mobe coordinators for the Chicago demonstrations. John Froines, a professor at Oregon State University, and Lee Weiners, a graduate student at Northwestern University, had played small organizational roles in Mobe during final preparations for the protests. The indictment of Froines and Weiners surprised many political commentators, as did the identity of the eighth defendant, **Black Panther** national chairman Bobby Seale. The Panthers had refused to participate in the demonstrations, and Seale had spent only a few hours in Chicago, where he gave an angry speech that was open to a variety of interpretations by the two or three thousand protesters who heard it.

Davis, Hayden, Hoffman, and Rubin had warned antiwar activists that the convention-week demonstrations were likely to turn violent, but they called on demonstrators to express their dissent peacefully and stated publicly that they expected any violence to be initiated by the police. Daniel Walker, author of the official report published by the National Commission on the Causes and Prevention of Violence appointed

Chicago police clashing with antiwar protestors during the 1968 Democratic National Convention (UPI/Bettmann Newsphotos)

by President Lyndon B. Johnson, concluded that only a small number of protesters deliberately provoked the police and that police response, amounting to a "police riot," far exceeded necessary force; most of the more than one thousand people injured were peaceful demonstrators, innocent bystanders, or journalists covering the protests.

The protest leaders had hoped that the televised beatings of demonstrators would mobilize new antiwar activists, and millions of Americans did indeed rally to the cause. Yet public-opinion polls conducted immediately after the convention all indicated that the majority of Americans thought Chicago authorities had responded to the disruption of law and order appropriately.

At their trial, which began in September 1969, the Chicago 8 soon became the Chicago 7. After repeatedly asserting his right to be defended by himself or an attorney of his own choosing, rather than by the lawyers representing the other defendants, Seale was tied to his chair and gagged for three days on orders from the presiding judge, Julius Hoffman. The next week Judge Hoffman declared a mistrial in Seale's case and sentenced him to jail for contempt of court.

The trial of the remaining defendants lasted more than six months. They and their attorneys frequently and loudly interrupted to protest Judge Hoffman's rulings. Finally, after five days of deliberation, the jury found Dellinger, Davis, Hayden, Hoffmann, and Rubin not guilty of conspiracy but guilty of incitement to riot, and they were each sentenced to five years in prison. Froines and Weiners were found not guilty on both counts, but Judge Hoffman sentenced all seven defendants and their attorneys to terms of varying lengths for contempt of court. In 1972 the U.S. Court of Appeals reversed all the convictions, citing Judge Hoffman's numerous legal errors and his "antagonistic" behavior toward the defendants.

REFERENCES:

Todd Gitlin, *The Sixties: Years of Hope, Days of Rage* (New York, London, Sydney & Auckland: Bantam, 1987);

Tom Hayden, *Reunion: A Memoir* (New York: Random House, 1988);

Norman Mailer, *Miami and the Siege of Chicago: An Informal History of the Republican and Democratic Conventions of 1968* (New York: World, 1968);

James Miller, *"Democracy Is in the Streets": From Port Huron to the Siege of Chicago* (New York: Simon & Schuster, 1987);

Daniel Walker, *Rights in Conflict: Convention Week in Chicago, August 25–29, 1968* (New York: Dutton, 1968).

– K.L.R.

CHICAGO LYRIC OPERA

Established in 1954 as the Lyric Theatre of Chicago, the Chcago Lyric Opera assumed its present name two years later and has since become one of the top opera companies in the United States.

Its origin can be traced to the 1910 founding of the Chicago Grand Opera Company, which featured many **New York Metropolitan Opera** stars on its roster. It premiered Sergey Prokofiev's *The Love of Three Oranges* in 1921. The ensemble was reorganized in 1922 as the Civic Opera Company and lasted until 1932, when the Great Depression caused it to founder. The present company was revitalized after World War II by Carol Fox and Lawrence Kelly, who persuaded the reigning diva of Italian opera, **Maria Callas,** to appear there in her American debut. The work selected for this occasion was Vincenzo Bellini's *Norma* (1831), and Callas's success insured the future viability of the Chicago Lyric Opera.

For most of its existence, the company has drawn largely from nineteenth-century Italian opera for its performances, adding an occasional German or French opera for variety. In recent years, the company has broadened its range to include older works such as Christoph Willibald von Gluck's *Alceste* (1767) in 1991 as well as contemporary operas as part of its "Toward the 21st Century" campaign. These productions include Dominick Argento's *The Voyage of Edgar Allan Poe* (1976) in 1991 and a new opera, *McTeague,* commissioned in 1992. Based on Frank Norris's 1899 novel, *McTeague* was composed by **William Bolcom** and directed by **Robert Altman.**

Chicago Lyric Opera performances are given at the Civic Opera House downtown. The season is relatively brief — thirteen weeks — because of performers' commitments to other companies (particularly the New York Metropolitan Opera) in the United States and abroad. Still, the Chicago Lyric Opera produces eight works every season. During the summer, resident members perform standard opera excerpts at outdoor concerts, often as part of the annual Ravinia Festival.

REFERENCE:

The Lyric Opera Companion: The History, Lore, and Stories of the World's Greatest Operas (Kansas City: Andrews & McMeel, 1991).

– L.D.S.

CHICAGO SYMPHONY ORCHESTRA

One of the oldest orchestras in the United States, the Chicago Symphony Orchestra, founded in 1891, is in the first rank of American musical ensembles and is respected throughout the world. Its international fame is based on its recordings and its tours abroad.

Much of its success during its first century of existence may be credited to an unusually strong line of conductors and music directors. During the last forty years they have included Fritz Reiner (1953–1963), Jean Martinon (1963–1968), and Sir Georg Solti (1969–1991). Reiner and Solti were responsible for helping to build the reputation the orchestra enjoys today, often with nineteenth-century German works featured in the repertoire. The present music director is Daniel Barenboim, who has been serving since 1991. Under his direction, the orchestra has begun to perform contemporary works more frequently in addition to the classical canon.

When performing in Chicago, the orchestra usually plays in Orchestra Hall, but the majority of its highly acclaimed recordings are made in nearby Medinah Temple, which is favored by sound technicians. The acoustics of this structure enhance the sound of the brass section, reputed by many music critics and concertgoers to be "without peer" anywhere in the world.

REFERENCE:

William Barry Furlong, *Season with Solti: A Year in the Life of the Chicago Symphony* (New York: Macmillan, 1974).

– L.D.S.

CHRISTO

Christo Javacheff (1935–), who goes by his first name only, is well known for his creation of earthworks — outdoor, usually large-scale works of art in which the artist makes use of the elements of the environment. In sympathy with the ideas of **conceptual art, earth artists** — also including Robert Smithson and Robert Morris — challenged the notion of the art object as a marketable commodity. With earthworks the plans and photographic records of their production (the artistic process) become at least as important as the final product itself.

Residing in America since 1964, Bulgarian-born Christo first began creating his major outdoor artworks in Paris. In one of these early projects, *Wall of Oil Drums* (1962), he completely blocked a Paris street with rows of oil drums. He later gained renown with his wrapping projects, commenting on American society's preoccupation with consumer packaging. Using plastic sheeting, Christo encased entire buildings so that they looked like giant packages, revealing the influence of Surrealism in his transformation of these familiar objects in order to stimulate both conscious reflection and unconscious association. In the 1980s he wrapped eleven islands off the coast of Miami in bright pink fabric.

An important project was *Running Fence,* on which he worked from 1972 to 1976. The fence was composed of nylon panels attached to steel posts, and it rolled across twenty-four miles of northern California countryside. Projects such as *Running Fence* usually take years of planning and when completed sometimes remain standing for only several weeks, again placing more importance on the artistic process than on the final art object. Christo and his business manager/wife, Jeanne-Claude, together work out every detail of these vast art projects. Because of the nature of this type of project, they must constantly deal with such legal issues as property rights and environmental concerns. Christo often finances these expensive endeavors by selling drawings of the proposed work. During installation he goes to great length to involve as many people as possible, using both hired workers and volunteers, including many local residents. Christo's most recent project was his 1991–1992 installation of giant yellow and blue umbrellas along the coasts of California and Japan.

REFERENCE:

David Bourdon, *Christo* (New York: Abrams, 1972).

– C.S.

CINEMA VERITÉ

Cinema verité, French for "film truth," is a documentary style of filmmaking developed in the 1960s by filmmakers who aimed to record events with minimal interference. Used mostly in documentary films, the techniques of cinema verité have also been used in fictional films since the 1960s.

Though it has its roots in Dziga Vertov's *kinopravda* newsreels of the 1920s, cinema verité was made possible only with the advent of lightweight portable cameras, zoom lenses, and on-site recording that allowed for spontaneity and movement. The term was first used by French filmmaker Jean Rouch to describe his and Edgar Morin's documentary *Chronique d'un été* (1961), in which they interviewed Parisians about life in the city. While a cinema verité movement progressed in France, another thrived independently in America. Sometimes called "direct cinema," it dispensed with offscreen narrators and any other devices that would indicate directorial manipulation of the reality being documented. The first American example is *Primary* (1960), a behind-the-scenes documentary about the 1960 Democratic presidential primary filmed for television by Drew Associates. Richard Leacock, the cinematographer, was a leading advocate of cinema verité in the 1960s. Two of the most important practitioners were Albert and David Maysles, who made *Salesman* (1969) with Charlotte Zwerin. In this film they covered four Bible salesmen on their rounds. The Maysleses' *Gimme Shelter* (1970) followed the **Rolling Stones** on tour, including footage of a Hell's Angel killing someone at a 1969 concert. One of the most eminent cinema verité filmmakers in America is Frederick Wiseman, who has documented American institutions for thirty years in controversial films such as *Titicut Follies* (1967), about a Massachusetts mental hospital, and *High School* (1968), *Welfare* (1975), and *Near Death* (1989).

Critics of cinema verité question its supporters' claims of the ability of filmmakers to capture "truth," asserting that objectivity is distorted by the presence of the camera and the selectivity of the editing process. Cinema verité ceased to be an active movement in America by the 1980s. However, its techniques have become part of the filmmaking repertoire in both documentaries and fictional films, particularly the use of handheld cameras for moving shots as in Wayne Wang's *Chan Is Missing* (1983) and **Woody Allen**'s *Husbands and Wives* (1992).

REFERENCES:

M. Ali Issari, *Cinema Verité* (East Lansing: Michigan State University Press, 1971);

Stephen Mamber, *Cinema Verité in America: Studies in Uncontrolled Documentary* (Cambridge, Mass.: MIT Press, 1974).

– I.R.H.

THE CIVIL RIGHTS MOVEMENT

The civil rights movement is the campaign by various individuals and organizations throughout the twentieth century, particularly in the 1950s and 1960s, to attain equality for American blacks.

Leadership of the movement was assumed early on by the National Association for the Advancement of Colored People (NAACP). Founded in 1910, the NAACP sought to achieve equality for blacks through the political system, by legal means. Though it was the best-financed and most-effective civil rights organization through the first half of the twentieth century, the NAACP was not a popularly based, grassroots movement.

The National Urban League, founded in 1911, sought to support blacks who had migrated to the cities. It led boycotts against businesses which refused to employ blacks and initiated programs to train blacks for jobs and to help them adjust to urban living. It also worked to improve relations between blacks and labor unions, which were not always harmonious.

The Congress of Racial Equality (CORE), founded in Chicago in 1942, took a more activist approach, believing that legal means alone would not bring about equality. CORE advocated nonviolent direct-action tactics, staging sit-ins as early as 1943 in Chicago and the first "freedom ride" (intended to test the putative desegregation of interstate busing) through the South in 1947. CORE was responsible for other public protests in the 1940s, portending the direction of the civil rights movement after the mid 1950s.

By the 1940s small but noticeable civil rights gains were evident. The armed forces were integrated by President Harry S Truman (1948), and the U.S. Supreme Court issued decisions voiding race-restrictive real-estate covenants and abolishing all-white primary elections. The court also began chipping away at segregation in graduate and professional education.

The major breakthrough for the movement occurred on 17 May 1954, when the Supreme Court, in *Brown* v. *Board of Education, Topeka, Kansas,* unanimously struck down the "separate but equal" doctrine that had legitimized segregated schools, which predominated in the South, since 1896. Resistance to school integration was widespread and often violent, occasionally requiring the use of federal troops, as was the case in Little Rock, Arkansas, in 1957. Not until the early 1970s were integrated schools the norm throughout the South.

In the years after *Brown*, the civil rights movement took a new direction, turning more often to the streets rather than the courts for results. The successful Montgomery, Alabama, bus boycott in 1956 brought Dr. **Martin Luther King, Jr.,** to the fore of the movement. He organized the Southern Christian Leadership Conference in Atlanta in 1957. Committed to nonviolent civil disobedience, the charismatic King gave direction and leadership to the movement until his assassination on 4 April 1968. King also helped to organize

Civil rights demonstrators arriving in Montgomery, Alabama, at the end of a fifty-mile march organized by Martin Luther King, Jr., protesting efforts by state officials to prevent blacks from registering to vote, March 1965

the Student Nonviolent Coordinating Committee (SNCC), founded in North Carolina in 1960. Borrowing many tactics from CORE, SNCC was responsible for many of the lunch-counter sit-ins and freedom rides that became commonplace in the early 1960s.

After the successful march on Washington of 28 August 1963, during which King delivered his famous "I Have a Dream" speech, the civil rights movement began to make progress in the political arena. President Lyndon B. Johnson was sympathetic to the movement and instrumental in the passage of the 1964 Civil Rights Act, which forbade discrimination in most public facilities. Blacks also found it easier to participate in politics after the passage of the Voting Rights Act in 1965 made it more difficult for state and local governments to deny them the franchise.

But just as these successes were being achieved, the movement began to fragment. King had tried with only marginal success to bridge the gap between those in the movement who advocated legal action and the radicals who by the mid 1960s were advocating violence. To many, civil rights laws were of little relevance to unemployed and undereducated inner-city blacks, a fact underscored by the rioting in the Watts section of Los Angeles in 1965. Malcolm X attracted a large following with his advocacy of militant black pride and of change "by any means necessary." Stokely Carmichael, who took over as chairman of SNCC in 1966, promoted black power, advocated retaliatory violence, and rejected integration into white society. CORE stopped describing itself as a "multiracial" organization in 1967, and its leader, Floyd McKissick, declared the civil rights movement dead and the "black revolution" begun.

In summer 1967 riots in Newark, Detroit, and thirty other cities left more than one hundred dead. Widespread rioting broke out again in 1968 after King was assassinated. Congress responded by authorizing spending for cities but also passing antiriot legislation. Tensions between young blacks and police erupted into violence on many occasions from 1968 to 1970.

In the 1970s the enactment of affirmative-action programs was a key goal of civil rights leaders, who turned their attention to overcoming the effects of past discrimination and improving the economic status of African Americans. But this has proved difficult, with many black leaders contending that social conditions for black Americans worsened in the 1980s and 1990s.

REFERENCES:

Kermit L. Hall, ed., *Civil Liberties in American History* (New York: Garland, 1987);

Jeannine Swift, ed., *Dream and Reality: The Modern Black Struggle for Freedom and Equality* (New York: Greenwood Press, 1991).

– W.L.T.

CLEVELAND ORCHESTRA

Founded in 1918, the Cleveland Orchestra is one of the most highly regarded orchestras in America. Its early success proved that it was possible for a premier orchestra to exist outside the major cultural centers in the United States.

The orchestra took up its current residence in Severance Hall in 1931 and has been fortunate in securing the lengthy services of several outstanding music directors and conductors. Among these are Artur Rodzinski (1933–1943), Erich Leinsdorf (1943–1946), George Szell (1946–1970), **Lorin Maazel** (1972–1982), and Christoph von Dohnányi (1984–). In particular, Szell is credited with improving and solidifying the international reputation of the orchestra by perfecting its characteristically precise and balanced

sound. Szell also emphasized the strengths of the orchestra in performing classical and Romantic works as well as twentieth-century compositions. For instance, in 1962 the Cleveland Orchestra premiered **Samuel Barber**'s Concerto for Piano and Orchestra. Its reputation is also based on the success of several renowned recordings and taped performances broadcast on nationwide radio since 1965.

Since 1952 the orchestra has maintained a chorus (and since 1967 a children's chorus). Today the Cleveland Orchestra Chorus includes about two hundred volunteer members. In addition to its regular season, the orchestra has also performed during the summer at Blossom Music Center in Cuyahoga Falls, Ohio, since 1968.

REFERENCE:

Robert C. Marsh, *The Cleveland Orchestra* (Cleveland & New York: World, 1967).

– L.D.S.

CLEVELAND QUARTET

Founded at the Marlboro Music Festival in Vermont in 1968, the Cleveland Quartet is one of the best-known string ensembles in America. The group tours extensively and has received many awards for its numerous recordings, most notably for its performance of the Brahms quartets.

The original members were Donald Weilerstein, first violin; Peter Salaff, second violin; Martha Strongin Katz, viola; and Paul Katz, cello. Presently, the group includes Salaff; Paul Katz; violinist William Preucil, formerly concertmaster of the Atlanta Symphony Orchestra; and James Dunham on viola. Primarily a teaching ensemble, the Cleveland Quartet has held residencies at the Cleveland Institute, the State University of New York at Buffalo, and the Eastman School of Music at the University of Rochester, in addition to many festival and summer residencies. Its repertory is based heavily upon nineteenth-century Romantic string literature.

REFERENCE:

R. Maycock, "The Cleveland Quartet," *Music and Musicians*, 22, no. 12 (1974): 10.

– L.D.S.

VAN CLIBURN

Van Cliburn (1934–) achieved instant fame as a great American concert pianist when he won the gold medal at the first International Tchaikovsky Competition, held in Moscow in 1958. He has used the fortune he earned as a performer from 1958 to 1978 to provide primary support for the Van Cliburn International Piano Competition, one of the most prestigious of such events.

Born in Shreveport, Louisiana, Harvey Lavan Cliburn grew up in Texas, where, at age three, he was first taught piano by his mother; he appeared in his first recital at four and his first concert in 1946. In 1951 he began studying with Rosina Lhévinne at the Juilliard School of Music in New York, from which he graduated in 1954, the year he first performed with the New York Philharmonic. His 1958 victory in Moscow during the height of the **Cold War** made Cliburn an American hero. From the ticker-tape parade with which he was greeted in New York, he went on to a lucrative concert and recording career. Admired for his technical prowess, Cliburn focused on Romantic works; this repertory and his increasingly showy style were admired by fans but derided by critics.

In 1978 Cliburn retired from performing to concentrate on the work of the Van Cliburn Foundation, the main sponsor of the Van Cliburn International Piano Competition, which has been held every four years in Fort Worth, Texas, since 1962. The winner receives twelve thousand dollars along with a recording contract and a two-year concert tour. Cliburn resumed performing in 1987 and today plays a handful of engagements each year.

REFERENCES:

Abram Chasins, *The Van Cliburn Legend* (Garden City, N.Y.: Doubleday, 1959);

Howard Reich, *Van Cliburn* (Nashville: T. Nelson, 1993).

– L.D.S.

Montgomery Clift

Along with **Marlon Brando** and **James Dean**, Montgomery Clift (1920–1966) epitomized the sensitive, tortured, nonconformist male in the first decade of postwar films. A stage actor since age fourteen, he made his screen debut in *The Search* (1948). Roles in *Red River* (1948), *The Heiress* (1949), *A Place in the Sun* (1951), and *From Here to Eternity* (1953) established him as a matinee idol and a delineator of troubled masculinity. His offscreen life was troubled as well: he was haunted by confusion over his sexuality and abused alcohol and drugs. A serious automobile accident in 1957 scarred his face and ruined his romantic image. Nevertheless he continued his career in nonromantic character roles in films such as *Lonelyhearts* (1958), *Suddenly Last*

Summer (1959), *The Misfits* (1961), and *Judgment at Nuremberg* (1961). Appropriately, given his association with neurotic characters, he played the lead in the film biography of Sigmund Freud in 1962. He performed in only one more film, *L'Espion* (1966), before his death of a heart attack at the age of forty-five.

REFERENCES:

Patricia Bosworth, *Montgomery Clift: A Biography* (New York: Harcourt Brace Jovanovich, 1978);

Robert LaGuardia, *Monty: A Biography of Montgomery Clift* (New York: Arbor House, 1977).

– I.R.H.

CNN

CNN (Cable News Network), the first cable network to offer twenty-four-hour news coverage, began broadcasting in 1980. It was the creation of millionaire **Ted Turner** and became, along with cable networks TBS and TNT, one of the cornerstones of his media empire. For decades the major networks had contended that the viewing public was satisfied with a half-hour daily summary of the news. CNN got off to a rocky start as its staff struggled with the complications of a continuous news broadcast, but the network steadily improved, and it has frequently been able to offer more-extensive coverage of important events than the major networks. In 1982 Turner launched CNN Headline News, which condensed the news into more-traditional half-hour summaries updated throughout the day.

During the 1989 massacre of protesting Chinese students in Tiananmen Square, Beijing, CNN was the only network able to provide live footage. CNN's efforts to continue coverage against orders from Chinese authorities were nearly as big a story as the massacre itself.

CNN coverage also surpassed that of the major networks in 1990, when the United States armed forces confronted Iraqi forces in the Persian Gulf. By that time CNN had grown considerably, with twenty-four bureaus around the world; it reached fifty-three million American homes and eighty-four countries. CNN covered the conflict without interruption, frequently bringing live footage directly to the viewer as it was received and providing the most spectacular and dramatic footage of the war. Occasionally, in fact, CNN coverage was deemed too dramatic by some military personnel, who felt that explicit footage of the conflict played into the hands of Iraqi propagandists' charges of American brutality.

REFERENCES:
Porter Bibb, *It Ain't As Easy As It Looks: Ted Turner's Amazing Story* (New York: Crown, 1993);
Perry M. Smith, *How CNN Fought the War* (New York: Birch Lane Press, 1991);
Hank Whittemore, *CNN: The Inside Story* (Boston: Little, Brown, 1989).

– C.D.B.

IMOGENE COCA

Imogene Coca (1908–) costarred with **Sid Caesar** on *Your Show of Shows* (1950–1954), a live ninety-minute program that has been called the greatest comedy-variety television show of all time.

Coca made her stage debut at age nine as a vaudeville tap dancer. Her first Broadway appearance was in the chorus of a short-lived musical, *When You Smile* (1925). Over the next two and a half decades she worked in vaudeville, on Broadway, and in nightclubs, but her talents were not widely recognized until she began to appear on the **NBC** comedy-variety show *Admiral Broadway Revue* (1949) and its popular successor on NBC, *Your Show of Shows*. The diminutive, saucer-eyed Coca won over audiences with her antic mugging, comic dancing, character sketches, and celebrity impersonations. In 1951 she was often called the "finest comedienne in America today."

Although Coca never again achieved the success she had with *Your Show of Shows,* she continued to work steadily on stage, screen, and television, often playing variations of the "dotty old aunt." She made one such appearance in a memorable 1972 episode of *The Brady Bunch.* In 1983 she won praise from film critics as Edna, the surly aunt in *National Lampoon's Vacation.* During the late 1980s she appeared in Polident commercials with Martha Raye and toured in a stage revue with Caesar.

REFERENCE:
Ted Sennett, *Your Show of Shows* (New York: Macmillan, 1977).

– D.M.J.

COFFEEHOUSES

During the 1950s and 1960s coffeehouses were gathering places for college-age Americans attracted to the **Beat** movement and various forms of antiestablishment protest. Poetry reading and jazz music were the entertainments of choice in coffeehouses, where patrons, who considered themselves in the avant-garde, drank strong nonalcoholic brews (though wine was sometimes served) and discussed art. Outsiders assumed that coffeehouse patrons used marijuana rather than liquor as an intoxicant, and so coffeehouses attracted the suspicion of parents and civil authorities. As the Beat movement faded, coffeehouses, which could serve draft-age customers too young to be admitted to bars, became centers of social protest, especially against the **Vietnam War.**

– R.L.

COLD WAR

The Cold War is the name given to the complex set of international tensions beginning just after the end of World War II and ending with the breakup of Soviet domination in Eastern Europe. The war referred to was a war of political, social, and economic ideologies marked by military posturing between the two superpowers, the United States and the Soviet Union, and the allies of each. It was a time of unparalleled tensions, when it seemed at several points that World War III was imminent and had the potential to destroy entire nations, if not the world. Ironically, peace was maintained because each superpower was well enough armed to inhibit the expansionist ambitions of the other.

Benjamin Frankel has observed that "the Cold War .... did not break out: it evolved." By the same token, it did not end: it faded away. As the influence of the Soviet Union diminished, due largely to economic strife, the bipolar character of world politics that was the essence of the Cold War began to dissolve, and the rules of international diplomacy changed accordingly. On 25 December 1991, when Soviet president Mikhail Gorbachev resigned and the Soviet flag over the Kremlin in Moscow was replaced by the flag of the Russian Republic, the change was complete.

People refer to the Cold War in several contexts. In terms of ideology, it was the tension caused by the clash of democracy and communism, socialism and capitalism. In terms of military strategy, it was the policies of mutual assured destruction (called MAD), massive retaliation, containment, and flexible response. In terms of diplomatic policy, it was the domino theory, Ostpolitik, containment, and linkage. In terms of conflicts, it was the Berlin Crisis, the Korean War, the Cuban Missile Crisis, the Suez Crisis, the U-2 affair, and the *Mayaguez* Crisis, among many others. The Cold War refers to the state of world affairs over some forty years. The term does not lend itself to simple definition.

REFERENCES:
Benjamin Frankel, *The Cold War,* 3 volumes (Detroit: Manly/Gale Research, 1992);

John Lewis Gaddis, *The Long Peace: Inquiries into the History of the Cold War* (New York: Oxford University Press, 1987).
                                                                – R.L.

NAT "KING" COLE

Singer and pianist Nat "King" Cole (1919–1965) is still admired by many jazz and popular-music fans more than a quarter century after his death. He is remembered for his romantic, velvety renditions of sentimental songs.

Born Nathaniel Adams Coles in Montgomery, Alabama, Cole came from a musical family and made his first public appearance in a Chicago talent competition at age four. He began his career as a pianist, forming the King Cole Trio in 1939 with guitarist Oscar Moore and bass player Wesley Prince. At first their style was influenced by jazz pianist Earl Hines. Starting in 1941 Cole added singing to their performances. As they began to record hits such as "It's Only a Paper Moon" (1945) and "For Sentimental Reasons" (1946), Cole began to use orchestral accompaniments for his solos, abandoning piano and jazz altogether. He disbanded the trio in 1950, the year he recorded the popular song "Mona Lisa," a **crossover** hit on the pop and rhythm-and-blues charts. In the early 1950s he appeared in shows, on television, and as a musician in several unremarkable films. His popularity led to a television show, *The Nat King Cole Show* (1956–1957). He continued to record such hits as "When I Fall in Love" (1957) and to appear in films, including *St. Louis Blues* (1958), in which he portrayed blues popularizer W. C. Handy, and the Western comedy *Cat Ballou* (1965) before his death from lung cancer.

REFERENCE:

Leslie Gourse, *Unforgettable: The Life and Mystique of Nat King Cole* (New York: St. Martin's Press, 1991).
                                                                – L.D.S.

ORNETTE COLEMAN

Ornette Coleman (1930-) is a jazz saxophonist (and later in his career, violinist and trumpet player as well) who is regarded with **Louis Armstrong** and **Charlie Parker** as among the most significant innovators in modern jazz. Largely unschooled and playing a white plastic alto saxophone, he developed a style of improvisation in the mid to late 1950s known as "free jazz," in which the melodic line of a composition is freed from a predetermined chord structure and rhythm is determined by group intuition. Some early

Ornette Coleman (photograph by David D. Spitzer)

audiences found free jazz so offensive that they physically attacked Coleman, thinking him a fraud.

Interaction was a key aspect of Coleman's music, and because his ideas were so revolutionary, he had difficulty finding musicians who accepted or understood his musical demands. Traditionalists ridiculed him, and modernists often had difficulty accepting the degree of freedom Coleman offered. His groups were restricted early on to trumpeter Donald Cherry (playing a miniature instrument called a pocket trumpet), bassist Charlie Haden, and drummers Ed Blackwell or Billy Higgins. As Coleman and his groups began to command respect within the jazz community, he recorded with other modernists, notably Freddie Hubbard, Eric Dolphy, and Pharoah Sanders.

In the mid 1960s Coleman added his ten-year-old son, Ornette Denardo, as his group's drummer, a move that renewed charges that free jazz was not serious music. He had by that time recorded ten records without, he says, ever having received a royalty check large enough to pay his monthly phone bill.

Coleman is a composer as well as a musician; though his works were not well received, they have been characterized as artistic successes. By the 1970s

Coleman had retreated into seclusion, if not retirement, but his influence was widely acknowledged.

REFERENCES:

John Litweiler, *Ornette Coleman: A Life in Harmolodics* (New York: Morrow, 1993);

A. B. Spellman, *Four Lives in the Bebop Business* (New York: Pantheon, 1966).

                                                                                    – R.L.

JUDY COLLINS

Initially trained for a career as a classical pianist, Judy Collins (1939–) instead became one of the brightest stars in the genres of popular and **folk music.** Known for her clear soprano voice and her combined repertoire of folk, popular, and theatrical tunes, she has been a promoter of new songwriters, including **Bob Dylan,** Leonard Cohen, Joni Mitchell, and Tom Paxton.

Born in Seattle, Washington, Collins began playing classical piano soon after her father, a bandleader and disc jockey, moved the family to Los Angeles. Then five years old, she was considered a child prodigy. After relocating to Denver, Colorado, she studied piano from 1953 to 1956 with conductor Antonia Brico, about whom she later produced and directed the film *Antonia: A Portrait of the Woman* (1974), which was nominated for an Academy Award as best documentary.

In the mid 1950s Collins became attracted to the increasingly popular folk-music scene. At sixteen she learned to play the guitar to accompany her singing and then began appearing in **coffeehouses** and clubs throughout the country. In 1960 Collins moved to Greenwich Village in New York, where she began to perform in clubs, and the next year she was signed to Elektra Records. Her first two albums, *Maid of Constant Sorrow* (1961) and *Golden Apples of the Sun* (1962), with songs such as "Hey Nellie Nellie" and "Wild Mountain Thyme," reflect a traditional folk repertoire. Her concerts became popular events, and she drew large crowds to such places in New York as Carnegie Hall and Town Hall, where her album *Judy Collins in Concert* was recorded in 1964. This album, as well as the previous *Judy Collins No. 3* (1963), features lyrics by new songwriters, such as Bob Dylan's "Masters of War" and Tom Paxton's "The Last Thing on My Mind." During these years Collins was active in the **civil rights movement,** participating in marches and fund-raising events, although she was not as outspoken as fellow folk performers **Joan Baez** or Dylan.

In the late 1960s Collins changed her style. The songs on *In My Life* (1966) are a mix of folk, pop, and theater music, including **The Beatles'** "In My Life," Jacques Brel's "La Colombe," and Kurt Weill and Bertolt Brecht's "Pirate Jenny." Her next two albums, *Wildflowers* (1967) and *Who Knows Where the Time Goes* (1968), both earned gold records; the former features a rendition of Joni Mitchell's "Both Sides Now," which won Collins a Grammy Award for best single in 1968, as well as the first songs that Collins wrote herself. Collins continued to make the charts in 1969 with "Turn, Turn, Turn," and in 1971 she released her biggest hit, an a cappella version of "Amazing Grace," a best-seller in Britain as well as the United States. *True Stories and Other Dreams* (1973) includes several of Collins's songs, many of them reflecting her support of the **feminist** movement. Her next big hit was her rendition of **Stephen Sondheim**'s "Send in the Clowns" on the gold-record album *Judith* (1975). The single was nominated for best female vocal effort at the 1975 Grammy Awards ceremony.

Collins dropped out of the spotlight for several years until releasing *Hard Times for Lovers* in 1979, but many critics thought her voice had diminished in quality and range. She made three more albums in the 1980s; the latest, *Trust Your Heart* (1987), has the same title as her autobiography.

REFERENCES:

Judy Collins, *Trust Your Heart: An Autobiography* (Boston: Houghton Mifflin, 1987);

Irwin Stambler and Grelun Landon, *Encyclopedia of Folk, Country, and Western Music,* second edition (New York: St. Martin's Press, 1984).

                                                                                    –J.E.F. and L.D.S.

JOHN COLTRANE

Along with Sonny Rollins and, perhaps, Stan Getz, John Coltrane (1926-1967) dominated jazz saxophone playing in America during the 1960s and 1970s. He had a solid background in **bebop,** which provided a base for his experiments with Eastern musical forms and unusual chord structures. Because Coltrane played a lot of notes in his improvised solos, he was often criticized for not being able to choose the ones he wanted; however, that was the style. His "sheets of sound" were characteristic of his musical expression, which was at once startlingly emotional and dauntingly complex, layering chord upon related chord.

Beginning in 1955 he played for a year and a half with the celebrated **Miles Davis** quintet, where he began exploring modal music. He then played for a year with **Thelonious Monk,** whom he called "a musical architect of the highest order," before joining Davis again, along with Cannonball Adderley, for the *Kind of Blue* sessions (early 1959), which are among the most admired jazz recordings of the post–World War II era. By the time his milestone record album *Giant Steps* was released later that year he was generally recognized as one of the most important innovators and performers in modern jazz. The title song on *Giant Steps* is so complex harmonically that the piano player gives up trying to improvise to its chord structure.

In 1960 Coltrane, who was by then playing both tenor and soprano saxophone, began recording with pianist McCoy Tyner and drummer Elvin Jones. With bass player Jimmy Garrison they formed the group that played Coltrane's most innovative music, which had as its goal the expression of a cosmic spiritual awareness. *A Love Supreme* (1964) was considered the best expression of Coltrane's spiritually inspired modal music, characterized by long improvisations and a confluence of sound. In 1966 Coltrane's wife, Alice Coltrane, began playing piano with him, which she continued to do until his death from cancer at the age of forty-one.

REFERENCES:

William Shadrack Cole, *John Coltrane* (New York: Schirmer, 1976);

Cuthbert Ormond Simpkins, *Coltrane: A Biography* (New York: Herndon House, 1975);

J. C. Thomas, *Chasin' the Trane: The Music and Mystique of John Coltrane* (Garden City, N.Y.: Doubleday, 1975).

– R.L.

BETTY COMDEN AND ADOLPH GREEN

Betty Comden (1919–) and Adolph Green (1915–) are among the most-acclaimed writing teams in the history of Broadway. They have written the books or lyrics for sixteen **Broadway musicals** and the screenplays for nine movies.

Comden and Green first met as students at New York University in the late 1930s. They began to work together in 1939 on a nightclub act called *The Revuers,* which they eventually performed at Radio City Music Hall, in the Rainbow Room, and on **NBC** radio. The success of the act led composer **Leonard Bernstein** to ask them to write the book and lyrics for a musical comedy based on *Fancy Free,* a ballet by Bernstein and choreographer **Jerome Robbins**. *On the Town* opened on Broadway in 1944 and was a smash hit. Comden and Green also wrote the screenplay for the 1949 screen version, which starred **Gene Kelly** and **Frank Sinatra**.

During their six-decade career Comden and Green have had an almost unbroken string of Broadway successes, including *Billion Dollar Baby* (1945), *Bonanza Bound* (1947), *Two on the Aisle* (1951), *Wonderful Town* (1953), *Peter Pan* (1954), *Bells Are Ringing* (1956), *Say, Darling* (1958), *A Party with Betty Comden and Adolph Green* (1958), *Do Re Mi* (1960), *Fade Out — Fade In* (1964), *Hallelujah, Baby* (1967), *Applause* (1970), *Lorelei* (1974), and *On the Twentieth Century* (1978). One of their few failures was *A Doll's Life* (1982), which was based on Henrik Ibsen's *A Doll's House* (1879).

Comden and Green's screen writing credits include *The Barkleys of Broadway* (1949), *On the Town* (1949), *Singin' in the Rain* (1952), and *The Band Wagon* (1953). They have also acted in films such as *My Favorite Year* (1982) and *Garbo Talks* (1984).

–J.W.H.

CONCEPTUAL ART

A broad term covering a variety of artistic activities that emerged in the mid to late 1960s, *conceptual art* was based on the premise that an artist's ideas are the defining feature of a work of art. In the United States conceptual art came at least partially in response to the dominance of **minimalism** in the New York art world. Reacting against minimalism's paring down of art to its formal elements, some artists began to question the necessity for making permanent art objects altogether. Instead, they called attention to the artist's thought process and to an open-ended view of what could be considered art.

In place of creating paintings or sculpture, conceptual artists devised transitory activities that could be performed by themselves or by others, as well as presentations of information that documented the artists' ideas, relying on photographs and/or text for their structure. The minimalist artist Sol LeWitt formulated a new strategy for his own work in the influential essay "Paragraphs on Conceptual Art," published in the June 1967 issue of *Artforum*. LeWitt not only introduced the term *conceptual art* but offered an explanation of how the process worked in his own case: "When an artist uses a conceptual form of art, it means that all of the planning and decisions are made beforehand and the execution is a perfunctory affair. The idea becomes a machine that make art."

In Europe Joseph Beuys and others were experimenting with non-object-based art, some of it involving **performance,** at the same time that Americans were beginning to pioneer conceptual activities in New York, California, and elsewhere. It has been noted that conceptual art was partly a reaction against the surfeit of material goods in American culture — not only regular commodities but also the large and ever-increasing number of gallery-sold paintings and sculptures. In an often-quoted statement Douglas Huebler, a pioneering American conceptual artist, wrote in 1969: "The world is filled with objects, more or less interesting; I do not wish to add any more...."

Along with rejecting the commercialization of art and the artist, some American conceptual artists also implied a sense of futility when considering the artist's role in society. Reduced aspirations concerning the artist's power to advance consciousness — which had once been an underlying assumption of modernism — was an undercurrent in some early conceptual work. It is important, however, not to assume that conceptual artists shared a unifying philosophy. Many had, or have, little in common apart from a tendency to treat ideas as the substance of art, as well as a lack of interest in producing traditional painting or sculpture.

Aspects of conceptual art were foreshadowed in the work of **Marcel Duchamp,** the activities of artists associated with Fluxus, Nam June Paik's early experiments with video, some of **Robert Rauschenberg**'s early works, and aspects of **Pop Art.** Conceptual art is now seen as central to the transition from modernism to postmodernism in the visual arts. Although rooted in the 1960s, conceptual art has been absorbed in some way by most important American artists, and it continues to be a significant factor in describing much contemporary work. Artists associated with the beginnings of conceptual art in the United States include Joseph Kosuth, Mel Bochner, Douglas Huebler, Lawrence Weiner, **Edward Ruscha,** Sol LeWitt, Bruce Nauman, **John Baldessari,** and **Hans Haacke.**

REFERENCE:
Ursula Meyer, *Conceptual Art* (New York: Dutton, 1972).
– K.B.

Confessional Poetry

Confessional poetry came to the literary forefront in the early 1960s and changed the direction of American poetry for the rest of the century. In "Tradition and the Individual Talent" (1919) T. S. Eliot had written, "Poetry is not a turning loose of emotion, but an escape from emotion; it is not an expression of personality, but an escape from personality." By the late 1950s **Robert Lowell, Theodore Roethke, Allen Ginsberg, John Berryman, Sylvia Plath, Anne Sexton,** and W. D. Snodgrass had begun to turn this widely accepted definition on its head, abandoning objectivity to write out-

pourings of emotion that reveal their inner torments, humiliations, and unresolved guilt. Though the degree of intensity varied, these poets — who, with the exception of Ginsberg, were part of a network of friends and students — embraced the romantic notion of the link between madness and creativity, seeming to glorify life on the brink of suicide. (Berryman, Plath, and Sexton did kill themselves; these three, as well as Ginsberg, Lowell, and Roethke, spent time in mental hospitals.) Yet the best of their confessional poems display therapeutic moral courage.

The long-term effect of the confessional revolution extended beyond the immediate influence of these confessional poets. It laid the groundwork for the intensely personal tone and the agonizing self-examination that have come to characterize much of contemporary American writing, often blurring or obliterating the distinction between fiction and nonfiction.

REFERENCES:
Jeffrey Meyers, *Manic Power: Robert Lowell and his Circle* (New York: Arbor House, 1987);
Robert Phillips, *The Confessional Poets* (Carbondale & Edwardsville: Southern Illinois University Press, 1973).
– K.L.R.

Sean Connery

Sean Connery (1930–   ) achieved American film stardom playing the popular-culture hero James Bond during the 1960s and then transcended typecasting to win critical acclaim and box-office success with a variety of other roles during a career that has spanned thirty years.

Born Thomas Connery in Edinburgh to a truck driver and a charwoman, Connery joined the British navy at age fifteen. After military service he worked at manual-labor jobs before his interest in bodybuilding led to modeling work and a part in the chorus of the 1951 London production of *South Pacific.* The male romantic lead in **Walt Disney**'s *Darby O'Gill and the Little People* (1959) was his most important role until he was cast as Bond in *Dr. No* (1962). Connery played the sexy, debonair spy in seven films, quitting after *Diamonds Are Forever* (1971), but returning for an encore with *Never Say Never Again* (1983).

Even while he was doing the Bond series, Connery was expanding his range with gritty, unglamorous character portrayals. After starring in the prison-camp drama *The Hill* (1965), he played a nineteenth-century coal miner/terrorist in *The Molly Maguires* (1970). Connery's post-Bond career has included historical adventures such as *The Wind and the Lion* (1975), *The*

Man Who Would Be King (1975), *Robin and Marian* (1976), and *The Name of the Rose* (1986). He has also made science-fiction films such as *Zardoz* (1974) and *Outland* (1981).

In 1987 Connery accepted a secondary role in *The Untouchables* and won an Academy Award (Oscar) for Best Supporting Actor. This achievement reaffirmed his credentials as an actor and led to starring parts in big-budget films such as *The Hunt for Red October* (1990), *The Russia House* (1990), *Medicine Man* (1992), and *Rising Sun* (1993).

REFERENCES:

John Parker, *Sean Connery* (Chicago: Contemporary Books, 1993);

Andrew Yule, *Sean Connery: From 007 to Hollywood Icon* (New York: Fine, 1992).

– I.R.H.

AARON COPLAND

With **Leonard Bernstein,** Aaron Copland (1900–1990) was one of the most popular composers of serious music in America in the twentieth century. Copland's most successful works with audiences and critics combine his distinctive harmonic arrangements and colorful instrumentation with elements of American folk and popular music such as hymns and Western tunes. He was the first American composer whose work was regarded internationally as American rather than as an extension of the European tradition.

Copland studied music theory and composition and completed his first symphony in 1924. The dissonant piece led to his first commission, from the **Boston Symphony Orchestra,** a year later, resulting in *Music for the Theater.* In this work and another Boston Symphony commission, his Piano Concerto (1927), Copland began to introduce elements of jazz to his work. In the 1930s he turned away from jazz-influenced compositions and toward two stylistic trends: works influenced by **atonal** composers such as Arnold Schoenberg, and more-accessible pieces drawing on popular American music. His folk-inspired compositions include the ballets *Billy the Kid* (1938); *Rodeo* (1942), based on a scenario by Agnes de Mille; and the Pulitzer Prize–winning *Appalachian Spring* (1944), derived from a Shaker hymn and choreographed by **Martha Graham.** All three were also arranged as orchestral suites. Other popular compositions by Copland include his *Fanfare for the Common Man* (1942) and his scores for films such as *Of Mice and Men* (1939), *Our Town* (1940), *The*

Red Pony (1948), and *The Heiress* (1949), for which he won an Academy Award (Oscar) in 1950.

Copland's earlier compositions are known and performed more than most of his works written after World War II. He continued writing complex compositions such as his Piano Quartet (1950) and Piano Fantasy (1957) and his **serial** pieces *Connotations* (1962) and *Inscape* (1967) as well as "popular" pieces such as his arrangements of *Old American Songs* in 1950 and 1952. After 1970 Copland devoted most of his time to promoting American classical music through conducting, teaching, and writing. In 1957 he revised his most noteworthy book, *What to Listen for in Music* (1939). He received the Presidential Medal of Freedom in 1964 and the Congressional Medal of Honor in 1977.

REFERENCES:

Arthur Berger, *Aaron Copland* (Westport, Conn.: Greenwood Press, 1971);

Aaron Copland and Vivian Perlis, *Copland: 1900 through 1942* (New York: St. Martin's Press, 1987);

Copland and Perlis, *Copland: Since 1943* (New York: St. Martin's Press, 1989).

– D.H.-F.

FRANCIS FORD COPPOLA

Best known for his *Godfather* films, Francis Ford Coppola (1939–) is one of the most talented, if erratic, American film directors of the second half of the twentieth century.

During an apprenticeship with **Roger Corman,** Coppola directed and wrote the screenplay for the horror film *Dementia 13* (1963). His first complimentary reviews were for the low-budget feature *You're a Big Boy Now* (1967). He wrote the screen adaptation and directed the film, which he submitted to complete the requirements for an M.F.A. in filmmaking from the University of California, Los Angeles.

Coppola's first major recognition came at the 1970 Academy Award (Oscar) ceremonies, when he and Edmund H. North won an Oscar for their screenplay for *Patton.* Coppola won a second screen-writing Oscar in 1972, when he and Mario Puzo shared the award for their adaptation of Puzo's best-selling novel, *The Godfather.* Coppola also directed the film, which won the Academy Award for best picture. Its major critical and box-office success made Coppola one of the highest-paid and most sought-after directors in the world. *The Godfather, Part II* (1974) and *The Conversation* (1974) further enhanced his reputation.

In the late 1970s Coppola encountered financial problems connected with American Zoetrope, a production company he had founded in 1969, and budget overruns on his much-delayed Vietnam War epic *Apocalypse Now* (1979). The ambitious film, loosely based on Joseph Conrad's *Heart of Darkness* (1902), was well received, but its many expensive production problems dimmed Hollywood's regard for Coppola. The experimental *One from the Heart* (1982) bankrupted American Zoetrope. Although all the films Coppola has directed since that time have considerable artistic interest, none — not even the long-awaited *Godfather, Part III* (1990) — has had critical and box-office success to match his films of the 1970s.

REFERENCES:

Jeffrey Chown, *Hollywood Auteur: Francis Ford Coppola* (New York: Praeger, 1988);

Michael Goodwin, *On the Edge: The Life and Times of Francis Coppola* (New York: Morrow, 1989).

– I.R.H.

JOHN CORIGLIANO

The son of musicians, John Corigliano (1938–) is, according to **Aaron Copland,** "one of the most talented composers on the scene today." In his deliberately accessible compositions, Corigliano attempts to use conventional approaches to melody and harmony in innovative ways.

Corigliano studied music in college and worked as assistant music director at **CBS** (1961–1972) before beginning a teaching career. He received respectful attention for early works such as his Violin Sonata (1963) and *The Naked Carmen* (1970), an "electric rock opera" inspired by Georges Bizet's masterpiece. His reputation as a major American composer began with his acclaimed Clarinet Concerto in 1977. Since 1980, when he composed the score for the film *Altered States,* Corigliano has produced an eclectic variety of compositions. These include his *Promenade Overture* (1981), commissioned by the **Boston Symphony Orchestra** for its one hundreth anniversary, and the *Pied Piper Fantasy* (1982), a flute concerto commissioned by James Galway that ends with young flutists from the audience responding to the soloist and following him down the aisle out of the auditorium. Corigliano's Symphony No. 1 (1990), inspired by the **AIDS** crisis, was premiered by the **Chicago Symphony Orchestra,** and *The Ghosts of Versailles* (1992) was commissioned by the **New York Metropolitan Opera.** In all of these pieces, Corigliano's primary stylistic features — lyricism with a sophisticated sense of rhythm — are readily evident.

– L.D.S.

ROGER CORMAN

During the 1950s and 1960s Roger Corman (1926–) was the most prolific and successful director and producer of American low-budget films.

In 1954 Corman became a silent partner in American Releasing Corporation (which became American International Pictures in 1956). He made pictures for the youth market: horror, science-fiction, and crime films, as well as movies about high-school and college students. His *Little Shop of Horrors* (1960), a takeoff on some of his own movies, developed a substantial cult following and eventually became the basis for a successful Off-Broadway musical, followed by a film version, directed by Frank Oz, in 1986.

In 1970 Corman formed his own production company, New World Pictures, which not only turned out Corman's movies but also served as American distributor for some of the most respected foreign art films of the decade. In 1983 Corman sold the company and started a new one, Millennium Films.

As a director, Corman is noted for his stylish series of Edgar Allan Poe films starring Vincent Price: *The Fall of the House of Usher* (1960), *The Pit and the Pendulum* (1961), *The Premature Burial* (1961), *Tales of Terror* (1961), *The Raven* (1962), *The Haunted Palace* (1963), *The Masque of the Red Death* (1964), and *The Tomb of Ligeia* (1964). Corman's film companies have also provided first opportunities in the film business to directors **Francis Ford Coppola,** Peter Bogdanovich, **Martin Scorsese,** and Jonathan Demme; actors **Robert De Niro** and **Jack Nicholson;** and other individuals who went on to achieve prominence in the industry.

REFERENCES:

Gary Morris, *Roger Corman* (Boston: Twayne, 1985);

Paul Willeman, David Pirie, David Wills, and Linda Myles, *Roger Corman: The Millennic Vision* (Edinburgh: Edinburgh Film Festival, 1970).

– I.R.H.

KEVIN COSTNER

Film actor Kevin Costner (1957–) is often compared to Gary Cooper and other straight-arrow, romantic leading men of Hollywood films from the 1930s, 1940s, and early 1950s.

Costner began playing small film roles in 1981 and had a key supporting part in *Testament* (1983). He thought he had his big break when he signed to play in *The Big Chill* (1983) as the man whose suicide brings together a group of his friends for his funeral,

James Gould Cozzens in the mid 1960s

but all his scenes were cut. Director Lawrence Kasdan compensated Costner by giving him a substantial role in *Silverado* (1985). When Costner played Eliot Ness in *The Untouchables* (1987), comparisons to Gary Cooper started appearing in the press. Costner solidified his all-American image in two baseball films, *Bull Durham* (1988) and *Field of Dreams* (1989). He then decided, against conventional Hollywood wisdom, to produce, direct, and star in *Dances with Wolves* (1990), an epic, revisionist Western about an isolated and disillusioned U.S. Cavalry officer who becomes part of a tribe of Sioux Indians. The film was a critical and commercial success, winning an Academy Award (Oscar) for best picture and earning Costner an Oscar for best director.

Costner went on to play leading roles in *Robin Hood, Prince of Thieves* (1991), *JFK* (1991), and *The Bodyguard* (1992). His portrayal of an escaped convict opposite **Clint Eastwood** in *A Perfect World* (1993) was praised by reviewers, but the film was not as successful as critics predicted. Some critics suggested that the public did not want to see Costner playing a "bad guy."

REFERENCES:

Todd Keith, *Kevin Costner: The Unauthorized Biography* (London: Ikonprint, 1991);

Adrian Wright, *Kevin Costner: A Life on Film* (London: Hale, 1992).

– I.R.H.

JAMES GOULD COZZENS

In 1957 James Gould Cozzens (1903–1978) became one of the best-known novelists in America. Just as his twelfth novel, *By Love Possessed,* was published, his picture appeared on the cover of *Time* magazine. The novel was on the *New York Times* **best-seller list** for thirty-four weeks, most of that time as number one. By 1959 nearly five hundred thousand copies had sold.

Before writing about a lawyer in *By Love Possessed,* Cozzens had had some financial and critical success with his earlier novels delineating the lives and moral dilemmas of middle-class professional men: *The Last Adam* (1933), about a small-town doctor; *Men and Brethren* (1936), often called the best American novel about a clergyman; and *The Just and the Unjust* (1942), about a small-town district attorney, Cozzens's greatest commercial and critical success before *By Love Possessed*.

Yet neither substantial sales nor good reviews had brought him the sort of lasting respect that builds literary reputations. Cozzens's relative obscurity was due in part to his reclusiveness but also in part to the kind of fiction he wrote. His well-written novels of manners, objective examinations of human values and behavior, do not lend themselves to the sort of in-depth explication favored by college professors under the sway of the **New Critics,** whose literary values and methods dominated literary scholarship in the 1940s and 1950s.

His first postwar novel, *Guard of Honor* (1948), drew on his stateside service in the U.S. Army Air Corps during World War II. (Cozzens's diaries from this period and some of the official memos he drafted were published in 1984 as *A Time of War*.) *Guard of Honor* was greeted by respectful but unenthusiastic reviews, and sales were only moderate, even after it earned Cozzens a Pulitzer Prize in 1949, beating out two other war novels of 1948, Norman Mailer's *The Naked and the Dead* and Irwin Shaw's *The Young Lions*, both of which had been best-sellers. The prize did generate a revival of interest in Cozzens's work. In the early 1950s several well-known critics wrote respectful assessments charging that Cozzens's novels were being unjustly neglected.

The story of an upper-middle-class lawyer who must confront personal and professional problems resulting from various kinds of love ranging from sacred to profane, *By Love Possessed* was greeted with an outpouring of positive reviews. John Fischer in *Harper's* suggested that Cozzens should receive the Nobel Prize.

Reaction to Cozzens's success came quickly. Some attacked Cozzens's complex sentence structure, which he defended as necessary to convey the complexity of the behavior he was describing. Others were disturbed by Cozzens's objective description of sex, which is tame by the standards of the 1990s. The most disturbing charges came from critics who interpreted views expressed by characters as Cozzens's own and charged him with anti-Semitism and anti-Catholicism. By 1963 Cozzens had once again become, in the eyes of some critics, "America's best unread novelist."

His last completed novel, *Morning Noon and Night* (1967), narrated by an aging management consultant, was his most philosophical, including long set passages ruminating in a didactic eighteenth-century tone on topics such as vocation, puritanism, and writers. (The period in

which he wrote this novel is covered in his *Selected Notebooks, 1960–1967,* published in 1984.) The novel was out of touch with the mood of the 1960s and, despite its acknowledged merits, did little to enhance Cozzens's reputation. Cozzens began another novel but set it aside and abandoned fiction writing entirely. He continues to have admirers, but attempts to spark wider interest in his fiction have so far proved unsuccessful.

REFERENCES:
Matthew J. Bruccoli, *James Gould Cozzens: A Descriptive Bibliography* (Pittsburgh: University of Pittsburgh Press, 1981);

Bruccoli, *James Gould Cozzens: A Life Apart* (San Diego, New York & London: Harcourt Brace Jovanovich, 1983);

Bruccoli, ed., *James Gould Cozzens: New Acquist of True Experience* (Carbondale & Edwardsville: Southern Illinois University Press, 1979);

Bruccoli, ed. *Just Representations: A James Gould Cozzens Reader* (Carbondale & Edwardsville: Southern Illinois University Press / New York & London: Harcourt Brace Jovanovich, 1978).

– K.L.R.

CREATIVE-WRITING PROGRAMS

Creative writing as a course of study in universities is largely a post–World War II development. There are at least three reasons it took so long, all related to academic conservatism. The first is that creative-writing courses imply the availability of a respectable occupation for graduates. Until late in the nineteenth century, creative writing was considered an acceptable hobby for an educated man, but those who wrote for a living were generally thought of as hacks. Professional writing, said to have started in America with James Fenimore Cooper early in the nineteenth century, was slow to achieve respectability. Except for undergraduate composition courses that concentrated on rhetoric and syntax, the art of writing was not emphasized in college classrooms, and young writers who required tutelage typically turned to newspaper jobs. The second reason is that contemporary literature has mostly been ignored by literature professors, who have traditionally argued that the perspective of time is prerequisite to serious literary criticism (which for them is synonymous with appreciation). Third, American literature of any period was not widely considered worthy of serious study until the middle of the twentieth century. Creative writing in the United States, being both American and contemporary, was thus looked upon with particular disdain in academic circles.

The American public's attitude toward professional writers changed markedly during the first half of the twentieth century as the success of **book clubs** and popular magazines that published fiction and po-

Artist Dan Rice and poet Robert Creeley at Black Mountain College, 1955 (photograph by Jonathan Williams)

etry brought celebrity status to novelists such as **F. Scott Fitzgerald** and **Ernest Hemingway** and poets such as **Robert Frost** and Carl Sandburg. American universities were predictably slow to respond to these trends. With some exceptions — most notably the **Iowa Writers' Workshop** — most colleges and universities did not institute creative-writing programs until after World War II. As these programs proliferated, the market for distinguished writers who would enhance a university's reputation kept pace. One of the earliest and most prestigious postwar programs was the **Stanford Writing Program,** founded in 1947 by Wallace Stegner, a product of the Iowa Writers' Workshop. There are now more than three hundred graduate and undergraduate writing programs at American colleges and universities.

REFERENCE:

D. W. Fenza and Beth Jarock. eds., *The AWP Official Guide to Writing Programs,* sixth edition (Norfolk, Va.: Associated Writing Programs, Old Dominion University, 1992).

                                          – R.L.

ROBERT CREELEY

Robert Creeley (1926–), with **Charles Olson** and **Robert Duncan,** is considered one of the major writers to emerge from the overlapping **Projective** and **Black Mountain** schools of poetry. Olson, who began exchanging ideas with Creeley in 1950, acknowledged Creeley's contribution to Projectivist theory.

Creeley shared Olson's admiration for Hart Crane, **Ezra Pound,** and **William Carlos Williams,** including a preference for Williams over Pound. While Creeley's poems frequently reveal his knowledge of literature, he has never shared Olson's love for peppering his poems with allusions to his extensive research. Creeley's verse exhibits his admiration for jazz musicians such as **Charlie Parker** and **Miles Davis** and employs slang terms that Creeley sometimes had to define for Olson (who was sixteen years older than Creeley). Shorter than Olson's (or Duncan's), Creeley's poems are carefully crafted, often personal Projectivist lyrics. *The Collected Poems of Robert Creeley, 1945–1975* appeared in 1982. Poems from books published since 1975, as well as some earlier poems, are included in *Selected Poems* (1991).

REFERENCES:

Tom Clark, *Robert Creeley and The Genius of the American Common Place, Together with the Poet's Own Autobiography* (New York: New Directions, 1993);

John Wilson, ed., *Robert Creeley's Life and Work: A Sense of Increment* (Ann Arbor: University of Michigan Press, 1987).

– K.L.R.

WALTER CRONKITE

Walter Cronkite (1916–   ) is one of the most respected figures in the history of television journalism. As the anchorman of *The CBS Evening News* from 1962 to 1986, he interpreted the events of the day for millions of Americans for more than two decades.

Born in Missouri, Cronkite dropped out of college and spent several rootless years before finding work with the United Press wire service. In 1942 he became a UP war correspondent in Europe. In 1950 he was recruited by **Edward R. Murrow** for **CBS** television. Cronkite quickly became one of the stars of the network news department, hosting a variety of shows, covering such events as the coronation of Queen Elizabeth II in 1952, and anchoring CBS coverage of the 1956 and 1960 presidential conventions. In 1962 Cronkite was chosen to host *The CBS Evening News,* competing directly against popular **NBC** newsmen Chet Huntley and David Brinkley.

Cronkite was one of the most trusted men in America during the 1960s, and in 1968 he decided to "cash in all this trust people say they have for me" by speaking the truth as he saw it about the **Vietnam War.** Cronkite visited the war-torn country himself that year, and on a special report he contradicted the claims of generals and politicians by predicting no better possible outcome than a stalemate. Watching the report, President Lyndon Johnson supposedly told an aide, "Well, if I've lost Cronkite, I've lost middle America."

Cronkite retired from his news-anchor position in 1986 but remained active, hosting a variety of documentaries and specials for CBS and **PBS** (Public Broadcasting System). Over his career he has received nearly every honor the industry could give him, including several Emmy awards and induction into the Academy of Television Arts and Sciences Hall of Fame in 1985.

REFERENCE:

Doug James, *Cronkite: His Life & Times* (Brentwood, Tenn.: J. M. Press, 1991).

– C.D.B.

CROSSOVER MUSIC

Coined in the early 1950s, the term *crossover music* refers to a song or recording that appears in one category of music chart (such as those in ***Billboard***) after reaching the chart in another category. Crossovers were prevalent in the 1950s, when **rock 'n' roll** emerged on popular musical charts as an amalgam of rhythm and blues, country and western music, and other influences.

The foundation for crossover music was laid after 1950 as record distribution among categories approached equality and *Billboard* made charts for separate categories identical. For most of the 1950s these charts were based on record sales and on what disc jockeys played on the radio. An early crossover was **Hank Williams**'s "Cold Cold Heart" (1950): after it appeared on the country charts, it was recorded by Tony Bennett, whose version reached the pop charts in 1951; later that year Dinah Washington produced an interpretation that hit the rhythm-and-blues chart. Another example, in which the same recording crossed charts, was **Nat "King" Cole**'s "Mona Lisa" (1950), which did well in both pop and rhythm and blues.

This musical cross-fertilization proved especially productive in early rock 'n' roll. For instance, **Chuck Berry**'s "Maybellene" was a hit on pop and ryhthm-and-blues charts in 1955, and the song was recorded later that year by Marty Robbins and appeared on the country chart. Also in 1955, "Rock around the Clock," performed by Bill Haley and the Comets, was a pop/rhythm-and-blues hit. A frequent crossover rock 'n' roll artist was **Elvis Presley,** who had roots in country, **gospel,** and rhythm and blues.

Crossovers have remained fairly common since the 1950s, with artists and producers enjoying the increase in sales brought by crossover hits.

REFERENCE:

Philip H. Ennis, *The Seventh Stream: The Emergence of Rocknroll in American Popular Music* (Hanover, N.H. & London: Wesleyan University Press — University Press of New England, 1992).

– D.H.-F.

BOSLEY CROWTHER

Bosley Crowther (1905–1981), chief film critic for the *New York Times* from 1940 to 1968, was the most influential arbiter of movie taste during the middle decades of the twentieth century.

Crowther joined the *Times* in 1928 as a general reporter and rewrite man. Before becoming film critic, he worked as assistant drama editor and assistant screen editor. He was a prolific writer, usually seeing and reviewing three or four movies per week in addition to writing a weekly essay for the Sunday edition of the *Times*. Long an advocate of free speech, Crowther was one of the most vocal opponents of Sen. **Joseph McCarthy** during his attacks on the film industry in the 1950s.

Crowther was president of the New York Film Critics three times and the first film critic to be honored by the Screen Directors Guild, receiving a special award in 1954. He was also known as a champion of foreign filmmakers, helping to establish the reputations of Ingmar Bergman and Federico Fellini in the United States. As the American film industry changed with the decline of the studio system in the 1950s, Crowther was thought by many to be old-fashioned and out of touch with the new sensibilities. The most c ted example is his review of Arthur Penn's *Bonnie and Clyde* (1967), which blasted the film for its excessive violence while other critics were praising it as a modern classic. The controversy over the film and his opinions contributed to his retirement from the *Times* in 1968.

In addition to reviewing films, Crowther wrote *The Lion's Share* (1957), a history of M-G-M Studios, and *Hollywood Rajah* (1960), a biography of the founder of M-G-M, Louis B. Mayer.

More than anyone, Crowther was responsible for creating the perception that film critics at the *New York Times* are capable of making or breaking a movie.

REFERENCE:
Frank E. Beaver, ed., *Bosley Crowther: Social Critic of the Film* (Ann Arbor: University of Michigan Press, 1970).

—I.R.H.

George Crumb

George Crumb (1929–), an important American composer and teacher, is most renowned for works that include avant-garde experiments with timbre (quality of musical sound) and orchestration. To this end he frequently incorporated sounds of unusual instruments as well as those of traditional instruments altered either mechanically or electronically. For example, his *Ancient Voices of Children* (1970) for soprano and boy soprano is scored for such nontraditional orchestral instruments as toy piano, musical saw, Japanese temple bells, and mandolin along with more-standard instruments amplified electronically.

Combining diverse mystical elements, exoticism, symbolic programs, and the darker side of emotionalism, Crumb is thought to have been an early representative of the neoromantic tendency of the 1980s. In *Black Angels: Thirteen Images from the Dark Land* (1970), written for electronically amplified string quartet, the four performers are at various times called to play the maracas, the tam-tam, and even crystal goblets (tuned with various levels of water) by bowing across the tops. According to the composer, the piece describes three stages in the journey of the soul — the fall from grace ("Departure," Images 1–5), spiritual emptiness ("Absence," Images 6–9), and redemption ("Return," Images 10–13) — and employs symbolically mystical groupings of notes and rhythms into units of seven and thirteen. His *Makrokosmos I* (1972), for amplified piano, is a set of twelve short pieces, each describing a sign of the zodiac as well as a friend born under that particular sign.

Although most of Crumb's pieces are somewhat theatrical in nature, his *Vox Balanae* (Voice of the Whale, 1971) — for amplified flute, violoncello, and piano — epitomizes the composer's bent toward **performance art.** The piece calls for the performers to wear masks on a stage under blue lighting, eliciting dreamlike effects reminiscent of the darker side of Surrealism. Crumb's more recent works are often intended to convey the struggle between evil and good — as in his *Haunted Landscapes* (1984), which pits harsh sounds from the brass and percussion against a lyrical hymn for the strings.

Currently on the faculty of the University of Pennsylvania, Crumb has won many awards and honors, including a 1968 Pulitzer Prize for his *Echoes of Time and the River* (1967).

REFERENCE:
Edith Borroff, *Three American Composers* (Lanham, Md.: University Press of America, 1986).

—J.M.H.

Cultural Literacy

Although the term *cultural literacy* did not come into common usage until the publication in 1987 of E. D. Hirsch's book *Cultural Literacy: What Every American Needs to Know*, the concern implicit in the phrase — that many people are ignorant of key works and ideas forming the foundation of what we call education — has a long tradition. In the period after World War II, the alarm was first sounded by Robert M. Hutchins, president of the University of Chicago. His Great Books Program (founded in 1947), which organized discussion groups for general audiences about classic works of literature, stimulated debate about what an educated person should know. By 1950, when only six percent of adults had college educations, there were about twelve hundred Great Books Clubs throughout the country. The idea of great books proved more alluring than the reading of them, and the popularity of the clubs faded with time. But the anxiety they addressed did not. Various forms of adult education and autodidacts' guides took their place. In the decades after World War II such scholars as Howard Mumford Jones and Jacques Barzun in America, C. P. Snow and F. R. Leavis in Great Britain, led the debate about what people should know.

Prof. Hirsch entered the field of cultural literacy with a conservative argument calling for the preservation of a tradition-bound curriculum at a time when radical academicians were questioning whether the classics have any relevance at all to modern life. (By 1987 19.9 percent of all American adults had gone to college for four years, though there was a consensus that many of them emerged uneducated.) Hirsch's book, which includes a list of terms, without definition or description, that educated people should know, was attacked by progressive colleagues, while it was being eagerly purchased by anxious middle-class readers hoping for a quick refresher course in what they ought to know. Many readers were frustrated by the lack of definitions for the terms that were supposed to be commonly understood, so Hirsch supplied what his audience wanted with *The Dictionary of Cultural Literacy* (1988): a humanities crib sheet for people who missed something in college.

REFERENCES:

E. D. Hirsch, *Cultural Literacy: What Every American Needs to Know* (Boston: Houghton Mifflin, 1987);

Hirsch, *The Dictionary of Cultural Literacy* (Boston: Houghton Mifflin, 1988);

Robert M. Hutchens, ed., *The Great Books of the Western World,* 24 volumes (New York: Encyclopaedia Britannica, 1952).

                                 – R.L.

MERCE CUNNINGHAM

Dancer and choreographer Merce Cunningham (1919–   ) is one of the most influential and innovative figures in modern dance. His avant-garde dances, in which "anything can follow anything," have surprised and shocked audiences since the 1940s but have gradually become widely accepted.

Born in Centralia, Washington, Cunningham attended the Cornish School for the Arts in Seattle in the late 1930s. He studied modern dance with Bonnie Bird,

Merce Cunningham (photograph by Jack Mitchell)

who had been a member of **Martha Graham**'s company. In the summer of 1939 he studied with Graham herself at Mills College in Oakland and was invited to join her company. He was the second male dancer to do so and remained with her until 1945, performing in dances such as **Aaron Copland**'s *Appalachian Spring* (1944) while also beginning to present dances of his own. Accompanied by **John Cage,** whom he had met at Mills in 1938, he began giving solo recitals and choreographing his own works in the 1940s. He formed his own company in 1953.

Cunningham's most significant innovation was his break with the strong narrative orientation of mainstream modern dance, as exemplified by Graham's work, while maintaining traditional dance techniques. With linear narrative abandoned, he developed a style of composition that allowed for chance or random elements to dictate movement or the order of various dance selections, as in *Sixteen Dances for Soloist and Company of Three* (1951). Costuming was freed from the necessity of suggesting specific characters, and stage settings did not need to reflect any specific locale. Since no "acting" was required by the dancers, attention was focused on the movement itself and the patterns it formed. He also abandoned the traditional centering of stage space in favor of spreading the dancers' movements to all points on the stage, and dancers in his works often move independent of the direction they face, of each other, or of the musical accompaniment.

His innovative method of working with musicians and set and costume designers has produced some of the most striking collaborations in contemporary dance. Musicians are told the nature and length of the new work, set and costume designers only a description. Usually the choreography, accompaniment, sets, and costumes come together for the first time at the opening performance. Artists with whom Cunningham has worked include **Jasper Johns, Robert Rauschenberg,** and **Andy Warhol.** Cage was Cunningham's most frequent collaborator, and in "How to Pass Kick Fall and Run" (1965) Cage provided the accompaniment for the dance by reading from his writings on stage.

Cunningham continues to supply the entire repertoire for his company. Dancers and choreographers who have worked under him include **Paul Taylor** and **Twyla Tharp.**

REFERENCES:

Merce Cunningham, *The Dancer and the Dance* (New York & London: Marion Boyars, 1989);

Don McDonagh, *The Rise and Fall and Rise of Modern Dance,* revised edition (Pennington, N. J.: A Cappella Books, 1990).
                                                                                    – D.M.

D

Mario Davidovsky

Composer Mario Davidovsky (1934–) is best known for his work in **electronic music.** These pieces and his many orchestral and chamber works are frequently performed in contemporary-music concerts.

Born in Buenos Aires, Argentina, Davidovsky came to the United States in 1958 to study with **Milton Babbitt** at the Berkshire Music Center in Massachusetts. Davidovsky settled in New York in 1960, and during the early 1960s he pursued additional training at the Columbia-Princeton Electronic Music Center, where he now teaches. In 1971 he won a Pulitzer Prize for *Synchronism No. 6,* for piano and taped electronic music. The eight works in his *Synchronism* series (1963–1974) combine conventional instruments with electronic media.

REFERENCE:

Nicholas E. Tawa, *A Most Wondrous Babble: American Art Composers, Their Music, and the American Scene, 1950–1985* (New York: Greenwood Press, 1987).

– L.D.S.

Miles Davis and John Coltrane playing together in the mid 1950s and Davis in the 1970s (photograph on right by Veryl Oakland)

Miles Davis

By any reasonable measure, Miles Davis (1926–1993) is the most influential jazz musician of the postwar period. His importance as a soloist and a creative influence extended from 1950 until his death in 1993. He was for much of that time the highest-paid jazz musician in the world for both concert appearances ($30,000-$50,000 in the mid 1980s) and recordings (a three-year, $300,000, plus royalties, contract from Columbia in the 1971); by 1970 he claimed to be making $350,000-$400,000 a year. His influence was enormous and wide ranging, from hard bop, to "cool jazz" (which he was credited with creating), to modal jazz, to **fusion**, to **rock**. As a young musician Davis impressed his elders with his economy of style, his musical intelligence, and his distincive, often muted, tone. As a senior musician he was praised by young artists for his open-minded approach to new forms, his powerful melodic sense, and his distinctive style.

Miles Davis was born to middle-class parents in Alton, Illinois. He studied trumpet formally from the age of thirteen and served his musical apprenticeship in jam sessions on 52nd Street in Manhattan with **The-**

91

lonious Monk, **Dizzy Gillespie,** and **Charlie Parker,** and at the Juilliard School of Music a few blocks uptown, where he studied formal music theory. He began recording in 1945 with Charlie Parker, and, with a notable break from 1975 to 1980 due to ill health, he continued to be a successful recording artist for the next forty-eight years.

The musical milestones of his career can are marked with influential recordings: "Birth of the Cool" (recorded in winter 1949–1950 and released in various forms before the LP of that name in 1957) in which he introduced what came to be called West Coast or cool jazz that saxophonist Lee Konitz and trumpeter Chet Baker adopted; *Milestones* (1958) and *Kind of Blue* (1959), in which his legendary group, including **John Coltrane** (beginning in 1955) and later Cannonball Adderley set the standard for mainstream jazz of the period; *Porgy and Bess* (1958) and *Sketches of Spain* (1959), in which he teamed with the orchestra of Gil Evans to provide haunting solos to classic works; *ESP* (1965) and *Miles Smiles* (1966), in which he pioneered modal jazz; *On the Corner,* (1972), which marked the "Africanization" of his music, and *Tutu* (1986), dedicated to Bishop Desmond Tutu, featuring a song by rock star Prince.

Style was important to Davis. He drove Ferraris or a Lamborghini (until he wrecked it); and he dressed flamboyantly, wielding as much influence in the clothes as in the music of jazzmen. As signifcant as his musical innovations was the sense of dignity — some would say arrogance — he brought to jazz musicans. He insisted on respect for his artistic achievement, and he refused to cater to audiences, often turning his back to them as he played. Only his music was important to him, he explained.

REFERENCES:

Ian Carr, *Miles Davis: A Biography* (New York: Morrow, 1982);

Miles Davis, *Miles: The Autobiography* (New York: Simon & Schuster, 1989).

– R.L.

Doris Day

Doris Day (1924–   ), is best known for her film roles as a perky, blonde, virginal girl-next-door.

Born Doris von Kappelhoff in Cincinnati, Ohio, she began a career as a singer in the 1940s, performing on radio and with the Bob Crosby and Les Brown bands. She broke into films in *Romance on the High Seas* (1948) and starred in a string of musicals and romantic comedies that extended into the mid 1950s. She also had more complex roles in *Love Me or Leave*

Me (1955) and **Alfred Hitchcock**'s *The Man Who Knew Too Much* (1956). In 1959 *Pillow Talk* launched her in a series of sexual farces (without the sex) that solidified her screen image and tied it to that of her *Pillow Talk* costar Rock Hudson, with whom she made three films. Her last film was *With Six You Get Eggroll* in 1968. After the death of her husband and manager, Martin Melcher, in that same year, she discovered that he had mishandled their finances and left her deeply in debt. A successful television series, *The Doris Day Show* (1968–1972), paid the bills. Day then retired from performing to devote herself to helping abandoned and abused animals.

REFERENCE:

Doris Day with A. E. Hotchner, *Doris Day: Her Own Story* (New York: Morrow, 1976).

– I.R.H.

James Dean

Having established himself as the quintessential alienated youth in *Rebel Without a Cause* (1955), James Dean (1931–1955) became a cult figure of rarely matched proportions when he was killed in a car crash right after the film was released.

He began his career in 1950, acting in television commercials and playing bit parts in films. He went to New York in 1952, observed classes at the **Actors Studio,** and gained parts in two Broadway plays — *See the*

James Dean beside the silver Porsche in which he was killed

Jaguar (1952) and *The Immoralist* (1954) — and several live television dramas. Warner Bros. called him to Hollywood for a screen test in 1954 and gave him the part of the rebellious Cal in **Elia Kazan**'s film version of John Steinbeck's novel *East of Eden* (1955). *Rebel Without a Cause* was followed by *Giant,* which was released in 1956 after Dean's death. His enduring status as a screen legend is especially remarkable because it is based on only three films.

REFERENCES:
Leith Adams and Keith Burns, eds., *James Dean, Behind the Scenes* (New York: Birch Lane Press, 1990);
David Dalton, *James Dean, The Mutant King*, revised edition (New York: St. Martin's Press, 1983);
Joe Hyams, with Jay Hyams, *James Dean: Little Boy Lost* (New York: Warner Books, 1992).

– I.R.H.

Roy De Carava

Roy De Carava (1919–) is probably the best-known African-American photographer of the post–World War II period. Trained as a painter, he began taking pictures in 1946 to document his own work. Gradually, he devoted himself entirely to photography and had his first one-person exhibition at Mark Perper's gallery in New York City in 1950. Perper was so impressed with De Carava's work that he invited the renowned photographer Eugene Steichen to the opening of the exhibition. Steichen, also impressed, offered to sponsor De Carava's application for a Guggenheim Fellowship. In 1952 De Carava was the first black artist ever to receive that fellowship.

The subjects of De Carava's photographs were most often scenes of everyday life in Harlem, with a direct and sensitive focus on the lives of blacks, from children to great jazz musicians. He was particularly conscious of the relationship of individuals to their surroundings, expressing in his work the notion that a subject's ugliness is only a reflection of the environment that created it. He came to public attention in 1955 with the publication of *The Sweet Flypaper of Life,* a book about life in Harlem combining his photographs with text by Langston Hughes.

In 1964 De Carava and fellow black photographers founded the Kamoinge (a Kikuyu word meaning "group effort") workshop, an organization with the purpose of working together to develop and promote the talent of other black photographers. In 1975 he became an associate professor of art at Hunter College in New York City, where he continues to teach photography classes.

REFERENCE:
Elton C. Fax, *Seventeen Black Artists* (New York: Dodd, Mead, 1971).

– K.B.

Deconstruction

Deconstruction seems to mean different things to different people. The term has become to laymen a catchword for the radical trend toward discrediting conventional ideas about literature, its significance, and its study. To practitioners, deconstruction, a form of **poststructuralism** closely related to philosophy, is the process of stripping the artifice, including the implication of absolute meaning, from literature. That process requires a close scrutiny of literary constructs, such as rhetoric, to determine variable meanings of a literary text that the author was probably unaware of. Often the ambiguities of meaning that the critic uncovers involve the discovery of cultural or tradition-based assumptions by the author or by influential readers that affect how the work is construed. The critic who can strip away the literary constructs before assigning new significance to a literary work is, for deconstructionists, at least equal in importance to the author. The term *deconstruction* was coined in the 1960s by French philosopher-critic Jacques Derrida, and its chief advocates in America are Paul de Man, J. Hillis Miller, Geoffrey Hartman, and Jonathan Culler.

REFERENCES:
Paul de Man, *Blindness and Insight: Essays in the Rhetoric of Contemporary Criticism*, enlarged edition (Minneapolis: University of Minnesota Press, 1983);
Geoffrey Hartman, *Saving the Text: Literature/ Derrida/ Philosophy* (Baltimore: Johns Hopkins University Press, 1981);
David Lehman, *Signs of the Times: Deconstruction and the Fall of Paul de Man* (New York: Poseidon, 1991);
J. Hillis Miller, *The Ethics of Reading: Kant, de Man, Eliot, James and Benjamin* (New York: Columbia University Press, 1987).

– R.L.

Willem de Kooning

Willem de Kooning (1904–), an original member of the **Abstract Expressionist** group, is one of the most important American painters of the twentieth century. Born and trained as an art student in Rotterdam, Netherlands, de Kooning arrived as a stowaway in Hoboken, New Jersey, in 1926. After a brief stint there as a housepainter, he moved to New York City, joined the Federal Art Project of the Works Progress Administration (WPA), and eventually became acquainted with

William de Kooning in his studio, 1972 (photograph by Hans Namuth)

other young, avant-garde artists such as **Jackson Pollock** and Arshile Gorky. In 1936 he met Elaine Fried, whom he married in 1943 (Elaine de Kooning would also become an active painter in the Abstract Expressionist style). He had his first one-person show in 1948, the same year that Pollock exhibited his drip paintings. De Kooning's reputation as a painter of national importance was established in 1951 with his one-person show at the Charles Egan Gallery and inclusion in the Museum of Modern Art exhibition Abstract Painting and Sculpture in America. This image was perpetuated by eminent art critic **Harold Rosenberg** in his highly publicized debates with **Clement Greenberg** regarding the abstract painting style.

In the early 1950s de Kooning began painting with greater spontaneity and speed than earlier, layering his canvases with heavy, overlapping brushstrokes and building up his paintings with numerous revisions and reworkings. Like Pollock's, de Kooning's mature painting style was eventually described by critics as

"gestural" or as "action painting." This designation was made popular by Rosenberg in his 1952 article "The American Action Painters," in which he alludes to contemporary painters for whom "the canvas began to appear as an arena in which to act. . . . What was to go on the canvas was not a picture but an event."

Unlike most of the paintings of his fellow Abstract Expressionists, de Kooning's works — although essentially abstract — often contain images that are representationally connected to objects in the visible world, mainly the human figure or landscape. Around 1950 he began a series of paintings on the theme of women, in which the female figure in various degrees of abstraction is a recurrent motif. The most famous is probably his first one, *Woman I* (1950–1952), in which a large-chested, ferocious woman glares out with huge, menacing eyes and teeth. There is no background or foreground; her body sits amid violent swirls of color and loose drips of paint. When first exhibited in 1953, it caused mixed reactions. Many Abstract Expressionists were shocked that de Kooning had reintroduced the human figure into an art movement that championed nonrepresentational work, while others found the grotesqueness of his archetypical woman disturbing. De Kooning continued this woman motif from 1953 to 1955 and then returned to it in the 1960s.

In 1963, with an improved financial situation, he moved permanently to East Hampton, Long Island, where previously he had only spent summers. His paintings subsequently began to reflect the space and light in nature that now surrounded him. During this period de Kooning's work won many new admirers because of its increased lyricism, freshness, and softness of colors. He continued to paint in his large studio there, with commercial success, through the 1970s and 1980s. In 1989, however, de Kooning was diagnosed with Alzheimer's disease. This disclosure suddenly threw into question the value of his most recent work and spawned a debate over whether or not a painter with this illness can be considered a productive artist as critical faculties begin to disappear.

Alongside the styles of the other first-generation Abstract Expressionists, de Kooning's gestural, emotive approach had perhaps the most profound and widespread influence on younger painters throughout the 1950s and early 1960s. For many years his style was almost synonymous with the concept of abstract art in the United States.

REFERENCES:

Harry F. Gaugh, *Willem de Kooning* (New York: Abbeville Press, 1983);

Thomas B. Hess, *Willem de Kooning* (New York: Museum of Modern Art, 1969);

Harold Rosenberg, *De Kooning* (New York: Abrams, 1974).

– K.B.

ROBERT DE NIRO

Robert De Niro (1943–) is widely considered the acting virtuoso of his generation.

The son and namesake of a respected artist, De Niro was born in New York, where he studied acting with **Stella Adler** and with Lee Strasberg at **Actors Studio.** He began performing in films in 1968. He first achieved notice in 1973, when he played a dying, slow-witted baseball player in *Bang the Drum Slowly* and a crazy street punk in *Mean Streets,* the first of seven films he made with director **Martin Scorsese.** His reputation was solidified after he won an Academy Award (Oscar) for best supporting actor as the young Vito Corleone in *The Godfather, Part II* (1974). He gave other highly acclaimed performances in *Taxi Driver*

(1976) and *Raging Bull* (1980). Widely regarded as one of the finest actors in films, De Niro puts himself through grueling regimens to become immersed in the physicality of a role; despite his star status, he is willing to play second leads or cameo roles (*Backdraft,* 1991) if a part interests him. Well-known for playing violent, psychotic men in films from *Mean Streets* to *Cape Fear* (1991), De Niro can convincingly play vulnerable or comedic characters as well. The few films in which he has starred as a "regular guy" (*Falling in Love,* 1984; *Guilty by Suspicion,* 1991) have had little commercial success. De Niro entered the film production business in the 1990s with the founding of his TriBeCa studio complex.

REFERENCE:

Douglas Brode, *The Films of Robert De Niro* (Secaucus, N.J.: Carol Publishing Group, 1993).

– I.R.H.

DIANETICS/SCIENTOLOGY

Founded by **science-fiction** writer L. Ron Hubbard (1911–1986), the Church of Scientology is based on Hubbard's "science" of *dianetics,* a term he defined as "what the soul is doing to the body." Hubbard first explained dianetics in the May 1950 issue of *Astounding Science Fiction,* followed later that year with *Dianetics: The Modern Science of Mental Health,* one of the **best-selling** self-help books in history.

Hubbard's followers have found dianetics, later expanded as "scientology," attractive for its simplicity and promise of personal improvement. Hubbard announced scientology as an advancement on dianetics in his 1952 book *This Is Scientology: The Science of Certainty.* In 1955 the Founding Church of Scientology was incorporated — according to critics, as a tax dodge and to escape criticism from doctors and psychologists who challenged dianetics. Scientologists claim that humans are the descendants of an omnipotent race called "thetans." Having created the universe for their own amusement, thetans soon lost interest in spiritual matters and came to believe that they were nothing more than the bodies they inhabited — which, according to Hubbard, is the current state of humanity. To awaken thetan powers of enhanced intelligence and physical healing, one must overcome all mental blocks, or "engrams," caused by living in the material universe. New members are therefore questioned by an "auditor," or spiritual adviser, in an effort to locate and rid themselves of engrams. Having undergone auditing, one becomes "clear" and works toward becoming an "operating thetan." This variation on psychotherapy includes both the subject's lifetime traumas and those from previous incarnations, according to believers.

The Church of Scientology has been accused of being a cult and of bilking members of millions of dollars. Scientologists have used lawsuits to silence critics. The church has extended its operations beyond its Los Angeles headquarters but has found a hostile reception in England, France, and Australia, as well as from the Internal Revenue Service. In an effort to win public approval, the church has published Hubbard's later science-fiction novels and his nonfiction books through its Bridge Publications and has participated in charitable activities, including hunger-relief and nonprofit drug-rehabilitation programs.

The church boasts a membership of millions, though this number is likely an exaggeration. It has drawn celebrities in the entertainment industry, including John Travolta, Kirstie Alley, Tom Cruise, and Sonny Bono. **William S. Burroughs** was a member in the late 1960s and even served as an auditor before leaving the church, which in recent years he has criticized.

REFERENCES:

Jon Atack, *A Piece of Blue Sky: Scientology, Dianetics, and L. Ron Hubbard Exposed* (New York: Lyle Stuart, 1990);

L. Ron Hubbard, *Scientology: The Fundamentals of Thought* (London: Hubbard Association of Scientologists International, 1956);

Russell Miller, *Bare-Faced Messiah: The True Story of L. Ron Hubbard* (New York: Holt, 1987).

– R.T.

JAMES DICKEY

James Dickey (1923–) became well known to the American public after his first novel, *Deliverance* (1970), became a best-seller and was made into a successful movie starring Jon Voight and Burt Reynolds. Dickey wrote the screenplay for the movie, which received an Academy Award nomination for best film of 1972. Yet Dickey's enduring reputation is most likely to rest on his accomplishments as a poet, including some of the finest war poems in American literature.

In poems such as "The Performance," "Drinking from a Helmet," and "The Firebombing" Dickey drew on his experiences in the U. S. Army Air Corps during World War II, when he took part in more than one hundred bombing missions in the South Pacific. Looking back with a sense of guilt over living when so many comrades as well as enemies have died, Dickey has described himself as "the poet of *survival*."

Though he had begun writing poetry by the late 1940s, Dickey's first collection of poems was not published until 1960, when he was thirty-seven. By the time his fourth collection, *Buckdancer's Choice* (1965), earned him a National Book Award in 1966, he had become a widely respected poet.

Like many poets of his generation, Dickey rebelled against the **New Critics**' prescriptions for the "well-made poem," rejecting outright one of their central rules: **T. S. Eliot**'s statement that poetry should be "not the expression of personality but an escape from personality." Believing that the poet's personality cannot, and should not, be separated from his writings, Dickey has nonetheless disassociated himself from the **confessional poets** (especially **Sylvia Plath** and **Anne Sexton**), as well as from other postwar schools of avant-garde poetry. The self in Dickey's poems actively confronts the world, using its imaginative, visionary powers to merge temporarily with other beings — human and animal, living and dead — and in the process to experience renewal. The importance of nature in an age when humanity is becoming increasingly removed from the land is apparent throughout Dickey's writings, including "The Strength of Fields," the poem wrote for President Jimmy Carter's inauguration in 1977. *The Whole Motion: Collected Poems 1945–1992*, published in 1992, brings together poems from his earlier books and some previously unpublished early poems.

Since *Deliverance,* Dickey has published two more novels, *Alnilam* (1987) and *To the White Sea* (1993). Both draw on his military experience, not only during World War II but as an instructor of pilots during the Korean War. He is also a perceptive literary critic, who is quick to point out artificiality or condescension.

REFERENCES:

Ronald Baughman, *Understanding James Dickey* (Columbia: University of South Carolina Press, 1985);

Ernest Suaarez, *James Dickey and the Politics of Canon* (Columbia: University of Missouri Press, 1993).

– K.L.R.

JOAN DIDION

Novelist and essayist Joan Didion (1934–) is known for her pessimistic view of contemporary American life, which she sees as lacking morality and meaning.

In 1963 Didion published her first novel, *Run River,* about the aimless, destructive lives of a family in her native California. Like her later novels, *Run River* is filled with brief scenes rich in descriptive detail and possessing a somewhat nightmarish quality. As in her later novels, plot is less significant than mood. In *Play It As It Lays* (1970), Didion's most successful novel, a former Hollywood model finds herself unable to cope with life and becomes institutionalized, while in *A Book of Common Prayer* (1977) the personal disintegration of an American woman in a fictional Central American country reflects the larger national chaos around her. This connection between personal and cultural anxiety, common in Didion's fiction and nonfiction, also appears in *Democracy* (1984), a **metafictional** novel involving love and murder in a troubled American family after the **Vietnam War**. She has also published a collection of stories, *After Henry* (1992).

While Didion's novels have received mixed reviews, critics have praised her collections of magazine essays for their **New Journalistic** impressions of American life. *Slouching towards Bethlehem* (1968) includes understated, often sardonic essays on California lifestyles, Las Vegas weddings, Alcatraz, cultural icons such as **John Wayne** and **Joan Baez**, herself, and living in New York and Los Angeles. She includes more of her own experience in *The White Album* (1979), which relates her own life to events in the late 1960s and the early 1970s. Her later efforts at nonfiction, her impressions of El Salvador in *Salvador* (1983) and *Miami* (1987), were less well-received.

Didion has also collaborated with her husband, novelist John Gregory Dunne, on screenplays for *Panic in Needle Park* (1971), *Play It As It Lays* (1972), and an adaptation of his 1977 novel *True Confessions* (1981). She has written for magazines such as *Esquire, The New Yorker,* and the *New York Times Review of Books.*

REFERENCES:

Ellen Friedman, ed., *Joan Didion: Essays and Conversations* (Princeton, N. J.: Ontario Review Press, 1984);

Mark Royden Winchell, *Joan Didion,* revised edition (Boston: Twayne, 1989).

– D.H.-F.

RICHARD DIEBENKORN

Known primarily for his abstract paintings that derive from West Coast outdoor scenes, Richard Diebenkorn (1922–1993) is important for his synthesis of the two major divisions of **Abstract Expressionism** — color-field painting and gestural (action) painting. His associations with **Mark Rothko** in the 1940s at the California School of Fine Arts introduced him to the former practice, while his exposure to the works of

Willem de Kooning in New York City in 1948 influenced him in the latter.

Diebenkorn began his career as an artist in the late 1940s, quickly becoming fairly prominent in various artistic circles as an abstract painter. Interestingly, when abstract painting became the fashion in the art world of the mid 1950s, Diebenkorn switched to painting representational works in the expressionist style of Fauvist painter Henri Matisse — a style he would continue for more than a decade. In the paintings of this figurative period, however, many of the figures' details have been reduced almost to the point of abstraction. In *Man and Woman in Large Room* (1957), for example, the subject is not really the two figures mentioned in the title but rather the way in which structural planes of subdued color interpenetrate to define both physical space and emotional atmosphere. The formal elements become more important than the incidental "subject."

This emphasis on the formal aspects of painting led Diebenkorn quite naturally back to an abstract style. In 1967, a year after he had moved from the San Francisco area in order to teach at the University of California, Los Angeles, he began his most famous work: the Ocean Park series, named after the Santa Monica community where he kept an art studio. By the end of his lifetime this series comprised more than 140 paintings, each an abstraction based on his experiences of light and color of the Ocean Park area. These paintings are characterized by muted colors in semitransparent layers that are expansive yet controlled by a superimposed linear structure of verticals, horizontals, and diagonals. Diebenkorn has been especially praised for his ability to create a pictorial space that, while flat, gives the illusion of a permeating inner light.

For all of his works, both figurative and abstract, Diebenkorn established what he called a "dialogue" with the canvas. Like the action painters, he would make no preliminary designs; rather, he would paint a few dabs of color on the canvas and then allow the demands of form to lead him through the creative process.

REFERENCE:

John Gruen, "Richard Diebenkorn: The Idea Is To Get Everything Right," *ARTnews,* 85 (November 1986): 80–87.

–J.M.H.

DISCO

A combination of rhythm and blues and Latin rhythms, disco music originated in the gay dance clubs of New York City during the early 1970s. By the end of the decade the "disco craze" had crossed over to the mainstream, inspiring movies, television series, and fashions.

The term *disco* is from "discotheque," the name used in the 1960s to designate any establishment that played prerecorded music for dancing. By 1969 "disco" was most often used to refer to the music of nightclubs in the Greenwich Village section of New York City. Disco dancing was an uninhibited celebration of the freer sensuality of the time. Songs such as Barry White's "Can't Get Enough of Your Love, Baby" (1974) or K.C. and the Sunshine Band's "That's the Way I Like It" (1975) were fun, exuberant, provocative responses to the dreary, economically troubled 1970s. Other singles, such as the Village People's "Y.M.C.A." (1975) openly endorsed the gay lifestyle.

Disco reached a national audience in 1977 with the enormous success of the movie *Saturday Night Fever* and its soundtrack. The film chronicles the lives of young, lower-middle-class New Yorkers seeking something like celebrity in the dance clubs, and it made its star, John Travolta, the heartthrob of the growing fad. Another movie, *Thank God It's Friday* (1978), introduced the other major disco star, Donna Summer, whose Oscar-winning disco anthem, "Last Dance," is featured in that film.

Saturday Night Fever was imitated in the theater, on television, and in hundreds of nightclubs around the country. But by the early 1980s national interest in disco was already fading. Hard rock and especially punk rock reacted against what was seen to be the shallow, monotonous pop-music sound of disco and the glitzy, equally shallow lifestyle that had grown up around it. In the 1990s, however, disco music and fashions enjoyed a resurgence of popularity.

REFERENCES:

Albert Goldman, *Disco* (New York: Hawthorn, 1977);

Hugh Mooney, "Disco: A Music for the 1980s?," in *American Popular Music: Readings from the Popular Press Volume II: The Age of Rock,* edited by Timothy E. Scheurer (Bowling Green, Ohio: Bowling Green State University Popular Press, 1989), pp. 240-251.

– C.D.B.

WALT DISNEY PRODUCTIONS

Since the 1930s, Walt Disney Productions has captured the imaginations of children with some of the best-known and most-beloved fictional characters in the world.

Walt Disney (1901–1966) began to build his financial empire in 1928, with a cartoon animal named Mickey Mouse. After his *Snow White and the Seven Dwarfs* (1937), the first animated feature film, made the then-considerable sum of $8 million dollars, Disney was inspired to make other full-length animated films.

To finance their company during the lean early years, Walt Disney and his brother Roy began licensing their popular cartoon characters to companies that wanted to use them on their products. Over time the royalties from licensing agents were substantial, but more important, products bearing Disney characters were extremely effective advertising for Disney movies. The company followed the same practice when it began to make live-action and television shows in the 1950s, and in 1987 it began opening its own Disney Stores in shopping malls nationwide.

Disney suffered financially during World War II, but by the early 1950s the company began to show regular profits, helped by backing from **ABC**. In October 1954 ABC began to televise *Disneyland,* an hour-long, weekly show that broadcast holdings from the Disney animated-film library and live-action adventure serials, including the extremely popular *Davy Crockett,* starring Fess Parker, which started a nationwide craze for coonskin hats (sold, of course, by a Disney licensee). The show aired continuously, under a variety of series titles (including *Walt Disney Presents* and *Walt Disney's World*), until 1983 (moving to **NBC** in 1961 and **CBS** in 1981). In October 1956 ABC began to air another popular Disney series, *The Mickey Mouse Club* (1955–1959), featuring "Mouseketeers," young performers (including the extremely popular Annette Funicello) wearing hats with Mickey Mouse ears, as well as Disney cartoons, news features, and adventure serials.

Initially, the Disney television shows helped to publicize Disneyland, the first movie-inspired theme park, which opened in Anaheim, California, in July 1955. In 1956 Disneyland made $10 million dollars, one-third of the company's gross revenues.

While Walt Disney Productions was venturing into other forms of entertainment in the 1950s, its filmmaking division, Walt Disney Studios, was expanding its offerings. It began making family-oriented nature films and live-action adventure films. Many of these films were initially more popular than Disney's feature-length cartoons of the 1950s. Yet, in the long run, as Disney periodically re-released its feature cartoons, movies such as *Cinderella* (1950), *Peter Pan* (1953), *Lady and the Tramp* (1955), and *Sleeping Beauty* (1959) have been big money makers.

Disney had two hit film in the 1960s: *Mary Poppins* (1964), which mixed live-action and animation, and a live-action comedy, *The Love Bug* (1969). After

Walt Disney at the opening of Disneyland, 17 July 1955

Walt Disney's death in 1966, the film division began to flounder. During the 1970s its most profitable movies were the old ones it re-released. The families who used to go to Disney movies were staying home to watch television, and Disney Studios failed to adapt to the tastes of 1970s theatergoers.

Walt Disney Productions continued to prosper through most of the decade, however, thanks in great part to the success of Disney World, a larger, more-elaborate version of Disneyland, which opened near Orlando, Florida, in 1971. Yet by 1979 the company was in trouble. The fuel shortage of the late 1970s and a nationwide economic slump in the early 1980s, reduced attendance at both Disney parks, and construction at Disney World of Walt Disney's idea of utopia, EPCOT (Experimental Prototype Community of Tomorrow), was costing hundreds of millions of dollars more than original estimates. When Epcot opened in 1982, it arrested the downward trend for a year, but in 1983 attendance at Disney World started slipping again. The only bright spot was Tokyo Disneyland, which opened in Japan in 1983 and was immediately profitable. The Disney Channel on **cable television,** launched in 1982, was a forward-looking and eventu-

ally profitable venture, but it went $100 million in the red before it finally broke even several years later.

Realizing that the Disney name had become so associated with children's movies that teens and young adults were avoiding them, the film division launched Touchstone Pictures, geared toward the audience it had lost. Its first release, *Splash* (1984), a comedy starring Daryl Hannah as a mermaid, showed more skin than any previous Disney film though it was still rated PG. The movie brought in more than $69 million, becoming the highest-grossing Disney picture to that date.

Later that year Michael Eisner became chairman and chief executive officer of Walt Disney Productions (which became the Walt Disney Company in 1985), bringing with him Jeffrey Katzenberg to head Disney Studios. This new management began by making the most of the company's chief asset: its huge library of old films, earning millions from its old animated features by timing their re-release to theaters and their appearance on video cassette so that one did not cut into the profits from the other. Disney Studios also made new animated features that, for the first time in two decades, matched the Disney "classics" in quality, and it entered the Saturday-morning and after-school television market for the first time ever with several successful cartoon series.

At the same time Disney Studios continued to pursue the teen and young-adult market with the Disney MGM Studio Tour, which opened at Disney World in 1989, and with Touchstone films. In 1988 *Three Men and a Baby, Good Morning Vietnam,* and *Who Framed Roger Rabbit?* each made more than $100 million; no other studio had ever had even two films that exceeded that mark in one year. *Pretty Woman,* released by Touchstone in 1990, earned $180 million, a new Disney record. By 1991 Disney had been a top-three money-making studio for five years.

REFERENCES:

Joe Flower, *Prince of the Magic Kingdom: Michael Eisner and the Re-Making of Disney* (New York, Chichester, Brisbane, Toronto & Singapore: Wiley, 1991);

Ron Grover, *The Disney Touch: How a Daring Management Team Revived an Entertainment Empire* (Homewood, Ill.: Business One Irwin, 1991);

Richard Schickel, *The Disney Version: The Life, Times, Art, and Commerce of Walt Disney* (New York: Simon & Schuster, 1968);

John Taylor, *Storming the Magic Kingdom: Wall Street, the Raiders, and the Battle for Disney* (New York: Knopf, 1987).

– K.L.R.

E. L. DOCTOROW

Fiction writer E. L. Doctorow (1931–) has achieved critical and popular success with his best-selling novel *Ragtime* (1975) and other imaginative re-inventions of American history.

Though all his fiction blends traditional realism and modern literary techniques, critics have frequently observed that no two Doctorow novels are alike. In his first, *Welcome to Hard Times* (1960), the story of a massacre in the Dakota Territory during the 1870s, Doctorow plays with the conventions of western fiction made popular over the years by writers such as Owen Wister and Louis L'Amour. Similarly, *Big as Life* (1966) takes on another staple of genre fiction: the invasion-from-outer-space story that has its roots in H. G. Wells's *The War of the Worlds* (1898).

His next novel, *The Book of Daniel* (1971), established Doctorow's reputation and marks the beginning of his preoccupation with American "history as imagery and therefore as a resource for writing." Based on the trial and execution of **Julius and Ethel Rosenberg** for espionage in the 1950s, the novel looks back at **Cold War** tension of the 1950s from the perspective of 1967, in the midst of the **Vietnam War.**

The American Dream gone sour, a frequent theme for Doctorow, is especially apparent in *Ragtime* (1975). Set mainly during 1908–1915, it links three families — white Anglo-Saxon Protestant, Jewish, and black — with historical figures, portraying America when it was still a nation of small towns and marking the decline of American optimism and idealism, finally shattered by the events of World War I, in the early twentieth century. While his later novels have been well received by critics and scholars, none has matched the popularity of *Ragtime*.

Doctorow's novels of the 1980s — *Loon Lake* (1980), *World's Fair* (1985), and *Billy Bathgate* (1989) — are all set in the 1930s. *Loon Lake* focuses on a working-class young man on a quest for the elusive American Dream. *World's Fair* draws on Doctorow's childhood in a Jewish-American family in the Bronx during the late 1930s for an evocative picture of family life during the Depression, while *Billy Bathgate* follows the fortunes of a fictional teenager who hooks up with the notorious real-life gangster Dutch Schultz. Four films have been based on Doctorow novels: *Welcome to Hard Times* (1967), *Ragtime* (1981), *Daniel* (1983), and *Billy Bathgate* (1991).

REFERENCES:

Douglas Fowler, *Understanding E. L. Doctorow* (Columbia: University of South Carolina Press, 1992);

Carol C. Harter and James R. Thompson, *E. L. Doctorow* (Boston: Twayne, 1990).

– D.H.-F.

KIRK DOUGLAS

Kirk Douglas (1916–) is a versatile actor who has been widely respected for his willingness to play unsympathetic roles.

Born Issur Danielovitch (later changed to Isadore Demsky) in Amsterdam, New York, to an impoverished family of Russian-Jewish immigrants, Douglas was the only son among seven children. He worked his way through St. Lawrence University (B.A., 1940), studied acting at the American Academy of Dramatic Arts in 1941, and landed two small Broadway roles before serving in the U.S. Navy during World War II. He returned to New York in 1944 and played a few larger parts on Broadway before going to Hollywood for a screen test. He was cast as the weak, alcoholic husband of femme fatale Barbara Stanwyck in his first film, *The Strange Love of Martha Ivers* (1946), and he played mostly neurotics or gangsters until his role as a boxer in *Champion* (1949) opened up more virile, action-oriented heroes to him. Yet the characters he played in *Ace in the Hole* (1951), *The Bad and the Beautiful* (1952), *Lust for Life* (1956), *Gunfight at the O.K. Corral* (1957), *The Vikings* (1958), *Lonely Are the Brave* (1962), *The List of Adrian Messenger* (1963), and *There Was a Crooked Man* (1970), retain a touch of the unscrupulous rogue or the tormented neurotic. Douglas was more conventionally heroic in *Paths of Glory* (1957), *Seven Days in May* (1964), *Cast a Giant Shadow* (1966), and *Spartacus* (1960), in which he gave what is probably his most memorable performance.

Resisting the traditional studio contract, Douglas took charge of shaping his career and headed his own production company, Bryna (named for his mother). After *Tough Guys* (1986), which he made with frequent screen partner **Burt Lancaster,** Douglas worked in television movies and wrote his autobiography, *The Ragman's Son* (1988), which was a best-seller and received far more-respectful reviews than the usual Hollywood autobiography. He received the American Film Institute Life Achievement Award in 1991. In his most-recent movie, the comedy *Greedy* (1994), Douglas plays a wealthy old man whose nieces and nephews are competing to inherit his money.

REFERENCE:

Kirk Douglas, *The Ragman's Son: An Autobiography* (New York, London, Toronto, Sydney & Tokyo: Simon & Schuster, 1988).

– I.R.H.

DOWN BEAT

Intended for musicians, *Down Beat* magazine has also appealed to music fans, and it is among the most widely read music periodicals in the United States. It is especially known for its coverage of jazz. Its annual polls provide a reliable indication of the success of jazz musicians and other popular performers, and the magazine also promotes the careers of younger musicians as well as professionals.

Down Beat was founded in 1934 by Glenn Burrs and Carl Cons as a monthly tabloid covering swing jazz and national radio programs; it switched to newspaper format in 1936. By 1937 it had achieved a circulation of 35,000. The magazine became biweekly in 1939, and by 1944 its circulation had grown to 70,000. Burrs and Cons shifted the coverage of the magazine from traditional jazz to modern jazz in the 1940s. In 1946 they sold the magazine to John Maher. He and his associates have published the magazine since then, with a series of editors responsible for its contents.

The first annual readers poll appeared in *Down Beat* in 1937 to gauge the most popular performers in different categories of jazz. Since 1952 these polls have provided the basis for the *Down Beat* Hall of Fame. In 1961 the magazine added a critics poll. *Down Beat* also features reviews of albums and live performances as well as stories and interviews. Since the 1970s these have dealt mostly with modern jazz, blues, and jazz-influenced **rock** musicians. *Down Beat* returned to monthly publication in 1979 and currently has a circulation of approximately 100,000.

REFERENCE:
Robert Byler, "*Down Beat,*" *International Music Journals,* edited by Linda M. Fidler and Richard S. James (New York: Greenwood Press, 1990).

– D.H.-F.

DRAFT RESISTANCE

One of the most powerful images of the **Vietnam War** protest movement was the sight of young men burning their draft-registration cards. While draft resisters during World War II and the Korean War were mostly conscientious objectors opposing all wars on moral and religious grounds, most of the young men who refused to serve during the Vietnam War considered that specific conflict and the draft system unjust and immoral.

Organized draft protests began in 1964, when "We Won't Go" petitions began to circulate. In 1965, after the first public draft-card burnings, Congress outlawed destruction of draft cards. The Supreme Court upheld the law in 1968, ruling that it was not an unconstitutional abridgment of free speech.

Full-scale resistance began in 1967, when groups such as The Resistance in San Francisco, Cadre in Chicago, and Draft Denial were founded and began to work together to coordinate draft-protest activities nationwide. That April in New York nearly two hundred young men burned their draft cards during a demonstration in Central Park. The following October, during the first Stop the Draft Week, nearly fifteen hundred draft cards were collected in eighteen cities and sent back to the Selective Service offices that had issued them.

Opposition to military conscription was not limited to those eligible to be drafted. In December 1967 seventy people, many of whom were too old to be drafted, were arrested during a sit-in outside an induction center in New York. Among them were the well-known pediatrician Dr. Benjamin Spock, Yale chaplain William Sloane Coffin, writer Mitchell Goodman, Resistance organizer Michael Ferber, and Marcus Raskin, a scholar at the liberal Institute for Policy Studies in Washington, D.C. These five men were later indicted on federal charges for counseling young men on how to avoid being drafted and for interfering with the operation of the Selective Service System. Though all but Raskin were found guilty, their convictions were later overturned.

The most radical protests were carried out by a group of Roman Catholic priests and nuns led by two brothers, Daniel and Philip Berrigan. In October 1967 Philip Berrigan and other protesters entered the Baltimore Selective Service office and — in an act of civil disobedience copied elsewhere — poured a substance they claimed was blood on official files. The Berrigans took their protest still further in May 1968, when they and seven others removed records from the Catonsville, Maryland, draft-board office and burned them. Labeled the Catonsville 9, they all served prison time for destroying federal property.

By the time President Richard M. Nixon began to phase out the draft in 1972–1973, at least five thousand draft cards had been turned in during public protests; others burned their cards or turned them in privately. Between 1967 and 1972 about ten thousand draftees went underground, often to Canada, to avoid induction. About a quarter of a million draft-age men never registered. One hundred seventy-two thousand successfully fulfilled the rigorous requirements to be classed as conscientious objectors. Ironically, of the more than two hundred thousand accused of draft offenses, fewer than nine thousand were ever convicted, and only four thousand spent any time behind bars. In

1977 President Jimmy Carter granted unconditional amnesty to all Vietnam-era draft evaders.

REFERENCES:

Todd Gitlin, *The Sixties: Years of Hope, Days of Rage* (Toronto, New York, London, Sydney & Auckland: Bantam, 1987);

Massimo Teodori, ed., *The New Left: A Documentary History* (Indianapolis & New York: Bobbs-Merrill, 1969).

– K.L.R.

Drive-in Theaters

The drive-in movie theater is a popular phenomenon of the post–World War II years, during which Americans moved to the suburbs and became dependent on the automobile.

The first drive-in opened in June 1933 in Camden, New Jersey. There were only twenty-five in existence by the end of World War II, but they boomed in the 1950s, just as conventional, indoor theaters in the central city were closing. By the early 1960s one in every five movie admissions sold was to a drive-in.

The viewing conditions at drive-ins were never ideal, with limited visibility through windshields of cars parked at a considerable distance from the screen and individual car speakers that often malfunctioned. Most drive-ins compensated by offering a large variety of food, playgrounds, and even laundromats. Drive-in owners frequently attracted customers with cheap, one-fee-per-car admissions. Drive-ins also offered privacy, not just for busy families but for dating couples seeking a "passion pit."

The number of drive-ins in the United States peaked in the early 1960s at roughly six thousand and has declined ever since. In the 1970s owners of the large tracts of land on which drive-ins were located discovered that they could generate higher profits by selling the land to developers than by maintaining their property as outdoor movie theaters. The development of the videocassette recorder (VCR) in the mid 1970s and the rise of video-rental businesses offering cassettes of recent films for home viewing contributed to a decline in drive-in patronage. By 1990 fewer than a thousand drive-ins remained.

REFERENCE:

Kerry Segrave, *Drive-In Theaters: A History from their Inception in 1933* (Jefferson, N.C.: McFarland, 1992).

– I.R.H.

Marcel Duchamp

By the mid 1960s it was becoming clear that the French artist Marcel Duchamp (1887–1968), then in his late seventies and living in New York City, was one of the most influential artists of the twentieth century. His status was paradoxical: for the previous several decades he had done little to perpetuate this reputation. Preferring privacy, he sustained the widely believed myth that he had retired from art to devote himself to his true love — the game of chess. Upon his death, however, it was discovered that Duchamp had, in fact, devoted some twenty of the last years of his life to his last major work, *Etant donnés* (1946–1966), a room-sized, mixed-media tableau, which he created in secrecy. It was subsequently installed as a permanent exhibit in the Philadelphia Museum of Art, behind a massive wooden door with two peepholes bored into it.

Duchamp began his artistic career in the early 1900s in France as a painter. He soon became famous in America after his *Nude Descending a Staircase, No. 2* (1912), which was shown in the 1913 Armory Show in New York City, scandalized the American public.

Painting, in general, struck him as overly concerned with pleasing the eye, so he abandoned this medium in favor of other, more effective means of stimulating the human intellect, but still retaining the iconoclastic bent of his painted works. He began to create works that challenged society's reverence for traditional art based on elitist criteria. To this end, one of his most significant contributions to the subsequent development of all twentieth-century art was the readymade, a work of art created by taking a previously manufactured object and simply titling and signing it. His *Bottle Rack* of 1914, for example, is nothing more than a bottle-drying rack that he purchased and subsequently designated as art, thereby rejecting the artificial hierarchy that defines what can be considered high art. Although Duchamp never declared himself a Dadaist, his anti-art philosophies and slyly humorous, often elusive procedures profoundly influenced the Dada movement as well as the chance art of Surrealism.

From 1915 on, Duchamp frequently lived in New York City, and in 1955 he became an American citizen. His original readymades served as an early prototype for the practice of artistic appropriation that surfaced in the 1980s. But more generally, they fundamentally redefined the role of the artist from a maker of objects to a creator of thoughts for objects. This redefinition was to express itself in most of the art movements of the late twentieth century, particularly **conceptual art.**

REFERENCES:

Anne D'Harnoncourt, *Marcel Duchamp* (Munich: Prestel, 1989);

Rudolf E. Kuenzli and Francis M. Naumann, *Marcel Duchamp: Artist of the Century* (Cambridge, Mass.: MIT Press, 1989).

– K.B.

ROBERT DUNCAN

Robert Duncan (1919–1988), is best known — with **Charles Olson** and **Robert Creeley** — as one of the major writers of **Projective Verse**, but his poetic associations were broader than Olson's or Creeley's. Like them, Duncan acknowledged the influence of **William Carlos Williams** and **Ezra Pound**, as well as Walt Whitman. He was also one of the young San Francisco poets gathered around Kenneth Rexroth in the mid 1940s, a group that later became affiliated with the **Beat** movement.

Duncan aligned himself with the Projectivists in the mid 1950s. The three important books in what is now recognized as his first major phase — *The Opening of the Field* (1960), *Roots and Branches* (1964), and *Bending the Bow* (1968) — are Projectivist poems. (The title of the first book alludes to the term *open field*, which Olson used in his 1950 manifesto "Projective Verse.") *The Opening of the Field* includes the first poems of an ongoing, interrelated series that Duncan called *The Structure of Rhyme*, displaying Duncan's fascination with myth and mysticism while demonstrating his interpretation of Projectivist theory. *Bending the Bow* includes the first poems in an even more ambitious series, *Passages*, an epic in the tradition of Pound's *Cantos* (1917–1969), Williams's *Paterson* (1946–1963), and Olson's *Maximus Poems* (1953–1975). Further poems in *Passages* are in *Ground Work: Before the War* (1984) and *Ground Work II: In the Dark* (1987), which appeared after a self-imposed moratorium on publishing his poetry that Duncan announced in 1972.

REFERENCES:

Ekbert Faas, *Young Robert Duncan: Portrait of the Poet as Homosexual in Society* (Santa Barbara:Black Sparrow Press, 1983);

Mark Andrew Johnson, *Robert Duncan* (Boston: Twayne, 1988).

– K.L.R.

Bob Dylan at the grave of Jack Kerouac (photograph by Ken Regan)

BOB DYLAN

Singer and songwriter Bob Dylan (1941–) was the central figure of the **folk-music** phenomenon of the 1960s. He was among the first to combine folk elements with **rock 'n' roll music,** and his often poetic lyrics and protest songs encouraged a seriousness in rock that was previously lacking. He was one of the most important popular songwriters of the 1960s, influencing groups such as **The Beatles** and **The Rolling Stones** later in the decade.

Born Robert Allen Zimmerman in Duluth, Minnesota, he became interested in folk music and leftist politics in college during the late 1950s and changed his name to Bob Dylan. He moved to New York in 1960 and began performing in **coffeehouses,** accompanying himself on guitar and harmonica. His first album, *Bob Dylan* (1962), was influenced by **Woody Guthrie** and includes mostly traditional American and British folk songs. In 1962 Dylan wrote "Blowin' in the Wind" to express his support for the **civil rights movement.** The best-selling 1963 recording of the song by **Peter, Paul & Mary** led to national attention for Dylan, and his 1963 album *The Freewheelin' Bob Dylan* marked his reputation as a protest poet with songs such as "Blowin' in the Wind," "A Hard Rain's a-Gonna Fall," and "Masters of War." This reputation was solidified further with *The Times They Are a-Changin'* (1964). He offers a different image of himself in *Another Side of Bob Dylan* (1964) with songs about love instead of politics, and in the popular song "Like a Rolling Stone" (*Highway 61 Revisited,* 1965) he began to feature rock more prominently in his folk style. While some fans criticized Dylan for introducing electric instruments into his music, many performers followed his example, including the Animals, the Byrds, and Sonny and Cher.

Dylan stopped touring for seven years after a motorcycle accident in 1966, but he continued to record. *Blonde on Blonde* (1966), a mixture of poetry and psychedelic rock, received little positive attention, but his return to his folk origins — in *John Wesley Harding*

(1968) and the country-influenced *Nashville Skyline* (1969), which includes the successful single "Lay Lady Lay" — were more favorably received.

Dylan's most successful period was the 1960s, and his many recordings since 1970 have received mixed reviews, but he has continued to write and record occasional hits such as "Knockin' on Heaven's Door" (1973) and his 1975 album *Blood on the Tracks.* In addition to his recordings and tours, he appeared with George Harrison, Tom Petty, Roy Orbison, and Jeff Lynne in the group the Traveling Wilburys during the late 1980s. In 1988 Dylan was admitted to the Rock and Roll Hall of Fame, and he received a Grammy Award for Lifetime Achievement in 1991.

REFERENCES:

Clinton Heylin, *Bob Dylan: Behind the Shades — A Biography* (New York: Summit Books, 1991);

Robert Shelton, *No Direction Home: The Life and Music of Bob Dylan* (New York & London: Morrow, 1986).

– D.H.-F.

E

EARTH ART

Earth art became a prominent art movement in the late 1960s when artists began to resist the increasing commercialization of the art market signaled by a proliferation of art sales by galleries and dealers. In reaction, some artists began to create large-scale sculptural works that made use of elements of the natural environment. Their work emphasized the importance of art as a personal experience rather than as a commodity. Earth art was at its peak in the 1970s but continued to attract attention afterward. Earthworks are made for specific, often isolated, locations, and their vast size and site-specific nature make it impossible for them to be bought and sold.

Many earth-art projects require resources, such as bulldozers and plows, which must be financed by the artists. In order to fund their projects earth artists rely heavily on sales to the public of sketches, preparatory drawings, models, and other types of documentation. Above all other media, photography is crucial to earth art. Photographs document the entire process and progress of the artwork, and more important, because earth artists often choose sites far removed from cities and populated areas, more people actually know earthworks from photographs than from viewing them firsthand.

In its forms, ideas, and processes, earth art contains elements of **minimalism, conceptual art,** and **performance art.** Yet its roots can be traced from archaeological monuments, such as Stonehenge, Egyptian temples, and ancient burial mounds, through the long traditions of sculpture gardens, parks, and some early-twentieth-century site-specific projects.

Earth artists Robert Smithson and Walter De Maria began by making "non-sites," sculptures in which they took natural materials from an outdoor site and brought them indoors into a gallery setting. In 1969 Smithson shifted from non-sites to working at actual outdoor sites. His best-known earthwork, *Spiral Jetty* (1969–1970), was a 1,500-foot curl of limestone, black basalt, earth, and red algae projecting into the Great Salt Lake in Utah. The work, which now lies underwater, symbolically confronted the issue of time and its endless cycle of erosion and change. Smithson died accidentally in an airplane crash while viewing a potential earthwork site.

Like *Spiral Jetty,* most earthworks are created and then left to evolve according to natural changes in the environment. This theme of infinite change is evident in the transient earthworks of Dennis Oppenheim. In *Cancelled Crop* (1969) Oppenheim plowed a giant *X* into a 422-by-709-foot wheat field. As new seeds sprouted, grain was harvested, and the field was plowed over, the artwork continually evolved until it finally disappeared altogether. The earthworks of Smithson's wife, Nancy Holt, deal with the passing of time on a universal scale. Works such as *Tunnels* (1973–1976), a series of four nine-foot-tall concrete tubes placed in the Utah desert, have holes cut into their sides through which viewers can look at various constellations. Many of Holt's earthworks have "eyes" that witness the eternal cycle of the earth's rotation. Michael Heizer has been one of the most adamant among the earth artists in advocating large-scale works away from galleries and museums. *Double Negative* (1969–1970), in which Heizer and his crew made two 50-foot-deep cuts into the Mormon Mesa in Overton, Nevada, creates a profound experience of space, confronting the viewer with overwhelming volumes of mass and void.

Earth art often depends on the psychological responses and physical movements of the viewer through the work, as in the creations of Mary Miss and Alice Aycock. In *Blind* (1976), by Miss, spectators enter a huge circular ring and descend underground through a series of concentric, layered flights of steps until the surrounding landscape is no longer visible. Aycock's *Low Building with Dirt Roof (for Mary)* (1973) evokes a strong sense of history and is meant to trigger old memories. Aycock, more than any other earth artist, promotes a narrative aspect in her creations.

Other artists who have participated in the earth-art movement include **Christo**, Jan Dibbets, Richard Long, Robert Morris, Charles Simonds, Michael Singer, Alan Sonfist, Michele Stuart, and George Trakas.

REFERENCE:

John Beardsley, "Traditional Aspects of New Land Art," *Art Journal*, special issue (Fall 1982): 226–232.

– C.S.

CLINT EASTWOOD

Clint Eastwood (1930–), the laconic star of Western and police-action films, has gradually earned critical respect for his acting and directing.

Born in San Francisco and raised on the road by his father, who worked in various places as a gas-station attendant, Eastwood settled in Los Angeles in 1955 and began to get acting roles. He became well known when he played the handsome young cowboy Rowdy Yates in the television series *Rawhide* (1958–1965). In the mid 1960s he became an international star as "The Man with No Name" in Sergio Leone's *A Fistful of Dollars* (1964), *For a Few Dollars More* (1965), and *The Good, the Bad, and the Ugly* (1967) — movies called "spaghetti Westerns" because they were filmed cheaply in Italy.

Eastwood returned to Hollywood to star in similar American films, and in the 1970s he became identified with rogue cop Harry Callahan, the character he played in *Dirty Harry* (1971), *Magnum Force* (1973), *The Enforcer* (1976), and *Sudden Impact* (1983), the last of which he directed. He had begun directing for his Malpaso production company with *Play Misty for Me* (1971).

Critics were impressed with *Bird*, the film biography of jazz musician **Charlie Parker**, directed by Eastwood in 1988. His directing and acting in *Unforgiven* (1992) brought him the major recognition that many felt was long overdue. The film, which exposes the myths surrounding the sort of cowboy hero Eastwood played in his early movies, won an Academy Award (Oscar) for best picture and earned Eastwood an Oscar for best director. He went on to direct and play opposite **Kevin Costner** in *A Perfect World* (1993). The critics praised the film, but it was not as successful at the box office as they predicted.

During the 1980s Eastwood became active in politics and was elected to serve a term as mayor of Carmel, California, in 1986.

REFERENCES:

Iain Johnstone, *The Man with No Name: The Clint Eastwood Biography* (New York: Morrow, 1981; revised, 1989);
Paul Smith, *Clint Eastwood: A Cultural Production* (Minneapolis: University of Minnesota Press, 1993).

– I.R.H.

THE ED SULLIVAN SHOW

One of the most popular television programs in history, *The Ed Sullivan Show* was standard Sunday-night entertainment for more than two decades, from 1948 to 1971. It debuted on **CBS** as *Toast of the Town*, one of the many variety series of early television. Ed Sullivan, a newspaperman, had an acute sense of what talent would strike a chord with the public. He mixed every type of entertainment, from opera and ballet to scenes from **Broadway musicals** to dancing bears and Topo Gigio, a mouse puppet that spoke with a funny accent. Many viewers tuned in each week to see what strange, new lineup Sullivan would present. Sullivan became a celebrity himself, his awkward stage presence and unusual diction somehow adding to his appeal.

Many famous performers appeared on the New York stage of the program, which was renamed *The Ed Sullivan Show* in 1955. Sullivan also introduced to the American viewing public superstars such as **Elvis Presley** in 1956 and **The Beatles** in 1964. When Presley appeared on the show he was shown from the waist up

Ed Sullivan talking to the puppet Topo Gigio, who often appeared on Sullivan's Sunday-night variety show

only in order to hide his suggestive hip movements from television viewers.

Although the show still ranked high in the ratings, by 1971 its audience was aging. Because the entertainment industry was no longer centered in New York, the program became more expensive to produce. It was cancelled by CBS in an attempt to modernize network programming. The series has been remembered as the greatest of all variety shows. Sullivan died in 1974.

– C.D.B.

ELECTRONIC MUSIC

Sporadic musical experiments using electronic devices occurred early in the twentieth century, but electronic music developed fully only with the increase in sophisticated equipment available to composers after World War II. Today it has an important role in virtually all kinds of music, including **rock** and jazz. While the term designates the use of electronic devices such as tape recorders and synthesizers, it implies the creative use of the equipment for musical composition or improvisation rather than simply the amplification of sound, as with an electric guitar or keyboard.

Experiments with the electronic manipulation of sound began soon after tape recorders became available in the 1940s. In Europe these experiments were conducted in radio studios, and the first compositions of *musique concrète* in France in the late 1940s resulted from storing, modifying, and combining natural sounds on tape. At the same time *Elektronische Musik* was created in Germany by using only electronically generated sounds. In 1956 German composer Karlheinz Stockhausen combined both approaches in *Gesang der Jünglinge,* in which a boy's electronically altered voice on tape was mixed with electronically produced sounds.

John Cage was among the first American composers to experiment with electronic music. His *Imaginary Landscape No. 1* (1939) employs variable-speed phonograph turntables, tape, piano, and cymbal, while *Imaginary Landscape No. 5* (1952) uses mixed tape recordings. **Edgard Varèse** added taped sounds to woodwinds and percussion for *Déserts* (1954). Other composers worked in electronic-music laboratories established at several universities in the 1950s. The best known is the Columbia-Princeton Electronic Music Center, founded in 1959. There **Otto Luening** and Vladimir Ussachevsky first produced "tape music" by playing musical passages on a tape that was then played backward or forward at different speeds on multiple tracks and passed through filters, reverberators, and modulators or cut and spliced into loops.

Other prominent composers to make use of the new medium included **David Tudor** and Earle Brown.

In 1958 the new RCA Synthesizer, capable of combining in one machine all the procedures accomplished with elaborate means before, expanded the possibilities for electronic music. When transistor technology became available in the 1960s, smaller, cheaper synthesizers were developed, first by Robert Moog and Donald Buchla. These synthesizers allowed for live performance and inspired compositions such as **Milton Babbitt**'s *Ensembles for Synthesizer* (1964). Keyboard-controlled synthesizers are now used in all kinds of art music and popular music for composing, improvising, and arranging, and especially for background music in film and television. Since pure tape or electronic music usually lacks audience appeal in concert, it was used more often for ballet, multimedia **Happenings** or **performance art,** or in combination with live music in the 1960s. Groups such as FLUXUS, Musica Elettronica Viva, and Sonic Arts Union created sophisticated ensembles of electronic music, and in the 1960s and 1970s **minimalist** composers **Philip Glass** and **Steve Reich** combined synthesizers with other instruments. **Mario Davidovsky**'s *Synchronism* series (1963–1974) as well as Babbitt's *Philomel* (1964) require artful interaction between live singers or instrumentalists and recorded music.

Computer music is a more recent development of electronic music. Like a synthesizer, the computer can generate sound, duplicate or extend the qualities of musical instruments, and explore new sounds. It can also be programmed to compose: Lejaren Hiller and Leonard Isaacson, for instance, programmed rules of sixteenth-century counterpoint and twentieth-century **serial music** into a computer and produced the *Illiac Suite for String Quartet* (1957). Composers also use computers for writing their compositions much as writers use word processors.

REFERENCES:

David Ernst, *The Evolution of Electronic Music* (New York: Schirmer-Macmillan, 1977);

Herbert S. Howe, Jr., *Electronic Music Synthesis: Concepts, Facilities, Techniques* (New York: Norton, 1975);

Peter Manning, *Electronic and Computer Music* (Oxford: Clarendon Press, 1985);

Barry Schrader, *Introduction to Electro-Acoustic Music* (Englewood Cliffs, N.J.: Prentice-Hall, 1982).

– L.E.P.

T. S. ELIOT

One of the chief architects of modernist literature, T. S. Eliot (1888–1965), who was awarded the Nobel Prize for Literature in 1948, distinguished himself as poet, essayist, and playwright.

Born in Saint Louis, Missouri, and educated at Harvard University (A.B., 1909; A.M., 1910), Thomas Stearns Eliot lived in England from 1914 until his death in 1965, returning to the United States only for visits and becoming a British subject in 1927. His long poem *The Waste Land* (1922) earned him a reputation as a major experimental poet, a leader with **Ezra Pound** and James Joyce in the new modernist movement. The poem bewildered many readers at first, but in less than a decade it was being widely imitated by young poets.

Eliot's *Four Quartets* (1936–1942) — four long poems meditating on time, art, history, love, and religion — were among the most admired poems of the World War II era. In the 1940s and 1950s Eliot devoted himself almost exclusively to playwriting. His verse play *The Cocktail Party* (1950) had long runs in London and New York.

With the rise of **New Criticism** in the 1940s Eliot became a dominant influence in the college classroom. The many layers of allusions in his poems were ideally suited to the sort of close reading practiced by academics schooled in the methods of New Criticism, and those methods were in large part indebted to Eliot's critical essays, especially those written during the years 1917–1922.

Yet by the mid 1950s some poets were beginning to challenge the chief tenets of modernism, which had looked so radical to earlier generations, even as the New Critics were continuing to uphold them in the classroom. At the heart of modernism and New Criticism was an idea expressed in Eliot's "Tradition and the Individual Talent" (1919): "Poetry is not a turning loose of emotion, but an escape from emotion; it is not the expression of personality, but an escape from personality." While hundreds of poets accepted the notion of poetic impersonality as a cardinal rule of verse writing, others rejected it; **Projective** poets such as **Charles Olson** and **Robert Creeley, Beat** poet **Allen Ginsberg,** and **confessional poets,** including **Robert Lowell,** found the models for their writing in the less formal and more personal poetry of Eliot's contemporary **William Carlos Williams.**

Eliot's poems and essays are still read in the college classroom, but as examples of poetic excellence and intellectual insight, not as prescriptives for modern literature. Ironically, he may now be best known for a book of children's verse. His *Old Possum's Book of Practical Cats* (1939) is the basis for Andrew Lloyd Webber's musical *Cats,* which has run continually on Broadway since it opened in 1981.

REFERENCES:

Peter Ackroyd, *T. S. Eliot: A Life* (New York: Simon & Schuster, 1984);

Lyndall Gordon, *Eliot's New Life* (Oxford: Oxford University Press, 1988).

– R.T.

DUKE ELLINGTON

Nicknamed "Duke" for his elegant stage manner, Edward Kennedy Ellington (1899–1974) was an outstanding American pianist, bandleader, and composer. Considered by many the greatest of all jazz composers, with more than two thousand musical works to his credit, he pioneered a sophisticated orchestral approach to jazz, and after World War II he was the dominant force internationally in big-band jazz, or "American music," as he insisted on calling his work.

During 1927–1932 Ellington and his first band, the Washingtonians, were featured at the famous Cotton Club in Harlem, where performances promoted as "jungle music" to attract an audience for radio broadcasts were successful. The band's exotic arrangements, featuring mutes, growling brass solos, and tom-toms were contrasted with Ellington's solicitously polite and meticulously stylish stage manner. Both his music and his stage personality evolved gracefully over his fifty-year career.

Early Ellington hits include "Black and Tan Fantasy" (1927), "Creole Love Call" (1928), and one of his best-known compositions, "Mood Indigo" (1930). Some historians believe his 1932 song "It Don't Mean a Thing If It Ain't Got That Swing" is the source for the term *swing jazz,* orchestrated, dance-oriented jazz with a steady beat played by big bands. Ellington and his band became famous during this period through performances for radio and for films. He increased the size of the band — now called Duke Ellington's Orchestra — and began touring in 1933.

Composer and pianist Billy Strayhorn joined Ellington in 1940 and wrote several hits, including "Passion Flower" (1941) and "Take the A Train" (1941), which became a signature piece for the band. In 1943 Ellington was commissioned to write a concert work for the band's first performance at Carnegie Hall; the result, *Black, Brown, and Beige,* deals with black heritage by drawing on black musical history in America. During the 1940s and early 1950s Ellington composed several such extended pieces, including *Deep South Suite* (1946) and *Liberian Suite* (1947), both of which premiered at Carnegie Hall.

In the late 1940s and early 1950s Ellington and his band, though they still commanded a respectful

Duke Ellington and Count Basie in 1961, during the recording of *First Time! The Count Meets the Duke,* an album on which their bands played together

following, declined in reputation, overshadowed by recent developments in jazz such as **bebop** while they maintained their big-band style. A partial comeback began in 1956, when Ellington was elected to the *Down Beat* Hall of Fame and the band gave a legendary performance at the Newport Jazz Festival in Rhode Island. Asked about his age afterward, he replied "I was born in 1956." After his rebirth, he was acclaimed internationally as a musical innovator of primary importance. In his later years, Ellington continued performing with his orchestra and concentrated on composing long works for various settings, such as the film score for *Paris Blues* (1961); music for the **Alvin Ailey** ballet *The River* (1970), which was premiered by **American Ballet Theatre;** and a series of religious works, particularly his three Sacred Concerts (1965–1973), the last of which was performed at Westminster Abbey in London. Among his many awards is the Presidential Medal of Honor.

During his career, Ellington employed some eight hundred musicians in his bands. "I give the musicians the money and I get the kicks," he said. After his death, Ellington's band was led by his son Mercer Ellington (1919–).

REFERENCES:

James Lincoln Collier, *Duke Ellington* (New York & Oxford: Oxford University Press, 1987);

Derek Jewell, *Duke: A Portrait of Duke Ellington* (New York: Norton, 1977);

Ken Rattenbury, *Duke Ellington: Jazz Composer* (New Haven: Yale University Press, 1990).

– L.D.S.

RALPH ELLISON

Ralph Ellison (1914–1994) became famous for his only published novel, *Invisible Man* (1952), an intellectual statement in fiction on the plight of African Americans in a society controlled by white people. The novel, which earned Ellison the National Book Award for fiction in 1953, was a powerful voice in support of the **civil rights movement** and is now considered a modern American literary classic.

Relying on complex symbolism, *Invisible Man* is narrated by an unnamed black man living in an underground room. As he looks back over the events that led to his "hibernation," he describes a search for self in a society that refuses to accept his existence as an individual. Ellison has called this search "*the* American theme," and in discovery of his identity as a black man Ellison's narrator realizes that he is also an American, "snarled inextricably" in the "veins and sinews" of American culture. This view of America as the sum of many interwoven ethnic influences is illustrated as well in Ellison's employing the techniques of European literary modernism to describe the African-American experience.

The success of *Invisible Man* brought about a new interest in African-American fiction. Yet Ellison has been criticized by some black writers for claiming all American culture as his rightful heritage rather than joining the writers of the **Black Arts Movement** in looking to Africa for his artistic roots.

In his two nonfiction collections, *Shadow and Act* (1964) and *Going to the Territory* (1986), Ellison continued the explore the nature of "Americanness," arguing in *Going to the Territory* that "we are . . . the inheritors, creators, and creations of a culture of cultures."

In the late 1950s Ellison started a second novel. Parts appeared in magazines during the 1960s and 1970s, but he was still working on it when he died.

REFERENCES:

John Hersey, ed., *Ralph Ellison: A Collection of Critical Essays* (Englewood Cliffs, N. J.: Prentice-Hall, 1974);

Robert G. O'Meally, *The Craft of Ralph Ellison* (Cambridge, Mass.: Harvard University Press, 1980).

– D.H.-F.

ENVIRONMENTS

Environments, also called environmental art, are a type of artwork that was pioneered in the late 1950s by a small group of avant-garde artists, including **Claes Oldenburg,** Jim Dine, and Allan Kaprow. Kaprow, who had previously been experimenting with the process of **assemblage,** was immersed in using found objects, often debris from the streets of New York City, to make three-dimensional works of art that either hung from the wall or stood on the floor. He eventually extended this concept to create the environment by filling up entire spaces with found objects. The viewer, instead of walking around the artwork, was now surrounded by it, the entire exhibition space becoming the work of art. In Kaprow's 1958 installation at the Hansa Gallery in New York City, for example, viewers had to navigate through sheets of plastic and strips of painted fabric suspended in rows from the ceiling along with Christmas lights and crumpled cellophane.

The objects crowded together in Oldenburg's environments tended to have a handmade and painted quality. *The Street* — first installed in 1960 in the Judson Gallery at Judson Memorial Church in New York City — was constructed with ragged, blackened cutouts of people and things, suggesting life in the slums of the Lower East Side. Oldenburg even welcomed visitors to add their own bits of junk to the floor.

Once these artists had established room-sized environments in which viewers were forced into such a close physical and psychological relationship with the work of art, the development of the **Happening,** led once again by Kaprow, was next inevitable step. Happenings were simply environments that had become settings for live, often theatrical performances by artists in their studios or noncommercial galleries. Environments and happenings, because of their emphasis away from the art object as well as their sheer physical dimensions, challenged the notion of art as a marketable commodity.

REFERENCE:

Allan Kaprow, *Assemblage, Environments & Happenings* (New York: Abrams, 1966).

– K.B.

ESQUIRE

Founded in 1933, *Esquire* magazine offered high-quality fiction and nonfiction to a readership of mostly middle- and upper-class, educated men. In the 1960s it became known as a pioneer in publishing innovative works of **New Journalism** by writers such as **Tom Wolfe,** Gay Talese, and **Norman Mailer.**

Arnold Gingrich (1903–1976), who edited *Esquire* from its founding until 1946 and again in 1952–1962 and 1974–1976, established high standards in the 1930s by publishing the writings of well-known authors, including **F. Scott Fitzgerald**'s "The Crack-Up" (February–April 1936), **Ernest Hemingway**'s "The Snows of Kilimanjaro" (August 1936), and five excerpts from John Dos Passos's *The Big Money* (Fall 1933–May 1936), as well as his reports on the Spanish Civil War. In the late 1950s Gingrich hired a group of young editors who went on to determine the course of the magazine through the 1970s. They included Harold Hayes (who edited the magazine from 1963 to 1973), Clay Felker (editor in 1978–1979), Rust Hills (fiction editor since 1957), and Ralph Ginzburg (articles editor in 1956–1958).

Since World War II *Esquire* has published fiction by writers such as **Truman Capote, John Updike, Kurt Vonnegut,** Norman Mailer, and **Raymond Carver.** Mailer, who covered the 1960 Democratic convention for *Esquire,* and Gay Talese, who wrote celebrity profiles for the magazine in the early 1960s, used their *Esquire* articles to develop techniques of New Journalism. The title article in Tom Wolfe's *The Kandy-Kolored Tangerine-Flake Streamline Baby* (1963), which helped to establish the popularity of New Journalism, was first published in *Esquire.*

In 1967 *Esquire* began to publish Michael Kerr's innovative reports on the **Vietnam War,** later collected as *Dispatches* (1977). *Esquire* war coverage also included a series of 1970 interviews with Lt. William L. Calley, who was convicted in 1971 of ordering the execution of unarmed villagers in the My Lai Massacre of 1968.

Phillip Moffitt became editor of *Esquire* in June 1979 and held the post until May 1984, when Lee Eisenberg, the current editor, replaced him.

REFERENCES:

50 Who Made the Difference: A Celebration of Fifty American Originals, Golden Anniversary Collector's Issue, *Esquire,* 100 (December 1983);

Dean Howd, *"Esquire,"* in *American Mass-Market Magazines,* edited by Alan Nourie and Barbara Nourie (New York: Greenwood Press, 1990), pp. 108–115;

60 Things Every Man Should Know, Sixtieth-Anniversary Collector's Issue, *Esquire,* 120 (October 1993).

– R.T.

EST

In 1976 *Newsweek* called EST (Erhard Seminars Training) "the Reader's Digest of the consciousness movement — a distillation of every self-help technique from Dale Carnegie to Zen packaged for quick consumption." California salesman Werner Erhard (his real name was John Paul Rosenberg) claimed that he "received" the EST concept while driving his wife's Mustang near the Golden Gate Bridge. He turned the idea into a multimillion-dollar empire.

In the early 1970s Erhard and his staff began teaching the EST philosophy in a series of highly publicized motivational sessions that led to a wave of interest in what was called "human potentiality," or instruction of people in how to make their lives better. The seminars, which mixed nihilistic philosophy, Eastern religious thought, **Scientology,** and motivational psychology, were abusive weekend sessions in which the audience was insulted, humiliated, and, finally, exhorted to take responsibility for creating every element of their individual worlds. During the 1970s some eight-hundred thousand customers paid $250–$625 for seminars that were typically held over two weekends. The virtue of the experience was hailed by such culture figures as singer John Denver (who called Erhard "a god") and political activist Jerry Rubin.

In the early 1980s Erhard pronounced EST dead and began selling The Forum — EST seminars under a different name tailored for businesses seeking to motivate their employees. Seminars in The Forum lasted from 9 AM to 11:30 PM on two consecutive weekends and three hours on one weeknight. The cost was $525 per person. In 1985 Erhard organized an international corporation to sell his seminars abroad.

The empire began to crumble in 1988 when Erhard's wife divorced him for using EST-like abuse in the family. In quick succession, his business was found to be unstable, and he was sued by a handful of former employees and seminar takers alleging harm from his abusive treatment. By 1991 Erhard was largely discredited though advocates stubbornly maintained the value of EST.

REFERENCES:

David Gelman with Pamela Abramson and Elizabeth Ann Leonard, "The Sorrows of Werner," *Newsweek,* 117 (18 February 1991): 72;

J. Leo, "est: 'There is Nothing to Get'," *Time*, 107 (7 June 1976): 53-54, 58-59.

– R.L.

EVANGELICALISM

Formerly a term for Protestant Christianity, evangelicalism now refers to the beliefs and actions of moder-

ately conservative Protestants who apply their theology not just to their own lives and churches but also to American society as a whole. In addition to evangelism — spreading the Christian gospel — evangelicals are concerned with defending and promoting their religious and moral values against what they perceive as the threat of an increasingly secular American culture.

Contemporary evangelicalism began in 1941 with the start of the Neo-Evangelical movement at the Moody Bible Institute in Chicago. Those in the movement criticized what they saw as anti-Christian trends in modern American life while rejecting the reactionary excesses of fundamentalism. Evangelicals from the 1940s to the 1960s also criticized mainline churches for selling out to contemporary culture and liberal political causes.

The most prominent figure of American evangelicalism during this period was Billy Graham, who began preaching at revival meetings across the country in 1947 and received national attention with a highly publicized appearance in Los Angeles in 1949. In 1951 he aired his first televised "crusade." Though criticized by fundamentalists for his inclusive approach, Graham was enormously popular among evangelicals. Graham also became known as the unofficial chaplain of presidents, from Dwight D. Eisenhower in the 1950s to Jimmy Carter in the 1970s. Graham helped to establish *Christianity Today* in 1957; this evangelical magazine is the best-selling Christian periodical in America.

The social changes and experiments of the 1960s and the early 1970s — particularly the banning of organized prayer and Bible readings in public schools in the early 1960s, the teaching of evolution, and the nationwide legalization of abortion in 1973 — provided a catalyst for a more-vocal evangelical response. In 1963, for instance, Graham unsuccessfully lobbied for a constitutional amendment restoring prayer in public schools. Blaming "secular humanism" for social problems, evangelicals sought to "restore" America as a "Christian nation" by turning their faith into public and political action. Like Graham, they turned to radio and especially television to promote their message, and by the 1970s television evangelists, or televangelists, were common.

Contemporary Christian musicians became popular during the 1970s, and Christian publishers sold millions of books. Hal Lindsey's apocalyptic *The Late Great Planet Earth* (1970) alone sold more than twelve million copies during the 1970s. During this period many private Christian schools were founded to provide an alternative to the "secularizing" influence of public schools, which many evangelicals blamed for declining moral values and student performance. These developments and the presidential election of evangelical Southern Baptist Jimmy Carter in 1976 led both *Newsweek* and *Time* to proclaim 1976 "The Year of the Evangelical." Evangelicals had rallied for Carter, a Democrat, but when he failed to promote their agendas many turned to the Republican party. Fundamentalist televangelist Jerry Falwell, who had criticized Carter in 1976 for being interviewed in *Playboy,* formed the Moral Majority in 1979. The group, along with other fundamentalists and evangelicals, actively campaigned for Ronald Reagan and other conservative candidates and helped to defeat both the ratification of the Equal Rights Amendment by its 1982 deadline and local legislation for **gay rights.** In his 1980 book *Listen, America!* Falwell urges the country to return "back to basics, back to values, back to biblical morality, back to sensibility, and back to patriotism." In detail, this meant support for Israel and attacks on abortion, pornography, evolution, and **feminism.**

While never the majority they claimed to be, evangelicals and related groups achieved a considerable impact on American culture in the 1980s. Despite embarrassments such as Oral Roberts's "vision" of a 900-foot Jesus or Falwell's reference to **AIDS** as a "gay plague," the evangelical movement was at its strongest in the early 1980s, claiming approximately forty million followers in America. The televangelists were especially successful: Falwell, Rex Humbard, and Jimmy Swaggart were popular with thousands of viewers, and Pat Robertson's The *700 Club* on his **cable-television** Christian Broadcasting Network (CBN) and Jim and Tammy Faye Bakker's cable PTL Network ("for Praise the Lord" or "People That Love") each drew millions of dollars in viewer contributions. Many televangelists began preaching a "gospel of prosperity" and practiced it themselves.

The influence of evangelicalism started to decline in the late 1980s with several scandals and other evidence of un-Christian behavior. Changing the name of the Moral Majority to the Liberty Foundation in 1986, Falwell effectively backed out of politics after the Iran-Contra affair involving President Reagan. The worst year was 1987: Roberts provoked ridicule with his claim that God would "bring me home" if he did not receive eight million dollars in contributions, and PTL became known as "Pass the Loot" and "Pay the Lady," with highly publicized stories about financial abuses and the use of money from contributions to keep a woman with whom Jim Bakker had an affair from telling the truth. Swaggart condemned the Bakkers, only to have his own sexual improprieties with a prostitute revealed later that year. None of this no-

toriety helped Robertson's presidential campaign, launched in 1987, though he and other evangelists such as Graham remained above the scandals. Since the late 1980s, evangelicals have tried to recover from the damage and are using their current decline in favor to take stock of their position in American culture.

REFERENCES:

Jeffrey K. Hadden and Anson Shupe, *Televangelism: Power and Politics on God's Frontier* (New York: Holt, 1988);

George M. Marsden, *Understanding Fundamentalism and Evangelicalism* (Grand Rapids, Mich.: Eerdmans, 1991);

Martin E. Marty, *Pilgrims in Their Own Land: 500 Years of Religion in America* (Boston & Toronto: Little, Brown, 1984).

– D.H.-F.

EVERGREEN REVIEW

Evergreen Review (1957–1973) was the best-known avant-garde literary journal of the 1950s and 1960s. Edited by Barney Rosset and Donald Allen (who were later joined by Richard Seaver and Fred Jordan) and published by **Grove Press,** the magazine provided a national forum for radical and experimental authors and artists whose work was ignored by mainstream literary markets.

In the second number of *Evergreen Review,* a special "San Francisco Scene" issue, editor Donald Allen gave **Allen Ginsberg**'s *Howl* (1956) its first national exposure. The issue also included the work of other **Beat Generation** writers, such as Kenneth Rexroth, **Lawrence Ferlinghetti,** and **Jack Kerouac,** and the magazine continued to be a major outlet for the Beats.

Over the course of its existence *Evergreen Review* published poetry by **Charles Olson,** Frank O'Hara, Gary Snyder, and Gregory Corso; fiction by Alain Robbe-Grillet, John Rechy, Henry Miller, **William S. Burroughs,** Hubert Selby, Jr., and Amos Tutuola; drama by Fernando Arrabal, Friedrich Durrenmatt, and Tom Stoppard; and art by Jean-Claude Forest and Salvador Dali. *Evergreen Review* ceased publication in 1973 because Grove Press was in financial trouble.

REFERENCE:

David A. Bower and Carol Campbell Strempek, *Index to Evergreen Review (1957-1970)* (Metuchen, N. J.: Scarecrow Press, 1972).

– S.B.

F

FARM AID

During his performance at **Live Aid,** the July 1985 rock benefit for Ethiopian famine victims, **Bob Dylan** suggested that some of the money raised could be used to support American farmers who were burdened by mortgages and debt. Inspired by Dylan's comment and the success of Live Aid, country performer Willie Nelson, with the help of **rock** musicians John Cougar Mellencamp and Neil Young, organized Farm Aid, a fifteen-hour concert that took place on 22 September 1985 in the University of Illinois football stadium.

Billed as a "Concert for America," Americans performing to benefit Americans, the concert attracted an audience of eighty thousand people, who heard a balanced selection of country and rock music. In addition to Nelson, Mellencamp, and Young, well-known country performers such as **Johnny Cash, Loretta Lynn,** Emmylou Harris, **Merle Haggard,** the group Alabama, and **folk** musician **Arlo Guthrie** shared the stage with rock and pop musicians including John Fogerty, Don Henley, Lou Reed, Tom Petty and the Heartbreakers, Van Halen, and X. Rhythm-and-blues musicians B. B. King and country singer Charley Pride were the only African-Americans who performed. Young and Dylan were criticized because they lobbied openly for Iowa Democrat Sen. Tom Harkin's controversial Farm Policy Reform Act, which was defeated later that year.

Televised in North America on the **cable television** Nashville Network, the benefit raised approximately fourteen million dollars. Though this money did not significantly decrease the U.S. farm debt, it did finance food assistance as well as legal and psychological counseling for American farmers.

REFERENCE:

David Gates, "Farm Aid: From Merle Haggard to X, they played to save the farm," *Rolling Stone,* no. 460 (7 November 1985): 24-28, 67-69.

– H.G.

SUZANNE FARRELL

Suzanne Farrell (1945–), one of the most talented ballerinas in America, epitomized the trademark style of her mentor **George Balanchine.**

Born in Cincinnati, Farrell was discovered by **New York City Ballet** ballerina Diana Adams in 1960 and recommended for a Ford Foundation Fellowship. She was admitted to the School of American Ballet and joined New York City Ballet in 1961. Her success came rapidly. In 1963 John Taras cast her in the female lead of his *Arcade,* and that same year Balanchine, the artistic director of the company, had her fill in for Adams in his new ballet *Movements for Piano and Orchestra.* She soon became Balanchine's chief inspiration. During her career he created twenty-six ballets for her, and her expressive skills as a dancer effectively set the standard for the female members of the company.

Farrell excelled in the roles of Titania in *A Midsummer Night's Dream* (1964) and Dulcinea in *Don Quixote* (1965). She and Balanchine, as Dulcinea and Quixote, were featured on the cover of the 23 August 1965 *Life* magazine. She was equally adept at the plotless roles he created for her, including the emotional *Meditation* (1963) and *Mestastaseis & Pithoprakta* (1967).

Rumors of Balanchine's attraction to Farrell circulated for years, and because of his anger over her marriage she and her husband, Paul Mejia, left New York City Ballet in 1969 and danced with Maurice

Béjart's Ballet of the Twentieth Century in Belgium for five years. She returned to New York City Ballet in 1975, and until his death in 1983 Balanchine once again created new roles for her such as the lead in his version of *Mozartiana* (1981). She has since taught at the School of American Ballet and staged ballets.

REFERENCE:

Suzanne Farrell with Toni Bentley, *Holding on to the Air: An Autobiography* (New York, London, Toronto, Sydney, Tokyo & Singapore: Summit Books, 1990).

– D.M.

WILLIAM FAULKNER

The winner of the Nobel Prize for Literature in 1950, William Faulkner (1897–1962) wrote highly regarded modernist fiction. Characterized by long, complicated sentences, the use of Southern history and myth, and experiments with time and point of view, nearly all his work is set in the fictional Yoknapatawpha County, located in his native Mississippi.

By 1945 Faulkner had written the novels that are generally considered his masterpieces, including *The Sound and the Fury* (1929) and *Absalom, Absalom!* (1936). In 1945, however, most of his books were out of print. Though he was highly regarded by many writers and critics, he was generally unappreciated by the reading public. During World War II he worked as a screenwriter in Hollywood to earn money.

Faulkner's fortunes improved dramatically in the late 1940s, beginning when Malcolm Cowley edited *The Portable Faulkner* (1946), which contributed to a substantial reassessment of Faulkner's work. His 1948 novel about a Southern black family, *Intruder in the Dust,* was well received, as was his 1950 *Collected Stories,* which gathered much of his short fiction.

Faulkner's work after he received the Nobel Prize in 1950 is usually considered less noteworthy. His 1951 novel *Requiem for a Nun* offers a more sympathetic look at the character Temple Drake than he presented in his controversial novel *Sanctuary* (1931). Faulkner's next novel, *A Fable* (1954), departs from his fictional South, taking place in France during World War I. He returned to his Southern setting with *The Town* (1957) and *The Mansion* (1959); these two novels complete Faulkner's trilogy about the acquisitive Snopes clan that began with *The Hamlet* in 1940. *The Reivers* (1962), Faulkner's last novel, provides a comic, nostalgic farewell to Yoknapatawpha County. Though none of these novels were as well received as Faulkner's earlier efforts, he continued to be recog-

nized as a major author throughout the rest of his life and beyond. With **F. Scott Fitzgerald** and **Ernest Hemingway,** Faulkner became lionized in American college classrooms. The intricacies of his work particularly attracted the **New Critics,** many of whom — including Cleanth Brooks and **Robert Penn Warren** — were also Southerners. Faulkner has influenced several generations of American writers, especially Southerners such as **Eudora Welty** and **Flannery O'Connor.**

REFERENCE:

Joseph Blotner, *Faulkner: A Biography,* 2 volumes (New York: Random House, 1974).

– D.H.-F.

FEMINISM

The feminist movement in America can be traced to the eighteenth century, but no period in the history of the movement provided more concrete reforms than the quarter-century beginning in the early 1960s. A critical tenet of the feminist movement is the insistence that the patriarchal societies of history have institutionalized male domination in social structures such as the economy, the government, the family, and religion. Feminist demands for changes in those institutions gained focus with publication of *The Feminine Mystique* by **Betty Friedan** in 1963. That book advanced the theory that the modern American woman had been trapped by the pervasive belief that the only desirable role for her was wife, mother, and housekeeper — a distorted image that had arrested her intellectual growth, threatened domestic relations, and stifled her potential.

Concerned women, including Friedan, created the National Organization for Women (NOW) in October 1966, with a charter membership of three hundred, intending "to take action to bring women into full participation in the mainstream of American society *now,* exercising all the privileges and responsibilities thereof in truly equal partnership with men." In November 1967, at the second national conference of NOW, a women's bill of rights was drawn up in order to outline the demands of modern feminists: "an equal rights constitutional amendment, the enforcement of laws banning sex discrimination in employment, maternity leave rights in employment and in social security benefits, tax deduction for home and child care expenses for working parents, child care centers, equal and unsegregated education, equal job training opportunities and allowances for women in poverty, and the right of women to control their reproductive lives." Thus, the feminist movement identified three primary

Feminists demonstrating in front of the White House, 1969 (UPI/Bettmann Newsphotos)

issues involved in their struggle: socio-economic oppression, sexuality/reproductive freedom, and cultural oppression.

The Equal Rights Amendment (ERA), which had been included in party platforms since 1940, was a proposed amendment to the U.S. Constitution which explicitly guaranteed women equality under the law. Advocates argued that it would guarantee prohibition of sex-segregated public schools, discrimination in university admissions policies, discrimination by government at all levels against women in public employment and job-training programs, and the unequal treatment of women in the military. The ERA was passed by Congress on 22 March 1972, but failed to achieve ratification by its deadline in 1982.

Forty years after winning suffrage in 1920, few women held high elected or appointed offices — only seventeen women served in the U.S. Congress. In an attempt to promote the election of women to political offices of all levels, the National Women's Political Caucus (NWPC) was founded in 1971 by Shirley Chisholm, Bella Abzug, and **Gloria Steinem,** who became a recognized spokesperson for the feminist movement through her publication of *Ms.* magazine.

Within the educational and professional realms, women were competing in a man's world. Despite the fact that in 1965 more than 200,000 women received

bachelor's degrees (of 530,000 total degrees conferred), when a woman entered the workforce she found discrimination, less pay than her male coworkers, and fewer chances for promotion. Women protested this discrimination to the Equal Employment Opportunity Commission (EEOC). They demanded enforcement of Title VII of the Civil Rights Act of 1964, which forbade all discrimination based on sex in private-sector employment. NOW acted as a major force in the enforcement of the provisions of Title VII and other provisions of the Civil Rights Act; however, the battle against sexual discrimination in the workplace continued into the 1990s.

By the early 1980s some feminists were insisting that the struggle for equality could not be resolved by participation in the executive and governmental worlds alone — nor by simple participation in committees and special organizations — nor by declarations of purpose and faraway lobbying and protesting. In rejection of the abstract, though radical, theorizing of the male-dominated **New Left,** and with attention to the use of political theory as a guide for action, radical feminists developed the technique of consciousness-raising (CR). The first CR groups (or rap groups) consisted of women gathered to discuss problems and grievances. These feminists discovered that their discussions led to increased awareness and the development of theory, analysis, and criticism, all of which spurred action. By this method, individual women in all parts of the nation and of all feminist schools were able to involve themselves in the movement and help to bring about action and change.

Women in rap groups learned to take pride in their sex. An example was the Boston Women's Health Collective, whose consciousness-raising led to complete awareness of women with their bodies and the publication of works such as *Our Bodies, Ourselves* (1973), information compiled from a course offered by the collective on women's bodies and health. Along with this emphasis on self-health arose the insistence on reproductive freedom for women and the fight for the right to voluntary interruption of pregnancy.

In the early 1970s, with the new emphasis on feminine sexuality and reproductive freedom, lesbians in America began speaking for equality in the name of feminism. Because of the activism of lesbians, many Americans began mistakenly to equate feminism with lesbianism, although some lesbian groups, who considered their sexual preference to be a political choice, maintained their existence independently from mainstream feminist groups such as NOW. The issue of sexual perference has caused a political dilemma for feminists. Another divisive voice within the feminist movement as a whole was that of minority women, the "triply oppressed" — nonwhite, poor, and female. Class and race often became more significant issues for these women than gender.

Modern feminism has been marked by a division of women into feminist radicals and radical feminists based on ideologies and demands for the future. However, all feminists persist in their belief that women have a lower status than men; that women are victims of social, economic, and political discrimination; and that this status quo is unjustified and must change. Feminist radicals devote themselves to working within the system (through women's studies programs in the arts and through reform-oriented activism). Radical feminists understand that if they want to address women's issues they will have to do so outside the existing radical movement. Male radicals have excluded themselves from feminism; thus radical feminists moved toward hatred of men. This radicalism arises as a protest against a society that "routes all human beings on their lifepath on the basis of sex." A modern "pattern for agreement" is presented by the revolutionary "androgyny theory," which rests on the idea that men and women are humans, above all, and that sexual equality exists in mutual reciprocity.

REFERENCES:

Ginette Castro, *Radioscopie du féminisme américain* (Paris: Presses de la Fondation Nationale des Sciences Politiques, 1984); translated by Elizabeth Loverde-Bagwell as *American Feminism* (New York & London: New York University Press, 1990);

Judith Freeman Clark, *Almanac of American Women in the 20th Century* (New York: Prentice Hall Press, 1987);

Barbara Sinclair Deckard, *The Women's Movement: Political, Socioeconomic, and Psychological Issues,* second edition (New York: Harper & Row, 1979).

– L.M.G.

FEMINIST ART

By 1970 reverberations from the women's movement were felt in all aspects of society. Feminist art raised a host of questions: Is there such a thing as a distinctly feminine art with feminine imagery? Are female artists judged differently from their male counterparts? Why are so few woman artists represented in museums, galleries, and art-history textbooks? Feminist art questioned the distinction between the "high" arts of painting and sculpture and the "low" arts, which consisted of traditionally female-dominated crafts such as needlework, ceramics, and miniatures. It also called attention to the large role that women had played throughout the history of art — as collectors, patrons, dealers, and, of course, subject matter — but questioned why women rarely received recognition as artists in their own right.

In reaction to the predominately male art world, feminists boycotted museums, formed their own cooperative galleries and studios, and explored women's concerns in their artwork. In addition, the feminist art movement gave birth to a new generation of important critics, such as Linda Nochlin and Lucy Lippard. Nochlin's cornerstone essay "Why Have There Been No Great Women Artists?" (*ARTnews,* 1971), that challenged the assumptions and preconceptions of the white male–dominated field of art.

Feminist art took many forms was but was epitomized by the work of Judy Chicago and Miriam Schapiro, who together established the first women's art program at the California Institute of Arts in 1970. In their 1972 project *Womanhouse.* They and their students converted an old, run-down house into a series of spaces, each constituting a particular feminist artistic expression. From the "Nurturant Kitchen" to the "Menstruation Bathroom," each room of *Womanhouse* addressed and attacked the oppressive roles placed on women by society.

Chicago's best-known work is her *Dinner Party* (1971–1975), a triangular table that features place settings for 39 influential women throughout history. The names of another 999 women are inscribed on the tile floor below. A collaborative effort, it was worked on by Chicago and hundreds of volunteers who helped produce the ceramic plates and needlework table runners. Intended to celebrate and reclaim women's influential heritage, *The Dinner Party* provoked a storm of controversy, mostly centered around Chicago's use of explicit sexual imagery in the plate designs.

Schapiro currently works in a highly personal form of collage that she calls *femmage,* a combination of the words *female* and *image.* Using material commonly associated with women in history — such as fabric, lace, yarn, rickrack, buttons, sequins, and tea towels — she creates rich and intricate compositions.

Feminist art explores experiences that are unique to women and their bodies, and **performance art** has become a natural outlet for expression. Works such as *Interior Scroll* (1975), by Carolee Schneemann, in which she pulled a text from her vagina, graphically confronted perceptions of the female nude in art.

With the rise of **multiculturalism,** feminist art continues to exert a strong presence on the contemporary art scene. In 1985 a group of women from the art world formed the Guerrilla Girls. Wearing gorilla masks to ensure their anonymity, they plaster city walls with inflammatory posters charging rampant sexism and racism within the art community. The Women's Action Coalition (WAC) was formed by a group of female artists in 1991, in response to several well-publicized rape and sexual-harassment trials.

REFERENCES:
Wendy Beckett, *Contemporary Women Artists* (New York: Universe, 1988);
Whitney Chadwick, *Women, Art, and Society* (New York: Thames & Hudson, 1990).

– C.S.

FEMINIST CRITICISM

Feminist criticism draws on **feminism** for its theoretical underpinnings, critiquing how literature and culture reflect the status of women. It originated in the 1960s with the second wave of twentieth-century feminism.

Feminist critics engage in the historical and theoretical analysis of gender representation. They reject the notion that "the nature of women" is biologically determined, insisting instead that womanhood is a social, political, linguistic, and psychological construct imposed by a patriarchal system. In contrast to theories of the **New Critics,** on the wane by the 1960s, and structuralistic and psychoanalytical critics in the 1960s

and early 1970s, feminist critics insist on the significance of cultural contexts.

An early example of feminist criticism is Mary Ellmann's *Thinking about Women* (1968). More broadly political was Kate Millett's *Sexual Politics* (1969), which analyzes relationships between the sexes, surveys the history of feminism, and examines sexual politics in literature. Like Ellmann and other early feminist critics, Millett focuses more on literary content than on form, investigating images of women in the works of male writers. In the early 1970s, college courses on images of women in literature (mostly works by men) were popular. Feminist critics of this period often dealt with nineteenth- and twentieth-century realism as an expression of the representation of women.

In the 1970s feminist critics began to concentrate on women as writers and readers. For instance, in *A Literature of Their Own: British Women Novelists from Brontë to Lessing* (1977), Elaine Showalter examines forgotten or neglected writers as well as canonical authors. Sandra M. Gilbert and Susan Gubar's *The Madwoman in the Attic: The Woman Writer and the Nineteenth-Century Imagination* (1979) analyzes the strategies women authors have used to evade and subvert patriarchal authority while seeming to follow its expectations. These classics of feminist criticism and others proved popular with students and teachers, which helped gain feminist criticism a place in academe for which it had struggled since the 1960s.

In the 1980s, feminist criticism was attacked from within for its focus on white, middle-class women to the exclusion of poor women, minorities, and lesbians. In response, much recent feminist criticism parallels **multiculturalism** in exploring relationships among gender, class, and race. It has also drawn increasingly on **poststructuralist** critical theories and has expanded its attention to other literary periods and forms. Recent prominent feminist critics include Carolyn G. Heilbrun, Alice Jardine, and Annette Kolodny.

Though some scholars accuse feminist critics of reading literature and culture through a narrow ideology, feminist perspectives have significantly contributed to literary and cultural studies by challenging "objectivity" by recognizing that the critic, like the author, writes from a personal, cultural, and political position, and by revising and re-evaluating the literary canon.

REFERENCES:
Toril Moi, *Sexual/Textual Politics: Feminist Literary Theory* (London & New York: Methuen, 1985);
K. K. Ruthven, *Feminist Literary Studies: An Introduction* (Cambridge: Cambridge University Press, 1984).

– D.H.-F.

Lawrence Ferlinghetti in front of his City Lights Bookshop in San Francisco, 1957, when he was on trial for publishing Allen Ginsberg's *Howl* (courtesy of Lawrence Ferlinghetti)

LAWRENCE FERLINGHETTI

Poet and publisher Lawrence Ferlinghetti (1919–) was one of the key figures in the **Beat Generation.** With co-owner Peter Martin, he founded San Francisco's City Lights Pocket Bookshop in 1953. The first bookshop in the country to deal exclusively in paperbacks, City Lights also had a policy of stocking hard-to-find works by controversial authors and of championing modernist — especially Beat movement — works.

Ferlinghetti began publishing his Pocket Poets Series under the City Lights Books imprint in 1955, starting with a collection of his own poetry, *Pictures of the Gone World*. Number four in the series appeared in 1956; it was the first publication of **Allen Ginsberg**'s *Howl and Other Poems*. A shipment of the second printing of *Howl* was seized by a U.S. Customs agent in 1957, and Ferlinghetti was subsequently arrested on obscenity charges. The court case drew international attention throughout the summer of 1957. By the time *Howl* was exonerated the entire world was aware of the literary revolution taking place in America and perceived Ferlinghetti and Ginsberg to be at its forefront.

In 1958 **New Directions** published Ferlinghetti's second book of poems, *A Coney Island of the Mind*. This collection remains Ferlinghetti's biggest popular success and is in fact one of the best-known and most widely read volumes of poetry to be published since 1950. The collection exhibits Ferlinghetti's radical, populist political vision, as well as such technical trademarks as the use of accessible imagery and allusions and a heavy reliance on oral patterns of language.

REFERENCES:

Neeli Cherkovski, *Ferlinghetti: A Biography* (Garden City, N.Y.: Doubleday, 1979);

Barry Silesky, *Ferlinghetti: The Artist in His Time* (New York: Warner Books, 1990);

Michael Skau, *Constantly Risking Absurdity: Essays on the Writings of Lawrence Ferlinghetti* (Troy, N.Y.: Whitston, 1989).

                                                        – S.B.

LESLIE FIEDLER

Since June 1948, when his "Come Back to the Raft Ag'in, Huck Honey!" appeared in the *Partisan Review*, Leslie Fiedler (1917–) has challenged, and often outraged, the American literary establishment with his Freudian/Marxist interpretations of major American writers such as James Fenimore Cooper, Herman Melville, Samuel Clemens (Mark Twain), **Ernest Hemingway,** and **William Faulkner.** Beginning in 1948 with Twain's *Huckleberry Finn* (1884), Fiedler has examined "the myth of interethnic male bonding" with what he calls "almost monomaniacal exclusivity" for most of his career.

In *Love and Death in the American Novel* (1960), *Waiting for the End* (1964), *The Return of the Vanishing American* (1968), and elsewhere Fiedler has developed and expanded his theory of homoerotic undertones in friendships such as those of Huck Finn and the runaway slave Jim or frontier scout Natty Bumppo and the Indian Chingachgook in Cooper's *Last of the Mohicans* (1826). Fiedler calls these relationships presexual rather than homosexual and argues that the central works of American literature are stories of arrested adolescents who choose life in the wilderness. These innocents see women as the governors of civilization, and they view mature heterosexual relationships as threats to their freedom, a means of forcing them to play responsible roles in civilized society. Also, Fiedler asserts, the fantasies of friendship between the races give the white man a way of compensating for his guilt over the way nonwhites have actually been treated in America.

Fiedler has been accused of ignoring important characters and plot elements when they do not support his theses. He has also been charged with reducing all literature, good and bad, to the same common denominator. Yet his provocative arguments have inspired scholars to take a fresh look at some of the American classics.

Fiedler, who has enjoyed being labeled the "wild man of American literary criticism," gained another sort of notoriety after he was arrested in 1967 for "maintaining premises where marijuana is used." Although he was found guilty, his conviction was later reversed. In *Being Busted* (1969) Fiedler charged that the police framed him because of his involvement in the movement to legalize marijuana. The episode made him a media celebrity, and he was looked upon as a spokesman for student radicals.

REFERENCE:
Mark Royden Winchell, *Leslie Fiedler* (Boston: Twayne, 1985).
– K.L.R.

HARVEY FIERSTEIN

The growing liberalization of attitudes toward sexuality in the 1970s and 1980s allowed Harvey Fierstein (1954–) to write and stage successful plays that look

Harvey Fierstein as Arnold Beckoff, the drag queen in *Torchsong Trilogy* (photograph by Gerry Goodstein)

at problems of love and family life from an openly homosexual perspective. While Mart Crowley's 1968 hit play *Boys in the Band* (1968) depicted homosexuals apart from society as a whole, Fierstein broke new ground by examining their relationships with heterosexuals as well as other homosexuals in plays that address concerns shared by many adult Americans in the late twentieth century.

Fierstein began acting and writing as an adolescent and developed a busy, if unconventional, career, including work as a female impersonator. He made his professional acting debut in Andy Warhol's *Pork* (1971), playing the lead role, an obese, asthmatic, lesbian maid. He acted in other plays throughout the 1970s. He also wrote and played the lead in three semi-autobiographical one-act plays: *The International Stud*

(1976), *Fugue in the Nursery* (1979), and *Widows and Children First* (1979). These plays were produced Off-Off-Broadway in 1981 and on Broadway in 1982 as *Torch Song Trilogy*. This trilogy chronicles the life of Arnold Beckoff, a Jewish homosexual who works as a "drag-queen" singer in a New York nightclub. He falls in love with a bisexual male schoolteacher and is abandoned for a woman; another lover is murdered by gay bashers; and he tries to help his mother accept his homosexuality while struggling to raise a gay teenager he has rescued from the street. *Torch Song Trilogy* won Fierstein two Antoinette Perry (Tony) Awards (for best play and best actor), as well as Drama Desk and Off Broadway (Obie) awards. Fierstein wrote the screenplay for the film version of *Torch Song Trilogy* (1988), in which he once again played the lead.

After his first Broadway success, Fierstein wrote the book for the Broadway musical version of the French farce *La Cage aux Folles* (1982). While the French play broadly caricatures the main characters, a pair of homosexual lovers named Georges and Albin, as well as the performers at Georges's transvestite nightclub, Fierstein treats them sentimentally. He focuses on the family crisis that develops when Georges's heterosexual son is ashamed to have his fiancée and her parents meet Albin, the flamboyant transvestite who has substituted for the boy's absent mother in raising him.

The **AIDS** epidemic spawned a new genre, the AIDS play, whose practitioners include Larry Kramer, William Hoffman, and Tony Kushner, as well as Fierstein. Fierstein's contribution to the genre is *Safe Sex* (1987), another trilogy of one-act plays: *Manny and Jake, Safe Sex,* and *On Tidy Endings.* The last of these, centering on the conflict between the former wife and bereaved male lover of a man who has just died of AIDS, has been the most praised of the three.

– I.R.H.

FILM NOIR

French for "black film," film noir is an American style of filmmaking that arose in Hollywood in the mid 1940s and early 1950s. In contrast to most earlier Hollywood movies, film noir rejected bright settings and happy endings in favor of dim lighting and dark moods. Most films noirs were crime/detective films or melodramas. The term was coined by French critics who saw similarities between these American films and *La série noire,* a paperback series of hardboiled detective fiction that became the basis for some of the best-known examples of film noir, such as Raymond Chandler's *The Big Sleep* (1939) and James M. Cain's *The Postman Always Rings Twice* (1934) and *Double Indemnity* (1943).

In film noir, paranoia and entrapment are common. Corrupt men and scheming women are driven by lust, greed, and betrayal. Many critics see these themes as reflections of uncertainty and disillusionment occasioned by World War II and its aftermath. Hollywood directors with backgrounds in German expressionistic film brought that style to film noir, especially in its nocturnal, urban settings where the only light comes from streetlights, neon signs, headlights, and other artificial sources of illumination. Voice-over narration and flashbacks are frequent plot devices in film noir.

Among the first examples of film noir was **Billy Wilder**'s *Double Indemnity* (1944), for which he wrote the screenplay with Chandler. Other notable examples include Tay Garnett's *The Postman Always Rings Twice* (1946), Howard Hawks's *The Big Sleep* (1946), Orson Welles's *The Lady from Shanghai* (1948), and Fritz Lang's *The Big Heat* (1953). The last example of film noir made during the period of its greatest popularity was Welles's *Touch of Evil* (1958). Film noir influenced the French New Wave films of the late 1950s and the 1960s as well as later films such as Roman Polanski's *Chinatown* (1974) and Ridley Scott's *Blade Runner* (1982).

REFERENCE:

Alan Silver and Elizabeth Ward, eds., *Film Noir: An Encyclopedic Reference to the American Style* (Woodstock, N.Y.: Overlook Press, 1979);

– I.R.H.

ELLA FITZGERALD

Ella Fitzgerald (1918–) is regarded as one of the finest African-American jazz singers of the twentieth century. Born in Newport News, Virginia, she began her professional career in small Harlem nightclubs during the 1930s and was discovered by the popular black bandleader Chick Webb, whose ensemble she joined in 1935. Her first hit record, "A-Tisket, A-Tasket" (1938) was recorded with Webb's orchestra. After his death in 1939, Fitzgerald led the group until 1942, when she decided to become a freelance singer. She has appeared with a long list of important jazz bands. One of the first so-called scat singers, Fitzgerald proved equally at ease in swing, **bebop,** and free improvisational styles. She has recorded extensively and has received many accolades for her work, including a National Medal of Arts in 1987.

REFERENCES:

Bud Kliment, *Ella Fitzgerald* (New York: Chelsea House, 1988).

– L.D.S.

F. Scott Fitzgerald

Since the Fitzgerald revival began in the 1950s, F. Scott Fitzgerald (1896–1940) has been considered a major twentieth-century novelist. He is one of a handful of important American writers whose works are read and enjoyed outside the classroom, and he is popular worldwide.

Yet at the end of his life Fitzgerald was regarded as a popular or commercial writer. During his lifetime readers failed to recognize that his major novels — *The Great Gatsby* (1925) and *Tender Is the Night* (1934) — were serious considerations of American character and values. They tended to see Fitzgerald's 4 novels and 160 short stories as superficial tales of the rich in the Jazz Age of the 1920s. During the 1930s that impression was reinforced by critics looking for fiction that overtly addressed the social ills of the Depression.

Reexamination of Fitzgerald's work as serious literature beyond its value as social history began soon after his death in December 1940. Critic Edmund Wilson prepared an edition of *The Last Tycoon* (1941), the novel Fitzgerald had left unfinished at his death. Wilson considered this Hollywood novel Fitzgerald's "most mature piece of work." Most critics agreed. Among the overwhelmingly positive reviews, perhaps the most eloquent was Stephen Vincent Benét's, which ends with this prediction: "You can take your hats off now, gentlemen, and I think perhaps you had better. This is not a legend, this is a reputation — and seen in perspective, it may well be one of the most secure reputations of our time" (*Saturday Review,* 6 December 1941).

The revival of Fitzgerald's critical reputation was spurred by the publication of *The Crack-Up* (1945), a collection of Fitzgerald's articles and tributes to him. By the 1950s serious academic scholarship on Fitzgerald's life and works had begun.

Today Fitzgerald's reputation as a major American writer is virtually unchallenged. *The Great Gatsby* is the most widely read American novel in the world. Readers have come to agree with **John O'Hara**, who said of Fitzgerald: "All he was was our best novelist, one of our best novella-ists, and one of our finest writers of short stories."

REFERENCES:

Matthew J. Bruccoli, *F. Scott Fitzgerald: A Descriptive Bibliography,* revised edition (Pittsburgh: University of Pittsburgh Press, 1987);

Bruccoli, *Some Sort of Epic Grandeur: The Life of F. Scott Fitzgerald,* revised edition (New York: Carroll & Graf, 1993);

Scottie Fitzgerald Smith, Bruccoli, and Joan P. Kerr, eds., *The Romantic Egoists* (New York: Scribners, 1974).

– R.T.

Folk Music

Though there is a rich tradition of folk music in America, including black blues, **bluegrass,** mountain music, and country music, the term *folk music* in popular usage has referred narrowly to traditional white rural music and new popular music after that style. To purists, folksingers were performers who sang and played, usually on an acoustic guitar, meaningful songs in which the words had at least equal importance with the music. Solo performers were most common.

The **hippie** movement of the 1960s had at its core a back-to-the-earth philosophy that promoted simple values and traditional folkways. One aspect of the movement was a folk-music revival that lionized social protest singers of the near past, such as Woody Guthrie (see **Arlo Guthrie**) and the Weavers (which included Pete Seeger). The new generation in this vein was led by **Bob Dylan, Joan Baez,** and **Peter, Paul & Mary,** who found ample material for songs of protest during the **Vietnam War** and an eager audience among militant college students.

A popularized — some would say vulgarized — form of this new folk music, as sung by such performers as the Kingston Trio, the Chad Mitchell Trio, and John Denver, appealed to more-docile college audiences. These singers avoided controversial material, opting for humorous new songs in the folk tradition and pleasing tunes with common themes. Hootenannies — folk sing-alongs — were popular among this audience, and a 1963 **ABC** television show called *Hootenanny* was a showcase for these generic folk singers.

Driven by a sense of purpose, the folksingers with a message were more enduring. Inspired by Bob Dylan, who shocked purists at the 1965 Newport folk festival by playing an electric guitar, the boundaries between folk music and **rock 'n' roll** began to blur later in the decade and in the 1970s into a form called folk-rock. Such electric groups as Crosby, Stills, Nash and Young, the Byrds, and The Lovin' Spoonful merged the energy of rock 'n' roll with the social consciousness of folk music; but as the spirit of the innovators gave way to imitation, folk-rock degenerated into what was called soft rock, which typically lacked both drive and message. In the mid 1980s the "folk aesthetique" began to show signs of renewed popularity with the success of such folk-rock performers as the Indigo Girls, Tracy Chapman, and Michelle Shocked.

REFERENCES:

Kristin Baggelaar and Donald Milton, *Folk Music: More Than a Song* (New York: Crowell, 1976);

Craig Harris, *The New Folk Music* (Crown Point, Ind.: White Cliffs Media Company, 1991);

Sarah Lifton, *The Listener's Guide to Folk Music* (New York: Facts On File, 1983);

Eric von Schmidt and Jim Rooney, *Baby, Let Me Follow You Down: The Illustrated History of the Cambridge Folk Years* (Garden City, N.Y.: Anchor/Doubleday, 1979).

—J.E.F.

JANE FONDA

Jane Fonda (1937–), talented daughter of the talented actor Henry Fonda, has been a popular and gifted actress as well as a controversial political activist.

After Fonda studied with Lee Strasberg at **Actors Studio,** she made her film debut in *Tall Story* and her Broadway debut in *There Was a Little Girl* in 1960. She performed in several romantic stage and film comedies in the first years of that decade. In 1965 she married French director Roger Vadim, who tried to mold her into a successor to French actress Brigitte Bardot, casting Fonda in the erotic science-fiction-fantasy film *Barbarella* (1968). In the late 1960s Fonda left Vadim (they were divorced in 1973), and in the early 1970s she became active in the **Vietnam War** protest effort, earning the nickname "Hanoi Jane" for her trip to the North Vietnam capital. Despite her controversial public persona, Fonda reached the height of her popularity as an actress. She won Academy Awards (Oscars) for best actress for her performances in *Klute* (1971) and *Coming Home* (1978) and was nominated for the same award for her roles in *They Shoot Horses, Don't They?* (1969) and *Julia* (1977). In the 1980s she acted in fewer films, a highlight being her only pairing with her father in *On Golden Pond* (1981), which won him his only Academy Award, for best actor. Instead she concentrated on her highly successful exercise videotapes. In 1992 she divorced antiwar activist Tom Hayden, whom she had married in 1973, and married media mogul **Ted Turner.**

REFERENCES:

Christopher P. Anderson, *Citizen Jane: The Turbulent Life of Jane Fonda* (New York: Holt, 1990);

Michael Freedland, *Jane Fonda: A Biography* (New York: St. Martin's Press, 1988);

Fred Lawrence Guiles, *Jane Fonda: The Actress in Her Time* (Garden City, N.Y.: Doubleday, 1982).

—I.R.H.

HARRISON FORD

Harrison Ford (1942–) starred for producer **George Lucas** as Han Solo in *Star Wars* (1977), *The Empire Strikes Back* (1980), and *Return of the Jedi* (1983) and as Indiana Jones in *Raiders of the Lost Ark* (1981), *Indiana Jones and the Temple of Doom* (1984), and *Indiana Jones and the Last Crusade* (1989) — two of the most lucrative movie series of the 1970s and 1980s.

Ford started out as a contract player for Columbia and Universal, doing television and small parts in feature films. Disgusted with the slow progress of his career, he virtually quit acting to work as a carpenter. But Lucas's casting him as drag racer Bob Falfa in *American Graffiti* (1973) brought him the recognition that led to his part in *Star Wars* and its two sequels. After he played Indiana Jones in *Raiders of the Lost Ark,* his position as the premiere wise-cracking action star was assured. Ford played law-enforcement officers in *Blade Runner* (1982) and *Witness* (1985), a lawyer in *Presumed Innocent* (1990), and a CIA operative in *Patriot Games* (1992). In *The Fugitive* (1993) — a reprise of the popular television show — he played a wrongfully convicted escapee in search of his wife's real murderer. He has also played in softer, more romantic fare such as *Hanover Street* (1979), *Working Girl* (1988), and *Regarding Henry* (1991).

REFERENCES:

Minty Clinch, *Harrison Ford: A Biography* (London: New English Library, 1987);

Ethlie Ann Yare and Mary Toledo, *Harrison Ford* (New York: St. Martin's Press, 1988).

—I.R.H.

LUKAS FOSS

Like his friend **Leonard Bernstein,** Lukas Foss (1922–) has had a multifaceted career as a pianist, composer, conductor, and teacher. Foss is known for using a variety of traditional and experimental techniques in his compositions and for promoting contemporary music as a conductor.

Born in Berlin, Lukas Fuchs moved with his family to Paris in 1933 to escape the Hitler regime; in 1937 they settled in America, changing their last name to Foss. A musical prodigy in his youth, Foss studied composition under Paul Hindemith and conducting under Serge Koussevitzky at Tanglewood (1940–1943). In 1943 Foss became the youngest composer to have a work performed by the **Boston Symphony Orchestra** with the premiere of the symphonic suite based on his 1943 cantata *The Prairie*. The next year, after performing his Piano Concerto No. 1 with the Boston Symphony, Foss joined the orchestra as a pianist, remaining until 1950. A Fulbright fellowship enabled him to study and write in Rome for three years (1950–1952), and in 1953 he succeeded Arnold Schoenberg as professor of composition at the University of Califor-

Bob Fosse conducting a rehearsal for a dance number in his 1965 musical *Pleasures and Palaces*, which closed before reaching Broadway (Bettmann Archives)

nia at Los Angeles. In 1962 Foss became director of the Buffalo Philharmonic Orchestra. His advocacy of new music gave the orchestra a worldwide reputation for its performances of contemporary works. Foss has also conducted the Brooklyn Philharmonic Orchestra (1971–1990), where he premiered **Ned Rorem**'s *Six Songs for High Voice and Orchestra* (1978) and **William Bolcom**'s *Songs of Innocence and Experience* (1987), and the Milwaukee Symphony Orchestra (1981–1986), which in 1984 premiered both **John Adams**'s *The Chairman Dances* and **John Corigliano**'s *Creations*.

Foss's early, traditional compositions include his one-act opera *The Celebrated Jumping Frog of Calaveras County* (1949), based on a short story by Mark Twain. Since the 1950s he has drawn on a wide range of techniques, including **aleatory music, electronic music,** and **serial music.** He also experimented with incorporating improvisation in his work: during 1957–1963 he worked with the Improvisation Chamber Ensemble, which he founded, writing scores allowing improvisation within an established framework. In his composition for soprano and orchestra called *Time Cycle* (1960), Foss included improvised sections for the

ensemble between the four songs. Other examples of Foss's eclectic compositions include the highly dissonant orchestral work *Echoi* (1963) and his Cello Concert (1967), which employs taped recordings as well as live instruments, quotes from compositions by other composers, and uses aleatory elements and improvisation. Similarly, *Baroque Variations* (1967) draws on themes by George Frideric Handel, Domenico Scarlatti, and Johann Sebastian Bach but alters them and occasionally makes them inaudible, with musicians going through the motions of playing.

REFERENCE:

Karen L. Perone, *Lukas Foss: A Bio-Bibliography* (New York & Westport, Conn.: Greenwood Press, 1991).

– L.D.S.

BOB FOSSE

Dancer, choreographer, and director Bob Fosse (1927–1987) helped to reshape **Broadway musicals** after World War II with his jazzy, sensual dance numbers. In 1973 he became the first person to win high honors in

1973 he became the first person to win high honors in film, Broadway, and television in the same year, receiving an Academy Award (Oscar) for directing *Cabaret,* two Antoinette Perry (Tony) Awards for directing and choreographing *Pippin,* and three Emmys for producing, directing, and choreographing a television special on Liza Minnelli, *Liza with a Z.*

Robert Louis Fosse made his first Broadway appearance in a revue, *Dance Me a Song* (1950). In 1954 he received his first assignment as a choreographer, *The Pajama Game,* for which he received a Tony Award. In this musical, especially in the "Steam Heat" number, Fosse pioneered a dance style characterized by angular, sexually charged movements heavily influenced by jazz dancing. He also choreographed the film version in 1957. Fosse repeated this pattern with his Tony Award–winning choreography for *Damn Yankees* (1955) and the film (1958). *Redhead* (1959) was his first venture as a Broadway director.

During the 1960s Fosse directed and choreographed a series of successful Broadway shows, including *How to Succeed in Business Without Really Trying* (1962) and *Sweet Charity* (1966). The 1969 film version of *Sweet Charity,* starring Shirley MacLaine, was the first movie Fosse directed. It received poor reviews, but he had a hit with *Cabaret* (1972), a musical about Berlin in the 1930s, which he directed and choreographed. Fosse's next film, *Lenny* (1974), was a downbeat, nonmusical biography of comedian Lenny Bruce with **Dustin Hoffman** in the title role.

In his Broadway work of the 1970s, Fosse turned away from strict musical comedy to productions centered less on plot and more on music, dance, and spectacle such as *Pippin* (1972), *Chicago* (1975), and *Dancin'* (1978). In 1979 he directed *All That Jazz,* an unflattering semi-autobiographical film about a hard-working, hard-living choreographer and director whose lifestyle eventually kills him. In the 1980s Fosse remained active on Broadway and directed *Star 80* (1983), a film about the late *Playboy* model and actress Dorothy Stratten. He died of a heart attack in 1987.

REFERENCES:

Martin Gottfried, *All His Jazz: The Life and Death of Bob Fosse* (New York: Bantam, 1990);

Kevin Boyd Grubb, *Razzle Dazzle: The Life and Work of Bob Fosse* (New York: St. Martin's Press, 1989).

– I.R.H. and D.M.

VIRGIL FOX

Combining showmanship and a high degree of technical skill, organist Virgil Keel Fox (1912–1980) attracted millions of Americans to organ music through his popular concerts. Unlike **E. Power Biggs,** Fox promoted the use of electronic organs in concert and was as much an entertainer as a performer.

At age ten Fox became the organist of a church in his hometown of Princeton, Illinois. He continued to study organ in his teens in America and Europe. Fox joined the faculty of the Peabody Conservatory in Baltimore and became head of the organ department in 1938. During 1946–1965 he was organist at Riverside Church in New York, where the pipe organ was designed to his specifications.

From the late 1960s to his death Fox toured Europe and America. He was the first American to perform on the organ at Thomaskirche in Leipzig, Germany, where Johann Sebastian Bach, his favorite composer, was once organist. In the United States he toured with his own organ; sometimes his performances were accompanied by light shows. His playing style was deliberately extravagant, and he often appeared on stage in a red cape and rhinestone-studded shoes. He sought to play even more-restrained Baroque masterpieces with a new freedom of expression, and he frequently addressed audiences to explain his ideas about the music. Fox's critics found his style excessive, but his performances usually filled concert halls.

– L.D.S.

ROBERT FRANK

Robert Frank (1924–), a Swiss-born photographer and film maker, is known primarily for a body of photographs taken on a ten-thousand-mile road trip through the United States in 1955–1956. Eighty-five images culled from his thousands of black-and-white negatives were published in book form in 1958 as *The Americans.* Now considered one of the most influential photographic projects of the second half of the twentieth century, *The Americans* represented a radical departure from the mainstream aesthetic in documentary photography, examples of which dominated the popular Family of Man touring exhibition organized by the **Museum of Modern Art** in 1954. Those photographs presented an optimistic, often sentimental view of a world society bound by common aspirations and values that answered a postwar longing for inspiration, healing, and a renewed faith in humankind. Frank's vision of his adopted country, on the other hand, was neither optimistic nor especially affirmative. Rather than echoing the stereotype of the affluent melting pot, which Americans had come to expect, Frank presented a social grab bag filled with scenes of alienation, loneliness, and a strangely bleak and unforgiving environment.

Frank's perspective was that of an outsider: not only was he foreign born, having immigrated to New York at age twenty-three, but he was also intellectually distanced from the bourgeois American mainstream, preferring the lifestyle and company of the **Beats.** His friend **Jack Kerouac** wrote the introduction to the American edition of Frank's book, noting that "After seeing these pictures you end up finally not knowing any more whether a jukebox is sadder than a coffin," and praising "The humor, the sadness, the EVERY-THING-ness and the American-ness of these pictures!" Frank had uncovered, as curator John Szarkowski later wrote, "whole segments of life that nobody had thought the proper concern of art." The book found a largely hostile reception when it first appeared.

Frank's work pioneered a more overt level of personal subjectivity than usually applied to the traditionally objective and "truth-seeking" documentary mode at that time. Stylistically, his imagery broke new ground by having a more spontaneous, seemingly uncontrolled and crude quality than was the norm for professional photography. All these innovations proved to be seminal for the direction of American photography.

During the late 1950s Frank began to turn away from photography in favor of film making. His first film, *Pull My Daisy* (1958), was created in collaboration with painter Alfred Leslie and narrated by Kerouac; it is now considered a classic of American independent cinema. He continued making films through the 1960s and in 1969 left New York for Nova Scotia, where he lives with his wife, June Leaf.

– K.B.

HELEN FRANKENTHALER

Helen Frankenthaler (1928–), one of the first women to achieve a distinguished and durable reputation in post–World War II American art, was originally associated with the second generation of **Abstract Expressionists.** In the early 1950s, influenced by **Jackson Pollock**'s "drip" paintings, she developed the technique of staining canvases with thinned-out paint rather than applying the paint with brushes. The unprimed canvases, which she would tack to the floor, allowed the colors to soak through and reveal the canvas's natural texture. This aspect of her style was encouraged by art critic **Clement Greenberg,** who believed the artist should reaffirm the flatness of the canvas rather than create the illusion of three-dimensional space.

Frankenthaler's style of abstract expression included the use of symbolic imagery, although it was seldom explicit. In *Mountains and Sea* (1952), her historic painting first using this staining technique, color forms evoke images of landscape — an iconography that became a trademark of the majority of her works throughout her career. In the 1960s she switched from oil paints to acrylics, and her works of this period are characterized by more-intensely saturated colors and larger-scale forms that reduce the still-extant landscape imagery even farther toward complete abstraction. In the late 1960s she began to experiment frequently with color combinations, allowing thin veils of paint to overlap. In *Movable Blue* (1973), for example, the translucent layers of paint evoke vague images of sky, clouds, and water.

Frankenthaler's style marks a transition between the gestural painting of the Abstract Expressionists and the stain-technique painting of the **Post-Painterly Abstract** artists, most notably Morris Louis and Kenneth Noland. She and Abstract Expressionist **Robert Motherwell** were married from 1958 to 1971.

REFERENCE:
John Elderfield, *Frankenthaler* (New York: Abrams, 1987).
– K.B. and J.M.H.

ARETHA FRANKLIN

Known as the "Queen of Soul," Aretha Franklin (1942–) is one of the most prominent African-American singers performing today.

Born in Memphis and raised in Detroit, she was a daughter of the Reverend C. L. Franklin, pastor of the New Bethel Baptist Church, whose powerful oratorical skills led to national distribution of his recorded sermons and a successful traveling revival show. During her childhood, many famous black performers — such as Mahalia Jackson, Sam Cooke, and Dinah Washington — visited her family. Detroit contemporaries included her close friend Smokey Robinson and **Diana Ross.** Franklin started out singing **gospel.** When she was twelve she became a soloist at her father's church, and in 1955 she began traveling with his revival show. She quickly became so well known for her expressive, flexible voice that Chess Records recorded her *Songs of Faith* (1956) when she was only fourteen. The album has since been released as *The Gospel Sound of Aretha Franklin* (1964) and *Aretha Gospel* (1982).

In 1958 Franklin turned her attention to the blues, and by early 1960 she had moved to New York City. Her recording of "Today I Sing the Blues" won her a contract with Columbia Records, which released her first jazz/blues album, *Aretha,* in 1961. "Today I Sing the Blues," the first cut from the album, reached the top ten on rhythm-and-blues (R&B) charts. Franklin recorded ten albums with Columbia. *The Electrifying Aretha Franklin* (1961) includes the only **Top 40** single she made while under contract to Columbia: "Rock-A-Bye Your Baby With a Dixie Melody." Her Columbia albums of jazz, blues, pop, show tunes, and ballads failed to win her recognition because her producers lacked focus in marketing them.

In 1966 Franklin signed with Atlantic Records, where producer Jerry Wexler encouraged her to change her style dramatically. She developed a heartfelt delivery that helped to redefine the music scene in the late 1960s. Her first Atlantic album, *I Never Loved a Man The Way I Love You* (1967), catapulted her to international stardom. The title track reached number nine on the ***Billboard*** charts, number one on the R&B charts, and became her first million-seller. Two months later she released the most successful single of her career, "Respect," which became a number-one pop and R&B hit and broke into the British top ten.

From February 1967 to February 1968 Franklin released an unprecedented six top-ten pop-hit singles and three top-ten albums, including "Baby I Love You" from *Aretha Arrives,* and "A Natural Woman (You Make Me Feel Like)" and "Chain of Fools" from *Lady Soul.* Franklin went on to win a record-breaking fifteen Grammy Awards, including consecutive wins for best female R&B performance from 1967 to 1974. She continued to celebrate her gospel roots with albums such as *Young, Gifted and Black* (1972) and *Amazing Grace* (1972). She also worked with other well-known musicians, producing *Hey Now Hey* (1973) with **Quincy Jones** and *Jump to It* (1982) with Luther Vandross, and recording duets with the Four Tops, **James Brown,** and Elton John. In 1985, thirty years after her first recording, *Who's Zoomin' Who?* (1985), which includes the Grammy-winning "Freeway of Love," went platinum. The next year, *Aretha* (1986), with Franklin and George Michael's Grammy-winning duet "I Knew You Were Waiting (For Me)" went gold.

REFERENCES:

Mark Bego, *Aretha Franklin: The Queen of Soul* (New York: St. Martin's Press, 1989);

Hettie Jones, *Big Star Fallin' Mama: Five Women in Black Music* (New York: Viking, 1974).

– J.E.F. and L.D.S.

FREE SPEECH MOVEMENT, BERKELEY

In September 1964 a dispute over a twenty-six-by-sixty-foot strip of sidewalk belonging to the Berkeley campus of the University of California precipitated a semester-long protest that established the climate and the methods for the flood of student demonstrations that swept through American college campuses in the late 1960s and early 1970s.

University of California regulations prohibited on-campus political activities such as speech making, passing out leaflets, and soliciting funds or recruiting members for political parties or social-action groups. Yet for about three years beginning in 1961 the university allowed such activities on the sidewalk out-

Mario Savio addressing demonstrators during a Free Speech Movement sit-in at the Berkeley administration building, 2 December 1964 (photograph by Don Kechely)

side the campus gate at the corner of Telegraph Avenue and Bancroft Way, even though this narrow strip of pavement was university property. At the beginning of the fall 1964 semester when Berkeley administrators attempted to halt political activities on that sidewalk, students responded by forming a coalition of campus groups with a whole spectrum of political views, from far right to far left. Representatives of **civil rights** organizations, including Mario Savio and Jack Weinberg, emerged as the leaders of this Free Speech Movement (FSM), employing methods of nonviolent protest they had learned from their work with the Student Nonviolent Coordination Committee (SNCC) and the Congress of Racial Equality (CORE).

As FSM set up tables in defiance of the ban and held rallies and sit-ins at the administration building, the administration responded with internal disciplinary action and legal action against individual demonstrators. Gradually the issues broadened; FSM began to advocate unrestricted freedom of expression on the entire campus and to question other areas of university control over student life, such as dormitory regulations. They also criticized the "multiuniversity" for relegating the instruction of undergraduates to graduate students while faculty members did research funded by lucrative contracts from government and big business.

Folksinger **Joan Baez** voiced her support for FSM, singing at two of their rallies and participating in the administration-building sit-ins that followed. In December FSM started a four-day student strike, in which roughly 48 percent of the student body participated, and the faculty senate voted 824–115 in support of the FSM position.

By the beginning of the spring semester, Berkeley had a new chancellor whose position on campus politics was in line with the protesters', and FSM was officially disbanded. Ironically, before the FSM protest ever began, a series of U.S. Supreme Court decisions had rendered unconstitutional the regulations that University of California administrators spent a semester trying to uphold. By the time they discovered their error, FSM had build up so much momentum that it could not be prevented from extending its influence beyond its original purpose. Veterans of the movement went on to challenge the administration on other issues and to play active roles in the antiwar movement that began to coalesce in the San Francisco area in autumn 1965. Students across the country followed FSM's example in challenging university control over student life and adopted FSM's methods in organizing to protest the **Vietnam War.**

REFERENCES:

David Lance Goines, *The Free Speech Movement: Coming of Age in the 1960s* (Berkeley, Cal.: Ten Speed Press, 1993);

Max Heirich, *The Beginning: Berkeley, 1964* (New York & London: Columbia University Press, 1970); enlarged as *The Spiral of Conflict: Berkeley, 1964* (New York & London: Columbia University Press, 1971);

Seymour Martin Lipset and Sheldon S. Wolin, eds. *The Berkeley Student Revolt: Facts and Interpretations* (Garden City, N.Y.: Doubleday, 1965);

Michael V. Miller and Susan Gilmore, eds., *Revolution at Berkeley* (New York: Dial, 1965).

                                                               – K.L.R.

BETTY FRIEDAN

Betty Friedan became known as the "founding mother" of the **feminist** movement that arose in the United States after *The Feminine Mystique* was published in 1963. The book revived women's rights sentiments that had lain virtually dormant since American women were granted the right to vote in 1920.

Friedan got the idea for *The Feminine Mystique* after she compiled the results from a 1957 reunion questionnaire she had sent to fellow members of the Smith College class of 1942. She was surprised by her classmates' frustration and boredom with their lives as wives and mothers; yet she understood their dissatisfaction. Friedan herself had discovered in the early 1950s that she had no legal recourse when she was fired from a newspaper job because she was pregnant, but she had accepted the prevailing belief that she should devote herself to her husband and children and had settled into life as a suburban housewife.

Betty Friedan (right) and Kathryn Clarenbach, an officer of the National Organization for Women (NOW) announcing NOW's adoption of a women's bill of rights, 1967 (UPI/Bettmann Newsphoto)

The questionnaire changed her mind. Five years of extensive research into the history of feminism led Friedan to isolate the present view of woman's role as a post–World War II phenomenon enforced by psychologists, advertisers, and women's magazines: femininity was equated with marriage and motherhood. Friedan believed this "feminine mystique" was forcing American women to deny their true abilities and causing society to waste potential talent.

After the book was published, Friedan became a controversial national figure. In 1966 she helped found the National Organization for Women (NOW), which demanded "full equality for women, in fully equal partnership with men." As its first president, Friedan led the organization in fighting subtle and overt discrimination against women by working toward widely accepted goals, such as guaranteed maternity leave and the Equal Rights Amendment (ERA).

By 1970, when she organized the Women's Strike for Equality March in New York City, more-radical factions of the feminist movement had developed. Many of these groups viewed men as enemies, an opinion Friedan did not share. She stepped down as president of NOW and resigned from the Women's Strike Coalition. In 1971 she helped **Gloria Steinem** and Bella Abzug form the National Women's Political Caucus (NWPC), but later disagreements on the purpose of the women's movement led to a rift between her and these feminist leaders.

In 1976 Friedan published *It Changed My Life,* an account of her involvement in the women's movement. In *The Second Stage* (1981) she again provoked controversy by reacting against radical feminism and continuing to maintain that women and men should work together to build a harmonious society based on equality of the sexes. The book met with a barrage of criticism, infuriating many feminists. After the ERA was defeated in 1982, some even accused the book of supporting the backlash against feminism.

During the 1980s Friedan turned her attention to the problems of aging: after ten years of extensive research, she published *The Fountain of Age* (1993). She hoped to dispel the "mystique" of age, or American society's view of old age as a time of physical and mental decline. Friedan celebrated this part of life as an exciting period with the potential for continued intellectual and personal development.

While she is best known for her major role in reenergizing the American woman's rights movement, Friedan's feminism is just one manifestation of her vision of a society built on equal opportunity for all people.

REFERENCES:

David Halberstam, *The Fifties* (New York: Villard Books, 1993);
Sondra Henry and Emily Taitz, *Betty Friedan: Fighter for Women's Rights* (Hillside, N. J.: Enslow Publishers, 1990).

– J.E.F.

ROBERT FROST

Robert Frost (1874–1963) entered the post–World War II era as the best-known living poet in America, having won an unprecedented fourth Pulitzer Prize for *A Witness Tree* (1942).

To the American public Frost was the wise, down-to-earth farmer-poet — an image he had spent decades cultivating through a series of college and university appointments and wide-ranging reading tours. Though critics noticed a decline in quality in his first postwar book, *A Steeple Bush* (1947), and though he wrote fewer and fewer poems during the final decade of his life, his fame grew. It reached its height when he read "The Gift Outright" at the inauguration of President John F. Kennedy (20 January 1961) and visited the Soviet Union in 1962 on a goodwill tour with U.S. Interior Secretary Stuart Udall.

Frost's carefully created public image tended to work against his reputation with the **New Critics,** whose methods dominated college classrooms during the 1940s and 1950s. Having been viewed as an experimental poet when his *North of Boston* (1914) broke away from the musicality of his contemporaries' verse to employ the natural patterns of everyday speech, Frost was now often considered an old-fashioned poet whose verse was too superficial to merit the New Critics' in-depth analysis. That perception was challenged by prominent critics such as **Randall Jarrell** and Lionel Trilling, whose careful readings revealed the complexity and modern sensibility of Frost's poetry. Their serious considerations, among others, led to a reevaluation of Frost's work, and his stature as a major modern American poet has remained secure since his death.

REFERENCES:

Lawrance Thompson, *Robert Frost: The Early Years, 1874–1915* (New York, Chicago & San Francisco: Holt, Rinehart & Winston, 1966); *Robert Frost: The Years of Triumph, 1915–1938* (New York, Chicago & San Francisco: Holt, Rinehart & Winston, 1970); Thompson and R. H. Winnick, *Robert Frost: The Later Years, 1938–1963* (New York: Holt, Rinehart & Winston, 1976); these three volumes abridged by Edward Connery Lathem, with Winnick, as *Robert Frost: A Biography* (New York: Holt, Rinehart & Winston, 1982);
William H. Pritchard, *Frost: A Literary Life Reconsidered* (New York: Oxford University Press, 1984).

– K.L.R.

Buckminster Fuller with one version of his Dymaxion Car

BUCKMINSTER FULLER

Richard Buckminster Fuller (1895–1983) — whose wide-ranging areas of expertise and achievement included mathematics, engineering, economics, philosophy, social science, cartography, environmentalism, and even the authorship of published prose and poetry — was seen by many of his contemporaries as an eccentric, though brilliant, inventor. Much of his popular renown is based on his design of the geodesic dome erected as the United States Pavilion for Expo '67 in Montreal.

Fuller was largely self-taught, viewing the traditional educational system as stifling. After brief, unsuccessful stints at Harvard University, he worked at various jobs, including positions as a millwright at a textile company and a manager in a meatpacking company. In those jobs and others, Fuller developed an acute mechanical ability and an interest in efficient resource management.

Fuller's inventions and conceptual designs have their philosophical origins in his view that progress comes from a technological upheaval characterized by the radical, but reasoned, rejection of those conventions that fail to address changing needs adequately.

The sole purpose of technology, Fuller believed, was to make human life as efficient (or, to use his word, *dymaxion*) as possible. Scientific breakthroughs with no purpose aside from scholarly cogitation were pointless to Fuller, whose bent toward the social sciences distinguished him from many of his exact-science peers. His desire to improve the human condition through technological means — by making it as "dymaxion" as possible — is affirmed in his designs for the pole-suspended Dymaxion House (1927), the Dymaxion Car (1932), and the Dymaxion Air-Ocean World Map (1943). In the Dymaxion Car, for example, Fuller used three wheels instead of the usual four and streamlined the shape of the body from the traditional box shape, which was a carryover from the horse-drawn carriage — both rejections of technological conventions that were no longer the most efficient for vehicles that traveled at much higher speeds than earlier ones.

By 1947 Fuller had developed the conceptual design for his most important invention: the geodesic dome. This geodesic design (comprised of light structural parts held in tension) was Fuller's solution to what he saw as the inefficient use of structural technology. Instead of relying on a large, strong base to support the downward-directed weight (compressional force) of the building, Fuller's new type of architecture exploited the heretofore-underused tensional forces (pulling forces, which direct weight outward rather than downward) by constructing domes out of interlocking triangular shapes. He used lighter materials to create grandiose forms that, according to some observers, appeared magically transparent, due to the minimal structural support that allowed more glass to be used.

Fuller's Geodesics, Inc., earned him a fortune when thousands of these domes were erected as exhibition pavilions, auditoriums, and cold-climate radar protectors as well as for many other purposes. He even drew up designs for his proposal to enclose a one-mile radius section of Manhattan (from Twenty-second Street to Sixty-second Street, between the Hudson and East rivers) within a geodesic dome for protection from the weather, control of air quality, and reduction of heating and cooling costs.

Fuller's eccentric image and his rejection of traditional methods of learning have gained him a substantial following in the twentieth-century counterculture. This antiestablishment reputation both led to and was fostered by his sojourns at the **Black Mountain College** summer institutes, where he gave informal lectures, participated in **performance-art** pieces, and, in fact, constructed his first large-scale geodesic model in 1948, with the help of several students.

REFERENCES:

Robert W. Marks, *The Dymaxion World of Buckminster Fuller* (New York: Reinhold, 1960);

Lloyd Steven Sieden, *Buckminster Fuller's Universe: An Appreciation* (New York & London: Plenum, 1989).

– J.M.H.

FUSION MUSIC

Fusion music is a synthesis of jazz and **rock** styles, elements of the former being combined with the electronic instruments of the latter. In vogue during the 1970s, fusion music is also characterized by its combination of ostinato (repeated) harmonies with rock and Latin dance rhythms. One of the best-known fusion groups is Spyro Gyra.

REFERENCE:

Joachim Ernst Berendt, *The Jazz Book: From Ragtime to Fusion and Beyond* (Westport, Conn.: Hill, 1982).

– L.D.S.

G

GAME SHOWS

Game shows, in which contestants are given a chance to win money and prizes by luck or skill, have been a staple of American entertainment since the days of radio. The enormous popularity of the new medium of television in the 1950s brought in huge revenues for networks and sponsors, allowing television game shows to offer extravagant payoffs to contestants The first of these big-money game shows, *The $64,000 Question* (1955–1958), was an immediate sensation when it premiered on **CBS** in 1955. Americans followed the fortunes of a series of ordinary people. A policeman who knew Shakespeare, a housewife who specialized in the Bible, and an opera-loving shoe repairman were some of the show's early champions.

The success of *The $64,000 Question* inspired a host of imitators, all with increasingly large jackpots. In 1958 a shocked public learned that the producers of many game shows had been rigging their outcomes by providing contestants with answers and even ordering some champions to lose intentionally. Among those implicated in the scandal was Charles Van Doren, a charismatic young member of a well-known family of American intellectuals. Van Doren, who had become a national celebrity after he had been the all-time money winner on the show *Twenty-One* (1956–1958), testified before a House of Representatives subcommittee that he had been coached before every appearance on the show.

The networks promised to exercise greater controls over game-show producers, but the shows lost considerable prestige in the wake of the scandal. Public confidence in television was shaken. Game shows were largely relegated to daytime programming, and big-money winnings were eliminated. To hold the interest of American housewives, appliances, furs, and vacations were frequently offered as prizes. Many game shows also had celebrities on hand to help the contestants and add to the excitement. Some of the most enduring daytime successes are *The Price Is Right* (which premiered in prime time in 1956), *The $25,000 Pyramid* (later *The $10,000 Pyramid,* 1973–), and *The Hollywood Squares* (1966–1981, 1986–).

Other game shows, most notably *Wheel of Fortune* (1975–), *Family Feud* (1976–1985, 1993–), and *Jeopardy!* (1964–1979, 1984–) have had success in syndication with evening audiences, demonstrating that the genre still holds considerable interest for a wide range of television viewers.

REFERENCE:

Thomas A. DeLong, *Quiz Craze: America's Infatuation with Game Shows* (New York: Praeger, 1991).

– C.D.B.

AVA GARDNER

Ava Gardner (1922–1990) reigned as America's number-one sex goddess between the decline of Rita Hayworth in the late 1940s and the ascendancy of Marilyn Monroe in the mid 1950s.

Born to a poor farming family in Smithfield, North Carolina, Gardner was brought to Hollywood in 1940 by M-G-M after her brother-in-law sent a photograph of her to their casting department. She was known primarily for her brief marriage to Mickey Rooney in 1942, until *The Killers* (1946), based on a short story by Ernest Hemingway, made her a star. Cast as the woman with a past or the straight-talking voice of mature sexual experience, Gardner made an ideal Hemingway heroine and went on to play in screen versions of his *Snows of Kilimanjaro* (1952) and *The Sun Also Rises* (1957). She played other notable roles in *Show Boat* (1951), *Mogambo* (1953), *The Barefoot Contessa* (1954), and *The Night of the Iguana* (1964).

Frequently cast in films with exotic foreign locations, Gardner lived the life of an international jet-setter after her divorce in 1957 from her third husband, Frank Sinatra. By the late 1960s she was no longer a top star, but kept busy for the next decade in all-star-cast films from *The Bible* (1966) to *Earthquake* (1974) to *The Cassandra Crossing* (1977). Gardner made her final feature film in 1981 and died in 1990, after a long period of ill health.

REFERENCES:

Ava Gardner, *My Story* (New York & London: Bantam, 1990);
Jane E. Wayne, *Ava's Men: The Private Life of Ava Gardner* (New York: St. Martin's Press, 1990).

– I.R.H.

Henry Louis Gates, Jr.

Henry Louis Gates, Jr. (1950–) is an outspoken advocate of **multiculturalism** in his efforts to expand the American literary canon to include often-overlooked works by African-American writers. Gates was a thirty-year-old professor at Yale University when he received a prestigious MacArthur Foundation Fellowship in 1981. The following year he discovered Harriet E. Wilson's *Our Nig* (1859) and republished it with an introduction that documented its place as the first African-American novel.

Currently the W. E. B. Du Bois Professor of the Humanities at Harvard University, Gates argues for the autonomy of African-American studies, but he also believes that the cultures of African Americans and other ethnic groups should be introduced into existing curricula. He has thus been attacked by Afrocentrists, who advocate separatism, and by conservatives, who defend the traditional literary canon. His essays on this subject are collected in *Loose Canons: Notes on the Culture Wars* (1992).

Gates agrees with proponents of the **Black Aesthetic** that African-American culture is significant for its own sake; yet he argues with their emphasis on its African roots. African-American literature, Gates claims, is more influenced by the pluralistic American culture of which it is a part than it is by African culture. He does not dismiss its Africanness, however. In *The Signifying Monkey: A Theory of Afro-American Literary Criticism* (1988) he employs methods of **poststructuralism** to develop the concept of "signifying" as a playful and subversive use of language by black writers and speakers that has its roots in African culture and myth.

REFERENCE:

Adam Begley, "Henry Louis Gates, Jr.: Black Studies' New Star," *New York Times Sunday Magazine*, 4 April 1990, pp. 25–26, 48–50.

– D.H.-F.

The Gay-Rights Movement

Though homosexuality arguably has existed throughout history, what became known as the gay-rights movement had its origin in the riot at Stonewall Inn, a New York City gay bar, in 1969. From that beginning the movement steadily gathered strength. On 25 April 1993, a march on Washington, D.C., drew anywhere from 300,000 to 1.1 million participants.

The incident at Stonewall was in response to a police raid to arrest homosexuals. Though such raids were common then, the reaction of the people inside was not. Both gay men and lesbians fought back by kicking, punching, and throwing stones and bottles at the police. Three days of riots and demonstrations followed, out of which emerged the gay-rights movement.

Until then homosexuals had lived an almost entirely closeted existence, out of sight and out of mind to mainstream America. Homosexuality was commonly regarded as perversion or sickness, police harassment was common, and to be exposed as a homosexual meant almost certain dismissal from one's job, or even a prison sentence.

The aims of the gay-rights movement are many, ranging from the repeal of what gays and lesbians regard as unjust laws to a general desire to increase their visibility in American culture. Gays and lesbians also seek a change in societal attitudes, to end both popular stereotypes about homosexuals and violence against homosexuals, commonly referred to as gay bashing. Specifically, gay-rights advocates seek the repeal of sodomy statutes (laws criminalizing homosexual sex acts between consenting adults), enactment of laws banning discrimination in employment and housing, the lifting of the U.S. military ban that prevents open homosexuals from serving in its ranks, and laws granting homosexual unions the same recognition and privileges as heterosexual unions, especially regarding marriage, insurance benefits, and inheritance rights.

Far from being monolithic, the gay-rights movement lacks unifying leadership. Many groups and organizations, whose specific goals, tactics, and leadership are often at odds, are active in the gay-rights movement. Mainstream organizations, such as the National Gay and Lesbian Task Force, seek change through the political system by lobbying and political organizing, while more militant groups, such as ACTUP and Queer Nation, try to get their message across through street demonstrations and acts of civil disobedience.

The proliferation of **AIDS** has had a profound impact on the gay-rights movement. Its effects have been manifold: though AIDS has been tragic for those afflicted with the disease, their friends, and their family members, in some ways its effects on the gay-rights movement have proved ironically positive. It has forced homosexuality into the open for many Americans (both homosexual and heterosexual), making them confront a painful issue that many would rather avoid. It has galvanized the gay and lesbian community into political action and involvement. But at the same time AIDS has drained the gay community of energy and funds that could have been used in the general fight for gay rights, in addition to increasing the paranoia and backlash among many heterosexual Americans.

In the quarter century since it first emerged, the gay-rights movement has been remarkably successful in increasing gay and lesbian visibility. Homosexuals are out of the closet in unprecedented numbers, and the homosexual presence in American culture — in literature, film, music, theater — is undeniable. But in the political arena success has proved elusive. As of 1994 sodomy laws are still on the books in twenty-three states, laws that were upheld by the U.S. Supreme Court in *Bowers* v. *Hardwick* in 1986. No state recognizes homosexual marriages. Eight states and more than one hundred municipalities have enacted anti-discrimination laws, but in most locales an individual can still be fired from a job or evicted from an apartment simply for being homosexual. Men and women in the military can be discharged for admitting their homosexuality. Gay rights is still a contentious issue whenever and wherever it arises, invariably provoking an angry backlash from conservatives. This fact was borne out by the anti-gay-rights ballot initiatives of 1992 in Colorado and Oregon. As lesbian activist Donna Minkowitz wrote in 1989, "there are almost as many reasons for us to riot as there were [in 1969]."

Like many social issues, gay rights has been divisive, with American society being "torn between a basic impulse to be tolerant and a visceral discomfort with gay culture." People on both sides of the debate are in agreement that it is a polarizing issue without much middle ground and nowhere close to resolution. Southern Baptist leader and gay-rights opponent Morris Chapman predicted the future of the debate: "in the

1990s homosexuality will be what the abortion issue has been in the 1980s."

REFERENCES:

Victoria A. Brownworth, "Stonewall + 20," *Nation,* 249 (3 July 1989): 5–6;

William Hayes, "Out With the Boys," *Mother Jones,* 15 (July/August 1990): 46–47;

Donna Minkowitz, "Why Heterosexuals Need to Support Gay Rights," *Village Voice,* 27 June 1989, p. 32;

James D.Wilson, "Gays Under Fire," *Newsweek,* 120 (14 September 1992): 34–41;

Rist Darnell Yates, "AIDS as Apocalypse: The Deadly Costs of an Obsession," *Nation,* 248 (13 February 1989): 181+.

– W.L.T.

FRANK GEHRY

In the early 1980s Frank Gehry (1929–), whose career had been underway for nearly thirty years, became internationally known as one of the most innovative, expressive, and quietly iconoclastic architects in the United States. He has practiced mainly in southern California, often collaborating with artists and collectors, and his work has ranged from individual residences to shopping malls, amphitheaters, museum installations, and experimental furniture. His aesthetic position is in contrast to those of architects such as **I. M. Pei and Richard Meier,** who tend toward a modernist vocabulary of rational forms and pure materials. Instead, Gehry has stated that he prefers the look of buildings under construction to finished ones and that he is interested in how one can make a building "look like it's in process." To this end, he introduced the use of pedestrian building materials such as chain-link fencing, corrugated metal, and raw wood into architectural contexts that previously would not have allowed them. His most famous and controversial project is undoubtedly his own home — the Gehry House (1978), in Santa Monica, California, in which he enclosed a small, pink bungalow on three sides with an ambiguous open shell, blurring the distinctions between old and new, inside and outside, and, as he said, "real and surreal." With this project, Gehry was not interested in making "a big or precious statement about architecture or trying to do an important work: I was trying to build a lot of ideas."

REFERENCES:

Peter Arnell and Ted Bickford, eds., *Frank Gehry: Buildings and Projects* (New York: Rizzoli, 1985);

Carol Burns, "The Gehry Phenomenon," *Thinking the Present: Recent American Architecture,* edited by K. Michael Hays and Burns (New York: Princeton Architectural Press, 1990) pp. 72–88.

– K.B.

GI Bill

The GI Bill was the popular name for the Servicemen's Readjustment Act of 1944. It provided unemployment benefits, educational expenses, and low-interest loans to demobilized soldiers after World War II. Though the GI Bill was first intended as a one-time aid package from a thankful citizenry to returning soldiers, the benefits it offered came to be considered the due of war veterans and eventually of all who completed military service. After the Korean War, the Veteran's Readjustment Act of 1952 was passed; Vietnam War veterans were served by the Veterans Readjustment Benefits Act of 1966; and members of the all-volunteer army received benefits from the Post-Vietnam Era Veterans' Education Assistance Act of 1977 and the New GI Bill of 1985.

While the benefits to recipients were substantial, amounting to $55 billion between 1944 and 1985 and providing educational programs for 18.2 million veterans during that time, the real benefits of the GI Bills were broader. They helped to reduce the tension traditionally felt by soldiers returning from service to face the troubling transition to civilian life. After World War II, the Korean War, and the Vietnam War, they helped to reduce unemployment by funneling demobilized veterans into educational training programs while the national economy adjusted to the wars' ends. They provided federal support for industries that needed revitalization after the war, particularly home construction and education. Most of all, they provided a useful perk for military recruitment.

REFERENCE:

U.S. Army Recruiting Command, *The Army and the GI Bill: Educating America* (Washington, D.C.: U.S. Government Printing Office, 1986).

– R.L.

Dizzy Gillespie

John Birks ("Dizzy") Gillespie (1917–1993) had a reputation that superseded his prominence as a musician. Over his long career, his engaging personality, coupled with his mastery of the trumpet, thrust him into the role of jazz ambassador, promoting modern jazz, especially **bebop,** to general audiences both in the United States and abroad. Horn-rimmed glasses, a beret, a goatee, and a broad smile were the elements of Gillespie's stage personality. He played a trumpet of his own invention with the bell bent upward, puffing his cheeks comically; yet his virtuosity was unquestioned.

Dizzy Gillespie (United Press International)

Born in Cheraw, South Carolina, Gillespie grew up in the segregated South before heading north, after graduation from high school, to pursue a musical career. He acquired his nickname in Philadelphia in 1935 for his playful antics on stage. By 1939 he was playing with the Cab Calloway Orchestra and was at ease among the best musicians of the day. That same year he began joining the jam sessions at Minton's Playhouse, and in 1940 he met **Charlie Parker,** beginning a close personal and musical relationship that lasted until Parker's death in 1955. Along with Parker and **Thelonious Monk,** Gillespie was credited as one of the founding fathers of bebop. His "A Night in Tunisia" (1942) became a bop showpiece for him and Parker; Gillespie's "Salt Peanuts," which he composed the same year, and later "Swing Low, Sweet Cadillac" (after the tune of "Swing Low, Sweet Chariot") were staples of stage performances demonstrating his playful appeal. He was a leader among modern jazz figures who appropriated Latin rhythms to their music.

Alone among the brooding stars of bebop, Gillespie was an endearing figure. He was invited to the White House by three presidents, and in 1989 he was awarded the National Medal of the Arts. He was among the most celebrated jazz musicians of his time.

REFERENCES:

Dizzy Gillespie with Al Fraser, *to BE, or not . . . to BOP: Memoirs* (Garden City, N.Y.: Doubleday, 1979);

Raymond Horricks, *Dizzy Gillespie and the Be-bop Revolution* (New York : Hippocrene, 1984).

– R.L.

Allen Ginsberg

A central figure in the **Beat Generation** that emerged in the 1950s, Allen Ginsberg (1926–) has often been

134

Allen Ginsberg (third from left) at the Human Be-In, Golden Gate Park, San Francisco, 1966 (photograph by Lisa Law)

recognized as part of a line of major American poets that begins with Walt Whitman and extends through **William Carlos Williams** to Ginsberg and **Robert Lowell.** Yet Ginsberg's controversial public stands on political and social issues have at times overshadowed his accomplishments as a writer, and in some cases his desire to influence public opinion has clouded his artistic judgment.

The title poem in Ginsberg's first published book, *Howl and Other Poems* (1956), which begins with the words "I saw the best minds of my generation destroyed by madness," is an angry indictment of American society but also a celebration of the Beats — nonconformist, "angelheaded hipsters burning for the ancient heavenly connection to the starry dynamo in the machinery of night." Ginsberg's quest for this connection had begun in 1948, when he had a vision of William Blake reciting poems from his *Songs of Innocence* (1789) and *Songs of Experience* (1794) and felt "a sudden awakening into a totally deeper real universe than I'd been existing in." He first sought to re-create this sense of cosmic unity through the use of drugs, including LSD (which he took with Timothy Leary in the 1960s).

The controversy surrounding the obscenity trial of **Lawrence Ferlinghetti,** publisher of *Howl and Other Poems,* made Ginsberg's first book a best-seller (see the entry on **The Beat Generation**). Ginsberg used his newfound fame to promote the works of his friends, helping **William S. Burroughs, Jack Kerouac,** and oth-

ers to find publishers for works that had earlier been rejected and considered too controversial. The powerful title poem in Ginsberg's *Kaddish and Other Poems, 1958–1960* is a long confessional elegy for his mother, who had suffered from paranoid delusions and died in a mental hospital in 1956.

Much of Ginsberg's later poetry has failed to achieve the standards set by *Howl* and *Kaddish,* poems that had seminal importance in the **confessional-poetry** movement that emerged in the late 1950s and early 1960s. In the 1960s, as his spiritual quest led Ginsberg to the study of Buddhism, audiences who expected to hear him reading his poetry often heard Ginsberg and his lover Peter Orlovsky chanting mantras instead. Writing poetry was also subordinated to Ginsberg's social concerns. As a leader in the nonviolent protest of American involvement in the **Vietnam War**, he became well known to many Americans who had never read his poetry. Yet with *The Fall of America* (1972), which earned him a National Book Award in 1974, he once again created powerful protest poetry in a sequence that has been favorably compared to Whitman's *Leaves of Grass* (1855). Although *Howl* and *Kaddish* may always be considered Ginsberg's highest achievements, the reassessment of his work that followed the publication of his *Collected Poems, 1947–1980* (1984) led many critics to conclude that Ginsberg has written poems of considerable merit throughout his career and deserves to be ranked as one of the major poets of his generation.

REFERENCES:

Barry Miles, *Ginsberg: A Biography* (New York, London, Toronto, Sydney & Tokyo: Simon & Schuster, 1989);

Michael Schumacher, *Dharma Lion: A Biography of Allen Ginsberg* (New York: St. Martin's Press, 1992).

– K.L.R.

NIKKI GIOVANNI

Responding at first to the call from the **Black Arts Movement** for poetry that advanced its militant agenda in language accessible to all black people, Nikki Giovanni (1943–) has become a popular poet who attracts standing-room-only crowds to her many public appearances. She has been was widely recognized as a poet of the African-American experience whose work creates a bridge between black culture and mainstream America.

Born Yolande Cornelia Giovanni, Jr., she emerged as a poet in the late 1960s, at the height of the Black Arts Movement, and organized the first Cincinnati Black Arts Festival in 1967. Her first book, *Black Feeling, Black Talk* (1968), which sold more than ten thousand copies within months of its appearance, includes angry poems such as "The True Import of the Present Dialogue, Black vs. Negro." Her next book, *Black Judgement* (1969), also includes poems filled with revolutionary rhetoric. Yet other poems in the volume examine the sort of personal and domestic issues that are the focus of her later poetry.

As she moved away from advocating militant social action, Giovanni was rejected and vilified by the Black Arts Movement because of her refusal to adhere to their ideology. She became embroiled in controversy during the mid 1980s, when she refused to support a boycott of South Africa because she felt that people should be more concerned with the problems of blacks in America. She was falsely accused of having performed in South Africa, and her life was threatened. (She had visited the country briefly in 1973 as a required stop on a United States Information Agency tour of Africa, but she had not spoken there.)

Giovanni has been extremely successful at reading her poetry before large audiences. Her 1971 album, *Truth Is On Its Way,* a recording of a program in which she reads her poetry to the accompaniment of **gospel music** before an enthusiastic crowd of fifteen hundred people at a church in Harlem. A popular and critical success, the album received an award from the National Association of Television and Radio Announcers in 1972.

Giovanni has often been dismissed as merely a popular poet. Yet her admirers compare her to Langston Hughes, who also took his poetry to the people.

REFERENCES:

Virginia Fowler, *Nikki Giovanni* (New York: Twayne, 1992);

Fowler, ed., *Conversations with Nikki Giovanni* (Jackson: University Press of Mississippi, 1992).

– W.W.D.

PHILIP GLASS

Philip Glass (1938–) is one of the most popular composers of serious music in America, one of only a few composers who have had premiere performances of their work at the **New York Metropolitan Opera,** and the only one who has appeared as musical guest on *Saturday Night Live*. Identified as **minimalist,** his music relies heavily on rhythmic and melodic repetitions and variations that listeners often find either hypnotic or maddening. Glass is especially known for his untraditional operas.

Glass, who studied at the Juilliard School in New York and with Nadia Boulanger in Paris in the 1960s, was introduced to Indian music, which influenced his approach to composition, by sitar player Ravi Shankar. Returning to New York in 1966, he became involved in experiments with minimalist music, and in 1968 he formed the Philip Glass Ensemble to perform his work on electronic keyboards and woodwinds. He struggled to find an audience in the late 1960s and early 1970s, but he became famous with his first opera, *Einstein on the Beach* (1976). The four-hour piece, which premiered at the New York Metropolitan Opera, is based on the life of Albert Einstein, but it lacks a plot, and its text uses mostly nonsense syllables. Glass's next opera, *Satyagraha* (1980), is more conventional, dealing with Mohandas Gandhi, while his third, *Akhnaten* (1984), is about an Egyptian pharaoh. Other Glass operas include *The Making of the Representative of Planet 8* (1988), based on a novel by Doris Lessing, and *The Voyage* (1992), commissioned by the Metropolitan Opera to commemorate the five-hundreth anniversary of Christopher Columbus's voyage.

Glass's nonoperatic compositions provide an indication of his diversity and popularity. He wrote the music for the torch-lighting ceremony at the 1984 Summer Olympics in Los Angeles, and in 1986 he composed the music for a rock album, *Songs from Liquid Days,* with lyrics by **Laurie Anderson,** David Byrne of Talking Heads, **Paul Simon,** and others. He has also composed scores for films, including *Mishima* (1984), *The Thin Blue Line* (1988), and *A Brief History of Time*

(1990), based on the 1988 book by physicist Stephen Hawking.

REFERENCES:

Philip Glass, *Music by Philip Glass* (New York: Harper & Row, 1987);

Wim Mertens, *American Minimal Music: LaMonte Young, Terry Riley, Steve Reich, Philip Glass,* translated by J. Hautekiet (London: Kahn & Averill / New York: Broude, 1983).
                                                                      – D.H.-F.

JACKIE GLEASON

Known as "The Great One," Jackie Gleason (1916–1987) was famous for his portrayal of perpetually frustrated bus driver Ralph Kramden in the television comedy *The Honeymooners,* which has become a classic in syndication. On the show, which was originally broadcast live, Kramden generally got into scrapes with his doltish neighbor Ed Norton (Art Carney) and battled with his wife Alice (Audrey Meadows).

Gleason began his career in his teens as an emcee at clubs, where he launched his comedy routines in the 1930s. He had small roles in films in the early 1940s and spent most of the decade performing in clubs and in Broadway revues such as *Along Fifth Avenue* (1949), which led to his television debut in *Cavalcade of Stars* (1950–1952), where he introduced a large repertoire of comic characters. Also during the 1940s he established a reputation for carousing and heavy drinking that would follow him for most of his life.

The Honeymooners first appeared as a sketch on the show in 1951 and was a recurring segment on his **CBS** variety program *The Jackie Gleason Show* (1952–1955). The early sketches, which focused exclusively on Ralph and Alice Kramden, were bitter portrayals of domestic strife with little comedy. As the characters evolved, the mood lightened, especially after the introduction of Carney as Kramden's best friend. *The Honeymooners* was broadcast as a half-hour situation comedy during 1955–1956 but met with a lukewarm response. It appeared again in segments on the new *Jackie Gleason Show* (1957–1959). Gleason tried to revive the series with Carney and two new actresses playing Alice Kramden and Trixie Norton in 1966, but the original half-hour episodes are viewers' favorites. The key to their success is the hilarious interplay between the blustering Gleason and the goofy Carney. Their slapstick relieves the pair's otherwise dreary lower-class existence. In 1985 Gleason received more than $5 million for rights to the "lost" episodes of *The Honeymooners,* sketches from his variety shows. They added more than seventy new episodes for syndication to the thirty-nine first aired during 1955–1956.

From 1962 to 1966 Gleason appeared in skits on *American Scene Magazine.* Yet another version of *The Jackie Gleason Show* aired on CBS from 1966 to 1970. Gleason also appeared in several movies. In *The Hustler* (1961), he played pool shark Minnesota Fats, his most praised role, and he played a soft-hearted hobo in *Gigot* (1962). In the 1970s he reversed his declining fame with his comic portrayal of the redneck sheriff Buford T. Justice in *Smokey and the Bandit* (1977), and in *Nothing in Common* (1986) he played a serious role as an aging father.

REFERENCES:

James Bacon, *How Sweet It Is: The Jackie Gleason Story* (New York: St. Martin's Press, 1985);

William A. Henry III, *The Great One: The Life and Legend of Jackie Gleason* (New York: Doubleday, 1992).
                                                             – D.M.J. and C.D.B.

GOSPEL MUSIC

The term *gospel music* generally refers to the music of African-American churches. It became popular with white Americans after World War II. Gospel was also influential in the development of rhythm and blues and **rock 'n' roll. Soul-music** performers such as **James Brown** and **Aretha Franklin** began as gospel singers.

Gospel music originated from slave spirituals and Christian hymns of the eighteenth and nineteenth centuries; spirituals such as "Nobody Knows the Trouble I've Seen" and "Swing Low, Sweet Chariot" were popular in the late nineteenth century. In gospel music songs like these are embellished with swaying motions, syncopated clapping, and exclamations, which gives the music a driven, emotional feel. While gospel music is usually sung by choirs, soloists and smaller groups also perform it.

Gospel music in black churches was extensively recorded during the 1930s. It was promoted by the African-American musician Thomas A. Dorsey (1899–1993), who is credited with coining the term and who wrote more than one thousand songs, including "Precious Lord, Take My Hand" (1938) and "Peace in the Valley" (1939). Though first considered a form of jazz or blues, gospel music became a distinct category after World War II with its own record labels, radio stations, and performers. The most famous gospel soloist was Mahalia Jackson (1911–1972), who crossed over to white audiences in the 1950s with her concerts and recordings. She sang "Take My Hand, Precious Lord" at **Martin Luther King, Jr.**'s funeral in 1968; Aretha Franklin sang the same piece at Jackson's funeral.

Other important gospel performers since 1945 include Sister Rosetta Tharpe and the Dixie Hummingbirds.

White Southern gospel music is derived from the Anglo-American evangelical hymn tradition and is closely connected to country music; country performers such as **Johnny Cash,** Tennessee Ernie Ford, and **Bill Monroe** have often included gospel selections in their repertoires. **Elvis Presley** was influenced by both black and white gospel in his rock 'n' roll music and recorded many religious songs. A development since the 1970s in white Christian music is the use of contemporary rock and pop styles by performers such as the Imperials, Amy Grant, and Petra.

REFERENCES:

Lois Blackwell, *The Wings of the Dove: The Story of Gospel Music in America* (Norfolk, Va.: Donning, 1970);

Don Cusic, *The Sound of Light: A History of Gospel Music* (Bowling Green, Ohio: Bowling Green State University Popular Press, 1990).

– L.D.S.

GOTHIC FICTION

For two centuries American writers have exploited the Gothic-fiction tradition for some of their finest works. Following in the footsteps of **William Faulkner,** mainstream post–World War II novelists as seemingly diverse as Carson McCullers, **Joyce Carol Oates, John Irving,** and **Anne Tyler** have reshaped Gothicism to suit the needs of their individual worldviews.

The origins of Gothic fiction in English may be traced to Horace Walpole's *The Castle of Otranto* (1765) and other eighteenth-century British novels that created a vogue for tales of terrifying supernatural happenings in isolated decaying castles or monasteries, of heroes or heroines pursued by physically grotesque villains through catacombs or secret passageways and out into the tangled night-time forest. Major nineteenth-century American fiction writers such as Edgar Allan Poe, Nathaniel Hawthorne, and Herman Melville recognized that Gothic images could be powerful symbols of the human psyche. This trend in American fiction reached is best exemplified by Henry James's ambiguous ghost story *The Turn of the Screw* (1898).

There are three Gothic strains in twentieth-century American fiction. Gothic romance (see **romance fiction**) displays only vague outlines of its Gothic origins. In contrast, **horror fiction** by writers such as **Stephen King, Anne Rice,** and Peter Straub remains close to its eighteenth- and nineteenth-century roots. Mainstream novelist Oates has written three novels —

Bellefleur (1980), *A Bloodsmoor Romance* (1982), and *Mysteries of Winterthurn* (1984) — that consciously follow in this nineteenth-century Gothic tradition, exploiting its conventions (as does Rice) for social commentary. The third strain, running through mainstream American fiction, demonstrates how innovative modern writers have reinvented the Gothic to mirror contemporary realities. Instead of terrorizing readers with the seemingly supernatural, writers such as **Flannery O'Connor,** John Hawkes, and — in most of her fiction — Oates shock readers by depicting the same sort of random violence reported in the news every day.

By far the most enduring legacy of Gothicism is the employment of grotesque characters. The fiction of Faulkner, O'Connor, Hawkes, Irving, and Tyler — among others — is filled with characters with varying degrees of physical oddities, some self-inflicted, often exaggerated for humorous effect. Yet these writers, as well as writers such as Oates, McCullers, and **Truman Capote,** also create characters who are mentally or spiritually deformed, heightening their neuroses and eccentricities to emphasize their inner torments and self-obsession. Replacing the castle haunted by ghosts or vampires, the family home, haunted instead by memories of a past that cannot be changed, often serves as a symbol of the narcissism these characters seem unable to escape.

REFERENCE:

Irving Malin, *New American Gothic* (Carbondale & Edwardsville: Southern Illinois University Press, 1962).

– K.L.R.

MORTON GOULD

Morton Gould (1913–) is unusual among American composers for his successful dual careers in popular and art music. Though he achieved recognition late in life because critics thought his work too simplistic, Gould has since been praised as one of the best composers in the United States.

In his teens Gould worked as a pianist for vaudeville acts to help support his family, and in 1931, at age eighteen, he became the pianist for the new Radio City Music Hall. He was in charge of the *Music for Today* series broadcast over the Mutual Radio Network (1934–1942). These positions had an effect upon Gould's compositions, many of which combine popular and serious elements such as his jazz-influenced *American Symphonette* No. 1 (*Swing*) (1935) and his 1952 concerto for tap dancer and orchestra. He also wrote music for **Broadway**

Graffiti painted on a subway car by Paze and Fome (photograph by Martha Cooper)

musicals such as *Billion Dollar Baby* (1945) and *Arms and the Girl* (1950) as well as for the ballets *Interplay* (1943), choreographed by **Jerome Robbins,** and Agnes de Mille's *Fall River Legend* (1947). Both were debuted by **American Ballet Theatre.** Recent commisioned pieces include *I'm Old Fashioned (Astaire Variations)* (1983) for **New York City Ballet** and a Flute Concerto (1985) for the **Chicago Symphony Orchestra.**

A talented guest conductor as well, Gould has led several orchestras, and his recording of **Charles Ives**'s First Symphony with the Chicago Symphony won the 1966 Grammy for best classical recording. He has also served as president of the American Society of Composers, Authors, and Publishers (ASCAP) since 1986.

– L.D.S.

GRAFFITI ART

From the early 1970s through the mid 1980s New Yorkers in subway stations were the primary audience for graffiti art, which was probably more of a social phenomenon than an art movement. This sort of art was produced by streetwise teenagers and preteenagers from Brooklyn and the Bronx, who worked both individually and in groups. Mostly untrained, they surreptitiously and illegally used aerosol paint to adorn subway cars with vivid, cartoonlike imagery and writing.

Graffiti began to develop into graffiti art when these youths turned their elaborate "tags," or stylized names, into works that covered entire subway cars and included messages and images drawn from music, television, comic books, and other popular media. The reactions of viewers, who most often saw the work in motion, were mixed. **Pop artist Claes Oldenburg** said that graffiti art brightened the gray and gloomy stations "like a big bouquet from Latin America." Others, including the city government of New York, did not agree: a long and eventually successful campaign was launched to eliminate the graffiti.

By the 1980s, however, several new storefront art galleries in New York's East Village became venues for the works of artists who had begun to translate their graffiti imagery from trains to the canvas, attracting the interest of some collectors. In 1980 the Times Square Show, featuring graffiti art and other new-wave styles, also captured the interest of the New York art world. Graffiti artists were commissioned to create theater settings, advertisements, and album covers in the early 1980s. Jean-Michel Basquiat, who died in 1988, made the transition from being one of the original subway-and-street graffiti artists (using the tag Samo) to being a painter of considerable promise and prestige; in 1985 one of his paintings sold at auction for more than twenty thousand dollars. **Keith Haring,** a trained artist who experimented with graffiti art early in his career, retained the influence of the style in his later work. Despite such successes, however, the long-range reputations of other graffiti artists have yet to be seen.

REFERENCES:

Martha Cooper and Henry Chalfant, *Subway Art* (New York: Holt, Rinehart & Winston, 1984);

Chalfant and James Prigoff, *Spraycan Art* (London: Thames & Hudson, 1987).

– H.K.

MARTHA GRAHAM

Dancer and choreographer Martha Graham (1894–1991) was the most influential figure in modern dance. Her innovative techniques are the base from which the majority of later choreographers have worked, and they are more widely taught than any other Western theater dance outside of ballet. In addition to this technical development, the more than two hundred dances that Graham created constitute the backbone of modern dance as one of the fine arts.

Graham started dance training in 1916 at the Denishawn School in Los Angeles. In 1923 she began an independent career, appearing in Broadway revues. She established her own company in 1926 and began forming her own style. Rejecting the exotic orientalism of Denishawn, Graham explored the use of spare sets and movements as a means of expressing emotion and social themes. While not strictly narrative like ballet, her dances were dramatic, and she took her artistry seriously. Her first work to employ this style was *Heretic* (1929), and her innovations were indeed new and shocking. By the premiere of *Primitive Mysteries* in 1931, however, critics and audiences began to recognize Graham's talent and her contributions to modern dance.

Graham introduced men into her company in 1938 and began to choreograph several works drawing on American themes. *Letter to the World* (1940) is based on the life and poetry of Emily Dickinson, and her famous *Appalachian Spring* (1944) features music by **Aaron Copland.** Such pieces won her a wider public. In the late 1940s she grew attracted to myth and created a series of dances based on Greek and Hebrew themes, including *Errand in the Maze* (1947), *Judith* (1951), *Clytemnestra* (1958), and *Circe* (1963). By this time the Graham technique was firmly established and accepted, and she devoted

Martha Graham (photograph by Barbara Morgan)

herself to its continuation through teaching and new creations such as *Lucifer* and *The Scarlet Letter,* both choreographed in 1975 for Rudolf Nureyev. During 1953–1954 she and her company toured extensively for the State Department. She stopped performing in 1969 at age seventy-six but continued to choreograph until a year before her death.

REFERENCES:

Marian Horosko, comp., *Martha Graham: The Evolution of Her Dance Theory and Training, 1926–1991* (Chicago: Chicago Review Press, 1991);

Don McDonagh, *Martha Graham: A Biography* (New York: Praeger, 1973).

– D.M.

CARY GRANT

The epitome of the debonair leading man, Cary Grant (1904–1986) became well established as a movie star in farces and romantic comedies during the 1930s and remained a sought-after performer and box-office draw throughout the 1950s.

Born Archibald Leach in Bristol, England, he began performing at age six with Bob Pender's vaudeville troupe, specializing in clowning, acrobatics, and stilt walking. The troupe came to New York in 1920, Grant, who wanted to remain in America, began working with other vaudeville acts. By the end of the decade he was appearing on Broadway as an actor.

When he moved to Hollywood and signed a contract with Paramount in 1932, the studio made him change his name, and he became Cary Grant. After roles in a few forgettable films, he got his first break when Mae West cast him as her love interest in *She Done Him Wrong* (1933). Grant's screen personality in screwball comedies was established in *Topper* (1937), *The Awful Truth* (1937), and *Bringing Up Baby* (1938), the first of five pictures he made with Howard Hawks.

Director **Alfred Hitchcock** recognized Grant as the perfect lead for romantic thrillers, casting him in *Suspicion* (1941), *Notorious* (1946), *To Catch a Thief* (1955), and *North by Northwest* (1959). In the 1960s he played a similar role in Stanley Donen's *Charade* (1963) before being cast against type as an unshaven, reclusive South Sea island bum in *Father Goose* (1964). Even at sixty he was still the romantic lead, winning the character played by the much younger Leslie Caron. In *Walk Don't Run* (1966), however, he was an avuncular businessman playing matchmaker to his younger costars, Samantha Eggar and Jim Hutton. The film was Grant's last. In 1970 he received a special Academy Award (Oscar) for lifetime achievement.

REFERENCES:

Lionel Godfrey, *Cary Grant: The Light Touch* (New York: St. Martin's Press, 1981);

Charles Higham and Ray Moseley, *Cary Grant: The Lonely Heart* (San Diego, New York & London: Harcourt Brace Jovanovich, 1989).

– I.R.H.

Graphic Notation

One of many innovations in musical notation designed to accommodate new concepts after World War II, graphic notation is a way in which some composers attempt to reveal insights into their music to performers through visual images other than traditional notation.

Sometimes combined with conventional musical notation or verbal instructions, graphic notation offers composers more choices of methods by which to communicate their musical goals effectively, including designs, symbols, maps, and other illustrations. At the most extreme, such scores can seem more artistic than useful, particularly to performers trained primarily in reading traditional notation. Graphic notation is used most often in **aleatory music,** in which the composer includes chance elements in the work, and in indeter-

minate music, in which choices are offered to the performers. Graphic notation was first used by American composers such as Morton Feldman for his chamber piece *Projections* (1951) and Earle Brown for *December 1952* (1952). Both composers were influenced by **John Cage,** who later used graphic notation himself, as well as by the patterns and visual forms of **Abstract Expressionist** painting.

REFERENCE:

Reginald Smith Brindle, *The New Music: The Avant-Garde Since 1945,* second edition (Oxford & New York: Oxford University Press, 1987).

– L.D.S.

The Grateful Dead

Formed in 1965 in the **Haight-Ashbury** district of San Francisco, the Grateful Dead virtually invented psychedelic rock and continues to have a loyal following nearly three decades later.

Jerry Garcia (lead guitar), Ron ("Pigpen") McKernan (electric organ), Bob Weir (rhythm guitar), and Bill Kreutzmann (drums) — who had played together in an acoustic **bluegrass** group in Palo Alto — settled in Haight-Ashbury in early 1965 and formed an electric rhythm-and-blues group called the Warlocks. Later that year they added bass player Phil Lesh to the group and changed its name to the Grateful Dead. The band's participation in the multimedia Acid Tests staged sporadically by **Ken Kesey** and his Merry Pranksters in 1965–1966 inspired them to improvise with musical effects that could be made with electronic instruments, creating psychedelic rock, a musical style that has been copied by other bands. These performances, which were among the first to be accompanied by light shows (see Haight-Ashbury), made the group the most popular band in San Francisco.

After it was featured in Bill Graham's dance shows at the Fillmore Auditorium in San Francisco, the Grateful Dead was signed by M-G-M to record the single "Don't Ease Me In" (1966). The next year the group moved to Warner Brothers. Its national record sales were low until the release of the concert album *Live/Dead* (1969), which conveyed the innovative, often improvisational, nature of the band's performances — an energy that could not be conveyed in studio recordings. The Grateful Dead participated in **Woodstock** that year and in 1970 released the celebrated studio album *Workingman's Dead,* which includes the single "Uncle John's Band." The group's success led to longer tours and more concerts. The

The Grateful Dead in Haight-Ashbury, 1967: Bob Weir, Ron (Pigpen) McKernan, Jerry Garcia, Bill Kreutzmann, and Phil Lesh (photograph by Herb Green)

major blues influence of the band was lost, however, when McKernan died of a liver ailment in 1973.

During the band's nearly thirty years of existence the other core members have remained. They have been joined at various times by other musicians, most notably Mickey Hart, who played drums with the group in the late 1960s and again from 1975 to the present; Keith Godchaux, who replaced McKernan on the keyboard in 1971 and whose wife, Donna, became a vocalist with the band in 1972; and keyboard player Brent Mydland, who joined the band in 1979 after the Godchauxs left and remained with the group until his death in 1990.

By the early 1970s an intensely supportive group of "Dead Heads" were following the Grateful Dead from one concert to another. Many of them are known for experimenting with psychedelic drugs and supporting their bohemian lifestyle by selling T-shirts and jewelery in parking lots outside concerts. The Grateful Dead's live performances became increasingly popular as the band continued to make innovative use of electronic amplification for their trademark "wall of sound." The group did not release a recording from 1981 until 1987, preferring to showcase new songs in concert and, increasingly, to replay songs of the 1960s and 1970s from its own and other artists' albums. The group appeared to have become mainstream when its

1987 album, *In the Dark,* became a million-seller, and the single "Touch of Grey" was the group's first top-ten hit. In 1989 *Amusement Business* called the group one of the top-grossing musical entertainments in the country, able to earn as much as two million dollars in a weeklong series of concerts.

REFERENCES:

Gene Anthony, *The Summer of Love: Haight-Ashbury at its highest* (Berkeley, Cal.: Celestial Arts, 1980);

Paul Grushkin, Cynthia Bassett, and Jonas Grushkin, *Grateful Dead: The Official Book of the Dead Heads* (New York: Quill, 1983);

William Ruhlmann, *The History of the Grateful Dead* (New York: Gallery Books, 1990).

–J.E.F.

MICHAEL GRAVES

Michael Graves (1934–) has played a key role in the establishment and development of the **postmodern** style in architecture. He started his first architectural firm in 1964 in Princeton, New Jersey, and his early works, such as the Hanselmann House (1967) in Fort Wayne, Indiana, evince his aesthetic and stylistic association with the New York School of modernist architecture.

In the 1970s, however, Graves moved away from the impersonal Bauhaus-inspired modernist style to begin designing works in what is now called the postmodern style. Rather than the modernist basing of forms on a building's function, Graves's postmodern style gave a new importance to the idea of formal beauty for its own sake and included a revival of elements of ornamentation from classical and other historical styles. His Portland Public Services Building (1980–1982), for example, is designed in three distinct sections that suggest the base, shaft, and column of classical orders. Color is a central concern of his designs: that same building, for instance, is ornamented with color articulations of green, beige, and brown. In many of his works the placement of color is governed by its natural place in the environment, with earth tones near the bottom of the building working up to brighter blues closer to the top. He called this concept "representational" color.

Another characteristic of Graves's work is an emphasis on the entranceway. Whereas modernist architects had sought to integrate the interior and exterior worlds of a building — de-emphasizing the difference by using nondistinct entranceways as well as a light, skeletal structure with a large amount of glass — Graves dramatized this passage from outdoors to indoors. His design for the Clos Pegase Winery (1984) in

Napa Valley, California, for example, articulates an oversize entranceway with an imposing single column that supports a lintel and quasi arch.

Other works, such as the Swan and Dolphin resort hotels (1987) for Walt Disney World and numerous office buildings, museums, and residences throughout the world, have earned Graves widespread acclaim. His major accomplishment is his success in incorporating diverse elements from styles of the past into an urban grand-scale context. Since 1962 Graves has been the Schirmer Professor of Architecture at Princeton University.

REFERENCES:

David Dunster, ed., *Michael Graves,* Architectural Monographs 5 (New York: Rizzoli, 1979);

Karen Vogel Nichols, Patrick J. Burke, and Caroline Hancock, eds., *Michael Graves: Buildings and Projects, 1982–1989,* with essays by Robert Maxwell and Christian Norberg-Schulz (New York: Princeton Architectural Press, 1990).

–J.M.H.

CLEMENT GREENBERG

By the mid twentieth century many people found art difficult to understand because of its often-complex philosophical basis. Viewers of art, and frequently the artists themselves, increasingly turned to the art critic for explanations of existing art forms. In the United States in the late 1940s the **Abstract Expressionist** style particularly seemed to call for such an art authority. Art critic Clement Greenberg (1909–1994) rose to the occasion, offering forceful guidance as to what should be considered good modern art.

Greenberg is most significant for developing the idea of formalist art criticism, which evaluates the artwork on the basis of the artist's manipulation of formal elements — such as color, line, and composition — rather than its expression of some external symbolic meaning. Greenberg felt that expressionism, with its highly subjective nature, had become decadent, particularly in Europe. He urged American painters to become more "modern" in their art. To Greenberg, this modernism could be achieved only by reducing art to its basic formal properties. The artwork should divest itself of literary or symbolic connections as well as any characteristic that de-emphasized the two-dimensional nature of the canvas, such as the illusion of spatial depth.

Greenberg, therefore, approved of the abstract component of Abstract Expressionism but felt that the expressionist part weakened the ideological purity of the style. In fact, Greenberg became notorious for his well-publicized debates with art critic **Harold Rosen-**

berg on the subject of abstract painting — especially regarding **Jackson Pollock** and **Willem de Kooning,** the two major abstract painters of the time. Rosenberg championed de Kooning as the leading abstract artist because of the highly expressive quality of his painterly style, while Greenberg favored Pollock for his more completely abstract style.

In the 1950s Greenberg's formalist views increasingly began to influence artists. Early in that decade, at Greenberg's urgings, artist **Helen Frankenthaler** began to use a staining method rather than a paintbrush to apply color to the canvas. This technique separated the formal element of color even more from the expressionist gesture of the brushstroke and served to reaffirm the flatness of the canvas. By the early 1960s several artists — most notably Morris Louis, Kenneth Noland, and Jules Olitski — had begun to incorporate this staining technique in their paintings to form a loosely defined stylistic movement, which Greenberg named **Post-Painterly Abstraction.** In general, however, his formalist ideas have influenced the direction and interpretation of every abstract style since World War II.

REFERENCE:

Donald B. Kuspit, *Clement Greenberg: Art Critic* (Madison: University of Wisconsin Press, 1979).

–J.M.H.

GROVE PRESS

Founded in New York in 1949, Grove Press became one of the most influential literary publishing houses in America after Barnet (Barney) Lee Rosset, Jr., bought it in 1952. Grove was the foremost American champion of avant-garde literature during the 1950s and 1960s, and its battles against attempts to censor several of its books led to a new, more liberal, legal definition of the term *obscenity* by American courts.

During the 1950s and 1960s Grove published the work of authors such as Samuel Beckett, Jean Genet, **Jack Kerouac, Allen Ginsberg,** Jorge Luis Borges, Alain Robbe-Grillet, Hubert Selby, Jr., and LeRoi Jones (**Amiri Baraka**) in book form or in its influential literary journal, *Evergreen Review.*

In 1959, after Grove published the first unexpurgated American edition of D. H. Lawrence's *Lady Chatterley's Lover,* the U.S. Post Office seized 164 copies of the book in New York on the grounds that it was pornographic and could thus be barred from the mails. Grove challenged the post office, and later that year a federal court ruled in Grove's favor. Grove's publication of the first American edition of Henry Miller's

Tropic of Cancer in 1961 involved the company in more than sixty **censorship** actions. The publishers persevered, and in 1964 the U.S. Supreme Court decided that Miller's book was not obscene. Grove once again faced obscenity charges after it published the first American edition of **William S. Burroughs**'s *Naked Lunch* in 1962, but they successfully defeated attempts to ban the novel. These battles against censorship had powerful ramifications, not just for the publishing industry but for other entertainment and information media as well.

In 1986 Rosset sold Grove Press to Ann Getty. It merged with Atlantic Monthly Press in 1993.

REFERENCE:

Charles Rembar, *The End of Obscenity: The Trials of Lady Chatterley, Tropic of Cancer, and Fanny Hill* (New York: Random House, 1968).

– S.B.

JOHN GUARE

Since the late 1960s playwright John Guare (1938–) has been dramatizing the yearning for fame and money that lies at the heart of American culture.

Guare began his professional play writing career in 1964, with one-act dramas produced Off-Off-Broadway. He became known as a promising young dramatist after one of them, *Muzeeka,* won an Obie Award in 1968.

A few years later his growing reputation received a decided boost when his first full-length play, *The House of Blue Leaves* (1971), earned an Obie, as well as a New York Drama Critics Circle Award. The play mixes farcical humor and absurdist violence in a poignant look at the life of zoo keeper Artie Shaughnessy, who dreams of escaping his suffocating existence by committing his mentally ill wife, Bananas, to a hospital for the insane and becoming a song writer in Hollywood. Set in their Queens apartment on the day the pope is visiting New York, the play attacks religion and show business for encouraging unrealistic dreams and false hopes. Artie's son seeks instant fame by attempting to kill the pope with a homemade bomb and blows up two nuns instead. Artie is rejected by his oldest friend, the famous film director he had planned to join in Hollywood. At the end of the play he strangles Bananas and withdraws totally from reality. Frequently revived, *The House of Blue Leaves* remains Guare's best-known work.

That same season he wrote the book for a musical version of *Two Gentlemen of Verona,* which won an Antoinette Perry (Tony) Award and other honors in 1972. New York productions of Guare's next plays —

including *Marco Polo Sings a Solo* (1973), *Landscape of the Body* (1977), *Bosoms of Neglect* (1979), and *Lydie Breeze* (1982) — were greeted with less critical enthusiasm than *The House of Blue Leaves* and *Two Gentlemen of Verona.* Yet toward the end of this period he had success in another medium, writing the highly regarded screenplay for the Louis Malle film *Atlantic City* (1980). Focusing on the fantasies of a waitress in an Atlantic City casino and the positive results of her relationship with an aging, minor Mafia functionary, the film brought renewed esteem for Guare's skill in conveying the desperate hopes of "unimportant" people in a culture obsessed with the rich and famous.

In 1990 Guare produced a fresh treatment of this theme in *Six Degrees of Separation,* a major dramatic achievement. Inspired by an actual incident, the play depicts the attempt of a young, gay black man to ingratiate himself with a wealthy New York couple by pretending to be the son of Sidney Poitier and a schoolmate of their children. After the couple discovers that the young man has duped them and other well-to-do New Yorkers, they begin to recognize the emotional emptiness of their life. At the same time the play reveals the yearnings of those on the margins of American society to have such a life.

When Guare's *Four Baboons Adoring the Sun* opened in New York in 1992, reviewers called it interesting but flawed.

– I.R.H.

GUNSMOKE

Gunsmoke was the first and longest-lived of the television shows called "adult" westerns, as distinguished from children's adventure shows such as *The Lone Ranger. Gunsmoke* aired from 1955 to 1975, the longest run to date of any dramatic series with continuing characters, and its success inspired the creation of many other television westerns in the late 1950s. At one time there were thirty prime-time western series on the air.

Gunsmoke began as a radio series on the **CBS** network in 1952, with veteran character actor William Conrad in the role of Matt Dillon, sheriff of Dodge City, Kansas. When the show moved to television, James Arness assumed the role. (He had been recommended to the producers by the first choice for the part, **John Wayne.**) Arness and Milburn Stone, who played the town's doctor, "Doc" Adams, were the only cast members to appear for the entire series. Amanda Blake, who played Kitty Russell, proprietor of the Longbranch Saloon was with the series from the beginning but left one year before it finished its run. Other central characters were Matt's deputies, first Chester (Dennis Weaver) and then Festus (Ken Curtis). Burt Reynolds, appeared on the show from 1962 to 1965.

The show expanded from a half-hour to an hour in 1961, and toward the end of the decade — like many other series — it developed a social conscience, tackling issues such as civil rights. The one constant on the show was the character of Matt, who was the epitome of the incorruptible, solitary television western hero.

– C.D.B.

A. R. GURNEY

Albert Ramsdell Gurney (1930–   ) became well known in the 1980s with a series of innovative plays that dissect life in the increasingly isolated world of rich, white Anglo-Saxon Protestant (WASP) Americans.

Gurney had been writing plays — and having some of them produced Off-Broadway — for more than two decades before he gained public recognition with *The Dining Room* (1982), which examines four generations of a wealthy family through their table conversations in the same dining room. The ritual of social drinking provides the background for *The Perfect Party* (1986), in which entertaining is a vehicle for social climbing. In *The Cocktail Hour* (1988) a well-to-do family that has managed to avoid reality with the help of alcohol fears public humiliation after their son writes a play critical of their social class.

One of Gurney's favorite themes is how WASP social codes prevent emotional fulfillment. In *Sweet Sue* (1987), his first play to reach Broadway, an older woman who considers having an affair with her son's college roommate and the young man who is the object of her desires, are each played by two actors to illustrate their divided sensibilities. Gurney's best-known play is probably *Love Letters* (1989), which traces the relationship of an upper-class man and woman through the correspondence that has passed between them since childhood. Staged as readers' theater with the two performers seated facing the audience, the play is a moving dramatization of the damaging effect that hereditary privilege can have on the individual psyche.

– I.R.H.

PHILIP GUSTON

Canadian-born artist Philip Guston (1913–1980) is best known for his highly symbolic figurative works in an often crudely rendered style. In 1919 he moved with his family to Los Angeles, where he later attended Manual Arts High School with his friend **Jackson Pollock.** In

1935 the two young artists went to New York City to join the Federal Art Project of the Works Progress Administration (WPA). Guston was an active mural painter for the WPA until the early 1940s, when he switched to doing easel paintings.

His early paintings are in a figurative style and often treat social and political themes. His *Martial Memory* (1941), in which four children are engaged in an argument over their particular roles in a mock battle, becomes an allegory for the roles typically played in real warfare. In Guston's early works, figures are generally framed by strongly articulated, miniaturized architectural forms and imbued with an uncanny psychological aura, a combination reminiscent of the early works of Giorgio De Chirico.

In the late 1940s Guston began to reduce his figures to more-abstract images lacking the spatial depth of his earlier works. By the 1950s he had eliminated figures in favor of expressionist, painterly brushstrokes that shape overlapping color densities. However, many of these abstract paintings, such as *The Mirror* (1957), evoke a sense of a hidden presence, an almost-figurative image buried deep within the dense layers of paint.

In the late 1960s Guston completely changed his style again — this time to figurative works with images painted in a crudely outlined manner that has often been called cartoonlike. Many **Abstract Expressionist** artists who had admired Guston's abstract paintings scorned this new stylistic direction. The change also signaled his return to the allegorical treatment of social and political themes that had characterized his early works. The paintings of this last period often contain recurring symbolic images, such as the Ku Klux Klan hood — one he had begun to use in the 1930s — and the suitcase and the pile of shoes, which symbolize the transport of Jews with their belongings to concentration camps during the **Holocaust.**

REFERENCES:

Arts Magazine, 63 (November 1988): 40–71;

Philip Guston (New York: Braziller/San Francisco Museum of Modern Art, 1980).

–J.M.H.

ARLO GUTHRIE

Folk singer Arlo Guthrie (1947–   ) was a major figure in the **folk-music** phenomenon of the late 1960s. From that time he has used his music and celebrity status to promote liberal causes and political protest.

His father, the famous folk musician Woody Guthrie (1912–1967), wrote populist songs such as "This Land Is Your Land" (1944) and advocated leftist causes in the 1930s and 1940s. Although the elder Guthrie was incapacitated by Huntington's disease for the last fifteen years of his life, his work influenced many younger folk performers in the late 1950s and the 1960s, including Pete Seeger and **Bob Dylan.** Seeger served as a mentor to Arlo Guthrie as he began his own career in folk music in the mid 1960s, and the two often performed and recorded together. Like his father, Guthrie took up social concerns in his work, but he did so using self-deprecating humor in addition to singing and storytelling. This tone is most evident in the song that made him famous, "Alice's Restaurant" (1967). The eighteen-minute song is based on Guthrie's arrest on Thanksgiving Day 1965 for leaving trash outside the closed city dump for a restaurant in Stockbridge, Massachusetts, that attracted young hippies, and how this kept him from being drafted to serve in the **Vietnam War.** The song, which criticized the war, became an anthem of rebellion and protest in the late 1960s. Guthrie appeared in *Alice's Restaurant,* a film based on the song, in 1969.

Guthrie has continued to record and tour while supporting environmental causes and assistance to farmers, the homeless, and people with **AIDS.** In 1992 he purchased the church that housed the original Alice's Restaurant as a base for his projects and his Rising Son Records.

REFERENCES:

Janet Enright, "Remembering Alice," *Maclean's,* 99 (17 March 1986): 10–11;

Claudia Dreifus, "Arlo Guthrie," *Progressive* (February 1993): 32–35.

– D.H.-F.

GUTHRIE THEATER

The first major non–East Coast repertory theater in the United States, the Guthrie Theater in Minneapolis, Minnesota, is one of the most respected regional theaters in the country. It is known for its generally conservative repertoire and for its high technical standards.

It was founded as the Minnesota Theatre Company by Irish actor-director Tyrone Guthrie, producer Oliver Rea, and theatrical designer Peter Zeisler, who began planning the project in 1959 and saw its culmination in the 7 May 1963 opening of the 1,441-seat semicircular auditorium with its unique seven-sided thrust stage. Guthrie organized the project to allow American performers the repertory experience he had enjoyed in various theaters in the United Kingdom and Canada, and the theater has always devoted itself to nurturing younger talent. Guthrie left after the 1965–1966 season. The theater was renamed in his honor in 1970.

Since the beginning, the Guthrie Theater has presented classic dramas and comedies along with at least one major American play each season. During its first season, for instance, the theater offered William Shakespeare's *Hamlet,* Molière's *The Miser,* Anton Chekhov's *The Three Sisters,* and **Arthur Miller**'s *Death of a Salesman* with Hume Cronyn and Jessica Tandy as Willy Loman and his wife, Linda. Cronyn and Tandy also appeared in the American premiere of Cronyn and Susan Cooper's *Foxfire* in 1981. Since the 1970s the Guthrie Theater has added contemporary works, often by foreign playwrights, to its repertoire.

REFERENCES:

Tyrone Guthrie, *A New Theatre* (New York, Toronto, & London: McGraw-Hill, 1964);

Alfred Rossi, *Minneapolis Rehearsals: Tyrone Guthrie Directs Hamlet* (Berkeley: University of California Press, 1970).

– I.R.H.

H

HANS HAACKE

German-born artist Hans Haacke (1936–), a resident of New York City since 1962, is important for his **conceptual art** projects. His early work focused on the process of artistic creation rather than a final product and in the 1960s included a series of transparent, fluid-filled boxes he called "condensation cubes." The fluid in these cubes would fluctuate with temperature and air pressure so that the creation was never actually complete.

Since the early 1970s Haacke has engaged in art projects aimed at exposing immoral or ethically ambiguous situations to public view. His major conceptual works have focused on the practices of international corporations and well-established institutions such as museums. For example, in his piece in the 1970 Information exhibition at the **Museum of Modern Art,** Haacke polled museum visitors concerning the question of Governor Nelson Rockefeller's position on President Richard Nixon's policy in Indochina. Because Rockefeller and several of his family, friends, and business associates were major benefactors of and held important official positions at the MoMA, the conceptual project not only addressed the political issue but also challenged the ability of a museum to function as a neutral exhibition space. Similarly, Haacke probes the value of public institutions by exhibiting relevant documentary photographs and text that have often revealed telling truths about particular institutions or individuals.

REFERENCES:

Bruce D. Kurtz, *Contemporary Art 1965–1990* (Englewood Cliffs, N. J.: Prentice-Hall, 1992);

Brian Wallis, *Hans Haacke: Unfinished Business* New York: New Museum of Contemporary Art / Cambridge, Mass. & London: MIT Press, 1986).

– K.B.

MERLE HAGGARD

During the 1960s and 1970s singer, guitarist, and fiddler Merle Haggard (1937–) was one of the top talents in country music. Since 1966 he has had nearly forty number-one hit singles on the country charts. He is best known for his song "Okie from Muskogee" (1969), which became an anthem of reactionary backlash against hippie lifestyles and liberal attitudes in the late 1960s and early 1970s.

Many of Haggard's realistically gritty songs are based on his experiences of childhood poverty and adolescent crime. In the late 1950s he served almost three years in San Quentin prison for burglary. (He received a pardon from California governor Ronald Reagan in 1972.) After being paroled in 1960, Haggard began his career as a country musician. In 1965 he founded a band, the Strangers, and began recording extensively, touring the country, and appearing on television. In 1966 Haggard had his first number-one country hit, "I'm a Lonesome Fugitive," written by Liz Anderson. None of his successes, however, wove itself so effectively into American culture as did "Okie from Muskogee," with its celebration of small-town values and criticism of longhaired youth and "women practicing politics." As Haggard realized, "I had more than just a song on my hands." Since 1970 Haggard has continued to write, record, and perform, and in 1974 he achieved his only **crossover** hit, the recession-inspired song "If We Make It through December." He has also appeared in a handful of films, including *Bronco Billy* (1980) with **Clint Eastwood.**

REFERENCE:

Merle Haggard with Peggy Russell, *Sing Me Back Home: My Story* (New York: Times Books, 1981).

– D.H.-F.

HAIGHT-ASHBURY

In 1965–1967 Haight-Ashbury, a San Francisco neighborhood of run-down Victorian houses, became the birthplace of the **hippie** movement, whose influence spread worldwide, making a significant and lasting impact on twentieth-century culture.

Because of its inexpensive rental housing, Haight-Ashbury had been popular with students at San Francisco State College since the 1950s. In the 1960s the area also attracted writers and artists fleeing from raised rents and tourists in North Beach, the San Francisco home of the West Coast **Beat Movement.** Between October 1965 and June 1966 the estimated number of hippies in Haight-Ashbury rose from fewer than one thousand to about fifteen thousand. What made the hippies more that just a second-generation carbon copy of the Beats was the Haight-Ashbury drug of choice. Though the neighborhood was jokingly called "Hashbury" in reference to the widespread availability of illegal drugs such as hashish and marijuana, the drug at the root of the Haight-Ashbury lifestyle was LSD (lysergic acid diethylamide), which was legal until October 1966, when a California law making possession of the drug a misdemeanor went into effect.

For the original hippies, taking LSD was part of a serious search for self-knowledge and expanded consciousness that went along with the rejection of capitalist economics for communal living and shared resources. Among the most committed practitioners of this way of life were the Diggers, who gathered up neighborhood surpluses for redistribution. They prepared and served free food to anyone who wanted it and ran the Free Store, where clothing and other necessities were available at no charge and with no questions asked.

The Diggers, who "clerked" their store on roller skates, were practitioners of improvised, absurdist street theater. After tourist buses started driving through Haight-Ashbury so the passengers could stare at the "freaks," the Diggers passed out mirrors for local residents to hold up to the tourists. Some of the original Diggers were members of the San Francisco Mime Troupe. Founded in 1959, it was the oldest of the radical theater groups that flourished during the 1960s. In the mid 1960s the troupe's **mixed-media** presentations, in which colored slides were projected onto the bodies of dancers, were probably some of the earliest attempts to re-create the psychedelic, or mind-altering, sensation of an LSD trip.

As the use of LSD became openly recreational, **performance art** in Haight-Ashbury began not only began to mimic the drug's effects but also to create a congenial atmosphere in which to take it. In 1965 the short-lived band the Charlatans teamed up with artist Bill Ham, who was familiar with the Mime Troupe's use of light and movement, to create the first psychedelic rock performance. While the band performed, Ham projected huge swirls of color onto the walls of the room, causing the shapes to pulsate in rhythm with the music.

This innovation caught on with others, most notably with **Ken Kesey** and his Merry Pranksters, who used light shows at their Acid Tests in 1965–1966. These public LSD parties featured another Haight-Ashbury group, the **Grateful Dead,** who quickly became known as the ultimate psychedelic rock band, the one other musicians imitated. They were among the first bands booked by Bill Graham, who was just beginning his career as a rock entrepreneur, for his "dance concerts" at the Fillmore Auditorium. Among the other Haight-Ashbury bands Graham introduced to San Francisco and then the world were **Jefferson Airplane,** with lead singer Grace Slick; Big Brother and the Holding Company, with lead singer Janis Joplin; and Quicksilver Messenger Service. The posters for these concerts and other Haight-Ashbury events soon became collector's items, examples of a recognizable Haight-Ashbury style that may generally be described as a blend of elements from Aubrey Beardsley drawings and the religious art of Hinduism and Indian Buddhism.

The biggest Haight-Ashbury event was the Gathering of the Tribes for a Human Be-In on 14 January 1967 in nearby Golden Gate Park. The event was a collaboration between hippies and antiwar activists from Berkeley, veterans of the **Free Speech Movement** who considered the Haight-Ashbury "flower children" politically naive for their belief that they could change society simply by dropping out and meditating. Described as not just an antiwar protest but a celebration of peace and love, the rally was planned by Haight-Ashbury artist Michael Bowen and other neighborhood leaders with Berkeley **New Left** activist Jerry Rubin and West Coast Beat poet Gary Snyder. About twenty thousand people showed up to hear speeches from LSD guru **Timothy Leary,** Rubin, comedian/political activist Dick Gregory, and others. **Allen Ginsberg** read his poetry and led the crowd in chanting a Hindu mantra along with Beat poets **Lawrence Ferlinghetti,** Michael McClure, and Lenore Kandel. All the popular Haight-Ashbury rock groups performed as well. The meeting of generations and ideologies was judged a major success and spawned a whole series of "be-ins" and "love-ins."

Ironically, the Human Be-In marked the end of Haight-Ashbury's heyday. Encouraged by its positive results, the publishers of the *Oracle,* the Haight-Ashbury hippie newspaper, invited the world to San Francisco for a Summer of Love. Hordes of young people from all over the country followed the advice of singer Scott McKenzie, whose popular song told them "If you come to San Francisco, be sure to wear some flowers in your hair....summertime will be a love-in there." So many would-be hippies arrived, and stayed, that the Diggers could not feed them or find housing for them. Haight-Ashbury became a haven for runaways, and most of the people who had made it a real community with its own shops, newspaper, and support systems went elsewhere.

Yet by 1967 hippies were no longer a San Francisco phenomenon. Young people all over the country were forming their own hippie communes. The rock groups had national followings, and their performance style was imitated by others. Psychedelic posters were for sale nationwide, and bright, "psychedelic" colored clothing was in fashion. In fact, Haight-Ashbury culture had touched the lives of Americans who would never dream of trying LSD or joining communes.

REFERENCES:

Gene Anthony, *The Summer of Love: Haight-Ashbury at its highest* (Berkeley, Cal.: Celestial Arts, 1980);

Charles Perry, *The Haight-Ashbury: A History* (New York: Random House, 1984);

Helen Swick Perry, *The Human Be-In* (New York & London: Basic Books, 1970);

Jay Stevens, *Storming Heaven: LSD and the American Dream* (New York: Atlantic Monthly Press, 1987).

– K.L.R.

DAVID HAMMONS

After many years of creating art on the streets of New York City for an audience of people passing by, and showing his work in nonprofit community galleries, David Hammons (1943–   ) eventually came to national prominence at the end of the 1980s as one of the most important African-American artists in the United States.

Hammons's work consistently refers to African-American concerns. His works during the 1970s and 1980s were both poignant and radical and included materials evocative of African-American roots and realities, such as the hair of African Americans collected from barbershops, elephant dung wrapped with gold leaf, bottle caps folded to look like shells, and discarded wine bottles found around Harlem. He did a series of large sculptural pieces on the theme of the basketball hoop, all of which underline the game's symbolic associations as one of the few exit routes out of the ghetto for black males. One of these works, *Higher*

Goals (1983), consisted of a basketball hoop set atop a fifty-five-foot telephone pole, urging young black males to realize that "basketball is not the only road to success." Originally exhibited in a parking lot in Harlem, this work was eventually torn down by angry spectators. Other works of his have elicited such a strong reaction as well. His portrait of a white, blond-haired, blue-eyed Jesse Jackson — labeled boldly with the question "HOW YA LIKE ME NOW?" — was smashed down by ten angry men with sledgehammers moments after it was installed on a Washington, D.C., street.

Hammons was given a full-career survey, Rousing the Rubble, at the alternative space P.S. 1 in 1990, and his work has been featured in major exhibitions in the United States and Europe since then, principally in the context of site-specific **installations.** He has been a resident of Rome since 1989, although he works extensively on installation projects in the United States.

– K.B.

LORRAINE HANSBERRY

Lorraine Hansberry (1930–1965) was the first African-American woman to have a play produced on Broadway. In 1959 that play, *A Raisin in the Sun,* won the New York Drama Critics Circle Award for best American play of the year. It ran on Broadway for 580 performances and is now a classic of the American repertoire. Hansberry wrote the screenplay for the film version, released in 1961.

Born and raised in Chicago, Hansberry came from a family that was far more prosperous than the Youngers in *A Raisin in the Sun,* but she was no stranger to the sort of racism that keeps the Youngers from leaving a Chicago tenement for their own home in a white neighborhood. The greatest strength of the play, however, is not its social commentary but its dramatization of the conflict between parents and children with differing goals and desires. The theme of warring generations has had a long tradition on the American stage. Hansberry's second play, *The Sign in Sidney Brustein's Window,* has a far less conventional theme. Its protagonist is a white, Jewish intellectual who sees through everyone's pretensions but his own in his dealings with an assortment of characters that includes a prostitute, a black radical activist, and a homosexual writer.

By the time the play opened in October 1964, Hansberry was gravely ill with cancer, and she died a few months later. Her husband, Robert Nemiroff, gathered together selections from her finished and unfinished dramatic and nondramatic writings as *To Be*

Young, Gifted, and Black (1969), which ran in New York for more than a year. Nemiroff and Charlotte Zatzberg worked with lyricist Robert Brittan and composer Judd Woldin to adapt *A Raisin in the Sun* into the musical *Raisin* (1973), which ran on Broadway for nearly three years.

REFERENCE:

Anne Cheney, *Lorraine Hansberry* (Boston: Twayne, 1984).

– I.R.H.

HAPPENINGS

Happenings emerged in the New York art scene at the end of the 1950s as quasi-theatrical events created by artists for small public audiences. They ranged from tightly scripted pieces performed by artists and their friends in studios and art galleries to less-planned, outdoor events involving audience participation. Using bizarre, often-crude props — frequently including perishable goods from the urban environment — and discontinuous, illogical sequences of action and dialogue, creators of happenings did away with the traditional separations between art forms. Happenings provided a means by which artists could explore not only painting and sculpture but also theater, music, and other artistic mediums.

Allan Kaprow, the leading figure in the inception of the happening, coined the term and essentially created the form with his ninety-minute piece *18 Happenings in 6 Parts* (1959), a group of separate artistic events that was presented at the opening of the Reuben Gallery in downtown Manhattan. Several young artists (some eventually well known as **pop artists**) followed with their own versions of the happening, including Red Grooms's *Burning Building* (1959), Jim Dine's *Smiling Workman* (1960), and Robert Whitman's *American Moon* (1960). Although happenings became highly popular among many avant-garde artists, they did not receive serious critical attention. By the mid 1960s many of the artists originally involved with happenings went in other artistic directions; the happening as a vital art form had run its course. Many of its concepts, however, foreshadowed **performance art.**

Historical roots include the performances of Dadaists, Surrealists, and Futurists, as well as an evening of theater, poetry, and music organized by **John Cage** at **Black Mountain College** in 1952. Cage's philosophy, which advocated the "blurring of the distinction between art and life" and favored chance operations and audience involvement, was central to the momentum behind happenings, as were the artistic concepts already developed through the creation of **assemblage** and **environments.**

REFERENCES:

Barbara Haskell, *Blam! The Explosion of Pop, Minimalism and Performance 1958–1964* (New York: Norton/Whitney Museum of American Art, 1984);

Adrian Henri, *Environments and Happenings* (London: Thames & Hudson, 1974):

Allan Kaprow, *Assemblage, Environments & Happenings* (New York: Abrams, 1966).

– K.B.

KEITH HARING

When he died of **AIDS** in 1990 at age thirty-one, Keith Haring (1958–1990) was internationally known for an exuberant body of work based entirely on cartoonlike images that he drew and painted with enormous speed, agility, and spontaneity. Because he often drew in public, his practice as an artist sometimes extended into the realm of **performance**; by the time of his death it also incorporated themes of social activism and AIDS awareness.

Haring arrived in New York in the late 1970s as an art student, but he ignored the official avant-garde, instead finding inspiration in the **graffiti art** then widespread throughout the city. He began making chalk drawings in subway stations, often attracting crowds of bemused onlookers. Over the next five years he executed, by his own count, about five thousand subway drawings while also pioneering alternative formats for reproducing his work, such as on button pins, which he often gave away. Throughout the 1980s Haring's images proliferated, ultimately appearing on T-shirts, billboards, advertisements, and watches; on ghetto murals painted by him in collaboration with groups of teenagers and in museum and gallery exhibitions in Europe and the United States.

Haring sought a "democratic" form of contemporary art — one that was highly accessible to the general public. He said that this sort of art was "a lot closer to the way it was in primitive cultures when art was everywhere. . . ." He laid claim to a huge artistic vocabulary derived from a variety of sources, including folk art, cartooning and animation, graffiti, European and American painters, and **conceptual** art. **Andy Warhol** and **Walt Disney** were two of his idols.

Haring created an ever-expanding vocabulary of simple, iconic figures and rhythmic patterns. His humans are archetypal and universal, not usually possessing race, age, or gender. While his imagery appeared graphically primitive — such as the famous "Radiant Child," a crawling baby with short lines radiating from

Keith Haring executing a chalk drawing on a Tokyo sidewalk, 1988
(Estate of Tseng Kwong Chi)

its body — it nonetheless embodied a well-defined aesthetic, sexual, and political sensibility. Although visually playful, Haring's message was pointed: he was against nuclear weapons, drugs, racism, sexual discrimination, and insensitivity to victims of AIDS.

REFERENCES:

Germano Celant, ed., *Keith Haring* (Munich: Prestel-Verlag, 1992);

Bruce K. Kurtz, ed., *Keith Haring, Andy Warhol and Walt Disney* (Munich: Prestel-Verlag/Phoenix Art Museum, 1992).

–K.B.

HARPER'S MAGAZINE

Harper's Magazine is one of the oldest magazines in America. It was founded in 1850 by the Harper and Brothers publishing house because it had extra time to fill on their presses; by the end of the nineteenth century it was one of the most successful general magazines in America, distinguished by its intelligent and influential literary coverage.

In the twentieth century *Harper's* began publishing less fiction and more nonfiction; by the 1950s nonfiction dominated, with only one or two stories and a few poems in each issue. By the 1960s the magazine market had changed and the tradition-bound *Harper's* had trouble keeping its position. In 1967 Willie Morris, then only thirty-two, was appointed editor-in-chief. He virtually reinvented the magazine. *Harper's* became known for its publication of controversial articles, such as Norman Mailer's "The Steps of the Pentagon" (published in book form as *Armies of the Night*), which appeared in the March 1968 issue. In the May 1970 issue *Harper's* published Seymour M. Hersh's thirty-thousand word article, "My Lai: The First Detailed

Account of the Vietnam Massacre." Despite his success in boosting circulation, Morris was, in effect, forced to resign after printing Mailer's attack on feminism, "Prisoner of Sex," in the March 1971 number, which set a single-issue sales record for *Harper's*. Lewis Lapham became editor in 1976 and saw the magazine into the 1990s.

After Morris's departure, *Harper's* began a rapid financial decline and was nearly dissolved in 1980. It was saved from extinction by the John D. and Catherine T. MacArthur Foundation and Atlantic Richfield Foundation, which set up a nonprofit foundation to own and administer the affairs of the magazine. A scaled-down, rigidly departmentalized *Harper's* appeared in the 1980s. The "Harper's Index," a section of quirky statistics, was especially popular and widely quoted.

REFERENCES:

Lewis Lapham, "Advertisements for Themselves: A Letter from Lewis Lapham," *New York Times Book Review,* 24 October 1993, pp. 3, 39;

Willie Morris, *New York Days* (Boston: Little, Brown, 1993).

– R.T.

HEAVY METAL

Heavy metal is a type of hard rock that uses loud electric guitars, drums, and vocals. Featuring guitar solos and driving beats, the songs usually deal with adolescent rebellion, sex, and violence. These topics, along with occasional songs about death or the occult, have made heavy metal controversial. Heavy metal is especially popular among white, middle-class teens, particularly males. Its fans are called "headbangers."

Precursors of heavy metal in the late 1960s included **acid-rock** performer **Jimi Hendrix** and hard-rock groups such as The Who and **Led Zeppelin,** all of whom used highly amplified guitars. The term *heavy metal* comes from the band Steppenwolf's 1968 song "Born To Be Wild," which borrowed the phrase "heavy metal thunder" from **William S. Burroughs**'s novel *Naked Lunch* (1959). A British and American phenomenon, heavy metal was identified as a separate style of rock in the early 1970s; prominent heavy-metal performers included British groups such as Deep Purple and Black Sabbath and American performers such as Grand Funk Railroad (in the early part of the group's career), Aerosmith, and Ted Nugent, who said of his music, "If it's too loud, you're too old." Major heavy-metal hits of the 1970s included Aerosmith's "Walk This Way" (1976) and Nugent's "Cat Scratch Fever" (1977). An Australian band, AC/DC, was also

popular in America, where their song "Highway to Hell" (1979) and album *Back in Black* (1980) sold well.

Heavy-metal albums were popular in the 1970s, but the music was seldom played by mainstream radio stations because of its content. During the 1980s heavy metal became more diverse, and "pop-metal" musicians began to get air time on radio and especially **MTV.** By 1989 heavy metal was one of the best-selling kinds of rock, popularized through accessible groups such as the British band Def Leppard and the American groups **Van Halen,** Poison, and Bon Jovi. Heavy metal has retained its hard edge in "speed metal," "thrash metal," and "death metal." Popular groups in these categories include Guns N' Roses, Iron Maiden, Megadeath, Metallica, and Mötley Crüe.

Heavy-metal performers are as famous for their look and lifestyle as for their music. They tend to cultivate an image of being hard-living "bad boys," and they usually have long hair and tattoos and dress in leather and chains. Their live performances often include bizarre stage acts; Ozzy Osbourne, then with the group Black Sabbath, once reportedly bit the head off a live bat. The excesses of heavy metal were satirized in Rob Reiner's "rockumentary" parody *This Is Spinal Tap* (1984). Some heavy-metal fans at first thought the fictional band Spinal Tap was a real group, and even after they discovered that the film was ridiculing their favorite music, they continued to advocate both the film and the band.

REFERENCES:

Philip Bashe, *Heavy Metal Thunder* (Garden City, N.Y.: Doubleday, 1985);

J. D. Considine, "Metal Mania," *Rolling Stone,* no. 591 (15 November 1990): 100–104;

Jennifer Foote, "Making It in Metal Mecca," *Newsweek,* 114 (7 August 1989): 56–58.

– D.H.-F.

JASCHA HEIFETZ

For most of the twentieth century violin virtuoso Jascha Heifetz (1901–1987) was widely considered one of the best violinists in America.

Born in Vilnius, Lithuania, Heifetz began studying violin at age three and made his first public appearance there at six. Two years later he became a pupil of the renowned teacher Leopold Auer in St. Petersburg, and in 1911 he appeared in concerts in Berlin under conductor Artur Nikisch before embarking on a European tour. Leaving Russia because of the Bolshevik Revolution, Heifetz and his family immigrated to the United States in 1917, and he made his American debut in Carnegie Hall later that year. He was an immediate success. He became an American citizen in 1925 and toured and recorded extensively until the 1960s. During his long career, Heifetz was celebrated for his technically perfect playing, which he made to seem effortless through his extremely reserved style of performing. He was best known for his performances of Romantic works, especially the standard violin concertos such as those by Felix Mendelssohn and Pyotr Ilich Tchaikovsky. Though conservative in his musical tastes, he commissioned new concertos from Erich Gruenberg, Sir William Walton, Mario Castelnuovo-Tedesco, and others. He taught at the University of Southern California from 1961 to 1972, performing more often with chamber groups than as a soloist during these years. He retired as a solo performer in 1972. Heifetz also arranged and transcribed popular-music pieces for the violin.

REFERENCES:

Harold C. Schonberg, *The Glorious Ones: Classical Music's Greatest Performers* (New York: Times Books, 1985), pp. 368–381;

Artur Weschler-Vered, *Jascha Heifetz* (New York: Schirmer, 1986).

– L.D.S.

ROBERT A. HEINLEIN

Robert A. Heinlein (1907–1988) was one of the influential American **science-fiction** writers responsible for the expansion of the market for the genre beyond the pulp magazines. Some credit him with predicting or encouraging technological developments in his fiction decades before they became fact.

Heinlein began writing in the late 1930s and quickly became one of the top names of science fiction, producing dozens of stories for science-fiction magazines. His early stories and novels depicted realistic, imaginative futures in a readable, engaging style. After World War II he wrote increasingly for the slick, mass-market periodicals, turning his back on the pulp magazines, and set his sights on book publication. Between 1947 and 1963 he wrote fourteen well-received juvenile novels (see **young adult literature**), including *Starship Troopers* (1959), which was controversial for its militarism. During the 1950s Heinlein also wrote novels for adults. In addition, he helped with media adaptations of his work, such as the film *Destination Moon* (1950).

His best-known work, *Stranger in a Strange Land* (1961), was the first science-fiction novel to appear on the *New York Times* **bestseller list.** The story of a young man who is brought to Earth after being

Robert Heinlein and his wife, Virginia, on the set of *Destination Moon* (1950), a science-fiction movie for which he wrote the screenplay (collection of Virginia Heinlein)

raised by Martians, it became a cult phenomenon on campuses in the 1960s. The controversial treatment of sex and religion through lengthy dialogues in *Stranger in a Strange Land* established Heinlein's approach in most of his subsequent novels such as *I Will Fear No Evil* (1970), in which a man's brain is transplanted in a female body, as well as *Time Enough for Love . . .* (1973), *The Number of the Beast* (1980), *Friday* (1982), and *Job: A Comedy of Justice* (1984). With the exception of his more tightly plotted novel *The Moon Is a Harsh Mistress* (1966), critics generally find these efforts less appealing than his stories for juveniles. Yet when Heinlein died, his books had sold more than forty million copies around the world, and they remain popular.

REFERENCES:

H. Bruce Franklin, *Robert A. Heinlein: America as Science Fiction* (New York: Oxford University Press, 1980);

Joseph H. Olander and Martin Harry Greenberg, eds., *Robert A. Heinlein* (New York: Taplinger, 1978).

– D.H.-F.

JOSEPH HELLER

Joseph Heller (1923–) is considered a major American writer primarily on the basis of his first novel, *Catch-22* (1961). The title has become part of the English language as a term referring to paradoxical, self-reversing logic that creates a no-win situation.

Based on Heller's experiences in World War II, *Catch-22* deals with the efforts of its protagonist, Yossarian, not to be killed for a cause he cannot understand. The novel had mediocre sales and reviews when it was published in 1961. Yet later in the decade, its antiwar theme and its indictment of established institutions made it favorite reading for young people disaffected by government handling of the **Vietnam War.** Their enthusiasm led to new assessments of the novel and widespread critical acclaim. **Mike Nichols** directed a popular film version of the novel in 1970. In 1994 Heller completed *Closing Time,* a sequel to *Catch-22* that reveals what has happened to characters such as Yossarian and Milo Minderbinder, the corrupt mess officer, in the 1990s.

Heller's other novels — *Something Happened* (1974), *Good as Gold* (1979), *God Knows* (1984), and *Picture This* (1988) — share the **black humor** approach of his first novel to the search for sanity and identity within insane institutions and the subversion of language as a weapon of social control. Heller has also written plays, including *We Bombed in New Haven* (1968), *Catch-22: A Dramatization* (1971), and *Clevinger's Trial* (1973; based on chapter 8 of *Catch-22*). *No Laughing Matter* (1986), by Heller and Speed Vogel, is an account of Heller's successful battle with Guillain-Barré syndrome, a debilitating disease of the nervous system.

REFERENCES:

Robert Merrill, *Joseph Heller* (Boston: Twayne, 1987);

Sanford Pinsker, *Understanding Joseph Heller* (Columbia: University of South Carolina Press, 1991);

Stephen W. Potts, *Catch-22: Antiheroic Antinovel* (Boston: Twayne, 1989).

– D.H.-F.

LILLIAN HELLMAN

Before World War II Lillian Hellman (1906–1984) was the most accomplished female playwright of her time, and she had an unmatched record of hits on Broadway — including *The Children's Hour* (1936), *The Little Foxes* (1939), and *Watch on the Rhine* (1941). After the war she assumed the mantle of intellectual, particularly in political matters. She was the doyenne of the American literary left.

Hellman continued to write successful plays after the war, notably *The Autumn Garden* (1951), which was not a hit but which she, along with critics, considered her best play, and *Toys in the Attic* (1960), but she was best known for her nonfiction memoirs, *An Unfinished Woman* (1969) and *Pentimento* (1973), which recounted, among other friendships, her long-time relationship with Dashiell Hammett, played loose with the facts in portraying Hellman as a truth seeker willing to sacrifice all for her beliefs. That image relied largely on her highly publicized testimony in 1952 before the House Un-American Activities Committee, in which she, like several witnesses before her, agreed to testify about her own activities but refused to implicate others. Hellman successfully took her case to the court of public opinion, though: "I can not and will not cut my conscience to fit this year's fashions," she wrote in a widely published letter to the committee chairman. Her image was reinforced in the section "Julia" from *Pentimento,* a heroic — and largely fabricated — portrait of Hellman's defiance of the Nazis during World War II. In the acclaimed movie adaptation of the same name, Hellman was played by **Jane Fonda.**

REFERENCES:

Carl Rollyson, *Lillian Hellman: Her Legend and Her Legacy* (New York: St. Martin's Press, 1988);

William Wright, *Lillian Hellman: The Image, the Woman* (New York: Simon & Schuster, 1986).

– R.L.

ERNEST HEMINGWAY

By the time of World War II Ernest Hemingway (1899–1961) had already written his best work, but his reputation, which he cultivated as carefully as his literary ideas, grew steadily until his death. He was the best known and most highly regarded American writer in the world. His rugged good looks, hard-boiled attitude, and adventure-seeking persona attracted a large, loyal audience who looked to Hemingway as the literary spokesman of the time.

The high point of his career after the war was the publication of *The Old Man and the Sea,* a novel about an old fisherman struggling against hard times. *Life* magazine, which published the novel in full in its September 1952 issue, printed five million copies in anticipation of reader demand. The same month the novel was one-half of a dual featured selection of the Book-of-the-Month Club, and in its trade edition it remained on best-seller lists for a year and a half. The novel won a Pulitzer Prize for fiction and reaffirmed Hemingway as a leading candidate for the Nobel Prize, which he won in 1954.

Hemingway was too ill to travel to Stockholm to receive the Nobel Prize. He sent a statement to be read at the ceremony: "A Writer should write what he has to say and not speak it." By 1954, having endured two highly publicized plane crashes during his 1953 African safari, Hemingway was broken, both physically and mentally. His work reflected his anguish, and he slipped slowly into a depression that consumed him. He committed suicide on 2 July 1961.

The new writers of the postwar period, led by **Norman Mailer** and **James Jones,** were directly influenced by Hemingway. He was admired as an outstanding prose stylist and a tough-minded artist whose achievement shaped the postwar literary environment.

REFERENCES:

Carlos Baker, *Ernest Hemingway: A Life Story* (New York: Scribners, 1969);

Baker, ed., *Ernest Hemingway: Selected Letters, 1917-1961* (New York: Scribners, 1981).

– R.L.

JIMI HENDRIX

The most influential electric guitarist in rock music since the late 1960s, Jimi Hendrix (1942–1970) helped to create **acid rock** through his exploration of new playing techniques and sounds, particularly the use of feedback and other intentional distortions. Though many blacks were popular **rock 'n' roll** performers, Hendrix was the first black star of the innovative rock music that followed.

Born James Marshall Hendrix in Seattle, he taught himself to play guitar in his teens from listening to blues recordings. He began his career in the early 1960s as a studio musician and as a band member for touring performers. He formed his own band, Jimmy James and the Blue Flames, in 1965. The following year he created the Jimi Hendrix Experience with bassist Noel Redding and drummer Mitch Mitchell. Though fans who elevated the Jimi Hendrix Experience to cult status appreciated their albums, the group did not become widely known until after its performance at the Monterey Pop Festival in July 1967. Hendrix's stage antics — such as playing the guitar behind his back or with his teeth, or setting it on fire — often attracted more attention than songs such as "Purple Haze"

(1967) or their only **Top 40** hit in America, their version of **Bob Dylan**'s "All Along the Watchtower" (1968). Hendrix's image as a flamboyant showman was reinforced by D. A. Pennebaker's successful documentary *Monterey Pop* (1968).

With the 1968 double album *Electric Ladyland,* Hendrix began to focus more on experimenting with studio effects than on live performance. He also tried to remain innovative by forming a new group, Band of Gypsies, with bassist Billy Cox and drummer Buddy Miles. He performed with this group at **Woodstock** in 1969, where he closed with a shockingly distorted version of "The Star-Spangled Banner." In 1970 he died of asphixiation due to a drug overdose.

REFERENCES:

Curtis Knight, *Jimi: An Intimate Biography of Jimi Hendrix* (New York: Praeger, 1974);

Charles Shaar Murray, *Crosstown Traffic: Jimi Hendrix and the Post-War Rock 'N' Roll Revolution* (New York: St. Martin's Press, 1989).

– D.H.-F.

BETH HENLEY

Beth Henley (1952–) became a widely celebrated young playwright when her first full-length play, *Crimes of the Heart,* opened on Broadway in 1980 and won both a New York Drama Critics Circle Award and a Pulitzer Prize. Her reputation as a dramatist rests primarily on her funny and incisive probing of the stereotypes associated with Southern women.

A Southern **gothic** farce set in Henley's native Mississippi, *Crimes of the Heart,* which had premiered at the **Actors Theatre of Louisville,** is above all a showcase for acting talents in the roles of three distinctly different sisters: Lenny, Meg, and Babe MaGrath. The MaGrath family has been plagued by grotesque tragedies, beginning when their mother hanged herself and the family cat and continuing, as the play opens, with the news that the youngest sister, Babe, has shot her husband because she did not like his looks.

Henley's *The Miss Firecracker Contest* — which had a short run Off-Broadway in 1980, before the Broadway success of *Crimes of the Heart* — is another humorous study of quirky Southern women, this time centering on the competition to win a local beauty pageant. Henley has written other stage plays, most notably *The Wake of Jamey Foster,* which ran on Broadway in 1982, as well as screenplays, including the film version of *Crimes of the Heart* (1986), which earned her an Academy Award (Oscar) nomination for best adapted screenplay.

REFERENCE:
Billy J. Harbin, "Familial Bonds in the Plays of Beth Henley," *Southern Quarterly*, 25, no. 3 (1987): 81–94.

– I.R.H.

AUDREY HEPBURN

Audrey Hepburn (1929–1993) became an international film star in the 1950s, combining the grace and elegance of a ballerina with what reviewers repeatedly called a *gamine*, or playfully mischievous, quality, in a series of memorable roles.

Born Edda van Heemstra Hepburn-Huston in Brussels, Belgium, Hepburn was the daughter of a Dutch baroness and an English banker. She was educated for the most part in England but spent World War II in Holland, where she and her mother had gone on vacation and become trapped when the Germans invaded. After the war she returned to London, where she studied ballet and acting while working as a model. In 1951, the year she began playing small parts in British films, she met the French writer Colette, who insisted that Hepburn star in the stage adaptation of her novel *Gigi*, which opened on Broadway in November of that year. Hepburn's success led director William Wyler to cast her as the runaway princess in the film *Roman Holiday* (1953), for which she won an Academy Award (Oscar) for best actress in 1954. In that same year she was given an Antoinette Perry (Tony) Award for her performance in the Broadway production of *Ondine*.

Other noteworthy film roles followed these successes, including *Sabrina* (1954), *Funny Face* (1957), *The Nun's Story* (1959), *Breakfast at Tiffany's* (1961), *Charade* (1963), *My Fair Lady* (1964), and *Wait Until Dark* (1967). In 1968 Hepburn announced her retirement from films, but she returned to play an aging Maid Marian opposite Sean Connery as Robin Hood in *Robin and Marian* (1976). Though she subsequently had cameo roles in other films, Hepburn devoted most of her time after 1988 to working as a special ambassador for the United Nations Children's Fund (UNICEF). She visited young victims of famine in Somalia in 1992, only a few months before she was diagnosed with terminal colon cancer. In 1993, for her work with UNICEF, she was posthumously given the Jean Hersholt Humanitarian Award by the American Academy of Motion Picture Arts and Sciences.

REFERENCES:
Diana Maychick, *Audrey Hepburn: An Intimate Portrait* (Seacaucus, N. J.: Carol, 1993);

Ian Woodward, *Audrey Hepburn* (London: W. H. Allen, 1984).

– I.R.H.

JERRY HERMAN

Jerry Herman (1933–) has specialized in composing hummable hit tunes around which successful **Broadway musicals** such as *Hello, Dolly!* and *Mame* have been built.

Herman's first musical was *I Feel Wonderful* (1954), an Off-Broadway show for which he wrote the music and lyrics and also directed. After a successful revue, *Nightcap* (1958), and another unsuccessful musical, *Parade* (1960), Herman broke into Broadway in 1961 with two shows, *Milk and Honey* (1961) and *Madame Aphrodite*. His first solid hit was his music for *Hello, Dolly!* (1964). Both the show and the title song were popular. The musical, with the lead played by Carol Channing, had an original run of 2,844 performances, a record at that time, and it has been revived several times since, notably in a 1967 all-black production starring Pearl Bailey. **Barbra Streisand** played Dolly in the 1969 film, which featured **Louis Armstrong** singing the title song.

Herman repeated his success with the music for *Mame* (1966), which starred Angela Lansbury in the title role and ran for 1,508 performances. His next success came with the music for *La Cage aux Folles* (1983), by **Harvey Fierstein.**

REFERENCES:
Steven Suskin, *Show Tunes,* revised edition (New York: Limelight, 1992);

Mark White, *"You Must Remember This . . ."* (London: Frederick Warne, 1983).

– I.R.H.

EVA HESSE

Eva Hesse (1936–1970) is considered one of the most original sculptors of her generation, a reputation that has grown steadily since her early death at age thirty-four from a brain tumor. Born in Germany to Jewish parents, she fled with her family in 1939 to New York City and became an American citizen in 1945. After studying art at the Pratt Institute, the Art Students League, and Cooper Union, she received a B.F.A. from Yale University in 1959. Hesse worked first as a painter, making the transition to sculpture in the mid 1960s, while living in Germany.

Hesse's sculptural works are usually considered **postminimalist:** they often incorporate **minimalist** elements of repetition and limited color; yet they are imbued with a personal, evocative quality not present in most minimalist works. Hesse pioneered the use of nontraditional sculptural materials such as resins and fiberglass, employing them in highly original combinations to achieve sculptural forms that trigger visceral, often erotic, associations for the viewer. In *Contingent* (1969), for example, she hung from the ceiling eight large panels of cheesecloth coated with fiberglass and latex. As in many of her works, the thin, gracefully hanging forms have a sense of fragility and vulnerability in spite of their large scale. In *Untitled* (1970) she created seven large L-shaped, fiberglass-covered poles, which she grouped together on the floor. Their richly metaphoric presences suggest a host of possible associations, from trees to wormlike animals to ritualistic totems. Hesse's mature work — created over a period of only four years — is important for its exploration of both the formal and the expressive nature of absurdity, repetition, and other minimalism-derived extremes.

REFERENCES:

Helen A. Cooper, ed., *Eva Hesse: A Retrospective* (New Haven, Conn.: Yale University Press, 1992);

Lucy R. Lippard, *Eva Hesse* (New York: New York University Press, 1976).

– K.B.

CHARLTON HESTON

Ever since Charlton Heston (1924–) played Moses in Cecil B. DeMille's film *The Ten Commandments* (1956), the images of actor and biblical patriarch have been linked in the minds of American moviegoers.

In 1947 Heston began to get work in Broadway plays and on live television. After his first Hollywood film, *Dark City* (1950), he played the hard-driving circus boss in DeMille's *The Greatest Show on Earth* (1952), which won an Academy Award (Oscar) for best picture. Though Heston's screen identity has since been shaped by a series of parts as historical authority figures, the personality of this contemporary hero — admirable for his obsessive devotion to the circus and its employees — has also helped to define Heston's image.

Throughout the 1950s and 1960s Heston lent his authoritative presence to roles such as Michelangelo in *The Agony and the Ecstasy* (1965), John the Baptist in *The Greatest Story Ever Told* (1965), Mark Antony in *Julius Caesar* (1970), and the title roles in *El Cid* (1961) and *Ben-Hur* (1959, for which he won an Oscar for best actor). In the late 1960s and the 1970s he played in science-fiction films such as *Planet of the Apes* (1968) and *The Omega Man* (1971) and disaster movies such as *Earthquake* (1973). He even played a villain, Cardinal Richelieu, in *The Three Musketeers* (1974) and *The Four Musketeers* (1975). Heston had fewer film roles in

the 1980s and 1990s, but he remained busy on the stage and in television. In 1990 he played an appropriate cameo role, God, in *Almost an Angel,* a comedy starring Paul Hogan.

In 1963 Heston chaired a group of film and theater people supporting the **civil rights movement** and took part in **Martin Luther King, Jr.**'s march on Washington in August of that year. He has continued to lend his support to humanitarian causes, and in 1977 he received a special Oscar, the Jean Hersholt Humanitarian Award. He has also been a spokesman for the National Rifle Association as well as participating in film-industry politics, serving as president of the Screen Actors Guild (1965–1971) and chairman of the American Film Institute (1973).

REFERENCES:

Bruce Crowther, *Charlton Heston: The Epic Presence* (London: Columbus, 1986);

Charlton Heston, *The Actor's Life: Journals 1956–1976* (New York: Dutton, 1978).

– I.R.H.

JEROME HINES

Jerome Hines (1921–) is one of the best-known American opera singers of the twentieth century. He also used his resonant bass voice in recordings of religious music.

Hines made his professional debut in 1941, as Monterone in a San Francisco Opera production of Giuseppe Verdi's *Rigoletto*. As winner of the Caruso Award in 1946, Hines was invited to appear with the **New York Metropolitan Opera,** and his New York debut — as the Sergeant in Modest Mussorgsky's *Boris Godunov* — began what was to become the longest continuous vocal career at the Metropolitan, more than thirty-five years. Hines's voice captured the attention of maestro Arturo Toscanini, who invited him to sing and record performances of Ludwig van Beethoven's *Missa Solemnis*. These engagements helped to establish Hines as a concert singer as well. His performances of operatic roles are frequently studied by younger opera singers who wish to understand these characters, since Hines took a psychological and a historical approach in preparing for his stage roles. He also composed *I Am the Way* (1954), an opera based on the life of Jesus. It was produced at the Metropolitan in 1968. He published an autobiography, *This Is My Story, This Is My Song,* in 1968, and he wrote four one-act plays on Christian themes collected as *Tim Whosoever* (1970).

REFERENCES:

Jerome Hines, *This Is My Story, This Is My Song* (Westwood, N.J.: Revell, 1968);

Hines, *Great Singers on Great Singing* (Garden City, N.Y.: Doubleday, 1982).

– L.D.S.

HIPPIES

During the late 1960s and the early 1970s the young people who called themselves "hippies" urged a nation at war in **Vietnam** to put aside the quest for power and profit for a life grounded in their idealistic concepts of peace and love.

They were the successors to the **Beats,** who gave this younger generation of nonconformists the derisive label *hippies,* to indicate that they were junior "hipsters," one of the names the Beats applied to themselves. While the Beat movement started out in New York and later established an enclave on the West Coast, the hippie lifestyle had its genesis in California, especially in and around the **Haight-Ashbury** neighborhood of San Francisco, and spread eastward. While the term *hippie* was eventually applied to nearly anyone with long hair, the original hippies were linked not only by outward appearance but also by a social and personal philosophy that permeated every aspect of their daily existence.

Like the Beats, the hippies studied Eastern religion and used drugs in a search for inner peace and cosmic significance. Yet the hippies distinguished themselves from their elders by calling the Beats negative and accusing them of escapism. In contrast, the hippies shared the idealistic belief that they could change the world, mainly by following the dictum of LSD guru **Timothy Leary** to "turn on, tune in, and drop out." If people could find harmony with themselves and the universe through LSD and meditation, they would refuse to participate in mainstream society, which seemed to function to fulfill the demands of the military and big business. Then, the hippies believed, that power-hungry, profit-oriented society would cease to exist.

The hippies' experiments with communal living, vegetarian diet, and cooperative, nonprofit business ventures were advance outposts of the new society the hippies hoped to create. Only a few of their communes survived into the 1990s. Yet the hippies' influence is pervasive and ongoing. While the Beats were a literary movement that became a social phenomenon, the hippies began by creating a lifestyle that—especially in its early manifestation in Haight-Ashbury—made broad inroads into many aspects of American culture. In the

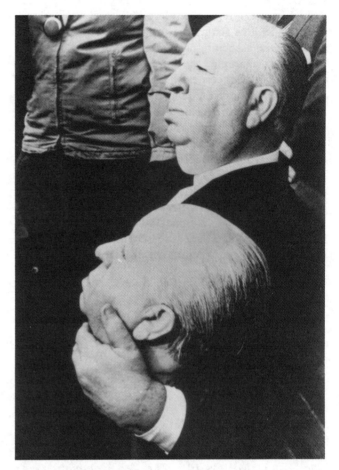

Alfred Hitchcock on the set of *Frenzy* (1972)

1990s its legacy is most apparent in the environmental movement, which draws on the reverence for and sense of connectedness with the natural world that were cornerstones of hippie philosophy.

– K.L.R.

ALFRED HITCHCOCK

Alfred Hitchcock (1899–1980) earned international recognition as a director of suspense thrillers in Britain in the 1930s and was brought to the United States by David O. Selznick in 1940. Although his first Selznick film, *Rebecca* (1940), was very successful, Hitchcock had trouble finding a distinctive touch for his American films in the 1940s. But *Strangers on a Train* (1951) began a decade-long creative burst during which he produced a string of masterpieces that made him one of the most admired filmmakers in the world: *Rear Window* (1954), *To Catch a Thief* (1955), *The Man Who Knew Too Much* (1956), *Vertigo* (1958), *North by Northwest* (1959), and *Psycho* (1960).

At this same time Hitchcock himself had become more recognizable than many of his stars because of his cameo appearances in his films and their trailers and, especially, through the droll introductions he provided as host of the television anthology series *Alfred Hitchcock Presents* (1955–1961). The combination of murder, suspense, romance, and black comedy in his films as well as their impeccable stylistic control — often employed to implicate the audience in the characters' guilt — have become the "Hitchcockian" standard imitated in countless succeeding films. Hitchcock made his last film, *Family Plot,* in 1976 and died in 1980, by which time he had received the 1979 American Film Institute Life Achievement Award and had been named a Knight Commander of the British Empire by Queen Elizabeth II.

REFERENCES:

Donald Spoto, *The Dark Side of Genius: The Life of Alfred Hitchcock* (Boston: Little, Brown, 1988);

Robin Wood, *Hitchcock's Films Revisited* (New York: Columbia University Press, 1989).

– I.R.H.

DUSTIN HOFFMAN

Dustin Hoffman (1937–) broke into films in the late 1960s, when antiheroic, ethnic actors without movie-star glamour were being given leading roles. Aided by a prodigious talent, Hoffman is still playing leads twenty-five years later.

Born in Los Angeles, he dropped out of Santa Monica City College to study acting at the Pasadena Playhouse. He then sought work on Broadway, where after many years of menial jobs and bit parts he gained critical acclaim for *The Journey of the Fifth Horse* and *Eh?* (both in 1966). Director Mike Nichols saw the former production and cast Hoffman in his career-making role as Benjamin Braddock in *The Graduate* (1967). When Hoffman revealed his acting range by playing a totally different character, the derelict Ratso Rizzo in *Midnight Cowboy* (1969), he earned his second straight Academy Award (Oscar) nomination and established himself as one of the most versatile performers in movies. Among his subsequent array of diverse characterizations are the picaresque Westerner adopted by Indians in *Little Big Man* (1970), comedian Lenny Bruce in *Lenny* (1974), Watergate reporter Carl Bernstein in *All the President's Men* (1976), the harried single father in *Kramer vs. Kramer* (1979), the starving actor who becomes a soap-opera star in drag in *Tootsie* (1982), the autistic savant in *Rain Man* (1988), and the title role in *Hook* (1991). Hoffman won best actor Oscars for both *Kramer vs. Kramer* and *Rain Man.*

REFERENCE:

Jeff Lenburg, *Dustin Hoffman: Hollywood's Anti-Hero* (New York: St. Martin's Press, 1983).

– I.R.H.

WILLIAM HOLDEN

Born William Franklin Beedle, Jr., film actor William Holden (1918–1981) played the average American guy, sometimes with a cynical twist on the type, from his first substantial role as the protagonist in *Golden Boy* (1939) to the world-weary television executive in *Network* (1976).

Holden signed to a contract with Paramount Pictures in 1938. After *Golden Boy,* his service in the army during World War II interrupted his career. His role in *Sunset Boulevard* (1950) as a struggling screenwriter manipulated by an aging film star (played by Gloria Swanson) elevated him to the first rank of Hollywood leading men, a position he retained throughout the 1950s. Holden's many notable films of the decade include *Stalag 17* (1953), for which he won an Academy Award (Oscar) for best actor; *The Country Girl* (1954); *Love Is a Many-Splendored Thing* (1955); and *The Bridge on the River Kwai* (1957). He continued to act in the 1960s and 1970s, but with the exception of his performances in *The Wild Bunch* (1969) and *Network,* most of his roles were no longer as significant. In 1981 he struck his head in a drunken fall and bled to death.

REFERENCES:

Laurence J. Quirk, *The Complete Films of William Holden* (Secaucus, N.J.: Citadel, 1986);

Bob Thomas, *Golden Boy: The Untold Story of William Holden* (New York: St. Martin's Press, 1984).

– I.R.H.

THE HOLOCAUST

The Holocaust was the systematic murder of European Jews by the Nazi regime of Adolf Hitler and collaborating governments before and during World War II. It is regarded as the most horrible occurrence of modern history. The Holocaust lasted some twelve years, beginning when the Nazis came to power in Germany in 1933. Jews were officially deprived of their basic rights in 1935, and on 9 November 1938, *Kristallnacht* (The Night of Broken Glass), the Nazis began a campaign of physical violence against Jews in Germany. In 1941 Hitler publicly proclaimed his "Final Solution," or *Endlosung*: the extermination of Jews and other undesirable elements of German society, including Gypsies, Communists, blacks, homosexuals, Jehovah's

Witnesses, and handicapped people. The Final Solution was formally adopted as government policy at the Wannsee Conference on 20 January 1942. Some six million Jews were executed and many others were forced into slavery at hundreds of concentration camps throughout Europe. Designated camps, notably Auschwitz in Poland, were devoted to mass executions, with factorylike gas chambers and cremetoriums. The Holocaust ended with the defeat of the Nazis in summer 1945.

Twenty-four principal Nazi leaders were tried for crimes against peace, humanity, and the laws of war by an International Military Tribunal at Nuremburg, Germany, in a showcase trial that lasted from 20 November 1945 to 1 October 1946. (Ten were hanged; one committed suicide on the eve of his execution; three were acquitted; and three escaped trial). In addition, the United States held a series of trials in the U.S. Occupation Zone during which 836,000 former Nazis were tried for various offenses; most of the 503,000 convicted received little more than token sentences.

For many Jews of the war generation, a central responsibility of their lives was to ensure that the memory of the Holocaust stayed alive, for all peoples, as the best means of preventing a recurrence. A body of Holocaust literature was created, including such popular works as the *Diary of Anne Frank* (1947), John Hersey's *The Wall* (1950), Leon Uris's *Mila 18* (1961), Saul Bellow's *Mr. Sammler's Planet* (1969) and William Styron's *Sophie's Choice* (1979). Death-camp survivor Elie Wiesel, whose parents and sister were exterminated, won the Nobel Peace Prize in 1986 for a canon marked by his intelligent obsession with the Holocaust. P.E.N., the international writers' organization, gives an annual award for the best work about the Holocaust. Yet, as a generation came of age that had no firsthand memory of World War II, the commemoration of the Holocaust seemed to fade, particularly in the view of Jewish elders, who remain convinced that to forget the horror was to risk repeating it. A 1992 public-opinion poll showed that 39 percent of all American high-school students and 28 percent of all adults were unaware of the Holocaust.

The U. S. Holocaust Memorial Museum in Washington, D.C., which opened in 1993, is dedicated to preserving the memory of the dead and of the abhorrent social conditions that led to their deaths.

REFERENCES:

Lucy Dawidowicz, *The War Against the Jews, 1933–1945* (New York: Free Press, 1975);

Martin Gilbert, *The Holocaust* (New York: Holt, 1985).

– R.L.

J. EDGAR HOOVER

From 1924 until his death, J. Edgar Hoover (1895–1972) was the director of the Federal Bureau of Investigation. Under his leadership the authority and scope of the FBI in crime fighting was greatly increased, and many improvements to police work and criminal investigations were introduced. But he also came under intense criticism for his management style and the authoritarianism of his leadership. Hoover built the FBI from a relatively obscure branch of the Justice Department into a formidable national police force with an internationally respected crime laboratory, a file of 191 million sets of fingerprints by the 1960s, and investigative reports on a huge number of suspected lawbreakers of all descriptions.

Hoover made a name for himself and the FBI through a largely successful campaign against organized crime in the 1920s and 1930s. When President Franklin D. Roosevelt gave the FBI broad powers in counterespionage and internal security in 1939, Hoover responded vigorously; countering espionage and subversion became a primary mission of the agency. It was a role that gained importance during the Cold War.

Hoover encountered his most vociferous criticism in the FBI's internal security functions. A friend of Sen. **Joseph McCarthy,** Hoover was a target of many of the same criticisms that were leveled against McCarthy. The FBI's counterintelligence program (Cointelpro), which Hoover established in 1956, was accused of widespread abuses of power. Under his direction, illegal wiretaps, infiltration of political groups deemed subversive, burglaries, kidnappings, and blacklisting occurred. Hoover was accused of using the agency to persecute his personal and political enemies; he kept files on the personal lives and sexual habits of many prominent political figures. Critics contended that Hoover exaggerated the threat of Communist subversion and manipulated crime statistics to further his own agenda and that his enforcement of federal civil-rights statutes was halfhearted.

Above all else Hoover was a masterful politician. For all the enemies he made in his long career, he had enough powerful friends in the political establishment to make his position secure. He was confirmed in his position by every president from Coolidge to Nixon. Despite the efforts of Attorney General Robert F. Kennedy to remove him and the constant acrimony that existed between the two in the early 1960s, Kennedy dared not fire him. Working under eight different presidents, who ranged from liberal to conservative, Hoover was indisputably one of the most powerful government officials of his time.

REFERENCES:

Ralph de Toledano, *J. Edgar Hoover: The Man in His Time* (New Rochelle, N.Y.: Arlington House, 1973);

Anthony Summers, *Official and Confidential: The Secret Life of J. Edgar Hoover* (New York: Putnam, 1993).

– W.L.T.

MARILYN HORNE

Marilyn Horne (1934–   ) is highly regarded as a major opera star. Her worldwide performances and numerous television appearances have helped to make opera popular with an audience far broader than the attendance at opera houses.

A mezzo-soprano, Horne first attracted widespread notice as the dubbed singing voice for Dorothy Dandridge in the 1954 film *Carmen Jones.* That year she made her operatic debut at the Los Angeles Guild Opera in Bedrich Smetana's *The Bartered Bride.* Horne perfected her singing technique in European opera companies from 1956 through 1959 and made her San Francisco Opera debut in 1960 as Marie in Alban Berg's *Wozzeck;* she also sang this role at her 1964

Marilyn Horne in a 1982 Ottawa production of George Frideric Handel's *Rinaldo* (photograph by Fernand R. LeClair)

London debut at the Royal Opera House, Covent Garden. In London, Horne became associated with the famous *bel canto* soprano Joan Sutherland and Sutherland's husband, conductor Richard Bonynge. They pointed Horne toward the nineteenth-century *bel canto* mezzo-soprano repertoire, with its emphasis on accuracy and tone rather than power, for which she has since become internationally renowned. One such role was Horne's **New York Metropolitan Opera** debut in 1970 as Adalgisa in Vincenzo Bellini's *Norma,* opposite Sutherland in the title role, conducted by Bonynge. This shift to *bel canto* was not surprising given the rare flexibility of Horne's voice, which allows her to sing different styles of music in the same recital and which critics have often cited as Horne's greatest asset. The Metropolitan Opera fired Horne in 1994, charging that she was difficult to work with.

REFERENCES:

Marilyn Horne with Jane Scovell, *Marilyn Horne: My Life* (New York: Atheneum, 1983);

Winthrop Sargeant, *Divas* (New York: Coward, McCann & Geoghegan, 1973).

– L.D.S.

VLADIMIR HOROWITZ

Vladimir Horowitz (1903–1989) was one of the most famous and respected classical pianists of the twentieth century. He successfully combined technical mastery and a reserved playing style with passionate interpretations of Romantic composers. His performances inspired scores of pianists, who often tried unsuccessfully to imitate his sound and his flat-fingered playing technique.

Born in Ukraine, Horowitz debuted in Russia in 1920 and began touring Europe in 1925. By his first performance in the United States in 1928, he had earned an international reputation. In 1933 Horowitz married Wanda Toscanini, daughter of Italian maestro Arturo Toscanini; both did much to further Horowitz's career in the West. Often unpredictable in temperament, Horowitz periodically quit performing during his career but continued to record prolifically. His first "retirement" came during 1936–1938. Horowitz's temperament also influenced his interpretations of standard piano works. He believed that interpretation was an activity for performers, not necessarily linked to the composer's directions on a printed score. Horowitz was thus most effective in pieces where his playing style was matched by the music, particularly in works by Franz Liszt, Sergey Prokofiev, and Sergey Rachmaninoff, as well as the Baroque composer Domenico Scarlatti.

Vladimir Horowitz practicing in Carnegie Hall for a 1965 concert

Horowitz settled in America in 1940 and became a United States citizen in 1945. He "retired" from concert tours again from 1953 to 1965, and his return to the stage was a media event. After his next "retirement" (1969–1974) he gave the first piano recital ever held at the **New York Metropolitan Opera** at Lincoln Center. As he resumed touring in the late 1970s, Horowitz became famous for his eccentricities, such as traveling with an entourage that included his wife, valet, secretary, piano tuner, recording engineers, and cook along with his beloved Steinway piano. Before his death, he returned to Russia for a 1986 tour.

REFERENCES:

David Dubal, *Evenings with Horowitz: A Personal Portrait* (New York: Birch Lane Press, 1991);

Glenn Plaskin, *Horowitz: A Biography of Vladimir Horowitz* (New York: Morrow, 1983);

Harold C. Schonberg, *Horowitz: His Life and Music* (New York, London, Toronto, Sydney, Tokyo, & Singapore: Simon & Schuster, 1992).

– L.D.S.

HORROR FICTION

Before World War II the audience for horror fiction was mostly confined to the readership of small-circulation pulp magazines, but by the late 1960s and early 1970s writers such as Ira Levin and **Stephen King** had attracted millions of new readers to the genre with **best-selling** novels published by large mainstream commercial publishers.

The supernatural frequently appears in horror fiction, therefore scholars often categorize it as a type of fantasy (see **science fiction and fantasy**). Horror fiction originated in the **Gothic fiction** of the late eighteenth and early nineteenth centuries, the tales of Edgar Allan Poe and Nathaniel Hawthorne, and the Victorian ghost story, but American horror fiction was equally shaped by horror films of the 1930s and pulp magazines specializing in genre fiction, especially *Weird Tales* (1923–1954), which published several writers of horror fiction including **Ray Bradbury** and Fritz Leiber. Horror fiction, mostly short stories, slowly began to enter mainstream American culture before 1945.

In the 1950s horror novels such as Richard Matheson's *I Am Legend* (1954) and Jack Finney's *The Body Snatchers* (1955) appeared, and Robert Bloch explored the boundary between normality and abnormality in *Psycho* (1959), the basis for **Alfred Hitchcock**'s famous film of the same name (1960). Despite the popularity of these books and others such as Shirley Jackson's *The Haunting of Hill House* (1959), horror fiction in general continued to have a relatively small readership and remained unprofitable for publishers during most of the 1960s. This situation began to change with the success of Ira Levin's *Rosemary's Baby* (1967), William Peter Blatty's *The Exorcist* (1971), and Thomas Tryon's *The Other* (1971). Levin's novel was groundbreaking as well for its contemporary setting and its humor — features incorporated in much horror fiction since then, including Stephen King's.

King followed his first novel, *Carrie* (1974), with several bestsellers; his incredible success transformed horror fiction into a distinct, profitable publishing category. Also, his example solidified the dominance of novels over short stories in the horror genre. Imitators capitalized on the market opened by the success of King and writers such as V. C. Andrews, whose *Flowers in the Attic* (1979) and its sequels were also bestsellers. Other significant horror writers who emerged in the 1970s include Dean R. Koontz, Robert R. McCammon, and especially **Anne Rice** for her modernizations of classic horror figures. Peter Straub uses several such motifs, with other horrors, in his 1979 novel *Ghost Story*.

After the commerical (if not critical) success of horror fiction in recent decades, some critics wonder if it has reached a dead end, through either repetition or a descent into gore, as in recent "splatterpunk" fiction. Still, academic attention to horror fiction has grown since the 1970s, and the genre continues to sell.

REFERENCES:

Neil Barron, ed., *Horror Literature: A Reader's Guide* (New York and London: Garland, 1990);

Stephen King, *Stephen King's Danse Macabre* (New York: Berkley, 1981).

– D.H.-F.

ALAN HOVHANESS

Alan Hovhaness (1911–) has consolidated the elements of his Armenian and Scottish ethnic background with non-Western music to produce a large body of work that is strikingly original.

Born Alan Hovhaness Chakmakjian in Massachusetts, Hovhaness began composing in the 1940s. His traditional early works gradually evolved into the hybrid style of most of his prolific output, which includes more than fifty symphonies alone. In the early 1940s he began to incorporate Armenian folk music into his own, and in the 1950s and 1960s he experimented with non-Western styles, especially Asian music. In his work since then Hovhaness has combined improvisation with repetition and fragmentation. Representative works include his *Fantasy on Japanese Woodprints* (1965) for xylophone and orchestra and his tone poem *And God Created Great Whales* (1970) for orchestra, with the actual sound of whales played on tape to accompany human performers.

– L.D.S.

THOMAS HOVING

During his ten years as director of the Metropolitan Museum of Art in New York, Thomas Hoving (1937–) combined forward-looking artistic vision with political savvy to revolutionize the concept and perception of American museums. Under Hoving's leadership, the museum drew an audience that represented a much wider cross-section of society than ever before.

After receiving a Ph.D. in art history from Princeton University in 1959, Hoving went to work on the curatorial staff of the Metropolitan Museum, soon becoming medieval curator of the Cloisters. He left the museum in 1965 to join Mayor John V. Lindsay's administration as commissioner of parks, making political connections that would later prove valuable. Two years later he was invited back to become the museum's director. Immediately he introduced programs reflecting his view that a museum should try to attract a wide audience — and to make money doing it. He developed the idea of the "blockbuster" exhibition, bringing together important groups of pieces from all over the world to be shown in spectacularly designed settings. The first of these shows was the In the Presence of Kings exhibition (1967), comprised of royal objects from many different cultures. Hoving and designer Stuart Silver created an extravaganza, with the objects displayed by category in "theme" galleries with walls painted in rich colors and flanked with cloth banners. Other blockbuster exhibitions included The Great Age of Fresco (1968–1969) and The Year 1200 (1970), all put together with the same pizzazz that has become Hoving's trademark. He was also largely responsible for bringing the historically important King Tutankhamen exhibition to the United States in 1975.

In 1968–1969 Hoving created controversy with his Harlem on My Mind show. A photographic documentary on the plight of black Americans, the exhibition was accompanied by a catalogue that many perceived as anti-Semitic. The trustees ordered the catalogue removed from sale at the exhibition, and several factions — including black and Jewish groups — protested the show. As with all of Hoving's important exhibitions, however, attendance was gratifying.

Hoving significantly enlarged the offerings of the museum shop, creating a relatively inexpensive way for consumer society to "purchase art," with sales of such items as replicas of coins and small statues, as well as jewelry and other items of personal apparel based on works in the museum's collections. Museums around the country imitated this successful venture. With his articulate, persuasive manner, he successfully courted such wealthy patrons as Nelson Rockefeller, Walter Annenberg, and Brooke Astor to fund expensive projects. Thus, he was often financially able to procure important artworks at phenomenal prices, such as Diego Velazquez's *Juan Pareja* for $5.5 million. After leaving the museum in 1977, Hoving remained in New York City, where he has written several nonfiction books as well two novels.

REFERENCE:

Thomas Hoving, *Making the Mummies Dance: Inside the Metropolitan Museum of Art* (New York: Simon & Schuster, 1993).

–J.M.H.

Elizabeth Taylor and Rock Hudson on the set of *Giant* (Kobal Collection)

TINA HOWE

Tina Howe (1937–) has written evocative plays about the white Anglo-Saxon Protestant (WASP) upper class in America, often from the perspective of a young female artist.

From a prominent New York family with New England roots, Howe wrote her first play as a student at Sarah Lawrence College (B.A., 1959) and continued writing others while teaching high school in the 1960s. Her first professionally produced play, *The Nest,* was staged in Provincetown, Massachusetts, in 1969 and Off-Broadway in 1970. *Birth and After Birth,* produced Off-Broadway in 1974, was followed by New York Shakespeare Festival productions of *Museum* in 1977 and *The Art of Dining* in 1979; these examinations of woman as artist brought her critical recognition. Howe's most highly regarded play to date, *Painting*

Churches, which premiered Off-Broadway in 1983 and earned her an Obie, focuses on a young woman portrait painter who realizes the complexity of her relationship with her parents when she encounters difficulties in getting representations of them "right" on canvas.

The central character in *Coastal Disturbances,* which opened Off-Broadway in late 1986 and transferred to Broadway in February 1987, is a female photographer who finds and loses love during a weekend at the beach. Howe has called *Approaching Zanzibar,* produced Off-Broadway in 1989, "a shockingly personal play" in which a family's crosscountry trip is "my own journey [to] face my own fears."

REFERENCE:

Ross Wetzsteon, "The Mad, Mad World Of Tina Howe: A Blue-Blood Playwright's Antic Vision, *New York,* 16 (28 November 1983): 58–71.

– I.R.H.

ROCK HUDSON

Tall, dark, and handsome, actor Rock Hudson (1925–1985) was a classic Hollywood leading man during the 1950s and 1960s, but he will also be remembered as the first major film star to die of **AIDS.** His death marked the beginning of celebrity involvement with AIDS as a cause and of greater public awareness about the disease.

Born Roy Harold Scherer, Jr., he later took the last name Fitzgerald when he was adopted by his stepfather. His agent renamed him Rock Hudson in 1947. Hudson's first film role was a small part in *Fighter Squadron* (1948). After he signed a contract with Universal Studios in 1949, he played several small parts in studio westerns and adventure films during the early 1950s. His good looks made him a fan favorite, and he began to get romantic leading roles in melodramas directed for Universal by Douglas Sirk, including *Magnificent Obsession* (1954), *All That Heaven Allows* (1956), *Written on the Wind* (1956), and *The Tarnished Angels* (1958). During this period he also starred in the Warner Bros. epic *Giant* (1956) with **Elizabeth Taylor** and **James Dean.** Hudson received his only Academy Award (Oscar) nomination for his portrayal of the flawed but admirable Bick Benedict in *Giant.*

Pillow Talk (1959), with **Doris Day,** was the first of many romantic comedies in which Hudson appeared. A more challenging dramatic role in *Seconds* (1966), now a cult film, did not translate into box-office success. By the 1970s Hudson had shifted his priorities from feature films to television, where his comic detective series *McMillan and Wife* (*McMillan* in the final season) ran from 1971 to 1976 on the *NBC Mystery Movie.* He had just completed a stint on the evening soap opera *Dynasty* in 1985 when his illness was revealed and his long-rumored homosexuality was confirmed publicly.

REFERENCES:

Rock Hudson with Sara Davidson, *Rock Hudson: His Story* (New York: Morrow, 1986);

Jerry Oppenheimer and Jack Vitek, *Idol: Rock Hudson — The True Story of an American Film Hero* (New York: Villard Books, 1986).
– I.R.H.

KAREL HUSA

Karel Husa (1921–), a Czech-American composer and conductor, has written extensively for concert band and orchestra. His works are direct in their appeal, many having been inspired by world events during the second half of the twentieth century.

He studied music at the conservatory in his native Prague (1941–1945) and from 1946 to 1949 in Paris, where his teachers included Nadia Boulanger and Arthur Honegger. He published his first composition, Sonatina for Piano, in 1943. Immigrating to the United States in 1954, Husa joined the music faculty of Cornell University, where he taught until retiring in 1992. He has written works in nearly every genre using a variety of styles and techniques, including **serial music** and **aleatory music.** He was awarded the Pulitzer Prize for his String Quartet No. 3 (1969). Two of his scores have been widely acclaimed: *Music for Prague 1968* (1968) was written in response to the Soviet invasion of Czechoslovakia, and *Apotheosis of This Earth* (1970) was inspired by the threat of world destruction. Both were written for concert band and later transcribed for orchestra, and *Music for Prague 1968* has received more than seven thousand performances worldwide.

REFERENCE:
Susan Hayes Hitchens, *Karel Husa: A Bio-Bibliography* (New York, Westport, Conn., & London: Greenwood Press, 1991).
– L.D.S.

JOHN HUSTON

John Huston (1906–1987), film director and screenwriter whose movies celebrate misfits, underdogs, losers, and obsessives, was the son of actor Walter Huston. He dropped out of school at fifteen to become a boxer and for the next twenty years led a restless, roistering life as an actor, cavalryman, and writer. In 1938 he signed a screenwriting contract with Warner Bros., and over the next three years he received a writer's credit on half a dozen films, including *Jezebel* (1938) and *Sergeant York* (1941), before he was given the assignment to direct *The Maltese Falcon* (1941) from his own screenplay. The movie is considered a classic, and for the rest of his career he directed all of his own screenplays, except for *Three Strangers* (1946).

During World War II Huston directed three prizewinning documentaries, and upon his return to civilian life he entered a period of remarkable creativity, directing and writing the screenplays for *The Treasure of Sierra Madre* (1948), for which he won two Academy Awards (Oscars), for best director and best screenplay; *The Asphalt Jungle* (1950), written with Ben Maddow and nominated for both the Writers Guild Award and the Academy Award for best screenplay; *The African Queen* (1951), written with James Agee and nominated for the Academy Award for best screenplay; and *Moulin Rouge* (1952), written with Anthony Veiller and nominated for a Writers Guild Award.

Beginning in the late 1950s Huston directed a series of movies in which he had no writing role. The quality of those works was erratic, but high achievements always compensated for the disappointments. Some of his best work (*The Man Who Would Be King*, 1975; *Wise Blood*, 1979; and *Prizzi's Honor*, 1985) was done when he was disabled with emphysema. Despite his illness Huston was brilliant in the role of the avaricious and perverse Noah Cross in *Chinatown* (1974). Huston was presented with the American Film Insti-

tute Life Achievement Award in 1982 and has the distinction of being the only filmmaker to direct both his father, director Walter Huston (in *The Treasure of Sierra Madre*), and his daughter, Anjelica Huston (in *Prizzi's Honor*), to Oscar-winning performances.

REFERENCES:

Scott Hammen, *John Huston* (Boston: Twayne, 1985);

Stuart Kaminsky, *John Huston: Maker of Magic* (Boston: Houghton Mifflin, 1978).

                                                              – I.R.H.

I

I Love Lucy

I Love Lucy was one of the most successful television shows in the history of American broadcasting. It ran originally for ten years (1951–1961) and has been on the air in syndication ever since. Its screwball depiction of married life set the pattern for half-hour-format situation comedies, which dominated the prime television viewing hours for decades.

The show starred Lucille Ball as Lucy Ricardo, a New York housewife, and Desi Arnaz as her husband, Ricky, a Cuban bandleader. Also featured were the Ricardos' landlords and best friends, Fred and Ethel Mertz (played by William Frawley and Vivian Vance). In 1957, while the series was still one of the highest rated on the air, the two stars ended regular production. Until 1961 the CBS network continued to show reruns of earlier episodes in prime time with occasional new hour-long episodes.

In 1950 Ball and Arnaz, who were married, created Desilu Productions, which produced *I Love Lucy* as well as other popular television series, notably *The*

Keith Thibodeaux, Desi Arnaz, Lucille Ball, William Frawley, and Vivian Vance, in a 1957 episode of *I Love Lucy* (© 1957 CBS, Inc.)

Untouchables (1959–1963) and *Star Trek* (1966–1969). Soon after their divorce in 1960, Arnaz sold his interest in the company to Ball, and she sold out to Gulf & Western in 1967. Ball starred in *The Lucy Show*, the first of several shows that would confirm her as the "first lady of American television." By the time the last of these, *Here's Lucy*, left the air in 1974, Ball had been entertaining television audiences for nearly twenty-five continuous years.

REFERENCES:

Bart Andrews, *Lucy & Ricky & Fred & Ethel: The Story of "I Love Lucy"* (New York: Dutton, 1976);

Coyne Steven Sanders and Tom Gilbert, *Desilu: The Story of Lucille Ball and Desi Arnaz* (New York: Morrow, 1993).

— C.D.B.

IMPRINT PUBLISHING

The term *imprint* refers to the designation of the publisher in a book. It may be the publishing house (Random House) or a division of the publishing house (The Modern Library). A personal imprint is the indication on the title page that the book is part of a group of books under the responsibility of a particular editor. Certain books published by Harcourt Brace Jovanovich bear the imprint "A Helen and Kurt Wolff Book"; and it is generally accepted that personal-imprint publishing was introduced by William Jovanovich when he offered a co-publishing arrangement to the Wolffs in 1961. The personal imprint may result from a partnership between an independent editor and the publishing house, or it may indicate that an editor employed by the house has special authority and responsibility for the books that carry his imprint.

Not all imprints are personal imprints; most imprints identify a series or line of titles. Thus Houghton Mifflin has fifteen imprints, of which three (preceded by asterisks below) are personal imprints: American Heritage Dictionaries, American Heritage Library, Cambridge Editions, Clarion Books, *A Peter Davison Book, Field Guide Series, *A Marc Jaffe Book, *Seymour Lawrence, Riverside Editions, Riverside Literature Series, Riverside Reading Series, Riverside Studies in Literature, Sandpiper Paperbacks, Sentry Editions, Travel Guides. A series imprint normally belongs to the publishing house, but a personal imprint may change houses.

— M.J.B.

WILLIAM INGE

During the 1950s William Inge (1913–1973) was the most popular serious playwright in the United States, with four Broadway hits dramatizing the dreams and frustrations of small-town Midwesterners. Yet after 1958 he never had another successful play, and his reputation as a dramatist has been eclipsed by his contemporaries **Arthur Miller** and **Tennessee Williams.**

A native of Kansas, Inge was living in St. Louis and working as a cultural reporter and critic for the *St. Louis Star-Times* when he interviewed and became friends with Tennessee Williams in 1944. Williams encouraged Inge's ambitions as a playwright, and Inge's first completed effort, the one-act *Farther off from Heaven* was produced by Margo Jones at her Dallas theater in 1947. He then transformed a short story he had been working on for some time into a full-length play, *Come Back Little Sheba,* the sympathetic portrait of a troubled marriage. Doc, an alcoholic chiropractor who gave up his dream of becoming a medical doctor to marry his pregnant girlfriend, Lola, who has become a bitter slattern after losing the baby in an incompetent delivery that has left her sterile. The Theatre Guild production of the play, which ends with a qualified hope of reconciliation, was a hit, due in part to Shirley Booth's strong performance as Lola.

The success of his first play, which ran for 190 performances, assured the Broadway production of Inge's second. *Picnic* (1953), which dramatizes the profound effect a twenty-four-hour visit from a virile, if none-too-bright young man has on a group of lonely, unfulfilled women, ran for more than a year on Broadway. It earned Inge a Pulitzer Prize and was voted best American play of the year by the New York Drama Critics Circle. *Bus Stop* (1955) — developed from *People in the Wind,* a one-act play he had written in the early 1950s — and *The Dark at the Top of the Stairs* (1957) — a reworking of *Farther off from Heaven* — had equally impressive runs on Broadway. These sympathetic treatments of lonely, purposeless characters who find the courage to embrace new possibilities were Inge's last hit plays. In 1959 *A Loss of Roses* closed after 25 performances on Broadway and uniformly negative reviews. Dismayed, Inge turned to film work, writing the script for *Splendor in the Grass* (1961), which won him an Academy Award (Oscar) for best original screenplay. Starring **Warren Beatty** and Natalie Wood, Inge's portrayal of young love destroyed by small-town puritanism and pressure to conform, was a box-office success. Though he continued to write for stage and screen, Inge never again had a critical or commercial hit in either medium. He began to feel that the subject he knew best, life in the rural Midwest, had become old-fashioned, and his attempts to write about "hip" urban characters met with failure. Troubled by inner conflicts about his homosexuality and increasingly dependent on drugs and alcohol, Inge sank into despair and finally committed suicide by carbon monoxide poisoning in 1973.

REFERENCES:

R. Baird Shuman, *William Inge,* revised edition (Boston: Twayne, 1989);

Ralph E. Voss, *A Life of William Inge: The Strains of Triumph* (Lawrence: University Press of Kansas, 1989).

                                                                    – I.R.H.

Insider Trading

Insider trading came to represent the greed, corruption, and conspicuous consumption associated with the 1980s. Specifically, the phrase describes the illegal activity of using information not available to the public to make a profit in the stock market. Since such profit ultimately comes at the expense of unwary stock holders, the practice is essentially theft.

Market manipulators and arbitrageurs, or traders who take advantage of inequities in the market, made huge fortunes during the 1980s. Led by head of high-yield securities at the investment-banking firm Drexel, Burnham, Lambert, Michael Milken — the "junk bond guru," as he was known because of his advocacy of high-risk, high-yield investments — corrupt investors created an atmosphere of deceit and corruption that symbolized the me-first attitude of the 1980s. Arbitrageur Ivan Boesky and investment bankers Martin Siegel and Dennis Levine were villainized as principals in sensationalized scams, but the problem was endemic. Whole investment houses during the decade artificially inflated stock and securities prices so they could take advantage of manipulated markets in schemes that violated securities laws.

The earnings were enormous and the money lust was insatiable. Milken earned $550 million in a single year and complained that it was not enough. It was estimated that his earnings by 1986 were in excess of $3 billion, leaving him enough to remain one of the richest men in the world even after he had pleaded guilty to securities fraud, paid a $600 million fine, and served three years of a ten-year jail sentence. Boesky, Siegel, and Levine also pleaded guilty to their crimes, paid substantial fines, and were banned from securities trading; Boesky and Siegel served short jail sentences. Though laws were tightened to prevent a recurrence, it was generally conceded that insider trading was so prevalent, the symptom of such a basic lapse of values,

Michael Milken giving a speech on Latin-American debt in front of a photograph of himself at a conference in Tijuana, Mexico (UPI)

that laws were inadequate to address the problem: the inside traders represented prevalent social attitudes.

REFERENCE:

James B. Stewart, *Den of Thieves* (New York: Simon & Schuster, 1991).

                                                                    – R.L.

International Style

Also known as "modernist architecture," the International Style dominated American urban architecture and city planning from the immediate post–World War II period to well into the 1970s. Its initial development took place in several different countries during the early part of the century. By the 1920s its leaders included Ludwig Mies van der Rohe and Walter Gropius in Germany and Le Corbusier in France. While many of his aesthetic aims were unrelated to those of the International Style, American architect Frank Lloyd Wright contributed to its development as well, particularly in his early work. The term *International Style* was coined by American architect **Philip Johnson** and architectural historian Henry Russell Hitchcock.

The sources of the International Style are complex and include early-twentieth-century European art movements as well as utopian social philosophies. In general, the progressive architects involved in the development of the International Style sought an alternative to the eclecticism of nineteenth-century academic building design. They objected particularly to the continued reliance on historical styles for types of surface design, which they considered obsolete, meaningless overornamentation when applied to twentieth-century urban architecture. The pioneers of modern architecture searched instead for an aesthetic that would be original to the twentieth century — based on functionalism and reflecting advances in industrial technology. In 1937 both Mies van der Rohe and Gropius immigrated to the United States and brought with them mature architectural styles that gave a new level of prestige to the evolving American modernist style. Gropius influenced several generations of American architects, including **I. M. Pei** and Johnson. Mies van der Rohe was also influential, producing buildings that were to have a profound impact on American architectural practices. These works included his seminal Farnsworth House (Plano, Illinois, 1946–1950) as well as the thirty-nine-story Seagram Building in New York City (with Johnson, 1956–1958), considered by many to be the paragon of postwar skyscraper design.

By the early 1950s the International Style was well entrenched in cities across the United States and had unmistakable characteristics that were clearly visible in the designs of many new skyscrapers: chiefly, the absence of decoration and ornament; the use of rectangular forms, flat roofs, exterior grid patterns, and curtain walls (rather than load-bearing walls); an extensive use of glass; and a preference for industrial materials such as the steel frame and reinforced concrete. The International Style became the style of choice for large corporations seeking a sleek, progressive appearance. Beginning with the creation of the Lever House (New York City, 1950–1952) by the firm Skidmore, Owings, and Merrill, the steel-and-glass box based on the principles of Mies van der Rohe became the signature style for business headquarters throughout the United States.

The popularity of the International Style highrise led, however, to a decline in many of the positive qualities it had originally represented. For example, Mies van der Rohe espoused the use of high-quality materials (such as the amber-tinted glass and bronze of the Seagram Building), the reduction of all elements to purified, rational forms, and the rigorous refinement of proportion and detailing. During the 1950s and 1960s his many imitators and their clients turned Miesian architectural principles into a deadening cliché. Too many impersonal glass boxes and sterile, antisocial spaces began to dominate the American urban landscape. Skepticism about modern architecture and its extreme uniformity began to appear in the mid 1960s in the form of **postmodernist** criticism. Among the most important critics of the International Style — or rather what it had become — was architect, teacher, and writer **Robert Venturi.** In a much-quoted statement, he took Mies van der Rohe's dictum regarding the formal elements in architecture — that "less is more" — and turned it around, stating that "less is a bore." Venturi's ideas, the work of other architects such as **Michael Graves** and **Frank Gehry,** and many other factors have had wide-ranging influence on the ongoing liberation of younger architects from the strictures of the International Style, helping to propel architectural theories of the late twentieth century into a far more open-ended, if yet uncharted, territory.

REFERENCES:

William J. R. Curtis, *Modern Architecture since 1900,* second edition (Englewood Cliffs, N.J.: Prentice-Hall, 1987);

Lawrence Wodehouse, *The Roots of International Style Architecture* (West Cornwall, Conn.: Locust Hill Press, 1991).

– K.B.

IOWA WRITERS' WORKSHOP

The oldest and probably the best college creative-writing program in the United States is the Writers' Workshop at the University of Iowa. Even before the official founding of the Writers' Workshop in 1939, Iowa was noted for its creative-writing courses. Novelist Wallace Stegner, who went on to win a Pulitzer Prize for *Angle of Repose* (1971) and a National Book Award for *The Spectator Bird* (1976), earned a master's degree in creative writing from Iowa in 1931, as did poet Paul Engle, who headed the Writers' Workshop for more than twenty years (1942–1965). Engle is usually credited with building the reputation that the program has today. Since his retirement George Starbuck (1965–1970), John Leggett (1970–1987), and Frank Conroy (1987–) have run the program.

A majority of the students in any writing program do not succeed as writers. Yet the number of Writers' Workshop students who do make names for themselves is unusually high. The impressive list of fiction writers who have attended the Writers' Workshop includes **Flannery O'Connor,** John Gardner, **Raymond Carver,** John Edgar Wideman, **John Irving,** Gail Godwin, and James Alan McPherson. Poets who have studied at the workshop include W. D. Snodgrass, Donald Justice, and **Robert Bly.**

The Writers' Workshop attracts good students with a faculty list that reads like a who's who of American literature. Over the years the opportunity to study with major poets, such as **Robert Lowell** and **John Berryman,** and notable fiction writers, such as **Philip Roth,** Vance Bourjaily, Richard Yates, **Kurt Vonnegut Jr.,**Robert Coover, and John Cheever, has attracted many talented young writers to Iowa. Several of them have either returned to the Writers' Workshop to teach, or taught creative writing at other colleges and universities, forming a network of friends and colleagues that can be an invaluable resource for the beginning writer.

REFERENCE:
Stephen Wilbers, *The Iowa Writers' Workshop: Origins, Emergence, & Growth* (Iowa City: University of Iowa Press, 1980).
                                                                                – K.L.R.

JOHN IRVING

John Irving (1942–), whom *Time* magazine hailed as the "most successful 'serious' young writer in America" (31 August 1981), presents a tragicomic picture of a modern world plagued by violence, terror, and sudden death. Though his novels include elements of the sort of **black humor** employed by fiction writers such as John Hawkes and **John Barth,** Irving rejects their experiments with narrative form to write fairly straightforward, accessible fiction, following the example of another black humor writer, **Kurt Vonnegut, Jr.** Tracing the origins of increasing modern violence to events immediately preceding World War II, Irving places his comic, eccentric characters in extreme situations, often with fatal consequences.

Irving's first three novels — *Setting Free the Bears* (1968), *The Water-Method Man* (1972), and *The 158-Pound Marriage* (1974) — were virtually ignored by the reading public. His fourth book, *The World According to Garp* (1976), however, sold 120,000 copies in hardback and more that 3 million paperback copies by 1979. The novel was on the *New York Times* **best-seller list** for twenty-five weeks, and its main character, writer T. S. Garp, became a sort of cult hero. Irving's next novels — *The Hotel New Hampshire* (1981), *The Cider House Rules* (1985), and *A Prayer*

for Owen Meany (1989) — did not match the popular success of *The World According to Garp,* but Irving continues to win respect from critics, who point out that his fiction is structurally and philosophically more complex than it seems to most casual readers.

Like **Joyce Carol Oates,** Irving has been accused of including too much violence in his fiction; yet Irving maintains that there is far more violence in the real world than in his novels. If anything, he believes, in conveying "how perilous and fragile our lives can be," his fiction should give readers "a strong incentive to live purposefully, to be determined about living well."

REFERENCES:
Carol C. Harter and James R. Thompson, *John Irving* (Boston: Twayne, 1986);
Edward C. Reilly, *Understanding John Irving* (Columbia: University of South Carolina Press, 1991).
                                                                                – R.T.

BURL IVES

Burl Ives's popular arrangements of **folk music** since the 1940s have helped to spread its appeal to a large audience. As an actor, he is especially remembered for his portrayal of Big Daddy in **Tennessee Williams's** play *Cat on a Hot Tin Roof* (1955) and in the 1958 film version. He was also the narrator of the animated Christmas television special *Rudolph, the Red-Nosed Reindeer* (1964), in which he introduced the now-classic "Holly Jolly Christmas."

Burl Icle Ivanhoe Ives (1909–) left college in the 1930s to travel North America as a folk singer. He settled in New York in 1937 and performed in clubs. He began appearing in small roles in **Broadway musicals,** starting with Richard Rodgers and Lorenz Hart's *The Boys from Syracuse* in 1938. From 1940 to 1942 he had his own radio program, *The Wayfaring Stranger,* on **CBS.** During the 1940s Ives was extremely popular, and he made many recordings, including songs such as "Blue Tail Fly" with the Andrews Sisters (1948) and "Riders in the Sky" (1949). Unlike Woody Guthrie, Ives performed his songs in a polished style, which led some critics to accuse him of turning folk songs into pop music. He also began arranging and preserving folk songs for collections such as *The Burl Ives Song Book* (1953) and *Song in America: Our Musical Heritage* (1962).

Ives's acting career prospered during the 1950s as he appeared in several productions, including a 1954 revival of the musical *Show Boat* and the Broadway premiere of *Cat on a Hot Tin Roof.* He received an

CHARLES IVES

Charles Ives (1874–1954) was a pioneer in the evolution of twentieth-century music. His experimental techniques and methods, anticipating those attributed to Arnold Schoenberg and Igor Stravinsky, placed him in the forefront of a distinctly American school of composition that later included **Aaron Copland,** Walter Piston, **Virgil Thomson,** and Roy Harris.

The son of a Connecticut band director, Ives studied composition while taking general coursework at Yale University (1894–1898). Upon graduation, he embarked on a business career that developed into a prosperous insurance partnership. Ives's music, which he wrote in his spare time, became increasingly distinctive, complex, and often surrealistic, employing extreme dissonance as well as polyrhythmic and polytonal devices. He often used American folk material and hymn tunes, sometimes unrecognizably embedded in the thick textures of the music. Ives's compositions, written mostly during the 1900s and 1910s, include four symphonies, four sonatas for violin and piano, two piano sonatas, two string quartets and other chamber works, more than a hundred songs, several choral works, and smaller pieces for piano and for orchestra. Although his symphonies are considered too difficult for most orchestras to play, orchestral suites such as *Three Places in New England* (1914) as well as piano and vocal works are commonly performed today.

Although virtually all of Ives's music was written between 1895 and 1930, it was not until decades later that most of his work was published, appreciated, or performed. His gargantuan *Concord Sonata* (*Piano Sonata No. 2 [Concord, Mass., 1840–1860],* 1915), considered by many to be his finest work, premiered in 1939 in New York, while his Third Symphony (1911) brought the composer a Pulitzer Prize in 1947. The Fourth Symphony (1916) finally received a complete performance in 1965 through a grant provided by the Rockefeller Foundation to compensate for the extra rehearsals needed before the musicians could play the difficult score. Though he was often overlooked during his lifetime, since his death Ives has become one of the most influential modern composers.

Burl Ives as Big Daddy in the Broadway premiere of Tennessee Williams's *Cat on a Hot Tin Roof* (photograph by Zinn Arthur)

Academy Award for best supporting actor in *The Big Country* (1958); his other films include *East of Eden* (1955), *Desire under the Elms* (1958), and *Our Man in Havana* (1959). In addition to his movies, Ives's career was helped by the folk-music revival of the late 1950s and the 1960s, and in 1962 he had three top-ten songs on the country-music charts. Since the 1960s Ives has continued to perform in concerts and on television and film.

REFERENCE:
Burl Ives, *Wayfaring Stranger* (New York: Whittelsey House, 1948).

– D.H.-F.

REFERENCES:
J. Peter Burkholder, *Charles Ives: The Ideas behind the Music* (New Haven and London: Yale University Press, 1985);

Henry and Sidney Cowell, *Charles Ives and His Music,* second edition (New York: Oxford University Press, 1969).

– E.M.M.

J

Michael Jackson

Michael Jackson (1958–   ) is one of the most successful popular-music stars of the twentieth century. Having sold more than thirty million copies worldwide, Jackson's album *Thriller* (1982) is the best-selling single album of all time, according to the *Guinness Book of World Records*. Jackson also holds the record for the number of Grammy Awards received in one year: eight in 1984.

Jackson began his musical career in 1965 as a singer with four of his brothers in a rhythm-and-blues group, the Jackson Five (the Jacksons after 1975). They had four hits in 1969 and 1970, including "ABC" and "I'll Be There." In 1971 Jackson also began to pursue a solo career, enjoying early hits with "Rockin' Robin" (1971) and "Ben" (1972). He remained with the group until the late 1970s, when his own career improved with his appearance as the Scarecrow in the 1978 film *The Wiz* and his 1979 album *Off the Wall* — the first of a series of albums produced by **Quincy Jones,** who helped to shift Jackson's style to pop and soul. The album featured hits such as "Don't Stop Till You Get Enough," "Rock with You," and "She's Out of My Life."

Jackson achieved superstardom with the release of *Thriller* in 1982. Its hit songs — including "Thriller," "Billie Jean," and "Beat It" — were promoted through popular music videos on **MTV** featuring Jackson's hyperkinetic dancing. He performed with other stars in **"We Are the World,"** a 1985 Grammy Award winner for best song, which he and Lionel Richie wrote in support of the African famine relief campaigns of the mid 1980s. Jackson starred in the short science-fiction film *Captain Eo,* which opened at Disneyland and Disneyworld in the late 1980s. His 1987 album *Bad* includes the song "The Way You Make Me Feel," and

Dangerous (1991) features "Black or White." He undertook a concert tour of the United States in 1988 and a world tour in 1993.

An intensely private and eccentric man, Jackson has been subjected to heavy media scrutiny since the early 1980s. This attention was heightened by his colorful outfits and dramatic changes in appearance. In 1993 Jackson's world tour was cut short amid widely publicized accusations that he had molested a thirteen-year-old boy. No criminal charges were filed after the boy's civil suit was resolved with a multimillion-dollar settlement out of court.

REFERENCES:

Paul Honeyford, *The Thrill of Michael Jackson* (New York: Quill, 1984);

Michael Jackson, *Moonwalk* (New York, London, Toronto, Sydney, & Auckland: Doubleday, 1988).

– L.D.S.

Randall Jarrell

Randall Jarrell (1914–1965) is best known for his World War II poems, especially "The Death of the Ball-Turret Gunner," which is frequently anthologized, and for children's books, such as *The Bat-Poet* (1964) and *The Animal Family* (1965), that depict a dream world underlying everyday reality. He also wrote *Pictures from an Institution* (1954), a novel based on his experiences while teaching at Sarah Lawrence College in 1946–1947, and influential literary criticism on poets such as **Robert Frost**, **William Carlos Williams**, **Wallace Stevens**, **Marianne Moore**, and **Robert Lowell**. His translations of fairy tales and works for adults are widely respected.

Poets Randall Jarrell and Robert Lowell with novelist Peter Taylor, 1948. The three writers became friends while they were studying under poet and New Critic John Crowe Ransom.

Although he studied under John Crowe Ransom, John Davidson, and **Robert Penn Warren** and counted Allen Tate among his mentors, Jarrell rejected the rural, conservative emphasis of these Fugitive Poets and **New Critics**. A poet of urban and suburban life in the United States, he considered himself a Freudian and a Marxist in his view of history but not politics. (He was a political liberal.)

Jarrell, who enlisted in the U.S. Army Air Force in 1942, spent most of World War II teaching celestial navigation in Texas. Though his poems reveal his first-hand knowledge of pilots and aircraft, he learned about the actual war through news dispatches.

In 1965 Jarrell died from injuries sustained when he was struck by a car. Although his death was ruled accidental, some witnesses said he "appeared to lunge" into the path of the car. His *Complete Poems* (1969) was posthumously published as were collections of his essays.

REFERENCES:

J. A. Bryant, Jr., *Understanding Randall Jarrell* (Columbia: University of South Carolina Press, 1986);

William H. Pritchard, *Randall Jarrell: A Literary Life* (New York: Farrar, Straus & Giroux, 1990).

– K.L.R.

JEFFERSON AIRPLANE

Formed in 1965, the Jefferson Airplane was one of the premier psychedelic-rock groups of the late 1960s. At its height the band was renowned for its creative songs rooted in the drug culture and radical politics.

Based in the **Haight-Ashbury** district of San Francisco, the group originally included Marty Balin, Paul Kantner, Signe Anderson, Jorma Kaukonen, Jack Casady, and Skip Spence. Beginning as a **hippie folk-music** group, the Jefferson Airplane gave its first performances at Bill Graham's dance concerts, most of which were staged at the Fillmore Auditorium in San Francisco. Their appearance at a folk-rock concert in Washington, D.C., led to a long-term contract at RCA in 1966. That year Anderson and Spence were replaced by Grace Slick and Spencer Dryden, and the group recorded its first album, *Jefferson Airplane Takes Off.* The band became more rock-oriented, as is evident in its 1967 album *Surrealistic Pillow,* which contained the band's signature hits "Somebody to Love" and "White Rabbit" — both written and sung by Slick. The Jefferson Airplane continued to experiment with their sound in the late 1960s, but their popularity and originality declined in the early 1970s with changing times and changing personnel.

Remaining members Kantner and Slick reorganized the band as Jefferson Starship in 1974. It endured for another decade, producing more conventional rock hits such as "Miracles" (1975) and "Runaway" (1978). In 1984, after Kantner left, Slick formed the group again as Starship, which had a number-one hit the following year with "We Built This City." Slick left Starship in 1989 to join Kantner, Balin, Casady, and Kaukonen, who toured and recorded once again as the Jefferson Airplane.

REFERENCE:

R. J. Gleason, *The Jefferson Airplane and the San Francisco Sound* (New York: Ballentine, 1969).

— L.D.S.

JOFFREY BALLET

Founded in 1956 by Robert Joffrey (1930–1988), the Joffrey Ballet is devoted to presenting twentieth-century works. It regularly commissions new ballets, many of them from Gerald Arpino, its resident choreographer and present artistic director, and neglected classics of the earlier twentieth century.

In 1956 Joffrey (born Abdullah Jaffa Anver Bey Khan) founded a six-member company that set out on a modest tour in a borrowed station wagon while he remained in New York teaching. The company grew slowly and toured the United States each year, attracting the patronage of Rebekah Harkness in 1962. In the early 1960s they danced new ballets such as **Alvin Ailey**'s *Feast of Ashes,* Arpino's *Incubus,* and Joffrey's *Gamelan.* During this period, it performed in the Middle East, and later in the Soviet Union with the sponsorship of the U.S. State Department. In 1964, following the Soviet tour, Harkness took over the company, changing its name to the Harkness Ballet and leaving Joffrey temporarily without a company of his own. With the assistance of a Ford Foundation grant, he

formed the City Center Joffrey Ballet, which presented its first season a year later, with Arpino as assistant director and choreographer.

The new company, which featured about forty dancers, soon gained a reputation for its energetic, dramatic productions, which often used special lighting effects and props and occasionally drew on rock music. Their new ballets included Joffrey's *Astarte* (1967), Eliot Feld's *Jive* (1973), and **Twyla Tharp**'s *Deuce Coupe* (1973). In addition, the company revived ballets by choreographers such as Frederick Ashton, **George Balanchine,** Kurt Jooss, Léonide Massine, and Vaslav Nijinsky. In the late 1980s, the company dissolved its Joffrey II apprentice company for financial reasons. It also established a second home outside New York with regular seasons in Los Angeles to increase its fundraising ability. Upon Joffrey's death Arpino assumed direction of the company.

REFERENCES:

John Gruen, *The Private World of Ballet* (New York: Viking, 1975), pp. 378–414;

Mary Whitney and Herbert Migdoll, *The Joffrey Ballet XXV* (Greenwich, Conn.: Steelograph, 1981).

— D.M.

JASPER JOHNS

Since his one-person exhibition at the Leo Castelli Gallery in New York City in 1958, Jasper Johns (1930–) has been one of the most formidable presences in contemporary American art. Although a young and relatively unknown painter when Castelli first introduced him, Johns was creating provocative, highly original work that many immediately recognized as charting new artistic territory. Johns's mostly figurative depictions of such matter-of-fact subjects as the American flag, circular targets, and sequences of numbers and alphabet letters were created during an era when abstract painting still dominated the American art scene. His work, in fact, can be seen as a transition between **Abstract Expressionism** and what would later independently emerge as **pop art.**

Johns was born in Augusta, Georgia, but grew up in South Carolina, raised largely by his grandmother. He studied art at the University of South Carolina but dropped out in 1949 to move to New York City, where he intended to become a working artist rather than simply a student. However, he was drafted into the army that year. Serving until 1952, he returned to New York and soon met **Robert Rauschenberg.** Besides becoming close friends, the two artists had common artistic goals in their move away from Abstract Expressionism toward a more-conceptual, pop-art aesthetic.

Initially using thick oil paints mixed with wax — a technique known as encaustic — Johns employed the gestural brushstroke of the Abstract Expressionists to create rich, sensuous painted surfaces that purposely avoided personal expression. He often chose objects that are flat — such as targets and numbers — for his early subject matter because these could actually be "created" on canvas rather than merely simulated using illusionistic techniques such as perspective. For example, when a tree or the sky is depicted on canvas, only an illusion of the real object is created; but a "real" target or a number 7 can actually be produced with paint. Johns's highly intellectual reasoning concerning the nature of illusion and reality marks him as a forerunner of **conceptual artists.** In fact, many of his works incorporate conceptual aspects of neo-Dadaism, showing the influence of **Marcel Duchamp,** whom Johns greatly admires.

In the late 1950s Johns began to create sculptural works, carrying his interest in the ambiguous distinction between illusionistic art and concrete objects into a new medium. Some of these works include ready-made objects combined with paint or bronze, while others are made of plaster or papier-mâché and painted to look like readymades. In the 1960s he began to attach handmade objects and readymades to painted canvases, again obscuring the line between reality and illusion. Paintings of the late 1960s and the 1970s introduced two new flat visual themes: flagstone walls and an all-over cross-hatching pattern.

Although Johns's work has been scrutinized and widely admired for the past thirty years, he remains one of the most enigmatic American painters, using his repertoire of imagery and techniques to create cryptic allusions to his private, subjective world.

REFERENCES:

Roberta Bernstein, *Jasper Johns' Paintings and Sculptures 1954–1974: "The Changing Focus of the Eye"* (Ann Arbor, Mich.: UMI Research, 1985);

Michael Crichton, *Jasper Johns* (New York: Abrams/Whitney Museum of American Art, 1977).

– K.B.

PHILIP JOHNSON

Architect, writer, curator, and art collector Philip Johnson (1906–) has had an influential place in American culture since the 1930s, when he founded and served as the first director of the architecture department at the **Museum of Modern Art** in New York City.

He has long been known as a proponent of the **International Style** in architecture. His own home — called the Glass House (New Canaan, Connecticut, 1957) — is based on a precedent set by Ludwig Mies van der Rohe, who exerted great influence on Johnson's early work. Johnson, in fact, did much to introduce the tenets of modernist architecture into the United States with the publication of his *International Style: Architecture since 1922* (1932, with Henry Russell Hitchcock) an important monograph (1941) on Mies van der Rohe.

In 1958 he collaborated with Mies van der Rohe on the Seagram Building in New York City, and he subsequently carried out other major architectural projects, including the New York State Theater at Lincoln Center (1964) and several important commissions in Houston, Texas, all done in a modernist vein. He therefore took the public by surprise in 1978 with his design for the AT&T corporate headquarters in New York City, for which he rejected the modernist glass-box formula in favor of flamboyant concessions to the new **postmodernist** trends. One of these included a decorative roof line in the shape of a broken pediment, which journalists compared to such things as a grandfather clock or a Chippendale highboy. That as well as other references to classical motifs sparked an ongoing controversy within the primarily modernist art world regarding the building's artistic merits. In any event, Johnson has demonstrated both in published statements and in his actual works that his thinking is open to the influence of new artistic currents, including the practices of such contemporary architects as **Frank Gehry, Michael Graves, Richard Meier,** and **Robert Venturi.**

REFERENCES:

Philip Johnson, *Johnson/Burgee: Architecture* (New York: Random House, 1979);

Carleton Knight, *Philip Johnson / John Burgee: Architecture 1979–1985* (New York: Rizzoli, 1985).

– K.B.

JAMES JONES

James Jones (1921–1977) wrote eleven books in a career that lasted more than twenty-five years, but he is most famous for his first, *From Here to Eternity* (1952), a novel about U.S. Army life in Hawaii before and during the bombing of Pearl Harbor. Along with his friends **Norman Mailer** and **Irwin Shaw,** Jones was considered one of the most gifted writers of the post–World War II era. Mailer called him "the only one of my contemporaries who I felt had more talent than

Quincy Jones, Michael Jackson, and Steven Spielberg

myself " and "the one writer of my time for whom I felt any love."

Having enlisted in the army, Jones was stationed in Hawaii when the war broke out; he was wounded on Guadalcanal a year later. His realistic, some said brutal, depiction of his army experience in *From Here to Eternity,* with its frank language, created a stir among readers. The novel won the National Book Award in 1952 and a film version in 1953 attracted further attention to Jones when it won eight Academy Awards, including best picture.

While Jones wrote on various aspects of American life, his main success came from his war novels. The story he began in *From Here to Eternity* continued in *The Thin Red Line* (1962), a depiction of the battle for Guadalcanal, and in the posthumously published *Whistle* (1978), the story of four wounded soldiers who return home to a country that has no place for them.

REFERENCES:

James R. Giles, *James Jones* (Boston: Twayne, 1981);

Frank MacShane, *Into Eternity: The Life of James Jones* (Boston: Houghton Mifflin, 1985).

       – R.T.

QUINCY JONES

Quincy Jones (1933–) has been one of the busiest and most influential figures in American jazz and popular music from the 1950s through the 1990s. He is respected as a composer and arranger in addition to his work as a producer.

Jones began his career in the early 1950s as an arranger for jazz performers such as **Dizzy Gillespie** and **Count Basie.** He also toured as a trumpeter with Lionel Hampton (1951–1953) and with Gillespie (1958). Jones led his own big band in the late 1950s, but it was financially unsuccessful. In 1961 he became a record producer, working with singers such as **Ray Charles, Frank Sinatra,** and Tony Bennett. Both as performer on his own jazz recordings and as producer, he has won more than twenty-five Grammy Awards for his albums. Jones was especially successful in promoting **Michael Jackson**'s career, beginning with *Off the Wall* in 1979. He also arranged and produced the number-one single **"We Are the World"** (1985), performed by about thirty popular-music stars as USA for Africa to raise money for famine victims.

In 1965 Jones began to compose scores for films. His many movie scores include *In the Heat of the Night* (1967), *In Cold Blood* (1967), and *The Color Purple* (1986). He has also written music for television series such as *Ironside* (1967–1975) and for the acclaimed mini-series *Roots* (1977).

REFERENCE:

R. Horricks, *Quincy Jones* (Tunbridge Wells: Spellmount, 1985).

       – I.R.H.

ERICA JONG

Poet and novelist Erica Jong (1942–) occupies a curious position between literary respectability and popular culture, due largely to the phenomenal success of her 1973 novel *Fear of Flying,* whose open treatment of sex led many to label Jong a writer of middlebrow erotica. Writing with insight and humor, Jong blends eroticism and **feminism** in her poetry and fiction.

Her career began with two poetry collections, *Fruits & Vegatables* (1971) and *Half-Lives* (1973). Both were well-received by critics. Though the success of *Fear of Flying* has overshadowed her accomplishments as a poet, Jong has continued to write **confessional poetry,** influenced by Walt Whitman, **Sylvia Plath,** and **Anne Sexton,** collecting her poems in books such as *Loveroot* (1975), *At the Edge of the Body* (1979), *Ordinary Miracles* (1983), and *Becoming Light* (1991).

Fear of Flying, a semi-autobiographical account of the adventures of Isadora Wing, sold millions of copies due to the controversy over its groundbreaking depiction of a woman's desires. Praised by Henry Miller and **John Updike** for presenting — as Jong said

— "a thinking woman who also had a sexual life," the novel became part of the vanguard of an increasingly candid portrayal of sex in mainstream fiction during the 1970s. Jong continued Isadora's saga in *How to Save Your Own Life* (1977) and *Parachutes and Kisses* (1984). Like *Fear of Flying,* these novels received mixed reviews, and they were not nearly as financially successful as their predecessor. Jong has also written two historical novels: *Fanny* (1980), a comic work about an eighteenth-century Englishwoman that is remarkable for its use of the conventions and style of the novel of that period; and *Serenissima* (1987), in which the setting shifts from present-day to sixteenth-century Venice. She returned to a contemporary setting in her latest novel, *Any Woman's Blues* (1990). In 1993 she published *The Devil at Large: Erica Jong on Henry Miller.*

REFERENCES:

"Over-40 Special," *Harper's Bazaar,* 122 (August 1989): 58+;

Ros Coward, "Coming Down," *New Statesman Society,* 3 (10 August 1990): 12–13.

– D.H.-F.

K

PAULINE KAEL

Pauline Kael (1919–) was the first postwar American film critic to achieve national recognition.

Kael became involved in analyzing films after graduating from the University of California, Berkeley, in 1940. She made weekly radio broadcasts about film over KPFA, the Pacifica Foundation radio network, and managed a Berkeley movie house, the first twin-screen art-film theater in the United States. The thousands of program notes she made for the films shown at the theater sharpened her critical skills and prose style. She began contributing film articles to popular and scholarly magazines, but she could not make a living as a film critic until her first collection of reviews and essays, provocatively titled *I Lost It at the Movies*, was published in 1965 and led to jobs as film critic for *Life* (1965) and *McCall's* (1965–1966). She also worked briefly for the *New Republic* (1966–1967) before becoming associated with the *New Yorker*, for which she wrote film reviews from 1968 through 1991, with time off in 1979–1980 when she worked as an executive consultant at Paramount Pictures. Before her stint in Hollywood Kael shared reviewing duties at the *New Yorker* with Penelope Gilliat, something of a sore point with Kael. When she returned to the *New Yorker* in 1980, Kael was named the sole film critic for the magazine.

Kael's *New Yorker* reviews are well-known for their densely argued, multi-page length and their sometimes idiosyncratic boosterism for film makers she particularly likes, such as **Robert Altman,** Jonathan Demme, Bernardo Bertolucci, and Brian De Palma. Her withering attack on the basic premise of the **auteur theory,** as promulgated by Andrew Sarris in 1962, is often included in anthologies of film criticism.

In addition to her 1965 book, Kael has collected her film criticism in *Kiss Kiss Bang Bang* (1968), *Going Steady* (1970), *Deeper into Movies* (1973, which won a National Book Award), *Reeling* (1976), *When the Lights Go Down* (1980), *State of the Art* (1985), *Hooked* (1989), and *Movie Love* (1992). She has also published *Five Thousand Nights at the Movies* (1982), a comprehensive film guide.

– I.R.H.

LOUIS KAHN

Although he had completed little more than one hundred buildings by the time of his death, Louis I. Kahn (1901–1974) is widely considered the major talent in post–World War II American architecture. Kahn was born in Estonia, immigrated with his family to Philadelphia in 1905, and became a U.S. citizen in 1915. He remained in Philadelphia as a student and later as a professor at the University of Pennsylvania School of Architecture. He was known as an inspiring, if somewhat mystical, lecturer and influenced a host of architecture students, including **Robert Venturi.**

Kahn is best known for his ability to combine an awareness of ancient forms of monumentality with an understanding of the social functions and pragmatic needs of modern-day buildings. Each of his designs emerged as a new solution to the problem at hand; his work therefore expresses a richly imaginative, personal approach rather than any one predictable style. In general, however, his buildings are large, solid masses suggesting timelessness and archaic simplicity.

Kahn's career got off to a slow start. His first significant commission was the Yale University Art Gallery (1951–1953), and other major projects did not come until he was asked to build the Richards Medical

Laboratories at the University of Pennsylvania (1957–1962). At the time, this undertaking stood out as an extraordinarily original stylistic statement that moved away from the then-dominant **International Style,** and the project established his professional reputation. Typically his designs focused on the creation of spaces that would foster social interaction and private contemplation within the context of an aesthetically pleasing environment. For example, the Jonas Salk Institute (La Jolla, California, 1959–1965), often cited as his masterpiece, was built for a community of scientists with a design that catered to an intense research environment. Other well-known commissions include the Kimball Art Museum (Fort Worth, Texas, 1972) — seen as one of the most enduringly successful art-museum buildings in the United States — and his master plan for the capitol at Dacca, East Pakistan (now Bangladesh), part of which was under construction when he died of a heart attack, at the height of his career, at age seventy-three.

REFERENCES:

John Lobell, *Between Silence and Light: Spirit in the Architecture of Louis I. Kahn* (Boulder: Random House, 1979);

Vincent Joseph Scully, *Louis I. Kahn* (New York: Braziller, 1962).
                                                                    – K.B.

GARSON KANIN

Actor, dramatist, and screenwriter Garson Kanin (1912–) wrote one of the first Broadway hit plays of the post–World War II era, *Born Yesterday,* which opened on Broadway in February 1946 and closed 1,642 performances later, in 1950.

Kanin began acting on Broadway in the 1930s, at the same time learning to direct plays by working as an assistant to **George Abbott.** Kanin went on to direct significant theatrical productions such as *Hitch Your Wagon* (1937, his directorial debut), *The Diary of Anne Frank* (1955), *A Hole in the Head* (1957), and *Funny Girl* (1964). During the late 1930s he also began writing screenplays and directing films. In the army during World War II he aided the war effort by making propaganda and documentary films. After his discharge in 1946 he wrote his first and most successful play, *Born Yesterday,* about corruption in Washington derailed by the awakening intelligence and commitment to democratic principles of Billie Dawn, the mistress of an industrialist attempting to bribe a senator. The play is still a classic of the American repertoire. Kanin collaborated on the screenplays for two film versions (1950 and 1993) and a television version (1956). Kanin's only other major dramatic success came in 1960, when he

adapted his novel *Do Re Mi* (1955) into the libretto for a hit musical, with a score by Jules Styne and lyrics by **Betty Comden and Adolph Green.**

During the late 1940s and early 1950s Kanin and his wife, actress Ruth Gordon, wrote the screenplays for five successful films, among them two Katharine Hepburn–Spencer Tracy comedies, *Adam's Rib* (1950) and *Pat and Mike* (1952). After the late 1950s Kanin's writings for stage and screen were less successful than his earlier efforts, but he remained a notable showbusiness figure and raconteur. He has written well-received film histories such as *Tracy and Hepburn* (1971) and *Hollywood* (1974), as well as several novels. One of them, *Moviola* (1979), was adapted as three made-for-television movies in 1980. In 1989 the Writers Guild of America gave Kanin and his brother Michael, a screenwriter, the Valentine Davies Award for lifetime achievement.

                                                                    – I.R.H.

ELIA KAZAN

Elia Kazan (1909–) was one of the most distinguished directors for both stage and screen in the 1940s and 1950s. His best work includes his stage productions of **Tennessee Williams's** *A Streetcar Named Desire* (1947) and **Arthur Miller's** *Death of a Salesman* (1949) and his films *On the Waterfront* (1954) and *East of Eden* (1955).

Born Elia Kazanjoglous, Kazan immigrated with his family to the United States from Turkey when he was four. He joined the leftist Group Theatre in 1932 as actor and assistant stage manager; in 1947 he joined other former members of the Group, which disbanded in 1940, in founding the **Actors Studio.** Kazan became an important Broadway director in the 1940s, directing successful plays such as *A Streetcar Named Desire,* **Robert Anderson's** *Tea and Sympathy* (1953), and Williams's *Cat on a Hot Tin Roof* (1955) — for each of which he received Antoinette Perry (Tony) Awards for directing. Between 1945 and 1969 Kazan directed several films. His first feature film, after an apprenticeship in documentaries, was *A Tree Grows in Brooklyn* (1945). He followed it with a string of impressive pictures addressing social problems, including *Gentleman's Agreement* (1947), which deals with unspoken discrimination against Jews; *Pinky* (1949), about a black woman who passes for white; and *A Face in the Crowd* (1957), about the effect of the media on politics. *Gentleman's Agreement* and *On the Waterfront* each received Academy Awards (Oscars) for best picture and best director.

In 1962 Kazan wrote about his family history in *America, America,* and he wrote his first novel, *The Arrangement,* in 1967. He made both into films in 1963 and 1969 respectively, but neither had the power of his earlier work. His directorial career ended in 1976 with the unsuccessful film version of **F. Scott Fitzgerald's** Hollywood novel, *The Last Tycoon* (1941). Kazan's later years were marked by published recriminations from former friends who believed he betrayed them to the House Un-American Activities Committee in his 1952 testimony.

REFERENCES:

Elia Kazan, *A Life* (New York: Knopf, 1988);

Thomas Pauly, *An American Odyssey: Elia Kazan and American Culture* (Philadelphia: Temple University Press, 1983).
　　　　　　　　　　　　　　　　　　– I.R.H.

ELLSWORTH KELLY

Ellsworth Kelly (1923–) is primarily known for his pioneering role in the development of Hard-Edge Painting, a branch of **minimalism** that incorporates flatly rendered colors in sharply defined geometric shapes. After beginning his artistic training at schools in Boston and Brooklyn, followed by some time in the army, he moved in 1948 to Paris, where he continued to study and practice. He lived there until 1954, when he moved back to New York, where many artists were becoming involved with **Abstract Expressionism.** Kelly, however, rejected this gesturally expressive art style, and he strove to rid his art of subjective personality and emotional content.

With this rapidly developing minimalist approach, Kelly used abstract forms in his paintings. He experimented by painting lines and patterns on small panels, then joining the panels together at random. Often his abstractions derive from relationships of color and form observed in everyday objects, and many of his paintings serve as highly concentrated presentations of particular visual phenomena. For example, he became enthralled with the shapes and patterns of certain casement windows that he saw around Paris, and he did a series of paintings based on these visual relationships. A trip to the Mediterranean in 1950 inspired Kelly to start painting in bright, sunny colors. At his first one-person show, in 1951 at the Arnaud Gallery in Paris, he exhibited a series of monochrome panels, each in a different color.

In the mid 1950s, after his return to New York, Kelly began to refine his style, creating works in the style of Hard-Edge Painting. In this mature style, Kelly produced paintings with smooth surfaces and clean geometric shapes, often using bright primary colors. Although his early works were on flat, rectangular canvases, he later began to work with various-shaped canvases as well as freestanding sculptures.

REFERENCES:

E. C. Goosen, *Ellsworth Kelly* (New York: Museum of Modern Art, 1973);

Diane Waldman, *Ellsworth Kelly* (Greenwich, Conn.: New York Graphic Society, 1971).
　　　　　　　　　　　　　　　　　　– C.S.

GENE KELLY

Dancer, choreographer, and director Gene Kelly (1912–) became the most celebrated male movie dancer after World War II, succeeding Fred Astaire. Kelly contributed substantially to the popularity of Hollywood musicals in the 1940s and 1950s not only through his dancing, which was both gymnastic and balletic, but also through his innovative choreography and directing, which helped to integrate dances as a part of the plot rather than as isolated production numbers.

Kelly made his Broadway debut in the chorus of *Leave It to Me!* in 1938. His breakthrough was his portrayal of the opportunistic heel Joey Evans in *Pal Joey* (1940), and he choreographed his first full show, *Best Foot Forward,* the following year. He starred in his first film, *For Me and My Gal,* in 1942 and went on to make a string of successful musicals. He received an Academy Award (Oscar) nomination for *Anchors Aweigh* (1946), which he choreographed. *The Pirate* (1948) is notable for his and Judy Garland's comic rendition of "Be a Clown." He also choreographed and starred in the film version of *On the Town* (1949), the first of three films he directed with Stanley Donen.

Kelly is best remembered for his performances in *An American in Paris* (1951) and *Singin' in the Rain* (1952), both of which feature his technical innovation of taking everyday objects and choreographing them into a routine, such as his use of an umbrella in a now-famous scene from *Singin' in the Rain.* He choreographed *An American in Paris,* which includes a dream ballet set among scenes from French impressionist paintings; he and Donen choreographed and directed *Singin' in the Rain.* Kelly regularly danced on television variety shows in the 1950s, and he directed a film, *Invitation to the Dance* (1956), that includes nothing but dancing. In 1958 he directed *Flower Drum Song* on Broadway. After his performance as the reporter in the film version of *Inherit the Wind* (1960) and his creation of a ballet, *Pas des Dieux,* for the Paris Opéra Ballet

Grace Kelly and Prince Rainier of Monaco attending a charity ball at the Waldorf-Astoria Hotel in New York on the night they announced their engagement, 6 January 1956

the same year, Kelly concentrated more on directing with films such as *Hello, Dolly!* (1969) and *40 Carats* (1973).

REFERENCES:

Clive Hirschorn, *Gene Kelly: A Biography,* revised edition (New York: St. Martin's Press, 1984);

Tony Thomas, *That's Dancing* (New York: Abrams, 1984).

– D.M. and I.R.H.

GRACE KELLY

Grace Kelly (1929–1982) was known for her patrician beauty, which led her first into movie stardom and then into a real-life fairy tale when she wed Prince Rainier of Monaco. As an actress, she typically was cast as an aloof yet passionate woman.

Born into mainline Philadelphia society, Kelly was educated at two preparatory schools and then went to New York to work as a model while studying at the American Academy of Dramatic Arts. After work in commercials, she made it to Broadway in 1949 and appeared in several plays and television shows. She had a small part in the film *Fourteen Hours* in 1951. Her next role, as Gary Cooper's Quaker wife in *High Noon* (1952), made her a star. She was nominated for an Academy Award for her role as an adulteress in her next film, *Mogambo* (1953), and won for *The Country Girl* in 1954. Kelly also became a favorite leading lady for **Alfred Hitchcock,** starring in his films *Dial M for Murder* (1954), *Rear Window* (1954), and *To Catch a Thief* (1955). During filming on the Riviera for *To Catch a Thief,* she met her future husband. They married in 1956, and Kelly retired from acting. *High Society* (1956), a musical remake of *The Philadelphia Story,* was her final film. She became well known for her devotion to humanitarian causes. Princess Grace died following an automobile accident in 1982.

REFERENCES:

Sarah Bradford, *Princess Grace* (London: Weidenfeld, 1984);

James Spada, *Grace: The Secret Lives of a Princess* (Garden City, N.Y.: Dolphin/Doubleday, 1987).

– I.R.H.

JOHN F. KENNEDY

Thirty years after his death, John F. Kennedy (1917-1963) is remembered as much for his furtive sexual liaisons with such luminaries as **Marilyn Monroe** as for his political achievements; yet his presidency had a symbolic significance of legendary dimensions. Kennedy was the television president, the first who took advantage of the image-hungry medium to project the personality of his administration. At his presidential inauguration, he boldly asserted that "the torch has been passed to a new generation of Americans," and, echoing Oliver Wendell Holmes, he exhorted them to "ask not what your country can do for you; ask what you can do for your country."

His image was youth, vigor, privilege, optimism, compassion, and confidence. He inspired his generation with the belief that the power of government could be marshaled to the benefit of people and that people, in turn, were duty bound to involve themselves in government. He established the Peace Corps and proposed VISTA to turn small armies of committed young Americans to social service. Kennedy inaugurated the era of **civil rights** and civil activism (though substantive civil rights reform came after his death, due to the efforts of Lyndon B. Johnson), and though he died before many of the elements of his "New Frontier" platform could be realized, Lyndon Johnson, his successor, pursued many of the domestic programs Kennedy initiated. Kennedy was the last president who balanced the national budget.

Kennedy was elected president in 1960. He had a heroic war record, a Harvard degree, an undistinguished but unblemished record as a congressman (in the House from 1947 to 1953; the Senate from 1953 to 1960). He was handsome; he had an attractive family; and he was very rich. Kennedy's election came in the wake of the eight-year presidency of the fatherly, but seemingly lethargic Dwight D. Eisenhower, and thus Kennedy's youthful energy was all the more apparent. The Kennedy clan, including the president, played touch football on the White House lawn and took photo-op sailing excursions on Cape Hatteras. Mrs. Kennedy provided an attractive image of good taste and active motherhood.

The time of the Kennedy presidency was called Camelot after the romantic play and movie based on Arthurian legend. John Kennedy was the benevolent king, who, with his alluring lady at his side, sent his faithful knights into the countryside to do battle with the forces of evil during their search for the Holy Grail that would bring peace and comfort to his kingdom. Kennedy's knights were his cabinet and staff, dubbed by journalists "The Best and the Brightest" because of their backgrounds as intellectuals in government and Ivy League universities.

Yet, for all its glamour, the Kennedy administration was marked by poor judgment, tragedy, and intense drama, especially in foreign affairs. Shortly after he assumed office, Kennedy authorized an amphibious invasion of Cuba at the Bay of Pigs, ninety miles south of Havana, by a CIA-trained and outfitted band of Cuban exiles. Although it was planned during Eisenhower's presidency, the invasion was an embarrassing failure for the new administration, and Kennedy was forced to apologize to his bitter enemy Fidel Castro of Cuba for the incursion. Three months later, when talks failed with Soviet Premier Nikita Khrushchev about German unification, the Soviets drew a firm line between East and West Berlin, marked it with a stone wall, and threatened world war if the Americans or their allies should cross it.

In October 1962 the tensions between the superpowers reached a crisis point when American intelligence revealed the presence of Soviet offensive missiles in Cuba capable of reaching U.S. soil. For nearly a month the stage was set for the final scene in which Kennedy called for a quarantine of Russian ships entering Cuba, which the Soviets vowed to resist. A Russian ship approached; it was stopped, searched, and found to have no weapons, so it was allowed to proceed. Other Soviet-bloc ships in the area turned away.

As the drama was played out on national television, it excited national tensions — and support for Kennedy's apparent sagacity (which subsequent scholarship questioned). Meanwhile, though, the Kennedy administration had been clumsily escalating the war in Southeast Asia and interfering clandestinely in the national politics of Vietnam. Kennedy was said to have been considering a withdrawal of American troops in the months before his death.

On 22 November 1963 Kennedy was assassinated by a lone gunman in Dallas. No event in modern American history has caused such national sorrow or prompted more intense scrutiny. After Kennedy's death, a debate raged about whether the assassin was in fact Lee Harvey Oswald, the gunman who was himself assassinated while in police custody two days after he killed the president. Conspiracy theories abounded over the next third of a century. But, for the time, the networks nationally televised the funeral, in which a riderless horse was led through the streets of Washington toward the burial site in Arlington National Cemetery to the sound of a funeral dirge; a beautiful young widow grieved with royal dignity; and two-year-old John-John Kennedy — his mother and his sister, Caroline, at his side — bravely yet tearfully saluted the casket of his father. This set of images was seared on the consciousness of the nation.

REFERENCES:

Doris Kearns Goodwin, *The Fitzgeralds and the Kennedys: An American Saga* (New York: Simon & Schuster, 1987);

William Manchester, *Portrait of a President: John F. Kennedy in Profile* (Boston: Little, Brown, 1962);

Theodore C. Sorensen, *The Kennedy Legacy* (New York: Macmillan, 1969).

                                                                        – R.L.

JACK KEROUAC

Jack Kerouac (1922–1969), who named the **Beat Generation** in 1948, became famous as the "King of the Beats" when his novel *On the Road* made the bestseller list in late 1957.

By the time *On the Road* appeared (six years after Kerouac finished typing the first complete draft in one paragraph on a long continuous roll of teletype paper), he had written more than twelve books, but only one, *The Town & the City* (1950), had been published. Publishers had been unwilling to take a chance on Kerouac's unorthodox portrayals of his friends' blatant rebellion against middle-class morality. While revising *On the Road* in late 1951, Kerouac had discovered a method of writing he called "sketching" or "spontaneous prose," comparing it to improvisation in jazz. He used this style in a few sections of *On the Road* and extensively in his later novels.

When *On the Road* was finally published, it profited from the publicity generated by a widely publicized censorship battle over **Allen Ginsberg**'s *Howl* (1956), which had everyone talking about the Beats. The book is narrated by Sal Paradise (Kerouac) and includes portraits of Ginsberg (Carlo Marx) and **William S. Burroughs** (Old Bull Lee), but the hero of the novel is Dean Moriarty, based on Neal Cassady, a charming con artist / car thief with whom Kerouac and Ginsberg had both become obsessed. For Kerouac, Cassady became the embodiment of the American dream betrayed by the materialistic, militaristic nation America had become.

Kerouac's next published novel, *The Subterraneans* (1958), based on, and written soon after, an affair he had with a young black woman in Greenwich Village (San Francisco in the novel) in late summer 1953, was also a best-seller. In November 1957, while *On the Road* was on the best-seller list, Kerouac responded to an editor's request for another book about his friends by writing *The Dharma Bums* (1958). Set on the West Coast during 1955–1956, the novel centers on Kerouac's (Ray Smith's) conversations about Buddhism with San Francisco Beat poet Gary Snyder (Japhy Ryder) and their climbing expedition in the Sierra Nevada.

After *The Dharma Bums*, Kerouac did not finish another novel for four years, but the books he had written earlier began to flood the market. (Seven were published in 1959 and 1960.) Kerouac's reputation as a writer — always a subject of debate — suffered from attacks on his spontaneous-prose method. The most notorious charge came in 1959 from **Truman Capote**, who said that what Kerouac did was not writing but "typing."

Unlike Ginsberg, who became a sort of guru for the generation of antiwar and human-rights activists that came along in the 1960s, Kerouac, a social and political conservative at heart, was unsympathic to the young **hippies** who modeled their lifestyles on the characters in his novels. He became increasingly reclusive and died from complications of alcoholism at age forty-seven.

REFERENCES:

Ann Charters, *Kerouac: A Biography* (San Francisco: Straight Arrow Books, 1973);

Tom Clark, *Jack Kerouac* (San Diego: Harcourt Brace Jovanovich, 1984);

Gerald Nicosia, *Memory Babe: A Critical Biography of Jack Kerouac* (New York: Grove Press, 1983).

– K.L.R.

WALTER KERR

As a New York drama critic for more than forty years, Walter Kerr (1913–) has been both praised and blamed for judging plays from the point of view of the typical Broadway theatergoer. Well known for his conservative tastes, he has little patience for social messages or the avant-garde.

Kerr began reviewing plays for *Commentary* in 1950. The next year he became theater critic for the *New York Herald Tribune*. When the *Tribune* ceased publication in 1966, Kerr was offered the post of drama critic for the daily and Sunday editions of the *New York Times*. Believing that writing all the reviews for the powerful *Times* gave one critic too much influence, Kerr agreed to the arrangement only until the paper could hire an additional reviewer. After **Clive Barnes** became daily drama critic in 1967, Kerr wrote the Sunday theater column and other occasional reviews until 1979, when he once again added daily reviewing to his responsibilities. He retired in July 1983 but continues to write occasional columns for the paper. In 1990 a Broadway theater, The Ritz, was restored and renamed for Kerr.

During his years as a daily reviewer, Kerr was credited with writing fewer positive reviews than any other newspaper critic covering Broadway. In 1965 he was given a *Village Voice* award for "outstanding disservice to the modern theatre." At the same time, however, he was considered the most readable of the New York critics. His criticism has earned him an award from the National Institute of Arts and Letters (1972) and a Pulitzer Prize (1978).

In addition to collections of his reviews, Kerr's books include *How Not to Write a Play* (1955), *Harold Pinter* (1967), and *Tragedy and Comedy* (1967). He has also written plays, some with his wife, Jean Kerr, whose *Please Don't Eat the Daisies,* a chronicle of their hectic family life, was a best-seller in 1957.

REFERENCES:

Roderick Bladel, *Walter Kerr: An Analysis of His Criticism* (Metuchen, N. J.: Scarecrow Press, 1976).

– I.R.H.

KEN KESEY

Though his literary reputation is based mainly on his first novel, *One Flew Over The Cuckoo's Nest* (1962), Ken Kesey (1935–) became well known as the foremost West Coast spokesman for the **hippie** generation. That reputation is due in large part to **New Journalist** Tom Wolfe's portrayal in *The Electric*

Members of Jefferson Airplane, the Grateful Dead, and others, riding on top of Ken Kesey's bus, 1966 (photograph by Gene Anthony)

Kool-Aid Acid Test (1968) of Kesey and his friends who called themselves the Merry Pranksters.

Kesey was twenty-seven when *One Flew Over The Cuckoo's Nest* was published to the applause of an iconoclastic generation of readers who mistook Randle J. McMurphy, an exuberant, free-spirited mental patient, for a model of heroic resistance to the restrictions of an unimaginative, conformist society. The consequences of McMurphy's attempt to impose his own idea of sanity on his fellow inmates were generally overlooked. The struggles against authority that McMurphy organizes result in the suicide of his most promising disciple, and McMurphy progressively erodes his own freedom by his irresponsible actions. McMurphy was elevated to the status of cultural icon after Jack Nicholson turned in an Academy Award–winning portrayal of him in the 1975 movie version of the novel.

Two years after *One Flew Over The Cuckoo's Nest,* Kesey's *Sometimes A Great Notion* (1964) was published with great fanfare and received mixed reviews. This dense, more ambitious novel is set in backwoods Oregon during a loggers' strike. By making his heroes the fiercely independent Stamper family, who break the strike, Kesey confounded his liberal fans and belied his nonconformist image by seeming to lionize

an anti-intellectual, anti-labor, anti-feminist, hard-rock conservative.

To celebrate the novel's publication Kesey and the Merry Pranksters staged a transcontinental drug party, traveling from Kesey's home in La Honda, California, to New York City in a school bus decorated with psychedelic images. Their bus driver was a well-known member of the **Beat Generation**, Neal Cassady, the model for Dean Moriarty in **Jack Kerouac**'s novel *On the Road* (1956). The trip reached a disappointing climax in Millbrook, New York, when Kesey and his fun-loving party met with sober-minded disapproval at the research compound of LSD guru **Timothy Leary**. Kesey, who had been taking LSD (lysergic acid diethylamide) since he was a volunteer subject in government-sponsored drug experiments in 1959, had hoped to be welcomed as a fellow researcher. Back in California, Kesey suspended his writing career and went about publicizing the benefits of the then-legal, mind-altering drug. In 1965–1966 he and the Merry Pranksters hosted a series of "Acid Tests," public gatherings that featured a new rock band, the **Grateful Dead,** and light shows as well as clips from the home movies the Merry Pranksters had taken on their cross-country trip — all to create a congenial atmosphere in which to take LSD.

In 1966 Kesey was convicted of possession of marijuana and served a five-month jail sentence. After his release he moved to a farm in Oregon. He lent his name and occasionally his talent to collaborations among his friends, including *The Last Supplement to the Whole Earth Catalog* (March 1971), *Kesey's Garage Sale* (1973), and the sporadically published journal *Spit In The Ocean* (1974–1981). He staged a minor literary comeback with *Demon Box* (1986), a collection of essays; two children's books, *Little Tricker the Squirrel Meets Big Double the Bear* (1990) and *The Sea Lion: A Story of the Sea Cliff People* (1991); and *The Further Inquiry* (1990), an extended mock conversation. His third novel, *Sailor Song* (1992), brought uneven reviews his fourth novel, *Last Go Round* (1994), is a multi-racial western in the style of the cowboy pulps.

The twenty-fifth anniversary of the Merry Pranksters' bus tour was commemorated with *On The Bus* (1990), a description of the trip with recollections by participants, and by the donation of the bus to the Smithsonian, an event that took on a Prankster-like quality when the authenticity of the donated bus was questioned by museum officials.

REFERENCES:

Paul Perry, *On The Bus: The Complete Guide to the Legendary Trip of Ken Kesey and the Merry Pranksters and the Birth of the Counterculture,* edited by Michael Schwartz and Neil Ortenberg (New York: Thunder's Mouth Press, 1990);

Tom Wolfe, *The Electric Kool-Aid Acid Test* (New York: Farrar Straus Giroux, 1968).

– R.L.

KINETIC SCULPTURE

Kinetic sculptures are three-dimensional constructions that incorporate actual movement by means such as motors, air power, and fluctuating light. Kinetic sculptors were primarily concerned with the movement of forms in space, as were the Futurist artists of the early twentieth century.

Although the creation of kinetic sculptures has occupied European artists more so than American artists, **Alexander Calder**'s kinetic sculptures — which he called "mobiles" — were important contributions. Kinetic sculpture came to the fore as an American art form in the 1960s with the work of artists such as George Rickey, who experimented with mostly outdoor pieces that relied on air power for motion. His *Two Lines Oblique* (1967–1968), for example, consists of two movable, bladelike rods attached to a twenty-five-foot-high Y-shaped pole and is gently set into motion by air currents. One of the most sensational pieces of kinetic sculpture to be seen in the United States was

by Swiss artist Jean Tingueley. His short-lived *Homage to New York* (1960) was built in the courtyard of the **Museum of Modern Art** from a ramshackle array of broken machines and other urban junkyard items. It was supposed to self-destruct dramatically before an audience, but, instead, it accidentally caught on fire ahead of time, requiring the assistance of New York City firemen.

Because kinetic sculptures continually change through motion, they serve to de-emphasize the importance of the completed art object, an aesthetic in common with the **conceptual artists.** The kinetic sculptor's interest in the dynamics of visual form was also shared by the near-contemporary **Op Artists,** though on a two-dimensional scale.

REFERENCES:

Frank J. Malina, comp., *Kinetic Art: Theory and Practice* (New York: Dover, 1974);

Frank Popper, *Origins and Development of Kinetic Art* (Greenwich, Conn.: New York Graphic Society, 1968).

– K.B.

MARTIN LUTHER KING, JR.

Martin Luther King, Jr. (1929-1968) was the preeminent civil rights activist of his era. Dedicated to the principal of passive resistance, he braved physical brutality and public humiliation in pursuit of his belief that nonviolent protest was the only responsible path to racial equality. He was thirty-five in 1964 when he became the youngest recipient ever of the Nobel Peace Prize. That was nine years after he had received a Ph.D. in theology from Boston University in 1955; eight years after he had organized a 382-day boycott of segregated public buses in Montgomery, Alabama, in 1956; seven years after he helped organize and served as first president of the Southern Christian Leadership Conference in 1957; three years after he joined his father in 1960 as co-pastor of the Ebenezer Baptist Church in Atlanta, a center of nonviolent civil rights protest; one year after he was jailed, for the twentieth time, in Birmingham, Alabama, in the wake of violent police reaction to his peaceful and successful protest in April-May 1963 against the city's segregationist policies.

On 28 August 1963 he inspired millions listening on radio and television as the stirring principal speaker (and one of ten organizers) at the March on Washington, called the largest protest in American history, drawing 200,000 marchers to the Lincoln Memorial to demand civil rights legislation. "Now is the time to rise from the dark and desolate valley of segregation to the sunlit path of racial justice," he told the Washington protesters in a speech punctuated by the refrain "I have a dream." After the longest debate in Senate history, the federal government took an important step toward the vision embodied in Rev. King's dream with passage of the Civil Rights Act of 1964, which outlawed segregation of public accommodations. Rev. King then began the arduous task of testing compliance with the law, promoting voter registration in Selma, Alabama, and open housing in Chicago in highly publicized campaigns.

The international acclaim of the Nobel Prize brought with it global responsibilities, and Rev. King felt compelled to broaden his vision after 1964. In a move criticized by members of the civil rights movement, he became an active critic of American involvement in Vietnam. His status as a Nobel laureate provided him a forum at the United Nations where he pleaded with the American government to stop bombing and withdraw troops. He enlisted in the war on poverty in 1967, planning an ambitious Poor People's Campaign in Washington, D.C., to push for antipoverty legislation. But the Rev. King's plans were cut short.

In April 1968, world weary beyond his thirty-nine years, he agreed to organize a protest march in Memphis, Tennessee, to support a strike by 1300 sanitation workers that had grown violent. He spoke to the strikers at the Mason Street Temple on 3 April, referring to threats against his life: "Like anybody I would like to live a long life. Longevity has its place. But I'm not concerned about that now. I just want to do God's will. And he's allowed me to go up to the mountain. And I've looked over, and I've seen the Promised Land. I may not get there with you, but I want you to know tonight that we as a people will get to the Promised Land. . . . I'm not fearing any man. Mine Eyes have seen the glory of the coming of the Lord." The next evening he was killed by James Earl Ray, who fired a single rifle shot at long-range.

News of the assassination prompted riots. In what was called the worst outbreak of arson in Washington, D.C., since the War of 1812, eleven people were killed, a thousand were injured, and eight thousand were arrested in a riot that was stilled by some thirteen thousand national guardsmen. Similar outbreaks of street violence occurred in other American cities, notably Chicago and Baltimore. They marked a turning point in American life. With the death of Rev. King, advocates of nonviolent protest lost the energizing spirit of their movement. More militant leaders took control.

REFERENCES:

Taylor Branch, *Parting the Waters: America in the King Years, 1954-1963* (New York: Simon & Schuster, 1988);

James A. Colaiaco, *Martin Luther King, Jr.: Apostle of Militant Nonviolence* (New York: St. Martin's Press, 1988);

Stephen B. Oates, *Let the Trumpet Sound: The Life of Martin Luther King, Jr.* (New York: Harper & Row, 1982).

– R.L.

STEPHEN KING

Horror writer Stephen King (1947–) is among the best-selling authors in history. A writer of novels, stories, and screenplays, King is so prolific that at one point he also published under the pseudonym Richard Bachman to avoid having too many books available under his name at once. Occasionally more than one King title has appeared on the bestseller lists at the same time, and several have been main selections of book clubs.

King's enormously popular books transcend the genre of **horror fiction** to which most of his work is assigned. Blending horror with humor and elements from genres such as detective fiction and the thriller, his fiction covers a vast spectrum of influences and references, both popular and literary. King's use of modern-day settings and problems, everyday language, and realistic technique combine with macabre events and page-turning plots in his novels.

King's first novel, *Carrie* (1974), is about an adolescent outcast who uses her telekinetic powers for vengeance. His next, *'Salem's Lot* (1975), updates the vampire story, while *Cycle of the Werewolf* (1983; later published as *Silver Bullet*) uses another classic horror trope. His third novel, *The Shining* (1977), involves a haunted house and a boy with paranormal abilities. *The Stand* (1978; revised edition 1990) mixes elements of **science fiction and fantasy,** as do *The Dead Zone* with its psychic protagonist and *The Talisman* (1984), King's collaboration with Peter Straub. Another main character with paranormal talents appears in *Firestarter* (1980). A dog provides the means of terror in *Cujo* (1981), and a car plays a similar role in *Christine* (1983).

King considers *Pet Sematary* (1983) one of his most terrifying works: it concerns the temptation of a father to bring his son back from the dead through the supernatural power of an ancient burial ground. *It* (1986) gathers many horrors into a single supernatural force, while the source of terror in *Misery* (1987) is human — a demented fan who holds her favorite writer hostage. *The Dark Half* (1989) is another King novel about a writer, this time one who finds his pseudonym harder to dismiss than he had believed. King's fantasy series, *The Dark Tower*, consists of *The Gunslinger* (1988), *The Drawing of the Three* (1989), and *The*

Gladys Knight and the Pips (Motown Record Corporation)

Waste Lands (1991). *Night Shift* (1978), *Different Seasons* (1982), *Skeleton Crew* (1985), *Four Past Midnight* (1990), and *Nightmares & Dreamscapes* (1993) are collections of King's stories. In the 1990s he continues to produce novels regularly, such as *Needful Things* (1991) and *Gerald's Game* (1992). He has also written a nonfiction book on horror, *Stephen King's Danse Macabre* (1981), which includes a good deal of autobiography.

Much of King's fiction has been made into movies, including *Carrie* (1976), directed by Brian De Palma; *The Shining* (1980), directed by **Stanley Kubrick**; and *Stand by Me* (1986) — based on the novella "The Body" — and *Misery* (1990), both directed by Rob Reiner. With the exception of Reiner's films, movies based on King's work are generally less effective than the books themselves.

REFERENCES:

George Beahm, ed., *The Stephen King Companion* (Kansas City & New York: Andrews & McMeel, 1989);

Tim Underwood and Chuck Miller, eds., *Kingdom of Fear: The World of Stephen King* (Los Angeles: Underwood-Miller, 1986).

                                    – D.H.-F.

GLADYS KNIGHT AND THE PIPS

Rhythm-and-blues singers Gladys Knight and the Pips have been among the leading popular vocalists in America since the 1950s. They have recorded several hit songs using Knight's **gospel**-influenced singing backed by the Pips' harmony.

Knight began singing in church choirs when she was four, and in 1952, at age eight, she won the grand prize on the television show *Ted Mack and the Original Amateur Hour*. In her early teens she formed the Pips with brother Merald Knight and cousins William Guest and Edward Patten. The group, later renamed Gladys Knight and the Pips, made its first record in 1958 and had its first major hit, "Every Beat of My Heart," in 1961. Gladys Knight and the Pips became especially popular after signing with **Motown** Records in 1966; their Motown hits include "I Heard It through the Grapevine" (1967), "Take Me in Your Arms and Love Me" (1967), and "Help Me Make It through the Night" (1972). They left Motown in 1973, the year of their popular song "Midnight Train to Georgia." The group split in 1977 but reunited in 1980. Since then, they have continued to perform in concerts and to record.

REFERENCE:

Don Waller, *The Motown Story* (New York: Scribners, 1985).

– L.D.S.

ARTHUR KOPIT

Arthur Kopit (1937–) has had the longest successful career of any American author of absurdist, **postmodern** plays.

Born in New York, he was an engineering major at Harvard University, but by the time he graduated in 1959 he had written seven plays and seen them through student productions. While traveling in Europe on a scholarship to study theater, he wrote the macabre **black-humor** farce *Oh Dad, Poor Dad, Mama's Hung You in the Closet and I'm Feelin' So Sad,* first performed at Harvard in 1960. After it was produced in London in 1961 and on Broadway in 1962, the play made Kopit's reputation as a brilliant young experimental playwright. Parodying dramatists as different as **Tennessee Williams** and Eugène Ionesco, Kopit's play is about two voracious, domineering women. A wealthy widow travels around the world with her dead husband's body in a coffin, two venus flytraps, a piranha fish that eats cats, and her son, whom she tries to protect by isolating him from the world. He ends up killing his predatory teenage babysitter after she tries to seduce him on his mother's bed.

Indians (1968), Kopit's next major success used the Buffalo Bill Wild West Show to demonstrate how the mythologizing tendencies of American culture have been used by whites to justify the genocide of native peoples. Among Kopit's other notable plays are *Wings* (1978), which takes place in the mind of an elderly female stroke victim whose speech and comprehension are so impaired that most of what she hears and says is gibberish, and *End of the World* (1983), a comedy about nuclear war. The controversial *Road to Nirvana* (1991) attacks Hollywood dealmakers and **David Mamet,** whose casting of box-office draw **Madonna** in his anti-Hollywood play, *Speed-the-Plow* (1988), seemed hypocritical to Kopit.

Despite their diverse subject matter Kopit's plays are united by his satirical treatment of American cultural mythology, his use of parody and the grotesque, and his avant-garde dialogue and staging techniques.

REFERENCE:

Doris Auerbach, *Sam Shepard, Arthur Kopit, and the Off Broadway Theater* (Boston: Twayne, 1982).

– I.R.H.

STANLEY KRAMER

Producer and director Stanley Kramer (1913–) is well known for his socially conscious "message" films, cloaking his liberal views in entertaining stories that drew audiences to movie theaters.

Born in New York, Kramer moved to Hollywood after graduating from New York University in 1933 and worked his way up through various film-industry jobs to executive assistant to David L. Loew in 1942. During World War II Kramer served in the U.S. Army Signal Corps, making army training films. He was discharged in 1945, and two years later he formed his own independent production company, which became an autonomous unit under the aegis of Columbia Pictures in 1951.

After his second film, *Champion* (1949), based on a boxing story by Ring Lardner, was a hit, Kramer produced other notable movies. *Home of the Brave* (1949) is the first American film to deal openly with the psychological effects of racial prejudice. *The Men* (1950), about a paraplegic war veteran, is one of the first movies to examine problems soldiers wounded in World War II faced at home. *High Noon* (1952), a classic Western, examines conventional notions of honor. *The Caine Mutiny* (1954), based on Herman Wouk's Pulitzer Prize-winning novel, angered some government officials for its implied criticism of the navy but was extremely popular with moviegoers.

Kramer began as a director with *Not as a Stranger* (1955), a realistic medical film, and had a string of worthy directorial achievements in the 1950s and 1960s. He examined American race relations in *The Defiant Ones* (1958), *Pressure Point* (1962), and *Guess Who's Coming to Dinner* (1967). One of his best-known films, *On the Beach* (1959), warned of the potential for nuclear holocaust at the height of public tension over the **Cold War.** *Judgment at Nuremberg* (1961) is a powerful treatment of the Nazi war-crime trial of 1945 and 1946. *It's a Mad, Mad, Mad, Mad World* (1963), a slapstick chase film, is atypical of Kramer's approach to delivering his message, in this case, American's obsession with money.

In 1961, at the height of his popularity, the Academy of Motion Picture Arts and Sciences gave Kramer the Irving Thalberg Award "for distinguished contributions to the American film industry." In the 1970s, however, his messages began to seem heavy handed and his understanding of issues superficial. He made his last film, *The Runner Stumbles,* in 1979.

REFERENCE:

Donald Spoto, *Stanley Kramer, Film Maker* (New York: Putnam, 1978).

– I.R.H.

Barbara Kruger

Barbara Kruger (1945–) is known for her black-and-white photographic images on which she superimposes texts that confront the viewer with social messages, primarily dealing with **feminist** topics. After studying in the fine-arts program at the Parsons School of Design (1965–1967), with photographers Martin Israel and **Diane Arbus** among her instructors, Kruger began her artistic career as a graphic designer for various Condé Nast magazines and also designed dust jackets for books. This experience with mass-media images was key to the development of her characteristic style in the late 1970s, when she began to combine photographs and text.

Kruger uses methods of **deconstruction** to strip away conventional meanings of clichéd phrases and sayings, putting them in a new context with photographic images. For example, in a 1988 work Kruger imposed on a photograph of a naked female doll with its head and limbs detached the familiar phrase, in bright red letters, "Use only as directed." As in many of her works, the traditionally neutral objects and phrase entice viewers, then assault them with a loaded message opposing male society's objectification and domination of women. In her more recent works Kruger has broadened her indictment of the subjugating effect of culture to address concerns such as the power of money and the traditional structures of society.

REFERENCES:

Barbara Kruger, *Love for Sale*, with text by Kate Linker (New York: Abrams, 1990);

Kruger, *Remote Control: Power, Cultures, and the World of Appearance* (Cambridge, Mass.: MIT Press, 1993).

–J.M.H.

Stanley Kubrick

A meticulous and fiercely independent film maker, Stanley Kubrick (1928–) has written, directed, and produced some of the most innovative and controversial movies of the post–World War II period.

Born in the Bronx, New York, Kubrick became a staff photographer at *Look* magazine soon after graduation from high school. In 1950, when RKO bought his first film, a short called *Day of the Fight*, Kubrick quit his job at *Look*. After directing another short for RKO and two low-budget features he financed himself, he captured the critics' attention with *The Killing* (1956), a **film-noir** treatment of a race-track robbery. His next film an adaptation of a World War I novel by Humphrey Cobb, established Kubrick's reputation as a significant American director, *Paths of Glory* (1957) is a searing indictment of French-army politics in an ac-

tual incident where an officer allowed three privates to be executed as scapegoats rather than admit that he had ordered his men to achieve an impossible military objective. The film starred **Kirk Douglas,** who was producing *Spartacus* (1960) and decided to fire the director, Anthony Mann. Douglas replaced him with Kubrick, who had already established the pattern of writing, directing, and producing his films. Disturbed by compromises he had to make while working for a major studio on *Spartacus*, Kubrick moved to England in 1961.

The 1960s was his most-productive decade. *Lolita* (1962), based on Vladimir Nabokov's best-selling but controversial novel about a grown man's obsession with a girl in her early teens, was not successful with the critics. *Dr. Strangelove; or, How I Learned to Stop Worrying and Love the Bomb* (1964), which Kubrick called "a nightmare comedy, where the things you laugh at most are really the heart of the paradoxical postures that make a nuclear war possible," was a critical and box-office success, and he followed it with the film for which he is now best known, *2001: A Space Odyssey* (1968). The film set a new, high standard for science-fiction movies and attracted a huge following of viewers who saw it again and again, despite the pronouncements of some critics, who called *2001* too long and "boring."

Kubrick's cynicism about human nature, implicit in *2001*, continues to inform the films he has made at increasingly longer intervals. *A Clockwork Orange* (1971), an innovative, highly regarded film, was controversial for its graphic depiction of sex and violence and disturbing for its warnings about the potential of government use of technology for purposes of mind control. *Barry Lyndon* (1975), based on William Makepeace Thackeray's 1844 novel, pleased most reviewers but was one of Kubrick's least profitable films. He had more financial success with *The Shining* (1980), based on a novel by **Stephen King.** *Full Metal Jacket* (1987), based on a novel by Gustave Hansford, was recognized as one of several important films about the **Vietnam War** that were released in the late 1980s.

Kubrick's films empty the heroism and humanity from romantic or melodramatic genres. He is one of the few major directors to have never made a film with a conventionally happy ending.

REFERENCES:

Thomas Nelson, *Kubrick: Inside a Film Artist's Maze* (Bloomington: Indiana University Press, 1982);

Gene Phillips, *Stanley Kubrick: A Filmmaker's Odyssey* (New York: Popular Library, 1975);

Alexander Walker, *Stanley Kubrick Directs,* expanded edition (New York: Harcourt Brace Jovanovich, 1972).

– I.R.H.

L

BURT LANCASTER

Well-known as an athletic star of gangster, western, and adventure films, Burt Lancaster (1913–) has also had parts as troubled protagonists in screen versions of plays by **Arthur Miller, William Inge,** and **Tennessee Williams.**

Lancaster was a sports star while attending De-Witt Clinton High School in New York City and earned an athletic scholarship to New York University, dropping out in 1932, after two years of school, to form the acrobatic team of Lang & Cravat with childhood friend Nick Cravat. After serving in the army during World War II, Lancaster returned to New York, where he had a chance meeting with a theatrical producer and was asked to read for a part in a Broadway war drama, *A Sound of Hunting (1945).* Lancaster got the part, which led to a Hollywood contract. The next year he made his film debut as Swede in the film version of **Ernest Hemingway**'s *The Killers* (1946) and became a star. In 1948, the same year he played the son of a factory owner in the film version of Miller's *All My Sons,* Lancaster and Harold Hecht formed their own production company, which made three popular swashbuckling adventure films, including *The Flame and the Arrow* (1950), in the early 1950s. During the same period he played the alcoholic husband in the film version of Inge's *Come Back Little Sheba* (1952) and an Italian truck driver in the screen adaptation of Williams's *The Rose Tattoo* (1955).

Among Lancaster's many memorable film roles are his portrayals of a tough sergeant in the film version of **James Jones**'s *From Here to Eternity* (1953); a ruthless columnist in another Williams adaptation, *Sweet Bird of Youth* (1957); a hypocritical evangelist in the film version of Sinclair Lewis's *Elmer Gantry* (1960; Lancaster won an Academy Award [Oscar] for best actor); a respected German judge on trial for Nazi war crimes in *Judgment at Nuremberg* (1961); and convicted murderer Robert Stroud in *Birdman of Alcatraz* (1962). His portrayal of an aging, small-time gangster in director Louis Malle's *Atlantic City* (1980) established Lancaster as a distinguished character actor. In 1990 a stroke forced him to retire just after he had completed an effective supporting role in *Field of Dreams* (1989).

REFERENCES:

Bruce Crowther, *Burt Lancaster: A Life in Films* (London: Hale, 1991);

Robert Windeler, *Burt Lancaster* (New York: St. Martin's Press, 1984).

–I.R.H.

LAUGH-IN

The brainchild of producer George Schlatter, *Rowan & Martin's Laugh-In* set the standard in the late 1960s for fast-paced, irreverent television comedy. The show combined sketches, blackouts, and one-liners with a satirical edge and was an instant success when it debuted on the **NBC** network in 1968. The hosts, Dan Rowan and Dick Martin, successful nightclub comedians, were only nominally the stars of the show. *Laugh-In* had a large cast of talented regulars, many of whom, such as Goldie Hawn, Lily Tomlin, Arte Johnson, and Henry Gibson, went on to greater stardom. Adding to the fun were surprise appearances by celebrities, including President Richard M. Nixon.

The show had many regular features that became viewer favorites: the "Fickle Finger of Fate" award; Arte Johnson's German soldier, who muttered "very interesting" in a comic German accent; Johnson and

Dictionary of Twentieth-Century Culture

Ruth Buzzi as an old couple on a park bench; "Laugh-In Looks at the News"; and jokes written on the bodies of bikini-clad girls. Phrases used on the show became part of the American vocabulary: "Sock it to me!" "You bet your bippy!" "Look that up in your Funk and Wagnall's!" *Laugh-In* was the highest-rated show on the air for its first two seasons, but as many of the favorite regulars left the series its popularity faded. It left the air in 1973 and was successfully revived in syndication in the 1980s.

– C.D.B.

JACOB LAWRENCE

Jacob Lawrence (1917–), considered one of the most important African-American painters, is best-known for figurative works that address the social and economic conditions of black Americans. His paintings are usually narrative, presenting series of scenes from contemporary society as well as black history. These series paintings are accompanied by descriptive texts that place them in historical context and often provide subtle commentary. Two of his best-known series focus on two nineteenth-century African-American heroes, Harriet Tubman and Frederick Douglass.

Lawrence was trained as an artist through his participation in the Federal Art Project of the Works Progress Administration (WPA) and was profoundly influenced by the artistically fertile Harlem Renaissance, which had begun in the 1920s. Established African-American artists such as Augusta Savage (1892–1962) and Charles Alston (1907–1977) had a significant impact on Lawrence's early development of color and design techniques. Lawrence's figurative style is characterized by bold colors, flat shapes, and a pervasive sense of pattern. As he often acknowledges, his stylistic debt to Cubism can be seen in his use of reductive geometric shapes, tilted planes, and strong, controlled outlines.

Since the 1941 exhibition of his Migration of the Negro series at the prestigious Downtown Gallery in New York City, Lawrence has received critical as well as public acclaim and has influenced the painting of many African-American artists. His work has been the subject of three retrospectives — by the American Federation of Arts (1960), the Whitney Museum of American Art (1974), and the Seattle Art Museum (1986). Lawrence is currently Professor Emeritus of Art at the University of Washington, Seattle.

REFERENCE:
Ellen Harkins Wheat, *Jacob Lawrence: American Painter* (Seattle: University of Washington Press in association with the Seattle Art Museum, 1986).

– A.A.

NORMAN LEAR

The producer of several of the most popular and controversial situation comedies of the 1970s, Norman Lear (1922–) broke into comedy writing in the 1950s and formed a production company with television director Bud Yorkin in 1959. After producing a series of mediocre theatrical films in the 1960s, the pair turned to television in 1971 with *All in the Family*. Lear peppered his script for the pilot with references to controversial issues and frank language that had long been taboo on television and resisted the efforts of network executives to soften his portrayals of these opinionated characters.

The series became one of the most popular and honored shows of the 1970s. The show was criticized by reviewers on the right — frequently the target of the show's satire — and the left — who accused Lear of trying to make bigotry comical. Following the success of *All in the Family*, Lear and Yorkin created several other popular series, including *Sanford and Son* (1972–1977), starring African-American comedian Redd Foxx, and *Maude* (1972–1978), a spinoff of *All in the Family* featuring Beatrice Arthur as Edith Bunker's cousin. These shows also featured arguing characters and sharp social commentary.

Lear's comedies of the 1970s brought a whole range of social issues, from racism and anti-Semitism to impotence and breast cancer, into the world of situation comedy. His attempts in the 1980s and early 1990s to recapture the success of those pioneering efforts did not catch on with viewing audiences. *704 Hauser*, about a black family living in Archie Bunker's old house, premiered in April 1994.

– C.D.B.

TIMOTHY LEARY

Timothy Leary (1920–) introduced the American public to LSD (lysergic acid diethylmide) and other psychedelic or hallucinogenic drugs. Although others — including writers Aldous Huxley, **Allen Ginsberg,** and **Ken Kesey** — discovered psychedelic drugs before him, it was Leary who established himself as chief guru of a vast **hippie** counterculture of young people disaffected from mainstream American society,

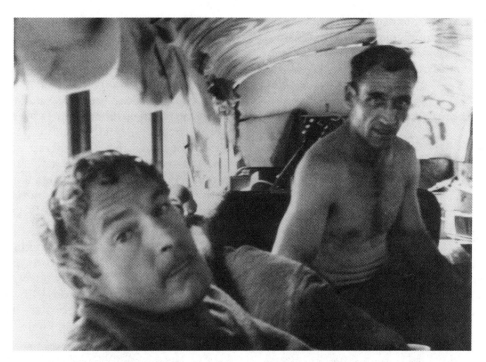

Timothy Leary and Neal Cassady on the bus Cassady drove for Ken Kesey and the Merry Pranksters on their 1964 cross-country trip, during which they visited Leary in Millbrook, New York (photograph by Allen Ginsberg)

largely because of the **Vietnam War.** They responded enthusiastically to Leary's credo: "turn on, tune in, and drop out."

Leary, who earned a Ph.D. in psychology from the University of California, Berkeley (1950), began research on psychedelic drugs in 1960 at Harvard University. He was particularly interested in the effects of these drugs on creative people and asked Ginsberg, who participated in Leary's project, to help him recruit other writers and artists. Among those who agreed to take part in 1961 were artists **Willem de Kooning** and Franz Kline, musicians **Dizzy Gillespie** and **Thelonious Monk,** and writers **Jack Kerouac** and **Robert Lowell.**

While Leary and his associate Richard Alpert (who in 1968 changed his name to Baba Ram Dass) began their investigations at Harvard with the same objective scientific approach employed by any well-designed research project, their methodology became increasingly casual. They began taking drugs with their research subjects and began to proselytize for the use of LSD and weaker hallucinogens such as mescaline, peyote, and psilocybin as a means of giving the individual a greatly heightened awareness of the inner self. By the time they were fired from Harvard in 1963 — Leary for neglect of his teaching duties, Alpert for giving LSD to an undergraduate — LSD was available on col-

lege campuses across the country, and by 1966 the U.S. Food and Drug Administration was estimating that ten percent of American college students had tried it.

In that same year Leary, who had set up a privately funded research group, predicted that LSD, marijuana, and other drugs would "be used in all schools ... to teach kids how to use their sense organs and their cellular equipment effectively...." After a trip to India in 1965, he declared himself a Hindu and called LSD "Western yoga," explaining, "The aim of all Eastern religion, like the aim of LSD, is ... to expand your consciousness and find ecstasy and revelation within." His presentations on the benefits of LSD, which attracted large crowds, were often compared to religious services. At the same time Congress was conducting hearings on psychedelic drugs, which at that time could be purchased legally for scientific research. Amid stories of bad LSD trips, psychedelic drugs were banned outright in late 1966.

In the late 1960s Leary was twice convicted for possession of marijuana and went to prison in March 1970. Six months later he escaped with the help of the **Weathermen** and ended up in Algeria, where he briefly joined forces with Weathermen and **Black Panthers**, who were also fugitives from the American justice system. In 1973 federal agents caught up with him in Afghanistan, and he was returned to prison. After his release in 1976, Leary founded the SMILE (Space Migration, Increased Intelligence, Life Extension) movement, advocating a link between self-development and exploration of outer space.

REFERENCES:

Timothy Leary, *Flashbacks: An Autobiography* (Los Angeles: Tarcher, 1983);

Jay Stevens, *Storming Heaven: LSD and the American Dream* (New York: Atlantic Monthly Press, 1987).

– K.L.R.

LED ZEPPELIN

Led Zeppelin was one of the most popular British rock groups to follow **The Beatles** in gaining a worldwide audience. In America it was one of the top rock bands of the 1970s and a major influence on **heavy-metal** music.

Founded in 1968 as the New Yardbirds, Led Zeppelin (the new name was suggested by Keith Moon of The Who) included Robert Plant, Jimmy Page, John Paul Jones, and John Bonham. The band's first album, *Led Zeppelin* (1968), featured blues-influenced rock and its trademark guitar solos and searing vocals. Led Zeppelin soon became known for mystical lyrics and innovative album covers and record sleeves. In 1973 the group made its first tour of the United States, where it had been popular since the late 1960s. The band's best-selling songs in America include "Immigrant Song" (1970) and "D'yer Mak'er" (1973). Their 1976 concert film, *The Song Remains the Same,* was also popular. Its most famous song was "Stairway to Heaven," from their 1972 untitled album (generally known as *Led Zeppelin IV*). The group disbanded upon Bonham's death in 1980. Plant and Page worked together with other musicians during the early 1980s as the Honeydrippers, recording the 1984 hit song "Sea of Love."

REFERENCE:

Stephen Davis, *Hammer of the Gods: The Led Zeppelin Saga* (New York: Morrow, 1985).

– L.D.S.

HARPER LEE

Southern writer Harper Lee (1926–) won the 1961 Pulitzer Prize for fiction with her only published novel, *To Kill a Mockingbird* (1960), a powerful plea for racial justice that helped to rally support for the growing **civil rights movement** in the United States.

Lee's novel is set during the 1930s in a small, rural Alabama town much like her hometown, Monroeville, Alabama, where one of her childhood friends was **Truman Capote** (the model for Dill in her novel). In *To Kill a Mockingbird* Jean Louise, nicknamed Scout, and her older brother, Jem, learn about racial prejudice firsthand after their lawyer father, Atticus Finch, agrees to defend Tom Robinson, a black man who has been falsely accused of raping a white woman. Taunted by classmates and neighbors about their father's "lawing for niggers," Jem and Scout inadvertently thwart plans to lynch Robinson, who is found guilty even though Atticus clearly proves him innocent.

Published in July 1960, *To Kill a Mockingbird* sold more than 500,000 copies over the next year, unusually large sales for a first novel. A film version (1962) starring **Gregory Peck,** with a screenplay by Horton Foote, was equally popular, earning Academy Awards (Oscars) for Peck and Foote.

In December 1959 Lee went to Kansas with Capote, who was beginning work on *In Cold Blood* (1966) and played an important role in the preliminary research for the book. By 1961 she had started another novel, but it remains unpublished and possibly unfinished.

– T.P.

SPIKE LEE

Spike Lee (1957–) was the first of several African-American film makers to prove that well-made movies about black people and so-called black political and social issues could be successful with people of all races.

Born in Atlanta, Georgia, Shelton Jackson Lee (called Spike since childhood) graduated from Morehouse University in 1979 and studied film making with **Martin Scorsese** at New York University, earning an M.A. in 1983. Lee produced, wrote, and performed in his first full-length film, the low-budget *She's Gotta Have It* (1986), shot in twelve days for $175,000. Avant-garde in style, this comic saga of an independent young black woman, who enters into sexual relationships with a series of stereotypical and unsatisfying men, earned critical praise (including comparisons between Lee and **Woody Allen**), attracted a substantial audience of both blacks and whites, and grossed several million dollars. Lee's next film, *School Daze* (1988), a musical comedy about life at a black college much like Morehouse, was controversial for its depiction of prejudice among light-skinned and dark-skinned African Americans.

Far more political than any of Allen's films, Lee's *Do the Right Thing* (1989), is generally considered his masterpiece, as well as one of the finest movies of the 1980s. Set on a sweltering summer day in a predominantly black Brooklyn neighborhood, which includes a pizzeria run by Italian-Americans and a Korean-owned grocery store, the film unsparingly dissects the motives of all races as ethnic tensions erupt in violence.

Lee's next film, *Mo' Better Blues* (1990), provoked charges of anti-Semitism — which Lee denied — with its portrayal of Jewish club owners exploiting black entertainers. Lee focused attention on the growing separation of blacks and whites in the United States with *Jungle Fever* (1991), about the troubled romantic relationship between a married black architect with a good job in an white-owned firm and a white secretary from a Brooklyn neighborhood known for racial intolerance. The critical and popular success of this film was overshadowed by the major media attention and lavish critical praise surrounding *Malcolm X* (1992), an epic film biography of the leader of the Nation of Islam.

REFERENCE:
Spike Lee, *Five to Five: The Films of Spike Lee* (New York: Workman, 1991).

                                                                        – I.R.H.

ANNIE LEIBOVITZ

Since the 1970s Annie Leibovitz (1950–) has maintained a high profile in American photojournalism with her portrait photographs of celebrities. Her professional success began almost immediately after she was hired by *Rolling Stone* magazine to photograph rock stars and other counterculture figures in the San Francisco Bay area. At that time she was a student at San Francisco Art Institute. Her first major out-of-town assignment for *Rolling Stone* came in 1971, a cover portrait of John Lennon. Initially Leibovitz used a 35-mm camera and shot crude, black-and-white images of celebrities as she found them — at home, in hotel rooms, on the road. Throughout her early career, she was strongly influenced by the work of Henri Cartier Bresson, **Robert Frank, Richard Avedon,** and **Irving Penn.**

In 1974 *Rolling Stone* began using full color and treating its unusually large front cover practically as a poster. With these new graphic-design opportunities, Leibovitz began to employ a more premeditated style, and her images became bolder and more stylized, with greater attention to lighting and staging. In 1984 she moved to the new *Vanity Fair,* under the editorial direction of Tina Brown. There she further expanded her

dramatic approach to celebrity portraiture by working with a group of stylists and technical assistants.

Leibovitz's portraits are usually the products of well-developed collaborations with her subjects, who are themselves creative individuals. Many of her best-known images are essentially performances pieces that combine her genius for inventing poses with the sitter's willingness to take risks (including self-parody). Her compositions often involve extensive conceptual preparations, such as having special costumes and rooms created, and planning the use of interesting props and locations. Images such as her portraits of David Byrne, Patti Smith, John Belushi, Mick Jagger, John Lennon, **Yoko Ono, Keith Haring,** and Steve Martin have become, for many, the quintessential representations of certain American popular-culture heroes and moments.

REFERENCES:
Charles Hagen, "Annie Leibovitz Reveals Herself," *ARTnews,* 91 (March 1992): 90–95;

Photographs / Annie Leibovitz (New York: Rolling Stone Press, 1983);

Photographs: Annie Leibovitz, 1970–1990 (New York: HarperCollins, 1991).

                                                                        – K.B.

JACK LEMMON

Although film actor Jack Lemmon (1925–) is generally considered a versatile light comedian, he has proved that he can play serious roles with equal effectiveness. In a career that spans more that forty years, Lemmon has had eight Academy Award (Oscar) nominations and won two Oscars, best supporting actor for his portrayal of Ensign Pulver in *Mr. Roberts* (1955) and best actor for his starring role in *Save the Tiger* (1973).

The son of a wealthy Irish-American Boston doughnut manufacturer, Lemmon graduated from Harvard University in 1946 (with seven months off in 1945 for wartime naval service). He worked in radio and television and on the New York stage before he was invited to Hollywood to co-star with Judy Holliday in *It Should Happen to You* (1954). In his third film, the screen version of Joshua Logan's hit play *Mr. Roberts,* his portrayal of the cringing, conniving, but ultimately rebellious Ensign Pulver made his reputation as a comic actor. He went on to play comic roles as hapless, put-upon, average guys in **Billy Wilder** movies such as *Some Like It Hot* (1959), *The Apartment* (1960), and *The Fortune Cookie* (1966) and in film versions of **Neil Simon** plays such as *The Odd Couple* (1968), *The Out-*

Frederick Loewe and Alan Jay Lerner in 1956, just after *My Fair Lady* opened on Broadway (AP/Wide World Photos)

of-Towners (1970), and *The Prisoner of Second Avenue* (1975).

Lemmon has also demonstrated his ability in serious dramatic parts: an alcoholic husband in *The Days of Wine and Roses* (1962), a financially strapped garment manufacturer in *Save the Tiger* (1973), a whistle-blowing nuclear-power-plant supervisor in *The China Syndrome* (1979), an anguished father in *Missing* (1982), a failing real-estate salesman in *Glengarry Glen Ross* (1992), and a man who walks out on his family, reappears twenty years later, and disappears again in **Robert Altman**'s *Short Cuts* (1993). After *Short Cuts* he returned to comedy in *Grumpy Old Men* (1994). The American Film Institute gave Lemmon its Life Achievement Award in 1987.

REFERENCE:
Michael Freedland, *Jack Lemmon* (New York: St. Martin's Press, 1985).

– I.R.H.

ALAN JAY LERNER AND FREDERICK LOEWE

The most successful creators of postwar **Broadway musicals** after **Rodgers and Hammerstein,** writer Alan Jay Lerner (1918–1986) and composer Frederick Loewe (1901–1988) combined sophisticated lyrics and romantic scores reminiscent of turn-of-the-century operettas in a series of musicals about apparently incompatible couples finding true love. Their most popular collaboration, *My Fair Lady,* was one of the most influential musicals of the 1950s with its extension of dialogue into the lyrics and the half-spoken singing style used by Rex Harrison as Professor Henry Higgins.

Lerner and Loewe met in 1942 and collaborated on a musical, *Life of the Party,* in Detroit that year. Their first successful musical, *Brigadoon* (1947), about a ghost village in Scotland, ran for 581 performances. Their next hit, *Paint Your Wagon* (1951), based on the California gold rush, had 289 performances. In 1956 they adapted George Bernard Shaw's 1913 play *Pygmalion* for Broadway as *My Fair Lady* — with a happier ending. A smash hit that ran for 2,717 performances over six years, longer than any musical up to that time, it starred Harrison, Julie Andrews, and Stanley Holloway. The show includes memorable songs such as "Why Can't the English," "Wouldn't It Be Loverly," "With a Little Bit of Luck," "I Could Have Danced All Night," "The Rain in Spain," and "I've Grown Accustomed to Her Face." The cast album has sold more than five million copies.

Their next collaboration was the film musical *Gigi* (1958), based on a novel by Colette. The movie received nine Academy Awards (Oscars), then a record, including awards for best screenplay and best song. They turned it into a stage musical in 1973. Their last musical, *Camelot* (1960), was inspired by T. H. White's retelling of the Arthurian legends. Starring **Richard Burton** and Andrews, the show ran for 873 performances. Loewe retired from composing after *Camelot,* and Lerner never again found so compatible a collaborator. Their last partnership was on the 1974 film *The Little Prince,* for which Lerner wrote the screenplay and Loewe, emerging from retirement, wrote the score.

REFERENCES:
Gene Lees, *Inventing Champagne: The Worlds of Lerner and Loewe* (New York: St. Martin's Press, 1990);
Alan Jay Lerner, *The Street Where I Live: The Story of My Fair Lady, Gigi and Camelot* (New York: Norton, 1978).

– I.R.H.

DENISE LEVERTOV

Denise Levertov (1923–) is the only well-known female poet among the practitioners of **Projective**

Verse, who also include **Charles Olson, Robert Duncan,** and **Robert Creeley.** Although she was never associated with **Black Mountain College,** Levertov has been called a Black Mountain Poet because Creeley published her poems in the *Black Mountain Review.*

Born in England, where her first book, *The Double Image,* was published in 1946, Levertov married American novelist Mitchell Goodman in 1947 and immigrated to the United States in 1948. (She became an American citizen in 1956.) After settling in New York City, she discovered the poetry of **William Carlos Williams,** became friends with Creeley and Duncan, read Olson's works, and consciously reshaped herself as an American poet.

In the 1960s Levertov attempted to use her poetry as a vehicle for social change, writing about events such as the 1967 riots in Detroit, civil war and starvation in Biafra, and the **Vietnam War.** (In 1968 her husband was tried with Dr. Benjamin Spock for conspiring to aid draft resisters.) Levertov's participation in antiwar protests culminated in her 1972 trip to Hanoi with poet Muriel Rukeyser and Jane Hart, wife of Sen. Philip Hart. By the time *The Freeing of the Dust* appeared in 1975, her poetry was beginning to signal a move away from the public arena, as she contemplated the disintegration of her marriage, which ended in divorce in 1972.

Since the late 1970s Levertov's poetry has been a spiritual quest through belief and doubt to define what she calls her own "Christian unorthodoxy."

REFERENCES:

Harry Marten, *Understanding Denise Levertov* (Columbia: University of South Carolina Press, 1988);

Audrey T. Rodgers, *Denise Levertov: The Poetry of Engagement* (Rutherford, N.J.: Fairleigh Dickinson University Press, 1993).

                                                                – K.L.R.

Jerry Lewis

Known in France as "le Roi du Crazy" (the King of Crazy), American comedian Jerry Lewis (1926–) is admired for his mugging antics and for hosting an annual telethon to raise money for a cure for muscular dystrophy. Despite his talent and substantial popularity American critics have found him tasteless, but he is virtually idolized in France.

Born Joseph Levitch, Lewis began working as a comedian in 1942 but had little success until he teamed up with singer Dean Martin in 1946. They soon became one of the top comedy teams in America and signed a contract with Paramount Pictures in 1949. They made

sixteen popular but critically unsuccessful films together before an acrimonious split in 1956. Their film formula was to have an idiotic Lewis threatening the romantic fortunes of his increasingly annoyed pal and straight man Martin — "a handsome man and a monkey," as Lewis described them. Lewis continued to star in films on his own, making his directorial debut with *The Bellboy* (1960), which he wrote. He also wrote, directed, and produced the Jekyll-and-Hyde comedy *The Nutty Professor* (1963), often regarded as his best film. His popularity declined in the late 1960s, but his 1981 film *Hardly Working* did well at the box office, and he gave an effective dramatic performance for **Martin Scorsese** as a comedian kidnapped by a deranged fan in *The King of Comedy* (1983). In 1972 he also starred as a clown who leads children to their deaths during the **Holocaust** in *The Day the Clown Cried,* which was not released due to legal complications.

Lewis has devoted a considerable share of his energies during the past decades to his charitable work for the Muscular Dystrophy Association. He began raising money for a cure in the late 1940s and appeared in his first local telethon in 1951. The first Labor Day telethon was held in New York in 1966.

REFERENCES:

Edward Edelson, *Funny Men of the Movies* (Garden City, N.Y.: Doubleday, 1970), pp. 116–120;

Jerry Lewis with Herb Gluck, *Jerry Lewis in Person* (New York: Atheneum, 1982).

                                                                – I.R.H.

Liberace

The flamboyant American entertainer Liberace (1919–1987) was as famous for his campy showmanship as for his showy piano interpretations of light classics (often in condensed form) and popular tunes. Though critics thought he wasted his talent, he had a loyal following.

Born Wladziu Valentino Liberace, he demonstrated early talent at the piano and considered a concert career. However, Liberace preferred working as a popular entertainer. He played in movie houses and nightclubs in the late 1930s and early 1940s. By 1945 he was famous. He toured the country and starred in a popular television program, *The Liberace Show* (1952–1956). Many of his performances after the 1950s were in Las Vegas, a location that suited the outrageous touches he added to his shows, such as placing a candelabrum on his piano and wearing a glittering array of sequined jackets and fur capes. At one point in the

1960s Liberace was the highest-paid performer in the world.

Liberace was the target of much speculation concerning his private life, especially his homosexuality, which he publicly denied. Upon his death (from complications of **AIDS**), much of his multimillion-dollar estate was bequeathed to charities throughout the world.

REFERENCE:

Bob Thomas, *Liberace: The True Story* (New York: St. Martin's Press, 1987).

– L.D.S.

ROY LICHTENSTEIN

A leader in the **Pop Art** movement of the 1960s, Roy Lichtenstein (1923–) is known primarily for his painted versions of popular comics. Lichtenstein's earliest cartoon paintings were based on bubble-gum wrappers that he collected from his children. In 1961 he began to take frames from well-known comic strips and paint the images, greatly enlarged, on canvas. *Look, Mickey* (1961) shows Mickey Mouse and Donald Duck fishing. Donald peers into the water, which resembles an abstract painting by **Jackson Pollock,** and exclaims, "Look, Mickey, I've hooked a big one!" Mickey laughs, realizing that Donald has hooked only himself. Although at first glance the painting seems devoid of any critical comment, Lichtenstein is actually poking fun at the **Abstract Expressionists.**

Though he differs from **minimalists** in his use of subjects from popular culture, Lichtenstein's artworks share many characteristics with the works of those artists. His images are simplified, impersonal, bereft of detail, and highly industrial. To produce this industrial effect in his art, Lichtenstein employs a technique that echoes the mechanical dot-printing process. His images are made up of carefully painted dots that look as if they were printed mechanically onto the canvas. Lichtenstein's comics are, in fact, more polished and neater than the originals that inspired them. Using this technique, Lichtenstein empties his paintings of any trace of personal style or emotion.

Critics, and Lichtenstein himself, rarely discuss the subjects of these early comic-strip works. Until his divorce in 1965, Lichtenstein seemed preoccupied with themes of love and war. His paintings based on love comics emphasize sappy sentimentality and include depictions of teary-eyed girls who spout silly melodramatic phrases such as "I don't care! I'd rather sink than call Brad for help!" Paintings inspired by war comics — such as *Takka Takka* (1962), *Whaam!* (1963), and

O.K. Hot-Shot (1963) — are heavily underscored with stereotypical battle noise and violence.

Since the late 1960s Lichtenstein's subjects have come more frequently from the realm of "high" art. He produced a series of paintings magnifying architectural entablatures and decorative moldings. He often takes works by famous artists — for example, Claude Monet's *Water Lilies* — and makes "pop" versions of them using his painted-dot process.

REFERENCES:

Lawrence Alloway, *Roy Lichtenstein* (New York: Abbeville Press, 1983);

Diane Waldman, *Roy Lichtenstein* (New York: Guggenheim Museum, 1993).

– C.S.

LITERARY HISTORY OF THE UNITED STATES

First published in 1948, *Literary History of the United States* (*LHUS*) is an important and comprehensive work that champions the national character of writing in the United States. For nearly three decades it had a major influence on the canon of American literature. Writers not included, such as Djuna Barnes, **James Gould Cozzens,** and **John O'Hara** generally were not taught in college classrooms, and writers of hardboiled detective fiction and **science fiction** were excluded entirely.

Robert E. Spiller, Willard Thorp, Thomas H. Johnson, and Henry Seidel Canby first met as the editorial board for *LHUS* in 1940 to plan a redefinition of the literary past of America that would supersede the *Cambridge History of American Literature* (1917, 1918). They assembled dozens of contributors to write essays on facets of American literature from colonial times to 1945. Macmillan published the first edition, composed of historical essays and an extensive primary and secondary bibliography, in 1948. The second edition (1953), the third (1963), and the fourth (1974) employed the same format. The later editions added chapters on literature after World War II and updated bibliographical material but made no substantial revisions to the original text.

Because the editors believed that literature is a reflection of culture, *LHUS* includes chapters on historical and intellectual backgrounds as well as on literature. In addition to the traditional genres of fiction, poetry, and drama, *LHUS* includes coverage of forms and subjects such as journals, pamphlets, writings on politics and religion, and folklore as well as journalism, publishing, and literary criticism. The editors strove to combine the various essays — by contributors such as R. P. Blackmur, Henry Steele Commager, Malcolm Cowley, F. O. Matthiessen, H. L. Mencken, and Carl Sandburg — into a unified narrative while permitting differences of opinion on the value of individual writers and works.

Such differences were minor, however, and *LHUS* demonstrates a remarkable consensus on American literary history concerning which writers belong in the literary canon. The diversity of opinion and subjects in contemporary literary studies, with challenges to the canon from **feminist critics** and advocates of **multiculturalism,** would make this consensus and a book such as *LHUS* unlikely in the 1980s or 1990s, as seen in the wide range of subjects and opinions in the *Columbia Literary History of the United States* (1987). Focusing on "great" writers in their historical contexts, *LHUS* celebrates a largely white, largely male canon of literature, which has caused some critics to call the work limited at best, elitist at worst due to its underrepresentation of major authors. Nonetheless, *LHUS* was a major achievement, impressive in size and scope, and students and scholars of American literature have found it an indispensable research tool for decades.

REFERENCE:

A. Walton Litz, "Literary Criticism," in *Harvard Guide to Contemporary American Writing,* edited by Daniel Hoffman (Cambridge, Mass. & London: Belknap/Harvard University Press, 1979), pp. 51–83.

– D.H.-F.

Live Aid

On 13 July 1985 Bob Geldof, new-wave singer for The Boomtown Rats, staged Live Aid — twin concerts in London and Philadelphia — to aid famine victims in Ethiopia. The event was an extension of the humanitarian efforts of Band Aid, a group of thirty-seven British pop stars assembled by Geldof to record "Do They Know It's Christmas?" (1984), a single which raised approximately $11 million for Ethiopian famine victims.

The largest rock benefit ever assembled, Live Aid included performances by more than sixty well-known figures in pop music. In London performers included Elton John, U2, Elvis Costello, Sting, David Bowie, and The Who; in Philadelphia, appearances were made by **Bob Dylan, The Beach Boys,** Mick Jagger, **Tina Turner, Madonna,** Robert Plant and Jimmy Page (formerly of **Led Zeppelin**), and Duran Duran. Seventy-two thousand concert goers showed up in London;

ninety thousand attended the concert in Philadelphia, organized by rock impresario Bill Graham.

The single-day event, described by Geldof as a "global jukebox," was televised in more than one-hundred countries — including Communist-bloc nations — and attracted 1.5 billion viewers, making it the most-watched live event in the history of television. Ticket sales, television rights, and donations raised more than $40 million for the famine victims of Ethiopia.

Many critics consider that Live Aid marked the renaissance of activism within the music community. Inspired by Geldof's efforts, Willie Nelson staged **Farm Aid** to benefit American farmers. Similar rock benefits have since been organized for social and political causes ranging from **AIDS** and Amnesty International to animal rights and environmentalism.

REFERENCES:

Jay Cocks, "Rocking the Global Village," *Time,* 126 (22 July 1985): 66-67;

David Fricke, "The Man Who Wouldn't Take No for an Answer," *Rolling Stone* (15 August 1985): 19-20+;

Michael Goldberg, "The Day the World Rocked," *Rolling Stone* (15 August 1985): 22-26+.

– H.G.

Frank Loesser

Frank Loesser (1910–1969) was a prolific songwriter for **Broadway musicals** and for the movies. He is known for his World War II morale booster "Praise the Lord and Pass the Ammunition" (1942) and for a series of popular musicals after the war, particularly *Guys and Dolls* (1950).

Loesser started writing songs in the early 1930s and spent most of the 1930s and 1940s as a successful lyricist for Hollywood films. He went to Broadway with **George Abbott**'s *Where's Charley?* (1948), for which he wrote the score and the lyrics. He continued to work in film, winning an Academy Award (Oscar) for "Baby, It's Cold Outside" from *Neptune's Daughter* (1949). He also wrote songs for *Hans Christian Andersen* (1951); some of them, such as "Thumbelina" and "The Ugly Duckling," have become children's classics.

Loesser's first hit on Broadway was *Guys and Dolls,* a musical based on stories by Damon Runyon, for which Loesser wrote the score and the lyrics. It ran for 1,200 performances and was filmed in 1955, starring **Marlon Brando** and **Frank Sinatra.** Loesser wrote the score and libretto for *The Most Happy Fella* (1956); based on Sidney Howard's play *They Knew What They Wanted,* the musical had 676 performances. He received a Pulitzer Prize for his score and lyrics for his most successful musical, *How to Succeed in Business Without Really Trying* (1961). The show ran for 1,417 performances. Acclaimed revivals of *Guys and Dolls* and *The Most Happy Fella* opened in the 1991–1992 Broadway season.

REFERENCE:

Susan Loesser, *A Most Remarkable Fella: Frank Loesser and the Guys and Dolls in His Life — A Portrait by His Daughter* (New York: Donald I. Fine, 1993).

– I.R.H.

ROBERT LOWELL

Robert Lowell (1917–1977) was widely acclaimed during his lifetime as a major poet in the generation of writers who came of age during the 1940s. He won a Pulitzer Prize for his first full-length book, *Lord Weary's Castle* (1946), and another for *The Dolphin* (1973). His *Life Studies* (1959), often called the genesis of the **confessional-poetry** movement, won a National Book Award.

A member of the prominent Lowell family of Boston, Robert Traill Spence Lowell — great-grandson and namesake of novelist Robert Lowell, great-grandnephew of poet James Russell Lowell, and a fourth cousin once removed of poet Amy Lowell — began his career under the influence of Allen Tate, John Crowe Ransom, Cleanth Brooks, and **Robert Penn Warren.** The lessons of these Fugitive poets / **New Critics** are apparent in Lowell's first two books, *Lord Weary's Castle* and *The Mills of the Kavanaughs* (1951). While the poems have autobiographical elements, they largely adhere to the impersonality, classical decorum, and traditional form preached by **T. S. Eliot** and taught to Lowell by Tate and Ransom. By the mid 1950s Lowell was beginning to find new models — including poems by his friend Elizabeth Bishop, the confessional poems of W. D. Snodgrass, and especially the free-verse, personal poems in simplified everyday diction that **William Carlos Williams** was writing in the 1950s. Though he was to return to formal verse on occasion, Lowell had by 1957 dropped all pretense of poetic objectivity or impersonality and had begun using his personal experiences in free-verse confessional poems.

Though Lowell quite rightly denied that he had invented confessional poetry, the publication of *Life Studies* in 1959 signaled a turning point in his career and initiated a revolution in American poetry. While continuing to open his life to the reader, Lowell extended his range to social commentary, beginning in 1960 by writing the title poem in his next book, *For the Union Dead* (1964). Later in the decade, Lowell — who had been imprisoned for six months in 1943–1944 after refusing to serve in the armed forces — became involved in protesting the **Vietnam War,** publicly turning down an invitation to read his poetry at the White House (1965), joined **Norman Mailer** and others in the March on the Pentagon (1967), and actively participating in Sen. **Eugene McCarthy**'s 1968 presidential campaign. The events of 1967–1968 form a framework for the free-verse "sonnets" in *Notebook, 1967–68* (1969, revised 1970), records of Lowell's private consciousness during this period. He continued to revise these poems and wrote more in the same form during the early 1970s. The irregular, free-verse poems in Lowell's *Day by Day* (1977), the last book published before his death from a heart attack in 1977, continue his poetic autobiography, chronicling his continuing battle with manic depression, for which he had been intermittently hospitalized since 1949.

Some literary scholars have called the 1960s and 1970s the Age of Lowell in American poetry.

REFERENCES:

Ian Hamilton, *Robert Lowell: A Biography* (New York: Random House, 1982);

Jeffrey Meyers, ed. *Robert Lowell, Interviews and Memoirs* (Ann Arbor: University of Michigan Press, 1988).

– K.L.R.

LP RECORDS

Columbia Records introduced the long-playing record (LP) as a medium for sound recordings in 1948. LPs produced better quality sound reproduction than 78 rpm records, providing listeners with a closer approximation of actual performance. For nearly four decades, LPs were the principal medium for recorded sound, especially music, though they were challenged by taped recordings such as reel-to-reel, eight-track, and cassette tapes.

Before 1948, commercial recordings were limited to shellac records played at 78 rpm (revolutions per minute). These records were easily damaged and could hold only four minutes of music per side. Constructed of vinyl, the LP was played at 33 1/3 rpm and could contain up to twenty-five minutes per side. In addition, the LP was unbreakable and scratched less easily than a 78. With the smaller and shorter 45 rpm records introduced by RCA Victor in 1949, LP records quickly eclipsed 78s. The development of high-fidelity (hi-fi) players in the early 1950s and the advent of stereophonic sound in 1958 further solidified the popularity of the LP by improving the quality of the sound, setting the recording industry stan-

Mark Hamill, George Lucas, and Harrison Ford during the filming of *Star Wars*

dard for decades. Improvements were introduced in the 1980s with digital recording. It was only with the appearance of the compact disc (CD) in the 1980s, with its even higher-quality digital sound, that the LP became less popular. By the early 1990s LPs had been superseded by CDs and cassette tapes.

REFERENCES:

Lawrence G. Goldsmith, "War in Three Speeds," *Nation,* 168 (7 May 1949): 523–525;

Ann M. Lingg, "Record Rumpus," *Reader's Digest,* 55 (December 1949): 139–142.

                          – L.D.S.

GEORGE LUCAS

The unexpected, blockbuster success of *Star Wars* (1977) gave its director, George Lucas (1944–), the freedom to create a cinema conglomerate that has made some of the most technically innovative American films of the twentieth century.

Born in Modesto, California, Lucas studied filmmaking at the University of Southern California (B.A., 1966; graduate study, 1967), winning the best dramatic film award at the Third National Student Film Festival with *THX 1138: 4EB* in 1967. In a Warner Bros. stu-

dent-apprenticeship program, he worked with **Francis Ford Coppola** on *Finian's Rainbow* (1968) and *The Rain People* (1969) before expanding his prize-winning student film into the visually impressive science-fiction feature *THX 1138* (1971).

In 1973 Lucas's low-budget film *American Graffiti* was a critical and box-office success. A nostalgic picture of one night in the lives of Modesto teenagers during summer 1962 as they "cruise" around town in their cars and ponder what to do after high school, the film includes a classic coming-of-age myth that may be found in *THX 1138* and *Star Wars* as well: a young man's quest to escape a sterile hometown environment and fulfill his true destiny.

The popularity of *Star Wars* freed Lucas from industry constraints, earning him enough money to give up film directing and shape his career on his own terms. He has produced two lucrative *Star Wars* sequels (with another film in the series on the way) and a trilogy of Indiana Jones films, which he persuaded his friend **Steven Spielberg** to direct. Among the strengths of these films and the original *Star Wars* are their striking and innovative visual effects, which are widely imitated but seldom equaled. These special effects were created by Industrial Light and Magic, part of the Lucas entertainment empire, which also includes

Otto Luening and Vladimir Ussachevsky at the Columbia-Princeton Electronic Music Center in New York, 1961

and his *Wisconsin Symphony* (1975) are among his most important nonelectronic works. Luening is best known, however, for his contributions to electronic music, beginning in 1952 with *Fantasy on Tape,* with flute altered on tape, and in 1954 with his and Ussachevsky's *Rhapsodic Variations for Tape Recorder and Orchestra,* the first extended composition to feature live performers with an electronically created background. He also collaborated with Ussachevsky on *A Poem in Cycles and Bells* (1954), which combines tape and orchestra. Such works placed Luening in the musical avant-garde, a position he has used to promote all sorts of contemporary American music.

REFERENCES:

Ralph Hartsock, *Otto Luening: A Bio-Bibliography* (New York, Westport, Conn., & London: Greenwood, 1991);

Otto Luening, *The Odyssey of an American Composer: The Autobiography of Otto Luening* (New York: Scribners, 1980).

– L.D.S.

Lucasfilm, Lucasarts, and the THX stereo system for motion-picture theaters. Although Lucas has not directed a feature film since *Star Wars,* he did direct several episodes of the television series *The Young Indiana Jones Chronicles* in 1992.

REFERENCE:

Dale Pollock, *Skywalking: The Life and Films of George Lucas* (New York: Harmony, 1983).

– I.R.H.

OTTO LUENING

Composer Otto Luening (1900–) began his long and productive career in the 1910s and is still composing in his nineties. He was one of the pioneers of **electronic music** in the United States.

Born in Milwaukee, Luening studied in Germany and Switzerland, becoming an accomplished flutist and conductor as well as a composer. He taught at several colleges in America before settling at Columbia University in 1944, where he codirected the Columbia-Princeton Electronic Music Center with Vladimir Ussachevsky from 1959 to 1980.

Employing traditional styles as well as innovative techniques in his work, Luening has written more than three hundred compositions, including pieces for younger performers. His opera *Evangeline* (1948), based on the poem by Henry Wadsworth Longfellow,

LORETTA LYNN

Loretta Lynn (1935–) has been one of the top female country-music singers and songwriters since the 1960s. The success of her traditional country songs, often about working-class women, and the popularity of her 1976 autobiography *Loretta Lynn: Coal Miner's Daughter,* the basis for an equally popular film in 1980, helped to return country music to its rural roots in the late 1970s and the 1980s.

Lynn grew up in Butcher Hollow, Kentucky, and married at age thirteen. She started singing and writing songs while raising her children, and she began to perform in the late 1950s. She and her husband promoted her first recording, "I'm a Honky Tonk Girl," by driving to radio stations across the country in 1960, which led to her debut at the Grand Ole Opry in Nashville that year. She quickly became one of the most successful performers in country music, recording several hits in the next two decades, including "Don't Come Home a-Drinkin' (With Lovin' on Your Mind)" (1966) and "Coal Miner's Daughter" (1970). In the 1970s she performed frequently with Conway Twitty, and since then she has continued to tour and record.

REFERENCE:

Loretta Lynn with George Vecsey, *Loretta Lynn: Coal Miner's Daughter* (Chicago: Regnery, 1976).

– D.H.-F.

M

Yo-Yo Ma

Yo-Yo Ma (1955–) is the most popular and talented of his generation of cellists. He has used his success to popularize the cello and to expand its repertoire through his transcriptions for cello from music for other instruments

Yo-Yo Ma rehearsing with Riccardo Muti and the Philadelphia Orchestra, 1988 (photograph by Jean E. Brubaker)

and by commissions for new works. Ma is especially noted for his technique and emotional playing style.

Born in Paris, Ma began playing an upturned viola like a cello at age four because an actual cello was larger than he was. Moving with his family to the United States at age seven, Ma was enrolled at the Juilliard School of Music two years later. In his twenties he became a celebrity by undertaking a whirlwind schedule of appearances, both as a soloist and with other performers as a chamber musician. He has also reached out to children through appearances on *Sesame Street* and *Mister Rogers' Neighborhood*.

REFERENCES:

David Blum, "A Process Larger Than Oneself," *New Yorker*, 65 (1 May 1989): 41, 42, 46, 48, 50–56, 61–66, 68–74;

Herbert Kupferberg, "Yo-Yo Ma," *Stereo Review*, 55 (April 1990): 70–72.

– L.D.S.

Lorin Maazel

Lorin Maazel (1930–) has become one of the most respected orchestral conductors of the second half of the twentieth century. His performances, though emotionally restrained, are noted for their vibrancy and attention to detail.

Maazel, who also showed an early gift for playing the violin, began studying conducting at age seven with Vladimir Bakaleinikoff, an assistant conductor of the Los Angeles Philharmonic Orchestra. One year later, Maazel conducted publicly for the first time, leading Bakaleinikoff's student orchestra through Franz Schubert's "Unfinished" Symphony. At age thirteen he conducted the New York Philharmonic Orchestra in an entire program. Maazel entered the University of Pitts-

Kenneth Millar (Ross MacDonald; right), with his wife, mystery writer Margaret Millar, and his publisher, Alfred A. Knopf (photograph by Hal Boucher)

burgh and the violin section of the Pittsburgh Symphony Orchestra when he was sixteen. A 1951 Fulbright scholarship allowed Maazel to study in Italy, and he made his formal adult debut as a conductor in 1953 in Catania, Sicily. Many worldwide engagements followed, including the Bayreuth Festival (where Maazel was the first American to conduct) in 1960 and the **New York Metropolitan Opera** in 1962. His conducting activities have included the artistic directorships of the Deutsche Oper in Berlin (1965–1971), the **Cleveland Orchestra** (1972–1982), and the Vienna Staatsoper (1982–1984). In 1986 Maazel assumed leadership of the Pittsburgh Symphony Orchestra, where he is still active.

REFERENCE:

Kathleen Hinton-Braaton, "Lorin Maazel: Master of His Craft," *Instrumentalist,* 38 (January 1984): 30–31.

– L.D.S.

Ross Macdonald

Ross Macdonald (1915-1983) led the second generation of hard-boiled detective novelists, heir to the literary innovations of Dashiell Hammett and Raymond Chandler. Macdonald used the genre to explore the workings of the human psyche in more than twenty novels and became one of the most successful American mystery writers in the post–World War II era.

Born Kenneth Millar, Macdonald published his first novel, the spy thriller *The Dark Tunnel* (1944), under his own name while working on his doctorate in English at the University of Michigan. By the time he received his degree in 1952, he had published six more novels, and had begun using the pseudonyms John Macdonald and John Ross Macdonald. Turning his back on an academic career, Macdonald continued writing, permanently adopting the Ross Macdonald by-line with *The Barbarous Coast* (1956) after fellow author John D. Macdonald complained that the similarity of their names was confusing.

Macdonald is most famous for his novels which feature Lew Archer, who premiered in *The Moving Target* (1949). Macdonald came into his own as a writer in the 1960s when he began writing more complexly plotted and emotionally driven works, reflecting his interest in social issues, particularly environmentalism. After **Eudora Welty** praised his work in her review of *The Underground Man* (1971) in the **New York Times**

Book Review, Macdonald broke free from categorization as a genre writer.

References

Matthew J. Bruccoli, *Kenneth Millar/Ross Macdonald: A Descriptive Bibliography* (Pittsburgh: University of Pittsburgh Press, 1983);

Bruccoli, *Ross Macdonald* (San Diego: Harcourt Brace Jovanovich, 1984).

– R.T.

MacDowell Colony

The MacDowell Colony, located on several hundred acres of secluded woodlands near Peterborough, Vermont, is one of the two most-prestigious artists' colonies in the United States. (The other is **Yaddo,** near Saratoga Springs, New York.) Marian MacDowell (1857–1956) established the MacDowell Colony on her Vermont estate in 1908 to honor the memory of her husband, pianist and composer Edward MacDowell (1861–1908).

Mrs. MacDowell raised funds and operated the colony for more than forty years, dedicating herself to maintaining a retreat where composers, writers, and artists could work undisturbed, freed temporarily from concerns about time or money. Among the many people who stayed at the colony before World War II were composer **Aaron Copland,** novelist Willa Cather, poet Edwin Arlington Robinson, and dramatist Thornton Wilder. Since 1945 the colony has been directed by an association and has hosted hundreds of creative people, among them writer **James Baldwin,** composer and conductor **Leonard Bernstein,** and artist **Louise Nevelson.**

REFERENCES:

William F. Claire, "Where Artists Do As They Please—And, Mostly, Work," *Smithsonian*, 8 (July 1977): 45–51;

Marya Mannes, "The MacDowell Colony," *Publishers Weekly*, 199 (17 May 1971): 32–34.

– D.H.-F.

Madonna

Singer and actress Madonna (1958–) was one of the most popular and controversial entertainers in American culture during the 1980s and early 1990s. She has had many number-one hits and cultivated a series of sultry, trend-setting images.

Madonna Louise Veronica Ciccone studied acting and dancing in her native Michigan, then moved to New York in 1978. She pursued multiple careers as an actress, model, and dancer. She became famous with two albums — *Madonna* (1983) and *Like A Virgin* (1985) — as well as a nationwide tour and videos on **MTV.** She established a catchy dance/pop style with songs such as "Holiday" from *Madonna* and "Into the Groove" from *Like a Virgin,* which also includes three number-one singles: "Like a Virgin," "Material Girl," and "Crazy for You." In 1985 she also appeared in her first commercial film, *Desperately Seeking Susan.*

Madonna's next album, *True Blue* (1986), an international success, was controversial for a song about teen pregnancy, "Papa Don't Preach." In 1987 she launched a highly successful world tour and starred in the film *Who's That Girl?* The video for the title song from her 1989 album *Like a Prayer* lost her an advertising contract with Pepsi-Cola due to its combination of religious and sexual imagery. Her 1990 Blond Ambition tour provided the basis for the documentary *Truth or Dare* (1991). Madonna continued to heat up her already sexy image in the 1990s with *Sex* (1992), a collection of erotic photographs and fantasies, and an accompanying album, *Erotica* (1992). She has also acted in films such as *Shanghai Surprise* (1986), with her then-husband Sean Penn; *Dick Tracy* (1990); *A League of Their Own* (1992); and *Body of Evidence* (1993).

REFERENCES:

Christopher Andersen, *Madonna: Unauthorized* (New York, London, Toronto, Sydney, Tokyo, & Singapore: Simon & Schuster, 1991);

Adam Sexton, ed., *Desperately Seeking Madonna: In Search of the Meaning of the World's Most Famous Woman* (New York: Delta, 1993).

– L.D.S.

Maharishi Mahesh Yogi

The Maharishi Mahesh Yogi (1918?–) became famous in 1967, when **The Beatles** announced they were giving up psychedelic drugs to study Transcendental Meditation (TM) at the Maharishi's ashram (Hindu religious retreat) in Rishikesh, on the banks of the Ganges in northern India. Actress Mia Farrow and popular singer Donovan were already studying TM with the Maharishi. By 1975 football player Joe Namath and entertainers such as Stevie Wonder, Peggy Lee, Shirley MacLaine, Efrem Zimbalist, Jr., and **The Beach Boys** were just a few of the nearly six hundred thousand Americans who had learned TM, which is basically a method of relaxing the mind and body.

The Maharishi Mahesh Yogi started teaching the technique in 1956. He came to the United States for

Norman Mailer and Muhammad Ali (Wide World)

the first time in 1959 and began to train American TM teachers in 1960. Fifteen years later six thousand American TM instructors were bringing in about $12 million a year ($125 from each new student). In TM each student is assigned a personal mantra, a Sanskrit word to be repeated continuously during twice-daily, twenty-minute meditation periods.

American interest in Eastern religions and meditative practices is largely an outgrowth of the **Beat** and **hippie** movements. The Maharishi was only one of many gurus with American followings in the late 1960s and early 1970s, but he attracted a broader spectrum of followers than the others because he insisted that TM was not a religion and required no changes in lifestyle. TM students ranged from hippies to suburbanites. Criticized by traditional practitioners of Hindu and Buddhist meditation as a "quick fix" that fails to bring true spiritual enlightenment, TM reached its peak around 1975 but is still attracting new followers in the 1990s.

REFERENCES:

Robert S. Ellwood and Harry B. Partin, *Religious and Spiritual Groups in Modern America,* second edition, revised (Englewood Cliffs, N.J.: Prentice-Hall, 1988), pp. 194–197;

Peter Russell, *The TM Technique: An Introduction to Transcendental Meditation and the Teachings of the Maharishi Mahesh Yogi* (London, Henley & Boston: Routledge & Kegan Paul, 1976).

– K.L.R.

NORMAN MAILER

No serious writer since World War II has attracted more media attention than Norman Mailer. A best-selling and award-winning author from the beginning of his skillfully managed career, he has concentrated on topics of contemporary interest, building his image as a macho intellectual along the way. *The Naked and the Dead* (1948), his much-acclaimed first novel, was about soldiers attempting to understand their place in a highly structured technological age represented by the war. *An American Dream* (1965), written five years after Mailer was arrested for stabbing his wife, is about a man who attains salvation by murdering his spouse and escaping from his old, conservative life. *Armies of the Night* (1968), winner of a National Book Award and a Pulitzer Prize, is based on Mailer's experiences protesting the **Vietnam War** and his arrest in the 1967 March on the Pentagon in Washington, D.C. *Prisoner of Sex* (1971) is Mailer's irreverent response to feminism. *Executioner's Song* (1979) is based on the highly publicized case of Utah murderer Gary Gilmore, who asked to be executed for his crime. In addition Mailer has written less celebrated works, including a pictoral biography of **Marilyn Monroe,** journalistic accounts of political conventions and boxing, a study of novelist Henry Miller, and a parodic detective novel.

Mailer was among the most visible authors after World War II. In 1955 he was one of the founders of the *Village Voice,* the successful Greenwich Village alternative newspaper, and he was active in the hipster movement of the day, dubbing himself in a celebrated essay a "white Negro." In 1969 he mounted a satirical campaign for mayor of New York City. In the 1960s and 1970s he often appeared on television talk shows, debating literary and political topics in an engaging enough way to interest general audiences, who were attracted by Mailer's boisterous image. The year after publication of *Executioner's Song,* he sponsored the parole of convicted murderer Jack Henry Abbott and publication of a book by him on the grounds that Abbott's unusual literary talent mitigated his offense. The scheme turned tragic when Abbott committed murder again. After that and after critics panned his long-awaited novel *Ancient Evenings* (1983), the 600-page first volume of a projected trilogy, Mailer seemed less inclined to seek the limelight.

REFERENCES:

Robert F. Lucid, *Norman Mailer: The Man and His Work* (Boston: Little, Brown, 1971);

Peter Manso, *Mailer: His Life and Times* (New York: Simon & Schuster, 1985).

　　　　　　　　　　　　　　　　　　　　　　　　　－R.T.

Bernard Malamud

Bernard Malamud (1914–1986) is highly regarded for his moralistic works, which he said were about "simple people struggling to make their lives better in a world of bad luck." Though he usually wrote about Jewish characters and was often compared to other Jewish-American writers such as **Saul Bellow** and **Philip Roth,** Malamud's treatment of people learning from suffering exemplified his contention that "all men are Jews."

Malamud was born in Brooklyn, New York, of working-class Russian-Jewish immigrants. He wrote his first novel, *The Natural,* in 1952. Like his later work, it deals with a character — a baseball player, in this case — who tries to make sense of his life. It also illustrates Malamud's frequent use of myth and literary allusion. A film version of the novel, directed by Barry Levinson and starring **Robert Redford,** appeared in 1984.

Malamud's second novel, *The Assistant* (1957), is widely regarded as one of his best. Set in New York, it concerns a Jewish grocer and his assistant, an anti-Semitic youth who learns about true morality from his employer and later helps the grocer and others in need. Malamud's next book, the short-story collection *The Magic Barrel* (1958), won a National Book Award. By the 1960s he was widely considered one of the best fiction writers in America.

The novel *A New Life* (1961), like much of Malamud's fiction, unites tragic and comic elements in its satire on university teaching. A darker tone pervades *The Fixer* (1966), one of his best-known works and a Pulitzer Prize–winner, which is based on the story of a Russian Jew accused of killing a Gentile child. A movie version of *The Fixer* was released in 1969. Malamud's next two novels deal with writers: *The Tenants* (1971) is about the relationship between a Jewish writer and a black writer in a New York ghetto, and *Dubin's Lives* (1979) features a biographer who escapes the complications of his own life by writing about others. Malamud's last novel, *God's Grace* (1982), is an exploration of morality and religion set in the near future, after a nuclear war survived by one man. Malamud collected the best of his short fiction in *The Stories of Bernard Malamud* (1983).

REFERENCES:

Richard Astro and Jackson J. Benson, eds., *The Fiction of Bernard Malamud* (Corvalis: Oregon State University Press, 1977);

Jeffrey Helterman, *Understanding Bernard Malamud* (Columbia: University of South Carolina Press, 1985).

　　　　　　　　　　　　　　　　　　　　　　　　　－D.H.-F.

David Mamet

The plays of David Mamet (1947–), one of the major new voices in the American theater during the 1970s and 1980s, have been praised for their heightened, naturalistic dialogue — proof of his sensitivity to urban American speech.

Born and raised in Chicago, Mamet attended Goddard College in Plainfield, Vermont (B.A., 1969), spending his junior year in New York, where he studied acting with Sanford Meisner, a former member of Group Theatre. Mamet's first plays were produced at Marlboro College in Vermont, where he taught in 1970–1971, and at Goddard, where he was artist-in-residence in 1971–1973 and helped to found the St. Nicholas Theater Company, which he took with him to Chicago in 1976.

Duck Variations (produced at Goddard in 1972) and *Sexual Perversity in Chicago* (staged in Chicago in 1974) opened as a double bill Off-Broadway in 1976 for an encouraging run of 273 performances and were included on the *New York Times* list of the ten best plays of the year. The 1977 Broadway premiere of *American Buffalo* brought still more acclaim. An indictment of American materialism, the play is set in a junk shop, where the owner and two other working-class men carry on a conversation about how to steal a coin collection that may or may not include a valuable American buffalo nickel. The play was voted the best American play of 1976–1977 by the New York Drama Critics Circle and in 1976 Mamet was awarded an Obie for distinguished play writing on the basis of this play and *Sexual Perversion in Chicago.*

After several other significant productions, including *A Life in the Theatre* (1977) and *The Water Engine* (1978), Mamet won a Pulitzer Prize for *Glengarry Glen Ross* (1983), an obscenity-laden portrayal of scheming, hustling real-estate salesmen.

Mamet's plays are populated by scam artists whose only reality consists of what they can fast-talk others — and themselves — into believing. Since the mid 1980s Mamet has worked repeatedly with actor Joe Mantegna, who seems to embody the quintessential Mamet protagonist. Mantegna acted with Ron Silver and **Madonna** in *Speed-the-Plow,* Mamet's exposé of Hollywood deal makers, which opened on Broadway in 1988. *Oleanna,* which uses a professor-student relationship to explore the politics of gender in the 1990s, opened Off-Broadway in 1992.

Mamet has written screenplays for and directed *House of Games* (1987), *Things Change* (1988), and *Homicide* (1990) — all starring Mantegna. He also wrote the screenplays for the 1981 film version of James M. Cain's *The Postman Always Rings Twice* as well as scripts for *The Verdict* (1982) and *The Untouchables* (1987).

REFERENCES:

Dennis Carroll, *David Mamet* (New York: St. Martin's Press, 1987);

Anne Dean, *David Mamet: Language as Dramatic Act* (Rutherford, Madison & Teaneck, N.J.: Fairleigh Dickinson University Press, 1990);

Leslie Kane, *David Mamet: A Casebook* (New York & London: Garland, 1992).

– I.R.H.

Henry Mancini

Henry Mancini (1924–) is one of the most popular and productive composers of film and television music in America. His work in the late 1950s and early 1960s introduced light jazz into movie and television scores and was part of a shift in such scores from background music to music that could be popular on its own.

In 1952 Mancini joined the staff of Universal-International Studios, where he attracted attention for his arrangements for *The Glenn Miller Story* (1954) and *The Benny Goodman Story* (1956) and for his jazz-influenced score for Orson Welles's *Touch of Evil* (1958). He became famous with his music for the tele-

vision series *Peter Gunn* (1958–1961); an album with music from the show became a best-seller. The producer of the show, Blake Edwards, hired Mancini to write the music for several films he directed, most notably *Breakfast at Tiffany's* (1961), *Days of Wine and Roses* (1963), and *The Pink Panther* (1964). Mancini received two Academy Awards (Oscars) for *Breakfast at Tiffany's,* one for best score and another for best song, "Moon River," with lyrics by Johnny Mercer. Mancini received another Oscar for the title song from *Days of Wine and Roses,* for which Mercer also wrote the words. He won another Academy Award for his score for Edwards's *Victor/Victoria* (1982). Mancini's theme for *The Pink Panther,* a **Top 40** hit, also was used in the popular cartoon series of the same name that first appeared in 1969.

REFERENCE:

Henry Mancini, *Sounds and Scores* (N.p.: Northridge, 1962).

– L.D.S. and I.R.H.

Robert Mapplethorpe

By the time of his death from **AIDS** at age forty-two, Robert Mapplethorpe (1946–1989) had become one of the most admired photographers in the United States — and perhaps the most controversial. He was trained as an artist at Pratt Institute (1963–1970), and his mature style was characterized by black-and-white images of impeccable craftsmanship, elegance, and tonal beauty — all exemplified in his well-known flower still lifes.

A master of studio lighting, he was considered one of the great portraitists of his generation, and he photographed influential clients from many walks of life. At the same time Mapplethorpe approached his subject matter — which often involved male and female nudes and suggested homoerotic themes — from a consistently radical position that shocked many viewers and ultimately tested the boundaries of fine art in America. In the 1970s his explicitly sexual images of black male models and racially mixed male couples charted new ground for subject matter in fine-art photography. Mapplethorpe's most controversial imagery by far, however, was the depiction of homosexual acts among his own friends and acquaintances, some of which suggested sadomasochism. The inclusions of several of these images in a traveling retrospective organized by the Institute of Contemporary Art in Philadelphia in 1988 caused a widely publicized debate over the definition of pornography and subsequently led to the resignation of one art-museum director and a court trial for another, who had defended the right of his museum to exhibit the works.

During the last year of his life, Mapplethorpe broke new ground with a series of portraits of himself dying of AIDS. Viewers were shocked to see those photographs of an emaciated Mapplethorpe, once known for his stylish good looks. He was among the victims of the first great wave of AIDS that swept the New York art world, and his courageous self-portraits opened up a discourse on the disease.

REFERENCES:

Janet Kardon, *Robert Mapplethorpe: The Perfect Moment* (Philadelphia: University of Pennsylvania, Institute of Contemporary Art, 1988);

Mapplethorpe (New York: Random House, 1992).

– K.B.

BRICE MARDEN

Brice Marden (1938–), who received his M.F.A. from Yale University in 1963, made his first experiments in painting in an **Abstract Expressionist** mode. A brilliant colorist, Marden often used a combination of oil paint and beeswax to create paintings with varying surface textures and color gradations. In the mid 1960s Marden became fascinated with Euclidian geometry. This interest led him more and more toward **minimalism**, and throughout his career he has created works that depict symmetrical shapes on blank color fields. For example, his *Elements III* (1983–1984) is a seven-by-three-foot painting consisting of four rectangles rendered in primary colors and carefully measured proportions.

Marden's first New York solo exhibition was in 1966 at Bykert Gallery, but American collectors were slow to accept his vacant wall-like canvases. Marden is an adamant opponent of figurative painting and expressionistic styles and continues to produce rigorously minimalist artworks. His art aims at achieving a calm, controlled balance and an overall sense of harmony.

REFERENCE:

Klaus Kertess, *Brice Marden, Paintings and Drawings* (New York: Abrams, 1992).

– C.S.

WYNTON MARSALIS

Equally at home with the classical repertoire and popular music, trumpet player Wynton Marsalis (1961–) is admired for his musical versatility and virtuosity. Marsalis began his trumpet studies at the age of six with his father, a talented jazz player in his own right, and later continued with the New Orleans teacher John Longo. Making his debut with the New Orleans Philharmonic at the age of fourteen in a performance of Joseph Haydn's *Trumpet Concerto in E-flat Major,* Marsalis also participated in jazz and rock ensembles while still a student. At seventeen he was selected to receive the Harvey Shapiro Award (as the most gifted brass player) while a student at the Berkshire Music Center at Tanglewood.

After completing his formal studies at the Juilliard School in 1981, Marsalis toured Europe — both as a soloist and as a member of various ensembles — which contributed decisively to his refined outlook on music. He later formed a quintet, which included his brother Branford (a talented saxophonist and leader of *The Tonight Show* orchestra) and also worked with **Miles Davis,** among many other well-established jazz artists. In 1984 Marsalis won Grammy Awards for classical and jazz recordings. He is admired for his ability to attract popular-music audiences to art music and for his ability as an articulate teacher of jazz history.

– L.D.S.

EUGENE MCCARTHY

On 30 November 1967, faced with the prospect that neither major political party would run an anti-**Vietnam War** candidate in the 1968 presidential election, Sen. Eugene J. McCarthy (1916–) announced that he would seek the Democratic Party nomination, promising a negotiated peace and charging that the war was draining "the material and moral resources of the country from our really pressing problems." His campaign attracted large numbers of young antiwar activists back into mainstream politics, where they got "Clean for Gene," cutting hair and shaving off beards to create a neat appearance as they went door to door to solicit votes for their candidate.

McCarthy was an unlikely figure to rally such support. His colleagues in the Senate saw him as scholarly and detached, even condescending. A native of Minnesota, he was a devout Roman Catholic who had even spent a few months in a monastery at one point before his election to the U.S. House of Representatives in 1948. In the House he established a liberal, pro-labor voting record and was considered an effective politician, but after he was elected to the U.S. Senate in 1958 he often seemed bored and inattentive to the practical matters that lead to legislative success. A member of the Senate Foreign Relations Committee, McCarthy supported the Gulf of Tonkin Resolution (August 1964), which gave President Lyndon B. Johnson authority to take whatever military steps he considered necessary to curb North Vietnamese aggression. Yet McCarthy became increasingly disturbed by the way in which the executive branch used a broad interpretation of that resolution to bypass Congress's Constitutional prerogative to declare war. He became a vocal opponent of Johnson's policies in early 1967.

When McCarthy first announced that he would run for president, most political observers believed that support for him would be negligible. In late January 1968 polls predicted that he would win 8–11 percent of the vote in the 12 March Democratic primary in New Hampshire, but the major Tet offensive launched by the North Vietnamese on 29 January shook public confidence in America's ability to win the war, and McCarthy's army of student volunteers (many of them under voting age, which was then twenty-one) conducted a thorough and effective grass-roots campaign that got their candidate's message to the people of New Hampshire. McCarthy shocked the nation by winning 42.4 percent of the Democratic vote (23,280). Johnson, who had not officially entered the primary got 49.5 percent (27,243) as a write-in candidate. When the write-in votes for both candidates from the New Hampshire Republican primary were added in, the results were even closer: Johnson beat McCarthy by only 230 votes.

McCarthy's victory was a major factor in Johnson's decision, announced on 31 March, not to seek reelection. Two days later, McCarthy, supported by some eight thousand student volunteers, beat Johnson in the Wisconsin primary, but Robert F. Kennedy had entered the presidential race a few days after the New Hampshire primary, dividing the pool of students and intellectuals who had supported McCarthy. Kennedy had a much broader political base than McCarthy, including minorities and working-class whites, and he beat McCarthy in several primaries before he was shot just after his major win in California and died on 6 June.

Much of Kennedy's minority support shifted to McCarthy, but in August at the Democratic National Convention in Chicago, where McCarthy's ineffectual efforts failed to win many Kennedy delegates, the nomination went to Vice-president Hubert H. Humphrey, who had entered no primaries but had the support of party regulars. Following a convention marred by dissent within and violent confrontations between police and antiwar demonstrators in the streets, the Democratic Party was in disarray. McCarthy refused to endorse Humphrey until just before the election, when his lukewarm support did little to bring antiwar voters back to the party. Humphrey was even more seriously hurt by the third-party candidacy of George Wallace,

who attracted conservative Democrats to his cause, especially in the South. As a result Republican Richard M. Nixon won an election that might well have been Humphrey's in a two-way race. Retiring from the Senate in 1971, McCarthy ran for president again in 1972 and 1976, and in 1982 he lost a bid to regain a seat in the Senate.

Although McCarthy had less influence on the outcome of the 1968 election than has often been attributed to him, he nonetheless played an important role in bringing about political change. After the 1968 election the Democratic Party reformed its candidate-selection process so that presidential hopefuls have to win delegates in primaries rather than having them delivered by party bosses. Moreover, McCarthy brought thousands of young antiwar activists back into the political system, where they became a force to be reckoned with in electoral politics. Finally, the strong show of support for McCarthy convinced Johnson, and Nixon after him, that the United States must take part in serious negotiations to end the war.

REFERENCES:

Jeremy Larner, *Nobody Knows: Reflections on the McCarthy Campaign of 1968* (New York: Macmillan, 1970);

Norman Mailer, *Miami and the Siege of Chicago: An Informal History of the Republican and Democratic National Conventions of 1968* (New York: New American Library, 1968);

Eugene J. McCarthy, *Up 'Til Now: A Memoir* (San Diego: Harcourt Brace Jovanovich, 1987);

Theodore H. White, *The Making of the President 1968* (New York: Atheneum, 1969).

– K.L.R.

JOSEPH McCARTHY

No politician since World War II has earned the level of contempt inspired by Joseph McCarthy (1909-1957). He was a liar, a character assassin and a charlatan; yet during a critical time in history he managed to dupe the American public into believing their worst fears: that federal agencies had been infiltrated by Communists seeking to overthrow the United States government. Many of his charges had an element of truth to them, but McCarthy distorted the facts shamelessly in self-serving maneuvers to gain political power.

After a couple of false starts into national politics, "Tail Gunner Joe," as he claimed to have been called during his World War II service in the South Pacific, ran against popular Wisconsin Sen. Robert La Follette, and, in a brilliant mud-slinging campaign, managed a narrow victory. In Washington, he moved aggressively to consolidate his power and marshal support by soliciting the favor of special interests, earning the bemused contempt of his fellow senators for his flamboyant actions and outrageous proposals. Reporters voted McCarthy the nation's worst senator in 1949. McCarthy's abrasive manner combined with the explosive issue of Communist infiltration of American government in 1950 to make him one of the most feared and most powerful members of Congress. In a 9 February 1950 address to the Ohio County Women's Republican Club in Wheeling, West Virginia, McCarthy claimed to have a list of 205 Communist Party members who worked in the State Department, and, he added, they were known to Secretary of State Dean Acheson. The charge caused a public uproar. Subsequent questioning of Senator McCarthy was inconclusive. He claimed to have proof of his allegations, which changed unaccountably from time to time, but refused to deliver it. An investigation by Senate Democrats into McCarthy's conduct was inconclusive.

During the next four years, McCarthy managed to stay in the limelight, making accusations recklessly. By June 1951 he had called President Truman a son of a bitch, the secretary of state a Kremlin lackey, and Secretary of Defense George C. Marshall, who was a truly distinguished figure in most people's eyes, a traitor; in the next two years McCarthy accused Presidents Roosevelt, Truman, and Eisenhower of treason. When President Eisenhower took office, he was determined to stifle McCarthy's sensational antics, partly because they were adding to the international tensions of Cold-War diplomacy. Working with leaders in the Senate, he managed to have McCarthy steered away from committee assignments that seemed to offer any power or visibility, and the senator was made chairman of the modest Committee on Government Operations, which had the responsibility of investigating petty charges against government officials. McCarthy parlayed that assignment into one of the most powerful in the Senate by forming a Permanent Investigations subcommittee, which he chaired. The committee had broad subpoena power, exercised with abandon by McCarthy, who staged sensational public hearings at which the Democratic Party was accused of coddling communists.

In spring 1953, McCarthy began an investigation into the procedures for security clearance at Fort Monmouth, New Jersey, and particularly into the circumstances surrounding promotion of a dentist who seemed, in fact, to have communist associations. The army countered that the McCarthy Committee's chief counsel, Roy Cohn, had sought preferential treatment for his recently drafted friend, David Schine, and had threatened to "wreck the army" if he did not get his way. McCarthy's committee agreed to an investigation of the entire affair, including the conduct of McCarthy and Cohn. The Army-McCarthy hearings were big

news, sensational enough to attract television coverage viewed in some two-thirds of all American homes with television sets. The culmination of the hearings, and of McCarthy's career, came in a confrontation with army chief counsel Joseph Welch, during which McCarthy accused a junior member of Welch's staff of being a Communist. Welsh's anguished question, "Have you no decency, sir, at long last?" represented what was, after fifty-seven days of hearings, a general sentiment. After that, McCarthy's public support eroded, and, on 2 December 1954 he was condemned by a 67 to 22 vote for contempt of a Senate committee investigating his conduct and financial affairs, for abuse of Senate members, and for insults to the Senate body. He was the fourth senator in history to be censured. He died in a Bethesda, Maryland, hospital of maladies caused by alcoholism.

REFERENCES:

Fred J. Cook, *The Nightmare Decade: The Life and Times of Joe McCarthy* (New York: Random House, 1971);

William Bragg Ewald, Jr., *Who Killed Joe McCarthy?* (New York: Simon & Schuster, 1984);

David M. Oshinsky, *A Conspiracy So Immense: The World of Joe McCarthy* (New York: Free Press/London: Collier Macmillan, 1983).

– R.L.

LARRY MCMURTRY

In reviving the western novel Larry McMurtry (1936–) draws on his west Texas heritage. His best-selling, critically successful fiction often satirizes the romantic myths that surround cattlemen, Indians, gunfighters, lawmen, and other iconographic figures of the American frontier. Many readers have discovered McMurtry through popular adaptations of his works for film and television.

McMurtry's first novel, *Horseman, Pass By* (1961), which explores the clash between old and new values on the modern American frontier, established its twenty-five-year-old author's reputation among critics of regional literature. The 1962 Academy Award-winning screen adaptation of the novel as *Hud* greatly enhanced the commercial success of the novel. McMurtry, however, has dismissed *Horseman, Pass By* and his second work, *Leaving Cheyenne* (1963), as the products of a young writer's immature artistic vision.

McMurtry's third novel, *The Last Picture Show* (1966), created a controversy when some critics charged that the novel was stereotypical in its rendering of small-town life and sensationalistic in its depiction of adolescent sex. Many people in McMurtry's hometown of Archer City, a model for town in the novel, agreed with these criticisms, and McMurtry later said that *The Last Picture Show* was too vindictive in its portrayal of Archer City. The novel was successfully adapted for the screen by McMurtry and director Peter Bogdanovich, who were nominated for an Academy Award (Oscar) for their screenplay. McMurtry published *Texasville*, a sequel to *The Last Picture Show*, in 1987.

In his "urban trilogy" — *Moving On* (1970), *All My Friends Are Going to Be Strangers* (1972), and *Terms of Endearment* (1975) — McMurtry concerns himself with the increasing urbanization of Texas life. During the late 1970s and early 1980s McMurtry ventured beyond the borders of his native state to find new settings and material for his novels. *Somebody's Darling* (1978), for instance, deals with life and work in Hollywood, and *Cadillac Jack* (1982) is set mainly in Washington, D.C. The 1985 publication of *Lonesome Dove* signaled McMurtry's return to the exploration of the pioneer ethos and frontier myth. The best-selling eight-hundred-page epic tells of a late nineteenth-century cattle drive, led by two former Texas Rangers, from the south Texas border to the grass lands of Montana. In this novel McMurtry undercuts the mythic pretensions of the romantically conceived frontier code with **black humor** and descriptions of violence that lend authenticity to the story. *Lonesome Dove* earned McMurtry a Pulitzer Prize in 1986. During the 1980s the popularity of McMurtry's fiction was further enhanced when James L. Brooks's screen adaptation of *Terms of Endearment* won the 1983 Oscar for best picture and *Lonesome Dove* was adapted as a highly successful television miniseries (1989). In 1993 McMurtry published *Streets of Laredo*, a sequel to *Lonesome Dove*.

Since 1970, McMurtry has lived in Washington, D.C., where he owns Booked Up Book Store; he continues to spend time at his Texas ranch. His book of nonfiction, *In a Narrow Grave: Essays on Texas* (1971) includes meditations on the mythic cowboy as well as a description of the filming of *Hud*.

REFERENCE:

Charles D. Peavy, *Larry McMurtry* (Boston: Twayne, 1977).
                                – D.L.

TERRENCE MCNALLY

Terrence McNally (1939–) began his career as a voice of Vietnam-era outrage, employing caustic, absurdist satire in the manner of **Arthur Kopit** and **Edward Albee** (with whom McNally shared an apartment in the early 1960s). McNally's later plays are more comedic than angry in their examination of American society.

McNally earned his first Broadway credit for reworking Giles Cooper's stage adaptation of *The Lady of the Camellias* for its short-lived New York production in 1963. His first original play to reach the stage, *And Things that Go Bump in the Night*, premiered at the **Guthrie Theatre** in Minneapolis in 1964, where it provoked controversy with its disturbing depiction of perversion and violence. The play reached Broadway in 1965 but ran for only sixteen performances. McNally was far more successful with *Next*, about an overweight forty-eight-year-old man who is drafted. It opened Off-Broadway in 1968 and ran for more than seven hundred performances on a double bill with Elaine May's *Adaptation*. Many critics consider *Where Has Tommy Flowers Gone?* (1971), a bizarre comedy about a young would-be actor who blows up various theaters at the Lincoln Center in New York, the best of McNally's early plays.

The Ritz, a substantial Broadway hit that opened in 1975 and ran for four hundred performances, marks McNally's departure from the angry social protest of his earlier works. The first of several plays in which McNally examines how the gay community lives, this comedy is about a heterosexual who is trying to avoid a Mafia hit man and hides in a bath house without knowing it is a homosexual hangout.

After a flop with *Broadway, Broadway*, which closed out of town in 1978, McNally wrote the book for an unsuccessful musical *The Rink*, in 1984. In the late 1980s and early 1990s he had several well-received plays. *Frankie and Johnny at the Clair de Lune* (1987), is about a sensitive waitress and an emotional short-order cook, who overcome past hurts and insecurity to form a romantic bond. *The Lisbon Traviata* (1989), in which one member of a homosexual love triangle is obsessed with obtaining a rare recording of **Maria Callas** performing in a Lisbon production of *La Traviata*, is the most notable of McNally's plays about homosexual life in America. In *Lips Together, Teeth Apart* (1992) a woman who has inherited a beach house from a brother dead of **AIDS** attempts to deal with tensions within her marriage while trying to recover from her brother's death and come to terms with his homosexuality. In 1993 McNally wrote the book for the musical version of Manuel Puig's novel *Kiss of the Spider Woman*, which received seven Antoinette Perry (Tony) Awards, including best musical and best book of a musical for McNally.

REFERENCES:

Samuel G. Freedman, "For McNally, a New Show and An Old Struggle," *New York Times*, 5 February 1984, II: 6;

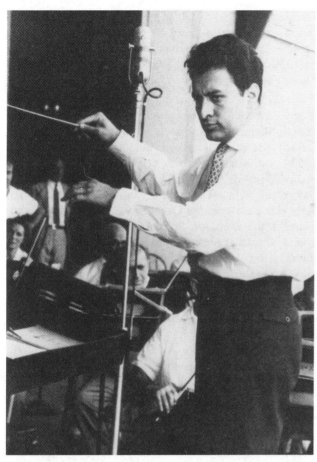

Zubin Mehta at his first rehearsal with the New York Philharmonic Orchestra, during summer 1960, when he was filling in for conductor Leopold Stokowski (photograph by Fred Fehl)

David Richards, "A Working Playwright Edges Into Fame," *New York Times,* 29 August 1993, C1, 5.

– I.R.H.

ZUBIN MEHTA

The youngest music director of a major American orchestra, Zubin Mehta (1936–) has been one of the most popular conductors in America during his lengthy career. Known for his passionate, expressive style, Mehta was especially successful in improving the orchestras he worked with and in championing contemporary works.

Born in Bombay, India, Mehta studied conducting at the Vienna State Academy of Music (1954–1960). A 1959 apprenticeship at the Berkshire Music Center at Tanglewood led to Mehta's first professional engagement as music director of the Montreal Symphony Orchestra (1960–1967). This experience led to

two of the longest conducting tenures ever held by a single person: Mehta first led the Los Angeles Philharmonic Orchestra for sixteen years (1962–1978), then capped his conducting career as music director of the New York Philharmonic Orchestra for thirteen years (1978–1991). In 1977 he also became the first music director of the Israel Philharmonic Orchestra, where he currently serves as guest conductor and musical adviser.

REFERENCE:

Martin Bookspan and Ross Yockey, *Zubin: The Zubin Mehta Story* (New York, Hagerstown, San Francisco, & London: Harper & Row, 1978).

– L.D.S.

RICHARD MEIER

Known primarily as a late-modernist or neo-modernist architect, Richard Meier (1934–) has maintained throughout his career a style related to the purism of the early **International Style,** particularly that of the modernist French architect Le Corbusier. Meier has tended toward the exclusive use of white for his buildings, which feature smooth, pristine surfaces, balanced arrangements of elementary geometric shapes, and natural lighting in the interiors. His career has focused on relatively small-scale public projects — such as art-museum buildings — and private homes; yet he has become widely known and is generally well received by critics and the public. In architectural criticism Meier is often associated with a group known briefly as the New York 5, which also included Peter Eisenman, Charles Gwathmey, John Hejduk, and **Michael Graves.** They were loosely united in the late 1960s by an admiration for the purist forms of the International Style — at a time when the aesthetic value of modernist architecture was being called into question and **postmodern** tendencies were on the rise.

REFERENCE:

Richard Meier, Architect, 1964/1984 (New York: Rizzoli, 1984).

– K.B.

GIAN CARLO MENOTTI

The first American citizen to have an opera produced in Italy, Gian Carlo Menotti (1911–) has enhanced the viability of American opera since World War II through the Broadway successes of his works, his highly popular opera *Amahl and the Night Visitors,* and his promotion of new works at the annual Spoleto

Festivals he established in Spoleto, Italy, and Charleston, South Carolina.

Menotti immigrated to America from Italy in 1928. His first produced opera, *Amelia Goes to the Ball* (1937), led to a commission for an **NBC** radio opera, *The Old Maid and the Thief* (1939). His first major success was *The Medium* (1946); with his comic opera *The Telephone* (1947), it ran on Broadway for 211 performances during the 1947–1948 season. Menotti's use of dramatic plots and melodic scores made his operas popular. *The Consul* (1950), about political bureaucracy in a modern police state, was even more successful than *The Medium,* receiving a Pulitzer Prize for music. In 1951 NBC commissioned Menotti to write the first opera for television, *Amahl and the Night Visitors,* about a boy who is healed when he gives his crutches to the Magi as a gift for the infant Jesus. It was first aired on Christmas Eve 1951 and became an annual event for thirteen years. Menotti received another Pulitzer Prize for *The Saint of Bleeker Street* (1954). He has written the librettos for his own operas and has collaborated as a writer with other composers, most notably for **Samuel Barber**'s opera *Vanessa* (1957).

Since the 1950s Menotti has written several other operas, including works for children, as well as choral works and orchestral and chamber pieces. He has also been active in the Festival of Two Worlds (better known as the Spoleto Festival), which he helped to found in Spoleto, Italy, in 1958. An American version of the arts festival began in Charleston, South Carolina, in 1977. (Menotti dissociated himself from the American festival in 1993.) The festivals present new works by established and younger artists as well as presentations of older works.

REFERENCES:

John Ardoin, *The Stages of Menotti* (Garden City, N.Y.: Doubleday, 1985);

John Gruen, *Menotti: A Biography* (New York: Macmillan/London: Collier Macmillan, 1978).

– L.D.S.

SIR YEHUDI MENUHIN

Sir Yehudi Menuhin (1916–) was one of the most popular violinists in America after World War II. He has also been active as a conductor and a promoter of musical education, and he has encouraged the performance of Indian and Russian music in the West.

Born in New York, Menuhin was a child prodigy on the violin. He made his public debut with the San Francisco Symphony Orchestra at age eight, and by eleven he had an international reputation. In 1932 he

recorded Sir Edward Elgar's violin concerto with the composer conducting, and he toured extensively with his sister, pianist Hephzibah Menuhin (1920–1981), in the 1930s. During World War II Menuhin played for soldiers in Europe.

Menuhin immigrated to England in 1959, was knighted in 1965, and became a British subject in 1985. He established three music festivals in Europe: the Yehudi Menuhin Festival in Gstaad, Switzerland (1957–), the Bath Festival (1959–1968), and the Festival of Windsor (1969–1971). He began conducting in 1957, often with his Menuhin Festival Orchestra (formerly the Bath Festival Orchestra). In 1963 he helped to create the Menuhin School of Music for musically gifted children at Stoke d'Abernon, Surrey. In his later years, he has been an outspoken advocate of human rights and internationalism.

REFERENCES:

Diana Menuhin, *Fiddler's Moll* (New York: St. Martin's Press, 1984);

Yehudi Menuhin, *Unfinished Journey* (New York: Knopf, 1977);

Tony Palmer, *Menuhin: A Family Portrait* (London: Faber, 1991).

– L.D.S.

METAFICTION

Metafiction is a type of **postmodern** literature in which the creation of fiction is itself the subject. Also labeled "surfiction" or "superfiction," metafiction consists of experimental works that are deliberately artificial in referring to themselves rather than attempting to mirror reality. They often parody fictional conventions and forms.

The self-reflexiveness of metafiction also appears in some earlier fiction, in particular Laurence Sterne's *Tristram Shandy* (1759–1767), but metafiction is a postwar phenomenon, differing from earlier works in its **poststructuralist** assumption that language cannot convey the truth of physical or psychological experience. In metafiction, all claims to knowledge are seen as artificial constructions rather than objective truth, and the narrative conventions of realism and modernism are rejected.

In his essay "The Literature of Exhaustion" (1967), **John Barth** argued that traditional narratives had reached a dead end; however, new possibilities for fiction resulted from confronting this impasse, leading to "novels which imitate the form of the Novel, by an author who imitates the role of Author." Such self-conscious artistry is evident in Barth's own novels *The Sot-Weed Factor* (1960) and *Giles Goat-Boy* (1966) and his collection *Lost in the Funhouse* (1968).

In addition to practicing theorists such as Barth and William H. Gass, the fiction of Irish-born French writer Samuel Beckett and Argentinian Jorge Luis Borges influenced American metafiction, as did **Vladimir Nabokov** with such novels as *Lolita* (1955), *Pale Fire* (1962), and *Ada* (1969). Donald Barthelme's *Snow White* (1967), presents itself as a self-conscious novel, including a questionnaire on the story's development. Robert Coover also uses myths and popular culture, especially in *Pricksongs and Descants* (1969), whose stories point out their fictionality to the reader. In **Kurt Vonnegut, Jr.**'s *Slaughterhouse-Five* (1969), the "author" of the book is also a character. Vonnegut goes further in *Breakfast of Champions* (1973), remarking how the novel is his own creation and how he can change things at will. Similarly, Raymond Federman's *Double or Nothing* (1971) is a complex novel about a writer preparing to write a story, while in his *The Twofold Vibration* (1982) the story of his fictionalized future self is "told" by three other fictionalized "author" selves.

Metafiction was in its prime in the 1960s and 1970s, but some authors continued afterwards to employ its techniques. Almost always intellectual and difficult, metafiction, with the exception of Vonnegut's novels, has attracted few readers but has garnered a considerable scholarly following.

REFERENCES:
Robert Scholes, *Fabulation and Metafiction* (Urbana: University of Illinois Press, 1979);

Patricia Waugh, *Metafiction: The Theory and Practice of Self-Conscious Fiction* (London & New York: Methuen, 1984).
– D.H.-F.

JAMES A. MICHENER

One of the most prolific and popular American novelists of the post–World War II era, James A. Michener (1907–) is best know as an author of historical fiction, but he began his career with well-received novels inspired by his experiences in the South Pacific and Asia during and just after World War II and has written nonfiction on subjects that extend from Japanese art to the American political system.

Michener wrote his first book while serving as a naval historian during World War II. His visits to some fifty Pacific islands were the basis for *Tales of the South Pacific* (1947), which won the Pulitzer Prize for fiction in 1948 and was adapted by **Richard Rodgers and Oscar Hammerstein II** into a successful Broadway musical, *South Pacific* (1949). Despite the popularity of this musical, Michener's book was not a **best-seller**.

Nor were the other novels he published before 1959. *The Bridges at Toko-Ri* (1953), based on an event he witnessed as a journalist during the Korean War, and *Sayonara* (1954), which draws on his visits to Japan between 1949 and 1954, were praised by critics and made into successful movies.

With *Hawaii* (1959) Michener found the format that made him a best-selling novelist: the epic narrative that follows generations of fictional families through centuries of actual history. *Hawaii,* which covers some eleven hundred years, begins with the volcanic origins of the islands and ends with their becoming the fiftieth state in 1959. This novel and the other massive sagas that followed it — including *The Source* (1965), *Centennial* (1974), *Chesapeake* (1978), *The Covenant* (1980), *Poland* (1983), *Texas* (1985), *Alaska* (1988), and *Caribbean* (1989) — rely on extensive research and Michener's travel experiences.

Reviewers have joked about the huge number of trees cut down to publish a Michener epic and the consequences of dropping it on one's foot, but there have been serious criticisms as well. Critics have faulted his post-1959 novels for one-dimensional characters and contrived plots. Others have charged that his research methods are unreliable and his facts are sometimes wrong. Yet each new Michener novel has been enthusiastically greeted by thousands of readers who like his combination of history and geography lessons with entertaining stories.

REFERENCES:
A. Grove Day, *James Michener* (Boston: Twayne, 1977);

John P. Hayes, *James A. Michener: A Biography* (Indianapolis & New York: Bobbs-Merrill, 1984).
– R.T.

ARTHUR MILLER

Arthur Miller (1915–), author of a classic American play, *Death of a Salesman* (1949), stands with Eugene O'Neill and **Tennessee Williams** in the first rank of American playwrights.

Miller's first play to reach Broadway, *The Man Who Had All the Luck* (1944), closed after four performances, but in 1947 *All My Sons* ran for almost a year, winning critical acclaim as well as the New York Drama Critics Circle Award for best American play. His next play was *Death of a Salesman,* winner of a New York Drama Critics Award, an Antoinette Perry (Tony) Award, and a Pulitzer Prize. The initial production ran for more than seven hundred performances on Broadway, and the play has been revived many times worldwide.

Profoundly influenced by Henrik Ibsen, Miller bases his plays in social realism, examining the individual's responsibilities in society. He frequently explores political and social themes through plots that revolve around troubled relationships between fathers and sons and competition between brothers for their father's approval. Joe Keller, who has knowingly shipped defective airplane parts to the United States military in *All My Sons,* for instance, is punished when one of his sons commits suicide because of his father's crime. At the end of the play Joe shoots himself. In *Death of a Salesman* Willy Loman, a down-and-out salesman who has just lost his job, kills himself with the hope that the insurance money will provide a legacy for his two sons, who have not lived up to his dreams for them. A realistic portrayal of the decline of one man, the play is also about the delusions inherent in the American dream.

After *Death of a Salesman,* Miller had another Broadway success with *The Crucible* (1953), about one man's refusal to give in to the witch-hunting hysteria in seventeenth-century Salem, Massachusetts, even at the cost of his life. The play, which won him another Tony and ran for nearly two hundred performances, was widely viewed as an allegory of the contemporary investigations of Sen. **Joseph McCarthy,** who alleged that Communists had infiltrated all aspects of American civilian and military life. *The Crucible* has been frequently revived.

During the years immediately following the Broadway premiere of this play, Miller went through a period of personal and political upheaval. He found himself under suspicion for ties to the Communist Party, and in 1956 he was called before the House Un-American Activities Committee (HUAC). He testified to having signed Communist-backed petitions and having attended Communist writers' meetings, but denied joining the party and refused to name others he had seen at those gatherings or believed to be Communists. This refusal led to his conviction on contempt of Congress charges in 1957. The conviction was overturned by a higher court in 1958. In 1955 Miller divorced Mary Grace Slattery, his wife of fifteen years, and in 1956 he married film actress **Marilyn Monroe.** During their troubled marriage, which ended in divorce in 1961, he wrote the screenplay for *The Misfits* (1961) for Monroe, who committed suicide in 1962, the year Miller married photographer Ingeborg Morath.

Miller's personal life figures in his next completed play, *After the Fall* (1964), which focuses on the protagonist's guilt over not having been caught up in the **Holocaust,** the suicide of his beautiful, neurotic wife, and his testimony before HUAC as a backdrop for examining people's responsibilities to each other.

Moral responsibility for the Nazi death camps is also the theme of *Incident at Vichy* (1964) and the television movie *Playing for Time* (1980). In *The Price* (1968), a return to the domestic theme of Miller's plays of the 1940s, two brothers — a policeman and a wealthy physician — meet for the first time in years and gradually reveal the influence their affluent father's financial failure has had on their lives. The play was Miller's last major Broadway success, running for more than a year. He returned to Broadway after a long absence with *The Last Yankee* in 1993.

REFERENCES:

Arthur Miller, *Timebends: A Life* (New York: Grove, 1987);

Dennis Welland, *Miller the Playwright,* second edition (London: Methuen, 1983).

– I.R.H.

Minimalism

The term *minimalism* refers to artistic movements, starting in the 1960s and 1970s, that emphasize stylistic spareness, cutting ornamentation in favor of a "bare bones" approach. Its "less is more" aesthetic theory had a profound effect on the development of contemporary art, music, and literature in the United States.

Minimalism became prominent as an art movement in the early 1960s. The term is credited to art critic Barbara Rose. Minimalist artists sought to remove all subject matter and all references to their own personalities or feelings from their art. Minimalism thus rejected **Abstract Expressionism,** which prized personal expression. It also challenged contemporary movements such as **Pop Art,** which referred to a complex cultural world outside itself. In minimalism, the work of art had no meaning or any reference to anything beyond itself as a concrete object.

In painting, minimalists stressed the importance of the basic physical nature of a painting — color applied to the flat surface of stretched canvas. Many art historians see **Post-Painterly Abstraction** as the first manifestation of minimalism in American painting, with its paintings of nothing more than color applied flatly and divorced even from the gestural expression of the brushstroke. The first painter called a minimalist was Frank Stella, who in 1959 began a controversial series of paintings consisting of a geometric progression of stripes. During the 1960s a group of painters emerged with their own distinctive versions of minimalism while adhering to the same general philosophy of pure, emotionless abstraction.

In sculpture, the most significant practitioners of minimalism in the 1960s were Carl Andre, Dan Flavin,

Donald Judd, and Robert Morris. Sol LeWitt was involved with minimalist sculpture at the beginning of his career. The basic premise of minimalist sculpture was that an artwork should not represent something; it should look like the material from which it was made, but in a definite shape. Andre, for instance, often used firebricks and square steel plates arranged on the floor. Judd often created his pieces out of metal sheets industrially fabricated into cubes or rectangles, while Flavin worked with simple arrangements of fluorescent tubes.

Minimalism in music, which may also be traced to the 1960s, refers to the composition methods of employing simplified instrumentation as well as repetition in musical phrases and rhythm, with subtle changes introduced in the course of the piece. Minimalist composers, many of whom were influenced by Asian and African music, rejected the complexity of much contemporary art music in favor of simplified yet musically sophisticated arrangements. Among the leaders of this style in the 1960s and 1970s were **Philip Glass, Steve Reich,** and Terry Riley; **John Adams** is a more recent minimalist composer.

Literary minimalism originated in the late 1970s and was labeled in the 1980s. It can be found in the work of **Raymond Carver** and other writers whose fiction exhibits a direct, detached style echoing that of **Ernest Hemingway.** Such fiction — usually short stories — relies heavily on dialogue, and often the spareness of the settings and plots reflects the emptiness of the characters' lives. Since Carver's death in 1988, minimalist fiction has appeared less frequently than during its height in the mid 1980s.

REFERENCES:

Kenneth Baker, *Minimalism: Art of Circumstance* (New York: Abbeville, 1988);

John Barth, "A Few Words about Minimalism," *New York Times Book Review* (28 December 1986): 1–2, 25;

Wim Mertens, *American Minimal Music: La Monte Young, Terry Riley, Steve Reich, Philip Glass,* translated by J. Hautekiet (London: Kahn & Averill/New York: Broude, 1983);

Mississippi Review, special issue on literary minimalism, edited by Kim A. Herzinger, 40/41 (Winter 1985);

Michael Nyman, *Experimental Music: Cage and Beyond* (New York: Schirmer, 1974).

– K.B., L.D.S., and D.H.-F.

ROBERT MITCHUM

Actor Robert Mitchum (1919–) has projected a sleepy-eyed detachment on and off screen so well that it is easy to forget that since 1943 he has played roles in more than two hundred films. (A 1972 biography of Mitchum is subtitled *"It Sure Beats Working."*) Mitchum dropped out

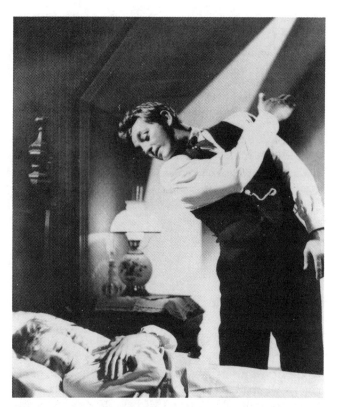

Shelley Winters and Robert Mitchum in *The Night of the Hunter* (Kobal Collection)

of high school at fourteen or fifteen and began drifting around the country during the Depression. He ended up in California, where he became interested in acting. In 1942 he decided to try film work, after having to quit his job at a Lockheed aircraft plant because working conditions threatened his health. He worked in nineteen films released in 1943 (among them nine westerns and six war movies) before signing a long-term contract with RKO in 1944. He won critical praise and an Academy Award (Oscar) nomination in 1945 for his supporting role in *The Story of GI Joe.* After serving eight months in the army during 1945, Mitchum returned to Hollywood, where many of his projects in the late 1940s were in the *film-noir* genre. At least one of these, *Out of the Past* (1947), is a minor classic. Mitchum survived the scandal surrounding his arrest and conviction for possession of marijuana. He spent two months of 1949 in jail, but continued to find work in Hollywood after his release. (His conviction was later overturned on the grounds of police entrapment.)

Never choosy about scripts, Mitchum has performed in many inferior films. His most unforgettable performance may be his portrayal of a demonic preacher terrorizing two young children in *The Night of the Hunter* (1955). His last substantial role was the lead in the mammoth television miniseries *The Winds of War* (1983) and its sequel *War and Remembrance* (1987). He had a supporting role in the second film version of *Cape Fear* (1991), which brought renewed interest in the original *Cape Fear* (1962), where Mitchum plays the sadistic ex-convict played by **Robert De Niro** in the 1991 film.

REFERENCES:

David Downing, *Robert Mitchum* (London: W. H. Allen, 1985);

Mike Tomkies, *The Robert Mitchum Story: "It Sure Beats Working"* (London: W. H. Allen, 1972).

– I.R.H.

DIMITRI MITROPOULOS

Conductor Dimitri Mitropoulos (1896–1960) helped to solidify the reputation of the New York Philharmonic Orchestra as a world-class ensemble. His intense, energetic style made him one of the most popular conductors in America during the 1940s and 1950s.

The Greek-born Mitropoulos began his conducting career at the Berlin State Opera in 1921. After conducting in Athens and Paris in the late 1920s and early 1930s, he appeared with the **Boston Symphony Orchestra** in 1936, which led to his engagement as music director of the Minneapolis Symphony Orchestra (now the Minnesota Orchestra). He conducted the orchestra from 1937 to 1949, when he assumed the directorship of the New York Philharmonic, for which he had been a guest conductor since 1940. Mitropoulos remained with the orchestra until 1958 and introduced many modern pieces to its audiences; he also selected and performed many concert versions of operas. His 1951 recording of Alban Berg's 1925 opera *Wozzeck* won audiences over to a work that had long been denounced by many for its stark realism and free use of **atonality.** During his years with the Philharmonic, Mitropoulos also conducted for the **New York Metropolitan Opera,** making his debut in 1954 with Richard Strauss's *Salome.* He conducted the world premiere of **Samuel Barber's** *Vanessa* in 1958.

REFERENCES:

Quaintance Eaton, *The Miracle of the Met: An Informal History of the Metropolitan Opera — 1883–1967* (New York: Meredith, 1968);

Howard Shanet, *Philharmonic: A History of New York's Orchestra* (Garden City, N.Y.: Doubleday, 1975).

– L.D.S.

MIXED MEDIA

Sometimes called "multimedia," the term *mixed media* refers to the combination of elements from different artistic forms into a single performance or presentation in theater, music, and art. Since World War II the proliferation of electronic media and its devices has increased the availability of mixed media techniques.

Mixed media has its origins in Richard Wagner's nineteenth-century concept of the *Gesamtkunstwerk* ("total work of art"), which he tried to achieve by combining music, poetry, dance, and art in what he called "music dramas." In addition to opera and ballet, other older examples include the experiments of some early-twentieth-century composers with blending music and visual elements.

Since World War II most mixed-media productions have combined elements of live sound, movement, film, tape, and/or setting, with occasional indeterminate elements such as audience participation. One of the most ambitious of such mixed-media events was **John Cage's** *HPSCHD* (1969): in its original form, it involved seven harpsichords, up to fifty-one tape machines, film clips and slides, and a light show. Light shows became part of the rock-music scene in the late 1960s (see **Haight-Ashbury**). The mixed-media applications of **performance art** were anticipated by some of the experiments of the **conceptual artists** as well as by the **happenings** of Allan Kaprow and Cage, while videos beginning in the 1980s merged film and music. In addition, some artists have used video or tape in conjunction with static images in their exhibits.

– L.D.S.

MODERN JAZZ QUARTET

Founded in 1952 by its leader and pianist, John Lewis, the Modern Jazz Quartet presented jazz as chamber music, combining, in the words of jazz critics Brian Case and Stan Britt, swing and delicacy. The musicians characteristically wore formal dress during performances. The ensemble included Milt Jackson (vibes), Percy Heath (bass), and Kenny Clarke (drums). Clarke was replaced by Connie Kay in 1954. Viewing jazz as an art form deserving sensitive, intense listening, the Modern Jazz Quartet fulfilled many of its expectations and goals via live performances and numerous recordings of its repertoire. Although the group formally disbanded in 1974, there have been several reunions of its personnel, mainly at jazz festivals throughout the world.

The Modern Jazz Quartet is noteworthy for its success in bringing attention to jazz as concert music.

– L.D.S.

THE MODERN LANGUAGE ASSOCIATION OF AMERICA

The Modern Language Association of America (MLA) is one of the largest academic organizations in the country. It was founded in 1883 by forty professors interested in promoting modern languages and literatures in higher education, which was then dominated by classical studies. The MLA aided in the establishment of these disciplines in academe; it now boasts a membership in the tens of thousands of professors, graduate students, and other scholars. Thousands attend the annual convention, either to choose among hundreds of paper presentations or for job interviews.

The MLA influences how modern languages and literatures are studied and taught and how the rest of America perceives these pursuits. Through its publications and its regional and national conventions, it has helped to shape the canon of modern literature, and since the 1960s it has encouraged the study of areas such as children's literature, critical theory, film, gay and lesbian studies, minority literatures, and women's studies. For this the MLA has been accused of abandoning the traditional study of literature in favor of theory and "political correctness." However, for its defenders it remains the primary forum for the study of modern languages and literatures in America.

Its most significant contributions to literary research include the journal *PMLA* (founded in 1884 as *Publications of the Modern Language Association*), a competitive and desirable venue for many scholars, and the *MLA Handbook for Writers of Research Papers* for students and the *MLA Style Manual* for scholars and publishers — both influential guides to the conventions of scholarly writing about literature. The annual MLA bibliography of scholarship and criticism is also an indispensable tool for students and scholars. The bibliography first appeared in 1921 in *PMLA* and featured American scholarship. By 1969 the *MLA International Bibliography,* as it was known after 1956, began to be published in book form. Computerization sped publication time beginning in 1981, and a substantial portion of the bibliography, past and present, is available on-line.

REFERENCE:

English Showalter, "The Modern Language Association of America Celebrates Its Centennial," in the *Dictionary of Literary*

Biography Yearbook: 1984, edited by Jean W. Ross (Detroit: Gale Research, 1985), pp. 63–67.

– D.H.-F.

THELONIOUS MONK

No other jazz pianist sounded remotely like Thelonious Monk (1917–1982). His creative vision was his alone, developed without regard for musical precedents or public acceptance. Even in the rarefied musical world of **bebop,** of which Monk was one of the founding members, he stood out for his talent, his genius, and his weird behavior. Monk's music had two dominant characteristics to the nonmusician: it was rhythmically surprising, requiring the listener to infer a steady beat as Monk used silence for emphasis and jerky, almost spastic, bursts to attack the convention of evenly spaced sound; and his music was harmonically dense, relying on chords that were atonal sound clusters, often rendered with his fist or the heel of his hand rather than his fingers. And yet he was the most rhythmic and melodic of performers. His influence was as great that of any modern-jazz musician; in the inner circle of bebop, he was highly respected as a teacher and mentor. He stands with **Duke Ellington, Miles Davis, Charlie Parker,** and **John Coltrane** as one of the most innovative jazz artists of his time.

Monk's accomplishment came despite a twelve-year period from 1945 to 1957, when he labored in obscurity, partly because he lost his cabaret license (the permit required in New York City of musicians playing in liquor-serving establishments) due to what was said to be a groundless drug charge. Monk was understandably suspect because of his characteristic behavior. He was given to wearing dark glasses and unusual hats, walking in a stumbling dance step, and mumbling enigmatic statements, such as "Writing about music is like dancing about architecture." He refused to leave New York to seek work, so he lived in near poverty devoting himself privately to his music. In the early 1960s he was discovered by Columbia Records, who skillfully promoted him and revived his career. With his new quartet, consisting of tenor saxophonist Charlie Rouse, drummer Frankie Dunlop, and bassists John Ore and later Wilbur Ware, Monk became an internationally prominent jazz star. His active career extended until the mid 1970s, when he fell ill. During his illness he was nursed by Countess Pannonica de Koenigswarter, who had attended Charlie Parker before his death.

Monk's greatest fame came posthumously, when **Clint Eastwood** produced a nationally released documentary movie about him, *Straight, No Chaser,* in 1989 and when he was awarded a Grammy for lifetime achievement in 1993.

– R.L.

BILL MONROE AND THE BLUE GRASS BOYS

Bluegrass music was named for the Blue Grass Boys, its most famous performers. The band's combination of traditional country music with a "high lonesome sound" played at high speed on acoustic string instruments earned it a prominent place in the Grand Ole Opry for forty years. In that time dozens of musicians played with the group, often moving on to form their own bands.

Bill Monroe (1911–), a mandolin player from Kentucky, formed the Blue Grass Boys in 1939. The group first performed on the Grand Ole Opry in 1940, the year they made their first record, "Mule Skinner Blues," an adaptation of an old song by Jimmie Rodgers. It quickly became associated with Monroe, who sang the lead, and the group recorded it again in 1950, 1971, and 1973. Popular Blue Grass Boys songs include "Orange Blossom Special," written in the 1930s by Chubby Wise and Ervin Rouse and first recorded by the group in 1941 and Monroe's "Kentucky Waltz," which he wrote in 1930 (adding lyrics in 1939) and recorded in 1946. His "Blue Moon of Kentucky," written and recorded in 1946 or 1947, became one of **Elvis Presley**'s first recordings in 1954. In 1970 Monroe was voted into the Country Music Hall of Fame. He continued to tour and make albums into the 1980s.

The Blue Grass Boys presented a traditional sound in country music; yet they were stylistically innovative in using the finger-picked mandolin, banjo, and guitar to carry the melody and harmony in most songs rather than using them for rhythm, which was supplied by fiddle and bass in most cases. The band was at its best in 1945 to 1948 when it included Earl Scruggs, "the fastest banjo picker in the world," and guitarist Lester Flatt. Though Flatt and Scruggs's Foggy Mountain Boys (1948–1969) and other groups provided competition for the Blue Grass Boys, Monroe's group remained the prototypical bluegrass band into the 1980s.

REFERENCES:

Jack Hurst, *Nashville's Grand Ole Opry* (New York: Abrams, 1975);

Neil V. Rosenberg, *Bluegrass: A History* (Urbana & Chicago: University of Illinois Press, 1985).

– D.H.-F.

MARILYN MONROE

Actress Marilyn Monroe (1926–1962) was the reigning sex-goddess of Hollywood films during the 1950s. Her legendary allure, troubled life, and premature death made her a popular icon like **Elvis Presley** and **The Beatles,** a source of apparently endless fascination to Americans.

Born in Los Angeles, Norma Jeane Mortenson (later called Norma Jeane Baker) was the illegitimate child of Gladys Monroe Baker Mortenson, who was diagnosed as a paranoid schizophrenic and hospitalized in 1934. Even before then, Monroe had been living with family friends, and she spent the rest of her childhood in an orphanage and foster care, where she was neglected and abused. To escape she married James Dougherty in 1942, just after her sixteenth birthday. (They were divorced in 1946.) In 1944 Monroe went to work in an aircraft factory, where a photographer who had come to photograph female war workers noticed her and used her for a pinup spread. These photographs led to her signing with a modeling agency in 1945. The next year 20th Century–Fox gave her a film contract — renaming her Marilyn Monroe — but dropped her after she played a minor part in *Dangerous Years* (1947) and a role that was cut from another movie. Columbia followed the same pattern, signing her in 1948 and dropping her after she played the second lead in *Ladies of the Chorus* (1949).

Marilyn Monroe, 1953

Monroe had small roles in two more films before **John Huston** gave her a featured role in *The Asphalt Jungle* (1950). Under Huston's direction she blossomed as an actress and won another important supporting part in *All About Eve* (1950), as well as a new contract with Fox. By 1952, Fox considered her ready for starring roles, including a sexy blonde wife who plots to murder her husband in *Niagara* (1953), the typical dumb blonde Lorelei Lee in *Gentlemen Prefer Blondes* (1953), and a near-sighted version of the same stereotype in *How to Marry a Millionaire* (1953). By 1954, the year she married baseball legend Joe DiMaggio, she was Fox's biggest star, but after *The Seven Year Itch* (1955) she tired of bimbo roles and left Hollywood to study with Lee Strasberg at the **Actors Studio** in New York. She divorced DiMaggio and began to mingle with intellectuals, one of whom, playwright **Arthur Miller,** she married in 1956.

Fox lured her back by making salary concessions and offering her more artistic control over her films. She made two of her finest movies, *Bus Stop* (1956) and *Some Like It Hot* (1959), but her life was crumbling amid bouts of depression and increasing dependence on drugs and alcohol. In her last completed film, *The Misfits* (1961), written for her by Miller, she appears to be in a narcotized stupor most of the time. She divorced Miller in January 1961 and was hospitalized for treatment of depression and drug abuse in February, just as the film was released. That June she began an affair with President **John F. Kennedy,** which continued on and off for several months. Later she became sexually involved with his brother Robert F. Kennedy. In June 1962, unhappy over script changes and other disputes with the director, Monroe was fired for lateness and absenteeism during the filming of *Something's Got to Give,* which was never completed. On 5 August she was found dead of an apparently intentional barbiturate overdose.

REFERENCES:

Fred L. Guiles, *Legend: The Life of Marilyn Monroe* (New York: Stein & Day, 1984);

Norman Mailer, *Marilyn* (New York: Grosset & Dunlap, 1973).
                                                            – I.R.H.

MARIANNE MOORE

Marianne Moore (1887–1972), whose poetry had been admired by readers of literary magazines since 1915, was virtually unknown to most Americans until she became a literary celebrity in the 1950s.

Moore settled in New York City with her mother in 1918, and except for employment at a branch of the New York Public Library and as editor of the *Dial* in the 1920s, she lived there quietly, devoting all her time to writing, for more than thirty years. Her life changed after her *Collected Poems* (1951) won a Pulitzer Prize, a National Book Award, and a Bollingen Prize; the *Newsweek* review of the book was titled "Best Living Poet" (24 December 1951). More honors followed, and in January 1953 the *Woman's Home Companion* named her one of the "Six Most Successful Women" of the previous year, launching her as a public personality.

Throughout the 1950s and 1960s newspapers and magazines published frequent articles and interviews, often accompanied by photographs of Moore wearing one of her signature tricorn hats. In 1955 the Ford Motor Company asked her to help them name a new car. Her suggestions included "Pastelogram" and "Utopian Turtletop"; the company decided to call it the Edsel. After her poem about the Brooklyn Dodgers appeared on page one of the *New York Herald Tribune* on 3 October 1956, the first day of the World Series, she became widely known as the poet who wrote about baseball. In 1968 she was invited to throw out the first ball on opening day at Yankee Stadium.

Moore's poetry of brilliant images and often esoteric words, moving from one idea to the next by process of association, might seem to make her an unlikely candidate for the celebrity she enjoyed. In fact, many people who recognized her as a famous poet and a lovable eccentric had read no more than a handful of her poems. Yet by the time the American public discovered Moore, poets such as **T. S. Eliot**, **Wallace Stevens**, and **William Carlos Williams** had been praising Moore's work for years, and she had influenced a new generation of poets that included **Richard Wilbur**, Elizabeth Bishop, and May Swenson.

REFERENCES:

Bernard F. Engel, *Marianne Moore*, revised edition (Boston: Twayne, 1989);

Charles Molesworth, *Marianne Moore: A Literary Life* (New York: Atheneum, 1990).
                                                            – K.L.R.

TONI MORRISON

Toni Morrison (1931–) is at the forefront of the group of black women writers who began to achieve recognition in the 1970s. In 1993 she was the first African American and the eighth woman to win the Nobel Prize for Literature. Her books are notable for their treatment of individuals within the context of African-American heritage, which she covers from the days of slavery to the present. Critics praise her evocative style, her sophisticated narratives, and her subtle blending of fantasy and realism.

Born Chloe Anthony Wofford in Ohio, Morrison promoted black authors as a book editor before her first novel, *The Bluest Eye,* appeared in 1970. The story of a black girl who wants to have blue eyes, the novel shows how racism and cultural ideals about beauty in a society dominated by whites can often lead to self-hatred among blacks. Though *The Bluest Eye* received respectful reviews, Morrison garnered more attention with her next novel, *Sula* (1973), which again explores the pain people inflict on each other, particularly across racial and gender lines. Against a background of unusual, often violent events, the novel deals with the friendship between Nel, who conforms to society's expectations, and Sula, who rejects them and becomes a catalyst for the town to unite against what they perceive as her evil nature. The occasional supernatural elements in *Sula* are even more apparent in Morrison's third novel, *Song of Solomon* (1977), in which reality and myth combine in the story of a man's spiritual self-discovery through tracing his heritage. In the eyes of many critics this novel marked the emergence of Morrison as a major American writer, and it was a Book-of-the-Month Club Main Selection — the first by a black author since Richard Wright's *Native Son* in 1940.

Morrison's next novel, *Tar Baby* (1981), also includes the supernatural. Mostly set on a Caribbean island, a shift from her earlier small-town settings, the novel treats a variety of conflicts: between young and old, men and women, and black and white. A beautiful young black woman, raised by her aunt and uncle and helped by their white employers, visits the island where they all live to reflect on her future. The household is visited by a young black drifter, whose honesty stands in contrast to the way the other characters control people and their environments. Morrison's most acclaimed work, for which she received a Pulitzer Prize, is *Beloved* (1987), a novel about a slave woman who escapes to Ohio and kills her daughter to keep her from being sold back into captivity. The mother, Sethe, is then haunted by her daughter's ghost, which later takes human form as a young woman, Beloved. Morrison's most recent work, *Jazz* (1992), is a **metafictional** novel tying together related stories set during Reconstruction and the 1920s. Morrison is also the author of *Playing in the Dark: Whiteness and the Literary Imagination* (1992), a study of the depiction of blacks in the work of white authors.

REFERENCES:

Trudier Harris, *Fiction and Folklore: The Novels of Toni Morrison* (Knoxville: University of Tennessee Press, 1991);

Nellie Y. McKay, ed., *Critical Essays on Toni Morrison* (Boston: G. K. Hall, 1988).

                                                                    – D.H.-F.

GRANDMA MOSES

As America's most-beloved folk artist, Grandma Moses (1860–1961) achieved success late, not beginning painting until her late seventies. Her interpretation of the American landscape celebrated a rustic way of life that, after World War II, was slowly fading away.

Born on her parents' farm in upstate New York, Anna Mary Robertson Moses received little education, and her childhood was devoted to daily farm chores. In her rare moments of free time she would draw, using juices from berries and grapes to color her works. From age twelve she spent fifteen years as a servant for various families until she married Thomas Salmon Moses in 1887. After eighteen years on a farm in Virginia, they bought a dairy farm in upstate New York.

When her husband died in 1927, Grandma Moses remained on the farm, where daily operations had been taken over by one of her sons. Too old to continue working outdoors, but believing that "idle hands make mischief," she began to sew worsted-yarn pictures. But her painful arthritis made stitching too difficult, and in the 1930s she took up painting.

Completely self-taught, Moses had never been to an art exhibit when she began painting although she had been inspired by the widely reproduced work of Currier and Ives. Brightly colored and patterned, Moses's paintings depict rolling country landscapes populated by small figures involved in everyday events such as farm chores, county fairs, and family gatherings. In a country obsessed with the machine and the ideas of progress and change, the paintings of Grandma Moses expressed a nostalgic yearning for a simpler time and preserved a sense of family tradition.

In 1938 New York art collector Louis Caldor discovered Moses's paintings hanging in a drugstore. She was given her first solo show in October 1940 at Galerie Etienne in New York, and the same show was then exhibited with much success in Gimbel's department store. In a short time Grandma Moses became extremely popular with the general public and the critics. Her art was avidly collected and exhibited around the world, and she received many commissions. In 1949 she was given the Women's National Press Club Award, which was presented to her by President Harry S Truman. President Dwight D. Eisenhower was also among her admirers.

Despite all the accolades bestowed on her, Grandma Moses remained a farm wife at heart. "If I didn't start painting," she once said, "I would have raised chickens. I could still do it now." Extremely prolific, Moses often completed as many as five paintings a week. When she died in 1961 at the age of 101, she had produced approximately sixteen hundred paintings.

REFERENCES:

Grandma Moses: Anna Mary Robertson Moses (1896–1961) (Washington, D.C.: National Gallery of Art, 1979)

Otto Kallir, *Grandma Moses* (New York: Harrison House/Abrams, 1984);

Kallir, ed., *Grandma Moses: American Primitive, 40 Paintings with Commentaries by Grandma Moses* (Garden City, N.Y.: Doubleday, 1947).

– C.S.

Robert Motherwell

The youngest member of the original group of artists who pioneered **Abstract Expressionism,** Robert Motherwell (1915–1991) served also as a spokesman for the movement, articulating their philosophies and visions through his paintings and writings.

Born in Aberdeen, Washington, Motherwell studied briefly at the California School of Fine Arts and earned a degree in philosophy from Stanford University (1937). After graduate study in philosophy at Harvard University and teaching art at the University of Oregon — Eugene, Motherwell studied art history at Columbia University. There his teacher Meyer Shapiro introduced him to prominent European artists in exile in New York during World War II, including Piet Mondrian and Surrealists Max Ernst, Yves Tanguy, Matta, and André Masson. Their influences are particularly evident in Motherwell's early works, in which a formal structure is imposed over quasi-Surrealistic automatic and intuitive brushstrokes.

Motherwell did not discover his true medium until 1943, when art patron Peggy Guggenheim asked him to participate in the first American exhibition devoted entirely to collage. The following year Motherwell was given his first major one-man show, at the Guggenheim's Art of This Century gallery. In 1949 Motherwell began work on his *Elegies to the Spanish Republic* series, a group of paintings and collages inspired by the Spanish Civil War. Dominated by stark rectangular and ovoid forms in black and white, the works were, Motherwell claimed, "general metaphors of the contrast between life and death." He eventually produced more than one hundred fifty paintings and collages based on this theme.

Simultaneously with the somber *Elegies to the Spanish Republic* series, Motherwell was producing collages that were filled with vibrant colors. In the early 1960s these vivid colors emerged boldly in his paintings as well, especially in his *Beside the Sea* series, which celebrates his love of the sea. Large textured areas of color and a window motif dominate Motherwell's *Open* series, begun in 1967.

By the 1970s Motherwell's paintings and collages had become quite large scale and ranged in tone from classical and dignified to violent and emotional. Throughout his life Motherwell produced art that seemed to bridge both action painting and color-field painting — the two major camps of Abstract Expressionism. He never abandoned collage, and his later works in this medium incorporate elements such as wine labels and postcards to produce a visual documentary of the artist's daily experiences.

One of the most respected American artists of the twentieth century, Motherwell was elected to the American Academy of Arts and Letters in 1986 and received the National Medal of Arts in 1990.

REFERENCE:
Jack Flam, *Motherwell* (New York: Rizzoli, 1991).

– C.S.

Motown

The Tamla Motown Company was the first major American recording company owned and operated by African Americans. Founded in 1959 in Detroit by Berry Gordy, Jr., to record and market African-American pop singers, the label was so successful that the music it released became known as the "Motown Sound." The music style was based on a simple, infectious beat backed by full orchestra and **rock 'n' roll** ensemble. Smoother than the music produced by the Chicago **soul** groups, such as Jerry Butler and the Impressions, and by the Stax and Atlantic label artists, such as **Aretha Franklin**, Otis Redding, and Wilson Pickett, Motown music dominated the **Top 40** charts in the 1960s. The label's success was a major influence in the integration of African-American popular music into the mainstream.

Among the many artists on the Motown roster to have multiple Top-10 hits were Smokey Robinson and the Miracles, the Four Tops, **Diana Ross and the Supremes,** the Jackson Five, **Michael Jackson,** Stevie Wonder, Marvin Gaye, the Temptations, and **Gladys Knight and the Pips.** During the 1970s the Motown sound became less distinctive. In 1971 Gordy moved the company to Los Angeles, where it became involved in the film industry. Despite some success in recording new artists, the main business of Motown

Performers in a 1965 Motown Revue: The Temptations (in light suits), Stevie Wonder (kneeling), The Miracles (in dark suits), Martha and the Vandellas (in white dresses), and the Supremes (in dark dresses) (Motown Record Corporation)

became the recycling of the great hits of the 1960s. In 1976 the name of the company was changed to the Motown Record Corporation; in 1988 it was sold by Gordy to MCA.

REFERENCES:

David Morse, *Motown & the Arrival of Black Music* (London: Studio Vista, 1971);

Don Waller, *The Motown Story* (New York: Scribners, 1985).

– L.D.S.

MTV

Music Television (MTV) began in 1981 as a cable network devoted to showing music videos, or short films set to the songs of popular artists. Targeting young viewers, MTV has had an enormous impact on the way popular-music performers and their recordings are promoted.

The network was the concept of John Lack, a young executive for Warner Cable company, who was convinced that it was possible to create a successful cable channel that showed nothing but video clips. The first video braodcast on MTV when the network had its debut at midnight, 1 August 1981 was appropriately "Video Killed the Radio Star" by the Buggles. At the

time few American recording artists or their record companies considered video a serious medium for artistic expression, and MTV was forced to rely on clips from British **New Wave** groups such as Duran Duran and Culture Club, whose flamboyant appearance made them naturals for the channel. Almost immediately, critics began to charge that the new network would lead the recording industry to value visual style over musical talent. The network weathered this criticism, as well as charges that it was sexist because of the imagery of many of the videos and racist because at first it did not show videos by black artists — a situation changed by the enormous success of **Michael Jackson**'s 1982 album *Thriller.*

By the mid 1980s MTV was available in most American cable markets, and the record industry was convinced of the necessity of providing striking videos to promote the latest singles of new and established artists. Network television shows such as **NBC**'s *Miami Vice* (1984–1989) and theatrical films such as *Flashdance* (1983) found great success by imitating the fast-paced video style. Other music-video networks also appeared, including ones devoted to country music (CMTV) and adult contemporary music (VH-1, also owned by MTV). After the mid 1980s MTV attempted to move away from its heavy reliance on a largely uninterrupted stream of video clips and began to develop series, including game shows and stand-up comedy shows. The network also began to group videos together into themed shows (*Yo! MTV Raps*).

In addition, MTV turned its attention to a variety of social issues, enlisting popular musicians for projects such as Rock Against Drugs and Rock the Vote, which encouraged viewers to become politically aware and register to vote. In 1992 the network provided extensive coverage of the presidential election. Arkansas governor William Clinton was the only one of the three major presidential candidates who saw the network as a medium for reaching young voters; his MTV appearances helped him capture that demographic group and contributed to his election as president.

REFERENCES:

R. Serge Denisoff, *Inside MTV* (New Brunswick, N.J. & Oxford: Transaction, 1988);

Andrew Goodwin, *Dancing in the Distraction Factory: Music Television and Popular Culture* (Minneapolis: University of Minnesota Press, 1992).

– C.D.B.

MULTICULTURALISM

Multiculturalism is a movement that aims to redress the neglect or misinterpretation of minority cultures through revisions in curricula, textbooks, and histories. Rather than promoting a "melting pot" attitude of assimilation, multiculturalism encourages a pluralistic view by celebrating the achievements of different groups — usually ethnic minorities.

Increased attention to ethnic, religious, and sexual identities in the 1960s provided the basis for multiculturalism, which appeared as a term in education theory in the 1970s. Educators began to scrutinize representations of groups such as ethnic minorities, the elderly, and the disabled in textbooks and children's literature, and publishers responded with books in which previously marginalized groups became more central. In children's literature, for instance, books based on folklore from other countries became popular in the late 1970s and the 1980s. Advocates of multiculturalism have said that it represents the diversity of America and promotes tolerance. In the 1980s multiculturalism became a popular subject as colleges and universities debated whether requiring students to study non-Western cultures was needed in order to counter the dominance of "Eurocentrism." Many literary and art critics turned their attention to minority cultures in the United States and the Third World, creating new fields such as cultural studies (which also deals with popular culture) and postcolonial studies.

By the early 1990s multiculturalism was a frequent topic in the media, which often focused on its critics' claims that it sought to divide American society by separating different cultures into isolated groups. Critics such as Dinesh D'Souza lambasted multiculturalism as a "politically correct" ideology imposed on students, while others found fault with exagerrated claims about the importance of distinct cultures and the tendency to regard all members of a culture as identical and as isolated from other groups. Nonetheless, multiculturalism has influenced American life profoundly by correcting previous distortions and oversights and by questioning the claims to universality of any given culture. In addition, while minority groups are still underrepresented and stereotyped in television and film, their presence has increased and their portrayals improved in recent decades.

REFERENCES:

Paul Berman, ed., *Debating P.C.: The Controversy over Political Correctness on College Campuses* (New York: Laurel, 1992);

Stephen Greenblatt and Giles Gunn, eds., *Redrawing the Boundaries: The Transformation of English and American Literary Studies* (New York: Modern Language Association of America, 1992);

Violet J. Harris, *Teaching Multicultural Literature in Grades K–8* (Norwood, Mass.: Christopher-Gordon, 1992).

– D.H.-F.

EDWARD R. MURROW

Broadcast journalist Edward R. Murrow (1922–1965) set the standards by which radio and television newscasters have been judged since World War II. He got his first radio job in 1935 when he was made "director of talks" (educational programs) for the Columbia Broadcasting System (CBS). Two years later he was sent to London as the director of the CBS European office. On the eve of World War II Murrow and his staff kept the network supplied with reports, analyses, and interviews. During the war he frequently went on the air himself at considerable personal risk. His live broadcasts from bomb-ravaged London in 1941–1942, from North Africa in 1943, and from bombers flying over Berlin in 1944 brought the sounds of the war into American homes with powerful immediacy.

After the war Murrow created the radio show *Hear It Now* with producer Fred Friendly in 1950. Television viewers were finally able to associate a face with Murrow's famous voice in 1951 when the show was adapted for television as *See It Now*. The series featured one-hour analyses of current events, narrated by Murrow, who always held a cigarette. The show addressed topics such as desegregation, the link between cigarettes and lung cancer, and the Korean War. The most memorable segments, however, were those devoted to exposing the tactics of communist witch hunters, including Sen. **Joseph McCarthy.** In March 1954 Murrow was the first television journalist to confront McCarthy himself, then at the height of his power, broadcasting without comment footage that revealed the senator's irrational, self-aggrandizing actions. Murrow ended the report with a direct appeal to viewers to resist political fear mongering.

Murrow left CBS in 1961 to become director of the United States Information Administration. He sought to bring journalistic standards of truth to the position, which carried the responsibility of portraying American values during the **Cold War.** Years of heavy smoking had begun to take their toll, however, and Murrow died of cancer in 1965.

REFERENCE:
Joseph E. Persico, *Edward R. Murrow: An American Original* (New York: McGraw-Hill, 1988).
                                                     – C.D.B.

Museum of Modern Art

The Museum of Modern Art (MoMA) in New York has played a major part both in lending authority to new trends in contemporary art — by daring to display even the most avant-garde works of twentieth-century artists — and in treating cinema as a legitimate branch of art. The impetus for forming the museum, as well as the funds for building its collection, came from three wealthy women: Abby Aldrich Rockefeller, Lillie P. Bliss, and Mary Quinn Sullivan. In 1929 the New York State Board of Regents granted a charter charging the institution with "establishing and maintaining a museum of modern art, encouraging and developing the study of modern arts and furnishing popular instruction." The Rockefellers donated the land on West Fifty-third Street where the museum was built.

Albert A. Barr, Jr., who served as director from 1929 to 1943 and remained at the museum until 1967, was largely responsible for shaping the museum's collections. While its holdings cover virtually all forms of modern art, MoMA has specialized on the post–World War II works of the **New York School** of painters (see also **Abstract Expressionism**), whose canvases constitute nearly a third of the collection. In 1935 a film department was established at MoMA, which now owns more than eight thousand films and more than three million still photographs. The museum screens its holdings regularly in its ground-floor auditorium; its film department was one of the first to begin renting 16-mm prints of classic films to film societies and educational institutions around the country.

REFERENCES:
Russell Lynes, *Good Old Modern: An Intimate Portrait of The Museum of Modern Art* (New York: Atheneum, 1973);
The Museum of Modern Art: The History and the Collection (New York: Abrams, 1984).
                                                     – I.R.H.

Muzak

Originally a trade name for background music intended for use in office buildings, factories, and other public areas, *Muzak* has become part of the English language as a generic term for any form of "piped-in" music in public places from radio or closed-circuit broadcast. Muzak and its imitations are often denigrated as bland instrumental arrangements of popular or light classical tunes. Some have characterized it as elevator music, referring to one of the places where one may hear it.

The Muzak Corporation, founded in 1934, was the first to provide recorded music via radio to subscribers such as hotels, restaurants, and supermarkets. It distributed its recordings of familiar songs to franchises across the country. In the 1940s Muzak began to program its music specifically to improve productivity in workplaces.

REFERENCE:
Jerri Ann Husch, "Music of the Workplace: A Study of MUZAK Culture," Ph.D. dissertation, University of Massachusetts, 1984.
                                                     – L.D.S.

N

VLADIMIR NABOKOV

The famed author of the novel *Lolita* (1955), Vladimir Nabokov (1899–1977) was born in Russia and educated at Trinity College, Cambridge. He settled in America in 1940, becoming a citizen in 1945. Nabokov (pronounced Na-BOW-kof) had already written novels, stories, plays and poems in Russian and French; after his immigration he wrote exclusively in English and translated many of his earlier works, sometimes aided by his son, Dmitri.

Nabokov's writing is often described as art about art. Some critics, including **John Updike,** have proclaimed Nabokov America's finest postwar novelist, praising his self-conscious, allusive style.

Little known in America during the 1940s, Nabokov supported his writing by teaching college. His lectures were published after his death. In 1947 his novel *Bend Sinister* appeared. This brilliant seriocomic work recounts a philosopher's oppression in a fictional totalitarian state that is stupid yet effectively brutal. His next novel published in America, *Pnin* (1957), is an affectionate portrayal of a Russian professor in the United States.

Nabokov's most famous — or infamous — book, *Lolita,* vaulted him to fame. Rejected by four American publishers due to its subject (a middle-aged man's lust for a twelve-year-old girl), it first appeared in 1955 from Olympia Press, an English-language French publishing house known mostly for pornography. The scandal over the novel continued when *Lolita* was published in America in 1958, becoming a best-seller. *Lolita* spurred interest in Nabokov's earlier work and established an audience for his later efforts.

Shortly after the success of *Lolita,* Nabokov moved to Switzerland. The best known of his later works include a four-volume translation, with commentary, of Aleksandr Pushkin's *Eugene Onegin* (1964). His novels from this period include *Pale Fire* (1962), featuring a 999-line poem and its "explication" by a crazed critic, and *Ada* (1969), a long, difficult book filled with allusions and multilingual puns.

REFERENCES:

Brian Boyd, *Vladimir Nabokov: The Russian Years* (Princeton, N.J.: Princeton University Press, 1990); *Vladimir Nabokov: The American Years* (Princeton, N.J.: Princeton University Press, 1991);

Michael Juliar, *Vladimir Nabokov: A Descriptive Bibliography* (New York: Garland, 1986);

Dmitri Nabokov and Matthew J. Bruccoli, eds., *Vladimir Nabokov: Selected Letters, 1940–1977* (San Diego: Harcourt Brace Jovanovich, 1989);

Stephen Jan Parker, *Understanding Vladimir Nabokov* (Columbia: University of South Carolina Press, 1987).

— D. H.-F.

NATIONAL EDUCATION ASSOCIATION

At one time the largest professional organization in the world, the National Education Association was formed in 1857, according to their constitution, to "elevate the character and advance the interests of the profession of teaching, and to promote the cause of popular education in the United States." It has since become extremely influential in shaping educational policies and curricula, defending teachers' rights, and lobbying for federal funding for public schools.

Founded as the National Teachers' Association, the first nationwide organization to unite state and local efforts at education reform, it was incorporated as the National Education Association in 1906. Through discussions and proposals concerning teaching methods and theories, curricula, and other practical matters at their annual conventions and in their publications, in its first hundred years the NEA helped to establish public schools as government agencies and to extend schooling from kindergarten to high school. It also encouraged a better understanding of how children learn and promoted hands-on instruction.

As the need for educators increased after World War II due to the Baby Boom, NEA leadership and emphasis shifted from administrators to teachers. Since 1945, the NEA has successfully lobbied for college training and certification of teachers, and as a union it has promoted improved salaries and benefits for teachers through collective bargaining. Becoming increasingly more powerful since the 1950s through lobbying efforts and skillful use of the media, the NEA also has promoted funding for education of mentally retarded and disabled children as well as racial integration of schools. In 1976 the NEA began endorsing sympathetic political candidates, part of a transition away from speaking out on matters pertaining solely to education that has led some critics to worry about the organization's power. While the NEA is clearly progressive in intent, it is also conservative in trying to preserve gains in education programs and the status of teachers, and since its inception it has defended education against criticisms of declining standards and performance.

REFERENCES:

Allan M. West, *The National Education Association: The Power Base for Education* (New York: Free Press–Macmillan / London: Collier Macmillan, 1980);

Edgar B. Wesley, *NEA: The First Hundred Years — The Building of the Teaching Profession* (New York: Harper, 1957).

– D.H.-F.

NATIONAL ENDOWMENT FOR THE HUMANITIES

The National Endowment for the Humanities was created as a government agency in 1965 in response to a perceived lack of government support for the humanities. It has since awarded more than $1 billion in grants and fellowships for research and publications, education, and public programs such as films and television shows, all related to languages and linguistics, literature, history, philosophy, comparative religion, archaeology, and other fields.

The NEH received little media attention in its first decade as it changed from a small government agency to a large institution. In the late 1970s and early 1980s, however, its funding was increasingly attacked by government officials and journalists, who criticized

the NEH for politicizing the agency and giving money for questionable projects. Despite setbacks caused by such scrutiny and the budget cuts that sometimes accompanied it, along with the more popular successes of the National Endowment for the Arts (also founded in 1965), the NEH has effectively supported research and teaching in the humanities and brought the humanities to a larger audience. Its many grants include partial backing for museums and libraries, individual research by scholars, reference books and other scholarly publications, including definitive texts of major American writers, and public television and radio programming.

REFERENCE:

Stephen Miller, *Excellence and Equity: The National Endowment for the Humanities* (Lexington: University Press of Kentucky, 1984).

– D.H.-F.

NATIVE AMERICANS

In 1950 Dillon S. Myer, the new U.S. Commissioner of Indian Affairs, initiated the policies of "Termination" and "Relocation," which were intended to end the complex of federal obligations to Native Americans that had grown out of 372 treaties, more than five thousand laws, and many presidential edicts. Termination sought to establish tribes as financially independent corporations, newly subject to taxation on their businesses and on their land. Between 1954 and 1962, Termination was imposed on sixty-one tribes, though most were eventually returned to federal status because of the economic hardship the program imposed. Relocation was a program to resettle reservation Indians in big cities, especially Seattle, Denver, Los Angeles, and Chicago. By 1957 approximately ten thousand Indians had been relocated to work at urban construction sites and in light industry; by 1960 about one-third of the nation's 525,000 Native Americans were designated "urban Indians" by the U.S. Census.

By the late 1950s most observers admitted that the Termination and Relocation policies were a mistake. The National Congress of American Indians organized numerous protests, in which representatives from more than eighty tribes participated, to draw attention to the failure of Bureau of Indian Afairs (BIA) policies. Though President **John F. Kennedy** reversed the Termination policy, tensions continued to build, and between 1964 and 1974 Native Americans staged a series of highly publicized demonstrations. The National Indian Youth Council was formed to educate the public, and support groups offered services such as legal assistance and counseling.

In the late 1960s Dennis Banks, Russell Means, and Vernon and Clyde Bellecourt founded the militant American Indian Movement (AIM). The group outfitted Indian patrol cars with two-way radios, cameras, and tape recorders to monitor police harassment of Native Americans in Chicago and Minneapolis-Saint Paul. They joined the nineteen-month Indian takeover of Alcatraz Island in November 1969. In the fall of 1972 AIM and others, in a protest they called "The Trail of Broken Treaties," drove in caravans to Washington, D.C., to present a twenty-point position paper to the BIA. When officials refused their demands, AIM occupied and trashed BIA headquarters. In February 1973 armed AIM members participated in a ten-week protest at Wounded Knee, South Dakota, at which two Indians were killed, and on 26 June 1975 two federal agents and one Indian died in a gun battle at the Pine Ridge Reservation in South Dakota. AIM member Leonard Peltier was convicted of the agents' murders. His claims of innocence spurred Indian protest during the 1980s and the 1990s.

Indian activism in the 1980s and into the 1990s focused on cultural revitalization. Leaders of AIM began emphasizing their religious traditions. Native American lawyers sought legal redress of their grievances and promoted economic development of tribes and tribal lands. Social and economic gains have been dramatic, but still Indians are an underprivileged ethnic group. Nearly one-third of all Native Americans live in poverty, as opposed to 13 percent of the general population, and unemployment on reservations averages 35 percent. However, by the 1990s two-thirds of Indian youths were graduating from high school, up from 55 percent a decade earlier. The main goals of Native American rights activists in the 1990s, cultural and economic independence, are gradually being obtained.

REFERENCES:

Dan Frost, "American Indians in the 1990s," *American Demographics*, 13(December 1991): 26–34;

Peter Matthiessen, *In the Spirit of Crazy Horse* (New York: Viking, 1991);

Peter Nabokov, ed., *Native American Testimony* (New York: Viking, 1991).

– D.W.E.

NBC

A subsidiary of the Radio Corporation of America (RCA), the National Broadcasting Company (NBC) was the largest of the "Big Three" networks that dominated commercial television for its first forty years. Under the leadership of David Sarnoff, NBC pioneered television as an entertainment medium. As early as 1933, NBC was experimenting with broadcasting images electronically from the fifty-third floor of the Empire State Building.

When serious development of television began after World War II, NBC set the pace, closely followed by its chief rival, **CBS.** CBS scored an early coup by luring away some of NBC's most popular radio stars, such as Burns & Allen and Jack Benny, by offering them their own television shows. But NBC still had its own share of successes in the new medium, including **Milton Berle** and the children's favorite *Howdy Doody* (1947–1960). NBC took an early lead in sports by broadcasting the first televised World Series, the classic 1947 Dodgers-Yankees match-up. The NBC news department also got off to a promising start, with *Meet the Press* (1947–) and the *Camel News Caravan* with anchorman John Cameron Swayze.

In the 1960s and 1970s NBC had more affiliates and higher revenues than either of its two rivals. NBC led in the development of color television technology, and in 1966 it became the first network to offer all of its programming in color. Some of the network's most popular shows of the period were *Bonanza* (1959–1973), *Laugh-In* (1968–1973), *The Tonight Show* (1954–), and *Dragnet* (1951–1959, 1967–1970). *Star Trek* (1966–1969) later became a cult favorite. The *Today* show, the longest-running and most-successful television morning show, debuted in 1952. In the 1980s the network offered the most critically acclaimed series of the decade, *Hill Street Blues* (1981–1987), as well as the most popular, *The Cosby Show* (1984–1992) and *Cheers* (1982–1993).

The "Big Three" all suffered in the 1980s with the growing success of cable. They became attractive targets for takeover by adventurous capitalists. NBC, whose policies had frequently been dictated by its large parent corporation, was absorbed into an even larger corporation when General Electric purchased RCA in 1985.

REFERENCES:

Erik Barnouw, *Tube of Plenty,* second revised edition (New York & Oxford: Oxford University Press, 1990);

Robert Campbell, *The Golden Years of Broadcasting: A Celebration of the First 50 Years of Radio and TV on NBC* (New York: Scribners, 1976).

– C.D.B.

New Age Music

New Age music emerged as a marketing category in the 1980s for an eclectic range of acoustic and electronic pieces in styles including classical, jazz, light rock, and non-Western music. Some people listen to the music as an aid to meditation or yoga. Natural sounds, such as rainfall, wind, ocean surf, songs of birds and whales, are occasionally included in the background of the works, which are always instrumental. Often considered contemporary mood music, it is sometimes ridiculed as "yuppie Muzak."

Many New Age musicians, among them pianists Liz Story and George Winston, appear on the Windham Hill recording label. Other well-known New Age artists are harpist Andreas Vollenweider and electronic keyboardists Yanni and Vangelis. Like many New Age musicians, the group Mannheim Steamroller has accomplished many of its innovations through skillful use of the synthesizer and sophisticated recording technology.

REFERENCE:

Nevill Drury, *Music for Inner Space: Techniques for Meditation and Visualization* (Dorset, U.K. & San Leandro, Cal.: Prism, 1985).

– L.D.S.

New Consciousness

The term *New Consciousness* refers to the ideas of a diverse set of individuals who share a belief in a present or approaching evolution of human consciousness. Challenging conventional models of knowledge and belief, New Consciousness stresses spirituality and intuition in addition to the material and the rational.

In New Consciousness mind, body, and spirit are distinct yet unified. While it encourages personal growth and wholeness, New Consciousness also emphasizes the interconnectedness of the individual and the world. Thus it urges cooperation rather than competition and an attitude of mutual respect and toleration. In the New Consciousness worldview people and the universe are innately good, and in its religious manifestations New Consciousness sees God within nature and each person. Some believers also find evidence of spiritual mystery in twentieth-century science, and many are interested in psychic phenomena. While there is a strong utopian streak in New Consciousness, its adherents seldom attempt to gain converts, preferring instead to lead by example.

Though proponents find elements of their beliefs in earlier religious ideas, they insist New Consciousness is or will be a modern phenomenon. In his best-selling book *The Greening of America* (1970), Charles A. Reich locates the origins of New Consciousness in the **hippie** culture of the 1960s. Examples from the

1970s include "personal growth" movements such as **EST** and books such as Fritjof Capra's *The Tao of Physics* (1975), which links the new physics with mysticism. In the 1980s much of the New Consciousness was absorbed by the New Age movement. In addition, New Age adherents often believe in past lives, psychic experiences, and healing caused by mental powers.

REFERENCES:

J. Gorton Melton, Jerome Clark, and Aidan A. Kelly, *New Age Encyclopedia: A Guide to the Beliefs, Concepts, Terms, People, and Organizations That Make Up the New Global Movement toward Spiritual Development, Health and Healing, Higher Consciousness, and Related Subjects* (Detroit: Gale Research, 1990);

Charles A. Reich, *The Greening of America* (New York: Random House, 1970);

Harold K. Schilling, *The New Consciousness in Science and Religion* (Philadelphia: Pilgrim Press/United Church Press, 1973).

– D.H.-F.

New Criticism

John Crowe Ransom's *The New Criticism* (1941) labeled the writings of a diverse group of literary critics who revolutionized American literary studies. Beginning in the 1920s, they shifted emphasis from the study of authors, periods, and categories to "close reading" of literary texts themselves. Arguing for the autonomy of literature, apart from historical, biographical, or other "extraliterary" concerns, the New Critics favored a formal analysis of the text, concentrating on the explication of verbal and metaphorical complexities. Irony, ambiguity, and paradox thus became values.

An important influence for the New Critics was the early criticism of I. A. Richards and **T. S. Eliot.** For instance, Eliot praised the synthesis of disparate experiences in poetry and disparaged literature as a forum for personal expression. Following Eliot's example, the New Critics sparked a re-evaluation of literary history and the canon. The criticism of Eliot and the early New Critics, most of whom were poets themselves, also served to explain and justify their intellectual, experimental modernist works.

In the 1930s New Critical analytic methods were defined further by critics such as R. P. Blackmur, William Empson, and Yvor Winters and became widespread with the success of *Understanding Poetry* (1938). This anthology with commentary by Cleanth Brooks and **Robert Penn Warren,** used in successive editions for decades, allowed college students to explicate poems without an extensive knowledge of their historical contexts. New Criticism was always most successful with poetry; Brooks and Warren's *Understanding Fiction* (1943) made less of an impact.

In the first years after World War II, the New Criticism dominated American literary criticism. Its positions were defended in Brooks's *The Well Wrought Urn* (1947), René Wellek and Austin Warren's *Theory of Literature* (1949), and in two influential essays, "The Intentional Fallacy" (1946) and "The Affective Fallacy" (1949), by William K. Wimsatt and Monroe C. Beardsley, who claimed that neither the author's intention (real or perceived) nor the effect of the work on the reader should influence interpretation.

The New Criticism influenced a new generation of American poets in the 1940s and early 1950s, among them **John Berryman, Randall Jarrell, Robert Lowell**, W. S. Merwin, **Sylvia Plath,** Adrienne Rich, and **Richard Wilbur**. Though some of these poets later rejected the strictures of the New Critics, especially in their emphasis on impersonality, early on they reflected New Critical practices in writing ironic, allusive poems loaded with interconnected ideas and imagery.

In the 1950s the New Criticism became institutionalized and formulaic, and by the 1960s it was passé, superseded by structuralism and other methodologies that defied the limitations of the isolated text. Its influence persists, however, in the insistence on close, careful reading in literary criticism, and, more than any other school of critical thought, it helped to improve the status of literary studies in higher education after World War II.

REFERENCES:

Gerald Graff, *Professing Literature: An Institutional History* (Chicago & London: University of Chicago Press, 1987);

David Perkins, *A History of Modern Poetry: Modernism and After* (Cambridge, Mass. & London: Belknap/Harvard University Press, 1987);

William K. Wimsatt and Cleanth Brooks, *Literary Criticism: A Short History* (New York: Knopf, 1957).

                                                                    – D.H.-F.

NEW DIRECTIONS

Founded by the poet and steel-fortune heir James Laughlin in 1936, New Directions Publishing Corporation has made its reputation by publishing innovative literature.

After studying in 1934 with Gertrude Stein and **Ezra Pound,** Laughlin began publishing at Pound's suggestion in 1936. New Directions was considered a publisher of avant-garde authors. Because the authors it published were not popular, the company did not make a profit in the first twenty-five years of its exis-

Ezra Pound and James Laughlin

tence. Despite limited sales, the company kept many books now considered important in print, thus giving them maximum exposure, especially in college classrooms.

New Directions has published some of the most talented and innovative authors of the century, including Pound, **William Carlos Williams,** Thomas Merton, and John Hawkes. **Lawrence Ferlinghetti**'s *A Coney Island of the Mind* (1958) was a best-seller for the firm. In addition, New Directions has done much to expose American readers to foreign writers, publishing in translation the works of authors such as Jean Cocteau, Pablo Neruda, and Octavio Paz.

REFERENCE:

D.W. Faulkner, et al., "New Directions Publishing Corporation," in *Dictionary of Literary Biography*, volume 46: *American Literary Publishing Houses, 1900-1980: Trade and Paperback* (Detroit: Gale Research, 1986), pp. 255-260.

                                                                    – R.T.

New Formalism

New formalism is a label applied after the fact to the works of those post–World War II poets who employ conventional, often complex, poetic forms. These poets have resisted the radical experiments with form and subject matter that characterize the work of postwar schools such as **projectivism, confessionalism,** and deep imagism. Following in the American tradition of **Robert Frost, Wallace Stevens,** and **T. S. Eliot,** poets who are frequently called new formalists include **Richard Wilbur,** Howard Nemerov, Elizabeth Bishop, Anthony Hecht, X. J. Kennedy, Donald Justice, and Mona Van Duyn. Most of these poets would probably agree with Wilbur, who once said that he could be labeled a new formalist if "it be understood that to try to revive the force of rhyme and other formal devices, by reconciling them with the experimental gains of the past several decades, is itself sufficiently experimental."

REFERENCE:

Wyatt Prunty, *"Fallen from the Symboled World": Precedents for the New Formalism* (New York & Oxford: Oxford University Press, 1990).

– K.L.R.

New Historicism

New Historicism is one example of the increasing prominence of critical theory in American literary studies since the 1960s. More a body of related scholarship than a school, New Historicism emerged in the late 1970s and early 1980s as a methodology focusing on the relationship of literature to the historical conditions in which it is produced and received.

What distinguishes New Historicism from other historical approaches to literature is its rejection of cause-and-effect historicism (as in Marxist criticism) and its avoidance of universal or definitive claims. New Historicist critics attempt not to recreate the past but to construct an approximation of it from textual materials.

In this and other respects, New Historicism is indebted to **poststructuralism** with its undermining of claims to knowledge. Following the French philosopher Michel Foucault's explorations into the history of sexuality and other social structures, New Historicist critics view history as a complex relationship of institutions and ideologies struggling for power — not only political power, but also control over language. In any given culture, New Historicism asserts, competing "discourses" — ways of thinking and living — interact and conflict. These discourses inform rather than reflect the thought and literature of an age; in New Historicism, therefore, culture is deterministic and the role of the author is less significant than how historical factors uniquely condition his or her writing.

New Historicism views literature as part of a larger cultural and social picture; an understanding of this context, its advocates maintain, is necessary to understand any work of literature fully. To assemble this picture, critics examine the physical and economic conditions of literary production, audience and critical reception, and both literary and nonliterary texts. In this way New Historicism challenges established divisions between high and low culture, literature and historical documents, and canonical and noncanonical works. Examples of New Historicism include Stephen Greenblatt's books on Renaissance literature such as *Shakespearean Negotiations* (1988), in which he analyzes "cultural poetics" as the "study of the collective making of distinct cultural practices and inquiry into the relations among these practices." Since the 1980s New Historicism has had a major influence in the American academy.

REFERENCE:

H. Aram Veeser, ed., *The New Historicism* (New York & London: Routledge, 1989).

– D.H.-F.

New Image Painting

The New Image Painters were a disparate group of artists who in the 1970s began to reject the excessive refinement and formalism of such abstract styles as **minimalism** in favor of a more figurative, expressive art. While still keeping to a relatively abstract style, these artists introduced a narrative content into their work — a combination recalling the expressive methods of Surrealism and German Expressionism. For example, while the paintings of Susan Rothenberg include representations of animal and human forms as well as other figures, they clearly do not deny the expressive power of the formal, abstract aspect of painting in itself. In 1978 the Whitney Museum of American Art organized an exhibition, New Image Painting, which gave the movement its name and at the same time underscored the diversity of the individual approaches it included. The late paintings of **Philip Guston** are sometimes seen as an important precursor to New Image Painting both in style and in the tendency toward social comment that often occupied the New Image artists. Other important artists associated with New Image Painting include Neil Jenney, Nicholas Africano, and Jonathan Borofsky.

REFERENCE:

Richard Marshall, *New Image Painting* (New York: Whitney Museum of American Art, 1978).

– K.B.

NEW JOURNALISM

The New Journalism, a popular and controversial trend in reporting, revolutionized journalism with its appropriation of fictional technique and its use of unconventional subjects and styles. Though its experiments were never fully accepted by journalists and readers even during its prime in the 1960s and early 1970s, the New Journalism succeeded in expanding the possibilities open to the reporter.

The New Journalists sought to wed the research of journalism with the techniques of fiction, particularly by developing stories through scenes rather than narration; extensive use of dialogue; relating parts of the story through a subject's perspective (based on interviews) or through the writer's own (sometimes subjective) point of view; detailed descriptions of people and places; and self-conscious style, ranging from realism to stream of consciousness.

Early practitioners of the New Journalism began as traditional journalists. Gay Talese's magazine pieces and Jimmy Breslin's columns for the *New York Herald Tribune* in the early 1960s, which read like short stories, were among the first to exhibit characteristics of what would be labeled the New Journalism in the mid 1960s. **Tom Wolfe** stretched the boundaries of journalism even further beginning in 1963 with a series of articles for *Esquire* and the *Herald Tribune* Sunday supplement that employed shifting points of view and eccentric punctuation, vocabulary, and typography. Wolfe became the unofficial spokesman of the New Journalism, promoting it as the heir to the novelistic tradition of social realism. It flourished in magazines such as *Esquire*, *Rolling Stone,* and the *Village Voice*.

In the late 1960s and early 1970s, Wolfe's essay collections such as *The Electric Kool-Aid Acid Test* (1968) and other books combining reportorial and fictional strategies helped to establish the techniques of the New Journalism. These books generally drew on personal experience and research and, like most New Journalism, showed readers the story behind the story. Three classics of New Journalism were published in 1966: **Hunter S. Thompson**'s *Hell's Angels: A Strange and Terrible Saga*, the product of a year and a half with a motorcycle gang; George Plimpton's *Paper Lion*, chronicling how he trained with a professional football team and played in an exhibition game; and **Truman Capote**'s enormously successful *In Cold Blood*, a "non-fiction novel" about a pair of murderers. Capote's approach, also labeled "faction" by some critics, is similar to **Norman Mailer**'s account of his participation in a 1967 protest march on the Pentagon, *The Armies of the Night: History as the Novel, the Novel as History* (1968). Other examples of New Journalism include **Joan Didion**'s essay collection *Slouching towards Bethlehem* (1968), Joe McGinnis's *The Selling of the President, 1968* (1969), and Talese's *Honor Thy Father* (1971), an inside view of the Mafia.

REFERENCE:

Tom Wolfe and E. W. Johnson, eds., *The New Journalism* (New York: Harper & Row, 1973).

– D.H.-F.

NEW LEFT

The first homegrown leftist movement in America, the New Left was created in the early 1960s by activists in the **civil rights movement.** Later in the decade the New Left became a major force in opposition to the **Vietnam War.** At the height of its influence, however, the New Left broke into competing factions. By the end of 1970 it had essentially ceased to exist, never having extended its power base much beyond college and university campuses.

The history of the New Left begins with the founding of Students for a Democratic Society (SDS) at the University of Michigan in 1960. By June 1962, when it held its national conference at Port Huron, Michigan, SDS had about 800 members in chapters at 10 colleges and universities. In 1968 it had 350 official campus chapters and around 100,000 members. In addition to operating its own programs, SDS officially or unofficially cooperated with other groups concerned with issues such as civil rights, students' rights, freedom of speech, poverty, and peace. By 1969–1970 the New Left as a whole had at least 150,000 active participants in various protests, while more than one million young people expressed sympathy for its goals.

The forty-three voting members at the Port Huron meeting saw SDS as a way to generate nationwide support for the civil rights activities in the South, but they also wanted to give poor people in northern cities a voice in governmental decisions that affected their lives. Tom Hayden, who drafted the first declaration of SDS policy, *The Port Huron Statement* (1962), was one of several SDS leaders heavily influenced by sociologist C. Wright Mills (1916–1962). In *The Power Elite* (1956) Mills had charged that the United States was governed by individuals in the top ranks of big business, the military, and politics, leaving the interests

Paul Potter, fourth president (1964-1965) of Students for a Democratic Society (SDS), and Tom Hayden, second president (1962-1963), at an SDS planning session in spring 1964

of most Americans unrepresented. *The Port Huron Statement* echoed Mills when it proclaimed, "we seek the establishment of a democracy of individual participation."

In his "Letter to the New Left" (1960) Mills rejected the Marxist idea that the working class would revolutionize society by seizing control of the means of production, arguing instead that young intellectuals were the "real live agencies of historic change." Following Mills's lead, *The Port Huron Statement* deplored "unreasoning anticommunism" but declared the "basic opposition [of SDS] to the communist system." The statement also criticized the unions as "too quiescent" to participate in reforming society. In cutting themselves off from the Old Left and from one of the most powerful forces in the Democratic Party, the idealists of the New Left inadvertently limited their influence from the start.

The first generation of SDS, including Hayden and Rennie Davis, applied the concept of participatory democracy to community-organization projects in cities such as Chicago, Baltimore, Cleveland, and Newark, New Jersey. Most of the New Left followed the lead of SDS in supporting Lyndon B. Johnson over Barry Goldwater in the 1964 presidential election, but in 1965, as the war in Vietnam began to escalate, the

movement started to lose faith in politics as usual. Its attention focused almost exclusively on antiwar protest and draft resistance, the New Left had entered a new phase by 1967. The most radical members of this generation of activists looked not to Mills but to Frantz Fanon (1916–1961), a member of the Algerian National Front during its war for liberation from France (1954–1962), who in *The Wretched of the Earth* (1961), had praised violent revolution as "a cleansing force."

After antiwar demonstrators were attacked by Chicago police during the 1968 Democratic National Convention (see **Chicago 8**), membership in SDS, which had played a small but inflammatory role in the events, increased significantly. Disparaging the "reformist" efforts of Hayden, Davis, and other SDS veterans working to organize the Chicago demonstrations, the current SDS leadership said the key to change was revolution. To the surprise of their elders, the number of college students who called themselves revolutionaries far exceeded the 100,000 members of SDS: a fall 1968 poll found approximately 368,000, while a survey taken two years later counted more than 1,170,000.

SDS leadership, which included individuals who would later become part of the militant **Weathermen,** began to talk optimistically about how SDS should "develop the seeds of revolution" and prepare for "armed struggle." Yet they failed. Over the next year two radical factions, the Weathermen and Progressive Labor Party (PL) members (adherents of the Chinese Communism of Mao Tse-tung), battled for control of SDS. In June 1969 it split into two groups, each claiming to be the real SDS. Less-radical members found they could support neither group and began to drop out.

The New Left splintered into dozens of small groups with differing agendas. SDS had held the New Left together by accommodating individuals with a wide range of political views, from traditional liberals to left-wing radicals.

Despite its brief life and violent end the New Left successfully challenged the conformity and conservatism of the 1950s. It was largely responsible for giving students a greater voice in determining university curricula and regulations governing campus life, and it played a major role in turning public opinion against the Vietnam War.

REFERENCES:

Todd Gitlin, *The Sixties: Years of Hope, Days of Rage* (Toronto, New York, London, Sydney & Auckland: Bantam, 1987);

Tom Hayden, *Reunion: A Memoir* (New York: Random House, 1988);

James Miller, *"Democracy Is in the Streets": From Port Huron to the Siege of Chicago* (New York: Simon & Schuster, 1987);

Kirkpatrick Sale, *SDS* (New York: Random House, 1973).

– K.L.R.

New Realist Painting

During the 1960s several artists began to paint in a figurative style rather than adhering to the avant-garde art world's general bent toward abstraction. Many of these New Realist artists had been trained in the **Abstract Expressionist** style. While ultimately rejecting that movement's exclusion of representational subject matter, the New Realist painters incorporated into their works many elements of Abstract Expressionist style — such as flattened pictorial space and reduced palette of colors. In his *Ada with Sunglasses* (1969), for example, Alex Katz renders the figurative subject with reduced shapes and flattened perspective — still maintaining, however, fidelity to realistic form. The New Realists often objectified their subjects by arbitrarily cropping them and avoiding sentimental treatment.

In the 1960s the New Realists' choice of subject matter, primarily portraits and nudes, seemed aesthetically retrograde to critics; yet many of these artists — such as Katz and Philip Pearlstein — eventually

achieved long-term critical acceptance. Other artists identified with New Realism include William Bailey, Jack Beal, Alice Neel, and **Fairfield Porter.**

– K.B.

New Wave Music

A type of American and British rock music, New Wave music has its roots in **punk rock** but lacks its consistently angry tone and amateurism. New Wave rock flourished in the late 1970s and early 1980s.

A reaction against prevailing rock styles such as **heavy metal,** punk, and so-called art rock, New Wave music is notable for its intelligent lyrics about relationships and social problems and for its use of basic rock forms and rhythms. British New Wave musicians popular in America include Elvis Costello, Dire Straits, and especially the Police with songs such as "Roxanne" (1978), "Message in a Bottle" (1979), and "Don't Stand So Close to Me" (1980). Talking Heads became the best-known New Wave group in America with such songs as "Psycho Killer" (1977) and "Burning Down the House" (1983).

REFERENCES:

Ira A. Robbins, ed., *The Trouser Press Guide to New Wave Records* (New York: Scribners, 1983);

David Bianco, ed., *Who's New Wave in Music: An Illustrated Encyclopedia, 1976–1982 (The First Wave)* (Ann Arbor: Pierian Press, 1985).

– L.D.S.

New York Metropolitan Opera

The New York Metropolitan Opera is the leading opera company in America and perhaps the world. From its original site on Broadway to its present location as part of the Lincoln Center for the Performing Arts, the Metropolitan Opera has successfully fended off numerous competitors for its position. The "Met" represents the pinnacle for any aspiring opera singer, conductor, designer, producer, or director.

Inaugurated on 22 October 1883 in what was once a brewery, the Metropolitan Opera now boasts a state-of-the-art facility that has been upgraded continually since opening on 16 September 1966 with the world premiere of **Samuel Barber**'s *Antony and Cleopatra,* one of its many notable premieres.

General manager Sir Rudolf Bing (1950–1972) was primarily responsible for modernizing the Met after World War II by improving settings and acting in new productions of classic operas. The current artistic

The New York Metropolitan Opera building at Lincoln Center (photograph by Bob Serating, Lincoln Center for the Performing Arts)

and musical director (as well as chief conductor) is James Levine, who has been associated with the company for more than twenty years. Affiliated organizations of the company include the Metropolitan Opera Guild, which publishes *Opera News*. Live performances of Metropolitan Opera productions have been broadcast on radio since 1932 and televised with increasing regularity on *Live from the Met* on **PBS** since the late 1970s.

REFERENCES:

Martin Mayer, *The Met: One Hundred Years of Grand Opera* (New York: Simon & Schuster, 1983);

Frank Merkling, John W. Freeman, Gerald Fitzgerald, and Arthur Solin, *The Golden Horseshoe: The Life and Times of the Metropolitan Opera House* (New York: Viking, 1965);

Francis Robinson, *Celebration: The Metropolitan Opera* (Garden City, N.Y.: Doubleday, 1979).

– L.D.S.

NEW YORK REVIEW OF BOOKS

The *New York Review of Books* (*NYR*) is among the most respected intellectual journals of culture and books in the United States. First published in February 1963 during a New York City newspaper strike, the *New York Review* was intended to replace the reviews and commentary usually published by the *New York Times* and the *New York Herald-Tribune*. The first issue of the journal was intended to be the only one, but after nearly one hundred thousand copies were sold, the backers decided to publish a second issue in May 1963. Since September 1963 the *New York Review* has been appearing twice monthly.

Jason Epstein, an editor at Random House, developed the idea for the *New York Review*. His wife, Barbara, and Robert Silvers, a former editor at *Harper's Magazine*, have edited the *NYR* since it was founded. During the first three decades of its existence, the journal has had an impressive list of contributors, including Edmund Wilson, Susan Sontag, V. S. Naipaul, W. H. Auden, Elizabeth Hardwick, Vaclav Havel, and Sir Isaiah Berlin. Intellectually sophisticated and politically to the left, the journal mainly publishes long book reviews and essays that usually address social, political, or cultural concerns.

REFERENCES:

Joseph Epstein, "Thirty Years of the 'New York Review'," *Commentary* 96 (December 1993): 39–43;

"Good Bet for a Baltic Baron," *Time* 81 (31 May 1963): 51–52.

–J.W.H.

NEW YORK SCHOOL

A label often applied to the **Abstract Expressionist** painters, the term *New York School* also refers to a group of young poets who were friends with these artists in New York City during the 1950s and early 1960s. These poets — most notably John Ashbery (1927–), Kenneth Koch (1925–), Frank O'Hara (1926–1966), and James Schuyler (1923–1991) — were part of a wide circle of New York artists, including **Willem de Kooning** and **Jackson Pollock. Ted Berrigan** has been called a second-generation New York School poet. O'Hara, Ashbery, Schuyler, and Berrigan all wrote reviews of museum and gallery shows for *ARTnews,* and O'Hara was on the staff of the **Museum of Modern Art.**

The term *New York Poets* was coined in Donald M. Allen's influential 1960 anthology *The New American Poetry.* Though each writer developed a unique voice, their poetry during the 1950s and 1960s shared certain traits. Like the painters who influenced them, these New York poets rejected realism in favor of art that revealed the conditions of its creation. Their idiosyncratic, often playful poems are spontaneous and include unexpected juxtapositions of language and imagery, spurning the deliberateness of poetry influenced by **T. S. Eliot** and the **New Critics** on the one hand and the **confessional poets** on the other. In their sometimes surrealistic poems, they attempted to capture the elusiveness of experience, particularly the energy and chaos of New York.

O'Hara, the central figure of the New York School, wrote poems in which he described everyday events and objects in dreamlike images. Koch advocated "formulalessness" in poetry, while Ashbery wrote witty, lyrical poems that defied logic or summary. After the "school" effectively ended with O'Hara's death in 1966, Koch became a celebrated teacher while continuing to write poetry, and Ashbery was eventually recognized as an important American poet.

REFERENCES:

Donald M. Allen, ed., *The New American Poetry* (New York: Grove / London: Evergreen, 1960);

John Gruen, *The Party's Over Now: Reminiscences of the Fifties — New York's Artists, Writers, Musicians, and Their Friends* (New York: Viking, 1972).

– D.H.-F.

NEW YORK TIMES BOOK REVIEW

The *New York Times Book Review* is the most influential book review in America. Its essays, reviews, and **best-seller lists** are read across the country. The tabloid-sized *NYTBR* is sold as part of the Sunday *New York Times* and separately to subscribers. Sometimes used by libraries and bookstores as an order catalogue, the *NYTBR* helps to sell books, even if the review is bad, because any notice in its pages is better than being ignored.

The *NYTBR* began publishing a weekly best-seller list in 1942. Described as "the list of lists," each weekly list is now based on reports from 2,000 bookstores across the nation. The separate **paperbacks** list also includes reports from wholesalers who cover 40,000 retail markets such as newsstands and supermarkets.

Before the 1960s, the publication remained fairly conservative and journalistic, dealing mostly with books on politics, history, and current events. In recent decades the focus has shifted to literature, and reviews are often extremely critical, though the editors try to reject patently unfair reviews beforehand. Critics of the periodical claim that it plays favorites (mostly Eastern writers) and that it is out of touch with the literary world, especially when it comes to reviewing poetry. Many readers feel, however, that the *NYTBR* does the best job possible, given the large number of books published and the incestuous nature of publishing, which insures that books are sometimes reviewed by an author's friend or enemy. In addition to commissioned reviews from authors, the *NYTBR* also has a small staff of critics. Between the reviews in the *NYTBR* and those that appear in the daily paper, the *Times* publishes the most book reviews in America. (*The Washington Post* is second.) In addition to literary books, the *NYTBR* covers popular genres such as **science fiction** in brief chronicle reviews, children's books, nonfiction, and books from university presses.

REFERENCES:

L. J. Davis, "The List of Lists," *Harper's,* 271 (August 1985): 60–61;

Christopher Surr, "The Most Powerful Book Review in America," in *Dictionary of Literary Biography Yearbook: 1982,* edited by Richard Ziegfeld, Jean W. Ross, and Lynne C. Zeigler (Detroit: Gale Research, 1983), pp. 29–34.

– D.H.-F.

THE NEW YORKER

Founded in 1925 by Harold Ross, the weekly magazine *The New Yorker* has become an icon of middle-highbrow American culture. The first cover and the cover of the annual anniversary issue published each February through 1993 features the fictional Eustace Tilley, dressed in morning coat and top hat and contemplating New York life through a raised eyeglass. Tilley has represented the editorial stance of the magazine since its inception, though new editorship in the 1990s indicates that he may require a makeover. The 21 February 1994 anniversary cover by satiric cartoon artist R. Crumb featured Elvis tilley, a scruffy, acne-ridden teenager contemplating an advertisement for an adult

Barnett Newman at the Guggenheim Museum exhibition of his *Stations of the Cross,* 1966 (photograph by Bernard Gotfryd)

video store. The magazine's format has changed little during its history. Such departments as "Notes and Comments," "Talk of the Town," "Reporter at Large," and a weekly summary of cultural activities in New York City, mixed with quality fiction, poetry, and in-depth nonfiction, witty cartoons from staff artists, and unusually interesting advertisements, with "news-breaks" (short, humorous infelicities from news sources) used as filler have been the expected elements of each issue. **John O'Hara, J.D. Salinger,** John Cheever, and **John Updike** are among the prominent authors associated with the postwar *New Yorker.*

The magazine has always had the reputation of being scrupulously edited, but under the editorship of William Shawn (who succeeded Ross in 1951), it came to be regarded as stuffy and outdated as well. A critic for *New York* magazine has noted that by the 1980s the magazine had become "far more admired than it is read, or relevant."

In 1985 the founding owners of the magazine sold a controlling interest in the magazine to media titan S.I. Newhouse, co-proprietor of Advance Publications, which controls a vast publishing empire. Concerned

about the *New Yorker*'s lagging ad revenue and flat circulation, Newhouse named Robert Gottlieb, editor in chief and president of the book publishing firm Knopf, as Shawn's successor. Respectful of the venerable *New Yorker* tradition, Gottlieb instituted little noticeable change in the format or material of the magazine and thus failed to deliver the results Newhouse expected.

In 1992 Gottlieb was replaced by Tina Brown, the thirty-three-year-old editor of *Vanity Fair,* a successful Newhouse revival of a sophisticated New York magazine that had failed in 1936. Brown had shocked and delighted *Vanity Fair* readers with her daring, hip editorial decisions, such as picturing the naked and very pregnant actress Demi Moore on a *Vanity Fair* cover. Brown's *New Yorker* was equally bold and irreverent. She enlisted the talents of a new generation of artists and writers, who produced lively, even relevant, creative art and timely editorial content. She introduced color and photography (by staff photographer **Richard Avedon**) to the magazine, and punctured the pretentious tone that had prevailed before her arrival. Traditionalists were horrified, but the initial response of readers supported the magazine's updated image.

REFERENCE:
Gigi Mahon, *The Last Days of The New Yorker* (New York: McGraw-Hill, 1988).
– D.L.

BARNETT NEWMAN

One of the few native New Yorkers involved in the formative years of **Abstract Expressionism,** Barnett Newman (1905–1970) was known for his polemical statements in defense of abstraction before he actually produced any major works. He graduated from the City College of New York in 1927, having also studied at the Art Students' League in New York (1922–1926, 1929–1930).

During the 1930s and most of the 1940s Newman destroyed his paintings almost as quickly as he painted them, believing that he had failed to make the radical break from the traditions of modern European painting that he felt was necessary. In 1948 he painted *Onement,* his first mature work. Newman covered his huge canvases with a single color and introduced a vertical strip, later known as the "zip," onto the field of color. Newman believed that his flat imagery held within it the possibility of transcendental experience for the viewer, an opportunity to confront the sublime. His major works include *Who's Afraid of Red, Yellow & Blue* (1969–1970) and *Vir Heroicus Sublimis* (1950–1951). The 1966 exhibition at the Solomon R. Guggenheim Museum of his *Stations of the Cross* (1958–1966) solidified his reputation, which had been slower to develop than those of other artists in the New York School.

REFERENCE:
John Philip O'Neill, ed., *Barnett Newman: Selected Writings and Interview* (New York: Knopf, 1990).
– K.B.

PAUL NEWMAN

Famed for his blue eyes and cocky smile, Paul Newman (1925-) played the wise-cracking outsider, charming heel, or persecuted marginal man in a series of excellent films from the 1950s through the 1980s. Newman studied acting at the Yale School of Drama and the **Actors Studio** in the early 1950s. His starring role in *Picnic* on Broadway in 1953 brought him a contract with Warner Bros. He soon established himself in films such as *Somebody Up There Likes Me* (1956), *The Left-Handed Gun* (1958), *Cat on a Hot Tin Roof* (1958), and *The Long Hot Summer* (1958). The last of these films was the first of nine in which Newman acted

with or directed his wife, Joanne Woodward. By the 1960s Newman was a top Hollywood star who enhanced his status with Academy Award (Oscar) nominations for *The Hustler* (1960), *Hud* (1963), and *Cool Hand Luke* (1967). After notable pairings with **Robert Redford** in *Butch Cassidy and the Sundance Kid* (1969) and *The Sting* (1973), Newman's career slowed, but it was reenergized by another Oscar nomination for *The Verdict* (1982) and, finally, an Oscar for the reprise of his *Hustler* role as Eddie Felson in *The Color of Money* (1986). Newman's and Woodward's portrayals of *Mr. and Mrs. Bridge* (1991) also received high praise. He played a greedy tycoon in the 1994 comedy *The Hudsucker Proxy.* When not acting, directing, and producing, Newman is active in liberal political causes, drives race cars, and oversees a successful line of food products, Newman's Own. In 1993 he was given the Jean Hersholt Humanitarian Award by the American Academy of Motion Picture Arts and Sciences.

REFERENCE:
J.C. Landry, *Paul Newman* (New York: McGraw-Hill, 1983).
– I.R.H.

MIKE NICHOLS

Mike Nichols (1931–) is a successful director in Hollywood and on Broadway. Most of his films and plays have met with popular success and critical acclaim.

Born Michael Igor Peschkowsky in Berlin, Nichols immigrated to America with his parents in 1938. He was a sophisticated sketch comedian in the 1950s, and by 1957 he and partner Elaine May were touring the country with their satiric revue. It appeared on Broadway in 1960 as *An Evening with Mike Nichols and Elaine May* and was a huge success. The act ended the following year. Nichols began directing with **Neil Simon**'s hit plays *Barefoot in the Park* (1963) and *The Odd Couple* (1965). He directed his first film, an adaptation of **Edward Albee**'s *Who's Afraid of Virginia Woolf?,* in 1966. His second movie, *The Graduate* (1967), helped revolutionize American film with its sexual themes and its comic critique of American materialism. It won him an Academy Award (Oscar). Other films Nichols directed offer a similarly satiric look at American society, including *Catch-22* (1970), *Heartburn* (1986), *Working Girl* (1988), and *Regarding Henry* (1991). Nichols's recent work for the stage includes *The Real Thing* (1982) and *Death and the Maiden* (1991).

REFERENCE:
H. Wayne Schuth, *Mike Nichols* (Boston: Twayne, 1978).
– I.R.H.

Roger Rowell, Ray Broussard, Murray Louis, Bill Frank, and Albert Reid in the first production of Alwin Nikolais's *Imago* (photograph by Robert Sosenko)

JACK NICHOLSON

Film actor Jack Nicholson (1937–   ) has been noted for his portrayals of idiosyncratic characters, often outsiders who threaten the establishment, for more than two decades.

Nicholson's early movie experiences, beginning in 1958, consisted largely of low-budget pictures for **Roger Corman;** the most famous of these roles is that of the masochistic dental patient in *Little Shop of Horrors* (1961). Nicholson's break came when he was cast as an alcoholic lawyer in Dennis Hopper's *Easy Rider* (1969), for which he received the first of his many Academy Award (Oscar) nominations. Impressive performances in *Five Easy Pieces* (1970), *The Last Detail* (1973), and *Chinatown* (1974) followed. This phase of his career culminated in his Academy Award-winning portrayal of McMurphy in the 1975 screen adaptation of **Ken Kesey**'s novel *One Flew Over the Cuckoo's Nest.*

In the 1980s and 1990s Nicholson's roles have been more varied. Although the devilish trickster type became his trademark with characters such as a deranged murderer in *The Shining* (1979), Satan in *The Witches of Eastwick* (1987), and the Joker in *Batman*

(1990), he has also succeeded in such challenging roles as playwright Eugene O'Neill in *Reds* (1981); the crude but romantic former astronaut in *Terms of Endearment* (1983), which resulted in a second Academy Award, for supporting actor; a Mafia hit man in *Prizzi's Honor* (1985); teamster boss Jimmy Hoffa in *Hoffa* (1992); and a brutal marine officer in *A Few Good Men* (1993).

REFERENCES:

Bruce Braithwaite, *The Films of Jack Nicholson* (Bembridge, U.K.: BCW, 1977);

John Parker, *The Joker's Wild: The Biography of Jack Nicholson* (London: Pan, 1991).

– I.R.H.

ALWIN NIKOLAIS

As a modern dance choreographer, Alwin Nikolais (1912–1993) created striking **multi-media** dance spectacles. In a career that spanned nearly six decades he choreographed more than eighty works, for most of which he also designed the costumes, lighting, and sets and composed their electronic scores.

Marsha Norman with Tom Moore, director of her Pulitzer Prize–winning play *'night Mother* (photograph by *Courier-Journal and Louisville Times*)

Born in Connecticut, Nikolais (pronounced NIK-oh-lye) acquired a taste for the stage as a child. In 1933 he saw a modern-dance performance by Mary Wigman and was intrigued by the percussion accompaniment. He sought out a former Wigman dancer, Truda Kaschmann, who encouraged him to study dance. Starting in 1936, he choreographed a dozen works (the first with Kaschmann) before serving in the U.S. Army Signal Corps during World War II. Like much modern dance in the 1930s and 1940s, these pieces centered around psychological dramas.

In 1948 Nikolais was invited to organize the dance department of the Henry Street Settlement Playhouse in New York. He stopped dancing professionally in 1953, turning his attention to choreographing increasingly abstract theatrical pieces. *Masks, Props, and Mobiles* (1953) was one of his first works to feature his new credo, "motion, not emotion." By 1956 he had trained his corps of seven dancers, and he began to create the mixed-media productions that became his artistic signature. The best known of these are *Kaleidoscope* (1953; revised, 1956) and his full-evening production *Imago* (1963). While Nikolais's dances are

nonrepresentational, many of them — such as *Tower* (1965) and *Tent* (1968) — symbolize the efforts of society to make individuals conform to its conventions.

REFERENCES:

Don McDonagh, *The Rise and Fall and Rise of Modern Dance* (Pennington, N.J.: A Capella, 1990);

Joseph H. Mazo, *Prime Movers: The Makers of Modern Dance in America* (New York: Morrow, 1977).

– D.M.

Marsha Norman

Marsha Norman (1947–), the playwright most closely associated with **Actors Theatre of Louisville,** specializes in plays about isolated, unhappy women. She has said in retrospect that she always writes about solitary confinement.

In 1976 Jon Jory, artistic director at Actors Theatre, urged Norman to write a play about a time when she was really frightened. Recalling her feelings and those of the disturbed children she had taught at Kentucky Central State Hospital in the early 1970s, Norman produced *Getting Out*, about a woman trying to forge a life for herself after a stint in prison. The play premiered at Actors Theatre in 1977, and in autumn 1978 it opened Off-Broadway, where it ran for eight months. After writing several other plays while she was playwright-in-residence at Actors Theatre in 1978–1979 and at the Mark Taper Forum in Los Angeles in 1979–1980, Norman achieved national prominence with *'night Mother* (1983), which portrays, in real time, the last hours in the life of a young woman who has decided to kill herself and wants to come to terms with her mother before she commits the act. Running for ten months on Broadway, the play earned Norman a Pulitzer Prize.

Norman's next major success came when she wrote the book for the Broadway musical version of Frances Hodgson Burnett's popular 1911 novel *The Secret Garden* (1990) and won an Antoinette Perry (Tony) Award in 1991.

REFERENCE:

Linda Kintz, *The Subject's Tragedy: Political Poetics, Feminist Theory, and Drama* (Ann Arbor: University of Michigan Press, 1992).

– I.R.H.

O

JOYCE CAROL OATES

Joyce Carol Oates is one of the best-selling seriously considered living fiction writers in the United States and undoubtedly the most prolific. In the thirty years since her first book appeared in 1963, she has published twenty-five novels and sixteen collections of short stories, as well as poetry, plays, and nonfiction prose including literary criticism and a book about boxing. As novelist **John Updike** has said in response to charges that she writes too quickly, "Single-mindedness and efficiency rather than haste underlie her prolificacy; if the phrase 'woman of letters' existed, she would be, foremost in this country, entitled to it" (*New Yorker,* 28 December 1987).

Oates was already a critically acclaimed writer in 1970, when she won a National Book Award for her fourth novel, *them* (1969), the final volume of a loosely connected trilogy that also includes *A Garden of Earthly Delights* (1967) and *Expensive People* (1968). These novels examine the emotionally and physically violent upheavals of contemporary American rural, suburban, and urban life. The climactic scenes in *them* are set during the summer 1967 race riots in Detroit, where Oates lived in 1962–1968.

In talking about her fiction, Oates distinguishes between "gothic" with a lowercase *g* and "Gothic" with a capital *G*. She defines the first as "a work in which extremes of emotion are unleashed." This type of fiction, she adds, is "not a literary tradition so much as a fairly realistic assessment of modern life." This definition applies to most of her fiction, including her 1960s trilogy, three highly regarded novels of the 1970s and 1980s — *Wonderland* (1971), *Son of Morning* (1978), and *Angel of Light* (1981) — and her most personal novels — *Marya: A Life* (1986) and *You Must Remem-*

ber This (1987) — as well as *Because It Is Bitter, and Because It Is My Heart* (1990).

Oates has also written three novels that she calls Gothic with a capital *G*: *Bellefleur* (1980), *A Bloodsmoor Romance* (1982), and *Mysteries of Winterthurn* (1984). In these novels she combines elements of **Gothic fiction** with realist presentation in examining life in nineteenth- and early-twentieth-century America. *Foxfire: Confessions of a Girl Gang* (1993), a small *g* gothic novel set in the present, also combines realism and fantasy.

Oates seems certain to maintain her reputation as an important American writer, despite charges from some critics that her fiction is too violent. She answers these charges by pointing out that "serious writers ... take for their natural subjects the complexity of the world, its evils as well as its good.... The serious writer, after all, bears witness."

REFERENCES:

Joanne V. Creighton, *Joyce Carol Oates* (Boston: Twayne, 1979);

Creighton, *Joyce Carol Oates: Novels of the Middle Years* (Boston: Twayne, 1992);

Greg Johnson, *Understanding Joyce Carol Oates* (Columbia: University of South Carolina Press, 1987).

–K.L.R.

FLANNERY O'CONNOR

Although the body of her work is relatively small — thirty-one short stories and two novels — Flannery O'Connor (1925–1964) is widely recognized as one of the foremost American writers of short stories in the twentieth century. Critics have compared her to such nineteenth-century writers as Nathaniel Hawthorne and Fyodor Dostoyevski. Because her stories deal with internally and externally grotesque characters and bizarre events in otherwise realistic Southern settings, they are often classified as Southern **Gothic fiction** and compared to the writings of other Southerners such as **William Faulkner** and Carson McCullers.

A devout Catholic who lived most of her life in the Protestant "Bible-Belt" region of southern Georgia, O'Connor took the grotesque to extremes to emphasize her central theme: the redeeming power of God's grace in a fallen world. At the pivotal point in all her stories, usually a horrifying act of violence, characters' illusions of self-determination are shattered and they must accept the unavoidable power of God. In the post–World War II era of scientific advancement and questioning of traditional religious beliefs, her works are unusual in their emphasis on orthodox Christian views, but her wickedly satiric method of delivering her message influenced writers of **black humor** and later Gothic fiction. Among O'Connor's best-known stories are "A Good Man Is Hard to Find," "Good Country People," "Everything That Rises Must Converge," "Greenleaf," and "Judgment Day."

Afflicted with the crippling disease lupus, O'Connor spent most of the last fourteen years of her life confined to her mother's home outside Milledgeville, Georgia, while publishing the novels *Wise Blood* (1952) and *The Violent Bear It Away* (1960) and the short-story collection *A Good Man Is Hard to Find* (1955). Another volume of short fiction, *Everything That Rises Must Converge* (1965), was published not long after her death at age thirty-nine. *The Complete Short Stories* (1971) earned her a posthumous National Book Award in 1972.

REFERENCES:

Josephine Hendin, *The World of Flannery O'Connor* (Bloomington: Indiana University Press, 1970);

Marion Montgomery, *Why Flannery O'Connor Stayed Home* (La Salle, Ill.: Sherwood, Sugden & Company, 1981);

Flannery O'Connor, *The Habit of Being: Letters,*, edited by Sally Fitzgerald (New York: Farrar, Straus & Giroux, 1979).
                                                              –J.E.F.

JOHN O'HARA

One of the most prolific American writers of the twentieth century, John O'Hara (1905-1970) produced thirty-four novels and short-story collections. During the 1950s and 1960s O'Hara's books had a large readership, and he was considered one of the most important American authors because of his unflinching realism and attention to social stratification and mores.

Many of O'Hara's works are set in or around the fictional town of Gibbsville, Pennsylvania, based on his hometown of Pottsville in the anthracite-coal region of southeast Pennsylvania. O'Hara referred to Gibbsville and its environs as his "Pennsylvania Protectorate," and the sense of time and place he achieved in creating this region makes it comparable to such fictional creations as **William Faulkner**'s Yoknapatawpha County and Thomas Wolfe's Altamount.

O'Hara published his first novel, *Appointment in Samarra,* in 1934. But he did not receive serious critical attention until after World War II with the publication of his fourth novel, *A Rage to Live* (1948).

The 1950s and 1960s were decades of triumph for O'Hara. In 1956 he won a National Book Award for his novel *Ten North Frederick* (1955). From 1958 until his death he published at least one book every year, including *From the Terrace* (1958) and *Ourselves to Know* (1960). During this time he also wrote most of his 400 short stories and novelettes, which constitute a major body of American literature.

Critics and professors of literature were put off by O'Hara's desire for critical and academic accolades. After his death O'Hara's reputation went into a decline. In his time, however, he was considered one of the best writers in America, striving always to represent accurately life as he saw it.

REFERENCES:

Matthew J. Bruccoli, *John O'Hara: A Descriptive Bibliography* (Pittsburgh: University of Pittsburgh Press, 1978);

Bruccoli, *The O'Hara Concern: A Biography of John O'Hara* (New York: Random House, 1975);

George V. Higgins, Preface to John O'Hara, *Gibbsville, PA,* edited by Bruccoli (New York: Carroll & Graf, 1992), pp. 11-16.
                                                              – R.T.

GEORGIA O'KEEFFE

From her first exhibit in 1917 until her death nearly seven decades later, Georgia O'Keeffe (1887–1986) enjoyed widespread public and critical acclaim, producing a body of artwork which has weathered the changing trends of modern art.

Born in Sun Prairie, Wisconsin, O'Keeffe studied art briefly at the Art Institute of Chicago and the Art Students League in New York. Later she enrolled in art classes at the University of Virginia and studied under painter Arthur Wesley Dow at Columbia University. O'Keeffe's earliest mature works, executed around 1915, are intimate abstract drawings and watercolors, striking for their use of simplified arched shapes and thick calligraphic lines. Her technique of applying wet coats of watercolor on top of each other resulted in delicate natural color gradations which seem to anticipate the lyrical abstractions of **Helen Frankenthaler.** O'Keeffe's sensitive handling of color and her subtle gestural effects gave her art an emotional impact which was enthusiastically embraced in the 1950s by artists and critics who saw her work as proto–**Abstract Expressionist.** Her experimentations with form and color also have affinities with such **Post-Painterly Abstraction** artists as **Ellsworth Kelly,** Morris Louis, and Kenneth Noland.

In 1917 photographer Alfred Stieglitz exhibited O'Keeffe's work at his 291 Gallery in New York. The two were married in 1924, and through Stieglitz O'Keeffe met artist Arthur Dove, whose organic abstractions of nature had a profound effect on her. For the rest of her life O'Keeffe's art would be motivated by her emotional responses to nature. Around 1919 she began painting flowers. Featuring isolated blossoms magnified almost to the point of abstraction, O'Keeffe's flower paintings are among her most enduring and controversial images. With the rise of **feminist art** in the 1970s, artists such as Judy Chicago saw in O'Keeffe's flower paintings explicit references to female genitalia and applauded what they interpreted to be O'Keeffe's "feminine" style. O'Keeffe, however, vehemently denied any sexual connotations in her art, saying instead that she painted large-scale flowers so that busy New Yorkers might take the time to stop and look at them,

During the 1920s O'Keeffe frequently vacationed in New Mexico, where she was mesmerized by the flat, arid landscape and endless horizon. In 1949, three years after Stieglitz's death, she moved there permanently. The paintings she produced in New Mexico are filled with magnified and abstracted southwestern motifs of sun-bleached animal bones and crude adobe buildings.

In the 1950s O'Keeffe traveled extensively, taking her first trip to Europe in 1953, visiting Peru and the Andes in 1956, and touring the Orient in 1959 at age seventy-one. Her travels and her many airplane flights inspired O'Keeffe to execute two series of paintings, one based on aerial views of rivers flowing through landscapes and another depicting "sky-above-the-clouds." After her eyesight began to fail in the 1970s, O'Keeffe devoted much of her time to organizing exhibitions of her life's work, although she never stopped painting. By the end of her life she had been the focus of numerous books, films, and retrospectives and had received many honors and awards, culminating in the United States Medal of Freedom, which she received in 1977.

REFERENCES:

Jan Garden Castro, *The Art and Life of Georgia O'Keeffe* (New York: Crown, 1985);

Lloyd Goodrich and Doris Bry, *Georgia O'Keeffe* (New York: Whitney Museum of Art, 1970).

– C.S.

CLAES OLDENBURG

Born in Sweden, **pop artist** Claes Oldenburg (1929–) studied at Yale University and the Art Institute of Chicago before moving to New York City in 1956. During his early years there, he exhibited works regularly at the Judson Gallery (in the basement of Judson Memorial Church) and the Reuben Gallery. By 1959 these galleries had become centers of avant-garde artistic activity, where Oldenburg became a friend and collaborator with a close-knit group of artists that included Red Grooms, George Brecht, Jim Dine, and Lucas Samaras. In 1959–1960 Oldenburg created papier-maché sculptures, and his association with Allan Kaprow at the same time influenced him to experiment with **Happenings.**

At the Judson Gallery Oldenburg installed *The Street* (1960), a ramshackle **environment** inspired by the slums of New York. Using dirty, discarded materials found on the Lower East Side — such as scraps of cardboard, burlap, and string — he created a gloomy atmosphere of human poverty and neglect. Once built, *The Street* became the setting for Oldenburg's Happening, *Snapshots from the City,* in which participants played the parts of stereotypical residents of the ghetto.

The somber mood of *The Street* is typical of Oldenburg's early work, whose brooding style reflects the inner searching that accompanied the Freudian psychoanalysis Oldenburg underwent in 1959–1961. His crude, childlike style rejected art that was too elegant and too refined, instead exposing the vulgarity that he saw in everyday life. After 1960 Oldenburg changed his approach to art somewhat. Instead of depicting depressing images of the world around him, his art took on a joyful exuberance that included elements of humor. Philosophically, he identified with the world of the working class, despising American popular culture that pandered to the upper and middle classes. In 1961 he opened *The Store,* an actual storefront where for two months Oldenburg sold "consumer products." Oldenburg's wares were not the neat, slickly packaged items found in most stores, however; instead they were his painted and sculpted versions of everyday products. Executed with thick, messy globs of paint and plaster, these normally anonymous, mass-produced consumer goods were transformed into unique, personal objects. Yet works such as *The White Slip* and *Four Pies in a Glass Case* were not meant to be worn or eaten. In 1962 Oldenburg began making soft sculptures, stuffed-cloth versions of his products. For example, he designed giant floppy hamburgers and cushiony, useless typewriters. In creating mass-market items divested of their traditional functions, Oldenburg made a strong statement on the negative aspects of consumer-oriented society.

Oldenburg has also translated his images into large-scale public monuments, creating social or political commentary related to the works setting. *Lipstick Ascending on Caterpillar Track* (1969), variously interpreted as a commemoration of the admission of women to Yale University, and a commentary on the **Vietnam War.** Oldenburg continues to work primarily on large-scale projects. Since 1976 he has collaborated with Dutch artist Coosje van Bruggen, whom he married in 1977.

REFERENCES:

Ellen H. Johnson, *Claes Oldenburg* (Baltimore: Penguin, 1971);

Barbara Rose, *Claes Oldenburg* (New York: Museum of Modern Art, 1970).

– C.S.

PAULINE OLIVEROS

Best known for her meditative **mixed-media** and **electronic** pieces, Pauline Oliveros (1932–) has expanded the boundaries of new music through her experiments with unusual sounds and instrumentations. A prolific composer, she also performs and records frequently.

Oliveros began composing in 1951 and started improvising in 1957 with **minimalist** composers Terry Riley and Loren Rush. From 1961 to 1967 she served as co-director and, later, director of the San Francisco Tape Music Center (now the Mills Tape Music Center), where she began many of her experimental projects, including mixed-media works such as a trio for flute, piano, and page turner in 1961 and a piece for wind octet, cash register, and tape. In the late 1980s and early 1990s Oliveros explored and expanded accordion music through unconventional techniques and electronic manipulation. She has written books on music and related subjects, including *Pauline's Proverbs* (1976) and *Software for People: Collected Writings 1963–80* (1984).

REFERENCES:

Kyle Gann, "Listening for Peace: Where Is the Male Pauline Oliveros?" *Village Voice,* 36 (12 March 1991): 73–74;

Heidi Von Gunden, *The Music of Pauline Oliveros* (Metuchen, N.J.: Scarecrow, 1983).

– L.D.S.

CHARLES OLSON

Charles Olson (1910–1970), originator of **Projective Verse,** is widely viewed as a major successor to **Ezra Pound** and **William Carlos Williams.** The influential leader of the loosely defined and overlapping schools of Projectivist and **Black Mountain** poets, Olson is best known for *The Maximus Poems* (1953–1975), which follow in the tradition of Pound's *Cantos* (1917–1969) and Williams's *Paterson* (1946–1963). Olson's inspiration for *The Maximus Poems* grew out of his decision, in early 1947, to outdo Pound's *Cantos,* which focus mainly on the Old World, by writing an epic of the New World.

In 1949, Olson found a reference to Maximus of Tyre, a little-known, second-century philosopher, and appropriated the name for the hero of his epic. (Olson was 6'8" tall.) Although he began writing his Maximus poems in 1950, it was not until 1953 that Olson realized these poems were becoming the New World epic he had thought about six years earlier. By then he had traveled to the Yucatan to study Mayan glyphs (research of key importance to *The Maximus Poems*) and was teaching at Black Mountain College, where his charismatic presence attracted a score of poetic disciples.

Charles Olson writing a Maximus poem, at Black Mountain College, 1951 (photograph by Jonathan Williams)

In *The Maximus Poems*, Maximus addresses the small seaport of Gloucester, Massachusetts, where Olson had spent summers during his childhood and — after Black Mountain College folded in 1956 — lived for most of the rest of his life. Maximus is a participant in the past and present of a Gloucester whose "history" includes not just local Massachusetts events but all Olson's gleanings from his vast reading and research (as well as his own dreams). In Olson's open-ended epic, Maximus absorbs and projects Gloucester as a microcosm in which the past and present of a New World are contemporaneous parts of a continuous process. Olson was still at work on *The Maximus Poems* when he died in 1970, and the last of the poems in the series were published posthumously in 1975. A complete edition was published in 1983.

REFERENCES:

George Butterick, *A Guide to the Maximus Poems of Charles Olson* (Berkeley, Los Angeles & London: University of California Press, 1978);

Tom Clark, *Charles Olson: The Allegory of a Poet's Life* (New York & London: Norton, 1991).

– K.L.R.

OMNIBUS

Omnibus marked the cultural high point of American television in the 1950s. Hosted by Alistair Cooke, the series aired on the **CBS** network on Sunday afternoons starting in November 1952.

The works of dramatists such as William Saroyan, W. S. Gilbert and Arthur S. Sullivan, and Maxwell Anderson were featured in the first season of the show. Because *Omnibus* was funded by a grant from the Ford Foundation, the series had no commercial sponsors and therefore no sponsor's demands or interruptions for advertisements.

Omnibus attempted to provide a broad spectrum of stimulating viewing. Adaptations of works by authors such as James Thurber, **Ernest Hemingway,** and **T. S. Eliot** were presented, starring the best actors of the American stage. Dancing, opera, and symphony were also featured prominently. *Omnibus* also broadcast informative documentaries, including one in January 1954 by then-unknown undersea explorer Jacques Cousteau.

In the 1956–1957 season *Omnibus* moved to the **ABC** network on Sunday nights. By the end of the season it had moved again, to **NBC.** It continued to appear irregularly on Sunday afternoons on that network until its final broadcast in 1961.

– C.D.B.

YOKO ONO

Japanese-American artist and vocalist Yoko Ono (1933–) is best known for her collaborations with former Beatle John Lennon (1940–1980), whom she married in 1969.

Ono was active in various avant-garde art and music groups in New York during the 1950s. She performed at Carnegie Hall in 1961, and in the early 1960s she worked briefly with composer **John Cage.** She met Lennon in 1966, and they began recording together in 1968. Their first album, *Unfinished Music No. 1: Two Virgins* (1969), featured a controversial photograph of the naked couple on the cover. They produced two more albums in 1969 and had a hit with "Give Peace a Chance" from *Wedding Album*. Some popular-music historians believe her artistic influence upon Lennon was one of the reasons for the breakup of **The Beatles** in 1970.

In the early 1970s they continued to work together as well as on their solo efforts. Lennon succeeded with the utopian "Imagine" (1971), while Ono's albums such as *Fly* (1971) and *Feeling the Space* (1973) found a limited audience. The couple's most successful collaboration, the album *Double Fantasy* (1980), appeared shortly before Lennon's assassination. She released several of their final collaborations as *Milk and Honey* (1984).

REFERENCES:

Jonathon Cott and Christine Doudna, eds., *The Ballad of John and Yoko* (Garden City, N.Y.: Doubleday, 1982);

Barbara Haskell, *Yoko Ono, Arias, and Objects* (Salt Lake City: Gibbs Smith, 1991);

David Sheff and C. Barry Golson, eds., *The Playboy Interviews with John Lennon and Yoko Ono* (New York: Playboy Press, 1981).

– L.D.S.

OP ART

Op Art, a style of abstract painting that creates the optical illusion of movement through the use of wavy lines and geometric shapes, moved from museum walls to the world of fashion in fabrics designed for clothing and home decoration in the late 1960s. Hungarian-born French painter Victor Vasarély and British artist Bridget Riley pioneered Op Art in the late 1940s, but it was introduced to the American public in 1965, when the **Museum of Modern Art** held a major international exhibition, The Responsive Eye. This show featured the works of two American Op artists, Larry Poons (1937–) and Richard Anuszkiewicz (1930–).

Division of Intensity (1964), by Richard Anuszkiewicz, one of the Americans whose work was included in the major exhibition of Op Art at the Museum of Modern Art in 1965

While Op Art delighted journalists and the general public, most art critics did not take it seriously.

REFERENCE:

Irving Sandler, *American Art of the 1960s* (New York: Harper & Row, 1988).

– K.B.

EUGENE ORMANDY

Eugene Ormandy (1899–1985) was conductor of the Philadelphia Orchestra for forty-four years (1936–1980), achieving the longest tenure ever held by a single conductor with the same orchestra. The orchestra became famous for its lush tone, known as the "Philadelphia sound," under his leadership.

Born Jenö Blau in Hungary, he was a violin prodigy and toured Europe in his youth. He immigrated to the United States in 1921 on the promise of a tour that never happened. Instead, he performed as concertmaster of the Capitol Theater Orchestra in New York, making his conducting debut in 1924. Ormandy led the Minneapolis Symphony Orchestra (now the Minnesota Orchestra) from 1931 to 1936 before joining Leopold Stokowski as music director of the Philadelphia Orchestra, which Stokowski had shaped into a world-class ensemble. After Stokowski left in 1938, Ormandy set the tone for the orchestra with his solidly conservative renditions of late Romantic and early modern works. After his retirement in 1980, Ormandy was succeeded by Riccardo Muti, who has made the orchestra more precise in its sound and has covered a wider repertoire.

REFERENCES:

Herbert Kupferberg, *Those Fabulous Philadelphians: The Life and Times of a Great Orchestra* (New York: Scribners, 1969);

Harold C. Schonberg, *The Great Conductors* (New York: Simon & Schuster, 1967).

– L.D.S.

P

AL PACINO

Al Pacino (1940–) has maintained a distinguished career as a stage and film actor.

Pacino grew up in the South Bronx and spent two years at the High School of Performing Arts in Manhattan, dropping out at the end of his sophomore year. He also studied acting with Charles Laughton at the Herbert Berghof Studio (1959) and with Lee Strasberg at **Actors Studio** (1966). Pacino began acting in children's theater in 1962, went on to Off-Broadway in 1963, and won an Obie Award in 1968 for his portrayal of a drug-addicted psychotic in Israel Horovitz's *The Indian Wants the Bronx*. In 1969 his Broadway debut, as another psychotic in Don Petersen's *Does a Tiger Wear a Necktie,* earned him an Antoinette Perry (Tony) Award.

He broke into movies with a small part in *Me, Natalie* (1969). His strong performance as a junkie in his second movie, *Panic in Needle Park* (1971), got him his most memorable role, Michael Corleone in *The Godfather,* parts 1–3 (1972, 1974, and 1990). He displayed his intense acting energy in his portrayals of a tough, honest cop in *Serpico* (1973) and a bisexual bank robber in *Dog Day Afternoon* (1975), before returning to the New York stage in 1977 to give a Tony-winning performance as the title character in **David Rabe**'s *The Basic Training of Pavlo Hummel.* Two years later he shocked New York audiences with a controversial interpretation of William Shakespeare's *Richard III.*

Pacino was miscast as a colonial American soldier in the historical epic *Revolution* (1986) but rebounded as a policeman in love with a possible killer in *Sea of Love* (1989). Critics praised his portrayal of Big Boy Caprice, his first comic film role, in *Dick Tracy* (1990), and he won an Academy Award (Oscar) as best actor for his role as a blind retired army officer in *Scent of a Woman* (1992). Also in

Al Pacino and producer Dino de Laurentiis on the set of *Serpico*

1992, he continued to take risks as a stage actor by playing King Herod in Oscar Wilde's *Salome* and a modern-day, forty-four-year-old struggling writer in Ira Lewis's *Chinese Coffee* on alternating nights at the Circle in the Square Theater in New York.

REFERENCE:

Andrew Yule, *Life on the Wire: The Life and Art of Al Pacino* (New York: Fine, 1991).

– I.R.H.

PAPERBACK BOOKS

The introduction of the mass-market paperback book in America, initiating what is often referred to as the "Paperback Revolution," roughly coincided with the outbreak of World War II in Europe. The consequences of the new format were far-reaching, changing the way Americans envisioned books and reading.

Books in paper covers had been marketed in the United States with varying degrees of success since the nineteenth century, but they tended to be either mass editions of formulaic fiction or editions aimed at a limited audience. But in 1939, inspired by the success of inexpensive European paperback reprints such as Penguin Books in Great Britain, Robert Fair de Graff created Pocket Books for an American audience. His intention was to issue inexpensive editions of successful and/or classic works for a mass market, and to make such a project viable he focused on reducing costs through lower reprint royalties, increasing dealer discounts, and economizing on production. Print runs were high to reduce the cost per unit. The covers were brightly illustrated, and the books received wide distribution on newsstands as well as in bookstores. They were an immediate success.

The first American paperback publisher to compete successfully with Pocket Books appeared in the fall of 1941. Avon Books was financed by the powerful American News Company, a national distribution group that held a virtual monopoly over newsstands in large cities.

Despite paper shortages following America's entry into World War II in 1941, the industry continued to grow. In 1943 two more important early paperback houses were launched — Popular Library and Dell Books — and in May the Council of Books in Wartime, formed by a coalition of publishers, reached an agreement with the army that resulted in the inauguration of Armed Services Editions, books in paperback format distributed gratis to American servicemen. Armed Services Editions were discontinued in 1947 after 1,322 titles and just under 123 million volumes.

The early postwar years saw several important events in the field. In December 1945 Ian Ballantine, the American manager of Penguin Books since 1939, began his own paperback imprint, Bantam Books, which would become a major force in paperback publishing. In 1946 Benjamin Spock's *Baby and Child Care* was published by Pocket Books and baby-boom mothers quickly turned it into the world's **best-selling** paperback, with consistent sales of one million copies per year through 1956.

Penguin's American branch spawned another important paperback house in 1948 when Victor Weybright and Kurt Enoch, resigned to establish the New American Library (NAL), with a Signet Books imprint for fiction and a Mentor Books imprint for nonfiction. Priced at 35 cents, Mentor Books also claimed the distinction of breaking the "25 cent barrier" — the uniform price for all mass-market paperbacks since the introduction of Pocket Books. A notable early success for Signet was the 1948 acquisition of reprint rights for **Mickey Spillane**'s *I, the Jury*. Spillane's violent detective novel had sold a few thousand hardback copies for Dutton, but the paperback edition was responsible for his amazing popular success, selling more than two million copies by 1950. Spillane replaced Erskine Caldwell (also on Signet's list) as the "world's bestselling author" — or so he was billed by his publishers.

After a test run in 1949, Gold Medal Books began regularly publishing paperback titles in 1950. Launched by Fawcett, a successful magazine publisher and distributor of NAL books since 1948, Gold Medal was important as the first to specialize in the paperback original rather than reprinting titles previously published in hardcover. The paperback original gradually became more common in the industry, and many authors began to submit books directly to paperback houses.

As part of the shift away from a reprint orientation in the industry, Ballantine left Bantam Books in 1952 to form Ballantine Books, designed to release paperback editions of titles simultaneously with a hardback release. In the same year, Ace Books launched a line of paperback "double novels" — one reprint and one original bound together, back to back, with two separate covers. A famous early example of the imprint is Ace D-15 (1953), which includes the first publication of *Junkie* by "William Lee" (**William S. Burroughs**), bound with Maurice Helbrant's *Narcotics Agent*. Both companies eventually shifted to more standard industry practices, and both became important publishers of **science fiction.**

The industry was shaken in 1952 by a House of Representatives probe of the paperback, magazine, and comics trade. Sen. E. C. Gathings headed a committee that targeted the "lurid and daring" covers prevalent in the paperback industry as one of its chief concerns. The committee's majority report was condemnatory, claiming that "the so-called pocket-size books, which originally started out as cheap reprints of standard works, have largely degenerated into media for the dissemination of artful appeals to sensuality, immorality, filth, perversion and degeneracy." Though no new laws resulted, the hearings inspired many local-level attacks on paperbacks, such as the systematic removal of "objectionable" titles from the racks of bookstores and newsstands. Soon, cover art for paperbacks began to be noticeably less provocative than during the late 1940s and early 1950s.

In the 1960s more authors approached paperback houses for first sales of manuscripts. The publishers sometimes released these works as paperback originals and sometimes sold first publication rights to hardback houses while retaining reprint rights. A third option was created by another trend in the industry — paperback houses began to establish their own hardback imprints, such as Trident Press (Pocket Books), Dial (Dell), and an NAL line of hardcover titles.

Paperbacks also provided a format for general-interest academic and scholarly titles. Pioneered by Anchor Books (founded in 1953), an imprint of Doubleday, large-format quality paperbacks with prices somewhere between mass-market paperbacks and hardback books targeted a market of price-conscious serious readers and students. The format, called trade paperbacks, was highly successful. Trade paperbacks flourised during the 1970s with the increase in retail bookstores serving a middle-class market.

The sums advanced by paperback publishers for reprint, or subsidiary rights grew throughout the 1960s, and in 1972 Avon Books set two consecutive records when it paid $1 million for rights to Thomas Harris's *I'm OK — You're OK* and then $1.11 million for Richard Bach's *Jonathan Livingston Seagull*. Both books became multimillion-dollar bestsellers, and Avon's business increased by more than 140 percent in 1973. The industry responded over the next decade with multimillion-dollar bidding at reprint rights auctions, and prices climbed to a record $3.2 million paid by Bantam in 1979 for Judith Krantz's *Princess Daisy*. Cover prices also rose over the decade to offset these enormous costs, and unit sales subsequently dropped, forcing further raising of prices.

The industry remained strong throughout the 1980s, but the spectacular, record-setting successes that paperback publishing had repeatedly experienced since its inception seemed to be a thing of the past in the wake of soaring cover prices.

REFERENCES:

Thomas L. Bonn, *Under Cover: An Illustrated History of American Mass Market Paperbacks* (Harmondsworth, U.K.: Penguin, 1982);

Kenneth C. Davis, *Two-Bit Culture: The Paperbacking of America* (Boston: Houghton Mifflin, 1984);

Piet Schreuders, *Paperbacks, U.S.A.: A Graphic History, 1939–1959* (San Diego: Blue Dolphin, 1981).

— S.B.

JOSEPH PAPP

Producer and director Joseph Papp (1921–1990) brought free Shakespeare plays to Central Park in New York and was the driving force behind the successful introduction of innovative new plays at the New York Shakespeare Festival Public Theatre.

A native of Brooklyn, New York, Papp studied acting at the Hollywood Actors Laboratory and served as its managing director in 1948–1950. In the early 1950s Papp moved back to New York, where he directed and produced plays Off-Broadway. In 1954 he founded the Shakespearean Theatre Workshop, which eventually became the New York Shakespeare Festival, and served as its director until his death in 1990. The group gave its first free outdoor summer performance of Shakespeare in 1956. In summer 1957 they began staging their free plays in Central Park, where a permanent outdoor location, the Delacorte Theatre, was completed for them in 1962.

In addition to luring big-name actors to perform Shakespeare under the stars every summer, Papp also staged new plays at the Shakespeare Festival Public Theatre, the former Astor Place Library, which was renovated as a theater and opened in 1967. Among the future Broadway hits that were launched there were Galt MacDermot, James Rado, and Gerome Ragni's *Hair* (1967); MacDermot and **John Guare**'s musical version of *Two Gentlemen of Verona* (1971); Jason Miller's *That Championship Season* (1972); and James Kirkwood, Nicholas Dante, and **Michael Bennett**'s *A Chorus Line* (1973). In 1973 Papp also took over the management of the Vivian Beaumont and Mitzi E. Newhouse theaters at Lincoln Center, where he introduced plays such as **David Rabe**'s *Boom Boom Room* (1973).

REFERENCE:

Stuart W. Little, *Enter Joseph Papp: In Search of a New American Theater* (New York: Coward, McCann & Geoghegan, 1974).

— I.R.H.

PARIS REVIEW

The *Paris Review* was founded in 1952 by Peter Matthiessen and Harold Humes to serve as a forum for "advance-guard Writing." Called "the biggest little magazine in history," it has given many talented writers and poets their first exposure.

George Plimpton has been the magazine's editor since its inception. He has published some of the best poets and fiction writers of the post–World War II era, including **Raymond Carver**, David Shapiro, Terry

Southern, Adrienne Rich, **Philip Roth,** Donald Hall, and X. J. Kennedy. (Hall and Kennedy also served as poetry editors.) The *Paris Review* has also introduced foreign authors to American readers.

The focus of the *Paris Review* is original literature, but since the beginning it has featured interviews with some of the most important writers of the time. Plimpton admits that the magazine wanted a famous name on the cover to attract readers. Over the years the magazine has interviewed such writers as **James Dickey, Ernest Hemingway, Truman Capote,** E. M. Forster, and **T. S. Eliot.** The best of the interviews have been collected in several volumes published by Viking Press under the title *Writers at Work: The Paris Review Interviews.*

REFERENCES:

Leonard C. Butts, "The Paris Review," in *American Literary Magazines: The Twentieth Century*, edited by Edward E. Chielens (Westport, Conn.: Greenwood Press, 1992), pp. 240–244;

George Plimpton, "Enterprise in the Service of Art," *The Little Magazine in America: A Modern Documentary History*, edited by Elliot Anderson and Mary Kinzie (Yonkers, N. Y.: Pushcart Press, 1978), pp. 524–535.

                                                        – R.T.

Charlie Parker

Charlie "Bird" Parker (1920–1955), a gifted saxophonist, was one of the foremost jazz figures of the century. With his legendary technical and improvisational abilities, Parker exploited the potential of the saxophone and exemplified the 1940–1955 jazz style known as **bebop.**

As a youth in Kansas City, Missouri, Parker was primarily influenced by his immediate predecessor, Lester Young. Parker's mature style, however, was the antithesis of his idol's mellow approach and was characterized by harsh, frenzied sound and driving rhythms. Despite his remarkable musical prowess, Parker was not accepted by the general public of the time; yet no one had a stronger impact on jazz.

Parker's early style developed from the preswing ambience of his hometown. By 1939 he had settled in New York and joined the Jay McShann band, a group specializing in the blues. Parker left McShann to work independently with Harlem jazzmen, and subsequently, between 1943 and 1946, he played with the Noble Sissle band and the Earl Hines band. In the last decade of his life, while fighting health problems resulting from drug abuse, he worked irregularly with big bands, such as Billy Eckstine's, and small ensembles that often included such bop principals as trumpeters

Dizzy Gillespie and **Miles Davis**, pianist Bud Powell, and drummer Max Roach.

Parker's best recorded work was done in small ensembles after 1944. Many of his recordings were released on Verve, notably "Now's the Time." In 1976 Arista Records reissued all of his recordings on the Savoy label, which were made between 1944 and 1948, in a thirty-side collection, *Charles Christopher Parker, Jr.: Bird/The Savoy Recordings.*

REFERENCES:

Lawrence O. Koch, *Yardbird Suite: A Compendium of the Music and Life of Charlie Parker* (Bowling Green, Ohio: Bowling Green University Popular Press, 1988);

Robert George Reisner, *Bird: The Legend of Charlie Parker* (New York: Da Capo, 1975).

                                                        – E.M.M.

Luciano Pavarotti

Luciano Pavarotti (1935–) arose from humble origins to become the most celebrated operatic tenor since Enrico Caruso early in the twentieth century. Pavarotti is famous even among Americans who know nothing about opera.

Pavarotti was born in Modena, Italy, and made his professional debut in 1961 in Reggio Emilia, where he played Rodolfo in Giacomo Puccini's *La Bohème,* his favorite role. Other Italian lyric opera roles in which Pavarotti has succeeded include the Duke in Giuseppe Verdi's *Rigoletto,* Edgardo in Gaetano Donizetti's *Lucia di Lammermoor,* and Tonio in Donizetti's *La fille du régiment.* This last role includes an aria with nine high C's, and by performing it successfully Pavarotti earned the nickname "King of the High C's."

Pavarotti first performed in America in a 1965 production of *Lucia di Lammermoor* in Miami. Since the 1970s he has become a celebrity in the United States through numerous television appearances, including the first *Live from the Met* telecast on **PBS** in 1977, as well as opera performances and recordings. His 1980 appearance in a concert version of *Rigoletto* with the **New York Metropolitan Opera** in Central Park drew approximately two hundred thousand people. In the 1980s Pavarotti began performing primarily in concerts and television specials on PBS.

REFERENCE:

Luciano Pavarotti with William Wright, *Pavarotti: My Own Story* (Garden City, N.Y.: Doubleday, 1981).

                                                        – L.D.S.

Loretta Lynn, Hal Holbrook, and Luciano Pavarotti on the 1980 ABC-television *Ominbus Special* (photograph by William Wright)

PBS

The value of noncommercial television, which eventually became unified as the Public Broadcasting System (PBS), has been appreciated since the early days of the medium, when the Ford Foundation developed National Educational Television (NET) in 1952.

The purpose of NET was to create educational and cultural television shows, providing a basic programming schedule for television stations that did not rely on commercial advertising. Although NET was designed to operate self-sufficiently, it could not; it would have folded without constant funding from the Ford Foundation. For the first several decades of television, only a few noncommercial stations attained any measure of success.

In the late 1960s industry leaders became concerned by what a 1967 poll called a "growing television boycott" among the college educated. An alternative to the sponsor-controlled networks seemed the most likely means of recapturing their interest in television. In the same year the Ford Foundation created the Public Broadcast Laboratory, which produced *PBL,* a series of plays and films with anti-establishment leanings. Two days after the debut of *PBL* Congress passed leg-

islation establishing a Corporation for Public Broadcasting (CPB), through which the federal government would subsidize the production of noncommercial programs broadcast on PBS. Critics feared, however, that the low level of funding ($4.5 million for the first year) and President Lyndon Johnson's appointment of a former General Dynamics chief executive to oversee the project would doom it from the start.

In 1969 PBS had its first major success with the children's show **Sesame Street.** Also popular on public stations were broadcasts of British television series, including *The Forsyte Saga* (1967) and *Upstairs, Downstairs* (1970–1975), one of the miniseries featured on the well-received *Masterpiece Theatre* (1971–). In the early 1970s public television shows such as *The Great American Dream Machine* were frequently critical of authority and particularly American involvement in the **Vietnam War.** In response President Richard M. Nixon recommended that the budget for the CPB be slashed, and for several years public television again had to struggle for existence. In 1973 the system received new life with its full coverage of the Watergate hearings, shown live and then rebroadcast in the evening.

Public broadcasting was still a low priority for federal funding in the 1980s, but PBS continued to offer informative, critically acclaimed programs. Frequently PBS series have been funded by independent stations and donations from viewers as well as the CPB. Several series have focused on science, such as *Nova* (1974–) or *Cosmos* (1980–1981), which was hosted by physicist Carl Sagan. Other shows during the 1980s chronicled historical events such as the Vietnam conflict and the **civil rights movement.** Another series, *American Playhouse* (1982–), has introduced viewers to the work of independent playwrights and filmmakers. *The MacNeil-Lehrer News Hour* has been praised for its searching analyses of current events. Despite the triumphs of public television, however, its relationship with the federal government has never been a particularly happy one. The question of whether the system should seek private funding has been debated fairly consistently over three decades.

REFERENCE:

Erik Barnouw, *Tube of Plenty,* second edition (New York & Oxford: Oxford University Press, 1990).

– C.D.B.

GREGORY PECK

Gregory Peck (1916–) has been the onscreen exemplar of American moral integrity for nearly half a century.

A California native, Peck started out as a pre-med major at the University of California, Berkeley, and got involved in acting when he was asked to try out for a student play because the director needed someone tall. After appearing in several college productions, Peck moved to New York in 1939 to study acting at the Neighborhood Playhouse. He had starring roles in three short-lived Broadway plays during 1942 and 1943 and then returned to Hollywood, where there was a dearth of leading men because of World War II. Peck, whose draft status was 4-F, made his film debut in *Days of Glory* (1944). He was nominated for an Academy Award (Oscar) for his portrayal of a Roman Catholic missionary to China in his second film, *The Keys to the Kingdom* (1945). By 1950 roles in films such as *Gentlemen's Agreement* (1947), *The Yearling* (1946), and *Twelve O'Clock High* (1950) had established Peck's screen persona as a Lincolnesque man of honor grappling with difficult ethical choices, a characterization that reached its apotheosis in his Oscar-winning performance as Atticus Finch in *To Kill a Mockingbird* (1962), based on the Pulitzer Prize–winning novel by **Harper Lee.**

Peck has also enjoyed playing conflicted protagonists who go over the edge, as in the two films he made with **Alfred Hitchcock,** *Spellbound* (1945) and *The Paradine Case* (1948), and later efforts such as *Moby Dick* (1957) and *The Bravados* (1958). Occasionally he has played outright villains, including Lute in *Duel in the Sun* (1947) and Josef Mengele in *The Boys from Brazil* (1978). Peck's last major film role was the Ambrose Bierce figure in *Old Gringo* (1989).

Peck has served as president of the **Academy of Motion Picture Arts and Sciences** (1967–1970), which gave him its Jean Hersholt Humanitarian Award in 1968; chairman of the board of trustees of the **American Film Institute** (1967–1969), which granted him its Life Achievement Award in 1989; and chairman of the American Cancer Society (1966). He received the Presidential Medal of Freedom in 1968 and a Kennedy Center Honor in 1991.

REFERENCE:

Michael Freedland, *Gregory Peck: A Biography* (London: W. H. Allen, 1980).

– I.R.H.

SAM PECKINPAH

Director/screenwriter Sam Peckinpah (1925–1984) eulogized the Old West in a series of highly acclaimed films during the 1960s but encountered difficulties with studio censors because of the violence in his movies.

After earning an M.A. in drama from the University of Southern California, in 1950, Peckinpah worked in a variety of theater and television jobs until he became an assistant to action-film director Don Siegel in 1954. During the 1950s he wrote regularly for television westerns such as *Gunsmoke* and *The Rifleman.*

After directing his first film, *The Deadly Companions,* in 1961, Peckinpah made his best-known westerns: *Ride the High Country* (1962), *Major Dundee* (1965), and his masterpiece, *The Wild Bunch* (1969). In 1971 he transferred the graphic violence that had worked effectively in his westerns to a contemporary setting in *Straw Dogs.* Although the film was well received by some critics, others characterized it as "fascist," "misogynist," and "brutal."

After his final western, *Pat Garrett and Billy the Kid* (1973), Peckinpah seemed to be indulging in onscreen gore for its own sake in *Bring Me the Head of Alfredo Garcia* (1974). He had always quarreled with the studios about the editing of his films, and backing for his projects began to decline. He made only five films during the final decade of his life, and none of them approaches the artistry of his movies of the 1960s.

REFERENCE:

Doug McKinney, *Sam Peckinpah* (Boston: Twayne, 1979).

– I.R.H.

I. M. PEI

Throughout a career spanning more than forty years architect Ieoh Ming Pei (1917–) has been known for ambitious projects, high-profile clients, and buildings that have met with mixed critical success. Already well-known in the United States, he achieved international renown during the 1980s as the architect chosen by French president François Mitterrand to create the new entrance to the Louvre in Paris, a controversial seventy-one-foot-high glass pyramid.

Born in pre–Communist China to well-to-do parents, Pei came to the United States in 1935 to study architecture. At the Harvard Graduate School of Design, from which he earned a Ph.D. in 1946, Pei studied and taught with Walter Gropius and Marcel Breuer, both of whom had been professors at Bauhaus, the revolutionary German school of design that had played a key role in the establishment and development of the modernist aesthetic in Europe. The clean lines and un-ornamented geometry of modernist architecture, disseminated in the United States Gropius and Breuer, have been the governing principles in Pei's designs.

Pei's first major success after establishing his own firm in 1960 was the National Center for Atmospheric Research near Boulder, Colorado (1961–1967). The John F. Kennedy Library commission (1964–1979) secured his national reputation but involved him in a fifteen-year controversy concerning the site of the library. It was initially intended to be built near Harvard University (Kennedy's alma mater) but ultimately was constructed at Columbia Point in Boston Harbor. Pei's first resounding critical success was his East Building of the National Gallery of Art in Washington, D.C. (1968–1978). Still considered one of his most successful buildings, it embodies the features for which his work is best known: a strong sense of geometry; bold, sculptural forms; and a pronounced concern with materials. Pei, who became an American citizen in 1955, has received every significant award in his field, as well as the Medal of Liberty in 1986 and the National Medal of Art in 1988.

REFERENCE:

Carter Wiseman, *I. M. Pei: A Profile in American Architecture* (New York: Abrams, 1990).

– K.B.

IRVING PENN

Irving Penn (1917–), trained in art and design at the Philadelphia Museum School, began as a fashion photographer for *Vogue* magazine in 1943. During the late 1940s and throughout the 1950s Penn, along with **Richard Avedon,** revolutionized fashion photography.

Unlike Avedon, whose work celebrated spontaneity, youthfulness, and motion, Penn favored a far more austere, serene, and sculptural approach to his subjects. His models were painstakingly posed and frozen in solitary moments of almost unnerving elegance. Penn's training as a painter and his interest in art history imbued his fashion photography with a strong sense of premeditated composition, lighting, and graphic design. These same qualities have characterized his portrait work from the 1940s, when he began traveling to remote parts of the world with a portable studio that could be set up anywhere. With his neutral gray studio backdrop, he banished all context of local geography and custom and photographed his subjects, who were often tribal peoples. In addition to work with this "ambulant studio," Penn has created monumental portraits of some of the most famous people in the world. In 1953 he opened his own commercial studio and has since become one of the most sought-after advertising photographers in the world. He has also produced a significant body of fine-art photography consisting of large handsomely printed images of objects usually considered unimportant — such as cigarette butts, used gloves, and other found urban detritus. These photographs underscore Penn's ability to create a graceful and indelible image out of any subject.

REFERENCE:

Irving Penn, *Passage: A Work Record* (New York: Knopf, 1991).

– K.B.

PERFORMANCE ART

The term *performance art* is an open-ended designation in use since the 1970s to describe a variety of situations in which visual artists perform before live audiences. Sometimes difficult to distinguish from avant-garde theater and dance, performance in the visual arts has been identified as such by its venues: art galleries, museums, art schools, and "alternative spaces." Its extensive historical roots include the performances of European artists involved in Futurism, Dada, Surrealism, Constructivism, and the Bauhaus, as well as Fluxus events, activities of the French New Realism group, and the "actions" of German artist Joseph Beuys.

The evolution of performance art in the United States has been complex and multifaceted. In general it began with the **Happenings** of the late 1950s and expanded in new directions with the idea-based activities of **conceptual art.** Also in the mid 1960s avant-garde dance groups influenced by the work of **John Cage** and **Merce Cunningham** — such as the Judson Dance Group in New York — provided an energized and highly creative milieu and resource for visual artists interested in performance. For example, the sculptor Robert Morris, who began experimenting with live performance in the mid 1960s, had previously worked with dancers Yvonne Rainer and Ann Halprin. In 1965 he collaborated with Carolee Schneemann on *Site,* a piece in which she posed nude mimicking Edouard Manet's painting *Olympia* while Morris manipulated the space around her by moving large boards into different positions. While artists such as Morris came to performance through an interest in the sculptural concerns of space and the body, other artists brought to it a variety of psychological, political, and aesthetic positions.

In the early 1970s conceptual artists such as Vito Acconci, Dennis Oppenheim, and Chris Burden explored the use of their own bodies as components of artworks or as the actual artwork itself. Their projects and those of several other artists working in a similar vein are also labeled **body art,** a related field of activity. Acconci, who has a background in poetry, created the notorious and influential *Seedbed* (1971), in which he lay hidden under a ramp in an art gallery, purportedly masturbating, while visitors walked around above him as his voice was transmitted via microphone. The implicit confrontation with the visitors and Acconci's deliberate attempt to embarrass them or create awkward feelings are an important part of the nature of performance art: it is a way for artists to deprive viewers of their traditionally passive role by creating situations in which their own self-consciousness is highlighted or in which strong reactions are elicited. Other important performance artists of the 1970s include Joan Jonas and **Laurie Anderson,** whose high-tech, multi-media music performances continued through the 1980s and into the 1990s. Her performance piece *United States Parts 1 and 2,* created in the early 1980s, is seen as a turningpoint in performance art. The technical complexity of the piece and its availability to large concert audiences began to break down the avant-garde aura of performance art and to place it, to an extent, in the larger context of popular culture. The 1970s also saw a great deal of performance art from artists in the **feminist** movement. Performance-art pieces of that decade, often presented in alternative spaces in New York such as Franklin Furnace, also include the work of versatile conceptual artists such as Bruce Nauman.

In the 1980s the performance artists Eric Bogosian, who was trained as an actor, and Karen Finley became known for controversial performances based on highly charged, abrasive monologues that were often critical of American media and society. Finley, whose anarchic spirit has influenced much contemporary performance, believes that the value of performance art lies in its ability to undermine the commodity status of art.

Performance art in the late 1980s and early 1990s has been influenced by **multiculturalism** and has seen an infusion of new performers from various backgrounds, not necessarily fine art, using the performance format to promote communication among disenfranchised groups. In Los Angeles, for example, the Highways Performance Space was created in 1989 to serve as a venue for "issue oriented" and "intercultural" performance art. On the East Coast performers such as the Blue Man Group in New York have blurred the distinction between performance art and entertainment, with satirical pieces aimed at the art world itself.

REFERENCES:

RoseLee Goldberg, *Performance Art: From Futurism to the Present* (New York: Abrams, 1988);

Margot Mifflin, "Performance Art: What is it and Where Is It Going?" *ARTnews,* 91 (April 1992): 84–89.

           – K.B.

ITZHAK PERLMAN

Israeli-American violinist Itzhak Perlman (1945–) is a popular classical musician who performs in hundreds of concerts annually.

Born in Tel Aviv, Israel, Perlman was striken with poliomyelitis at age four. A violin prodigy, he was discovered in his homeland by violinist **Isaac Stern** in 1958 and featured on *The Ed Sullivan Show* the following year. Perlman undertook advanced training at the Juilliard School of Music in the late 1950s and made his professional debut in 1963 at Carnegie Hall. He appeared with the New York Philharmonic Orchestra in 1964 and became a protégé of Stern, who did much to further his career in America. After successful tours of the United States, Europe, and elsewhere, Perlman's reputation as a major violinist was established through his skillful playing and showmanship. Perlman has performed the standard violin repertoire as a soloist and with many of the major orchestras in the world. He has also performed jazz, Cajun music, and ragtime.

REFERENCE:

Boris Schwarz, *Great Masters of the Violin: From Corelli and Vivaldi to Stern, Zukerman, and Perlman* (New York: Simon & Schuster, 1983).

– L.D.S.

PETER, PAUL & MARY

The **folk-music** trio Peter, Paul & Mary became popular during the 1960s for their advocacy of nonviolence and human rights as well as straightforward renditions of folk selections, particularly ballads, using harmony and acoustic guitars.

The group, formed in 1961, consisted of Peter Yarrow (1938–), Paul Stookey (1937–), and Mary Travers (1937–). They recorded the first of their ten albums during the 1960s, *Peter, Paul & Mary,* in 1962, the year they had a hit with Pete Seeger and Lee Hays's "If I Had a Hammer." By 1963 they were extremely popular with college students and liberals for their songs encouraging nonviolent resistance to the **Vietnam War** and the advancement of **civil rights** for all people. They led the singing at **Martin Luther King, Jr.**'s civil-rights march on Washington in 1963. Their best-known songs from this period include **Bob Dylan**'s "Blowin' in the Wind" (1963) and Yarrow's "Puff the Magic Dragon" (1963), a popular children's song despite allegations that it promoted drug use. Their only number-one hit came in 1969 with John Denver's "Leaving on a Jet Plane." After this success, Peter, Paul & Mary began issuing solo albums, and the trio disbanded in 1971. The group has reunited for several concerts and an album, *Reunion* (1978). In the 1980s and early 1990s they appeared in popular television specials on **PBS.**

REFERENCE:

Phil Hood, ed., *Artists of American Folk Music: The Legends of Traditional Folk, the Stars of the Sixties, the Virtuosi of New Acoustic Music* (New York: Morrow, 1986).

– L.D.S.

SYLVIA PLATH

Virtually unknown when she committed suicide at the age of thirty, Sylvia Plath (1932–1963) has attracted a loyal readership since the early 1970s, when her autobiographical novel, *The Bell Jar* (1963), and her intensely revealing **confessional poetry** were discovered by **feminists.**

Plath published only two books during her lifetime. The first, *The Colossus and Other Poems* (1960), was respectfully reviewed in England, where she was living with her husband, British poet Ted Hughes, but it was ignored in the United States. The second, *The Bell Jar*, published in England under the pseudonym Victoria Lucas during the month before Plath's death, is a slightly fictionalized account of Plath's experiences during her years as a student at Smith College in the early 1950s — a period that included a suicide attempt, hospitalization, and shock treatments. The novel was fairly well received in England.

Plath's authorship of *The Bell Jar* became widely known soon after her death, and her mother, fearing embarrassment to family members and friends, blocked its publication in the United States until 1971. The novel's examination of women's traditional roles and the heroine's rebellion against them spoke to the concerns of the feminist movement that had emerged in the late 1960s. The first American edition of *The Bell Jar* stayed on the *New York Times* best-seller list for twenty-four weeks. The American paperback edition (1972) sold more than a million copies in one month.

During the autumn and winter of 1962, while attempting to cope with a deteriorating marriage, Plath wrote her finest and most powerful poems — including "Ariel," "Lady Lazarus," and "Daddy" — in which she confronted the most intimate aspects of her present life and her unresolved, conflicting feelings about her father, who had died when she was eight. After her suicide in February 1963 they were published in *Ariel and Other Poems* (1965). The book prompted poet **Robert Lowell,** who had introduced Plath to confessional po-

Sylvia Plath and Ted Hughes

etry when she attended his writing class in 1959, to exclaim, "These poems are playing Russian roulette with six cartridges in the cylinder." By 1985 the book had sold more than half a million copies in Great Britain and the United States. Her *Collected Poems* (1981) won a Pulitzer Prize in 1982.

REFERENCES:

Paul Alexander, *Rough Magic: A Biography of Sylvia Plath* (New York: Viking, 1991);

Anne Stevenson, *Bitter Fame: A Life of Sylvia Plath* (Boston: Houghton Mifflin, 1989).

– K.L.R.

PLAYHOUSE 90

Playhouse 90 is the best-known example of the various anthology series that were staples of early American television. Each week the series produced a full-length drama featuring some of the most talented actors, writers, and directors of the time.

The series premiered in October 1956 on the **CBS** network and ran until 1961, appearing every other week beginning in 1959. It was the launching pad for young talents such as screenwriters **Rod Serling** and Reginald Rose and directors John Frankenheimer and George Roy Hill. Notable actors who appeared in *Playhouse 90* productions included Polly Bergen, Art Carney, Jack Palance, and Mickey Rooney. Several of the dramas, such as *Requiem for a Heavyweight, The Miracle Worker,* and *The Days of Wine and Roses,* were so popular that they were remade into equally successful motion-picture versions. Adaptations of works by writers such as **Ernest Hemingway** and **William Faulkner** were also featured.

Since most of the productions were performed live, the crew of the series, led by its principal director, Frankenheimer, were faced with logistical challenges involving sets, camera movements, and blocking. The uncertainty of working in a still-young medium, however, lent an air of excitement to the series and was part of the reason many artists became involved.

The dramas produced on *Playhouse 90* and similar anthology series stood in stark contrast to most of the network offerings of the time, with their sanitized depictions of American life. *Playhouse 90* productions were frequently hard-hitting character studies, designed to provoke thought rather than discourage it. Perhaps for that reason, such series were never very popular with sponsors, and consequently they had virtually disappeared from television by the mid 1960s.

REFERENCE:

Erik Barnouw, *Tube of Plenty: The Evolution of American Television,* second edition (New York: Oxford University Press, 1980).

– C.D.B.

POET LAUREATE OF THE UNITED STATES

The position of Poet Laureate of the United States was created by Congress in December 1985, and the following February **Robert Penn Warren** was appointed to serve the first one-year term, which is renewable once. Before the creation of the American laureateship, the Poetry Consultant to the Library of Congress, the first of whom was appointed in 1937, was informally considered poet laureate. The holder of the laureateship now holds the consultantship as well. Typically the duties of laureates and consultants have included: suggesting additions to the Library of Congress poetry collection, advising the library on literary programs, finding authors and collectors willing to donate manuscripts and books to the library, selecting poets to read their works for the library's Archive of Recorded Poetry and Literature, and delivering occasional lectures. The composition of poems for special state occasions, the original function of the laureate in England, is not required of the American laureate.

Consultants in Poetry	
Joseph Auslander	1937–1941
Allen Tate	1943–1944
Robert Penn Warren	1944–1945
Louise Bogan	1945–1946
Karl Shapiro	1946–1947
Robert Lowell	1947–1948
Léonie Adams	1948–1949
Elizabeth Bishop	1949–1950
Conrad Aiken	1950–1952
William Carlos Williams (appointed but did not serve)	1952
Randall Jarrell	1956–1958
Robert Frost	1958–1959
Richard Eberhart	1959–1961
Louis Untermeyer	1961–1963
Howard Nemerov	1963–1964
Reed Whittemore	1964–1965
Stephen Spender	1965–1966
James Dickey	1966–1968
William Jay Smith	1968–1970
William Stafford	1970–1971

Josephine Jacobson	1971–1973
Daniel Hoffman	1973–1974
Stanley Kunitz	1974–1976
Robert Hayden	1976–1978
William Meredith	1978–1980
Maxine Kumin	1981–1982
Anthony Hecht	1982–1984
Robert Fitzgerald	1984–1985
(appointed but did not serve)	
Reed Whittemore	1984–1985
Gwendolyn Brooks	1985–1986

Poets Laureate

Robert Penn Warren	1986–1987
Richard Wilbur	1987–1988
Howard Nemerov	1988–1990
Mark Strand	1990–1991
Joseph Brodsky	1991–1992
Mona Van Duyn	1992–1993
Rita Dove	1993–1994

– K.L.R.

SIDNEY POITIER

Sidney Poitier (1927–) was the first African-American actor to become a major Hollywood leading man.

Born in Miami, where his parents had gone to sell tomatoes they had grown on their farm in their native Bahamas, Poitier returned to the United States in 1943. After serving a little more than a year in the U.S. Army during 1944–1945, he discovered acting when he answered a newspaper advertisement for openings at the American Negro Theater in New York. A Broadway producer saw him in a student play there and signed him for a small part in an all-black Broadway production of *Lysistrata* (1946).

Poitier made his Hollywood film debut as a young doctor in *No Way Out* (1950). His early film roles usually cast him as an urban youth capable of "better things," as in *The Blackboard Jungle* (1955) and *Edge of the City* (1957), or as a troubled African, as in *Cry the Beloved Country* (1952) and *Something of Value* (1957). His move toward stardom came through three film roles: a black escaped convict handcuffed to a white escapee in **Stanley Kramer**'s *The Defiant Ones* (1958); Walter Lee Younger in *A Raisin in the Sun* (1961), a role he had first played in the Broadway stage version (1959) of **Lorraine Hansberry**'s play; and an itinerant carpenter who builds a church for a group of German nuns in *The Lilies of the Field* (1963), a performance that won him an Academy Award (Oscar) for best actor.

Aware of Poitier's potential as a role model, Hollywood cast him in improbably noble and dignified roles throughout the 1960s. He played such parts superbly in three 1967 films: *To Sir with Love, In the Heat of the Night,* and Kramer's *Guess Who's Coming to Dinner.* In the 1970s Poitier turned to directing less serious movies such as *Uptown Saturday Night* (1974), in which he also acted, and *Stir Crazy* (1980). Absent from the screen for much of the 1980s, he returned to acting in 1988 and enjoyed renewed success in *Shoot to Kill* (1988) and *Sneakers* (1992). He received the **American Film Institute** Life Achievement Award in 1990.

REFERENCES:
William Hoffman, *Sidney* (New York: Stuart, 1971);
Sidney Poitier, *This Life* (New York: Knopf, 1980).

– I.R.H.

POLICE PROCEDURAL

The police-procedural genre can be regarded as the other side of the private-detective genre. Whereas the private eye operates independently of — and often outside of — the law-enforcement establishment because the cops are incompetent or corrupt or irresponsible, the police procedural traces the step-by-step work of cops operating according to the book. Moreover, in contrast to the loner private eye, the police procedural frequently has a collective hero: the squad or the precinct or the investigative team.

In printed form the police procedural lends itself to series development because it provides the writer with the opportunity to recycle the same law group, and readers feel comfortable with familiar characters. The police procedural crosses national boundaries and is an international genre. In America the 87th Precinct novels of Ed McBain are perennially popular, but the productivity record is held by Elizabeth Linnington, whose series include the Detective Varallo novels (as Lesley Egan), the Sergeant Maddox novels (as Linnington), and the Lt. Mendoza novels (as Dell Shannon); Englishman John Creasey's Chief Superintendent West and the Commander Gideon novels of J.J. Marric (who is Creasey) have appealed to Americans; the Inspector Maigret novels of Georges Simenon published in France and translated into every language are the most widely recognized examples of the school.

Jackson Pollock at work on one of his "drip" paintings, 1950 (photograph by Rudolph Burckhardt)

The effectiveness of the police-procedural genre is not restricted to the book form, for it has provided material for successful movie and television treatments. Television is particularly well suited to police procedural series; *Hill Street Blues* (1981–1987) and *NYPD Blue* (1993–) are notable examples.

REFERENCES:

George N. Dove, *The Police Procedural* (Bowling Green, Ohio: Bowling Green University Popular Press, 1982);

Jacques Barzun and Wendell Hertig Taylor, *A Catalogue of Crime* (New York: Harper & Row, 1971).

– M.J.B.

JACKSON POLLOCK

The first American avant-garde painter to become a household word in the United States, Jackson Pollock (1912–1956), is now considered the central figure of the **Abstract Expressionist** movement.

Pollock's first mature paintings, such as *Guardians of the Spirit* (1943), reveal his intense interest in the role of the unconscious mind in artistic creation. In 1947 he began to work on the "drip" paintings for which he is best known. Tacking his canvas to the floor of his studio and working from all sides, Pollock dripped paint onto the surface while moving in a controlled, almost dancelike manner. Using broad sweeps of his arms he created what came to be known as an "all-over" surface of evenly distributed, weblike skeins of color and line. His most significant drip paintings, which were typically huge in scale, include *Full Fathom Five* (1947), *Lavender Mist* (no. 1, 1950) and *Blue Poles* (1952). The creation of the all-over painting is considered one of the major innovations in twentieth-century painting.

After years of struggle Pollock was catapulted into celebrity at age thirty-seven, when *Life* magazine published "Jackson Pollock: Is he the greatest living painter in the United States?" in its August 1949 issue. Major collectors and wealthy visitors attended the next exhibition of his paintings, and the avant-garde had been discovered. In the words of **Willem de Kooning**, Pollock had "finally broken the ice." His success, however, did not bring him peace of mind. Plagued by alcoholism and self-doubts and estranged from his wife, painter Lee Krasner, Pollock died at the wheel in an automobile accident not far from his rural home on eastern Long Island in August 1956. The first retrospective exhibition of his paintings was held at the Museum of Modern Art in 1956 and was followed by another in 1967.

REFERENCES:

Claude Cernushi, *Jackson Pollock: Meaning and Significance* (New York: Icon, 1992);

Ellen G. Landau, *Jackson Pollock* (New York: Abrams, 1989);

Steven W. Naifeh and Gregory White Smith, *Jackson Pollock: An American Saga* (New York: C. N. Potter, 1989).

– K.B.

REFERENCE:

Irving Sandler, *American Art of the 1960's* (New York: Harper & Row, 1988).

– K.B.

POP ART

At the end of the 1950s artists working in New York, such as **Andy Warhol, Claes Oldenburg,** James Rosenquist, and **Roy Lichtenstein,** began to look at popular culture — including billboards, comic strips, advertisements, and commercial art — as sources for painting and sculpture. By the early 1960s their individual efforts had blossomed into an avant-garde art movement of unprecedented popular appeal. Opinions among art critics were divided.

While Pop Art embraced a host of individual styles and media — from Warhol's screenprints of **Marilyn Monroe** to Oldenburg's "soft sculpture" of french fries — its tone was usually one of ironic humor and emotional distance. Pop Art was a reaction against the seriousness of the postwar years, particularly of **Abstract Expressionism.** It satirized, often through inversion, social and cultural stereotypes, including "high art" itself. Lichtenstein, for example, successfully proved that comic strips could be valid subjects for major works of art, while Tom Wesselman exploited a growing national tolerance for explicit sexual imagery and eroticism.

In general, Pop Artists embraced all urban consumer culture and current events as potential artistic subject matter and, in doing so, radically changed the avant-garde artist's role from social outsider to a participant in everyday life. Pop Art also commented on the growing economic power of the United States that was reflected in the proliferation of material goods and disposable commodities as well as media stars. Depending on the artist, Pop Art could be a celebration of American culture or a critique.

Stylistically, Pop Art appropriated techniques of commercial art. Paintings and prints tended toward a machine-made rather than a hand-made look. Stencil, silkscreen, and airbrush were some of the techniques used to create clean, crisply defined images that served to eliminate the artist's immediate presence as craftsman.

Other artists associated with Pop Art included Jim Dine, Robert Indiana, and Red Grooms in New York and Wayne Thiebaud and **Edward Ruscha** on the West Coast.

FAIRFIELD PORTER

Fairfield Porter (1907–1975), best known for his paintings in the **New Realist** style, was recognized by the 1960s as a leader among artists rejecting abstraction in favor of representation. His brother Elliott Porter is a well-known nature photographer.

Born in Winnetka, Illinois (near Chicago), to a well-to-do family, Porter earned an art-history degree from Harvard University (1928), where he first took an interest in painting. After studying for two years at the Art Students League in New York, he began teaching himself to paint. Great Spruce Head Island, the small island in Penobscot Bay, Maine, that his family bought in 1912, is a setting that provided inspiration for many of his serene landscapes and seascapes. The large but rustic family summer cottage there and the house and adjacent studio in the rural eastern Long Island village of Southampton, New York, where Porter moved with his wife and children in 1949, are settings for most of his interiors and portraits — usually of family members and friends.

Although he was a realist painter, Porter did not attempt an exact transcription of the objective world. His figures are drawn from reality, but Porter rendered them with a freedom of brushstroke, color, and spatial representation that recalls paintings by Edouard Vuillard and the early works of Henri Matisse. That interpretive freedom allowed him to convey to the viewer the relative importance of and the connections between various images in a particular painting. In *Lizzie with Wild Roses* (1960), for example, both the seated girl (his younger daughter) and the vase of flowers are clearly defined with a painterly brushstroke and bold splashes of red (for the dress and the roses), but the furniture on which each is sitting in this domestic interior has been reduced to such loose outlines and muted colors that everything but the "subjects" meld ambiguously into the wall and floor space. Porter sought to create representational works in which the resulting pattern of forms and colors was aesthetically pleasing in an abstract sense as well. This constant struggle between the virtues of figurative and abstract painting belies the truly complex nature of his tranquil seascapes, interiors, and portraits that have frequently been described as simplistic.

REFERENCES:

William C. Agee, *Fairfield Porter: An American Painter* (Southampton, N.Y.: Parrish Art Museum, 1993);

Fairfield Porter(1907–1975): Realist Painter in an Age of Abstraction (Boston: Museum of Fine Arts, 1982);

John T. Spike, *Fairfield Porter: An American Classic* (New York: Abrams, 1992).

–J.M.H.

POSTMINIMALISM

Postminimalism is a broad term used to cover a variety of sculpture that emerged just after **minimalism** in the late 1960s. Artists associated with postminimalism were interested in reinvesting sculpture with the self-expression and personal nuance that had been rejected by the minimalists. Also, unlike the minimalists, who favored the use of one simple material, postminimalists were drawn to unusual combinations of materials not usually associated with sculpture. They created a highly original, visually eccentric range of forms and pioneered the use of a variety of nontraditional, **mixed-media** material, such as poured latex, foam, fiberglass, vinyl-coated wire, vulcanized rubber, string wrapped around wood and then painted, hemp, gauze, and industrial felt.

The term *postminimalism* was coined by art critic Robert Pincus-Witten in his article, "Eva Hesse: Post-Minimalism into Sublime," which appeared in the November 1971 issue of *Artforum*. The article focused on the work of **Hesse** and Richard Serra. Robert Morris's work gravitated from minimalism into postminimalism. Other important artists who are often identified with postminimalism include Lucas Samaras, Lynda Benglis, Barry La Va, Jackie Winsor, Jackie Ferrara, Keith Sonnier, Richard Tuttle, and Joel Shapiro. Postminimalist sculpture was similar to minimalist sculpture in its tendency to engage the architectural space in which it was placed. As such, it foreshadowed elements of **site-specific installation** art.

–K.B.

POSTMODERNISM

The term *postmodernism* usually refers to a loosely defined body of work in European and American art and literature that followed the height of modernism. Postmodernism arose as a reaction to what many saw as the failure of modernism to reach its idealistic goals through strict formalism. While modernists sought purity in both style and aesthetic, postmodernist artists extolled the value of a nonidealistic art based on synthesis.

Modernist movements in art and literature, beginning in the late nineteenth century, rejected a realistic concentration on subject in favor of an emphasis on form as a means of reaching a truth beyond the surface of objects or events. Consequently, modernist art and literature were often experimental and nonrepresentational. By World War II modernism was the dominant aesthetic of high culture.

Disillusioned with a technologized society that allowed works of art to become easily marketable commodities through mass production, some postmodernists sought aesthetic and stylistic alternatives while others employed such techniques in order to critique them, as did **Pop Artists.** Among postmodernist writers, the response was the widely expressed assertion that all possible styles had been used and that the only viable option was to write about the impasse literature had reached. As a result, the modernist virtue of artistic originality lost much of its significance. For postmodernists, this de-emphasis on their role led to quotations, imitations, or parodies of earlier works and the use of chance in the creative process. Postmodernist works include **William S. Burroughs**'s "cut-up" novels, in which sections were arranged by chance, and the **aleatory music** of **John Cage** and others. Postmodernist art is sometimes described as "post-object art" for its emphasis away from a final art object. For instance, movements and styles such as **conceptual art,** process art, **body art, earth art,** and **performance art** emphasize artistic planning and process rather than final form.

Whereas modernists generally excluded past styles, social issues, and emotional concerns from their pure, autonomous artworks, postmodernists practiced a much more open-ended and pluralistic art. These artists sought to reinvest their work with a sense of subjectivity by reviving styles, genres, and subject matter from earlier periods. In architecture, this eclectic approach included the revival of elements from pre–**International Style** architecture. Classical arches and capitals began to be integrated into the modern skyscraper along with types of ornamentation considered impure and superfluous in modernist architecture. These postmodern architects, many of whom were trained in the International Style, include **Michael Graves, Philip Johnson,** Charles Moore, and **Robert Venturi.** Postmodernist artists often returned to representation, including landscape and historical painting — all of which had been scorned by modernist artists in favor of abstraction. In the late 1960s and through the 1970s several figurative styles began to appear, with names such as **New Realism, New Image Painting,** Photorealism, Neo-Expressionism, and Neo-Surrealism.

Postmodernist writers initially turned to fantasy and experiment during the 1960s, often as a means of questioning what is real and how meaning is constructed by culture. Influenced by Samuel Beckett, Jorge Luis Borges, **Vladimir Nabokov,** and the French *nouveau roman,* writers such as **Richard Brautigan, William S. Burroughs,** William Gaddis, and **Thomas Pynchon** created works of fiction whose formal chaos suggested a similarly chaotic worldview. Unlike modernism, which made a sharp separation between high art and mass culture, such works often allude extensively to popular culture. The best-known form of postmodernist writing during the 1960s was **metafiction,** in which writers referred to their own act of writing. These tendencies are also present in certain films since the 1960s. While postmodernism in poetry and drama has received comparatively little critical attention, examples can be found in the poetry of John Ashbery and the plays of **Edward Albee.**

In recent decades postmodernism has elicited responses, just as postmodernism itself was a reaction to modernism. In fiction, for instance, a revival of traditional realism paralleled postmodernist fiction during the 1970s and 1980s, while in music some composers returned to more-conventional melodic and harmonic arrangements. In the resulting dialogue, artists and critics continue to debate the nature and purpose of art.

REFERENCES:

Steven Connor, *Postmodernist Culture: An Introduction to Theories of the Contemporary* (Oxford: Blackwell, 1989);

Andreas Huyssen, *After the Great Divide: Modernism, Mass Culture, Postmodernism* (Bloomington: Indiana University Press, 1986);

John Carlos Rowe, "Postmodernist Studies," in *Redrawing the Boundaries: The Transformation of English and American Literary Studies,* edited by Stephen Greenblatt and Giles Gunn (New York: Modern Language Association of America, 1992), pp. 179–208;

Daniel Wheeler, *Art since Mid-Century: 1945 to the Present* (Englewood Cliffs, N.J.: Prentice-Hall / New York: Vendome, 1991), pp. 243–336.

                                                            –J.M.H. and D.H.-F.

POST-PAINTERLY ABSTRACTION

Post-painterly abstraction is a style of large-scale abstract painting in which paint is usually applied to the canvas by techniques other than paintbrush. By choosing to pour color onto the canvas, the artist could avoid the personal gesture of the brush stroke. This style was named and aggressively promoted by art critic **Clement Greenberg** from the mid 1950s through the 1960s. He saw post-painterly abstraction as the next stage after

Abstract Expressionism in the development of modern art because the absence of gestural expression in post-painterly abstraction further reduced color to its purely formal nature. The principle artists involved in the movement were Morris Louis (1912–1962), Kenneth Noland (1924–), and Jules Olitski (1922–).

In 1952 **Helen Frankenthaler** had begun pouring thinned-out acrylic paint directly onto unprimed cotton-duck canvases. This staining technique greatly influence the post-painterly abstract artists. In 1954 Louis began to stain his canvases, often controlling the paint flow by moving the canvas itself. His staining technique was characterized by the use of beautiful colors, and he often left large areas of canvas empty. His best-known series is *Veils,* painted first in 1954 and again in 1957–1960. Noland's works tend to have a more controlled and geometric quality than Louis's. His recurrent motifs include concentric circles, the chevron, or simply long horizontal bands. Jules Olitski typically uses a paint sprayer to create a hazy atmospheric effect with layers of pastel colors on large canvases. In general post-painterly abstraction consciously intended to eliminate all other creative concerns beyond the formal properties of color and shape on a flat surface.

                                                            – K.B.

POSTSTRUCTURALISM

The term *poststructuralism* applies to a broad range of theories in the humanities and the social sciences. Poststructuralism is the body of questions and assumptions that grew out of responses to structuralism, a set of ideas developed before World War II and popularized in the 1950s and 1960s in linguistics, anthropology, and literary criticism. While structuralists believe in the possibility of knowledge about structures that order language and culture, poststructuralists deny the possibility of absolute truth. Critics of poststructuralism denounce it as nihilistic and deliberately obscure, but proponents support it as difficult yet celebratory.

Structuralism and poststructuralism share a common ancestor: the Swiss linguist Ferdinand de Saussure, whose posthumously published notes suggest that language structures and conditions our experience of the world rather than naturally reflecting it. For Saussure, each element in language (and, for structuralists after him, in literature and culture) derives its meaning from its relationship to other elements; such structures are thus arbitrary and independent of "reality." However, structuralists believe that a deeper knowledge of reality can be gained through analysis of these structures.

In the late 1960s and the 1970s, several structuralists began to question the validity of their approach. The turning point came with the work of French writers such as literary critic Roland Barthes, philosopher Jacques Derrida, historian Michel Foucault, and psychoanalyst Jacques Lacan, all of whom challenged the notion of a structure or order transcending language or culture. Lacan, for instance, questioned the idea of a unified, knowable self; Foucault, the idea of a unified, knowable history. (Foucault's influence is especially evident in one school of poststructuralist literary criticism, **New Historicism.**) Derrida's concept of **deconstruction** holds that "texts" (networks of words or other cultural signifiers) lack determinate meanings by their very nature as linguistic constructions. For deconstructionists, not only does literature not relate to reality, it is inherently contradictory — texts destabilize their own meanings because language always points to more than its user may intend. In deconstruction and poststructuralism as a whole, texts cannot be pinned down to a single interpretation or meaning, and there is no privileged critical position.

From France poststructuralism was disseminated in American literary criticism through critics such as those at Yale University in the 1970s and 1980s, including Geoffrey Hartman, Barbara Johnson, J. Hillis Miller, and especially Paul de Man. Deconstruction has proved the most influential poststructuralist theory: its similarities to the previously reigning approach of **New Criticism,** such as close reading and a dismissal of authorial intention, help to explain how, for all its revolutionary rhetoric, it was so easily subsumed into the academy. In the United States, ironically, poststructuralism has been applied mainly to canonical texts. However, **feminist critics** drawing on poststructuralism have applied its subversion of established conventions more defiantly. The poststructuralist challenge to the boundaries of literature has also contributed to the growing field of cultural studies.

REFERENCES:

Terry Eagleton, *Literary Theory: An Introduction* (Oxford, England: Basil Blackwell, 1983);

Frank Lentricchia, *After the New Criticism* (Chicago: University of Chicago Press, 1980).

D. H.-F.

Ezra Pound

No single individual has had a wider influence on the course of twentieth-century American poetry than Ezra Pound (1885–1972). Yet his most influential work, *The Cantos* (1917–1969), is now probably read less than any other major American poem, and his personal reputation has been tarnished by his open support of Fascism during World War II.

During the first three decades of the twentieth century Pound was at the forefront of the revolution against the artificial diction and prudish morality pervasive in late nineteenth-century verse, defying its conventions in his own writings and championing other innovative poets such as Hilda Doolittle (H. D.), **William Carlos Williams, Robert Frost**, and **T. S. Eliot.** In the 1930s, overlooking the repression of individual liberties in Italy, he came to believe that the solution to the world's economic woes could be found in the fiscal and social-welfare reforms enacted there by Mussolini. During World War II Pound remained in Rapallo, Italy, where he had lived since 1924, and broadcast pro-Fascist, anti-Semitic speeches on an Italian radio program aimed at English-speaking countries.

Charged with treason, he was arrested by invading American troops in 1945. In February 1946 a federal court ruled him insane and confined him to St. Elizabeths Federal Hospital for the Insane in Washington, D.C., until such time as he was capable of standing trial. In the mid 1950s, amid charges that Pound had been confined in St. Elizabeths for a period longer than the sentence he might have received if found guilty, poet-attorney Archibald MacLeish enlisted Frost, Eliot, and **Ernest Hemingway** in a campaign to win Pound's release. In June 1958 he was allowed to return to Italy.

Pound's 1948 book, *The Pisan Cantos,* written during the nearly six months in 1945 that Pound spent in the U.S. Army Disciplinary Training Camp near Pisa while awaiting return to the United States for trial, was a controversial choice for the first Bollingen Prize in Poetry, awarded in 1949 by the Fellows in American Literature at the Library of Congress.

By the time *Drafts & Fragments of Cantos CX–CXVII* appeared in 1969, Pound had abandoned work on his verse epic. Critics and other poets have called this lack of an ending appropriate to a poem that veers back and forth between the present and various ages in the past as though all exist at the same time. This same open-endedness is apparent in Williams's *Paterson* (1946–1963), **Charles Olson**'s *Maximus Poems* (1953–1975), and **Robert Duncan**'s *Passages* (1968–1987). The authors of these epics also followed Pound's practice of incorporating in his work bits and pieces from his voluminous reading on whatever topic absorbed his attention at the moment. The later cantos, beginning with *The Pisan Cantos,* were also influential in their challenge to Eliot's dictum on the impersonality of the poet. The hero of these cantos is Pound, filtering historical as well as personal experience through his own eyes and paving the way for **confessional poetry.**

Pound's most pervasive influence on his own and succeeding generations of poets lies in what **James Dickey** has called "the highly personal and imaginative directness" of Pound's poetic images. The *Cantos* as a whole may be flawed by his anti-Semitism and his proselytizing on economics; their complex allusions and lack of chronological narrative structure may always put off more readers than they attract. Yet the brilliance of the language throughout all his poetry is likely to ensure his stature as a major American poet.

REFERENCES:

Humphrey Carpenter, *A Serious Character: The Life of Ezra Pound* (Boston: Houghton Mifflin, 1988);

James Dickey, *The Water-Bug's Mittens, Ezra Pound: What We Can Use* (Bloomfield Hills, Mich. & Columbia, S. C.: Bruccoli Clark, 1980);

Wendy Stallard Flory, *The American Ezra Pound* (New Haven & London: Yale University Press, 1989).

– K.L.R.

OTTO PREMINGER

Director/producer Otto Preminger (1906–1986) occasionally played Nazis onscreen and was accused of behaving like one by the actors in his films, but he kept coming back with "big" pictures after commercial and artistic failures.

Born in Vienna, Preminger gained his first experience with German play producer Max Reinhardt, he immigrated to the United States in 1935 to direct the Broadway version of *Libel,* which had been a hit in Vienna and had a successful run in New York as well. His first attempts at Hollywood directing — two B movies — were failures, but he was successful as an actor, playing a Prussian officer in *The Pied Piper* (1942). When asked to reprise his 1939 stage portrayal of a Nazi in the movie version of *Margin for Error* (1943), he insisted that he be allowed to direct the film as well.

Preminger's 1944 film *Laura,* which — like many of his films — he also produced, established his reputation as a director. This story of a rough-hewn police detective and an epicene newspaper columnist who are both obsessed with an apparently dead woman is probably Preminger's best, but during his forty-year directorial career he made many highly entertaining if overblown melodramas disguised as daring explorations of taboo subjects and controversial events. These movies include the murder thriller *Angel Face* (1953); *The Man with the Golden Arm* (1955), based on **Nelson Algren**'s novel about drug addiction; *Anatomy of a Murder*

(1959), a courtroom drama about a man who has murdered his wife's alleged rapist; *Exodus* (1960), based on Leon Uris's novel about the conflict that led to the birth of modern Israel; *Advise and Consent* (1962), based on Allen Drury's novel about the clash between a president and Congress over the appointment of a secretary of state; and *The Cardinal* (1963), about the rise to power of a Catholic churchman who looks the other way on important moral issues when speaking out would jeopardize his career. Even the inoffensive romantic farce *The Moon Is Blue* (1950), the first film made by Preminger's independent production company, was controversial for dialogue using then-forbidden words such as *virgin* and *pregnant.*

Preminger directed his last film,*The Human Factor,* in 1979, but during the final decade of his life he got more publicity for revealing that he was the father of stripper Gypsy Rose Lee's son Erik than for his films.

REFERENCES:

Gerald Pratley, *The Cinema of Otto Preminger* (New York: Castle Books, 1971);

Otto Preminger, *Preminger: An Autobiography* (Garden City, N.Y.: Doubleday, 1977).

– I.R.H.

ELVIS PRESLEY

Known as "the King" of **rock 'n' roll** for his major part in popularizing the new music of the 1950s, Elvis Presley (1935–1977) achieved an unprecedented level of fame and an unmatched impact on American culture during the 1950s and 1960s. At his death, more than 150 million of his records had been sold, and "Elvis" was a household name.

Elvis Aron Presley was born in Tupelo, Mississippi, and moved to Memphis, Tennessee, with his family in 1948. He was discovered by Sun Records when he recorded a song in their studios for his mother's birthday. His early music was a unique blend of black rhythm and blues with white country and **gospel** influences that was later called *rockabilly*. His first single, the blues tune "That's All Right, Mama" (1954), was introduced by disc jockeys who felt it necessary to explain that the singer was white. Presley became popular in the South in the mid 1950s through shows and radio performances.

In 1955 Presley's contract was purchased by RCA for a record $35,000, and "Colonel" Tom Parker became his manager. Parker and RCA succeeded in making him a star. That year Presley had the first of his eighteen number-one hits with "Heartbreak Hotel,"

Elvis Presley

songs such as "Return to Sender" (1962) and began performing softer, romantic ballads such as "It's Now or Never" (1960), "Are You Lonesome Tonight?" (1961), and "Can't Help Falling in Love with You" (1961) for the remainder of his career. At the same time he continued to star in a series of unremarkable films such as *Blue Hawaii* (1961) and *Viva Las Vegas* (1964). Presley maintained a loyal following into the 1970s, when he performed almost exclusively in Las Vegas, and his fans were devastated by his death in 1977 from a drug overdose. Claims that Presley is still alive have led to many jokes and tabloid headlines about "Elvis sightings." His Memphis home, Graceland, is a popular tourist attraction, and he has remained a part of American popular culture through Elvis memorabilia, scores of Elvis impersonators, and books and television shows about his life.

REFERENCES:

Patsy Guy Hammontree, *Elvis Presley: A Bio-Bibliography* (Westport, Conn. & London: Greenwood Press, 1985);

Jerry Hopkins, *Elvis: A Biography* (New York: Simon & Schuster, 1971);

Hopkins, *Elvis, the Final Years* (New York: St. Martin's Press, 1980);

Dave Marsh, *Elvis* (New York: Times Books, 1982).

– D.H.-F.

ANDRÉ PREVIN

Pianist, conductor, and composer André Previn (1929–) began his career as a film composer and conductor and then turned to orchestral conducting. He has written many popular and classical compositions and made several recordings as a jazz and classical pianist.

Born Andreas Ludwig Prewin in Berlin, Previn and his family fled Hitler's Germany in 1938 and settled in Los Angeles in 1939. At sixteen he began working as an arranger for M-G-M Studios, and from the late 1940s through the early 1970s he was an arranger, rehearsal conductor, composer, and conductor for dozens of movies, including *Kiss Me, Kate* (1953), *The Graduate* (1967), *Goodbye, Mr. Chips* (1969), *Catch-22* (1970), and *Jesus Christ Superstar* (1973). He received an impressive number of Academy Awards (Oscars) for films scores such as *Gigi* (1958), *Porgy and Bess* (1959, with Ken Darby), *Irma la Douce* (1963), and *My Fair Lady* (1964). He also composed the music for *Every Good Boy Deserves Favour* (1977) by British playwright Tom Stoppard.

Frequent appearances as a pianist led to numerous guest conducting engagements for Previn in the early 1960s. A series of highly publicized recordings,

which sold more than a million records. In 1956 he reached a national audience through appearances on *The Ed Sullivan Show,* famous for filming Presley only above the waist to hide the suggestive hip movements that earned him the nickname "Elvis the Pelvis." RCA sold a record ten million Presley singles in 1956, including "Hound Dog," "Blue Suede Shoes," and "Don't Be Cruel." That same year Presley starred in his first film, *Love Me Tender,* which introduced another hit song. By this time Elvis was everywhere — on television, in films, on merchandise — and his image of youthful rebellion set a fashion for white teens, who adopted leather jackets, slicked-back hair, and sideburns. In 1957 Presley's success continued with songs such as "Jailhouse Rock," from the movie of the same title, and "All Shook Up." His fans were shaken in 1958 when he was drafted.

By the time Presley was released from the service in 1960, the rock 'n' roll sound he had helped to establish was changing. While his work during the 1950s was extremely influential on 1960s rock performers such as **The Beatles** and **The Rolling Stones,** Presley kept to his rockabilly roots with beginning in 1964, increased his standing among conductors and opened up conducting positions with the Houston Symphony (1967–1969), the London Symphony Orchestra (1968–1979), the Pittsburgh Symphony Orchestra (1976–1984), and the Los Angeles Philharmonic Orchestra (1986–1990). He is the director of the Royal Philharmonic Orchestra in London (1985–   ).

REFERENCES:

Martin Bookspan and Ross Yockey, *André Previn: A Biography* (Garden City, N.Y.: Doubleday, 1981);

André Previn, *No Minor Chords: My Days in Hollywood* (New York: Doubleday, 1991);

Helen Drees Ruttencutter, *Previn* (New York: St. Martin's Press / Marek, 1985).

– L.D.S.

LEONTYNE PRICE

Like her predecessor and mentor **Marian Anderson,** Leontyne Price (1927–   ) rose from humble beginnings to establish herself as one of the leading American opera singers of the twentieth century. She has been called the perfect lyric soprano for the operas of Giuseppe Verdi.

Price was born in Laurel, Mississippi, and began her musical training in local church choirs. She won a full scholarship to the Juilliard School of Music, where **Virgil Thomson** heard her and selected her for a revival of his opera *Four Saints in Three Acts* in the early 1950s. After this engagement, Price embarked on a world tour as Bess in George Gershwin's opera *Porgy and Bess* (1953–1954), establishing herself as a favorite with foreign audiences. She also undertook a concert career in 1954. The following year she appeared in an **NBC**-TV production of Puccini's *Tosca*. The show was controversial for its casting of Price, an African American, in a still-segregated United States, but it was a success.

Price made formal operatic debuts during the late 1950s and early 1960s in the great opera houses of the world: **San Francisco,** Vienna, Covent Garden, La Scala, and — most significantly — the **New York Metropolitan Opera,** where she performed in Verdi's *Il Trovatore* in 1961. She then became a mainstay of the Metropolitan resident company. She was chosen by **Samuel Barber,** whose music she had long championed, to create the role of Cleopatra in the world premiere of his *Antony and Cleopatra* (1966) at the opening of the new Metropolitan Opera House at Lincoln Center. Price had many successful years at the Metropolitan Opera, making her farewell appearances in

1984 in the title role of Verdi's *Aida*. She is still active as a concert and recital artist.

REFERENCES:

Frank E. Smith and Audrey Warren, *Mississippians All* (New Orleans: Pelican, 1968), pp. 35–43;

Winthrop Sargeant, *Divas* (New York: Coward, McCann & Geoghegan, 1973), pp. 134–167.

– L.D.S.

HAROLD PRINCE

Harold (better known as Hal) Prince (1928–   ) was the greatest producer-director of Broadway musicals in the postwar period. He began as a co-producer of such 1950s hits as *The Pajama Game* (1954), *Damn Yankees* (1955), and *West Side Story* (1957). *West Side Story* was Prince's first association with **Stephen Sondheim,** its lyricist. Prince's second solo producing effort was Sondheim's first show as both lyricist and composer, *A Funny Thing Happened the Way to the Forum* (1962). Prince and Sondheim collaborated on six other musicals, including such ground-breaking projects as *Company* (1970), *Follies* (1971), and *Sweeney Todd* (1979). Other memorable Broadway hits that Prince produced, directed, or both, include the innovative *Fiddler on the Roof* (1964), *Cabaret* (1966), and *The Phantom of the Opera* (1986). Prince's trademarks include innovative deployment of the chorus, dynamic staging, and close unity between the meaning of the play and the style of the production.

REFERENCE:

Foster Hirsch, *Harold Prince and the American Musical Theatre* (Cambridge: Cambridge University Press, 1989).

–I.R.H.

PROGRESSIVE JAZZ

The outgrowth of an attempt to establish jazz as a permanent fixture of formal concert venues, progressive jazz evolved in the late 1940s and took its name from an ensemble — the Progressive Jazz Orchestra — organized by bandleader Stan Kenton. Among the features of this musical genre are complex, big-band-style arrangements in which a thick instrumentation is predominant. Attempts to link progressive jazz with art (or classical) music forms may be discerned from the titles of many selections in the progressive-jazz repertoire (Kenton's "Opus in Pastels," "Artistry in Bolero," and "Riff Rhapsody," for example). The Duke Ellington Orchestra is perhaps the best known of the full-fledged progressive jazz-ensembles, although

Stephen Sondheim and Hal Prince backstage on the opening night of their 1981 musical, *Merrily We Roll Along*

many smaller groups and individuals (notably **Gunther Schuller** and Charles Mingus) have been progressive jazz innovators.

– L.D.S.

PROJECTIVE VERSE

Projective Verse (or Open Verse), an important innovation in American poetry of the 1950s, developed from a theory propounded by **Charles Olson** in "Projective Verse," first published in *Poetry New York*, no. 3 (October 1950). Olson's manifesto defines the poem as "energy transferred from where the poet got it ... by way of the poem itself to the reader." In what Olson calls "Composition by Field," the poet must be constantly open to everything around him, allowing his writing to be a direct extension of his perceptions. He does not shape or rethink his experience; rather he is the passive transcriber who "projects" what he perceives onto the page.

Arguing against traditional form — in which line length, meter, rhyme, and stanza form are predetermined — Olson states "the law which presides conspic-

uously" over Projective Verse by quoting poet **Robert Creeley,** with whom he had corresponded about his theory: "FORM IS NEVER MORE THAN AN EXTENSION OF CONTENT." The form is not only unique to the individual poem but also "the only possible extension of content under hand." The shape of the poetic line is determined by "breath": The poet uses his breath to "push" his perceptions onto the page.

Olson developed his theory from ideas about organic form expressed by a long line of poets that extends from Samuel Taylor Coleridge through Ralph Waldo Emerson to Walt Whitman to **William Carlos Williams.** Williams, who called Olson's essay a "keystone," included a large portion of it in his *Autobiography* (1951). Olson's influence was widespread, even among poets who did not wholly subscribe to his manifesto. In addition to Olson and Creeley, poets who were influenced by Projectivist theory include **Robert Duncan, Denise Levertov,** Joel Oppenheimer, and LeRoi Jones (**Amiri Baraka**). Some Projectivists are called Black Mountain Poets because of their association with **Black Mountain College** or the *Black Mountain Review.*

REFERENCES:

Donald Allen, ed., *Human Universe and Other Essays,* by Charles Olson (New York: Grove Press, 1967);

Robert Creeley, ed., *Selected Writings of Charles Olson* (New York: New Directions, 1967);

Sherman Paul, *Olson's Push: Origin, Black Mountain, and Recent American Poetry* (Baton Rouge & London: Louisiana State University Press, 1978).

– K.L.R.

PUNK ROCK

Punk rock surfaced during the late 1960s in the New York underground-music scene and crystallized during the mid 1970s in London and New York. Seen by some critics as a form of social protest by youths rebelling against mainstream culture, punk rock is typically fast, rhythmic, dissonant, high-volume music. Performers and fans are known for engaging in aggressive antisocial behavior — spitting, shoving and kicking, and even self-mutilation. Punk is pessimistic and anarchistic. With lyrics detailing drug abuse, deviant sex, and other generally unaccepted behaviors, punk records have been censored, and performances have been banned. The roots of punk date to the late 1960s and early 1970s with the emergence of the New York underground-music groups the Velvet Underground (whose singer Lou Reed composed shocking songs such as "Heroin," 1966) and the New York Dolls (whose screaming made lyrics unintelligible). The Sex Pistols, a British group known for songs such as "Anarchy in the U.K." (1978), is frequently called the archetypal punk rock band.

Intending to shock and alienate the general public, many punk performers and fans dressed in mix-matched, ripped clothing and sadomasochistic bondage wear such as chains, spiked dog collars around necks and wrists, and even safety pins through noses, ears, cheeks, and other body parts. Their hair was often spiked and dyed in unnatural hues such as blue, green, and pink. Many punk fans also wore stark white and black make-up to imitate horror-movie monsters or corpses.

American performers who contributed to the development of punk during the mid to late 1970s include Patti Smith, who is credited with releasing the first punk-rock record single, "Hey Joe" with flip side "Piss Factory" (1974); Richard Hell and the Voidoids, who performed the punk song "(I Belong to) The Blank Generation" (1977); and the Ramones, who recorded "Now I Wanna Sniff Some Glue" (1976). Groups such as the Dead Kennedys, Blondie, and Black Flag continued to develop the punk style in the late 1970s and early 1980s. After the break-up of the Sex Pistols in 1979, punk rock lost much of its appeal, but elements of punk were incorporated into other musical styles, such as **New Wave,** hard-core, and **heavy-metal** music.

REFERENCES:

Tricia Henry, *Break All Rules!: Punk Rock and the Making of a Style* (Ann Arbor, Mich.: UMI Research, 1989);

Clinton Heylin, *From the Velvets to the Voidoids: A Pre-Punk History for a Post-Punk World* (New York: Penguin, 1993);

Greil Marcus, *Ranters & Crowd Pleasers: Punk in Pop Music, 1977-1992* (New York: Doubleday, 1993).

–J.E.F. and J.M.P.

MARTIN PURYEAR

Martin Puryear (1941–) rose to the forefront of the American art world during 1988–1989 as an abstract sculptor of large-scale simple, wood-based forms. After formal training at Catholic University (where he majored in painting), the Swedish Royal Academy of Art, and Yale University, he learned the traditional wood-carving techniques of West Africa while serving in the Peace Corps in Sierra Leone for two years in the 1960s. Although his works are abstract, Puryear intentionally creates forms that have an ambiguous biomorphic quality. For example, his *Lever #3* (1989), which at first glance seems **minimalist** in its reduced abstract form, offers vague suggestions of a birdlike or plantlike form.

In his choice of materials — including wood, tar, and wire mesh — and in his combination of the graceful forms of abstract art and the raw, expressively powerful style of tribal art, Puryear has proved the universal appeal of artworks with **multicultural** style and aesthetic references. In 1989 he was selected as official representative of the United States to the Sao Paolo Bienal in Brazil, marking the first occasion for an African American to do so in an international exhibition. At that event he was awarded the coveted grand prize for eight works that spanned his mature artistic development.

REFERENCE:

Neal Benezra, *Martin Puryear* (London: Thames & Hudson, 1992).

– A.A.

THOMAS PYNCHON

Thomas Pynchon (1937–) is one of America's most critically acclaimed novelists. His experimental works combine humor with serious themes in complex plots filled with allusions and information ranging from science and history to popular culture.

Pynchon's novels are absurdist, encyclopedic books that use a variety of styles and employ **black humor** and other types of comedy in conjunction with elements of **science fiction** and an impressive display of learning. His characters' attempts to decode their worlds mirror the reader's attempt to make sense of Pynchon's often difficult texts. Pynchon's characters seek knowledge in a world flooded with information and systems that ultimately break down into meaninglessness. Paranoia and conspiracy theories, frequent topics in Pynchon's fiction, are thus means of seeing order in a chaotic world.

In *V.* (1963), his first novel, Herbert Stencil searches for a mysterious woman whose identity cannot be pinned down; his futile efforts to achieve meaning from disorder are juxtaposed with the disorderly life of Benny Profane. Pynchon's talent was recognized immediately. While he has never had popular appeal, his work soon gained a cult following and became the subject of academic attention.

Oedipa Maas tries to unravel a complex conspiracy in *The Crying of Lot 49* (1966), Pynchon's next novel and his most accessible because, unlike most of his other works, it is short. Conspiracy also figures in his massive *Gravity's Rainbow* (1973), set during and after World War II. Many critics hailed it as a masterpiece; others said it was unreadable. With the exception of *Slow Learner* (1984), a collection of five early stories, Pynchon published nothing after *Gravity's Rainbow* until 1990, when his novel *Vineland* appeared. Less complex than his previous novels, the book was deemed less compelling by critics as well.

Pynchon is extremely private: his whereabouts since the beginning of his writing career have been shielded from the public, and the last published photograph of the author is from his high-school yearbook.

REFERENCES:

Judith Chambers, *Thomas Pynchon* (New York: Twayne, 1992);

Robert D. Newman, *Understanding Thomas Pynchon* (Columbia: University of South Carolina Press, 1986).

– D.H.-F.

R

DAVID RABE

In the 1970s David Rabe (1940–   ) became widely recognized as an important new playwright speaking for the Vietnam veteran.

Born in Dubuque, Iowa, Rabe had his graduate studies at Villanova University (M.A., 1968) interrupted by the draft in 1965. During the final eleven months of his two-year tour of duty, he worked in a support group attached to a U.S. Army hospital in Vietnam. This experience would provide the material for his most accomplished plays. The first to reach New York was *The Basic Training of Pavlo Hummel* (1971), which ran for 366 performances and brought Rabe Obie and Drama Desk Awards. His reputation was cemented six months later with the New York opening of *Sticks and Bones*, which won an Antoinette Perry (Tony) Award, a New York Drama Critics Circle Special Citation, and other honors. *Sticks and Bones* deals with an "All-American" family named after the Nelsons of the 1950s television comedy *The Adventures of Ozzie and Harriet.* Unable to cope with their blinded Vietnam-veteran son, David, the Nelsons persuade him to commit suicide and eagerly help him, onstage, to slit his wrists. Rabe's military series concluded in 1976 with *Streamers,* which won the New York Drama Critics Circle Award for best American play of 1976. Set in an army barracks, the play presents a microcosmic view of the collective American psyche during the mid 1960s.

Rabe had moderate success with two plays on subjects unrelated to army life, *In the Boom Boom Room* (1973) and *Hurly Burly* (1984). His most recent play, *Those the River Keeps,* premiered in 1990 in Princeton, New Jersey, and opened Off-Broadway on 31 January 1994. None of these plays has had the critical or popular success of his Vietnam trilogy, and he seems destined to be remembered primarily as the major American playwright of the **Vietnam War.**

REFERENCE:

Philip Kolin, *David Rabe: A Stage History and Primary and Secondary Bibliography* (New York: Garland, 1988).

– I.R.H.

RAMPARTS

Ramparts is best known as the most successful **New Left** magazine of the late 1960s and early 1970s. Published in the San Francisco Bay area, the periodical was widely distributed nationwide and became often a center of media attention.

Edward M. Keating founded *Ramparts* in 1962 as a liberal Catholic magazine devoted to literature and ideas for laity. While it published works by serious writers such as **Robert Lowell,** the magazine did not attract much attention until 1964, when it began to address Keating's growing social concerns and his discomfort with the Church's failure to remedy them. The October 1964 issue signaled a clear change of direction: the format and style became more colorful and **New Journalistic,** and the emphasis shifted from religion and literature to politics. In a month, circulation rose from 2,500 to 10,000. By 1965, it had increased to 50,000.

Warren Hinckle III edited *Ramparts* between 1965 and 1969, its most prosperous years: circulation was 165,000 in 1966 and peaked at 225,000 in 1969. The deliberately controversial magazine, from which Keating was eased out in 1967, published increasingly radical exposés and articles against war and racism and favoring environmentalism. It featured **Martin Luther King**'s **Vietnam War** protest and contributors such as

271

Tom Hayden and **Black Panther** Eldridge Cleaver. In the 1970s *Ramparts* advocated causes such as **feminism** and **gay rights.**

Even at its height *Ramparts* was published irregularly, suffering from financial problems created by its liberal spending and inability to attract advertisers. During the 1970s its prominence declined along with the protest movements it had supported earlier, and the magazine folded in 1975. The following year its heir, the slightly more mainstream *Mother Jones,* was founded by *Ramparts* editorial board member Adam Hochschild.

REFERENCES:

Warren Hinckle III, *If You Have a Lemon, Make Lemonade* (New York: Putnam, 1973);

Daniel Stroubel, "*Ramparts,*" *American Mass Market Magazines*, edited by Alan Nourie and Barbara Nourie (New York: Greenwood, 1990), pp. 419–425.

– D.H.-F.

RAP MUSIC

Rap music emerged from the hip-hop culture of the late 1970s as a strictly urban style of black music, but within a decade it spread across the country and crossed over to white listeners, becoming a major branch of American popular music. Rap relies on electronic equipment and instruments and is most distinctive for the spoken, usually rhymed lyrics that provide its name.

Bronx disc jockey Afrika Bambaataa coined the term *hip hop* in 1974 to refer to the black music scene — then dominated by funk music and **soul music** — and its attendant culture, which included dance, fashion, and occasionally **graffiti art.** Rap music began at dance clubs with disc jockeys mixing different records on multiple turntables and providing new effects by scratching records with the phonograph needle. Rapping was soon added to these new sounds, creating a different musical style. The background to these lyrics later included synthesizers, drum machines, and especially samplers. The latter, which enable musicians to take individual parts from recorded songs, provide one of the key elements of rap: samples, usually altered, from other music.

The first successful rap single was "Rapper's Delight" (1979) by the Sugar Hill Gang. Beginning in the late 1970s, Grandmaster Flash was one of the first artists to popularize rap, and it was often associated with breakdancing in the early 1980s. One of the first groups to achieve substantial success beyond New York was Run-D.M.C., the first rap artists to sell enough records

for a gold album (*Run-D.M.C.,* 1984), a platinum album (*King of Rock,* 1985), and a triple-platinum album (*Raising Hell,* 1986). They also had the first rap music video on **MTV** and the first rock/rap **crossover** hit, in collaboration with Aerosmith, with "Walk This Way" in 1986. That year the Beastie Boys, a white rap group, sold more than four million copies of their album *Licensed to Ill.*

As rap became an inescapable part of American culture in the mid 1980s, it also diversified. In addition to traditional boasting or insult lyrics, rappers began addressing social issues and problems with greater frequency, sometimes in a hard-edged style called "gangsta" rap. Rap stars, ranging from popular performers who were adopted into the mainstream to musicians controversial for songs with obscene lyrics, proliferated in the late 1980s. Among the best known are D. J. Jazzy Jeff and the Fresh Prince, L. L. Cool J, Queen Latifah, Salt-N-Pepa, and 2 Live Crew. Rap hits from the 1980s include N.W.A.'s "Boyz N the Hood" (1986) and Tone-Loc's "Wild Thing" (1988), while Public Enemy's "Fight the Power" was featured in **Spike Lee**'s 1989 film *Do the Right Thing.*

The first Grammy Awards for rap were presented in 1989, and the following year was a prosperous one: rap-album sales totaled more than $100 million, rap star Will Smith starred in the new television show *The Fresh Prince of Bel Air,* and rap was featured in the financially successful film *House Party.* By the early 1990s rap was increasingly used in films and in advertising, and hip-hop culture influenced dance styles, fashion, and other aspects of popular culture. Pop-oriented performers such as Hammer and Vanilla Ice became widely popular. At the same time, some found fault with songs such as Ice-T's "Cop Killer" (1992) and other lyrics, by performers such as Snoop Doggy Dog, that critics found violent, obscene, racist, or sexist. Others have found rap in general to be repetitive and nonmusical. However, its popular appeal and widespread cultural impact are undeniable.

REFERENCES:

Judy McCoy, *Rap Music in the 1980s: A Reference Guide* (Metuchen, N.J.: Scarecrow, 1992);

Michael Small, *Break It Down: The Inside Story from the New Leaders of Rap* (New York: Citadel Press, 1992);

David Toop, *The Rap Attack: African Jive to New York Hip Hop* (London & Leichhardt, New South Wales: Pluto Press, 1984).

– D.H.-F.

ROBERT RAUSCHENBERG

One of the most influential artists to emerge in the 1950s, Robert Rauschenberg (1925–) is best known for his revolutionary "combine" paintings, which include real objects as well as paint.

Rauschenberg settled in New York in 1949 and began working on a series of monochromatic canvases in black, white, or red. At about the same time he met artist **Jasper Johns** and composer **John Cage.** In 1952 Rauschenberg participated in Cage's **mixed-media** event at **Black Mountain College,** a spectacle that has been called a forerunner of **Happenings.**

Rauschenberg's first solo exhibit, in 1951 at Parsons Gallery in New York, received little attention, but in March 1958, at the Leo Castelli Gallery, Rauschenberg dismayed many in the art world by exhibiting the first of his "combine" paintings. Influenced by the Dadaists and **Marcel Duchamp,** these canvases were splashed with paint in an **Abstract Expressionist** style and had real objects fastened to them. The most startling example was *Bed* (1955), in which Rauschenberg had mounted a pillow and a quilt on a canvas and covered it with paint. In *Monogram* (1963) a stuffed goat wearing an automobile tire stands on a base painted with gestural brush strokes. Rauschenberg's art is important because it bridges the gap between the expressiveness and introspection of the Abstract Expressionists and the Pop artists' acknowledgment of the outside world.

In 1964 Rauschenberg became the first American painter to win the international prize in painting at the Venice Biennale. Throughout the 1960s and 1970s he dabbled in many different art forms, including Happenings, **performance art,** dance, and theater. He continues to create experimental collage canvases and to exert a major influence on contemporary artists.

REFERENCES:

Mary Lynn Kotz, *Rauschenberg, Art and Life* (New York: Abrams, 1990);

Calvin Tomkins, *Off the Wall: Robert Rauschenberg and the Art World of Our Time* (Garden City, N.Y.: Doubleday, 1980).

– C.S.

READER'S DIGEST CONDENSED BOOKS

Since 1950 the *Reader's Digest,* the magazine with the largest circulation in the world, has offered thousands of books in abridged form through anthologies available through the *Reader's Digest* Condensed Books Club. Though critics see such condensations as watered-down versions of the real thing, the abridgments have often increased sales of the original books and have placed books in the hands of people who otherwise are not frequent readers.

Established in 1922, the *Reader's Digest* began publishing condensations of magazine articles — a practice the magazine extended to books twelve years later. Though both the magazine and the club cover fiction and nonfiction, the magazine focuses mainly on nonfiction while the club deals mostly with novels, from major authors to the fairly obscure. Also, the book club offers books not previously condensed by the magazine. From the beginning, each anthology volume, averaging between five hundred and six hundred pages, included four or five condensed books in large type with color illustrations and attractive binding. The first volume was sent to 183,000 subscribers, a number that more than doubled within the first year and rose to 2.5 million within four years. Both the *Reader's Digest* and the club translated their publications for foreign sales in the millions. Also successful were club series, such as Best Loved Books for Young People (1966) in fourteen volumes and Great Biographies (1970) in twelve volumes. The *Reader's Digest* condensed version of the Bible, published separately in 1982, was more controversial.

REFERENCES:

John Heidenry, *Theirs Was the Kingdom: Lila and DeWitt Wallace and the Story of the* Reader's Digest (New York: Norton, 1993);

James Playsted Wood, *Of Lasting Interest: The Story of the Reader's Digest* (Garden City, N.Y.: Doubleday, 1958).

– D.H.-F.

ROBERT REDFORD

Robert Redford (1937–), a popular romantic leading man of the 1970s, became a respected director and environmental activist.

Redford made his Broadway debut in *Tall Story* (1959) and later played the young husband in the Broadway production of *Barefoot in the Park* (1965). During the early years of his career he also appeared in episodes of television shows such as *Twilight Zone, The Untouchables, Alfred Hitchcock Presents,* and *Playhouse 90.*

Redford made his first film appearance in *War Hunt* (1962). He had parts in four other movies, including the film version of *Barefoot in the Park,* before becoming a star with *Butch Cassidy and the Sundance Kid* (1969), in which he played the Sundance Kid opposite **Paul Newman**'s Butch Cassidy. The two actors teamed up again, with equal success, in *The Sting* (1973). Redford continued as a bankable star in popular movies such as *The Candidate* (1972), *The Way We Were* (1973), *All the President's Men* (1976), and *Out of Africa* (1985). His first directorial effort, *Ordinary*

People (1980), earned him an Academy Award (Oscar) for best director, and the film won an Oscar for best picture.

Redford has been an environmental activist since 1970, when he formed a group that blocked the building of an eight-lane highway through a canyon near his Utah ranch, and he has sometimes provoked controversy with his campaign to develop solar energy as an alternative to nuclear-power plants. During the late 1980s he scaled back his acting commitments to devote more time to projects such as his Sundance Institute for independent filmmakers, which has held workshops for directors and screenwriters every summer since 1981 at his Sundance Ski Resort in Utah. In 1992 commercial success as an actor in *Sneakers* and as director of *A River Runs Through It* returned Redford to prominence in Hollywood.

REFERENCES:

David Downing, *Robert Redford* (New York: St. Martin's Press, 1982);

James Spada, *The Films of Robert Redford* (Seacaucus, N.J.: Citadel, 1977).

– I.R.H.

REGGAE

Reggae, the popular music of black Jamaica, has its antecedents in a variety of West Indian styles as well as rock music. It became popular in America beginning in the early 1970s through the international success of Bob Marley and the Wailers.

With its repeated musical phrases, electric instruments and drums, and loose vocal style, reggae shares many traits with the **calypso** and other kinds of West Indian music along with rock and rhythm and blues. Heavy bass lines and syncopation are also characteristics of reggae, which is sometimes chanted rather than sung. Early lyrics deal with protest and rebellion and feature flexible, sophisticated metrical patterns. The music emerged as a distinct type in the late 1960s with 1969 hits such as Jimmy Cliff's "Wonderful World, Beautiful People" and Marley's "Duppy Conqueror" and "No Woman, No Cry." Due to Marley's impact, reggae was successfully assimilated into American popular music in the 1970s; one of his more commercial hits was "I Shot the Sheriff" (1973). Since the 1970s reggae has enjoyed a wide following in the United States and Europe, particularly in the United Kingdom. Important reggae artists of the 1980s and early 1990s include Marley's son Ziggy Marley and the British group UB40, which had a popular success in America with Neil Diamond's "Red Red Wine" in 1983.

REFERENCES:

Stephen Davis, *Bob Marley,* revised edition (Rochester, Vt.: Schenkman, 1985);

Davis, *Reggae Bloodlines: In Search of the Music and Culture of Jamaica,* revised edition (Garden City, N.Y.: Doubleday / Anchor, 1977).

– L.D.S.

STEVE REICH

Like **John Adams** and **Philip Glass,** composer Steve Reich (1936–) is best known for his work in **minimalist** music. In 1966 he founded his own performing group, for which he has written most of his work.

In the 1960s Reich began composing **electronic music** such as *Come Out* (1966), which uses tape loops, and minimalist pieces with traditional instrumentation such as *Piano Phase* (1967), for two pianos. In these pieces and others he experimented with what he called *phasing:* two musicians begin by playing identical rhythmic patterns, then one speeds up, gradually shifting "out of phase" with the other. In the early 1970s he studied Asian and African percussion instruments and playing techniques, resulting in his best-known piece, *Drumming* (1971). The work, written for bongos, marimbas, glockenspiels, and vocalists, features repeated motifs and variations. Since the 1970s Reich has built his compositions around such patterns and changes in rhythm, melody, and harmony. In collaboration with his wife, Beryl Korot, he wrote and produced a video opera, *The Cave* (1993), which traces the history of Judaism and Islam through a **mixed-media** approach.

REFERENCES:

Wim Mertens, *American Minimal Music: LaMonte Young, Terry Riley, Steve Reich, Philip Glass,* translated by J. Hautekiet (London: Kahn & Averill / New York: Broude, 1983);

Steve Reich, *Writings about Music* (Halifax: Press of the Nova Scotia College of Art and Design / New York: New York University Press, 1974).

– L.D.S.

ANNE RICE

Anne Rice (1941–) redefined the vampire in her first novel, *Interview With the Vampire* (1976), capturing the imaginations of an audience far broader than the usual horror-fiction readership.

Rice was not the first writer to create sophisticated, cerebral vampires and develop sympathy for them by allowing the reader to view events from their perspectives, but her vampires have a depth that ear-

Anne Rice, 1982 (photograph by Cynthia Rice Rodgers)

lier ones lack and are grounded in an extensive mythology of her own creation. Because of their complex psychological makeup, they are tortured, yet aroused, by their need for human blood, and they are given to existential meditations on the nature of evil and their own existence. Rice has since added three novels to her ongoing Vampire Chronicles. In *The Vampire Lestat* (1985), *The Queen of the Damned* (1988), and *The Tale of the Body Thief* (1992), she gave them a history stretching back to ancient Egypt, expanded their powers as well as their moral dilemmas, and used their experiences in contemporary America as vehicles for social commentary.

After the third Vampire Chronicle, Rice redefined another staple character of the horror genre in *The Mummy, or Ramses the Damned* (1989) and traced inherited supernatural powers of witchcraft through generations of a New Orleans family in *The Witching Hour* (1990). A sequel to this novel, *Lasher,* was published in 1993. Rice has also written two historical novels, *The Feast of All Saints* (1979) and *Cry to Heaven*

(1982), and erotica under the pseudonyms A. N. Roquelaure and Anne Rampling.

Many of Rice's novels are set in her native New Orleans. Her Catholic upbringing there and her subsequent loss of faith are at the heart of her fiction, in which stories of vampires, mummies, and witches are finally metaphorical approaches to questions of how to define good and evil when absolute answers no longer seem to exist. She considers herself a mainstream, Southern novelist who happens to write about vampires, and many readrs and reviewers agree. Filming for a movie version of *Interview With the Vampire,* with Tom Cruise as Lestat, began in autumn 1993.

REFERENCES:

Katherine Ramsland, *Prism of the Night: A Biography of Anne Rice* (New York: Dutton, 1991);

Ramsland, *The Vampire Companion: The Official Guide to Anne Rice's The Vampire Chronicles* (New York: Ballantine, 1993).

– K.L.R.

FRANK RICH

During his thirteen-year tenure in the powerful post of *New York Times* drama critic (1980–1993), Frank Rich (1949–) became know as "The Butcher of Broadway."

Rich started out as a film critic for the *New Times* (1973–1975) and the *New York Post* (1975–1977) and worked as a movie and television critic for *Time* (1977–1980) before he began reviewing plays for the *New York Times.* Like film critic John Simon, Rich received almost as much attention for how he conducted himself as a critic as for his actual opinions about specific play productions. Public feuds with producer David Merrick, playwright David Hare, and composer Andrew Lloyd Webber — among others — attracted the attention of the television news show *60 Minutes,* which did a segment on Rich. Yet Rich also championed new playwrights — including David Henry Hwang, **Beth Henley,** William Finn, **Marsha Norman,** and **August Wilson** — and he consistently supported established theater people such as **Sam Shepard, Michael Bennett, David Mamet, Lanford Wilson,** and Athol Fugard.

After he was succeeded as drama critic by David Richards, Rich became a columnist for the Op-Ed page of the *Times,* writing mostly on subjects other than the theater.

REFERENCE:

Frank Rich, "Exit the Critic: After 13 years of drama and farce . . . humming music and settling scores," *New York Times Sunday Magazine,* 13 February 1994, pp. 32–39, 50–53, 62, 66, 79.

– I.R.H.

JEROME ROBBINS

Dancer, choreographer, and director Jerome Robbins (1918–) has worked on a wide range of successful productions, from ballets to **Broadway musicals.** the dances he choreographs are notable for their inclusion of natural movements and gestures.

Born Jerome Rabinowitz, Robbins studied ballet, modern dance, and Asian and Spanish dance before starting his career as a dancer in 1938. Joining Ballet Theater (now **American Ballet Theater**) in 1940, he earned public recognition with his first choreographed ballet, *Fancy Free* (1944). The popularity of this piece about three sailors on shore leave was so great that Robbins and composer **Leonard Bernstein** were asked to adapted it as a Broadway musical, *On the Town* (1944), with writers **Betty Comden and Adolph Green** and director **George Abbott.**

In 1950 Robbins became associate artistic director of the New York City Ballet under **George Balanchine,** appearing as a dancer with that company and choreographing a variety of ballets for them until 1959. In 1958 he formed his own company, Ballets USA, which disbanded in 1961. He returned to the New York City Ballet in 1969 as balletmaster, a position he held until he retired in 1989. Among his best-known ballets are *Afternoon of a Faun* (1953), *Dances at a Gathering* (1969), *Afternoon of a Faun* (1971), *The Concert* (1971), and *Interplay* (1972). All of his works are based on the classic ballet but supplemented with movements drawn from other dance traditions. His works display theatrical mastery and are often humorous.

These qualities also appear in Robbins's work in musical theater. He won an Antoinette Perry (Tony) Award for his choreography in his first musical, *High Button Shoes* (1947). He choreographed the **Rodgers and Hammerstein** musical *The King and I* (1951), which includes a ballet sequence, "The Small House of Uncle Thomas." With Abbott he directed *The Pajama Game* (1954), and he directed and choreographed *Peter Pan,* starring Mary Martin — both on stage (1954) and on television (1955, 1956, 1960).

Robbins's biggest musical success came with *West Side Story,* which he choreographed with Peter Gennaro in 1957. Robbins also directed the play. His seamless combination of dance with the story influenced many later musicals. He also directed and choreographed the 1961 film version of the musical. In addition to an Academy Award for directing, he won the first Academy Award ever given for choreography.

Other successful Robbins musicals include *Gypsy* (1959) and *Fiddler on the Roof* (1964), both of which he directed and choreographed. Running for 3,242 per-

formances, then a record, *Fiddler on the Roof* was one of the most successful musicals in American theater history. After this show, Robbins essentially retired from the Broadway stage until 1990, when he prepared an anthology selection from his previous shows called *Jerome Robbins's Broadway.*

REFERENCE:

Christena L. Schlundt, *Dance in the Musical Theater: Jerome Robbins and His Peers, 1934–1965 — A Guide* (New York & London: Garland, 1989).

– D.M.

GEORGE ROCHBERG

American composer and teacher George Rochberg (1918–) is noted for his evolving musical style, which reflects the most modern musical trends while drawing on music of the past. His many compositions, include orchestral, chamber, vocal, and piano music.

Rochberg began composing seriously in the 1940s. His earliest works are modeled on the music of composers such as Béla Bartók and Igor Stravinsky, while his compositions of the 1950s and early 1960s were influenced by modernist approaches such as **serialism** (especially the twelve-tone method) and **atonality.**

Following his son's death at age twenty in 1964, Rochberg consciously rejected serialism for its inability, in his view, to express emotion, which he claimed was the purpose of music. Instead, he turned to a more Romantic style that nonetheless blends traditional and tonal elements with experiments in avant-garde styles. This combination may be heard in his works including numerous quotations from the music of other composers, such as *Contra Mortem et Tempus* (Against Death and Time, 1965) for flute, clarinet, violin, and piano.

The best known of Rochberg's compositions are his seven string quartets (1952–1979), which reveal his development as a composer. Of particular interest are the second quartet (1961), which includes a soprano singing the poetry of Rainer Maria Rilke, and the seventh (1979), for baritone, set to poetry by Rochberg's son. Another notable piece is his opera, *The Confidence Man,* based on Herman Melville's novel; the opera was premiered by the Santa Fe Opera Company in 1982.

REFERENCES:

Joan DeVee Dixon, *George Rochberg: A Bio-Bibliographic Guide to His Life and Works* (Stuyvesant, N.Y.: Pendragon Press, 1992);

Poster advertising one of Alan Freed's popular rock 'n' roll shows, summer 1957

George Rochberg, *The Aesthetics of Survival: A Composer's View of Twentieth-Century Music,* edited by William Bolcom (Ann Arbor: University of Michigan Press, 1984).

– L.D.S.

ROCK 'N' ROLL

Rock 'n' roll music emerged in the mid 1950s and quickly became the dominant form of popular music in America. Coined by disc jockey Alan Freed from an older rhythm-and-blues term for sex, *rock 'n' roll* refers specifically to dance music of the 1950s and early 1960s aimed at a teenage market. At the time it was also called *pop music.* Though sometimes *rock 'n' roll* is used to refer to all varieties of rock, since the mid 1960s the term *pop* has been used for lighter, more-commercial popular music descended from the earlier rock 'n' roll, while *rock* refers to the more innovative efforts.

In the early 1950s a strict distinction prevailed between white popular music, which consisted mainly of light jazz and songs by well-known performers such as **Frank Sinatra,** and black popular music (then called "race music"), dominated by rhythm and blues. At first

only a handful of disc jockeys, such as Freed, played black music for white teens. Encouraged by the success of black music in the white youth market, recording companies sought white performers who could sing black music. The new rock 'n' roll, first performed mostly by white musicians mainly for white teens, was essentially a watered-down version of black rhythm and blues, with **gospel,** boogie-woogie jazz, and country-music influences as well. Like rhythm and blues, rock 'n' roll had emotional lyrics, which appealed to its teenage audience, and a steady, danceable beat. The simple arrangements, played on electric guitars and drums, backed songs about young love and having a good time.

One of the first rock 'n' roll bands, Bill Haley and the Comets, began as a country-music group and came on the rock 'n' roll scene in 1955 with "Shake, Rattle, and Roll" in the film *The Blackboard Jungle,* which linked the music with adolescent rebellion. In same year they had another hit song, "Rock around the Clock." A remake of a rhythm-and-blues song about sex, "Rock around the Clock" was interpreted by white listeners as referring to dancing. Nevertheless, many adults were alarmed at the supposed immorality of rock 'n' roll, and in some cases they disapproved of

277

white teens listening to "black" music. Such concerns failed to impede the career of **Elvis Presley,** who was turned away from the Grand Ole Opry for playing "nigger music" but went on to become the most popular rock 'n' roll performer of the late 1950s and early 1960s, with songs such as "Heartbreak Hotel" (1955), the first single to sell more than a million copies; "All Shook Up" (1956); and "Jailhouse Rock" (1956). Presley was discovered by Sun Records, which specialized in *rockabilly,* a combination of rhythm and blues with country music.

Between 1955 and 1956, record sales of all sorts of music in the United States rose from $60 million to $331 million, largely on the strength of rock 'n' roll. By 1957 Danny and the Juniors could confidently claim that "Rock and Roll Is Here to Stay." Such a dramatic increase was due to new advances in technology — most significantly 45 rpm and **LP records,** inexpensive phonographs, and transistor radios — as well as to the disposable incomes of teenagers enjoying middle-class postwar prosperity. The popularity of rock 'n' roll also coincided with the gradual easing of racial barriers in the mid 1950s, allowing for **crossovers** between rock 'n' roll and rhythm and blues: soon black artists such as **Chuck Berry,** Chubby Checker, Fats Domino, and Little Richard joined white performers such as Bobby Darin, the Everly Brothers, Buddy Holly, and Jerry Lee Lewis on the charts.

Rock 'n' roll quickly spread to other countries, and by the mid 1960s British groups such as **The Beatles** and **The Rolling Stones** were introducing their musical innovations in America as part of a "British Invasion." By this time rock 'n' roll was beginning to split into pop and rock. Rock musicians experimented with new instrumentations; longer songs, often about serious topics; and studio mixing. Groups from the 1960s — including **The Beach Boys,** The Doors, **The Grateful Dead, Jefferson Airplane,** Simon and Garfunkel, and the influential Velvet Underground — illustrate the growing diversity of rock. In addition to **acid rock** and psychedelic rock, a popular variety during the 1960s was derived from the **folk-music** movement with performers such as **Joan Baez, Bob Dylan, Arlo Guthrie,** and **Peter, Paul & Mary.** Since the early 1970s the rock landscape has become even more diverse, with pop, soul and funk music, and rap as well as **heavy-metal, punk,** and **New Wave rock,** each claiming a portion of the rock audience, which includes adults who grew up with rock 'n' roll.

REFERENCES:

Philip H. Ennis, *The Seventh Stream: The Emergence of Rocknroll in American Popular Music* (Hanover, N.H. & London: Wesleyan University Press / University Press of New England, 1992);

Ed Ward, Geoffrey Stokes, and Ken Tucker, *Rock of Ages: The Rolling Stone History of Rock and Roll* (New York: Summit Books / Rolling Stone Press, 1986).

    – D.H.-F.

RICHARD RODGERS AND OSCAR HAMMERSTEIN II

With *Oklahoma!* (1943), their first collaboration, composer Richard Rodgers (1902–1979) and librettist and lyricist Oscar Hammerstein II (1895–1960) popularized the "integrated" musical — in which songs and dances advanced the story — that would break with the light operetta plots, scantily clad chorus girls, and musical comedies of urban society life of the past. Many of their shows were phenomenally successful, influencing **Broadway musicals** from the 1940s to the 1960s, and provided the basis for equally popular movies.

Rodgers and Hammerstein began their careers separately in the 1920s: Rodgers as a composer with writer Lorenz Hart, and Hammerstein with various composers, most notably Jerome Kern. (Their 1927 musical *Show Boat* was a precursor of the integrated Rodgers and Hammerstein formula.) *Oklahoma!* set the pattern for many of the hits that followed: a romance, another romance in a subplot, an inspirational older woman, a hint of tragedy, and a vividly evoked locale. Based on Lynn Riggs's play *Green Grow the Lilacs* (1931), *Oklahoma!* centers around the lives of farmers and ranchers — an unusual subject for a Broadway musical in 1943. Another innovation was its choreography by Agnes de Mille, which departed from the jazz-dance styles of earlier musicals. Like all of their hit shows, *Oklahoma!* includes many memorable songs, such as "Oh What a Beautiful Morning," "People Will Say We're in Love," and the title song. A successful cast album set a trend for popular recordings of musicals for the next two decades. The show ran in New York for 2,243 performances over nearly six years, a record unbroken until **Lerner and Loewe**'s *My Fair Lady* (1956). For two years *Oklahoma!* ran opposite Rodgers and Hammerstein's next musical, *Carousel.*

Carousel premiered in 1945 and had 890 Broadway performances. Adapting Ferenc Molnár's *Liliom* (1909) to late-nineteenth-century New England, the musical deals with a ne'er-do-well who dies and is able to return to earth to help his good-hearted wife and daughter. Two of its best-known songs are "June Is Bustin' Out All Over" and "You'll Never Walk Alone."

Rodgers and Hammerstein achieved one of their biggest hits with *South Pacific* (1949), which won a

Pulitzer Prize for drama. The book of the musical, written by Hammerstein and Joshua Logan, was based on two stories from **James A. Michener**'s *Tales of the South Pacific* (1947), set during World War II. The 1,925-show run of *South Pacific* was due to songs such as "Some Enchanted Evening" and "I'm Gonna Wash That Man Right out of My Hair" as well as to the unusual casting of an opera singer, Enzio Pinza from the **New York Metropolitan Opera,** and gimmicks such as Mary Martin actually washing her hair on stage.

The King and I (1951), which ran for 1,246 performances, was almost as successful as *South Pacific.* Drawn from Margaret Landon's *Anna and the King of Siam* (1944), the musical featured Yul Brynner as an Asian king who grudgingly learns about life and love from the English schoolmistress he hires to teach his children. Two popular songs from the show are "Getting to Know You" and "Shall We Dance?"

After *Me and Juliet* (1953), *Pipe Dream* (1955), and *Flower Drum Song* (1958) came Rodgers and Hammerstein's last collaboration, *The Sound of Music* (1959). Though some critics found it overly sentimental, the musical enjoyed 1,443 performances and was extremely popular for its depiction of the von Trapp family in the Austrian Alps during World War II and songs such as "My Favorite Things," "Climb Every Mountain," "Do-Re-Mi," and "Edelweiss."

Rodgers worked with other collaborators after Hammerstein's death, including **Stephen Sondheim,** but he never found another so compatible with the expressive new style he employed beginning with *Oklahoma!*

REFERENCES:

Stanley Green, *The Rodgers and Hammerstein Story* (New York: John Day, 1963);

Frederick Nolan, *The Sound of Their Music: The Story of Rodgers and Hammerstein* (New York: Walker, 1978).

                                                                    – I.R.H.

THEODORE ROETHKE

Successor to **Robert Frost** and **Wallace Stevens** in a line of American poets that traces its roots to Ralph Waldo Emerson, Theodore Roethke (1908–1963) wrote powerful poems that have been admired by poets as diverse as **James Dickey** and **Sylvia Plath**.

Roethke's poetry reveals a poet's search for mystical union with the natural world. He saw intensive exploration of his own psychological roots as a means of approaching this unity, through what Carl Jung called the collective unconscious — shared memories

of a prehuman existence locked away in each individual's mind. Focusing not on journey's end but on the process itself, his poetry brought him awards and honors such as a Pulitzer Prize for *The Waking, Poems: 1933–1953* (1953) and National Book Awards for *Words for the Wind* (1957) and *The Far Field* (1964).

Roethke's *Lost Son and Other Poems* (1948), often heralded as a precursor to the **confessional poetry** that emerged in the late 1950s, introduced the symbolic-journey motif that was to characterize all his mature poetry and includes some of his finest poems, such as the sequence called the Greenhouse Poems (his father and uncle had owned a large greenhouse business), "My Papa's Waltz," "Dolor," and the long title poem. The title of Roethke's next book, *Praise to the End!* (1951), is a quotation from the first book of William Wordsworth's *Prelude* and refers to the mystical unity of man and nature that both poets sought and that Roethke sometimes thought he had achieved when he was in the manic stage of the manic-depressive psychosis from which he suffered throughout his life.

Yet Roethke counted himself "among the happy poets," and the joy he found in his work is apparent in *The Waking, Poems: 1933–1953,* which includes the justly acclaimed title poem and the equally powerful "Four for Sir John Davies." Among the poems in *Words for the Wind* is "I Knew a Woman," one of the finest love poems by an American poet. Roethke was still revising his last book, *The Far Field*, when he died of a coronary occlusion in 1963.

REFERENCES:

Allan Seager,*The Glass House: The Life of Theodore Roethke* (New York: McGraw–Hill, 1968);

George Wolff, *Theodore Roethke* (Boston: Twayne, 1981).

                                                                    – K.L.R.

ROLLING STONE

Rolling Stone is among the first and, by a wide margin, the foremost of magazines focusing on the world of contemporary popular music. The magazine is characterized by a brash editorial voice that, especially in its early years, was heavily influenced by **New Journalism.** By the end of the 1960s *Rolling Stone* became a leading voice in rock culture, later broadening its scope to include articles on political and general social topics.

Rolling Stone was founded by Jann S. Wenner, who has been editor in chief since the first issue appeared in November 1967. Disgruntled by anesthetized, often faulty reporting on rock and the culture developing on its fringes, Wenner borrowed $7500 to start a magazine that would reflect the "changes related to **rock and roll.**" The first issue, published by Straight Arrow Press in San Francisco, was a twenty-four-page, black-and-white paper sold for a quarter. In its early years *Rolling Stone* was almost exclusively a rock music review. Although the first issue sold only 6,000 copies from a press-run of 40,000, by 1971 its circulation was 250,000, with most copies sold from newsstands. Describing the magazine in 1973, contributing editor Joe Eszterhas said, "truth and quality were the only standards. . . . *Rolling Stone* broke many of the old rules, flauntingly violated the no-nos." One of the most controversial issues — featuring the nude photos of John Lennon (see **The Beatles**) and **Yoko Ono** that appeared on the cover of their *Two Virgins* album — hit the stands on 23 November 1968.

Rolling Stone later became a slick, full-color magazine, and in 1977 the editorial offices were moved to New York City. After this relocation, the topics featured in the magazine broadened to include national affairs, presidential races, social concerns such as teen suicide and **AIDS**, and other cultural issues. Many well-known writers have contributed to the magazine, including **Truman Capote, Tom Wolfe,** and **Hunter S. Thompson.** In the 1990s *Rolling Stone* has two primary audiences: those interested in American popular culture from the 1960s to the present and rock-music fans ranging from adolescence to middle age. The advertisements, which take up 45 percent of each issue and generated $39 million in 1993, target mainly an age range of eighteen to thirty, promoting records, cars, cosmetics, liquor, and cigarettes.

In the early 1990s *Rolling Stone* had a circulation of more than a million copies in the United States and ninety-five foreign countries. Initially inspired by what the editors have called the "Cosmic Giggle," *Rolling Stone* became after a quarter of a century a mainstay of the rock-culture establishment.

REFERENCES:

Jann S. Wenner and others, "The ROLLING STONE Reader" (New York: Warner, 1974);

Sandra Wenner, *"Rolling Stone,"* in *American Mass Market Magazines,* edited by Alan Nourie and Barbara Nourie (New York: Greenwood Press, 1990), pp. 442–444.

                                                                    –J.E.F.

THE ROLLING STONES

Although never as popular as their English contemporaries, **the Beatles**, the Rolling Stones epitomized the blues-charged music and radical lifestyle that became associated with **rock 'n' roll** during the late 1960s and early 1970s.

The original group — Mick Jagger, lead vocalist; Keith Richards and Brian Jones, guitars; Bill Wyman, bass guitar; Charlie Watts, drums — formed in 1962 in London and signed their first recording contract with Decca Records in 1963. Taking their name from a blues song by Muddy Waters, the Rolling Stones recorded their first **LP record,** *The Rolling Stones,* in 1964. A collection of their versions of obscure rhythm-and-blues songs, the album underscored the differences between the group and the Beatles; whereas the Beatles were clean cut and melodic, the Stones were loud and raunchy.

Their first major success was in 1965 when two singles from the *Out of Our Heads* album, "(I Can't Get No) Satisfaction" and "Get Off My Cloud" reached number one on the **Top 40** chart in the United States. The group had a total of twelve top-ten singles during the 1960s. Their albums *Aftermath* (1966), *Between the Buttons* (1967), and *Beggars Banquet* (1968) are regarded as among the best of the decade.

In 1969 Brian Jones left the band and died in a drowning incident a few days later. He was replaced by Mick Taylor. The appearance by the Rolling Stones at the free concert at Altamont Speedway in California during the same year ended in violence as a fan was murdered by a Hell's Angels member who had been hired as a security guard. The concert was documented in the acclaimed film *Gimme Shelter* (1970). The four albums they recorded next — *Let It Bleed* (1970), *Get Your Ya-Yas Out* (1970), *Sticky Fingers* (1971), and *Exile on Main Street* (1972) — are widely believed to be their finest work.

In 1975 Ron Wood replaced Mick Taylor on guitar. After several lackluster albums, the group recorded *Some Girls* (1978), which yielded a number one single, *Miss You.* Their popularity revived, the group continued to work and tour during the late 1970s, 1980s, and 1990s. Their 1993 album, *Steel Wheels,* was the focus of a very successful United States concert tour. At tour's end, bassist Bill Wyman retired. In between albums and tours by the Rolling Stones, the current members have solo careers.

REFERENCES:

Stanley Booth, *Dance with the Devil: The Rolling Stones and Their Times* (New York: Random House, 1984);

Robert Greenfield, *Stones Touring Party* (London: Michael Joseph, 1974);

Philip Norman, *The Stones* (London: Elm Tree Books, 1984).

                                                                    –J.W.H.

ROMANCE FICTION

Popular with female readers since its origins in the eighteenth century, romance fiction became a major moneymaker for publishers on both sides of the Atlantic after World War II. Although these works are seldom reviewed by serious literary critics, two of the five best-selling authors in the world during the 1980s were romance writers: American Janet Dailey and Englishwoman Barbara Cartland. In 1991 about 40 percent of all mass-market paperbacks sold in the United States were romance novels. The American market has been dominated by British writers such as Cartland, Victoria Holt, and Georgette Heyer, but in the 1970s American writers began to claim a larger share.

Publishers often divide romance fiction into three categories (which overlap in many cases): contemporary romance, historical romance, and Gothic romance. All share a single focus: a love relationship between a man and a woman.

Contemporary romances and historical romances differ mainly in time period and are part of a tradition of "seduction fiction" that goes back to the eighteenth-century. In these romances a young woman who successfully defends her virtue is rewarded with marriage. Until the 1970s romance heroines who engaged in sex outside marriage were almost always punished for their defiance of conventional morality. Contemporary-romance writers such as Dailey have changed with the times, adding more sex to their fiction in the 1980s. In the 1990s the biggest trend among American romance-fiction writers, including LaVyrle Spencer, Sondra Sanford, and Constance O'Day-Flannery, is the treatment of contemporary issues such as alcoholism, wife abuse, **AIDS**, and incest within the traditional happy-ending romance formula.

Some historical romances — including those by well-known British historical-romance writers Cartland, Heyer, Dorothy Eden, and Mary Stewart, and Americans Kathleen Winsor and Anya Seton — demonstrate their authors' considerable knowledge of history. In other historical romances, derisively dubbed "costume dramas," modern characters wearing powdered wigs express contemporary ideas in dialogue filled with words such as "thee," "thou," and "forsooth."

From the early 1960s through most of the 1980s the most popular romance fiction in the United States and Britain was the Gothic romance, which still commands a large share of the market. The Gothic trend probably began with the extremely popular *Mistress of Mellyn* (1960) by Victoria Holt (one of several pen names used by British novelist Eleanor Alice Hibbert) and American writer Phyllis Whitney's *Thunder*

Heights (1960), which became a **paperback** best-seller after it was reprinted in 1963. Modern Gothics may be set either in the present (like Whitney's) or the past (like Holt's).

Like the tale of seduction, the Gothic tradition dates back to eighteenth-century England (see **Gothic fiction**), but most modern Gothic romances have only superficial ties to the eighteenth century and have their roots no further back than Daphne du Maurier's best-selling novel *Rebecca* (1938). In the typical modern Gothic romance a young, unattached woman (often an orphan) is placed in an isolated household where she faces hostility and a terrifying mystery — which she eventually manages to resolve, while winning the love of the master of the household. Though much romance fiction continues to be circumspect and traditional on the subject of sex, American publishers began to publish "erotic Gothics," or "bodice rippers," in the 1970s. The success of Kathleen Woodiwiss's *The Flame and the Flower* (1972) and Rosemary Rogers's *Sweet Savage Love* (1974), both of which include long erotic descriptions of sexual encounters, sparked a revolution in romance publishing.

Many popular romances, including Dailey's, are published as paperback originals. The leaders in this field have been Harlequin Books of Toronto, founded in 1949, and the Silhouette Romance series, founded in 1980 by American publisher Simon and Schuster as an imprint in its Pocket Books division. (After a few years of intense competition Harlequin and Silhouette merged in 1984.) Harlequin romances, with 120,000 retail outlets in the United States, had sales of $167.5 million in this country during 1991. Other American paperback publishers, including Ace, Dell, Berkley, and Bantam, also have romance series. All these books are aggressively marketed with expensive advertising campaigns backed by extensive research. There are subseries aimed at different segments of the women's market, and publishers provide their series writers with "formulas" based on their research findings.

REFERENCES:

Lesley Henderson, ed., *Twentieth-Century Romance and Historical Writers,* introduction by Kay Mussell, second edition (Chicago & New York: St. James Press, 1990);

Kay Mussell, *Women's Gothic and Romance Fiction: A Reference Guide* (Westport, Conn.: Greenwood Press, 1981).

– K.L.R.

NED ROREM

Also highly regarded for his candid, elegant published diaries, composer Ned Rorem (1923–) is best known for his many art songs, widely believed to be among the finest written in America since World War II.

Rorem began composing in the 1940s. During the period from 1949 to 1958, he lived in France and, for two years, in Morocco. His experience with other languages decisively shaped his philosophy of music, convincing him that all music must sing. Unlike the experiments of many of his contemporaries, Rorem's compositions — especially his operas, songs, and choral works — evince a natural lyricism and flow. He received a Pulitzer Prize for his 1976 orchestral piece *Air Music*.

Rorem's first published diaries, *The Paris Diary of Ned Rorem* (1966) and *The New York Diary* (1967) were sensational for their honesty about his homosexuality and the character flaws of French and American cultural figures. Since the 1960s Rorem has published a succession of later diaries, along with essays on music.

REFERENCE:
Arlys L. McDonald, *Ned Rorem: A Bio-Bibliography* (New York: Greenwood, 1989).

– L.D.S.

CHARLES ROSEN

Charles Rosen (1927–) is an accomplished American pianist and music scholar whose 1971 book, *The Classical Style: Haydn, Mozart, Beethoven,* earned him a National Book Award.

Rosen began piano lessons at age four and studied at the Juilliard School of Music from seven to eleven. He began his career as a concert pianist in 1951, the year he received a Ph.D. in French literature. As a pianist, he has received much acclaim for his performances of the standard repertoire from the Baroque period to the classical — particularly the works of Johann Sebastian Bach — as well as for his interpretations of the music of modern composers such as Arnold Schoenberg, Anton Webern, Pierre Boulez, and **Elliott Carter.** He performed in the premiere of Carter's *Double Concerto* for piano, harpsichord, and orchestra (1961). In addition to *The Classical Style,* Rosen has also written *Arnold Schoenberg* (1975) and *Sonata Forms* (1982), both highly praised.

– L.D.S.

HAROLD ROSENBERG

As a leading spokesman for the **Abstract Expressionist** movement, art critic Harold Rosenberg (1906–) was instrumental in shaping public opinion concerning twentieth-century art. Known for his eloquent commentary in

such journals as *Art Front* and *ARTnews,* Rosenberg is perhaps most important for his 1952 *ARTnews* article "The American Action Painters," the title of which provided the name for a branch of abstract expressionism.

According to Rosenberg, action painting turned the canvas into an "arena in which to act." Rather than reproduce premeditated objects — or even abstract emotional ideas that were already conceived — the action painter would use spontaneous gesture, coloring the canvas with paint according to the artistic needs of the moment. The painting became an autographic record of an "event" of expressive energy in a sort of dialogue with the canvas, rather than the success or failure to render a preconceived "picture." Naturally, the Abstract Expressionist **Jackson Pollock** fit Rosenberg's description of the action painter almost exactly, with his method of spilling paint onto a canvas tacked to the floor, using wide, flowing gestures of the arm. Rosenberg also championed **Willem de Kooning** for the spontaneous nature of his painting style, deeming him the leader of the abstract style and writing an important biography of him in 1974.

Like art critic **Clement Greenberg,** Rosenberg believed that art should be divested of both social concerns and representational subject matter, remaining autonomous as a form of purely artistic expression. Whereas Greenberg felt that the goal of abstract art was to reduce art to its basic formal elements in order to express more perfectly the relations of form, line and color, Rosenberg saw abstraction as a way to avoid hindering the expressive spontaneity of the gesture with the need to represent images. For Rosenberg, the manipulation of the formal elements was secondary to the event of the actual painting — or "acting"—process and the revelatory nature of the result.

REFERENCES:
Harold Rosenberg, "The American Action Painters," *ARTnews,* 60 (December 1952): 22–23+;
Rosenberg, *Discovering the Present: Three Decades in Art, Culture, and Politics* (Chicago: University of Chicago Press, 1973);
Rosenberg, *The Tradition of the New* (New York: Horizon Press, 1959).

–J.M.H.

JULIUS AND ETHEL ROSENBERG

Between summer 1950 and 18 June 1953, Julius and Ethel Rosenberg, along with a cast of supporting players, were the chief villains in a real-life drama of international espionage and intrigue. At the height of national fears of communist subversion and the destructive power of new types of atomic weapons, the Rosenbergs were

Diana Ross (center) and the Supremes, Cindy Birdsong and Mary Wilson, in the late 1960s (Motown Record Corporation)

accused of delivering national secrets about U.S. atomic weapons to the enemy.

In June 1950 Ethel Rosenberg's brother, David Greenglass, admitted to FBI agents that he had passed information about Manhattan Project atomic-bomb tests to a known spy. He implicated his sister in the affair, and the FBI found evidence that both Ethel and Julius Rosenberg, known to have been members of the Communist Party before World War II, had funneled classified military information to the Soviet Union.

In March and April 1951, the Rosenbergs, who steadfastly proclaimed their innocence, were tried for conspiracy to commit espionage rather than the more serious crime of treason. The jury found them guilty, and Judge Irving Kaufman, proclaiming that their crime was "worse than murder" because it had, in his view, caused the communist aggression in Korea that had claimed fifty thousand lives, sentenced the Rosenbergs to die in the electric chair. Appeals took two years and reached the U.S. Supreme Court. Meanwhile sympathizers who felt

the sentence should be commuted mounted demostrations throughout the world. The sentences stood, as the Rosenbergs reiterated their innocence. They were executed on 18 June 1953 at Sing Sing Prison in Ossining, New York. During the 1950s and afterward the case became a cause célèbre for American artists, who typically maintained that it was a conspicuous miscarriage of justice.

REFERENCES:

Alvin H. Goldstein, *The Unquiet Death of Ethel and Julius Rosenberg* (New York: Hill, 1975);

Joseph F. Sharlitt, *Fatal Error: The Miscarriage of Justice That Sealed the Rosenbergs' Fate* (New York: Scribners, 1989).

– R.L.

DIANA ROSS AND THE SUPREMES

Diana Ross and the Supremes were the most popular of the performers associated with the **Motown** record label during the 1960s and the most successful female singing group in the history of popular music.

The Supremes began in 1959 when Diana Ross, Barbara Martin, Cindy Wilson, and Florence Ballard, formed a quartet they called the Primettes. Berry Gordy, Jr., signed them to his Tamla Motown record label in 1960 and used them mainly as backup singers. Martin left the group in 1961 shortly after they changed their name to the Supremes.

In 1964 the Supremes began to record as a trio, with Ross singing lead vocals. They had eleven number-one hits between 1964 and 1969, including "Where Did Our Love Go?," "Stop! In The Name Of Love," "You Can't Hurry Love," "Love Child," and "Someday We'll Be Together." Gordy renamed the group Diana Ross and the Supremes in 1966. Ballard left the Supremes in 1967 and was replaced by Cindy Birdsong.

In 1969 Ross began a solo career, marketed by Gordy as a black **Barbra Streisand.** During the 1970s she played Billie Holiday in the feature film *Lady Sings the Blues* (1970) and had roles in the movies *Mahogany* (1975) and *The Wiz* (1978). Some of her other credits include the Broadway show *An Evening with Diana Ross* (1976) and the **ABC** television production *Out of Darkness* (1994).

The Supremes continued to record with Jean Terrell (1969–1972) and then Scherrie Payne (1972–1976) replacing Ross as lead singer, but the post-Ross Supremes had only minor chart success. The group officially disbanded in 1976.

Ross had eleven top-ten hits during the 1970s and early 1980s. Her last number-one hit was *Endless Love* (1981), a duet with Lionel Richie.

REFERENCE:
Geoff Brown, *Diana Ross* (New York: St. Martin's Press, 1981).
–J.W.H.

MSTISLAV ROSTROPOVICH

Mstislav Rostropovich (1927–) is the most renowned cellist of his generation. He is also well-known as a conductor and as an outspoken critic of the former Soviet regime.

Born in Baku, Azerbaijan, Rostropovich studied at the Moscow Conservatory (1937–1948), making his debut as a cellist in 1942. His friends included Russian composers Dmitry Shostakovich and Sergey Prokofiev, whose *Sinfonia Concertante* for cello and orchestra (1952) was written specifically for Rostropovich. Revered for his impeccable playing technique and full-bodied tone, Rostropovich has commissioned and pre-

miered several scores by composers such as Benjamin Britten and **Lukas Foss.** One of the first Soviet artists to appear in America, Rostropovich first performed in the United States in 1956.

Rostropovich has often served as accompanist for his wife, Russian soprano Galina Vishnevskaya, once a star of the Bolshoi Opera in Moscow. The couple spoke out in support of dissenters such as writer Aleksandr Solzhenitsyn and scientist Andrey Sakharov during the late 1960s and early 1970s. As a result the Soviet government imposed a three-year travel ban on the Rostropoviches. They left the U.S.S.R. in 1974 and were stripped of their citizenship in 1978. It was restored in 1990.

From 1977 to 1994 Rostropovich was principal conductor and music director of the National Symphony Orchestra in Washington, D.C. The recordings the orchestra made under his guidance introduced it to the international spotlight. Also active as a cellist, Rostropovich has promoted modernist Russian music, much of it unperformed during the Soviet years.
–L.D.S.

PHILIP ROTH

Philip Roth (1933–) is one of the most popular and influential postwar authors of Jewish-American fiction, along with **Saul Bellow**, **Bernard Malamud**, and **Isaac Bashevis Singer.** Exploring the nature of Jewish identity with characterstorn between traditional and modern American values, Roth's well-known stories and novels deal frankly with sex. In particular, his 1969 novel *Portnoy's Complaint* became a best-seller notable for its controversial treatment of adolescent masturbation.

Roth's highly praised first book, *Goodbye, Columbus* (1959), includes five stories and the title novella, all of which examine the relationships of modern urban Jews to each other and to American culture. His next two books received less acclaim from critics; many of them have felt that these novels and much of Roth's later work are a waste of his talent. *Letting Go* (1962) is a novel of manners set in a Chicago graduate school, while *When She Was Good* (1967) deals with a Gentile woman from the Midwest. Each is focused, as is much of Roth's fiction, on the conflict between traditional morality and personal freedom. Critical opinion was even more divided on *Portnoy's Complaint*: some saw it as a brilliant comic novel about the challenges of childhood and adulthood, others as anti-Semitic pornography.

Roth went on to write three wildly satirical novels — *Our Gang* (1971), based on the Nixon adminis-

Mark Rothko in front of his *Painting Number 7* (1960)

tration; *The Breast* (1972), a Kafkaesque fantasy; and *The Great American Novel* (1973), on baseball — before returning to a realistic treatment of modern topics with *My Life as a Man* (1974) and *The Professor of Desire* (1977).

The character of Nathan Zuckerman first appears in *My Life as a Man* as a fictional creation of another character, but in Roth's next four semi-autobiographical novels Zuckerman is the protagonist and a writer himself. *The Ghost Writer* (1979), *Zuckerman Unbound* (1981), and *The Anatomy Lesson* (1983) were collected in 1985 as *Zuckerman Bound*, along with an epilogue, "The Prague Orgy." Roth's last Zuckerman novel, *The Counterlife* (1986), enters the realm of **metafiction** in its blurring of the boundaries between art and life, truth and falsehood, as do most of his subsequent books, including his novels *Deception* (1990) and *Operation Shylock: A Confession* (1993). In *The Facts: A Novelist's Autobiography* (1988), for instance, letters from Zuckerman preface and end the book. Roth's account of his father's last days, *Patrimony: A True Story* (1991), is straightforwardly nonfiction.

REFERENCES:

Murray Baumgarten and Barbara Gottfried, *Understanding Philip Roth* (Columbia: University of South Carolina Press, 1990);

Jay L. Halio, *Philip Roth Revisited* (New York: Twayne, 1992).
                                                          – D.H.-F.

MARK ROTHKO

Mark Rothko (1903–1970) is important primarily for his role as a leader in color-field painting, which — along with gestural or "action" painting — is one of the two major branches of **Abstract Expressionism.** He was born in Latvia, and immigrated with his parents to the United States in 1913. He attended Yale University (1921–1923) and began to paint in 1925. Apart from study at the Art Students League in New York, he was largely self-taught.

Rothko emerged in the late 1940s as a member of the **New York School.** Initially influenced by the Surrealists, he experimented with painting shapes that suggest living organisms before achieving his mature style, creating large canvases on which soft-edged horizontal bands of color float one above the other as luminous, weightless clouds of saturated color. Rothko did not intend these works to be decorative. He wanted to cause the viewer to transcend ordinary experience and to get in touch with profound emotional and spiritual states: "I'm not interested in the relationship of color or form to anything else. I'm interested in expressing basic human emotions — tragedy, ecstasy, doom, and so on. The people who weep before my pictures are having the same religious experience I had when I painted them."

Rothko's belief that art could sustain the weight of timeless spiritual convictions, helped to establish the idea in the minds of many critics and historians that Abstract Expressionism could be a moral alternative to the growing materialism of American culture in the 1950s. Rothko's works are widely dispersed in museums throughout the United States and abroad. His best-known project is a series of huge canvases (1966) privately commissioned for the nondenominational chapel attached to Rice University in Houston. Rothko suffered from depression toward the end of his life and committed suicide in 1970.

REFERENCES:

James E. B. Breslin, *Mark Rothko: A Biography* (Chicago: University of Chicago Press, 1993);

Anna Chave, *Mark Rothko: Subjects in Abstraction* (New Haven: Yale University Press, 1989);

Diane Waldman, *Mark Rothko, 1903–1970: A Retrospective* (New York: Abrams, 1978).

– K.B.

EDWARD RUSCHA

Born in Omaha, Nebraska, and raised in Oklahoma, Edward Ruscha (1937–) was trained as an artist at the Chouinard Art Institute (1956–1960) in California and is most often associated with the **Pop Art** movement. His Pop works derived mainly from his observations during frequent road trips between Oklahoma and Los Angeles, depicting what he saw as the American "highway culture" of filling stations, roadside diners, and motels.

Ruscha's creation of artist's books in the early 1960s established him also as an early practitioner of **conceptual art,** as did his mature drawings and paintings, which often feature single words or phrases treated as representational subject matter. Irony, humor, and technical mastery of graphic-design methods characterize most of his artistic work. He has written many books — including *Every Building on the Sunset Strip* (1966) — that capture to the character of southern California, especially Los Angeles.

REFERENCE:

The Works of Edward Ruscha (New York: Hudson Hill Press / San Francisco: San Francisco Museum of Modern Art, 1982).

– K.B.

S

St. Mark's Church-in-the-Bowery

During the mid 1960s St. Mark's Church-in-the-Bowery, an Episcopal church on the Lower East Side of Manhattan, became the central meeting place in New York for the **hippie** counterculture poets who considered themselves successors to the **Beat Generation.** Known as the Lower East Side poets, they included **Ted Berrigan,** Ron Padgett, Anne Waldman, Lewis Warsh, Dick Gallup, and Ed Sanders.

These young poets — as well as holdovers from the Beat movement and some older poets whom **Allen Ginsberg** described as "antique 'delicatessen intellectuals' " of the 1930s and 1940s — began meeting informally at the church in 1963. Three years later part of a federal grant for work with "alienated youth" on the Lower East Side was used to fund the St. Mark's Poetry Project. **Black Mountain** poet Joel Oppenheimer, who ran the project in 1966–1968, established "open" Monday-night readings at which anyone who walked in off the street could have three or four minutes to present his or her work. Wednesday nights were for invited guests, including more-established writers such as Ginsberg and Black Mountain poet **Robert Creeley,** rock musicians Patti Smith and **Yoko Ono,** and avant-garde composers **John Cage** and **Philip Glass.** Although funding for the Poetry Project was cut in the 1980s, it is still in existence and continues to publish a newsletter.

REFERENCE:

Anne Waldman, ed. *Out of This World: An Anthology of the St. Mark's Poetry Project, 1966-1991,* foreword by Allen Ginsberg (New York: Crown, 1991).

– K.L.R.

J. D. Salinger

J. D. Salinger (1919–) is almost as famous for his self-imposed exile as he is for his only published novel, *The Catcher in the Rye* (1951), which many critics consider one of the most important American novels written after World War II. For at least a dozen or so years after the book was published, Salinger was a favorite author of high-school and college students, as well as many adults, who rejected the conformist mentality of American society in the 1950s.

The Catcher in the Rye is narrated by an adolescent prep-school student, Holden Caulfield, who in distinctive and memorable everyday language describes a series of adolescent crises and his rejection of the "phoniness" he detects in socially "successful" schoolmates and most of the adult world he is reluctant to enter. As in most of Salinger's short stories, the overriding theme of the novel is the search for love and value in a world where they are apparently absent. Though tame by contemporary standards, the use of mild profanity and episodes such as Holden's meeting with a prostitute (with whom he does not have sex) resulted in attempts to remove the book from some libraries (see **censorship**).

Salinger collected some of his short stories — many first published in the **New Yorker** and most about the fictional Glass family — in *Nine Stories* (1953), *Franny and Zooey* (1961), and *Raise High the Roofbeam, Carpenters and Seymour: An Introduction* (1963). Although it is said he is still writing, nothing by Salinger has appeared in print since 1965.

After the success of *The Catcher in the Rye,* Salinger was so disturbed by the hordes of curiosity seekers attracted by his sudden fame that he retreated to

Cornish, New Hampshire, where he carefully guards his personal, and literary, privacy. In 1974 he successfully sued to suppress a pirated edition of all his short stories, including some early, previously uncollected, magazine stories. Twelve years later, he was back in court and managed to delay publication of Ian Hamilton's unauthorized Salinger biography by refusing to let Hamilton quote or even paraphrase Salinger letters held in public archives.

REFERENCES:

Warren G. French, *J. D. Salinger, Revisited* (Boston: Twayne, 1988);

Ian Hamilton, *In Search of J. D. Salinger* (New York: Random House, 1988).

– D.H.-F.

SALSA

Often used as a term to describe a variety of Latin and West Indian musical styles, *salsa* is actually a popular musical style of Cuban origin derived from dance music and jazz. In addition to its periodic popularity in the United States, salsa has succeeded in Puerto Rico and in Central and South America.

Salsa emerged in the 1940s and 1950s in New York, brought there by Caribbean immigrants adept at combining jazz with Latin rhythms. The results were first called "Latin jazz"; the term *salsa* did not appear until the 1960s — often in songs such as Pupi Legarreta's "Salsa Nova" (1962) and "Llegó la Salsa" by Federico y su Combo Latino. A salsa composition typically employs singers, trumpets, percussion instruments, and high-pitched instruments such as flutes. Most salsa pieces include a straight melodic section, improvised vocals against a sung refrain, then a concluding *mambo* of different instrumental riffs. Many Latin-American dance forms have been incorporated into salsa, including the bolero, the cha-cha, and the mambo.

REFERENCE:

Vernon Boggs, *Salsiology: Afro-Cuban Music and the Evolution of Salsa in New York City* (New York: Greenwood Press, 1992).

– L.D.S.

SAN FRANCISCO OPERA

With the **New York Metropolitan Opera** and the **Chicago Lyric Opera,** the San Francisco Opera is one of the "Big Three" American opera companies. Many singers have made their debuts with the San Francisco

Opera, and it has featured opera stars such as Placido Domingo, **Luciano Pavarotti, Beverly Sills,** and Joan Sutherland.

The company was established in 1923 by Gaetano Merola, an Italian conductor and impresario who served as general manager for thirty years. His successors have included Kurt Herbert Adler (1953–1982), Terence McEwen (1982–1988), and Lofti Mansouri (1988–). Its formal season is brief, September and October of each year, mainly because many of its singers are also under contract to the New York Metropolitan Opera, and its musicians are from the San Francisco Symphony Orchestra. The shortage of musicians was a major reason for the company's concentration during its early years on traditional operas that could be presented with a minimum of rehearsal time. Since the 1960s the San Francisco Opera has expanded its resources, branching out into modern operas and revivals of little-known works. Part of this expansion was possible because of renovations to the company's home, the War Memorial Opera House, which was built in 1934.

REFERENCES:

Arthur Bloomfield, *Fifty Years of San Francisco Opera* (San Francisco: San Francisco Book Company, 1972);

Joan Chatfield-Taylor, *Backstage at the Opera* (San Francisco: Chronicle Books, 1982).

– L.D.S.

SATURDAY NIGHT LIVE

One of the most popular television programs of the 1970s and 1980s, *Saturday Night Live* has featured irreverent, often hilarious portrayals of contemporary American life and launched the careers of several well-known comic actors. Created by producer Lorne Michaels, the series has run at 11:30 on Saturday nights since October 1975. Each week, in addition to the ensemble of regulars, the show features a celebrity guest host who participates in that week's sketches. Guest hosts have included comedian Steve Martin, hockey star Wayne Gretzky, and legislator/civil-rights activist Julian Bond. Also featured each week are some of the best-known performers in popular music.

Blending sharp social satire with zany humor, the show has at times pushed the conventional limits of good taste. The first four seasons of *Saturday Night Live,* which featured the original "Not Ready for Prime Time Players," were the most successful. All talented comedians, the early cast brought to life such popular characters as the Blues Brothers and the Coneheads. Several members of that group — most notably Chevy

Chevy Chase, Jane Curtin, and Gilda Radner in a "Weekend Update" segment of *Saturday Night Live* (photograph © NBC)

Chase, Dan Aykroyd, John Belushi, and Bill Murray — achieved stardom in their own right. Beginning in 1980 regulars came and left with greater frequency, and the show lost much of its topical edge. The series still served as a launching pad, however, for such talented comdians as Eddie Murphy and Dana Carvey.

                                                        – C.D.B.

Gunther Schuller

Gunther Schuller (1925–) has had a brilliant career as a composer, conductor, writer, and teacher. As a composer, he has been influenced primarily by twentieth-century art music and jazz, which he sought to combine in his conception of the Third Stream, a term he coined in the 1950s.

Although this cross-fertilization was already accomplished in American art music before World War II by composers such as **Aaron Copland** and George Gershwin, or in **Duke Ellington**'s "symphonic jazz," Schuller wanted to restrict it largely to improvised forms in which twelve-tone principles as well as ethnic music traditions, such as Japanese or Greek, could be included. Examples from Schuller's work include *Variants* (1961), a ballet written for **George Balanchine** to be performed by jazz quartet and orchestra, and *The Visitation* (1966), an opera based on Franz Kafka's

1925 novel *The Trial.* In other compositions Schuller strives to fuse elements from the visual arts with music, as in his orchestral works *Seven Studies on Themes by Paul Klee* (1959) and *American Triptych* (1965), for which **Jackson Pollock**'s canvases and **Alexander Calder**'s mobiles provided the inspiration. In 1970 Schuller completed a children's opera based on a Grimm fairy tale, *The Fisherman and His Wife,* with a libretto by **John Updike.**

REFERENCES:

Mark C. Gridley, *Jazz Styles: History and Analysis,* fifth edition (Englewood Cliffs, N.J.: Prentice-Hall, 1994);

Gunther Schuller, *Musings: The Musical Worlds of Gunther Schuller* (New York: Oxford University Press, 1986).

                                                        – L.E.P.

Arnold Schwarzenegger

Arnold Schwarzenegger (1947–), whose thick Austrian accent seemed likely to prevent a career in the movies, used sheer ambition and shrewd self-promo-

Arnold Schwarzenegger when he won the 1967 Mr. Universe contest (Arax-Hankey)

tion to turn himself into one of the hottest box-office draws of the 1980s and 1990s. Schwarzenegger gained international fame through bodybuilding. He won the Mr. Universe title five times and the Mr. World competition once. He was featured in a 1976 documentary on bodybuilding, *Pumping Iron,* which alerted producers to his strong screen presence. The first significant turn in his career came in 1982, when his sword-and-sorcery adventure, *Conan the Barbarian,* was a commercial success. He elevated himself to stardom in the role of a relentless cyborg killing machine in *The Terminator* (1984). In the sequel, *Terminator 2: Judgment Day* (1991), he played a good cyborg. In the meantime he played in other action movies and showed his comic ability in the Ivan Reitman films *Twins* (1988) and *Kindergarten Cop* (1990). He combined his comic and action-adventure talents in the parodic *The Last Action Hero* (1993). Schwarzenegger married a niece of **John F. Kennedy,** television newscaster Maria Shriver.

REFERENCE:

Robert Lipsyte, *Arnold Schwarzenegger: Hercules in America* (New York: HarperCollins, 1993).

– I.R.H.

SCIENCE FICTION AND FANTASY

Modern science fiction and fantasy have always been closely linked, though considered distinct by their readers. Using the techniques of realism, these subgenres of fiction typically present worlds that do not exist. Settings are either scientifically plausible (in science fiction) or explained in terms of magic, the supernatural, or the otherworldly (in fantasy). *SF* is the abbreviation for science fiction preferred by those in the field, who usually look down on the term *sci fi.*

Since the 1950s SF and fantasy have gradually become part of the cultural landscape of America. Until the first few years after World War II SF and fantasy appeared mainly in pulp magazines. New digest-sized magazines, such as *The Magazine of Fantasy and Science Fiction* (1949–) and *Galaxy* (1950–1980), eschewed the pulp-magazine formats and formulas and challenged the predominance of established magazines such as *Astounding Science Fiction* (*Analog* since 1960). Other magazines have since emerged, either to disappear quickly or to thrive like *Isaac Asimov's Science Fiction Magazine* (1977–), but since 1945 other factors have lessened American SF and fantasy's dependence on the magazines.

In the late 1940s, magazine stories began to appear in hardcover anthologies, brought out first by presses run by fans and then by mainstream publishers such as Doubleday and Random House. *Astounding Science Fiction* authors such as **Isaac Asimov** and **Robert A. Heinlein** shifted from short stories to novels, and by the 1980s both writers appeared regularly on **bestseller lists,** as have several other SF and fantasy authors — an inconceivable feat in the 1940s.

The relative isolation of the genre carried over into the 1950s. Yet new publishing opportunities presented by the success of **paperbacks** encouraged new writers, many reacting to the **Cold War,** to enter the field. The influence of the Cold War may be seen as well in SF and fantasy films such as *The Day the Earth Stood Still* (1951). Significant authors of this period include Alfred Bester, Fritz Leiber, and Theodore Sturgeon. In the 1950s some writers began to gain attention beyond the confines of SF and fantasy readers: **Ray Bradbury** is the most notable example, and Walter M. Miller, Jr.'s SF novel *A Canticle for Leibowitz* (1959) attracted favorable reviews outside the field. In the 1960s **Kurt Vonnegut, Jr.,** who was identified early in his career as an SF writer, broke out of the ghetto of genre fiction even more dramatically, gaining acceptance as a "literary" author.

Science fiction and fantasy slowly gained mainstream acceptance in the 1950s and 1960s. Heinlein's novel *Stranger in a Strange Land* (1961) enjoyed enormous success, especially on college campuses, and the popularity of J. R. R. Tolkien's four Middle Earth novels (1937, 1954–1955) and Robert E. Howard's Conan books (1950–1954) spawned a fantasy renaissance in the United States that has continued. Sometimes called "dark fantasy" when it employs the supernatural, **horror fiction** has also found a faithful readership. In addition to the paperback revolution, another reason for the growth of science fiction was America's entry into the space race in the late 1950s.

Rod Serling's *The Twilight Zone* (1959–1964) and Gene Roddenberry's **Star Trek** (1966–1969) boldly introduced SF/fantasy to television audiences, and in 1968 **Stanley Kubrick** rejuvenated SF film with *2001: A Space Odyssey.* Since then some of the highest-grossing American films have been science fiction or science fantasy, among them **Steven Spielberg's** *Close Encounters of the Third Kind* (1977), *E.T.: The Extra-Terrestrial* (1982), and *Jurassic Park* (1993), and **George Lucas's** *Star Wars* trilogy (1977–1983).

In the 1960s, some writers began to experiment with techniques associated more with modern literature than the plot-driven narratives common to science fiction. This movement, known as the New Wave, was short-lived but resulted in a combination of style and substance found in most SF and fantasy since, including the SF cyberpunk movement begun in the mid

1980s, which features hard-edged writing about human-machine interactions, usually involving computers. Some of the most notable SF and fantasy writers since the 1960s are Samuel R. Delany, Philip K. Dick, Stephen R. Donaldson, Harlan Ellison, Philip José Farmer, Joe Haldeman, Ursula K. Le Guin, Frederik Pohl, Joanna Russ, Robert Silverberg, and Gene Wolfe. The work of these writers and their predecessors has often been the focus of the academic attention, as manifested in college courses and in scholarly books and journals such as *Extrapolation*.

REFERENCES:

Brian W. Aldiss with David Wingrove, *Trillion Year Spree: The History of Science Fiction* (New York: Atheneum, 1986);

Neil Barron, ed., *Anatomy of Wonder: A Critical Guide to Science Fiction*, third edition (New York: Bowker, 1987);

Barron, ed., *Fantasy Literature: A Reader's Guide* (New York: Garland, 1989).

– D.H.-F.

MARTIN SCORSESE

Martin Scorsese (1942–), among the most-acclaimed filmmakers of his generation, has specialized in searing portraits of lower-middle-class life in his native New York, where he grew up in the Little Italy section of Manhattan.

Scorsese, who studied filmmaking at New York University (B.S., 1964; M.A., 1966), worked in British and American television and served on the faculty of his alma mater (1968–1970). He also worked with several documentary filmmakers and with director **Roger Corman,** who hired him to work on *Boxcar Bertha* (1972).

Mean Streets (1973), Scorsese's critically hailed depiction of Italian-American petty hoodlums, began his association with actor **Robert De Niro,** who has appeared in most of the filmmaker's best work, including *Taxi Driver* (1976), *Raging Bull* (1980), *The King of Comedy* (1983), *Goodfellas* (1990), and *Cape Fear* (1991). Although the public associates Scorsese's name with stories of urban angst and paranoia featuring psychotic, violence-prone men, Scorsese has also worked in a variety of other genres, from the feminist romantic comedy *Alice Doesn't Live Here Anymore* (1975) to the musical *New York, New York* (1977), the documentary *The Last Waltz* (1978), the controversial biblical epic *The Last Temptation of Christ* (1988), and *The Age of Innocence* (1993), based on Edith Wharton's classic American novel of life in New York high society of the 1870s.

REFERENCES:

Lee Lourdeaux, "Martin Scorsese in Little Italy and Greater Manhattan, " in his *Italian and Irish Filmmakers in America* (Philadelphia: Temple University Press, 1990), pp. 217–266;

Martin Scorsese, *Scorsese on Scorsese* (London & Boston: Faber & Faber, 1990).

– I.R.H.

SEMIOTICS

Semiotics is the last active branch of structuralism in America. While structuralism proper analyzes how signs (words, signals, symbols, and so on) relate to each other (see **poststructuralism**), semiotics advances from this basis to analyze the conventions of communication and meaning in literature and culture.

The Swiss linguist Ferdinand de Saussure, the father of structuralism, conceived of what he called semiology, a study of signs and their systems, early in the twentieth century. Present-day semiotics is also foreshadowed in the work of American philosopher C. S. Peirce. Modern semiotics emerged during the 1960s in the work of European theorists such as Roland Barthes, Julia Kristeva, and Umberto Eco, whose literary and cultural criticism explored how a variety of signs — including language, body language, fashion, graphic signs and symbols, and the arts — communicate.

Semiotics has been adopted by many literary theorists and critics in America. Developing the semiotic tenet that sign systems are not simply communicative but evolve their own characteristics, such scholars investigate how signification in literature is often ambiguous, making a definitive reading of a text's "meaning" impossible, even in seemingly "realistic" works. In such claims, as well as in the belief that texts refer not to the outside world but to themselves and other texts (what Kristeva calls *intertextuality*), semiotics at times shades into poststructuralism.

REFERENCES:

Terry Eagleton, *Literary Theory: An Introduction* (Oxford: Blackwell, 1983);

Terence Hawkes, *Structuralism and Semiotics* (Berkeley & Los Angeles: University of California Press, 1977).

– D.H.-F.

MAURICE SENDAK

Maurice Sendak (1928–) attained national prominence as an author/illustrator of enormously popular and critically acclaimed children's picture books. Through their portrayal of threatening situations and

WHERE THE WILD THINGS ARE

STORY AND PICTURES BY MAURICE SENDAK

Cover for Sendak's most popular book, which disproved reviewers' predictions that it would frighten small children

of child protagonists with many of the shortcomings of real children, his stories were instrumental in changing notions of what a children's book should be.

Sendak was already a successful illustrator of picture books by other authors, when he began to illustrate his own stories with *Kenny's Window* (1956), which was followed by *Very Far Away* (1957), *The Sign On Rosie's Door* (1960), and a popular four-volume set of small books, *The Nutshell Library* (1962). Characters from some of these early books have been featured in *Really Rosie, Starring the Nutshell Kids* (1975), an animated television program. A theatrical production of *Really Rosie* opened in Washington, D.C., in 1978.

Sendak's most successful book, *Where the Wild Things Are* (1963), is about a naughty boy named Max who is sent to bed without his supper. Max fantasizes that he travels to a land of horrible monsters and becomes their king, but he becomes homesick and returns to find that his mother has brought supper to his room. Sendak portrayed the Wild Things with truly ferocious aspects — wild eyes and large, pointed fangs and claws — and although many critics praised Sendak's artistry, controversy arose because some thought the book would frighten small children. Sendak defended his work on the grounds that he wanted to address childhood fears honestly.

Readers seem to agree. *Where the Wild Things Are* has sold millions of copies. It won the prestigious Caldecott Medal in 1964, and it is now generally regarded as a modern children's classic. The book's images have become part of a cultural heritage shared by two generations of Americans. There is a version of the book available on videotape, as well as posters and stuffed-toy versions of Max and the monsters. In 1980 the Brussels Opera presented a musical version of *Where the Wild Things Are,* for which Sendak designed the sets and costumes and wrote the libretto.

Sendak's subsequent books — including *In the Night Kitchen* (1970) and *Outside Over There* (1981) — have also garnered critical praise and have a loyal following of children and adults.

REFERENCE:

Selma G. Lanes, *The Art of Maurice Sendak* (New York: Abrams, 1980).

— S.B.

SERIAL MUSIC

Serial music, a significant trend in twentieth-century music, has inspired many leading European and American composers to redefine traditional notions about music. Since it is usually **atonal** and dissonant, an appreciation of serial music often depends upon an understanding of its method: the organization of notes or other musical elements in predetermined series by the composer.

Taking their departure from Arnold Schoenberg's twelve-tone method of the 1920s, which organized the twelve notes in an octave (the chromatic scale) into a pattern, composers such as Anton Webern and Alban Berg introduced variations in such patterns by using fragments of series and manipulated patterns. In the 1940s Olivier Messiaen extended the serial concept to the duration of notes and rests.

The American composer **Milton Babbitt** employed serial means as early as 1947 and subsequently advocated *total serialism,* in which the composition is constructed from a matrix of serialized musical elements, including pitch, duration, volume, and tone color. The composition itself is thus largely predetermined and consists entirely of permutations on the series — the extreme opposite of **aleatory music.** Examples include Pierre Boulez's *Structures* for two pianos (1952), in which all elements are ordered in a single series of twelve numbers, and Karlheinz Stockhausen's *Gruppen* for three orchestras (1957), in which he set up numerical proportions to control the specific features of the composition. Other prominent American composers who have written serial music include **George Rochberg,** Donald Martino, and **Charles Wuorinen.** Igor Stravinsky's last works, including *In Memoriam Dylan Thomas* (1954), the ballet *Agon* (1957), and the cantata *Threni* (1958), are serially constructed.

REFERENCE:

George Perle, *Serial Composition and Atonality: An Introduction to the Music of Schoenberg, Berg, and Webern,* sixth edition (Los Angeles: University of California Press, 1991).

– L.E.P.

RUDOLF AND PETER SERKIN

Father and son Rudolf and Peter Serkin are two of the most acclaimed classical pianists of the twentieth century.

Born in Austria, Rudolf Serkin (1903–1991) studied piano in Vienna and became one of the top pianists in Europe before making his first American appearance with violinist Adolf Busch, his future father-in-law, in 1933. Serkin was a featured soloist with Arturo Toscanini and the **NBC** Symphony Orchestra in 1936. He settled in America in 1939 and resumed his international career after the end of World War II. As a performer, Serkin was renowned for his playing of the Viennese classics, particularly the works of Franz Joseph Haydn, Wolfgang Amadeus Mozart, and Ludwig van Beethoven. A member of the piano faculty at the prestigious Curtis Institute of Music in Philadelphia from 1939, Serkin served as director from 1968 to 1976. In 1950 he also helped to found the annual Marlboro Music Festival in Vermont.

Serkin's son Peter (1947–   ) studied at the Curtis Institute under his father and others (1958–1964) before making his debut as a solo pianist in 1965. He was the pianist in an eclectic chamber ensemble called Tashi from 1973 to 1980. Since 1980 he has had a solo career; he is best known for his performances of contemporary music, as well as many of the classics from his father's repertoire.

– L.D.S.

ROD SERLING

Rod Serling (1924–1975) is perhaps best remembered as the creator and host of *The Twilight Zone,* a weekly fantasy series that ran for five seasons between 1959 and 1964. That series brought an unusually high level of imagination and craft to network television, and is still considered one of the creative high points of television's Golden Age. Serling broke into television in 1951. Two of his teleplays, *Patterns* (1955) and *Requiem for a Heavyweight* (1956), were well received and adapted into movies.

The Twilight Zone debuted on **CBS** in October 1959 to immediate critical and popular success. Serling wrote many of the scripts himself, and became a television star in his own right, introducing and concluding each episode in a style that has been often imitated. The phrase *twilight zone,* Serling's distinctive voice, and the show's four-note theme song are still familiar to television viewers.

Despite his success, Serling was often frustrated by the constraints on his creativity imposed by network executives and sponsors. In 1970 Serling returned to the formula of *The Twilight Zone* with *Rod Serling's Night Gallery,* another fantasy series. He had far less creative control over this series, however, and it rarely reached the level of its predecessor.

REFERENCES:

Joel Engel, *Rod Serling: The Dreams and Nightmares of Life in the Twilight Zone* (Chicago: Contemporary, 1989);

Gordon F. Sander, *Serling: The Rise and Twilight of Television's Last Angry Man* (New York: Dutton, 1992);

Marc Scott Zicree, *The Twilight Zone Companion,* second edition, revised and expanded (New York: Bantam, 1989).

– C.D.B.

The original cast of *Sesame Street* with Muppets and visiting children

SESAME STREET

Sesame Street is one of the best-known children's television programs in history. Seamlessly blending preschool educational concepts with entertainment that even adults can appreciate, the hour-long show features a variety of cartoons, short films, and scenes with the multiethnic residents — children, adults, and Jim Henson's winsome puppets — and celebrity visitors of Sesame Street.

Produced by the Children's Television Workshop, *Sesame Street* became a household word shortly after its 1969 premiere on 180 independent public-television stations. The following year it was broadcast by **PBS** and became the backbone of the fledgling network created to unify local educational stations. Although many praised the show for its subtle encouragement of learning letters, numbers, and social skills, a key factor in its success was the Muppets. Created by Henson in the mid 1950s, Muppets combined puppetry with marionette techniques such as moving arms with strings or rods, allowing for a greater range of activity. Henson brought one of his first Muppets, Kermit the Frog, to *Sesame Street* and added others, including Bert and Ernie, Big Bird, the Cookie Monster, and Oscar

the Grouch. In addition to their work with *Sesame Street,* Henson and collaborator Frank Oz developed other Muppet characters in a series of television shows and films during the 1970s and 1980s.

From the beginning, *Sesame Street* has had its critics, who maintain that the show encourages early addiction to television, decreases attention spans, and promotes unrealistic expectations for school and the outside world. Its supporters have always outweighed its detractors, however, and the show continues to prosper. At the height of its popularity in the 1980s, versions of *Sesame Street* appeared in more than one hundred countries in fourteen languages.

REFERENCE:

Gerald S. Lesser, *Children and Television: Lessons from Sesame Street* (New York: Random House, 1974).

– D.H.-F.

ROGER SESSIONS

Like his contemporary Walter Piston, Roger Sessions (1896–1985) is remembered not only as a composer but also as a teacher who covered nearly every style of modern music. Sessions taught composition from 1935 to 1980, influencing several composers in his promotion of contemporary music.

Sessions began composing in his youth. In 1961 he and **Otto Luening** became codirectors of the Columbia-Princeton Electronic Music Center. Sessions's varied output as a composer — including nine symphonies, many concerti and sonatas, and an opera, *Montezuma* (1964) — reveals his characteristic use of multiple parts and complex **atonality** combined with occasional lyricism. Though his work is respected, performances are rare, due to the demands his compositions make on musicians and audiences. Sessions was awarded a special Pulitzer Prize for music in 1974, and he received a second Pulitzer in 1982 for his *Concerto for Orchestra* (1981).

REFERENCES:

Andrea Olmstead, *Roger Sessions and His Music* (Ann Arbor, Mich.: UMI Research Press, 1985);

Roger Sessions, *Conversations with Roger Sessions* (Boston: Northeastern University Press, 1987).

– L.D.S.

Dr. Seuss

"Probably the best-loved and certainly the best-selling children's book writer of all time" was how Robert Wilson of the *New York Times Book Review* described Theodor Geisel (1904–1991), better known to millions of readers by his pseudonym, Dr. Seuss. His fanciful characters are familiar even to those who have never read one of Dr. Seuss's books.

His first book, *And To Think That I Saw It on Mulberry Street!* (1937), was a celebration of unbridled imagination. Seuss's catchy doggerel verse and frenetic, cartoonlike illustrations constituted a radical departure from traditional children's books of the time. Seuss introduced fanciful creatures of his own devising in *McElligot's Pool* (1947), which won a Caldecott Honor Award in 1948, and he began to coin fantastic nonsense names for his creations in *If I Ran the Zoo* (1950). This combination of imaginary creatures and exaggerated, playful language became characteristic of Seuss's subsequent work.

With *The Cat in the Hat* (1957), Seuss introduced a new kind of primary reader. Using a vocabulary of only 237 words, he created a whimsical, knockabout story as a response to the bland "Dick and Jane" readers employed by educators. The enormous critical and popular success of *The Cat in the Hat* launched Beginner Books, the first publishing company to specialize in easy-to-read books for children. Geisel served as president of the company until his death. Seuss kept experimenting with restricted word lists. *Green Eggs and Ham* (1960) uses only 51 different words. This book has become Dr. Seuss's biggest seller, and according to some record keepers, the best-selling children's book of all time.

Geisel's successful exploitation of the television medium with animated versions of his *How the Grinch Stole Christmas!* (1966), *Horton Hears a Who* (1970), and *The Cat in the Hat* (1971) reinforced the popularity of his books and firmly entrenched the creations of Dr. Seuss in postwar American culture.

REFERENCE:

Ruth K. MacDonald, *Dr. Seuss* (Boston: Twayne, 1988).

– S.B.

Anne Sexton

Anne Sexton (1928–1974) began writing poems in 1956 as therapy after her first suicide attempt. By the time she killed herself in 1974, she had become well known for her revealing examinations of her own mental illness and family relationships.

In 1958 Sexton read in an anthology W. D. Snodgrass's "Heart's Needle," a poem that for her, as well as for **Robert Lowell**, introduced **confessional poetry**. Lowell, whose writing seminar at Boston University she attended in 1959, helped Sexton select the poems for *To Bedlam and Part Way Back* (1960). The book was nominated for a National Book Award, as was her second, *All My Pretty Ones* (1962).

By 1962 — while working on the poems that would be collected in *Live or Die* (1966) — Sexton was developing her own distinctive style. As she explained to her psychiatrist, she took "what my unconscious offers me." Though she reworked these poems later, they lack the formal logic of her earlier work, and Lowell, for one, thought she had gone too far. Winning a Pulitzer Prize for *Live or Die* confirmed her belief in her new method.

Sexton's next book, the sexually explicit *Love Poems* (1969), was her most commercially successful. *Transformations* (1971), seventeen long poems "retelling" fairy tales, sold nearly as well, but there was a decline in the quality of her poems as she neared the end of her career and revised her work less and less.

Though Sexton always had her share of detractors, those who disliked her early poetry tended to be unsympathetic to confessional poetry in general, but critics of her later work have compared it unfavorably to her earlier books. Today she is often considered a lesser poet than her friend **Sylvia Plath** — who, ironically, might never have written confessional poetry had she not read Sexton's poems when the two women studied under Lowell in 1959.

REFERENCES:

Caroline King Barnard Hall, *Anne Sexton* (Boston: Twayne, 1989);

Diane Wood Middlebrook, *Anne Sexton: A Biography* (Boston: Houghton Mifflin, 1991).

– K.L.R.

IRWIN SHAW

During the 1930s and 1940s Irwin Shaw (1913-1984) was recognized as a brilliant short-story writer and praised as the most talented writer of the socially conscious post-Jazz-Age generation. "Main Currents of American Thought," "Eighty-Yard Run," "The Girls in Their Summer Dresses," "Sailor off the Bremen," and "Act of Faith" are classics of the genre.

The Young Lions (1948) was the first major postwar American novel dealing with World War II and signaled an expansion of the scope of Shaw's material. Although he continued to write stories, much of his work for the rest of his life was given over to eleven novels—including *Rich Man, Poor Man* (1970) and *Beggarman, Thief* (1977). These novels were commercial successes but were condemned by critics as pot-

Irwin Shaw (photograph © 1981 Nancy Rica Schiff)

boilers. It was alleged that he had "sold out" to maintain his expensive standard of living in Europe.

At the time of his death Irwin Shaw had lost his once-high position in American letters. Nonetheless his best stories retain their worth.

REFERENCES:

James Giles, *Irwin Shaw* (Boston: Twayne, 1983);

Giles, *Irwin Shaw: A Study of the Short Fiction* (Boston: Twayne, 1991);

Michael Shnayerson, *Irwin Shaw: A Biography* (New York: Putnam, 1989).

– M.J.B.

SAM SHEPARD

An experimental playwright during the 1970s, Sam Shepard (1943–) gradually eased his way into the mainstream during the 1980s without abandoning his oblique, surrealistic vision of a mythic cowboys-and-Indians America portrayed through the turmoil of the dysfunctional family.

Born Samuel Shepard Rogers, Shepard dropped out of junior college after a year to join a traveling repertory-theater group. He arrived in New York in 1963 and found a job as a busboy at the Village Gate jazz club and a forum with the Theatre Genesis acting company, which produced many of his early plays, beginning with two one-acts, *Cowboys* and *The Rock Garden,* at **St. Mark's Church-in-the-Bowery** in 1964.

Between 1966 and 1979 ten of Shepard's Off- and Off-Off-Broadway plays won Obie Awards. The tenth Obie winner, *Buried Child* (1978), also earned him the 1979 Pulitzer Prize for drama and established Shepard's reputation as an important American playwright. In *Buried Child,* which admiring critics described in words such as "epitaph for the American family" and "requiem for America," a family that at first seems ordinary has a dirty secret of incest and murder. At the end of the play the long-dead child, conceived through incest and drowned by its father to cover up his sin, is disinterred from its backyard grave, and its decomposed body is carried onstage.

Shepard has continued to write major stage plays such as *True West* (1982); *Fool for Love* (1983), which won him another Obie; and *A Lie of the Mind* (1985), which earned him a New York Drama Critics Circle Award. He has also achieved prominence as a motion-picture actor, with an Academy Award nomination for his supporting role in *The Right Stuff* (1983), and as a screenwriter, especially for his script of the Wim Wenders film *Paris, Texas* (1984), which won a Golden

Palm Award at the Cannes Film Festival. He also wrote the screenplay for the film version of *Fool for Love* (1985), in which he played the lead role.

REFERENCES:

Ron Mottram, *Inner Landscapes: The Theater of Sam Shepard* (Columbia: University of Missouri Press, 1984);

Elena Ouamano, *Sam Shepard: The Life and Work of an American Dreamer* (New York: St. Martin's Press, 1986).

—I.R.H.

BEVERLY SILLS

Beverly Sills (1929–) was one of the first American opera singers to achieve international acclaim. After **Maria Callas**'s retirement in 1965, Sills became the most famous soprano in America, a position she maintained during the late 1960s and early 1970s.

Born Belle Miriam Silverman in New York, she was a child star on radio under the name "Bubbles," her lifelong nickname, and studied voice under Estelle Liebling from age seven. Sills made her operatic debut in 1947 as Micaela in Georges Bizet's *Carmen* with the Philadelphia Civic Opera. In 1955 she joined the New York City Opera, where she created the title role in Douglas Moore's *The Ballad of Baby Doe* (1956). Her 1966 performance in another of her well-known roles, Cleopatra in George Frideric Handel's *Giulio Cesare,* inaugurated the new theater at Lincoln Center for the New York City Opera and made Sills a star. Hailed for her acting ability as well as her voice, she became famous with the general public from her many television appearances, where her outgoing personality assured her popularity. In 1975 she gave a highly successful debut performance at the **New York Metropolitan Opera** as Pamira in Gioacchino Rossini's *Le siège de Corinthe.*

In 1979 Sills became director of the New York City Opera. She retired from singing the following year, after a farewell tour of the United States and one last performance, in a new role: the title character of **Gian Carlo Menotti**'s *La loca,* which he wrote especially for her. During her directorship of the New York City Opera (1979–1988), Sills promoted high standards of performance and production and revived neglected works. For a time the company seriously challenged the supremacy of the Metropolitan Opera.

REFERENCES:

Winthrop Sargeant, *Divas* (New York: Coward, McCann & Geoghegan, 1973), pp. 77–103;

Beverly Sills, *Bubbles: A Self-Portrait* (Indianapolis: Bobbs-Merrill, 1976);

Sills and Lawrence Linderman, *Beverly: An Autobiography* (Toronto & New York: Bantam, 1987).

—L.D.S.

NEIL SIMON

Beginning in 1961, Neil Simon (1927–) has had one of the longest runs of commercial success on Broadway of any post–World War II American playwright. Always adept at crafting hilarious one-liners, he increased the emotional depth in his plays of the 1980s and 1990s and gained critical recognition as well.

Simon's career began in 1948, when he and his older brother, Danny, began to write material for nightclub comedians and for radio and television performers such as Robert Q. Lewis and Phil Silvers. The brothers also wrote sketches for several theatrical revues. In 1956 Simon joined the writing team for the **Sid Caesar** television program *Your Show of Shows.* (Simon's 1993 play, *Laughter on the Twenty-Third Floor,* is based on his experiences while working for Caesar.)

Simon's first stage play, *Come Blow Your Horn* (1961), deals with two bachelor brothers trying to come to terms with a domineering father and meddlesome mother as well as the conflicting pulls of bachelor-playboy life and married domesticity. Like many of Simon's subsequent works, it is partially autobiographical, based on the time he and his brother moved from home to their first apartment. *Come Blow Your Horn* was a hit, as were *Barefoot in the Park* (1963), chronicling the rocky marital beginnings of newlyweds living in a fifth-floor walk-up apartment in Manhattan, and *The Odd Couple* (1965), which took the roommates-in-conflict theme to the extreme with the unforgettable characters of fussy, neatness-obsessed Felix Unger and slovenly Oscar Madison. During this initial period of stage success, Simon also wrote the books for the musicals *Little Me* (1962), *Sweet Charity* (1966), and *Promises, Promises* (1968). Starting with the film version of *Barefoot in the Park* (1967), Simon has written screen adaptations of nearly all his successful plays, as well as original screen treatments beginning with *After the Fox* (1966).

During the 1970s, *The Prisoner of Second Avenue* (1971), *The Sunshine Boys* (1972), and *California Suite* (1976) had long Broadway runs, but the decade was a difficult time for Simon. His 1977 play, *Chapter Two* draws on the period of recovery following the death of his first wife, Joan Baim, in 1973 and his marriage to actress Marsha Mason later that year. (He and Mason separated in 1983, and in 1986 he married Diana Lander.) For much of the 1970s Simon concentrated on writing films such as *Murder by Death* (1976), *The Goodbye Girl* (1977), and *The Cheap Detective* (1978), as well as screen adaptations of his plays.

In the 1980s Simon's reputation as a dramatist was reinvigorated by a trilogy of plays featuring his alter ego Eugene Morris Jerome. The first, *Brighton Beach Memoirs* (1983), draws on Simon's adolescence during the early years of World War II, while the second, *Biloxi Blues* (1983), for which he won an Antoinette Perry (Tony) Award, is based on his experiences as a New York Jew in basic training in the South. The third, *Broadway Bound* (1987), covers the years in which he and Danny had their first success as writers. Simon also mined personal experience for *Lost in Yonkers* (1990), about two young brothers left temporarily in the care of a termagant grandmother and a mentally retarded aunt. The play won a Tony Award as best play and a Pulitzer Prize. Even when tackling serious themes, Simon is basically an entertainer. He has been one of the most bankable playwrights in post–World War II America.

REFERENCE:

Robert K. Johnson, *Neil Simon* (Boston: Twayne, 1983).

– I.R.H.

PAUL SIMON

Singer and songwriter Paul Simon (1941–) is known for his partnership with Garfunkel (1942–) in Simon and Garfunkel, one of the most important folk-rock groups of the late 1960s, as well as for his successful solo career. His music, initially inspired by **rock 'n' roll** of the 1950s, was increasingly influenced by **world music** after the 1960s.

Simon began writing and performing in high school, where he met Art Garfunkel. They recorded their first song, "Hey Schoolgirl," as Tom and Jerry in 1957. After success eluded them in the early 1960s, they began combining **folk music** and rock in their smooth, harmonized sound with Simon's poetic, often forceful lyrics. Their first hit single, "The Sounds of Silence," was released in December 1965 and quickly reached number one. It was followed by other hits, including "Homeward Bound" (1966), "I Am a Rock" (1966), "Scarborough Fair" (1968), "Cecilia" (1970), and "Bridge over Troubled Water" (1970), their biggest hit. Their music was featured in the soundtrack of the highly successful 1967 film *The Graduate*, which introduced a new hit song, "Mrs. Robinson." By 1968 their fame was worldwide, and in June 1968 their songs held the top three positions on the charts.

Art Garfunkel and Paul Simon in 1966 (photograph by David Redfern)

When the duo split in 1971, Garfunkel pursued an acting career and Simon went solo. His albums, while still based in rock, began to incorporate influences such as **reggae,** Latin–American music, **gospel,** and cajun music. His hits from the 1970s include "Me and Julio Down by the Schoolyard" (1972), "Loves Me Like a Rock" (1973), "Fifty Ways to Leave Your Lover" (1976), and "Slip Slidin' Away" (1977). In 1977 he also had a small but substantial role in **Woody Allen**'s *Annie Hall*.

Simon and Garfunkel reunited in 1981 for a national tour, the highlight of which was a free concert in Central Park in New York that was recorded as a new album. Simon's next major project was his album *Graceland* (1986), which was controversial because he recorded it in South Africa during an unofficial artistic boycott protesting apartheid. The album was a commercial and critical success, particularly because of Simon's collaboration with the African group Ladysmith Black Mambazo. His next album, *Rhythm of the Saints,* was released in 1990, the year Simon and Garfunkel were inducted into the Rock and Roll Hall of Fame.

REFERENCE:
Patrick Humphries, *Paul Simon: Still Crazy after All These Years*
(New York: Doubleday, 1989).

–D.H.-F.

REFERENCES:
Richard W. Ackelson, *Frank Sinatra: A Complete Recording History of Techniques, Songs, Composers, Lyricists, Arrangers, Sessions, And First-Issue Albums, 1939–1984* (Jefferson, N.C.: McFarland, 1992);

E. J. Kahn, *The Voice: The Story of an American Phenomenon* (New York: Harper, 1946).

–J.W.H.

FRANK SINATRA

One of the firt singers to be idolized by teenage girls, Frank Sinatra (1915–   ) got his start singing with big bands before World War II and remained popular for his romantic ballads despite the rise of **rock 'n' roll** in the late 1950s.

Sinatra made his first recordings with Harry James's big band in 1939. He left James for the Tommy Dorsey Band in 1940 and sang on more than eighty of their recordings through 1942. He struck out on his own that year, and recorded forty top-ten hits — including "Dream" (1945), "Nancy (With the Laughing Face)" (1946), and "Day by Day" (1946) — between then and 1954.

Sinatra's popularity led to roles in movies such as *Las Vegas Nights* (1941), *Higher and Higher* (1943), *Miracle of the Bells* (1948), and *On The Town* (1949). After these mainly musical roles, his stature as an actor rose with his performance in *From Here to Eternity*, for which he won an Academy Award for best supporting actor. His other film credits include *The Man with the Golden Arm* (1955), *Guys and Dolls* (1956), and *The Manchurian Candidate* (1962).

In 1954 Sinatra began collaborating with arranger/conductors Nelson Riddle and Gordon Jenkins, producing many of his best recordings. His 1954 album *In the Wee Small Hours of the Morning* is regarded by many critics as his finest album. Other notable recordings of the 1950s include the albums *Songs for Young Lovers* (1954), *Swing Easy* (1954), *Songs for Swinging Lovers* (1956), *Only the Lonely* (1956), and *Come Dance with Me, Come Fly with Me* (1959) and the singles "Young at Heart" (1954), "(Love Is) The Tender Trap" (1955), "I've Got You Under My Skin" (1956), "All the Way" (1957), and "Witchcraft" (1958). In 1961 Sinatra began his own record label, Reprise. This label released albums by Dean Martin, Sammy Davis, Jr., and Bing Crosby, as well as Sinatra's own recordings, including the albums *Sinatra Swings* (1961), *It Might as Well Be Swing* (1964), and *September of My Years* (1965) and the singles "Strangers in the Night" (1966), "Somethin' Stupid" (1967), and his signature song "My Way" (1969).

Sinatra continued to work in the next three decades. The albums *Trilogy* (1980) and *Duets* (1993) were both chart successes. In 1994 he received an honorary Grammy Award for lifetime achievement.

ISAAC BASHEVIS SINGER

One of America's great fiction writers and one of the world's foremost Yiddish authors, Isaac Bashevis Singer (1904–1991) is known for his many stories, novels, and children's books about Jewish life in his native Poland and in America. The most significant of the many awards he received for his writing was the Nobel Prize for Literature in 1978.

Singer published his first story in 1927 and his first novel in 1935 in Poland. He immigrated to America that same year and went to work for the *Jewish Daily Forward* in New York. From the late 1940s until Singer's death more than four decades later this news-

Isaac Bashevis Singer

paper serialized most of his new work, written originally in Yiddish. During the 1950s translations of his books into English and other languages began to attract an ever increasing amount of attention from readers and critics worldwide. Drawing on life in *shtetls* (small Jewish towns in eastern Europe) and Jewish folklore, especially the supernatural, his writings typically deal with conflicts between religion and rationalism, tradition and progressiveness, and passions and obsessions, particularly those of religious faith and of love and sex.

His novel *The Family Moskat* (1950), like his related novels *The Manor* (1967) and *The Estate* (1969), is a realistic epic of Polish Jews over several generations, while *Satan in Goray* (1956), an English translation of his first novel, is set in seventeenth-century Poland and features demonic possession and a false messiah in a *shtetl*. *Enemies, A Love Story* (1972) is Singer's first novel with an American setting; like his other "American" stories, it details the disorientation of immigrants and relates how World War II decimated European Jewish culture. Set in New York, *Enemies* involves a Jewish man who has survived the **Holocaust** only to experience self-inflicted torments in the New World.

One of Singer's most widely read works is his much-anthologized story "Gimpel the Fool" (1953). Translated by **Saul Bellow** for *Partisan Review,* it is the tale of a "wise fool" who is deceived by everyone yet believes them and is rewarded for his faith. Singer wrote more than a hundred stories, which have been gathered in collections such as *The Spinoza of Market Street* (1961) and *Old Love* (1979).

In addition to four volumes of autobiography, much of Singer's later fiction is autobiographical, and some critics consider it repetitive. In the last decades of his career, Singer also wrote more than a dozen highly successful children's books based on folklore; his first, *Zlateh the Goat and Other Stories* (1966), was illustrated by **Maurice Sendak**.

REFERENCES:

Lawrence S. Friedman, *Understanding Isaac Bashevis Singer* (Columbia: University of South Carolina Press, 1988);

Paul Kresh, *Isaac Bashevis Singer: The Magician of West 89th Street — A Biography* (New York: Dial, 1979).

– D.H.-F.

GENE SISKEL AND ROGER EBERT

During the 1980s Roger Ebert (1942–) and Gene Siskel (1946–) became the best-known film critics in America, in large part because of their entertaining

wrangling over the merits of individual movies on their half-hour television program. Their trademark "Two Thumbs Up," awarded to movies they both liked, became a catchphrase nationwide. In 1976 Ebert, film critic for the *Chicago Sun-Times,* and Siskel, the film reviewer for the rival *Chicago Tribune,* were hired by the local educational television station, WTTW, to review each week's new movie releases on a program called *Sneak Previews,* which was syndicated nationally on **PBS.** The portly, droll Ebert and the earnest, balding Siskel contrast as much as personality types as they do in their opinions about films, and the program has a huge following. In 1982 Siskel and Ebert left PBS to star in the syndicated review program *At the Movies,* which became *Siskel and Ebert* in 1986.

– I.R.H.

SITE-SPECIFIC INSTALLATION ART

A broad term in use since the late 1980s, *site-specific installation art* refers to artists' projects created for a particular exhibition space. Considered more experimental than many other areas of international contemporary art, site-specific installations are closely related to the aesthetics of sculpture, as well as the idea-based strategies of **conceptual art.** Typically, site-specific pieces engage the entire space for which they are created, often transforming the original appearance of the site significantly. They are often temporary, existing only for the duration of an exhibition — thus avoiding classification as objects or commodities.

In contemporary practice sites have been both outdoor areas and interior spaces such as warehouses, rooms in private homes, and entire abandoned houses, as well as galleries and museums. Differing from studio-based artists in their working methods, site-specific artists often create their installations on the spot, using brought-in materials. The relationship between the site and the ensuing work of art depends on many variables, including the parameters of a given exhibition (such as the curator's directives), the artist's areas of concern and content, and the degree to which the artist is influenced by the history or ambiance of the site.

Site-specific installations are related to the general category of installation art, and the two terms are often used interchangably, creating some confusion. Installation art is usually less directly determined by the character of the site for which it is destined and uses the exhibition space more as neutral territory. Much installation art can, with adjustments, be moved and reinstalled in different places, but site-specific work is generally rooted to one place and time. Essentially hybrids of many currents in twentieth-century art, installation art and site-specific installations have precedents in **assemblage, environments,** the"sets" for **Happenings, Claes Oldenburg's** *Store* (1961), **earthworks, postminimalist** sculpture, **conceptual art,** Edward Kienholz's room-size tableaux, and **performance art.** American artists involved in installation art and site-specific installation art include Jonathan Borofsky, Ann Hamilton, **David Hammons,** Bruce Nauman, Elizabeth Newman, Dennis Oppenheim, **Hans Haacke,** David Ireland, Joseph Kosuth, Sol LeWitt, Judy Pfaff, Sandy Skoglund, James Turrell, and Bill Viola.

– K.B.

B. F. SKINNER

Psychologist and writer B. F. Skinner (1904–1990) was controversial for his promotion of behaviorism, the theory that all animals (including humans) are entirely conditioned by their environments. At the same time, his belief that behavior could be modified through positive reinforcement has proved extremely influential in psychology, education theory, and other fields.

An aspiring writer in college, Burrhus Frederic Skinner turned instead to science, particularly the study of behavior. His experiments with rats and pigeons during the 1930s and 1940s, in which he taught them how to perform specific tasks for rewards, convinced him that positive conditioning could make people happier. In 1943 he built an "air crib," an enclosed crib in which he raised one of his daughters for two and a half years. When he reported this fact in *Ladies' Home Journal* in 1945, he was attacked for experimenting on his own child (who suffered no ill effects) and for considering humans little better than animals.

Equally controversial was Skinner's 1948 novel *Walden Two,* a utopian application of behaviorist theory to an isolated human society. Though many readers found his critiques of contemporary politics and education valuable, others found fault with his dismissal of free will and human individuality, and some thought him naive for not considering how conditioning could be used negatively. Skinner's refusal to back down from his beliefs is evident from his other major work, *Beyond Freedom and Dignity* (1971), where he argues for social change based on the encouragement of productive behavior and the elimination of destructive responses.

REFERENCES:
Daniel W. Bjork, *B. F. Skinner: A Life* (New York: Basic–HarperCollins, 1993);
B. F. Skinner, *Particulars of My Life* (New York: Knopf, 1976);

Skinner, *The Shaping of a Behaviorist: Part Two of an Autobiography* (New York: Knopf, 1979);
Skinner, *A Matter of Consequences: Part Three of an Autobiography* (New York: New York University Press, 1985).

– D.H.-F.

DAVID SMITH

Often considered the most influential American sculptor of the post–World War II era, David Smith (1906–1965) began his career studying painting at the Art Students League in New York (1927–1932). During the 1930s Smith discovered the welded-metal sculpture of Pablo Picasso and Julio Gonzalez and began to produce his own constructed sculpture. Always socially conscious and sympathetic to the working man, Smith saw in metal the glories and the agonies of modern industry. To him metal symbolized progress and opportunity as well as an impersonal, destructive brutality.

Smith had his first solo exhibition in 1938 at East River Gallery. His early sculpture of the 1930s and 1940s was highly experimental. Influenced by surrealism, he produced open, linear works, described as "drawings in space." He also began incorporating machinery parts in his sculpture. In 1940 Smith decided to leave New York City and settle in a house and studio in Bolton Landing, New York, near Lake George. During the 1950s, after his second divorce left him alone at Bolton Landing, Smith began populating the fields around his home with large sculptures. He worked on several sculpture series in different styles, all intended to be placed outdoors. His best-known series, the *Cubi,* is a group of monolithic totems in geometric form, Consisting of simple cylindrical and cubic shapes, Smith's giant sculptures were applauded by formalists, who saw in them an elimination of subject in favor of an emphasis on pure form. However, Smith's works are never quite as anonymous as they appear. He took special care to polish and abrade the surface of each of his sculptures individually to give each a uniquely personal and fanciful effect.

REFERENCE:
Karen Wilkins, *David Smith* (New York: Abbeville Press, 1984).
– C.S.

STEPHEN SONDHEIM

Stephen Sondheim (1930–) is sometimes described as the thinking person's lyricist and composer for **Broadway musicals** and the most important and influential figure in the field since the 1970s. While his music has its detractors, his sophisticated lyrics have always received high praise. His "Send in the Clowns," from *A Little Night Music* (1973), has become a solo standard.

In 1940 Sondheim and his mother moved from New York to Doylestown, Pennsylvania, where he was taken under the wing of Oscar Hammerstein II during the time that the **Rodgers and Hammerstein** musicals were written. After completing a music major at Williams College in 1950, Sondheim studied composition with **Milton Babbitt** before receiving a break as the lyricist for *West Side Story* (1957), which features songs such as "Maria," "America," "Tonight," and "One Hand, One Heart" set to music by **Leonard Bernstein.** The success of this show led to an assignment to write the lyrics for Jule Styne's *Gypsy* (1959), based on the life of striptease artist Gypsy Rose Lee. A popular song from this musical was "Everything's Coming Up Roses."

Sondheim began writing both the music and the lyrics with the songs for *A Funny Thing Happened on the Way to the Forum* (1962), directed by **George Abbott.** In 1970, after a few unsuccessful musicals, Sondheim entered a successful partnership with producer and director **Harold Prince,** beginning with *Company,* the first of Sondheim's "concept musicals," in which themes such as marriage or revenge are as important as the plot. Sondheim received his first Antoinette Perry (Tony) Awards for this musical. *Follies* (1971) was acclaimed for its use of styles from earlier American musical theater, while *A Little Night Music* (1973), a sex comedy by Hugh Wheeler derived from Ingmar Bergman's 1955 film *Smiles of a Summer Night,* was notable for its exclusive use of 3/4 time or variations on it.

After the critically acclaimed but poorly attended *Pacific Overtures* (1976), Sondheim had one of his greatest successes with *Sweeney Todd* in 1979. Written by Wheeler and Christopher Bond, the nearly operatic musical is about a man's gruesome vengeance on those who had wrongly imprisoned him.

Sondheim's next major success was *Sunday in the Park with George* (1984), which won a Pulitzer Prize for him and writer/director James Lapine. The musical is a fantasy about the life of Georges Seurat and his pointillistic painting *A Sunday Afternoon on the Island of La Grande Jatte* (1886). By the mid 1980s Sondheim's earlier works were often revived on Broadway. His 1987 musical *Into the Woods,* based on classic fairy tales and influenced by the interpretations of Bruno Bettelheim, was also well-received.

REFERENCES:

Joanne Gordon, *Art Isn't Easy: The Theater of Stephen Sondheim,* revised edition (New York: Da Capo, 1992);

Craig Zadan, *Sondheim & Co.,* revised edition (New York: Harper & Row, 1989).

– I.R.H.

SOUL MUSIC

Soul music is African-American popular music that derives from the mingling of **gospel music** and blues. While not greatly different from rhythm and blues, soul music tends to emphasize the vocal aspects of the music, using many techniques of gospel music, including spoken delivery, call-and-response choruses, and shouts. The lyrics, however, are secular, focusing on love, sex, and personal relationships.

What is now called soul music first appeared in the late 1940s and early 1950s with the music of black vocal groups such as The Orioles, The Ravens, and the Five Satins. The success of the Drifters, who made their first recordings on the Atlantic label in 1953, was followed by that of other Atlantic soul artists such as **Ray Charles,** The Coasters, and Clyde McPhatter. Other record labels — including Chess, King, **Motown,** and Stax — began recording and marketing soul artists.

In the 1960s, artists from Atlantic, Motown, and Stax — Smokey Robinson and the Miracles, **Diana Ross and the Supremes,** Stevie Wonder, The Four Tops, The Jackson Five, Marvin Gaye, Wilson Pickett, Otis Redding, Sam and Dave, William Bell, and **Aretha Franklin** — dominated the pop and rhythm-and-blues charts.

By the 1970s, soul music had become less distinctive as it was integrated in mainstream music. The Spinners, Al Green, and the Stylistics continued in the soul tradition, but **funk,** rougher rhythm and blues, and later, **rap,** reduced the popularity and influence of soul music.

REFERENCES:

Michael Haralambos, *Right On: From Blues to Soul in Black America* (New York: Da Capo Press, 1979);

Gerri Hershey, *Nowhere to Run: The Story of Soul Music* (New York: Time Books, 1984).

–L.D.S.

STEVEN SPIELBERG

Gifted with the ability to create fantasy and adventure films that capture the popular imagination with their blend of tried-and-true plots and innovative cinematography, Steven Spielberg (1947–) has had more success at the box office than any other Hollywood director.

Henry Thomas and the title character in Steven Spielberg's *E.T.: The Extra Terrestrial* (Kobal Collection)

Spielberg gained recognition with the television movie *Duel* (1971), about a motorist menaced by a huge truck and its never-seen driver, before moving into feature films with *The Sugarland Express* (1974). He became a major Hollywood director with his next film, *Jaws* (1975), the first blockbuster of the 1970s. After the success of *Jaws*, Spielberg formed his own production company, Amblin' Entertainment, and fostered the careers of other young directors who shared his love for fantasy and adventure. By the mid 1980s Spielberg had directed more top money-making films than any other person in Hollywood history. His film successes included *E.T.: The Extra-Terrestrial* (1982), the biggest moneymaker of all time until it was surpassed by Spielberg's *Jurassic Park* in 1993, and three Indiana Jones films: *Raiders of the Lost Ark* (1981), *Indiana Jones and the Temple of Doom* (1984), and *Indiana Jones and the Last Crusade* (1989). An acknowledged master of visual story-telling and fast-paced montage, Spielberg has nevertheless received limited recognition from critics and his peers in the film industry. His first attempts at making serious films such as *The Color Purple* (1985), based on the novel by **Alice Walker,** and *Empire of the Sun* (1987), based on the novel by J. G. Ballard, were commercially unsuccessful. But *Schindler's List* (1993) was his most critically acclaimed film to date, winning seven Academy Awards, including best picture and best director.

REFERENCE:

Donald R. Mott and Cheryl McAllster Saunders, *Steven Spielberg* (Boston: Twayne, 1986).

– I.R.H.

MICKEY SPILLANE

As a writer of mystery, suspense, and detective novels, Mickey (Frank Morrison) Spillane (1918–) has sold more than 180 million copies of his books in sixteen languages since his first novel was published in 1947. He has also become a celebrity even among people who have never read his books through his appearances in motion pictures and on television, especially a series of popular beer commercials.

Spillane's first novel, *I, the Jury* (1947) was a moderate commercial success, selling several thousand copies, but when Signet published a paperback reprint in 1948, the book's sales skyrocketed, reaching more than two million copies by 1950. Soon Spillane's publishers were billing him as the "world's best-selling author."

The novel introduced Spillane's most popular character: the violent, amoral, and womanizing detective, Mike Hammer. Spillane drew on the tradition of the hardboiled detective, developed by John Carol Daly, Dashiell Hammett, and Raymond Chandler, but Hammer tended to be more violent and less concerned with laws than his predecessors, enforcing his own conception of justice on criminals.

Hammer's vigilantism and violence tended to offend reviewers, though his adventures obviously delighted readers, who quickly turned each new Spillane book into a best-seller. Spillane wrote six more novels by 1952, but after *Kiss Me, Deadly* (1952) he began a nine-year hiatus from novel writing.

He returned to novel writing with *The Deep* (1961), and fans bought copies of the book as soon as they were placed on the shelf. Although Spillane developed new characters, such as secret agent Tiger Mann, Mike Hammer remained his most popular creation. New novels appeared fairly regularly through 1973, after which Spillane's production has been infrequent. A measure of his celebrity is his appearance in a series of television beer commercials.

– S.B.

BRUCE SPRINGSTEEN

Nicknamed "the Boss," singer and songwriter Bruce Springsteen (1949–) has been a major figure in American popular music since the mid 1970s. His music — basic, hard-driving rock — often draws on working-class themes and social protest.

Springsteen began his career in the mid 1960s. He began performing with a backup group, the E-Street Band, in 1973. His first nationally successful album, *Born to Run* (1975), produced a **Top 40** hit with its title song. In the 1980s he became one of the top names in rock with albums such as *The River* (1980), which included the hit single "Hungry Heart," and *Nebraska* (1982). His next album, *Born in the U.S.A.* (1985), sold more than ten million copies and includes seven songs that reached the top ten on the charts, including "Born in the U.S.A.," "I'm on Fire," "Glory Days," and "My Hometown." Springsteen's live shows were particularly popular during the mid 1980s. Although his career stalled after he disbanded the E-Street Band in 1989, he received an Academy Award (Oscar) in 1994 for his song, "The Streets of Philadelphia," from the movie *Philadelphia* (1993).

REFERENCES:

Dave Marsh, *Born to Run: The Bruce Springsteen Story* (Garden City, N.Y.: Dolphin / Doubleday, 1979);

Marsh, *Glory Days: Bruce Springsteen in the 1980s* (New York: Pantheon, 1987).

– D.H.-F.

SYLVESTER STALLONE

Sylvester Stallone (1946–) created era-defining heroes in the 1970s and 1980s in the *Rocky* and *Rambo* movie series. Stallone had been doing bit parts in films for five years when he insisted on playing the title role in his screenplay about a never-was club fighter who gets a chance to challenge the heavyweight champion of the world. The studio took the gamble, and *Rocky* won the best picture Academy Award for 1976 and spawned numbered sequels in 1979, 1982, 1985, and 1990. Stallone played out-of-control Vietnam veteran John Rambo in *First Blood* (1982), *Rambo: First Blood II* (1985) and *Rambo: Part 3* (1988). In those parts Stallone was a model for the muscular, macho action stars that dominated the movies during the 1980s. Although Stallone has played in a wide variety of action films and occasional comedies, his enduring reputation is tied to his two signature roles.

REFERENCE:

Marsha Daly, *Sylvester Stallone: An Illustrated Life* (New York: St. Martin's Press, 1984).

– I.R.H.

STANFORD WRITING PROGRAM

One of the best-known and most successful creative writing workshops, the writing program at Stanford was founded in 1948 by novelist Wallace Stegner, one of the first graduates of the prestigious **Iowa Writers' Workshop**. Joining Stegner on the original Stanford creative-writing faculty were poet Yvor Winters and fiction writer Richard Scowcroft.

Among the fiction writers who have come out of the Stanford program are **Ken Kesey, Larry McMurtry, Raymond Carver,** Ernest J. Gaines, Robert Stone, George V. Higgins, and Tom McGuane. Poets who studied in the program include Donald Justice, Donald Hall, and Philip Levine. Since Stegner's retirement in 1971, the program faculty has included poets **Denise Levertov,** W. S. Di Piero, and Kenneth Fields and fiction writers John L'Heureux, Nancy Packer, and Gilbert Sorrentino.

REFERENCE:

"Wallace Stegner on the Stanford Writing Program," in *American Literary Almanac,* edited by Karen L. Rood (New York & Oxford: Facts on File, 1988), pp. 98–103.

                                                                    – K.L.R.

STAR TREK

Star Trek was one of the first television series to take an adult approach to science fiction, featuring intelligent scripts and well-developed characters. It languished near the bottom of the ratings during its original three-year run on **NBC** (1966–1969) but when *Star Trek* episodes began to run in syndication, it became one of the most popular series of all time. Its avid cult of followers, who call themselves "trekkies" or "trekkers," are a well-organized national group.

The series chronicles the voyages of the U.S.S. *Enterprise,* a starship in the fleet of an interplanetary diplomatic organization. Many episodes mirror the tense global politics of the late 1960s: the crew of the *Enterprise* tries to resolve local conflicts peacefully while also playing its part in a cold war between the peaceful Federation of Planets and the warlike Klingons. The series effectively mixes exotic planets, monsters, and rousing action with social consciousness and the spirit of discovery.

Contributing screenwriters for the series included respected science-fiction writers such as Harlan Ellison and Theodore Sturgeon. *Star Trek* also benefited from its strong ensemble cast, led by William Shatner (as Capt. James T. Kirk), Leonard Nimoy (as First Officer Spock, half-human and half-Vulcan, the series's most popular character), and DeForest Kelley (as "Bones" McCoy, the ship's doctor). In 1979 the first of a series of theatrical films on the continuing adventures of the *Star Trek* characters was released. In 1989 a new series, *Star Trek: The Next Generation,* debuted in syndication. It follows the adventures of a new *Enterprise* crew, with occasional guest appearances from the original cast members. *The Next Generation* has outlasted its predecessor's three-year run and developed a similar following of loyal viewers. A spin-off set on a space station, *Star Trek: Deep Space Nine,* premiered in 1993, and others were planned in 1994.

REFERENCES:

David Gerrold, *The World of Star Trek,* revised edition (New York: Blue Jay, 1984);

William Shatner, *Star Trek Memories* (New York: HarperCollins, 1993).

                                                                    – C.D.B.

JOHN STEINBECK

John Steinbeck (1902–1968) received the Nobel Prize for Literature in 1962, capping a four-decade career as one of America's most important writers. In addition, he was among the most popular American writers.

Steinbeck depicted ordinary people with sympathy and dignity. His readable fiction is generally realistic, although he occasionally uses poetic language and symbolism or allegory. Often critical of commercialism and institutions, his writing is concerned with the struggles of individuals and their relationships. Steinbeck's virtues are inseparable from his faults. Even in his best writing passion lapses into sentimentality; powerful writing is side by side with triteness. Many critics believe that Steinbeck sometimes aimed too high and that the negative elements dominate his later work.

Steinbeck's first postwar novel, *Cannery Row* (1945), is set in his native California and revolves around a likable group of vagabonds and their biologist mentor. The book sold well but critics thought it flawed and were less impressed by its sequel, *Sweet Thursday* (1954), the basis for the **Rodgers and Hammerstein** musical *Pipe Dream* (1955). Nor did his two 1947 novels, *The Pearl* and *The Wayward Bus,* win Steinbeck the same respect as earlier successes such as *Of Mice and Men* (1937) and *The Grapes of Wrath* (1939). His play *Burning Bright* (1950) closed after only thirteen performances. His screenwriting fared better: his films include adaptations of *The Pearl* (1948) and his 1937 novella *The Red Pony* (1949) and the successful *Viva Zapata!* (1952), directed by **Elia Kazan.**

One of Steinbeck's most ambitious and most flawed novels is *East of Eden* (1952). Based allegorically on the biblical story of the first family and filled with sometimes heavyhanded symbolism, it chronicles a California family's downfall. Though it told a good story and enjoyed good sales, it received mixed reviews and failed to reverse Steinbeck's declining literary reputation. At the same time, however, the popular 1954 film version starring **James Dean** enhanced Steinbeck's reputation with the public. His subsequent novels met the same fate as *East of Eden.* In his last years he wrote mostly nonfiction, including *Travels with Charley in Search of America* (1962), about his cross-country trip with his poodle.

REFERENCES:

Jackson J. Benson, *The True Adventures of John Steinbeck, Writer: A Biography* (New York: Viking, 1984);

Warren G. French, *John Steinbeck,* second edition (Boston: Twayne, 1975).

                                                                    – D.H.-F.

Gloria Steinem (center), with Patricia Carbine (left), who became publisher of *Ms.,* and *Washington Post* publisher Katharine Graham (right), who helped to fund the feminist magazine (UPI / Bettmann Newsphoto)

GLORIA STEINEM

As writer, lecturer, and founding editor of *Ms.,* Gloria Steinem (1934–) has been one of the most prominent advocates of **feminism** in America since the 1970s. Though she has often held controversial views, she has been perceived by the media and many Americans as a middle-of-the-road feminist.

Steinem became well-known as a free-lance journalist after she went undercover as a Playboy Bunny in 1963 to report on the opening of the New York City Playboy Club for *Show* magazine. While active in the **civil rights movement,** she was not particularly involved in women's rights issues during most of the 1960s. The turning point came in 1969, when she wrote a sympathetic article on abortion rights that surprised her male colleagues and followed it with an essay promoting feminism. The resulting backlash convinced her that only a magazine published by women could address women's issues adequately. In 1971 Steinem, **Betty Friedan,** and Congresswomen Shirley Chisholm and Bella Abzug formed the National Women's Political Caucus (NWPC) to lobby for feminist issues and encourage women to run for political office.

In 1968 Steinem had helped Clay Felker found *New York* magazine, to which she contributed a monthly column on politics. The partnership enabled her to establish *Ms.,* which was introduced as a thirty-page supplement in the 20 December 1971 issue of *New York.* The first separate issue of *Ms.,* published January 1972, sold its 300,000 print run in eight days. Steinem remained editor in chief until 1987, when the magazine was sold to an Australian media firm. *Ms.* became an independent, reader-supported magazine in 1990.

Steinem's 1983 collection of essays, *Outrageous Acts and Everyday Rebellions,* a **best-seller,** covers twenty years of her writing, including her account of how she became a feminist. She has also written *Marilyn* (1986), a feminist look at the life of **Marilyn Monroe.** *Revolution from Within: A Book of Self-Esteem* (1991) received negative reviews from critics who considered Steinem's remedies for low self-esteem overly simplistic.

REFERENCES:

Marcia Cohen, *The Sisterhood: The True Story of the Women Who Changed the World* (New York: Simon & Schuster, 1988);

Mark Hoff, *Gloria Steinem: The Women's Movement* (Brookfield, Conn.: New Directions / Millbrook Press, 1991).

– W.W.D.

ISAAC STERN

Isaac Stern (1920–) has been one of the best-known violinists in the world since World War II. His playing is noted for its expressiveness.

Brought to the United States from Russia as an infant, Stern was initially trained in music by his mother, a professional singer. He studied the violin under Louis Persinger (also the teacher of **Sir Yehudi Menuhin**) and Naoum Blinder, who became his principal teacher and adviser. Stern made his debut in 1935 at age fifteen playing Camille Saint-Saëns's Third Violin Concerto with the San Francisco Symphony Orchestra; he made his New York debut shortly thereafter. The first of his many appearances at Carnegie Hall was in February 1939, and he is among the artists credited with saving it from demolition in the 1960s. He has toured Europe many times since his 1948 debut at the Lucerne Festival. Since 1960 he has also been active in a trio with pianist Eugene Istomin and cellist Leonard Rose. Stern has championed aspiring musicians in his work with the America–Israel Cultural Foundation, through which he discovered violinist **Itzhak Perlman.** In 1991, during the Gulf War, Stern's impromtu solo performance of a Bach saraband in Jerusalem, after the Israel Philharmonic left the stage during a scud-missile attack, was among the most memorable events of his career.

REFERENCE:

Boris Schwarz, *Great Masters of the Violin: From Corelli and Vivaldi to Stern, Zukerman, and Perlman* (New York: Simon & Schuster, 1983).

– L.D.S.

WALLACE STEVENS

By 1945 Wallace Stevens (1879–1955) had played a major role in the reinvention of modern American poetry. Like **William Carlos Williams,** however, Stevens was respected by his fellow poets but little known to the American public. Even colleagues at the insurance company where he worked for most of his life, first as a staff attorney and later as vice-president, knew little of his writing. Many early reviewers considered his quiet rebellion against traditional language and his attempts to capture reality apart from prevailing conceptions and conventions intentionally difficult and overly "aesthetic."

Stevens had already written many of his best-known poems before the end of World War II, but the work of his last decade exhibits a power undiminished by age. The long poems of his later period, such as *Notes toward a Supreme Fiction* (1942) and *Esthétique du mal* (1945), began to delineate ideas about poetry and the imagination that Stevens had hinted at in his previous writings. These poems were included in his 1947 collection *Transport to Summer*. Central to his ideas is Stevens's theory of the "Supreme Fiction." An agnostic, Stevens sought "to believe beyond belief" through art, especially poetry. The artist, in his view, invents "Supreme Fictions" that fuse imagination and the external world, achieving a transcendent order from a chaotic world. Positing a godless universe but opposing skepticism and materialism, Stevens saw poets, as did the Romantics before him, as creators of meaning and beauty through language and imagination. He developed these ideas further in *The Necessary Angel: Essays on Reality and the Imagination* (1951) and the essays in *Opus Posthumous* (1957).

In his final years Stevens gained increasing recognition from critics, professors, and younger poets, especially after the publication of *The Auroras of Autumn* (1950) and his *Collected Poems* (1954). His reputation as a major American poet has continued to grow since his death, particularly among literary scholars. His influence on later poets is extensive, including American poets as different as A. R. Ammons, John Ashbery, **Robert Creeley, Theodore Roethke,** and **Richard Wilbur.** Though Stevens was viewed as an avant-garde poet during his lifetime, critics came to consider him a conservative due to the formalism of much of his work and to its reconstructed Romanticism, with its emphasis on individual imagination.

REFERENCES:

Peter Brazeau, *Parts of a World: Wallace Stevens Remembered: An Oral Biography* (New York: Random House, 1983);

Joan Richardson, *Wallace Stevens: The Early Years, 1879–1923* (New York: William Morrow / Beech Tree Books, 1986); *Wallace Stevens: The Later Years, 1923–1955* (New York: William Morrow / Beech Tree Books, 1988).

– D.H.-F.

OLIVER STONE

Film director Oliver Stone (1946-) has displayed his obsession with the 1960s and the **Vietnam War** in a series of critically and commercially successful films during the 1980s and 1990s.

Born in New York City to an affluent family, Stone dropped out of Yale University in 1965 to serve in Vietnam as a teacher at the Free Pacific Institute in

Cholon (1965–1966). After a stint in the U.S. Merchant Marines in 1966, he enlisted in the U.S. Army in 1967. Discharged in 1968, having earned a Purple Heart with an oakleaf cluster (signifying that he had been wounded twice) and a Bronze Star for bravery, he went to New York University to study film making under **Martin Scorsese** and earned a B.F.A. in 1971.

Stone's first film as a director was the little-known *Seizure* (1974). He began to gain recognition after he won an Academy Award (Oscar) for best screenplay and a Writer's Guild Award with his script for *Midnight Express* (1978). He continued during the 1980s to write action-film scripts for noted directors such as Brian de Palma, John Milius, and Michael Cimino. He then gained notice as a director for *Salvador* (1986) and *Platoon* (1986), both of which condemned U.S. military intervention in Third World countries. A brilliant evocation of the confusion and terror of jungle combat in Vietnam, *Platoon* won best picture and best director Oscars. Stone recreated its central conflict in a contemporary, civilian setting in *Wall Street* (1987), then returned to a Vietnam setting to win another best director Oscar for his film adaptation of the autobiography of Ron Kovic, a paralyzed Vietnam veteran turned antiwar activist, in *Born on the Fourth of July* (1989). His third Vietnam film, *Heaven and Earth* (1993), presents the war from the point of view of a young Vietnamese woman.

Stone's 1991 epic *JFK* is a controversial exploration of New Orleans district attorney James Garrison's failed quest to prove that a wide-ranging government conspiracy was behind the assassination of President **John F. Kennedy.** Highly suspect as history, the film once again proved the effectiveness of Stone's filmmaking talents as an expression of his anti-establishment political ideology.

– I.R.H.

MERYL STREEP

Meryl Streep (1949–) was one of America's best-known serious actresses in the late 1970s and the 1980s.

Interested in performing from the age of twelve, Streep majored in drama at Vassar College (A.B., 1971) and the Yale School of Drama (M.F.A., 1975). In autumn 1975 she got a small part in a New York Shakespeare Festival play at the Public Theatre, which led to larger roles there and on Broadway.

Streep made her film debut with a small part in *Julia* (1977). She got the first of her nine Academy Award (Oscar) nominations for her supporting role in her second film, *The Deer Hunter* (1978), and won an

Emmy for her role in the television miniseries *Holocaust* (1978). In 1979 she had secondary parts in three movies, most notably *Kramer vs. Kramer,* in which her sympathetic portrayal of a woman who leaves her husband and child earned her a best-supporting actress Oscar. This award launched her on a series of leading roles as beleaguered women in *The French Lieutenant's Woman* (1981), *Sophie's Choice* (1982), *Silkwood* (1983), *Plenty* (1985), *Out of Africa* (1985), *Ironweed* (1987), and *A Cry in the Dark* (1988). Her portrayal of a Nazi-death-camp survivor in *Sophie's Choice* earned her an Oscar for best actress.

In the late 1980s Streep began playing comedic roles, taking parts in movies such as *She-Devil* (1989), *Postcards from the Edge* (1990), and *Death Becomes Her* (1991). Only in her 1990 movie, a serious look at celebrity drug addiction that qualifies as a comedy because of its happy ending and its satire of film-industry phoniness, does her performance approach the success of her leading roles of the 1980s.

REFERENCE:

Diana Maychick, *Meryl Streep: The Reluctant Superstar* (New York: St. Martin's Press, 1984).

– I.R.H.

BARBRA STREISAND

Noted for her powerful voice, comedic talents, and dramatic personality, Barbra Streisand (1942–) has been one of the most famous performers in America since the 1960s.

Born in Brooklyn, New York, Streisand made her debut on Broadway in 1962 with a small but show-stealing role in the musical *I Can Get It for You Wholesale.* She became a star with her portrayal of vaudeville actress Fanny Brice in the musical *Funny Girl* (1964), which ran for 1,348 performances on Broadway. She also starred in the 1968 film version, which resulted in an Academy Award for best actress. Other films in which Streisand appeared include *Hello, Dolly!* (1969), *On a Clear Day You Can See Forever* (1970), *What's Up Doc?* (1972), and *The Way We Were* (1973). In addition to her role in *A Star Is Born* (1976), a remake of two earlier films of the same title, she won an Academy Award for its theme song, "Evergreen," which she wrote with Paul Williams. Streisand was producer, director, and co-author as well as the star of *Yentl* (1983), a movie about a woman who masquerades as a man in order to enter a yeshiva. She also produced, directed, and starred in the widely acclaimed film *The Prince of Tides* (1991).

As a popular singer, Streisand has recorded several award-winning albums of show tunes and contem-

Barbra Streisand on the set of *Yentl*

porary hits. *The Broadway Album* (1985) won a Grammy Award for best female popular vocal performance. One of her best-selling singles was "You Don't Bring Me Flowers" (1978), performed with Neil Diamond. Afflicted with stage fright, Streisand avoided live performances after 1968, but in 1994 she embarked on a lucrative comeback tour.

REFERENCE:

Shaun Considine, *Barbra Streisand: The Woman, the Myth, the Music* (New York: Delacorte, 1985).

– L.D.S.

WILLIAM STYRON

William Styron (1925–) writes carefully crafted and often controversial novels that deal with conflicts between individuals and institutions and the nature of evil. Though his output is small, Styron is widely recognized as an accomplished stylist and a major novelist.

Many critics considered *Lie Down in Darkness* (1951) a phenomenal first book by a twenty-five-year-old author. Influenced by the work of **William Faulkner, F. Scott Fitzgerald,** and **Robert Penn Warren,**

among others, the novel relates the decline of a Southern family and the suicide of a woman torn between her parents' conflicting expectations. Styron's next two novels were less successful: the novella *The Long March* (1956) was based on his military experiences at the end of World War II and during 1950–1951, while his years in France and Italy during the 1950s provided the basis for *Set This House on Fire* (1960), a novel about a painter in Europe who comes to terms with his Southern heritage and his guilt over murdering an evil man.

Styron's subsequent novels have been highly praised by many readers but controversial. He received a Pulitzer Prize for *The Confessions of Nat Turner* (1967), based on an actual slave rebellion in Virginia. Many black writers and intellectuals, along with some white liberals, castigated Styron, who is white, for presuming to write from the perspective of a black slave and accused Styron of misrepresenting facts about Turner and slavery. This response surprised Styron, who wrote the novel hoping to bring blacks and whites together. He was prepared for a similar controversy that never came with the publication of *Sophie's Choice* (1979) for its depiction of Jewish guilt over surviving **the Holocaust.** The novel instead became a

Jacqueline Susann with a poster promoting her 1970 novel

best-seller yet earned a mixed reception from critics. A 1982 film of the novel featured **Meryl Streep** in the title role.

Styron also helped to found the *Paris Review* and has published two books of nonfiction: *This Quiet Dust and Other Writings* (1982), a collection of essays, and *Darkness Visible* (1990), about his successful battle with depression.

REFERENCES:

Arthur D. Casciato and James L. W. West III, eds., *Critical Essays on William Styron* (Boston: G. K. Hall, 1982);

Robert K. Morris and Irving Malin, eds., *The Achievement of William Styron* (Athens: University of Georgia Press, 1981).
                                                                        – D.H.-F.

JACQUELINE SUSANN

Jacqueline Susann (1918–1974) was the first author to have three consecutive books reach the top of the *New York Times* **best-seller list:** *Valley of the Dolls* (1966), *The Love Machine* (1969), and *Once Is Not Enough* (1973). Her romans à clef, based on the lives of such celebrities as Judy Garland and **Marilyn Monroe,** feature scenes that were considered sexually daring.

Susann left her Philadelphia home at eighteen to become an actress in New York. Although she appeared in the original production of Clare Boothe Luce's *The Women* (1936) and other plays, she never made a great success in the theater. However, she befriended many stars and behind-the-scenes people who figured in her fiction.

Susann's novels were without literary pretensions. Their enormous popularity resulted from her ability to skillfully concoct appealing, easy-to-read plots using elements of sex, celebrity, and gossip. Susann accurately predicted the future of her pop-culture standing: "I think I'll be remembered as the voice of the 1960s…**Andy Warhol, the Beatles,** and me."

REFERENCES:

Irving Mansfield, *Life with Jackie* (New York: Bantam, 1983);

Barbara Seaman, *Lovely Me: The Life of Jacqueline Susann* (New York: Morrow, 1987).
                                                                        – D.M.J.

T

Elizabeth Taylor

Elizabeth Taylor (1932–) is one of a handful of popular child actors who have achieved fame as an adult, but her onscreen stardom has often been eclipsed by the melodrama of her personal life.

Born in London to American parents, she lived in England for the first seven years of her life, until the threat of German invasion persuaded her parents to return to the United States, where they settled in southern California. Taylor appeared in her first film — *There's One Born Every Minute* (1942), one of the *Our Gang* series — when she was ten. M-G-M signed her to a long-term contract the next year, and cast her first in *Lassie Come Home* (1943). From then on, she worked often as child actress, with her most famous part being in *National Velvet* (1943), where she played Velvet, the little girl who disguises herself as a boy to ride her horse in, and win, the Grand National horse race.

Taylor went directly into adult roles with no awkward transitional period. After a fine performance in *A Place in the Sun* (1951), she received Academy Award (Oscar) nominations for her roles in *Raintree County* (1957), *Cat on a Hot Tin Roof* (1958), and *Suddenly Last Summer* (1959). In 1958, after the death of her third husband, Mike Todd, Taylor caused a scandal by having an affair with singer Eddie Fisher, then married to popular performer Debbie Reynolds. Taylor and Fisher were married in 1959, and public opinion was softened by Taylor's near-fatal bout with pneumonia in March 1960, just before she won an Oscar for her portrayal of a disillusioned young woman in the 1959 film version of **John O'Hara**'s novel *Butterfield 8*.

Even greater notoriety surrounded the romance between Taylor and **Richard Burton** — both married to others — during the filming of the epic box-office ca-

Richard Burton and Elizabeth Taylor in *Cleopatra*

tastrophe *Cleopatra* (1963); two tempestuous marriages followed (1964–1974 and 1975–1976). Most of the films Taylor made during and after her marriage to Burton were undistinguished, but her performance opposite him in *Who's Afraid of Virginia Woolf* (1966), for which she won her second Oscar as best actress, may well be her finest. Her last starring role in a film was her portrayal of a fading movie star in *The Mirror Crack'd* (1980). Since the end of her seventh marriage (1976–1982), to Sen. John Warner, Taylor has overcome problems with obesity and substance abuse, survived another severe respiratory infection, become a powerful spokesperson and fund raiser for **AIDS** research, and married for an eighth time. She won the American Film Institute Life Achievement Award for 1992.

REFERENCES:

Kitty Kelley, *Elizabeth Taylor: The Last Star* (New York: Simon & Schuster, 1981);

Sheridan Morley, *Elizabeth Taylor* (London: Pavilion, 1988).

– I.R.H.

Paul Taylor

Dancer and choreographer Paul Taylor (1930–) is among the most respected figures in modern dance. His work has a bold, athletic assertiveness and a flowing quality that softens the aggressiveness. Many of his pieces demonstrate a sense of playfulness and joy rare in modern dance.

Taylor was an art student on a swimming scholarship at Syracuse University when he first encountered modern dance. A year later, in 1952, he attended the American Dance Festival at Connecticut College and was invited to join **Martha Graham**'s company.

While performing with the Graham Company, Taylor worked on his own choreography and presented annual concerts with the small dance company he formed in 1954. In 1957 he shocked the modern-dance establishment with *7 New Dances,* which broke with the strong narrative tradition of modern dance and included unorthodox accompaniment and staging. *Dance Observer* reviewed the performance with a quarter column of blank space, and the manager of the theater where Taylor's company had performed told Taylor that he would never again be allowed to rent it. He toured extensively with his company and established both a national and international reputation. When Graham and **George Balanchine** collaborated on *Episodes* in 1960, Balanchine selected Taylor to do an intricate solo devised for his special talents. Taylor left Graham's company in 1961.

Taylor's work has light and dark sides: he sees both nobility and baseness in human motivation and behavior. Starting with his *Three Epitaphs* (1960), which can be interpreted as pathetic or humorous depending on the viewer's perception, this duality has manifested itself in works such as *Insects and Heroes* (1961) and *Agathe's Tale* (1967).

In general, Taylor's work during the 1960s was more traditionally theatrical than his choreography of the 1950s. With its combination of balletic and modern-dance positions, *Aureole* (1962) became a signa-

ture piece for Taylor. The Royal Danish Ballet made it one of the first modern-dance pieces to be added to the repertory of a ballet company. He created his first full-evening work, *Orbs,* in 1966 and another, *American Genesis,* in 1973, but for the most part he continued to favor programs of several short pieces.

Years of touring took their toll in a variety of injuries that forced Taylor to retire from performing in 1974. The following year he choreographed one of his most popular dances, *Esplanade.* It consists of walking, running, and jumping in various combinations, and contains no conventional dance steps. Taylor remains active as a choreographer.

REFERENCE:

Paul Taylor, *Private Domain* (New York: Knopf, 1987).

– D.M.

Twyla Tharp

Twyla Tharp (1941–) is perhaps the best-known avant-garde choreographer in America. She combined modern dance and ballet in carefully planned dances that appear spontaneous. Her dances have a quirky, compact look: upper-body movements are frequently eccentric, though the lower half of the body is kept strictly controlled.

Tharp began her career as a dancer with the **Paul Taylor** company in 1963. She struck out on her own in 1965 with her first solo concert, which included *Tank Dive,* the first of her works performed to popular music. Shortly thereafter she formed a trio. Interested in formal structure, she had her dancers wear stopwatches around their necks to time their movements in *Re-Moves* (1966). *Medley* (1969) was a turning point for Tharp. Designed for a large outdoor space, it emphasizes the personalities of her dancers rather than its technical scheme.

Tharp rose to prominence during the 1970s with dances such as *Eight Jelly Rolls* (1970) and *Bix Pieces* (1972), both inspired by jazz of the 1920s. Their popularity resulted in a commission from the **Joffrey Ballet.** *Deuce Coupe* (1973), a piece performed to songs by **The Beach Boys,** featured Tharp's company with members of the Joffrey Ballet and incorporated popular dances from the 1960s. It was the first of a series of projects undertaken with the Joffrey Ballet, **American Ballet Theater,** and New York City Ballet. The most notable of these is *Push Comes to Shove* (1976), written for **Mikhail Baryshnikov** and American Ballet Theater. Tharp has also worked as a film choreographer, most significantly for *Hair* (1979) and *Amadeus* (1984).

Hunter S. Thompson (photograph © 1992 Michael Montfort / Michael Ochs Archives)

REFERENCE:
Twyla Tharp, *Push Comes to Shove* (New York: Bantam, 1992).
                                                                                    – D.M.

HUNTER S. THOMPSON

Hunter S. Thompson (1939–) is one of the best-known and most-eccentric practitioners of **New Journalism,** which subverts the conventions of journalistic objectivity and reportorial distance and uses the techniques of fiction to tell a nonfiction story.

Thompson began his career in 1959 as Caribbean correspondent for the *New York Herald Tribune,* where several other New Journalists, including Gay Talese, Jimmy Breslin, and Tom Wolfe, began their

innovative work. After serving as South American correspondent for the *National Observer* (1960–1964), Thompson became a free-lance writer, publishing articles in *Harper's,* the *Nation,* and elsewhere while beginning the research that led to his first book, *Hell's Angels: A Strange and Terrible Saga* (1966).

Thompson's research included several months of hanging out with the California branch of the Hell's Angels observing their actions and their lifestyle. Stylistically, *Hell's Angels* is Thompson's most conventional book: he diminishes his role in the story and focuses on the notorious motorcycle gang. Many reviewers called *Hell's Angels* the fairest and most informative book about the gang yet published.

In 1971 Thompson published his best-known book, *Fear and Loathing in Las Vegas: A Savage Journey to the Heart of the American Dream.* A fully realized work of New Journalism, which Thompson called "Gonzo Journalism," the book is ostensibly the story of Thompson's failure to write a magazine story on two events in Las Vegas: a motorcycle race and a conference on enforcement of narcotics laws. The main subject is the drug-crazed frenzies of Thompson and his companion, a 300-pound Samoan attorney (based on Chicano lawyer and writer Oscar Zeta Acosta).

Thompson followed this critical and commercial success with his version of the 1973 presidential campaign, *Fear and Loathing on the Campaign Trail '72* (1973). Not as successful as its predecessor, the book treats politics as a purely personal experience, complete with large doses of drugs and alcohol. Most of the reviews were positive, but some critics found Thompson's New Journalism techniques excessive.

Thompson's subsequent books — *The Great Shark Hunt* (1979), *The Curse of Lono* (1983), *Generation of Swine: Tales of Shame and Degradation in the '80s* (1988), *Songs of the Doomed: More Notes on the Death of the American Dream* (1990), and *Better Than Sex: Confessions of a Campaign Junkie* (1994) — have been avidly read by a loyal coterie of Thompson fans but have not received the same critical attention as his earlier books.

REFERENCE:
Paul Perry, *Fear and Loathing: The Strange and Terrible Saga of Hunter S. Thompson* (New York: Thunder's Mouth Press, 1992).
                                                                                    –J.W.H.

VIRGIL THOMSON

Perhaps better remembered for the perceptive music criticism he wrote after World War II than for his

Johnny Carson (right) interviewing Vice President Spiro Agnew on *The Tonight Show,* 1969 (photograph © NBC)

complex yet seemingly simple music, Virgil Thomson (1896–1989) nevertheless ranks as a major American composer.

Thomson began composing during the 1920s in Paris, where he met writer Gertrude Stein and worked with her in one of the most inspired musical-literary collaborations of the twentieth century. Stein provided the libretti for Thomson's best-known works, the operas *Four Saints in Three Acts* (1934), which featured an all-black cast, and *The Mother of Us All* (1947), based on the life of American suffragist Susan B. Anthony.

In general Thomson's music is noted for its embracing of American themes, particularly folk tunes and hymns. He wrote many film scores; the best-known example is his work for *Louisiana Story,* which earned him a Pulitzer Prize in 1948. In 1940 Thomson began a fourteen-year tenure as music critic for the *New York Herald Tribune.* As a critic, he quickly gained a reputation for his wit and insight as well as for the quality of his writing. He continued to compose, but the popularity of his music began to decline during the 1960s.

REFERENCES:

Kathleen Hoover and John Cage, *Virgil Thomson: His Life and Music* (New York: Yoseloff, 1959);

Michael Meckna, *Virgil Thomson: A Bio-Bibliography* (New York: Greenwood Press, 1986).

           – L.D.S.

THE TONIGHT SHOW

The Tonight Show, which premiered on **NBC** on 27 September 1954, was the first late-night show on network television. Over nearly four decades under a variety of hosts, most notably Johnny Carson, the popular show made the late-night schedule slot profitable, and until 1993 it faced little competition. The talk shows broadcast opposite it by rival networks **CBS** and **ABC** were canceled because of low ratings.

The Tonight Show was the brainchild of NBC executive Pat Weaver, who had created *The Today Show* in 1952. The two programs were meant to complement each other and to lock viewers to NBC from the earliest viewing hours to the latest. Weaver moved a local New York version of *The Tonight Show,* which had been on the air with **Steve Allen** as host since July 1953, to the national network. The show featured Allen's satiric humor and musical performances by regulars Steve Lawrence, Eydie Gorme, and Andy Williams.

In 1956 comedian Ernie Kovacs began to host *The Tonight Show* for two of the five nights each week. Ratings plummeted. The show was canceled in January 1957 but returned in July 1957 with Jack Paar as host. Paar's mercurial personality captured the imagination of the viewing audience, returning the show to the top of the late-night ratings. But Paar, who stalked off the show in February 1960 and stayed off for a month to protest network censorship of one of his jokes, was often at odds with network executives, and resigned in March 1962.

After six months of interim hosts, Johnny Carson officially replaced Paar as host of *The Tonight Show* in October 1962. During Carson's thirty years on the program *The Tonight Show* became a television institution, far outpacing all competing shows in the ratings. Carson's comedic talents and ability to attract celebrity guests kept viewers tuned in to NBC. When Carson retired in 1992, the new host, Jay Leno, had the advantage of having served as a guest host for several years. Yet the ratings for *The Tonight Show* have declined since Carson's departure because of competition from *The Late Show with David Letterman* on CBS.

REFERENCE:

Paul Corkery, *Carson: The Unauthorized Biography* (Ketchum, Idaho: Randt, 1987).

– J.W.H.

Top 40

Originally conceived during the mid 1950s by the major AM network radio stations as a way to unify popular-music programming standards and to attract new listeners (particularly young ones) and sponsors, the Top 40 is a listing of what are presumably the forty most popular songs at a given time. It is based largely on sales charts from ***Billboard*** and similar sources. The Top 40 reflects current listening preferences of a national radio audience and influences the success or failure of an artist's career. By the 1980s "Top 40 music" had become synonymous with mainstream pop or rock music, though **crossovers** to the list from other kinds of popular music sometimes occur.

REFERENCES:

David T. MacFarland, *The Development of the Top 40 Radio Format* (New York: Arno, 1979);

Joel Whitburn, *The Billboard Book of Top 40 Hits,* fifth edition (New York: Billboard Publications, 1992).

– L.D.S.

Joan Tower

As founder of the highly acclaimed Da Capo Chamber Players, composer and pianist Joan Tower (1938–) has steadily advanced contemporary music written for small ensembles in the United States. Her music, which also includes works for solo piano, has been described as attractive to the ear and easy to comprehend.

In 1969 Tower founded the Da Capo Chamber Players, for which she has written chamber pieces such as *Petroushskates* (1980) for flute, clarinet, violin, cello, and piano. She served as composer-in-residence with the St. Louis Symphony Orchestra from 1985 to 1987. She has also written works in larger forms, most recently her Violin Concerto (1992), premiered by the Utah Symphony Orchestra.

– L.D.S.

Antony Tudor

Dancer and choreographer Antony Tudor (1908–1987) added psychological motivation to classic ballet in works such as *Jardin aux Lilas, Pillar of Fire,* and *Undertow.* His body of work is relatively small, but its innovations made a large impact on American ballet after World War II. His work is performed by many ballet companies worldwide.

Tudor began choreographing in 1934 as a member of the Ballet Rambert in his native England. In 1940 he was invited to New York to join the new Ballet Theater (later **American Ballet Theatre**) as dancer and choreographer. He mounted several of his works that had been successful in England, including *Jardin aux Lilas* (1936), and began to cast them with dancers who understood and responded to his creative approach, which drew on the psychological emphasis (as well as some of the movements) of modern dance. It was with this group, known informally among the larger company as "Tudor dancers," that Tudor began work on *Pillar of Fire* (1942). The success of this work made him one of the brightest choreographic stars to emerge in the company. During the next several years he regularly brought out psychological dramas such as *Romeo and Juliet* (1943), *Dim Lustre* (1943), and *Undertow* (1945).

During the 1950s Tudor devoted much of his energy to his students, first at the combined school for the Ballet Theater and the **New York Metropolitan**

Opera and later at the Juilliard School. A commission from the Royal Ballet in London summoned a major effort from him, *Shadowplay* (1967), revealing his dramatic intensity on a larger scale than the one on which he had been working since the 1950s. In his later years Tudor focused more on revivals of earlier works than on creating new ones.

REFERENCE:

Donna Perlmutter, *Shadowplay: The Life of Antony Tudor* (New York: Viking, 1991).

                                                                — D.M.

DAVID TUDOR

As a pioneering performer of new music for keyboard instruments, David Tudor (1926–) has helped audiences understand difficult modern compositions through his enthusiastic approaches to the works of several twentieth-century composers, most notably **John Cage.** Tudor has commissioned and performed

David Tudor playing his composition *Untitled* on his electronic-music equipment, 1972 (photograph by Gordon Mumma)

many new works for piano, including pieces by Sylvano Bussotti and Pierre Boulez, and has developed new methods of dealing with the demands of such scores, such as donning thick leather gloves to play the tone clusters in Bussotti's *Five Piano Pieces for David Tudor* (1959).

A composer as well as a keyboard artist, Tudor — like Cage — has long been affiliated with the **Merce Cunningham** Dance Company, for which Tudor has written many pieces since 1953. During the 1950s and 1960s he worked extensively with Cage on various **electronic-music** experiments. In his compositions since the 1960s Tudor has tended to create **mixed-media** works such as *Rainforest I–IV* (1968–1973), combining music with lights, lasers, and video.

                                                                — L.D.S.

IKE AND TINA TURNER

For nearly twenty years Ike and Tina Turner were a popular team in rhythm and blues, **rock 'n' roll,** and rock. After their split in 1975 Tina Turner went on to a successful solo career.

Ike Turner (1931–) organized his Kings of Rhythm in high school. Anna Mae Bullock (1938–) joined the group in 1956 and married him in 1958, becoming Tina Turner. "Fool in Love" (1959) was their first hit. As the Ike and Tina Turner Revue, they toured and recorded extensively during the 1960s. Their biggest hit came in 1971 with their version of Creedence Clearwater Revival's "Proud Mary." This recording was also the beginning of Tina Turner's rise to stardom and the decline of Ike Turner's career. The couple separated in 1975 and were divorced the following year.

Tina Turner appeared as the Acid Queen in the film version of The Who's rock opera *Tommy* (1975). Her solo efforts languished until 1982, when she was a successful opening act for **The Rolling Stones** during their American tour. In 1984 her album *Private Dancer* sold more than ten million copies. One of the best-selling singles from the album was "What's Love Got to Do with It?" She appeared in the science-fiction film *Mad Max Beyond Thunderdome* in 1985 and performed a hit song from the film, "We Don't Need Another Hero." She went on a highly successful world tour in 1987.

In 1991 Ike and Tina Turner were elected to the Rock and Roll Hall of Fame. Their relationship and career were fictionalized in the 1993 film *What's Love Got to Do with It?*

Ike and Tina Turner (center) with backup singers Ann Thomas, Paulette Parker, Pat Powdrill, and Jean Brown, 1965 (photograph by Rhonda Graam)

REFERENCE:
Tina Turner with Kurt Loder, *I, Tina* (New York: Morrow, 1986).
                                                                    – L.D.S.

TED TURNER

Ted Turner (1938–   ), one of the most innovative and successful mass-media businessmen has built an international television conglomerate.

In 1960, after his father's suicide, Turner took over the family billboard firm in Atlanta, Georgia, and transformed the company into the Turner Communications Group (TCG), a profitable regional advertising firm. In 1970 he purchased a failing independent television station in Atlanta, and renamed it WTCG. In the early 1970s, seeing satellite and **cable television** as the wave of the future, he worked ceaselessly to get cable systems around the South to carry WTCG (later renamed WTBS).

In 1976, after Turner bought the Atlanta Braves baseball team and a controlling interest in the Atlanta Hawks basketball team, WTCG increased sports coverage, adding it to the reruns of old series and movies that filled the rest of the sched-ule. This lineup of shows proved popular, and Turner's "Superstation," was worth more than $40 million by 1978.

Turner's most innovative move was the 1980 formation of the Cable News Network (**CNN**), which has become the largest and most influential news operation in the world. His purchase of the MGM/United Artists movie studio and film library in 1986 greatly expanded the network's film holdings and provided programming for his expanding number of entertainment channels. In 1991 he bought the Hanna-Barbera animation studio and used its cartoon library in his programming. Other cable and satellite channels of the Turner Broadcasting System include Headline News (1982), Turner Network Television (TNT, 1986), the Airport Channel (1992), the Cartoon Network (1992), and Turner Classic Movies (1994).

Turner captained the winning vesssel in the 1977 America's Cup and married actress and activist **Jane Fonda** in 1992.

REFERENCE:
Porter Bibb, *It Ain't as Easy as It Looks: Ted Turner's Amazing Story* (New York: Crown, 1993).
                                                                    –J.W.H.

THE TWIST

The Twist, a social dance that emerged in the late 1950s, was the first of a flood of "no-touch" dances that nearly displaced the convention of partnered social dance inaugurated by the waltz one hundred and fifty years earlier.

The song "The Twist" was written by Hank Ballard and the Moonlighters in 1958, when it had some success on flip side of a hit. Chubby Checker recorded the song for his 1960 performance on the popular teen dance show *American Bandstand,* which launched the craze. He capitalized on the success of the dance a year later with "Let's Twist Again." While the dance rapidly gained popularity among young people, it was not widely performed by adults until fashionable patrons at the Peppermint Lounge in Manhattan began doing its characteristic pelvic gyrations to "The Peppermint Twist" (1961) by the club's house band, Joey Dee and the Starlighters.

"Killer" Joe Piro helped adults learn the dance by offering private instruction as well as exhibitions. The most popular twist song was "Twist and Shout," recorded in 1962 by the Isley Brothers and in 1964 by **The Beatles.**

The twist spawned a host of spin-off dances, including the Swim, the Locomotion, the Monkey, the Funky Chicken, the Mashed Potato, and the Frug. These dances were denounced by those who deplored their blatant display of "suggestive" movements. The fad for such dances continued throughout much of the 1960s.

– D.M.

ANNE TYLER

The popularity of Anne Tyler (1941–) has grown steadily since 1976, when **John Updike** announced in a review of her sixth novel, *Searching for Caleb:* "This writer is not merely good, she is *wickedly* good" (*New Yorker,* 29 March 1976). Tyler's tenth book, and first **best-seller,** *The Accidental Tourist* (1985), was the basis for a highly acclaimed, 1988 movie. Her next book, *Breathing Lessons* (1988), earned her a Pulitzer Prize.

Tyler considers herself a Southern writer and acknowledges the influence of **Eudora Welty,** whose fiction showed Tyler that one could write about the eccentricities of everyday people. Her first three novels — *If Morning Ever Comes* (1964), *The Tin Can Tree* (1968), and *A Slipping Down Life* (1970) — are set in North Carolina, where she spent most of her childhood. Beginning with *The Clock Winder* (1972), her novels have been set mostly in Baltimore, where she has lived since 1967 and which she has called "wonderful territory for a writer."

Tyler's fictional world is largely peopled by two sorts of characters: convention-bound, change-resistant, near recluses and disruptive tradition-flaunting lovers of change. In the novels mentioned above — as well as in *Celestial Navigation* (1974), *Earthly Possessions* (1977), *Morgan's Passing* (1980), *Dinner at the Homesick Restaurant* (1982), and *Saint Maybe* (1991) — Tyler portrays with humor and sympathy the strategies of her characters for ordering a contemporary chaos of random events and violent upheavals that seem beyond their control. Though families offer security, they are also sources of unresolved childhood conflicts that prevent individuals from becoming fully functional adults, and the agents of change are as capable of provoking tragedy as stimulating positive growth. At best Tyler's characters discover a limited, but real, ability to shape their own lives. As Justine learns in *Searching for Caleb,* choice is always possible "to *some* extent." She can even change the past to the degree that she can alter its hold on her in the present and future. Tyler once said, "I write about those offbeat characters and that blend of laughter and tears because in my experience, that's what real life consists of." The eccentricities of her characters are finally representations of the ways ordinary people approach everyday life.

REFERENCES:

Elizabeth Evans, *Anne Tyler* (New York: Twayne, 1993);

Alice Hall Petry, *Understanding Anne Tyler* (Columbia: University of South Carolina Press, 1990).

– K.L.R.

U

JOHN UPDIKE

John Updike (1932–) is one of the most prominent and prolific American novelists of the second half of the twentieth century. He is also an accomplished poet, playwright, essayist, and critic. Sometimes accused of writing baroque prose unbefitting of his subjects — which, his detractors claim, are too often the suburbs and sex — Updike has been called too slick a stylist and too limited in his artistic vision. He is, however, one of the few American authors of best-selling novels whose work is respected by academics.

Updike's first commercially published story, "Friends from Philadelphia," appeared in the 30 October 1954 issue of the *New Yorker,* and in 1955 he took a job as a staff reporter at that magazine, where he often wrote for the "Talk of the Town" section and contributed stories, poems, and cartoons. He left his staff position in 1957 to devote himself to full-time free-lance writing, but he continued to write for the magazine and became a regular book reviewer. As predominantly white, urban or suburban northeasterners, the *New Yorker* readership was a ready-made audience for Updike's subtle criticism of American suburban middle-class mores and values.

With the publication of his first novel, *The Poorhouse Fair* (1959), which examines the attitudes of a series of characters on the annual fair day at a New Jersey home for the destitute, Updike already had a readership familiar with his portrayal of culturally shared beliefs as increasingly secular, materialistic, and banal. Popular recognition for Updike began with the appearance of his second novel, *Rabbit, Run* (1960), and continued with three more Rabbit novels (1971–

John Updike reading one of his short stories to students and teachers at Governor Mifflin High School in Shillington, Massachusetts, 23 June 1968 (photograph by Richard J. Patrick)

1990). These novels focus on the life of Harry (Rabbit) Angstrom, who was a high-school basketball star in the 1950s and who laments lost glory and missed opportunities over the next three decades. Both *Rabbit, Run* and the second novel in the series, *Rabbit, Redux* (1971), enjoyed popular and critical success. The third book in the series, *Rabbit Is Rich* (1981), won a Pulitzer Prize, a National Book Critics Circle Award, and an American Book Award. Updike's appearance on the 18 October 1982 cover of *Time* gave further evidence of his popularity. The fourth Rabbit novel, *Rabbit at Rest* (1990), won a Pulitzer Prize and a National Book Critics Circle Award. Though Updike has writ-ten many other well-received novels, these four novels have received the most recognition.

Updike exhibited an unusual breadth of interest as a writer of and about literature and is respected as a man of letters.

REFERENCES:

Donald J. Greiner, *John Updike's Novels* (Athens: Ohio University Press, 1984);

Greiner, *The Other John Updike: Poems, Short Stories, Prose, Plays* (Athens: University of Ohio Press, 1981);

John Updike, *Self-Consciousness: Memoirs* (New York: Knopf, 1989).

–D.L.

V

EDGARD VARÈSE

Known in the 1930s and 1940s for his experiments with new musical sounds, composer Edgard Varèse (1883–1965) became a major proponent of **electronic music** after World War II.

Varèse immigrated to America from France in 1915, leaving most of his early compositions behind him. His new musical start came with *Amériques* (1921), an orchestral piece innovative for its use of dissonance, complex harmonies, and unconventional sounds. He continued his experiments along these lines until 1936, when he wrote *Density 21.5* for solo flute. After this work, he composed almost nothing until the development of the tape recorder in the early 1950s expanded the possibilities for electronic music.

His first piece to employ the new technology fully was *Déserts* (1954), for wind, percussion, and tape — one of the first compositions to use both live performers and electronic media. His best-known work is *Poème électronique,* composed for the Philips pavilion designed by Le Corbusier at the 1958 Brussels Exposition. Having conducted tape experiments at the Columbia-Princeton Electronic Music Center, Varèse created an eight-minute montage of sound that was relayed over more than four hundred loudspeakers at the pavilion. The piece was accompanied by (yet not synchronized to) projected images chosen by Le Corbusier, resulting in one of the first **mixed-media** events.

REFERENCES:

Jonathan W. Bernard, *The Music of Edgard Varése* (New Haven: Yale University Press, 1987);

Fernand Ouellette, *Edgard Varèse,* translated by Derek Coltman (New York: Orion Press, 1968).

                                                        — L.D.S.

SARAH VAUGHAN

Sarah Vaughan (1924-1990) was among the most beloved female jazz artists of the twentieth century. Born in Newark, New Jersey, she demonstrated an early talent for singing and playing the piano. After winning an amateur singing contest at the Apollo Theater in Harlem in 1942, Vaughan joined Earl Hines's band as a

Sarah Vaughan (photograph by Veryl Oakland)

singer and pianist. Later she appeared with the ensembles of Billy Eckstine and John Kirby before launching a solo career in which she performed both popular music and jazz. Called "The Divine One" and "Sassy" by her colleagues, Vaughan was renowned for her singing style, which reflected her association with the major **bebop** performers of the late 1940s and 1950s. She was lauded for her improvisational abilities and for her masterful control of vocal intonation. Vaughan is best remembered for her lithe renditions of "Misty," "A Foggy Day in London," "Tenderly," and "Poor Butterfly," as well as other popular songs.

REFERENCES:

Dennis Brown, *Sarah Vaughan: A Discography* (New York: Greenwood Press, 1991);

Leslie Grouse, *Sassy: The Life of Sarah Vaughan* (New York: Scribners, 1993).

– L.D.S.

ROBERT VENTURI

Robert Venturi (1925–) is considered one of the most important architects in the world, primarily because of his theoretical writings. He revolutionized thinking in architectural circles with his seminal book *Complexity and Contradiction in Architecture* (1966), in which he states that "architects can no longer afford to be intimidated by the puritanically moral language of orthodox modern architecture." Six years later he wrote *Learning from Las Vegas* with Denise Scott-Brown (1931–) — his business partner and wife — and Steven Izenour. Both works have greatly influenced the development of the **postmodern** movement in architecture. Venturi and Scott-Brown reject the aesthetic ideals of modernism — such as simplicity, rationality, and clarity — and propose instead an architecture that embraces complexity, ambiguity, and variety. Venturi and Scott-Brown have continued to advocate a nondoctrinaire approach to design that accepts historical precedents and contemporary vernacular forms as potential styles and sources. Unlike the autonomous nature of modernist formalism, this pluralistic approach enables them, and other postmodernist architects, to build structures that give consideration to site and context as well as the client's specific needs and wants. Consequently, the work of Venturi and Scott-Brown's own firm, which has included John Rausch since 1964, is wide ranging and often unpredictable.

REFERENCE:

Christopher Mead, ed., *The Architecture of Robert Venturi* (Albuquerque: University of New Mexico Press, 1989).

– K.B.

VIETNAM WAR

Reaction to the Vietnam War polarized the United States throughout the 1960s and into the 1970s. Draft-age youths were pitted against their elders as people aligned themselves into two camps: at one extreme were war supporters called "hawks," motivated by patriotism and **cold-war** anxiety; at the other extreme were peace advocates called "doves," who opposed the endangerment of American soldiers for a foreign cause. The positions were reduced to their simplest terms in bumperstickers: "My Country right or wrong" and "Love it or leave it" on the one hand; "Make Love, Not War" on the other. Not since the Civil War had the power of the government been so forcefully wielded, so rudely questioned, and so often resisted. Defiant college students publicly challenged authority, marching on Washington, D.C., to protest American foreign policy, burning their draft registration cards to protest forced military service in what they called an immoral war, and obscenely ridiculing government officials in the cause of peace and love.

Harry S Truman, in 1950, was the first U.S. president to commit forces to Vietnam, beginning the longest war in U.S. history. But most Americans were unaware of the war in Indochina or even the whereabouts of Vietnam until **John F. Kennedy** sent sixteen thousand American troops as advisers to South Vietnam in the early 1960s. The total area of North and South Vietnam is about half that of Johnson's home state of Texas, and yet over the course of his five-year presidency, from November 1963 to January 1969, President Lyndon B. Johnson increased American troop levels to half a million soldiers, largely draftees. Each year Americans were horrified at the cost of the Vietnam War, in terms of casualties, money, national integrity, and social cohesion.

Johnson, whose presidency was considered a success by most other measures, admitted that his failure to end the war cost him his political career. Late in his term he was greeted at public appearances by placard-waving protestors chanting, "Hey, Hey, LBJ. How many kids did you kill today?" His successor, Richard M. Nixon, moved decisively toward a negotiated peace and withdrew American troops in 1973, but by then the war had left a permanent scar on American culture. Veterans who returned alive were victimized by a national mood of embarrassment over the American role in what was widely regarded as an unjust, even shameful, war. It took a decade or more of reflection for Americans to accord heroes' status to Vietnam veterans. National remorse was institutionally recognized in the form of Vietnam War memorials all over the country. The national monument in Washington, D.C., de-

Photograph by John M. Del Vecchio, a U.S. Army combat journalist during the Vietnam War, who drew on his experiences with 101st Airborne Division for his first novel, *The 13th Valley* (1982)

signed by Yale architecture student Maya Lin and dedicated on 13 November 1982, is a black-granite wall on which is carved the names of the more than 58,000 Americans killed or missing in Vietnam.

Americans who lived through the period responded in a variety of fiercely personal ways. There were hundreds of songs, some promilitary, such as Sgt. Barry Sadler's popular hit "The Ballad of the Green Berets" (1966) celebrating the courage of men in special forces: "Fighting soldiers from the sky / Fearless men who'd jump and die / Men who mean just what they say / The brave men of the Green Berets." Most songs, though, were antiwar, like the **hippie** anthem "I-Feel-Like-I'm-Fixin'-to-Die Rag" (1967) by a band called Country Joe and the Fish: "One, Two, Three, what are we fighting for / Don't ask me 'cause I don't give a damn / Next stop is Vietnam / And it's five, six, seven, open up them pearly gates / Ain't no time to wonder why / Whoopee we're all gonna die."

Movies raised war issues and personalized them, combining depictions of real-world grief with screen-star glamour. *Coming Home* (1978), about a wounded soldier's return, starred Jon Voight and **Jane Fonda,** the award-winning actress who had earned the name Hanoi Jane and the boycott of nationalistic critics for her antiwar protest visit to North Vietnam. Among the dozens of national-release movies with war themes are *The Green Berets* (1968), *The Deer Hunter* (1978), *Apocalypse Now* (1979), *Birdy* (1984), *Platoon* (1986), *Full-Metal Jacket* (1987), *Gardens of Stone* (1987), *Good Morning, Vietnam* (1987), and *Hamburger Hill* (1987).

When the war was over, many Americans wanted it forgotten, but perceptions of the war and its effect on American society were the subjects of hundreds of books, such as *Born on the Fourth of July* (1976), a memoir by Ron Kovic, a soldier who was paralyzed by a bullet that severed his spinal cord and who mobilized other disaffected soldiers to fight for the respect given to veterans of previous wars. (In the movie of the same title based on the book [1989] Tom Cruise played Kovic.) *Vietnam War Literature,* a 1988 bibliography by John Newman and Ann Hilfinger, identifies more than four hundred literary works about the war. Vietnam Veterans Against the War, a national association that included war poets and fiction writers, published a series of anthologies presenting members' work.

Artists responded forcefully. **Jasper Johns**'s series of American flag paintings, for example, evoked the range of emotions that the official symbol of national pride had come to represent during the Vietnam years. To the horror of their parents who had lived through World War II, antiwar protestors publicly burned the once-hallowed flag and adapted it to such uses as patches on the seats of their pants. Traveling shows of works by artists who were also veterans attracted respectful attention by the 1980s. Among the most successful was *A Different War,* a 109-work exhibit mounted in 1990 by the Whatcom Museum in Seattle. In addition to a Johns flag painting, it included **Claes Oldenburg**'s *Lipstick (Ascending) on Caterpillar Track,* a huge, phallic sculpture mounted on a tank body suggesting the association between business, feminism, the macho ethic, and the military. The sculpture was presented to Yale University by a dissident student group in 1969. Another work in the exhibit was Duane Hanson's *Vietnam Scene,* realistic "life sculptures" of dead soldiers. Also included was a photograph of the Guerrilla Art Action Group's *Blood Bath* demonstration at the **Museum of Modern Art,** during which actors attacked one another and doused themselves with animal blood to act out their theory that art had no right to be enjoyable when the nation was indulging in what they called mass murder.

Certainly because it was so controversial and perhaps because of the vivid image Americans of the war generation had of television newscasters reporting the daily totals of dead and wounded in scoreboard fashion while showing gruesome videotapes of war action, producers of television drama largely avoided the war as a topic, except in documentaries and news specials.

Clearly the Vietnam War was the most important force in the shaping of American culture in the thirty-year period beginning in 1960. Just as clearly, the responses of creative people in the various arts provided an expression of natural sentiment and public dialogue that was critical in overcoming the trauma war inflicted on society.

REFERENCES:

Ronald Baughman, ed. *American Writers of the Vietnam War, Dictionary of Literary Biography Documentary Series,* volume 9 (Detroit: Gale Research, 1991);

Philip D. Biedler, *American Literature and the Experience of the Vietnam War* (Athens: University of Georgia Press, 1982);

Lucy R. Lippard, *A Different War: Vietnam in Art* (Seattle: Real Comet Press, 1990);

Michael McClear, *The Ten-Thousand Day War* (New York: Avon, 1982);

John Newman and Ann Hilfinger, *Vietnam War Literature* (New York: Scarecrow, 1988).

– R.L.

VILLAGE VOICE

The liberal New York weekly tabloid the *Village Voice* was founded in October 1955 to express the bohemian views and reflect the counter culture lifestyles of people in Greenwich Village. Founding editor Dan Wolf gave contributors and staff writers freedom to criticize politics and culture through personal narrative styles. As a result of Wolf's permissive editorial policies the *Voice* became a showcase for **New Journalism**, influencing the direction of American journalism and setting the standard for alternative and underground publications during the 1960s.

The rationale of the *Village Voice* was to "give the voiceless people a voice and encourage cultural diversity." Founded in 1955 by Wolf and Ed Fancher (chief publisher), it billed itself as "A Weekly Newspaper Designed to be Read," and the editors combined magazine content with newspaper format in an effort to reach beyond the normal readership for newspapers. **Norman Mailer**, a frequent contributor in the early years, contributed half of the ten-thousand dollars needed to launch the publication. Although the *Voice* lost almost six times that amount over the next seven years, its popularity increased during the 1960s, and by 1969 it had a circulation of 138,000 — of which about 100,000 copies were sold at newsstands and the rest through national distribution.

Despite low pay, many talented writers were attracted to the *Village Voice,* including **Allen Ginsberg, William S. Burroughs, Ezra Pound,** E. E. Cummings, Katherine Anne Porter, and Henry Miller. The letters-to-the-editor section contributed to the paper's reputation as a lively forum for both readers and writers. Under the leadership of Wolf and Fancher, the paper won several New York Press Association awards.

The *Village Voice* has been influential in both the political and art worlds. Offbeat columnists and outspoken reporters have been given free reign to rage against injustice, corruption, and social ills, and the paper has been a leader in minority-rights movements, particularly gay rights. It has earned respect for its coverage of avant-garde art, including underground film and other experimental visual and performing arts. The *Voice* was among the first newspapers to devote space to rock-music criticism. It was a leader in its coverage of Off-Broadway and Off-Off-Broadway drama and instituted the Obie Awards for the best Off-Broadway production. In 1981 *VLS*, a book-review supplement, was established.

In 1970 Wolf and Fancher sold The *Village Voice* and over the next fifteen years it underwent several editorial and managerial turnovers. In 1974 Clay Felker, an editor for *Esquire*, became editor and, by merging it with his magazine *New York*, refined the layout but lost readership by emphasizing personalities and lifestyles over political and cultural issues. Although the *Village Voice* never fully regained the influence it enjoyed during the 1960s, it influenced a wave of underground newspapers, including the *L.A. Free Press* and the *San Francisco Bay Guardian.*

REFERENCES:

Kevin McAuliffe, *The Great American Newspaper* (New York: Scribners, 1978);

Geoffrey Stokes, *The Village Voice Anthology: 1956–1980* (New York: Morrow, 1982).

–J.E.F.

Kurt Vonnegut, Jr.

KURT VONNEGUT, JR.

With his iconoclastic anti-establishment humor, novelist Kurt Vonnegut, Jr. (1922–) was considered the voice of reason by student readers in late 1960s and early 1970s. He sold his first story in 1950, but until the second half of the 1960s he remained obscure, either relegated to cult status or viewed as a writer of **science fiction**. He resisted this science-fiction label, only to admit later that some of his work is indeed in that genre.

Most of Vonnegut's fiction, narrated in a fragmented but accessible style, is characterized by wry social commentary, elements of science fiction, **black humor,** and a dark view of the world. As a critic of war, commercialism, stupidity, and cruelty, he presents human beings as lovable, promising creatures who rarely live up to their potential. Vonnegut's writing also deals with the interaction of reality and falsehood, fiction and fact, which has led to his identification by some scholars as a **postmodern** author.

His early novels were noticed by a few writers and critics, but for the most part they were overlooked

by reviewers. *Player Piano* (1952), satirizes soulless business practices and treats the loneliness of the individual in a mechanized society. *The Sirens of Titan* (1959), concerns a millionaire who encounters aliens and travels through the solar system, learning how insignificant humans are in the grand scale of things and what joy human life can offer. From the futuristic settings of these novels Vonnegut shifted to the events of World War II in *Mother Night* (1962), narrated by an American writer and spy who poses as a Nazi and wonders which he really is. Vonnegut returned to speculation about the future in *Cat's Cradle* (1963), with its invented religion and its depiction of the end of the world — by ice rather than fire. *God Bless You, Mr. Rosewater* (1965) continues Vonnegut's investigation of morals and reality in the modern world through its protagonist, Eliot Goldwater, and introduces Vonnegut's alter ego, the obscure, eccentric science-fiction writer Kilgore Trout, who appears in several novels.

With *Slaughterhouse-Five* (1969), Vonnegut's place in contemporary American fiction was assured.

Combining science fiction and his experiences in the army during World War II, the novel spoke to the sentiments of many college-age readers at the height of the **Vietnam War** with its depiction of war as brutal, senseless, and unglamorous. *Slaughterhouse-Five* became a critical and commercial success and launched Vonnegut to literary stardom. Vonnegut was at the height of his popularity in the late 1960s and the 1970s, His novels since then — such as *Breakfast of Champions* (1973), *Jailbird* (1979), *Galapagos* (1985), and *Hocus Pocus* (1990) — have sold well, but reviewers have noted that these books seem to lack the energy and inspiration of Vonnegut's best work.

REFERENCES:

William Rodney Allen, *Understanding Kurt Vonnegut* (Columbia: University of South Carolina Press, 1990);

Jerome Klinkowitz, *Kurt Vonnegut* (New York: Methuen, 1982);

Klinkowitz and Donald L. Lawler, eds., *Vonnegut in America* (New York: Delacorte, 1977).

– D.H.-F.

ALICE WALKER

Alice Walker (1944–) is an African-American writer whose fiction is widely admired for its descriptive style and positive focus on black women. She is also credited with bringing attention to other black women authors, in particular Zora Neale Hurston.

Walker's first novel, *The Third Life of Grange Copeland* (1970), describes the impact of racism on a Southern black family while *Meridian* (1976) is about the **civil rights movement.** Though she built a solid reputation, Walker was not widely known until *The Color Purple* (1982) was a popular and critical success and earned her a Pulitzer Prize. Depicting racism and sexism through letters written in black English by a poor, uneducated, but highly creative woman, the novel, like other works by Walker, reveals her belief that beauty and redemption are possible even in the hardest of circumstances. The popular 1985 film version, directed by **Steven Spielberg** and produced by **Quincy Jones,** further enhanced Walker's reputation. Her next novel, *The Temple of My Familiar* (1989), was a best-seller praised for it blending of dream and reality, black history and myth. *Possessing the Secret of Joy* (1992) was controversial for its treatment of female circumcision.

Walker, who has also written poetry, essays, and fiction for children, has sometimes been criticized for letting politics and her recent **New Age** beliefs dominate her work and for showing black males in a negative light.

REFERENCE:

Donna Haisty Winchell, *Alice Walker* (New York: Twayne / Toronto & New York: Macmillan, 1992).

– D.H.-F.

ANDY WARHOL

Andy Warhol (1930–1987) provided a model for the American celebrity artist of the 1960s, publicly pursuing profit, glamour, and fame. From lower-class beginnings in Pittsburgh, Pennsylvania, where he was born Andrew Warhola to Czech immigrant parents, Warhol became a successful commercial artist, achieving recognition for his whimsical drawings for shoe advertisements and discovering the power of marketing. Ultimately, he put this knowledge to use in packaging and marketing himself as an art phenomenon.

Complementing his businesslike approach, Warhol produced art that reflected the material world around him, becoming a leader in the **Pop Art** movement. He chose subjects from American popular culture — consumer products such as Campbell's Soup and Coca-Cola and portraits of celebrities such as **Marilyn Monroe** and **Elvis Presley.** He produced his paintings by silkscreening, a technique of printing an image on a canvas that eliminates the personal brushstrokes of the artist. Using silkscreen, Warhol could repeat an image many times on a single canvas or produce multiple canvases with the same image. The smooth surfaces and obvious imperfections in Warhol's works make his artworks look as if they were produced on an assembly line. In 1963 he opened The Factory, an art studio where he and his staff mass-produced his works.

Warhol's persona was as familiar to the public as his art. Thin, with a pale complexion, he always wore a silver wig and surrounded himself with a crowd of young, beautiful people. Stating that everyone was entitled to fifteen minutes of fame, he associated with celebrities and was often the subject of extensive media attention. In the mid 1960s he branched into film making and also managed the rock group Velvet Under-

Lorna Luft, Jerry Hall, Andy Warhol, Debbie Harry, Truman Capote, and Paloma Picasso at Studio 54 in New York, 1979 (photograph by Anton Perich)

ground. Ironically, the sign that Warhol had achieved the kind of cult fame he so craved came in 1968 when he barely survived an assassination attempt.

Critics have often suggested that Warhol's works critique or satirize contemporary society, but Warhol never had this intention. His art is an enthusiastic celebration of popular culture.

REFERENCES:

Victor Bockris, *The Life and Death of Andy Warhol* (New York: Bantam, 1989);

Kynaston McShine, ed., *Andy Warhol: A Retrospective* (New York: Museum of Modern Art, 1989).

– C.S.

ROBERT PENN WARREN

Robert Penn Warren (1905–1989) was one of the most versatile and productive American authors of the twentieth century. His first book was published in 1929; nearly sixty years later, in 1986, he became the first official **Poet Laureate of the United States.**

Warren's canon includes ten novels, sixteen books of poetry, and several books of literary criticism. The widely used college textbooks he edited with Cleanth Brooks, including *Understanding Poetry* (first edition, 1938; fourth edition, 1976) and *Understanding Fiction* (1943), were extremely influential in promoting the interpretative theories of the **New Criticism.**

A native of Kentucky, Warren rooted his writing in Southern history, and his work often deals with the progression from innocence to experience. His best-known book is the novel *All the King's Men* (1946), loosely based on the career of Louisiana governor Huey Long. Narrated by Jack Burden, who works for the populist governor Willie Stark, the novel relates Stark's rise and fall as well as Burden's realization of his own spiritual decline and its implications for his life. A popular success, *All the King's Men* also won a Pulitzer Prize. *World Enough and Time* (1950), Warren's next novel, is also based on history — on the Kentucky Tragedy, in which a woman encourages her husband to kill the man who seduced her. When the husband succeeds and is sentenced to death, both attempt suicide the night before the execution. She dies but the husband lives to be hanged the next day.

Warren also received two Pulitzer Prizes for his poetry, making him the only recipient of the award in both poetry and fiction. After the mid 1950s he concentrated mainly on writing poetry. He remained productive until his death: his *Selected Poems: 1923–1975* (1977) was followed by several more collections.

REFERENCES:

Charles Bohner, *Robert Penn Warren,* revised edition (Boston: Twayne, 1981);

James H. Justus, *The Achievement of Robert Penn Warren* (Baton Rouge: Louisiana State University Press, 1981).

– D.H.-F.

WENDY WASSERSTEIN

Wendy Wasserstein (1950–) became the dramatic voice for young women of the generation that reached adulthood after the re-emphasis on American **feminism** in the 1960s.

Wasserstein's first full-length play, *Uncommon Women and Others,* is an expanded version of the play she wrote to satisfy master's degree requirements at the Yale School of Drama (M.F.A., 1976), where she studied with Robert Brustein. The play, which brought Wasserstein instant acclaim when it was presented Off-Broadway in 1977, is set during a reunion luncheon at Mount Holyoke College (where Wasserstein earned a B.A. in 1971) and contrasts the exciting uncertainty of the women's futures as they imagined them in college with the mostly bleak facts of their lives several years after graduation. In her next play, *Isn't It Romantic?,* which opened Off-Broadway in 1981, Wasserstein focuses on the effect of the biological clock in compelling independent career women to enter into less-than-fulfilling marriages.

Wasserstein combined the best elements of her first two plays in *The Heidi Chronicles,* which opened Off-Broadway in 1988. She follows the career of art professor Heidi Holland, who tries to remain true to the idealism of the 1960s while most of her friends give way to the materialism of the 1980s. In the end Heidi adopts a baby and looks forward to the 1990s as a career woman and single mother. While overly schematic at times, *The Heidi Chronicles* was a major success, winning an Antoinette Perry (Tony) Award, a New York Drama Critics Circle Award, and a Pulitzer Prize in 1989. In that same year it became the first of Wasserstein's plays to be produced on Broadway.

Wasserstein's *The Sisters Rosensweig,* about the reunion of three accomplished sisters — each in a period of crisis — was a critical and commercial success on Broadway in 1992.

– I.R.H.

ANDRÉ WATTS

André Watts (1946–) is one of the most celebrated American pianists to emerge since World War II.

The son of an American soldier and a Hungarian mother, Watts was a child prodigy, making his formal public debut at the age of nine when he played Franz Joseph Haydn's D Major Concerto with the Philadelphia Orchestra in 1955. At sixteen he became a protégé of conductor-composer **Leonard Bernstein,** who helped to launch Watts at a televised performance with the New York Philharmonic Orchestra in 1963. Watts has remained a favorite with the public, giving worldwide concerts in which he has focused on performing Romantic composers, particularly Johannes Brahms and Franz Liszt.

REFERENCE:

Linda J. Noyle, ed., *Pianists on Playing: Interviews with Twelve Concert Pianists* (Metuchen, N.J.: Scarecrow, 1987).

– L.D.S.

JOHN WAYNE

John Wayne (1907–1979), nicknamed "The Duke," forged an onscreen identity as a gung-ho all-American male.

Born Marion Michael Morrison, he played football for the University of Southern California and got some bit parts in movies in the late 1920s. His leading role in *The Big Trail* (1930) typecast him as a B-western actor, but he became an A-movie star after he was cast as The Ringo Kid in director John Ford's *Stagecoach* (1939). Ford, with whom Wayne made fourteen movies, was instrumental in shaping Wayne's career. Wayne's onscreen western persona was solidified in Ford's cavalry trilogy — *Fort Apache* (1948), *She Wore a Yellow Ribbon* (1949), and *Rio Grande* (1950). In Ford's *The Searchers* (1956) and in Howard Hawks's *Red River* (1948), Wayne's performances prompted au-

John Wayne in *El Dorado,* 1967

diences to examine the darker implications of the American cowboy mentality. In *The Quiet Man* (1952) Ford provided Wayne with a romantic role.

The vast majority of Wayne's more than two hundred films are westerns or other historical dramas. When he played a contemporary figure, he was often in uniform. He played a marine in *Sands of Iwo Jima* (1949), a naval officer *In Harm's Way* (1965), and an airline pilot in *The High and the Mighty* (1954). Wayne directed *The Alamo* (1960) and *The Green Berets* (1968). These films, in which he also starred, reflect his conservative political views and his staunch support for the American military. Playing Rooster Cogburn in *True Grit* (1969) allowed Wayne to reprise his cowboy image and brought him an Academy Award for best actor. In his last film, *The Shootist* (1976), Wayne, who died of cancer in 1979, starred as an aging gunfighter dying of that same disease.

REFERENCES:

Emmanuel Levy, *John Wayne: Prophet of the American Way of Life* (Metuchen, N. J.: Scarecrow, 1988);

Richard D. McGhee, *John Wayne: Actor, Artist, Hero* (Jefferson, N.C.: McFarland, 1990);

Maurice Zolotow, *Shooting Star: A Biography of John Wayne* (New York: Simon & Schuster, 1974).

           – I.R.H.

"WE ARE THE WORLD"

"We Are the World," a song written by **Michael Jackson** and Lionel Richie to raise money for famine relief in Africa, promotes the idea that all the world's people are one family and responsible for each other. It was recorded in 1985 by United Support of Artists for Africa (USA for Africa). The all-star chorus, conducted by **Quincy Jones,** included Richie, Jackson, and most of his brothers and sisters, as well as Dan Aykroyd, **Harry Belafonte, Ray Charles, Bob Dylan,** Bob Geldof, Billy Joel, Cyndi Lauper, Bette Midler, Willie Nelson, The Pointer Sisters, Smokey Robinson, Kenny Rogers, **Diana Ross, Paul Simon, Bruce Springsteen, Tina Turner,** Dionne Warwick, and Stevie Wonder. The record and accompanying video raised millions to feed the hungry and inspired other efforts to help the needy, including Band Aid, **Farm Aid,** and **Live Aid.**

           – K.L.R.

THE WEATHERMEN

A radical offshoot of Students for a Democratic Society (SDS), the Weathermen were the most visible of the militant groups that split away from the **New Left** in the late 1960s at the height of antiwar-movement frustration over the continuing **Vietnam War.** The Weathermen saw themselves as the vanguard of a Red Army of young Americans who would join the oppressed peoples of the world in violently overthrowing American imperialism, but they overestimated their ability to muster troops and self-destructed in the early 1970s.

The Weathermen took their name from a line in **Bob Dylan**'s "Subterranean Homesick Blues" (1965): "You don't need a weatherman to know which way the wind blows." These words were the formal title of the "Weatherman" statement, presented at the June 1969 SDS national convention by a committee that included Mark Rudd, Bernardine Dohrn, and other future Weather leaders. Responding to a takeover move initiated in June 1968 by members of the Progressive Labor Party (PL), who supported the Chinese Communism of Mao Tsetung, the "Weatherman" statement proclaimed that "the main struggle going on in the world today is between US imperialism and the national liberation struggles against it" and asserted that white Americans must support Third World guerrillas abroad and "black liberation struggles" at home by any means necessary, including violent force.

The battle between PL and the Weathermen split SDS into two groups, neither of which represented the political views of a vast majority of SDS members. Yet the Weathermen seemed confident of picking up new followers and announced that they would take the war to the streets of Chicago. Their violent "Days of Rage" protest on 8–11 October 1969, during the trial of the **Chicago 8,** failed to mobilize the large number of local young people who had turned out for the August 1968 antiwar protest planned by the defendants. The Weathermen's wild spree of window breaking and people bashing resulted in the arrests of two hundred Weathermen, and more injuries and financial damage to themselves than to their targets. SDS members on college campuses rushed to disassociate themselves from the national organization controlled by Weathermen, causing SDS to collapse.

The Weathermen decided to go underground in small groups and transform themselves into a revolutionary army. In 1970–1972 they took credit for eight bombings, including a blast that inflicted major damage on the New York City Police headquarters in June 1970.

A few months earlier, on 6 March 1970 a Weatherman bomb factory in the basement of a Greenwich Village town house exploded, killing three Weathermen. The discovery that their arsenal included antipersonnel explosives, as well as bombs designed to damage property, destroyed public support for the New Left in general.

Under indictment for a variety of offenses, the Weathermen became fugitives, renaming themselves the Weather Underground. Some took on new identities; others ended up in Algeria, where they joined forces with **Black Panthers** who were also fugitives from American justice. Since the late 1970s various Weathermen have been reemerging and turning themselves in to authorities.

REFERENCES:

Todd Gitlin, *The Sixties: Years of Hope, Days of Rage* (Toronto, New York, London, Sydney & Auckland: Bantam, 1987);

Larry Grathwohl, as told to Frank Reagan, *Bringing Down America: An FBI Informer with the Weathermen* (New Rochelle, N.Y.: Arlington House, 1976);

Kirkpatrick Sale, *SDS* (New York: Random House, 1973);

Susan Stern, *With the Weathermen: The Personal Journal of a Revolutionary Woman* (Garden City, N.Y.: Doubleday, 1975).
                                                               – K.L.R.

LAWRENCE WELK

Lawrence Welk (1903–1992) was a popular musician among mature listeners for more than two decades after World War II. A native of Strasburg, North Dakota, Welk began his musical career as an accordionist with ethnic bands in the German-speaking communities near his home. He later formed his own groups, beginning with small combos and moving gradually to leadership of a full orchestra. The romantic style linked with his name was called "champagne music." "Bubbles in the Wine," which became Welk's theme song in 1939, introduced the *Lawrence Welk Show* (1955–1971), a weekly musical variety television show. As it was played soap bubbles were produced behind the orchestra or from the wings. Members of the **rock 'n' roll** generation often ridiculed Welk and his music as epitomizing naive musical values.

REFERENCES:

Mary Lewis Coakley, *Mister Music Maker, Lawrence Welk* (Garden City, N.Y.: Doubleday, 1958);

Lawrence Welk, *You're Never Too Young* (Englewood Cliffs, N.J.: Prentice-Hall, 1981).
                                                               – L.D.S.

EUDORA WELTY

Eudora Welty (1909–) is one of the most acclaimed American fiction writers. From the beginning of her career in 1936 her reputation has risen steadily.

Most of Welty's short stories and novels are set in her native Mississippi, where she has lived most of her life. Her work defies easy classification, including the label of regionalism. Instead, Welty has sought — as she describes in her essay "Place in Fiction" (1954) — to explore the mystery of life and other universal subjects through the particularity of a chosen location. In addition to Welty's strong sense of place, supported by her eye for detail and her ear for dialogue, she writes of individuals, white and black, and their relationships in affirmative, sympathetic fiction that often employs humor and myth. She has divided her fiction into two types: "outside" stories, such as "Petrified Man" (1941), are objective and rely extensively on dialogue, while "inside" stories, such as "Livvie" (1943) and *Delta Wedding* (1946), portray characters'

Eudora Welty (photograph © Jorge Gamio)

thoughts and feelings in an oblique, almost impressionistic style.

Early in her career Welty had difficulty getting her work published. After her breakthrough with the story "Death of a Traveling Salesman" in 1936, she came to the attention of writers, notably **Robert Penn Warren,** and publishers who promoted her career. Her first book, *A Curtain of Green* (1941), was a well-received collection of stories with an introduction by Katherine Anne Porter. A novella, *The Robber Bridegroom* (1942), was praised by fellow Mississippian **William Faulkner.** The book later served as the basis for a 1974 musical. Readers and critics also admired her next collection of stories, *The Wide Net* (1943), and *Delta Wedding,* a lyrical novel about love and family life. Many critics consider Welty's next collection, *The Golden Apples* (1949), her best; the stories cover forty years in a fictional Mississippi town.

After other successful books, Welty was virtually silent between 1955 and 1970 as she attended to family concerns. She returned in force with two best-selling novels, *Losing Battles* (1970) and *The Optimist's Daughter* (1972), and a collection of photographs, *One Time, One Place: Mississippi in the Depression* (1971), from the three years she spent with the Works Progress Administration (WPA) in the early 1930s. In 1984 she published a widely admired autobiography, *One Writer's Beginnings.*

REFERENCES:

Harold Bloom, ed., *Modern Critical Views: Eudora Welty* (New York: Chelsea House, 1986);

Ruth M. Vande Kieft, *Eudora Welty,* revised edition (New York: Twayne, 1987).

– D.H.-F.

Minor White

Although not well known to the general public, Minor White (1908–1976) is considered one of the most influential American photographers of the post–World War II period, largely because of his long career as a teacher. White — whose mature work was influenced by Eastern philosophies including Zen, the ideas of spiritualist G. I. Gurdjieff, and Gestalt psychology — developed a belief in the spiritual quality of the photographic image. His best-known works focus on details from nature photographed as black-and-white abstractions of great mystery and formal beauty. He is also known for exhibiting sequences of metaphorically related photographic images. White taught photography at several institutions, including the California School of Fine Arts (headed by **Ansel Adams**) in the mid

1940s, the Rochester Institute of Technology in the mid 1950s, and the Massachusetts Institute of Technology, from which he retired in 1974. With Adams, Beaumont and Nancy Newhall, and others, White founded the quarterly *Aperture* in 1952 and served as editor until 1975. That periodical is considered the most important American publication for serious photographers. In 1962 White became a founding member of the Society for Photographic Education.

– K.B.

Richard Wilbur

Following in the tradition of **Robert Frost** and **Wallace Stevens,** Richard Wilbur (1921–) is probably the foremost writer of formal verse in his generation and is the best known of those poets who are often called **New Formalists.**

While serving with the U.S. Army Infantry in Europe during some of the most brutal battles of World War II, Wilbur wrote most of the poems in his first book, *The Beautiful Changes and Other Poems* (1947), as a means of creating "some little pattern" in the frightening chaos around him. In a foxhole at Monte Cassino he read a paperback edition of Edgar Allan Poe's stories, becoming fascinated with Poe's symbolism. Yet Wilbur has characterized much of his poetry as "a public quarrel with the aesthetics of Edgar Allan Poe," objecting to Poe's dismissal of visible reality for the fantastic world of dreams. For all their exquisite, and sometimes extravagant, wordplay, Wilbur's mature poems ground flights of imagination in a firm recognition of outward reality.

A high point in Wilbur's career came in 1957: he won a Pulitzer Prize and a National Book Award for his third collection of poetry, *Things of This World* (1956); and **Lillian Hellman** and **Leonard Bernstein**'s comic-opera version of Voltaire's *Candide,* for which Wilbur wrote most of the lyrics, completed a successful New York run. By the time Wilbur's next collection of verse, *Advice to a Prophet and Other Poems,* appeared in 1961, **confessional poetry** and the flamboyantly autobiographical poetry of the **Beats** had captured the public's imagination. Wilbur's technical precision and verbal mastery were often overshadowed by their radical experiments, but he continued to win admirers and awards.

Walking to Sleep, New Poems and Translations (1969), which won a Bollingen Prize for Poetry in 1971, demonstrates what Wilbur calls his "partial shift from the ironic meditative lyric toward the dramatic poem." The title poems in this and his next book, *The Mind*

Reader: New Poems (1976), are much-admired dramatic monologues.

Wilbur's appointment as the second **Poet Laureate of the United States** in 1987 and the publication of his *New and Collected Poems* (1988), which won a Pulitzer Prize in 1989, brought a revival of interest in his work.

REFERENCES:

William Butts, ed., *Conversations with Richard Wilbur* (Jackson & London: University Press of Mississippi, 1990);

Bruce Michelson, *Wilbur's Poetry: Music in a Scattering Time* (Amherst: University Press of Massachusetts, 1991).

– K.L.R.

BILLY WILDER

As a screenwriter and director, Billy Wilder (1906–   ) expressed his cynical assessment of human nature in film classics from 1938 through the 1960s.

Born Samuel Wilder in Vienna, Austria, he was a successful screenwriter in Germany from 1929 until Adolf Hitler came to power in 1933. Wilder, who was a Jew, fled to Paris and then to Mexico, gaining entry into the United States in 1934. Before he could write American film scripts he had to master English. In 1938 he began a fruitful screen-writing partnership with Charles Brackett. Among the earliest of the fifteen pictures they wrote together are classics such as *Midnight* (1939), *Ninotchka* (1939), and *Ball of Fire* (1941). After these movies were directed by others, Wilder took over direction of their screenplays, among them the commercially and artistically successful **film noir** *Double Indemnity* (1944), on which he collaborated with Raymond Chandler; a searing study of alcoholism, *The Lost Weekend* (1945); and a story of a mad, former silent-movie star, *Sunset Boulevard* (1950). Wilder and Brackett won Academy Awards (Oscars) for the screenplays of *The Lost Weekend* and *Sunset Boulevard,* and Wilder won the best-director Oscar for *The Lost Weekend.* After *Sunset Boulevard,* the Brackett-Wilder team broke up.

Wilder wrote screenplays with other collaborators and continued to flourish as a director and producer for another decade, with films such as *Ace in the Hole* (1951; retitled *The Big Carnival*), *Stalag 17* (1953), and *Sabrina* (1954). In 1957, with *Love in the Afternoon,* he began writing scripts with I. A. L Diamond. Among their successful films were *Some Like It Hot* (1959) and *The Apartment* (1960). As censorship restrictions loosened, Wilder's movies, such as *Kiss Me Stupid* (1964) and his remake of *The Front Page* (1974), became more sexually explicit than his previous efforts and were criticized as tasteless. His last film was *Fedora* (1978).

REFERENCES:

Bernard Dick, *Billy Wilder* (Boston : Twayne, 1980);

Maurice Zolotow, *Billy Wilder in Hollywood* (New York: Putnam, 1977).

– I.R.H.

HANK WILLIAMS

Hank Williams, known as "King of the Hillbillies," was to country music what Elvis Presley was to **rock 'n' roll.** He was among the first country singers to achieve a national celebrity. Because, in the words of his son Hank Williams, Jr., "he lived the songs that he wrote," the elder Williams had a reputation that complemented his music, raising him to legendary status among country music fans.

Williams claimed to have learned to play guitar at the age of six in Georgiana, Alabama, from a black street musician named Teetot, while working as a shoeshine boy. After World War II, he had achieved a reputation in the South as a regular on two popular radio shows, *The Louisiana Hayride* and *The Grand Ole Opry.* By 1952 he had a string of tearjerking hits, including "Your Cheatin' Heart," "I'm So Lonesome I Could Cry," "Lovesick Blues," and "I'll Never Get out of This World Alive." During 1951 and 1952 there was rarely a month in which Williams did not have a song in the top-ten hits across the nation in its category.

During the same time, however, he was losing control of his life. A congenital back ailment caused him to be in constant pain, and unscrupulous physicians first allowed then nurtured his addiction to narcotics. He drank heavily and behaved recklessly, abusing associates, shooting up motel rooms, and announcing to audiences on occasion that he was too drunk to perform. The Grand Ole Opry banned him from its stage. The culmination of his behavior came on New Year's Eve 1953, when Williams died of a drug overdose in the backseat of a limousine on the way to a show. Twenty thousand fans attended his funeral. They paid homage to a man who was able to express his country values and his lonesome heartaches in music that spoke to them and for them.

REFERENCE:

Roger M. Williams, *Sing a Sad Song: The Life of Hank Williams* (Urbana: University of Illinois Press, 1981).

–R.L.

Hank Williams (AP / Wide World)

JOHN WILLIAMS

John Williams (1932–) is best known as a prolific composer of film scores and as conductor of the **Boston Pops Orchestra** from 1980 to 1993. Audiences enjoy his lush, romantic orchestrations, full of colorful effects that are often reminiscent of an earlier era in the cinema.

Williams began writing for television in the late 1950s and wrote his first film score in 1960. He received an Academy Award in 1971 for his arrangement of Sheldon Harnick and Jerry Bock's *Fiddler on the Roof.* He composed scores for dozens of movies before gaining recognition with his music for the action-adventure films *Jaws* (1975) and *Star Wars* (1977); he received Academy Awards for both scores. Williams also composed and conducted the music for the next two *Star Wars* films, as well as *Close Encounters of the Third Kind* (1977), *Superman* (1978), *Raiders of the Lost Ark* (1981) and its sequels, and *E.T.: The Extra-Terrestrial* (1982). He also wrote the theme music for the 1984 Summer Olympics.

– L.D.S.

TENNESSEE WILLIAMS

Tennessee Williams (1911–1983) was the first major American playwright to emerge during the period after World War II.

Born Thomas Lanier Williams, the delicate child of a Mississippi clergyman's daughter and a traveling salesman from Tennessee, he was disturbed by the family's move from rural Columbus, Mississippi, to St. Louis, Missouri, when he was seven years old. An unsuccessful sojourn at the University of Missouri (1929–1931), a mind-numbing job at a St. Louis shoe company (1931–1935), a nervous breakdown (1935), and the institutionalization and lobotomy of his schizophrenic sister, Rose, during the 1930s provided a further store of anguish that he would convert into powerful, lyrical dramas for the next four decades. After local productions of early plays in Memphis (1935) and St. Louis (1935–1937) while he was a student at Washington University, Williams went to study play writing at the University of Iowa (B.A., 1938).

Celebration of the first year in the Broadway run of Tennessee Williams's *A Streetcar Named Desire:* director Elia Kazan, Jessica Tandy (Blanche Du Bois), Williams, producer Irene Selznick, Karl Malden (Mitch), and Kim Hunter (Stella; photograph by Friedman-Engeler)

Special mention in a Group Theatre play-writing contest in 1939 launched Williams's career nationally. In 1945 the New York production of his autobiographical "memory play," *The Glass Menagerie,* which won a New York Drama Critics Circle Award and ran for almost two years on Broadway, established his reputation. The play focuses on the first of several characters Williams based on his sister: shy and withdrawn Laura, whose mistaken interpretation of friendly overtures from a "gentleman caller" results in a shattering blow to her fragile psyche.

Williams's next Broadway hit, *A Streetcar Named Desire* (1947), displays his talents to their greatest advantage. With its conflict between the brutally realistic, working-class Stanley Kowalski and his sister-in-law, Blanche DuBois, who lives in a world of illusion rather than accept her soiled gentility, *A Streetcar Named Desire* dramatizes the reduction of a wounded passionate soul to dependence on "the kindness of strangers" through effective use of symbolism and poetic dialogue. Prone in other works to exaggerate symbolism, rhetoric, and grotesque characterization, Williams was poignantly on target in *A Streetcar Named Desire,* which ran on Broadway for more than two years and earned him his first Pulitzer Prize.

Other notable dramas of vulnerable men and women, frequently Southerners — their passions denied, crushed, or perverted by an alienating social reality — followed: *Summer and Smoke* (1948), *The Rose Tattoo* (1951), *Camino Real* (1953), *Cat on a Hot Tin Roof* (1955), *Orpheus Descending* (1958, a reworking of his 1940 play *Battle of Angels*), *Sweet Bird of Youth* (1959), and *The Night of the Iguana* (1961) appeared on Broadway during the years of his greatest success as a playwright. He won his second Pulitzer Prize for *Cat on a Hot Tin Roof.*

Williams continued to write plays until his death in 1983, but none of his later plays approaches the artistry of his works of the 1940s and 1950s. *Small Craft Warnings* (1972) was his only commercial success after *The Night of the Iguana.* His earlier plays were frequently revived, securing his place as one of the great American dramatists.

REFERENCES:

Roger Boxill, *Tennessee Williams* (New York: St. Martin's Press, 1987);

Donald Spoto, *The Kindness of Strangers: The Life of Tennessee Williams* (New York: Ballantine, 1986).

— I.R.H.

WILLIAM CARLOS WILLIAMS

William Carlos Williams (1883–1963) has been acknowledged as a forerunner by nearly every avant-garde American poetry movement since World War II. **Confessional** poet **Robert Lowell, Beat** poet **Allen Ginsberg,** and **Projective** poets **Charles Olson, Robert Creeley,** and **Denise Levertov** are a few of the many writers who learned from Williams's works and profited from his friendship. Yet of all the major American poets whose careers began during the first half of the twentieth century, Williams was probably the least recognized by the American reading public, especially before 1950.

Williams spent most of his life quietly writing poetry and practicing medicine in Rutherford, New Jersey (near the city of Paterson). He retired from his medical practice in 1948, and despite increasing disability from the series of strokes he suffered during the final decade of his life, he produced some of his finest poems after World War II. The most influential is *Paterson.* Williams completed five parts of this long poem (1946–1958) and started part 6 in 1960 but abandoned it after writing a few pages. These drafts were published with parts 1–5 in 1963.

Paterson is a modern, fragmented verse epic in the tradition of the *Cantos* (1910–1969) of Williams's friend and mentor **Ezra Pound.** Quotations from local histories and letters from friends (including one from Ginsberg), are part of the mass of disparate material brought together in Williams's epic. The poem is unified by the presence of Mr. Paterson, both a personification of the city and a stand-in for Williams, the poet searching for a new American poetry that captures the essence of American speech and does not rely on traditional metrics and rhyme schemes inherited from the Old World. The technical innovations — as well as the personal tone — of *Paterson* and Williams's other late poems, such as "Of Asphodel, That Greeny Flower," were imitated and adapted by his contemporaries.

Williams will never be as widely known as his contemporary **T. S. Eliot,** whose conservative and widely accepted ideas about poetry led Williams to consider him an "enemy." Yet Williams's literary reputation continues to grow among scholars, and his influence has spread to several generations of American poets.

REFERENCES:

Paul Mariani, *William Carlos Williams: A New World Naked* (New York, Saint Louis, San Francisco, Toronto, Sydney, London, Mexico & Hamburg: McGraw-Hill, 1981);

Thomas R. Whitaker, *William Carlos Williams,* revised edition (Boston: Twayne, 1989).

       – K.L.R.

AUGUST WILSON

With his sequence of plays about the black experience in America during each decade of the twentieth century, August Wilson (1945–) has established himself as the pre-eminent African-American playwright of the 1980s and 1990s.

Wilson's white natural father never lived with the family, and Wilson was raised by his black mother and stepfather in Pittsburgh. His first writing was poetry, and his abiding interest in the blues led him to a careful reproduction of the musical rhythms of black speech in the dialogue of his plays. While involved in the **Black Arts Movement** Wilson began writing plays, founding the Black Horizon Theatre Company in Pittsburgh in 1968. In 1978 he was invited to write plays for a black theater group in St. Paul, Minnesota.

Wilson's first commercially produced play was *Jitney* (1982), set in a Pittsburgh gypsy-taxicab station. Success came to Wilson after *Ma Rainey's Black Bottom —* about a 1920s jazz singer resisting exploitation by the recording industry — premiered at the Yale Repertory Theatre in 1984, moved on to Broadway, and earned Wilson his first New York Drama Critics Circle Award. This play is the first of his projected ten-play series, which is unified by a concern with the oppressive burden of black history and a celebration of black heritage, as characters deal with the question of whether to exorcise or embrace the past. Like *Ma Rainey's Black Bottom,* all these plays to date have opened at the Yale Repertory Theatre, under the direction of Lloyd Richards, and then moved on to New York.

The next play in the series is Wilson's most acclaimed work, the Pulitzer Prize–winning *Fences,* the story of an embittered former Negro League baseball player in conflict with his wife and son during the 1950s. This play also won a New York Drama Critics Circle Award, as did *Joe Turner's Come and Gone* (1988), set in a Pittsburgh boardinghouse in 1911. Wilson won a second Pulitzer Prize for *The Piano Lesson* (1990), set in Pittsburgh in 1936 and focusing on a conflict over ownership of a piano that was once the price paid for two of the family's slave ancestors. The fifth play in the series, *Two Trains Running* (1991), is set in the 1940s.

REFERENCES:

Samuel G. Freedman, "A Voice from the Streets," *New York Times Magazine,* 15 March 1987, pp. 36, 38–40. 49, and 70;

Yvonne Shafer, "August Wilson: A New Approach to Black Drama," *Zeitschrift für Anglistik und Amerikanistik,* 39, no. 1 (1991): 17–27.

       – I.R.H.

LANFORD WILSON

Since the 1960s Lanford Wilson (1937–) has produced an impressive series of plays distinguished by a tolerance for losers.

Born in Missouri, Wilson worked as a graphic artist in Chicago before deciding that play writing was his true calling. After moving to New York in 1962, he caught the attention of Off-Off-Broadway impresario Joseph Cino, who produced several of Wilson's one-act plays at Caffe Cino. Throughout the 1960s Wilson's plays — including his first three full-length works: *Balm in Gilead* (1965), *The Rimers of Eldritch* (1966), and *Lemon Sky* (1968) — played Off-Off-Broadway or in regional theaters.

Wilson had his first commercial success in New York with *The Hot l Baltimore* (1973), staged by the Circle Repertory Company, which Wilson, Marshall Mason, Robert Thirkield, and Tanya Berezin founded in 1969 and which continues to stage many of Wilson's plays. The sympathetic portrait of a condemned skid-row hotel and its hard-luck tenants in *The Hot l Baltimore* includes many elements of the playwright's other works. Wilson's plays typically combine naturalistic subject matter with lyricism and antirealistic staging devices in dramatizing the plights of social outcasts.

Wilson has also received critical acclaim for *5th of July* (1978), *Talley's Folly* (1979), and *A Tale Told* (1981; revised as *Talley & Son,* 1985) — installments in a projected five-play, semi-autobiographical series about the Talley clan of southern Missouri. *Talley's Folly* has been the most successful of these plays so far, making it to Broadway in 1980 and winning a Pulitzer Prize. *Burn This!* (1987) also had a successful New York run. *Redwood Curtain,* which opened on Broadway in 1993, dramatizes the relationship between an Amerasian girl and an alienated **Vietnam War** veteran.

REFERENCE:
Gene A. Barnett, *Lanford Wilson* (Boston: Twayne, 1987).
– I.R.H.

TOM WOLFE

Author of books such as *The Kandy-Kolored Tangerine-Flake Streamline Baby* (1965), *The Electric Kool-Aid Acid Test* (1968), *The Painted Word* (1975), and *From Bauhaus to Our House* (1981), Tom Wolfe (1931–) is a respected commentator on American culture and the most popular practitioner of the **New Journalism.**

After earning a Ph.D. in American studies at Yale University, Wolfe worked as a journalist at the *New York Herald Tribune,* writing stories that read like fiction. His breakthrough came with an article on customized cars for *Esquire* in 1963 which became his title essay in his first book, *The Kandy-Kolored Tangerine-Flake Streamline Baby.* Unable to complete it, he typed his notes in rapid-fire succession, using scenes, dialogue, and impressionistic detail. *Esquire* published the work, introducing a new type of reportage variously viewed as groundbreaking or faddish. Most critics have conceded Wolfe's talent, however, and his books have been generally well-received.

Wolfe has stressed that, for all his stylistic exuberance and satirical tendencies, he has maintained a journalist's belief in exhaustive research. After the *Esquire* article, he continued to write magazine pieces and books in the same vein. *The Electric Kool-Aid Acid Test,* a book of nonfiction, is about **Ken Kesey** and his Merry Pranksters. Wolfe has reported on popular culture, art and architecture, and most notably on the early history of the American space program in his novelistic *The Right Stuff* (1979). He became a popular legend himself for his trademark white suits and for coining phrases such as "radical chic" and "the Me Decade" to describe the 1970s.

His only novel, *The Bonfire of the Vanities* (1987), first serialized in *Rolling Stone,* was a best-seller. Critics praised it for its realistic insights into class and race in contemporary urban society. After its publication, Wolfe wrote a controversial essay for *Harper's* in which he asserted that novelists should return to realism and abandon experimental techniques — an ironic argument from a writer whose experiments helped to reshape journalism.

REFERENCES:
Doug Shomette, ed., *The Critical Response to Tom Wolfe* (Westport, Conn. & London: Greenwood Press, 1992);
Tom Wolfe and E. W. Johnson, eds., *The New Journalism* (New York: Harper & Row, 1973).
– D.H.-F.

WOODSTOCK

The most famous popular-music concert of the twentieth century, the Woodstock Music and Art Fair, took place on 15–17 August 1969 at Max Yasgur's six-hundred-acre farm near Bethel, New York, in rural Sullivan County, about seventy miles northwest on New York City. The event was billed as "An Aquarian Exposition," a reference to the popular rock musical *Hair* (1967), which

Jimi Hendrix performing at Woodstock (photograph by Benno Friedman)

proclaimed "the dawning of the Age of Aquarius," a time of peace and love (see **Broadway Musicals**).

Woodstock attracted a crowd estimated at between three and five hundred thousand people, mostly between the ages of sixteen and thirty, to hear performers such as **Joan Baez,** Janis Joplin, **Jimi Hendrix, The Grateful Dead, Jefferson Airplane, Arlo Guthrie,** Ravi Shankar, The Who, The Band, Sly and the Family Stone, Canned Heat, Creedence Clearwater Revival, Crosby, Stills, Nash and Young, and Blood, Sweat and Tears. For most of the weekend traffic jams on the main routes leading to Bethel were ten to thirty miles long. The crowd arriving at the festival site was so overwhelming that Woodstock promoters, who had expected no more than two hundred thousand people, gave up on collecting admission.

There were shortages of food, water, and toilet facilities; torrential rainstorms cut short some of the performances. About eighty people were arrested for possession of LSD, barbituates, or amphetemines. Police overlooked marijuana users because, as one officer said, there were not enough jail cells "in Sullivan or the next three counties to put them in." About four thousand people were treated for illnesses, injuries, and adverse reactions to drugs. Two people died, and two babies were born. Yet no one was arrested for fighting.

Many political observers had feared that Woodstock would be a replay of the violent clash between police and antiwar demonstrators at the Democratic National Convention in Chicago the previous summer; yet the crowd camping out in Max Yasgur's muddy fields surprised authorities with its nonviolence. The gathering was also largely apolitical. Abbie Hoffman, there to represent the **Yippies** and other groups opposed to the **Vietnam War,** generated little interest. While some comentators at the time pointed to Woodstock as proof that young Americans had rejected the increasing violence of emerging **New Left** groups such as the **Weathermen,** these observers were making the common mistake of confusing two distinct groups of disaffected young people: idealistic **hippies** who believed in the power of meditation and pragmatic radicals who believed in taking direct action in the streets. While these two elements of the so-called counterculture sometimes came together — as the hippies of **Haight-Ashbury** and the New Leftists at Berkeley had united in 1966 to promote peace at the Human Be-in — their joint ventures were at best the product of an uneasy temporary truce.

REFERENCE:

Jack Curry, *Woodstock: The Summer of Our Lives* (New York: Weidenfeld & Nicolson, 1989).

                                                                – K.L.R.

World Music

Once known as exotic, ethnic, **folk,** or non–Western music, *world music* is the term used to designate the musics of all the people of the world other than Western art music and American popular music. World music thus includes African, Native American, and Australian aboriginal tribal music; the art music of Asian countries such as India, Indonesia, China, and Japan; and folk-music styles from anywhere outside the limits of European art music. In a commercial context, the term is mostly associated with popular styles and genres resulting from a fusion between Western mainstream and indigenous musical traditions, such as samba, **bossa nova, calypso,** Afro-Cuban jazz, and **reggae.** Many Third World countries have developed distinctive styles of popular music, either by playing their own music with Western instruments and arrangements or by adapting American rock and other Western styles to their own instruments and performance practices. Ethnomusicology is the systematic study of world music.

REFERENCES:

Bruno Nettl, *The Study of Ethnomusicology: Twenty-Nine Issues and Concepts* (Urbana: University of Illinois Press, 1983);

Timothy Rice and J. Potter, eds., *Garland Encyclopedia of World Music,* ten volumes (Hamden, Conn.: Garland, forthcoming 1994);

Jeff Todd Titon, ed., *Worlds of Music: An Introduction to the Music of the World's Peoples,* second edition (New York: Schirmer / Toronto: Collier Macmillan / New York: Maxwell Macmillan, 1984).

                                                                – L.E.P.

Charles Wuorinen

Like **Milton Babbitt,** composer Charles Wuorinen (1938–) is known primarily for his advancement of **serial-music** techniques beyond their initial boundary of pitch.

Born in New York of Finnish heritage, Wuorinen began taking piano lessons at age five, when he also began composing. He wrote his first orchestral score — *Into the Organ Pipes and Steeples* — at eighteen. His early works, based upon the neoclassicism of Igor Stravinsky, emphasize structure as well as linear counterpoint. Among the works written by the time he turned twenty-one are three symphonies. Wuorinen's first mature pieces are characterized by sonorities not organized into thematic lines, recalling the works of **Edgard Varèse,** whose *Poème électronique* (1958) is a forerunner of Wuorinen's *Time's Encomium.* Commissioned by Nonesuch Records and later adapted for orchestra, *Time's Encomium* (1969) was created on the synthesizer and won the 1970 Pulitzer Prize for music, the first awarded for an **electronic** composition. In this later style he has employed total serialism, in which pitch, time, and rhythm are related to each other in a system. Such a system also appears in his orchestral piece *Contrafactum* (1969), based on the same predetermined sets and structures of *Time's Encomium* but an entirely different work.

REFERENCE:

Charles Wuorinen, *Simple Composition* (New York: Longman, 1979).

                                                                – L.D.S.

Andrew Wyeth

Andrew Wyeth (1917–) is one of the most popular serious American artists of the twentieth century. He is known for his paintings of rustic landscapes and the people who live on and work the land.

Wyeth was born in Chadds Ford, Pennsylvania, a farming community that became the setting for many of his paintings. His father, N. C. Wyeth, was an accomplished artist who became well-known for his book illustrations. From his father he derived the meticulous realism that characterizes his works, which often take on a sense of the sublime and mysterious. Preferring to work in watercolor and tempera rather than oil, Wyeth most often uses a dry-brush technique (applying watercolor with a brush squeezed almost dry), which allows him to achieve a remarkable degree of precision and detail.

In addition to Chadds Ford, the fishing village of Cushing, Maine, where Wyeth has a summer home, is the setting for some of his paintings. It was in Maine that Wyeth produced his best-known work, *Christina's World* (1948), effectively suggesting the circumscribed existence of a paralyzed woman whose entire world is the fields surrounding her country home. Other well-known works include *The Trodden Wood* (1951), *Nicholas* (1955), and *Tenant Farmer* (1961) — as well as the series known as *The Helga Suite,* more than 240 drawings and paintings of a Chadds Ford neighbor, on which Wyeth worked in virtual secrecy for fifteen years (1971–1985).

In 1963 Wyeth became the first painter to receive the Presidential Medal of Freedom. In 1977 he was elected to the French Académie des Beaux-Arts, and in 1980 he became the first living American artist to be elected to the British Royal Academy. His son James Wyeth is also a highly regarded painter.

REFERENCES:

Wanda M. Corn, *The Art of Andrew Wyeth* (Greenwich, Conn.: Published for the Fine Arts Museums of San Francisco by the New York Graphic Society, 1973);

Thomas Hoving, *The Two Worlds of Andrew Wyeth: A Conversation with Andrew Wyeth* (Boston: Houghton Mifflin, 1978).

– W.L.T.

Y

YADDO

Yaddo is one of the two most distinguished artists' colonies in America. (The other is the **MacDowell Colony**.) Located on more than four hundred acres near Sarasota Springs, New York, Yaddo was founded by Elizabeth Ames in 1926, four years after Katrina Trask, widow of philanthropist Spencer Trask, left their elegant estate as a retreat for artists.

Yaddo offers writers, composers, and other artists a place to work free of distractions and concerns for a limited time. Though Yaddo has hosted composers such as **Ned Rorem** and **Virgil Thomson** and other artists, it especially has attracted writers, including John Cheever, Langston Hughes, **Robert Lowell, Bernard Malamud,** Jay McInerney, Dorothy Parker, **Sylvia Plath, Theodore Roethke,** and **William Carlos Williams.** Among the works of fiction that have been at least partially written at Yaddo are **Truman Capote**'s *Other Voices, Other Rooms* (1948), **Carson McCullers**'s *The Member of the Wedding* (1946) and *The Ballad of the Sad Café* (1951), **Flannery O'Connor**'s *Wise Blood* (1952), **James Baldwin**'s *Giovanni's Room* (1956), **Saul Bellow**'s *Henderson the Rain King* (1959), Katherine Anne Porter's *Ship of Fools* (1962), and **Philip Roth**'s *Portnoy's Complaint* (1969).

REFERENCES:

Roy Bongartz, "Yaddo at 60," *Publishers Weekly*, 229 (13 June 1986): 32–35;

William F. Claire, "Where Artists Do As They Please — And, Mostly, Work," *Smithsonian*, 8 (July 1977): 45–51.

— D.H.-F.

YIPPIES

The Yippies (short for Youth International Party) were a mock political party founded by Abbie Hoffman, Jerry Rubin, and other **New Left** anti–**Vietnam War** activists after their participation in the October 1967 March on the Pentagon. During that antiwar demonstration, Hoffman, who was gifted at using street-theater techniques inspired by the Diggers of **Haight-Ashbury,** had attracted media attention with an "Exorcism of the Pentagon," at which singing and chanting demonstrators surrounded the building in a comic attempt to levitate it. The Yippies, who nominated Pigasus the Pig as their presidential candidate, were invented to publicize the "Festival of Life" antiwar demonstrations that Hoffman and Rubin were planning to hold during the August 1968 Democratic National Convention in Chicago. Violence broke out between protesters and Chicago policemen, and Hoffman and Rubin were among the so-called **Chicago 8** who were arrested under a federal antiriot law. They and other Yippies disrupted the trial with absurd behavior designed to mock the judicial system, just as they had satirized a political system in which neither major party had nominated an antiwar presidential candidate.

REFERENCES:

David Farber, *Chicago '68* (Chicago & London: University of Chicago Press, 1987);

Todd Gitlin, *The Sixties: Years of Hope, Days of Rage* (Toronto, New York, London, Sydney & Auckland: Bantam, 1987);

David Lewis Stein, *Living in Revolution: The Yippies in Chicago* (Indianapolis & New York: Bobbs-Merrill, 1969).

— K.L.R.

Yippies campaigning for their presidential candidate, Pigasus the Pig, during the 1968 Democratic National Convention in Chicago (AP / Wide World)

YOUNG-ADULT FICTION

Young-adult (YA) or adolescent fiction features characters in the transition between childhood and adulthood, with its attendant physical and emotional changes.

Young-adult fiction (mostly novels) emerged as a distinct publishing category after World War II, reflecting a growing recognition of and interest in adolescence as a separate stage of human development and a need to address the concerns of teens and preteens at a level appropriate to them. The novels often treat adolescent difficulties with parents, peers, love and sex, and substance abuse, which has led to occasional controversy and attempts at **censorship.** Yet these books also deal with the sort of anxiety-producing situations experienced by real-life adolescents, showing them that they are not alone. While adolescent literature does not avoid negative aspects of life, it generally presents a positive side as well.

The subjects and language of young-adult fiction would have marked much of it as "adult" in the late 1940s and early 1950s; indeed there was some debate about how to classify **J. D. Salinger**'s *The Catcher in the Rye* (1951), which has influenced many young-adult writers. While Beverly Cleary's *Fifteen* (1956) and **Robert A. Heinlein**'s science-fiction "juveniles" (1947–1963) favor the traditional values of the 1950s, much adolescent fiction has echoed Salinger in focusing on teens seeking identity, values, and independence in contrast to questionable adult authority.

Significant young-adult novels include Emily Neville's *It's Like This, Cat* (1963); S. E. Hinton's *The Outsiders* (1967) and *Rumble Fish* (1975); Paul Zindel's *My Darling, My Hamburger* (1969); **Judy Blume**'s *Are You There God? It's Me, Margaret* (1970) and *Forever . . .* (1975); the anonymous *Go Ask Alice* (1971; author later revealed as Beatrice Sparks); Robert Cormier's *The Chocolate War* (1974) and *I Am the Cheese* (1977); and Katherine Paterson's *Jacob Have I Loved* (1980). In addition to such realistic works, **science fiction and fantasy** are also popular with teenagers, especially Ursula K. Le Guin's four Earthsea books and Madeleine L'Engle's "Time Fantasy" series.

REFERENCES:

Kenneth L. Donelson and Alleen Pace Nilsen, *Literature for Today's Young Adults*, third edition (Glenview, Ill. & London: Scott, Foresman, 1989);

Patricia E. Feehan and Pamela Petrick Barron, eds., *Writers on Writing for Young Adults: Exploring the Authors, the Genre, the Readers, the Issues, and the Critics of Young-Adult Literature, Together with Checklists of the Featured Writers* (Detroit: Omnigraphics, 1991).

– D.H.-F.

YUPPIE

Yuppie was a journalistic acronym used to designate young, upwardly mobile professionals in the 1980s. An ironic play on the term *yippie,* coined to describe young radical activists of previous decades, yuppie carried connotations of greed, conformity, and conspicuous consumption. As the implications of reckless spending during what was called the "me-decade" grew ominous, so did the negativity of term *yuppie.*

– R.L.

Z

FRANK ZAPPA

Frank Zappa (1940–1993) was a distinctive guitarist, composer, and producer of international acclaim. Characterized by eclectic styles, complex musical treatment, and intentionally shocking lyrics, his work attracted a cult following from the release of his first album, *Freak Out,* in 1966 until his death. A product of the anti-establishment movement of the 1960s, he was an active nonconformist throughout his career, satirizing social issues from **hippie** optimism in "We're Only in It for the Money" (1967) to **censorship** in "Frank Zappa Meets the Mothers of Prevention" (1985).

Zappa was a prolific composer, and with his band The Mothers of Invention he parodied pop strains such as doo-wop, big band, **heavy metal,** and jazz rock. His avant-garde symphonic and chamber compositions, influenced by works of Igor Stravinsky and **Edgard Varèse,** were performed by such eminent conductors as **Zubin Mehta** and Pierre Boulez, but these works gained him less recognition than his sixty-plus albums of popular music. However, the provocative nature of many of Zappa's works often limited their audience. His single **Top 40** hit, "Valley Girl" (1982), featured his daughter Moon Unit Zappa.

Zappa made his recording debut in 1960 writing scores for B movies. In 1964 he joined Ray Collins's band, The Soul Giants. Under Zappa's leadership, the group was renamed The Mothers of Invention in 1966. In 1969 Zappa disbanded the original group and began recruiting musicians with remarkable improvisational and technical skills to play his increasingly complex compositions. Throughout the 1970s his band attracted outstanding musicians such as bassist Roy Estrada, who founded Little Feat, and Adrian Belew, who went on to play guitar with David Bowie, King Crimson, and Talking Heads.

Frank Zappa (photograph by Greg Gorman)

Zappa entered the record-production business in 1968, founding two labels — Straight and Bizarre — on Reprise Records. The labels signed Alice Cooper and Captain Beefheart, whose *Trout Mask Replica,* produced by Zappa, influenced experimental and alternative rock groups. Zappa later established a new label, Zappa Records, through Mercury in 1979, as well as the Barking Pumpkin label in 1980. In addition to recordings, Zappa produced films featuring his own scores — *200 Motels* (1971) and *Baby Snakes* (1980) — and started Honker Video to release his films and videotapes in 1988. *Jazz from Hell* won him a Grammy Award for best rock instrumental performance in 1988.

REFERENCES:

David Fricke, "Frank Zappa," *Rolling Stone,* 674 (27 January 1994): 11–16;

David Walley, *No Commercial Potential: The Saga of Frank Zappa, Then and Now,* revised edition (New York: Dutton, 1980);

Frank Zappa with Peter Occhiogrosso, *The Real Frank Zappa Book* (New York: Poseidon, 1989).

– E.M.M.

Ellen Taaffe Zwilich

The first woman to win a Pulitzer Prize in music, Ellen Taaffe Zwilich (1939–   ) is one of the most celebrated contemporary American composers. Many critics have attributed her success to her balance between musical substance and audience appeal through her use of complex melodies, striking rhythms, and distinctive instrumentation.

After studying violin and composition at Florida State University, Zwilich entered the Juilliard School of Music in 1970 and studied with **Roger Sessions** and **Elliott Carter.** In 1975 she became the first woman to receive a doctorate in composition from the school. Among her works are *Symposium for Orchestra* (1973); Symphony No. 1 (Three Movements for Orchestra), for which she won the Pulitzer Prize in 1983; *Concerto Grosso 1985* (1985); and *Symbolom* (1988), the world premiere of which was performed by **Zubin Mehta** and the New York Philharmonic Orchestra in Leningrad during its 1988 world tour.

– L.D.S.

CONTRIBUTORS

DICTIONARY OF

TWENTIETH CENTURY CULTURE

American Culture After World War II

INDEX

A

B

I

L

O

P

ISBN 0-8103-8481-7